5.4 Perform preventative maintenance of networks including securing and protecting network cabling	
DOMAIN 6 SECURITY	
6.1 Identify the fundamental principles of security	
6.2 Install, configure, upgrade and optimize security	8, 10
6.3 Identify tools, diagnostic procedures and troubleshooting techniques for security	10, 11
6.4 Perform preventative maintenance for security	
DOMAIN 7 SAFETY & ENVIRONMENTAL ISSUES	
7.1 Identify potential hazards and proper safety procedures including power supply, display devices and environment (e.g. trip, liquid, situational, atmospheric hazards and high-voltage and moving equipment)	2, 11
DOMAIN 8 PROFESSIONALISM AND COMMUNICATION	
8.1 Use good communication skills including listening and tact/discretion, when communicating with customers and colleagues	
8.2 Use job-related professional behavior including notation of privacy, confidentiality and respect for the customer and customers' property	

CompTIA A+ 220-603

Objectives	Chapters
DOMAIN 1 PERSONAL COMPUTER COMPONENTS	
1.1 Install, configure, optimize, and upgrade personal computer components	8, 9, 10
1.2 Identify tools, diagnostic procedures, and troubleshooting techniques for personal computer components	2, 3, 4, 5, 6, 7 8, 9, 10, 11, 12
1.3 Perform preventative maintenance on personal computer components	2, 8, 9, 11, 12
DOMAIN 2 OPERATING SYSTEMS—UNLESS OTHERWISE NOTED, OPERATING SYSTEMS REFERRED TO WITHIN INCLUDE MICROSOFT WINDOWS 2000, XP PROFESSIONAL, XP HOME AND MEDIA CENTER.	
2.1 Identify the fundamental principles of using operating systems	10
2.2 Install, configure, optimize and upgrade operating systems	
2.3 Identify tools, diagnostic procedures and troubleshooting techniques for operating	2, 7, 8, 11, 12
2.4 Perform preventative maintenance for operating systems.	
DOMAIN 3 PRINTERS AND SCANNERS	
3.1 Identify the fundamental principles of using printers and scanners	12
3.2 Install, configure, optimize and upgrade printers and scanners.	12
3.3 Identify tools, diagnostic procedures and troubleshooting techniques for printers and scanners	12
DOMAIN 4 NETWORKS	
4.1 Identify the fundamental principles of networks	8, 10
4.2 Install, configure, optimize and upgrade networks	10, 11
4.3 Identify tools, diagnostic procedures and troubleshooting techniques for networks	10
DOMAIN 5 SECURITY	
5.1 Identify the fundamental principles of security	
5.2 Install, configure, optimizing and upgrade security	8, 10, 11
5.3 Identify tools, diagnostic procedures and troubleshooting techniques for security issues	10, 11
5.4 Perform preventative maintenance for security.	
DOMAIN 6 PROFESSIONALISM AND COMMUNICATION	
6.1 Use good communication skills, including listening and tact/discretion, when communicating with customers and colleagues	
6.2 Use job-related professional behavior including notation of privacy, confidentiality and respect for the customer and customers' property	

CompTIA A+ 220-604

Objectives	Chapters
DOMAIN 1 PERSONAL COMPUTER COMPONENTS	
1.1 Install, configure, optimize and upgrade personal computer components.	3, 4, 5, 6, 7, 8, 9, 10, 11
1.2 Identify tools, diagnostic procedures and troubleshooting techniques for personal computer components.	2, 3, 4, 5, 6, 8, 9, 10, 11, 12
1.3 Perform preventative maintenance of personal computer components.	2, 3, 4, 5, 8, 9, 10, 11, 12
DOMAIN 2 LAPTOPS AND PORTABLE DEVICES	
2.1 Identify the fundamental principles of using laptops and portable devices.	8, 10, 11
2.2 Install, configure, optimize and upgrade laptops and portable devices.	8, 11
2.3 Identify tools, diagnostic procedures and troubleshooting techniques for laptops and portable devices.	8, 10, 11
DOMAIN 3 PRINTERS AND SCANNERS	
3.1 Identify the fundamental principles of using printers and scanners.	12
3.2 Install, configure, optimize and upgrade printers and scanners.	12
3.3 Identify tools, diagnostic methods and troubleshooting procedures for printers and scanners.	12
3.4 Perform preventative maintenance of printer and scanner problems.	2, 12
DOMAIN 4 SECURITY	
4.1 Identify the names, purposes and characteristics of physical security devices and processes.	
4.2 Install hardware security	8, 11
DOMAIN 5 SAFETY AND ENVIRONMENTAL ISSUES	
5.1 Identify potential hazards & proper safety procedures including power supply, display devices and environment (e.g. trip, liquid, situational, atmospheric hazards, high-voltage and moving equipment).	2, 11

A+ Guide to Hardware:
Managing, Maintaining,
and Troubleshooting
FOURTH EDITION

Jean Andrews, Ph.D.

THOMSON

COURSE TECHNOLOGY

Australia • Canada • Mexico • Singapore • Spain • United Kingdom • United States

A+ Guide to Hardware: Managing, Maintaining, and Troubleshooting, FOURTH EDITION:
is published by Thomson Course Technology.

Executive Editor:
Steve Helba

Managing Editor:
Larry Main

Acquisitions Editor:
Nick Lombardi

Senior Product Manager:
Michelle Ruelos Cannistraci

Developmental Editor:
Jill Batistick

Marketing Manager:
Guy Baskaran

Editorial Assistant:
Jessica Reed

Proofreader:
John Bosco

Manufacturing Coordinator:
Susan Carroll

Content Project Manager:
Summer Hughes

Indexer:
Alexandra Nickerson

Quality Assurance:
Christian Kunciw

Cover Design:
Betsy Young

Interior Design:
Betsy Young

Compositor:
Integra, Inc.—Pondicherry

Printed in Canada
1 2 3 4 5 6 7 8 9 TC 10 09 08 07 06

For more information, contact
Thomson Course Technology, 25 Thomson Place, Boston, Massachusetts, 02210.

Or find us on the World Wide Web at:
www.course.com

Disclaimer
Thomson Course Technology reserves the right to revise this publication and make changes from time to time in its content without notice.

ISBN-10 0-619-21762-6
ISBN-13 978-0-619-21762-4

Instructor Edition ISBN-10 0-619-21771-5
Instructor Edition ISBN-13 978-0-619-21771-6

Table of Contents

CHAPTER 1

Hardware Needs Software to Work 1

CHAPTER 2

PC Repair Fundamentals 35

CHAPTER 3

Form Factors and Power Supplies 89

CHAPTER 9

Multimedia Devices and Mass Storage .381

CHAPTER 10

PCs on a Network 443

CHAPTER 11

Notebooks, Tablet PCs, and PDAs 507

CompTIA A+ Essentials
2006 Examination Objectives

DOMAIN 1 PERSONAL COMPUTER COMPONENTS

1.1 Identify the fundamental principles of using personal computers

OBJECTIVES	CHAPTERS	PAGE NUMBERS
Identify the names, purposes, and characteristics of storage devices		
◢ FDD	1, 7	7, 13–18/250–254
◢ HDD	1, 7	7, 13–18/257–276
◢ CD/DVD/RW (e.g. drive speeds, media types)	1, 9	7, 13–18/406–418
◢ Removable storage (e.g. tape drive, solid state such as thumb drives, flash and SD cards, USB, external CD-RW and hard drive)	7, 8, 9	257–276/349–354/ 419–427, 393–396, 406–418
Identify the names, purposes, and characteristics of motherboards		
◢ Form Factor (e.g. ATX/BTX, microATX/NLX)	3, 5	91–98/176–181
◢ Components		
• Integrated I/Os (e.g. sound, video, USB, serial, IEEE 1394/firewire, parallel, NIC, modem)	1, 5, 8, 9	8–9/176–180/342–358/ 382–385
• Memory slots (e.g. RIMM, DIMM)	1, 5, 6, 11	12–13/176–180/ 220–231/542–544
• Processor sockets	4, 5	148–150/176–180
• External cache memory	1, 4	12–13/134–137
• Bus architecture	1, 4, 5, 8	18–23/150–153/181–188/ 333–336
• Bus slots (e.g. PCI, AGP, PCIE, AMR, CNR)	1, 5, 8	18–23/181–188/333–336
• EIDE/PATA	1, 7	13–18/257–276
• SATA	1, 7	13–18/257–276
• SCSI Technology	7	272–222
◢ Chipsets	1, 4, 5	8–11/150–153/186,199–201
◢ BIOS/CMOS/Firmware	1, 2, 5	8–11, 26–27/71–72/ 188–201 More content in *A+ Guide to Software*
◢ Riser card/daughter board	3, 5	96–98/186–188
Identify the names, purposes and characteristics of power supplies, for example: AC adapter, ATX, proprietary, voltage	3, 5	90–100/176–181
Identify the names, purposes and characteristics of processor/CPUs		
◢ CPU chips (e.g. AMD, Intel)	1, 4	3–4, 10–11/130–150
◢ CPU technologies		
• Hyperthreading	4, 9	131–143/382
• Dual core	4, 9	133–134/382
• Throttling	4.5	133/195–199
• Micro code (MMX)	4, 9	150–153/382
• Overclocking	4, 5	132–133/195–199
• Cache	4	134–137
• VRM	4	157–159

1.2 Install, configure, optimize and upgrade personal computer components

1.3 Identify tools, diagnostic procedures and troubleshooting techniques for personal computer components

▲ Assess a problem systematically and divide large problems into smaller components to be analyzed individually	2, 7, 8, 12	72–78/295–304/ 366–374/617–619 More content in *A+ Guide to Software*
▲ Verify even the obvious, determine whether the problem is something simple and make no assumptions	2, 7, 8, 12	72–78/295–304/ 366–374/617–619 More content in *A+ Guide to Software*
▲ Research ideas and establish priorities	2, 7, 8, 12	72–78/295–304/ 366–374/617–619 More content in *A+ Guide to Software*
▲ Document findings, actions and outcomes	2, 8, 12	72–78/366/617–619 More content in *A+ Guide to Software*
Identify and apply basic diagnostic procedures and troubleshooting techniques for example: ▲ Identify the problem including questioning user and identifying user changes to computer	2, 7, 8, 11, 12	72–78/295–304/ 366–374/558–565/617–619 More content in *A+ Guide to Software*
▲ Analyze the problem including potential causes and make an initial determination of software and/or hardware problem	2, 7, 8, 11, 12	72–79/295–304/366–374/ 558–565/617–619 More content in *A+ Guide to Software*
▲ Test related components including inspection, connections, hardware/software configurations, device manager and consult vendor documentation	2, 7, 8, 11 12	72–79/295–304/366–374/ 558–565/617–619 More content in *A+ Guide to Software*
▲ Evaluate results and take additional steps if needed such as consultation, use of alternate resources, manuals	2, 7, 9, 11, 12	72–79/295–304/366–374/ 558–565/617–619/ More content in *A+ Guide to Software*
▲ Document activities and outcomes	2, 8, 11, 12	72–78/366/558–565/ 617–619 More content in *A+ Guide to Software*
Recognize and isolate issues with display, power, basic input devices, storage, memory, thermal, POST errors (e.g. BIOS, hardware)	2, 3, 4, 5, 6, 7, 8, 11, 12	78–83/115–121/167–169/ 210–213/243–244/295–304/ 366–374/558–565/ 617–619
Apply basic troubleshooting techniques to check for problems (e.g. thermal issues, error codes, power, connections including cables and/or pins, compatibility, functionality, software/drivers) with components for example: ▲ Motherboards	2, 4, 5, 11	78–83/167–169/210–213/ 558–565
▲ Power supply	2, 3, 5, 11	78–83/90–100, 95–96, 115–121/ 210–213/558–565
▲ Processor/CPUs	2, 4, 5	78–83/167–169/210–213
▲ Memory	2, 6, 11	78–83/243–244/ 558–565
▲ Display devices	2, 8, 11	78–83/366–374/558–565
▲ Input devices	2, 8, 11	78–83/366–374/ 558–565
▲ Adapter cards	2, 8, 10	78–83/366–374/497–501

Recognize the names, purposes, characteristics and appropriate application of tools for example: BIOS, self-test, hard drive self-test and software diagnostic test	1, 2, 5, 6, 7, 8, 11, 12	8–11, 26–27/66–72, 78–83/210–213/243–244/ 295–304/366–374/558–565/ 617–623

1.4 Perform preventative maintenance on personal computer components

OBJECTIVES	CHAPTERS	PAGE NUMBERS
Identify and apply basic aspects of preventative maintenance theory for example:		
◢ Visual/audio inspection	2, 8, 11, 12	40–48/314, 317 353, 358–366/509–518/ 606–613, 616–617
◢ Driver/firmware updates	5, 8, 11, 12 21	199–212/314, 317, 353, 358–366/509–518/ 606–613, 616–617, More content in *A+ Guide to Software*
◢ Scheduling preventative maintenance	2, 11, 12	40–48/509–518/ 606–613, 616–617 More content in *A+ Guide to Software*
◢ Use of appropriate repair tools and cleaning materials	2, 8, 9, 11, 12	36–40/314, 317/417–418, 424/509–518/ 606–613, 616–617
◢ Ensuring proper environment	2, 8, 11, 12	40–48/366–368/ 509–518/606–613, 616–617
Identify and apply common preventative maintenance techniques for devices such as input devices and batteries	2, 8, 11, 12	40–48/366–368/ 509–518/606–613, 616–617

DOMAIN 2 LAPTOPS AND PORTABLE DEVICES

2.1 Identify the fundamental principles of using laptops and portable devices

OBJECTIVES	CHAPTERS	PAGE NUMBERS
Identify names, purposes and characteristics of laptop-specific:		
◢ Form factors such as memory and hard drives	6, 11	222–231/542–549
◢ Peripherals (e.g. docking station, port replicator and media/accessory bay)	11	527–539
◢ Expansion slots (e.g. PCMCIA I, II and III, card and express bus)	11	527–539
◢ Ports (e.g. mini PCI slot)	11	527–539, 556–558
◢ Communication connections (e.g. Bluetooth, infrared, cellular WAN, Ethernet)	8, 10, 11	346–347/448–464/ 527–558
◢ Power and electrical input devices (e.g. auto-switching and fixed-input power supplies, batteries)	11	520–525
◢ LCD technologies (e.g. active and passive matrix, resolution such as XGA, SXGA+ , UXGA, WUXGA, contrast radio, native resolution)	8	322–328
◢ Input devices (e.g. stylus/digitizer, function (Fn) keys and pointing devices such as touch pad, point stick/track point)	8	314–318
Identify and distinguish between mobile and desktop motherboards and processors including throttling, power management and WiFi	10, 11	481–491/520–527

2.2 Install, configure, optimize and upgrade laptops and portable devices

OBJECTIVES	CHAPTERS	PAGE NUMBERS
Configure power management		
▲ Identify the features of BIOS-ACPI	3, 11	112–114/520–525
▲ Identify the difference between suspend, hibernate and standby	3, 11	112–114/520–525
Demonstrate safe removal of laptop-specific hardware such as peripherals, hot-swappable devices and non-hot-swappable devices	8, 11	349–354/527–539

2.3 Identify tools, basic diagnostic procedures and troubleshooting techniques for laptops and portable devices

OBJECTIVES	CHAPTERS	PAGE NUMBERS
Use procedures and techniques to diagnose power conditions, video, keyboard, pointer and wireless card issues, for example:	11	539–542
▲ Verify AC power (e.g. LEDs, swap AC adapter)	11	520–525, 558–565
▲ Verify DC power	11	520–525, 558–565
▲ Remove unneeded peripherals	11	520–525, 558–565
▲ Plug in external monitor	8, 11	368–374/560–561
▲ Toggle Fn keys	8, 11	368–374/560–561
▲ Check LCD cutoff switch	8, 11	368–374/560–561
▲ Verify backlight functionality and pixilation	8, 11	368–374/560–561
▲ Stylus issues (e.g. digitizer problems)	8, 11	366–368/558–565
▲ Unique laptop keypad issues	8, 11	368/560–561
▲ Antenna wires	10, 11	481–491/556–558

2.4 Perform preventative maintenance on laptops and portable devices

OBJECTIVES	CHAPTERS	PAGE NUMBERS
Identify and apply common preventative maintenance techniques for laptops and portable devices, for example: cooling devices, hardware and video cleaning materials, operating environments including temperature and air quality, storage, transportation and shipping.	2, 11	40–48/509–518

DOMAIN 3 OPERATING SYSTEMS—UNLESS OTHERWISE NOTED, OPERATING SYSTEMS REFERRED TO WITHIN INCLUDE MICROSOFT WINDOWS 2000, XP PROFESSIONAL, XP HOME AND MEDIA CENTER.

3.1 Identify the fundamentals of using operating systems

OBJECTIVES	CHAPTERS	PAGE NUMBERS
Identify differences between operating systems (e.g. Mac, Windows, Linux) and describe operating system revision levels including GIU, system requirements, application and hardware compatibility		See *A+ Guide to Software*
Identify names, purposes and characteristics of the primary operating system components including registry, virtual memory and file system		See *A+ Guide to Software*
Describe features of operating system interfaces, for example:		
▲ Windows Explorer		See *A+ Guide to Software*
▲ My Computer		See *A+ Guide to Software*
▲ Control Panel		See *A+ Guide to Software*
▲ Command Prompt		See *A+ Guide to Software*
▲ My Network Places	12	594–601
		More content in *A+ Guide to Software*

◢ Task bar/systray	12	587–594 More content in *A+ Guide to Software*
◢ Start Menu	12	587–594 More content in *A+ Guide to Software*
Identify the names, locations, purposes and characteristics of operating system files for example:		
◢ BOOT.INI		See *A+ Guide to Software*
◢ NTLDR		See *A+ Guide to Software*
◢ NTDETECT.COM		See *A+ Guide to Software*
◢ NTBOOTDD.SYS		See *A+ Guide to Software*
◢ Registry data files		See *A+ Guide to Software*
Identify concepts and procedures for creating, viewing, managing disks, directories and files in operating systems for example:		
◢ Disks (e.g. active, primary, extended and logical partitions)		See *A+ Guide to Software*
◢ File systems (e.g. FAT 32, NTFS)		See *A+ Guide to Software*
◢ Directory structures (e.g. create folders, navigate directory structures		See *A+ Guide to Software*
◢ Files (e.g. creation, extensions, attributes, permissions)		See *A+ Guide to Software*

3.2 **Install, configure, optimize and upgrade operating systems—references to upgrading from Windows 95 and NT may be made**

OBJECTIVES	CHAPTERS	PAGE NUMBERS
Identify procedures for installing operating systems including:		
◢ Verification of hardware compatibility and minimum requirements	11	513–517 More content in *A+ Guide to Software*
◢ Installation methods (e.g. boot media such as CD, floppy or USB, network installation, drive imaging)	11	513–517 More content in *A+ Guide to Software*
◢ Operating system installation options (e.g. attended/unattended, file system type, network configuration)		See *A+ Guide to Software*
◢ Disk preparation order (e.g. start installation, partition and format drive)		See *A+ Guide to Software*
◢ Device driver configuration (e.g. install and upload device drivers)	8	310, 357–366 More content in *A+ Guide to Software*
◢ Verification of installation	8	310, 357–366 More content in *A+ Guide to Software*
Identify procedures for upgrading operating systems including:		
◢ Upgrade considerations (e.g. hardware, application and/or network compatibility)		See *A+ Guide to Software*
◢ Implementation (e.g. backup data, install additional Windows components)		See *A+ Guide to Software*
Install/add a device including loading, adding device drivers and required software including:		See *A+ Guide to Software*
◢ Determine whether permissions are adequate for performing the task	8	310, 357–366 More content in *A+ Guide to Software*
◢ Device driver installation (e.g. automated and/or manual search and installation of device drivers)	8, 11, 12	310, 357–366/590–594 More content in *A+ Guide to Software*

DOMAIN 5 NETWORKS

5.1 Identify the fundamental principles of networks

DOMAIN 7 SAFETY AND ENVIRONMENTAL ISSUES

7.1 Describe the aspects and importance of safety and environmental issues

OBJECTIVES	CHAPTERS	PAGE NUMBERS
Identify potential safety hazards and take preventative action	2, 11	38–39, 44–46/517–518, 549–550
Use Material Safety Data Sheets (MSDS) or equivalent documentation and appropriate equipment documentation	2	38–39
Use appropriate repair tools	2, 11	36–40/549–550
Describe methods to handle environmental and human (e.g. electrical, chemical, physical) accidents including incident reporting	2	38–39 More content in *A+ Guide to Software*

7.2 Identify potential hazards and implement proper safety procedures including ESD precautions and procedures, safe work environment and equipment handling | 2, 11 | 44–46, 49–54/549–550

7.3 Identify proper disposal procedures for batteries, display devices and chemical solvents and cans | 2 | 49

DOMAIN 8 PROFESSIONALISM AND COMMUNICATION

8.1 Use good communication skills, including listening and tact/discretion, when communication with customers and colleagues | 2 | 73–74 More content in *A+ Guide to Software*

OBJECTIVES	CHAPTERS	PAGE NUMBERS
Use clear, concise and direct statements		See *A+ Guide to Software*
Allow the customer to complete statements— avoid interrupting		See *A+ Guide to Software*
Clarify customer statements—ask pertinent questions		See *A+ Guide to Software*
Avoid using jargon, abbreviations and acronyms		See *A+ Guide to Software*
Listen to customers		See *A+ Guide to Software*

8.2 Use job-related professional behavior including privacy, confidentiality and respect for the customer and customers' property (e.g. telephone, computer)

OBJECTIVES	CHAPTERS	PAGE NUMBERS
Behavior		
◢ Maintain a positive attitude and tone of voice		See *A+ Guide to Software*
◢ Avoid arguing with customers and/or becoming defensive		See *A+ Guide to Software*
◢ Do not minimize costumers' problems		See *A+ Guide to Software*
◢ Avoid being judgmental and/or insulting or calling the customer names		See *A+ Guide to Software*
◢ Avoid distractions and/or interruptions when talking with customers		See *A+ Guide to Software*
Property		
◢ Telephone, laptop, desktop computer, printer, monitor, etc.		See *A+ Guide to Software*

CompTIA A+ 220-602
2006 Examination Objectives

DOMAIN 1 PERSONAL COMPUTER COMPONENTS

1.1   Install, configure, optimize and upgrade personal computer components

OBJECTIVES	CHAPTERS	PAGE NUMBERS
Add, remove and configure personal computer components including selection and installation of appropriate components for example:		
◢ Storage devices	7, 9	255–257, 276–293/ 406–432
◢ Motherboards	5	199–210
◢ Power supplies	3	117–122
◢ Processors/CPUs	4	130–131, 157–169
◢ Memory	6	231–243
◢ Display devices	8	322–341
◢ Input devices (e.g. basic, specialty and multimedia)	8	258–322
◢ Adapter cards	8, 9, 10	331–341, 358–366/ 382–393/497–501
◢ Cooling systems	3, 4	118–121/157–169

1.2   Identify tools, diagnostic procedures and troubleshooting techniques for personal computer components

OBJECTIVES	CHAPTERS	PAGE NUMBERS
Identify and apply basic diagnostic procedures and troubleshooting techniques	2, 5, 8, 10, 11, 12	72–83/212–213/ 366–374/497–501/ 539–542, 1060–565/ 617–629
◢ Isolate and identify the problem using visual and audible inspection of components and minimum configuration	2, 5, 8, 11, 11, 12	72–83/212–213/366–374/ 432–436/1060–565/ 617–629
Recognize and isolate issues with peripherals, multimedia, specialty input devices, internal and external storage and CPUs	2, 4, 7, 8, 9, 11, 12	72–83/167–169/294–304/ 366–374/432–436/ 1060–565/617–629
Identify the steps used to troubleshoot components (e.g. check proper seating, installation, appropriate component, settings and current driver) for example:		
◢ Power supply	2, 3, 11	72–83/115–122/1060–565
◢ Processor/CPUs and motherboards	2, 4, 5, 11	72–83/167–169/210–213/ 1060–565
◢ Memory	2, 6, 11	72–83/243–244/ 1060–565
◢ Adapter cards	2, 8, 9 10, 11	72–83/366–374/432–436 497–501/1060–565
◢ Display and input devices	2, 8, 11	72–83/366–374/ 1060–565
Recognize names, purposes, characteristics and appropriate application of tools for example:		
◢ Multi-meter	11	559–560
◢ Anti-static pad and wrist strap	2, 11	49–54/549–550
◢ Specialty hardware/tools	2, 11	36–40/549–550

◢ Loop back plugs	2	38
◢ Cleaning products (e.g. vacuum, cleaning pads)	2, 8, 9, 11, 12	36–40/314, 317, 314–368/ 417–418, 424/517–518/ 606–613

1.3   Perform preventative maintenance of personal computer components

OBJECTIVES	CHAPTERS	PAGE NUMBERS
Identify and apply common preventative maintenance techniques for personal computer components, for example:		
◢ Display devices (e.g. cleaning, ventilation)	2, 8, 11	44–48/366–374/ 517–518
◢ Power devices (e.g. appropriate source such as power strip, surge protector, ventilation and cooling)	2, 3, 11	44–48/107–111, 115–122/ 520–525
◢ Input devices (e.g. covers)	2, 8	44–48/314, 317, 366–368
◢ Storage devices (e.g. software tools such as DEFRAG and cleaning of optics and tape heads)	2, 9	38–39/417–418, 424 More content in *A+ Guide to Software*
◢ Thermally sensitive devices such as motherboards, CPUs, adapter cards, memory (e.g. cleaning, air flow)	2, 3, 4, 5, 11	44–48/115–122/153–156, 167–169/210–213/ 517–518

DOMAIN 2 LAPTOPS AND PORTABLE DEVICES

2.1   Identify fundamental principles of using laptops and portable devices

OBJECTIVES	CHAPTERS	PAGE NUMBERS
Identify appropriate applications for laptop-specific communication connections such as Bluetooth, infrared, cellular WAN and Ethernet	8, 10, 11	346–347/448–464/ 536–539
Identify appropriate laptop-specific power and electrical input devices and determine how amperage and voltage can affect performance	11	520–525
Identify the major components of the LCD including inverter, screen and video card	8, 11	322–328/549

2.2   Install, configure, optimize and upgrade laptops and portable devices

OBJECTIVES	CHAPTERS	PAGE NUMBERS
Removal of laptop-specific hardware such as peripherals, hot-swappable and non-hot-swappable devices	8, 11	349–358/527–536
Describe how video sharing affects memory upgrades	11	542–544

2.3   Use tools, diagnostic procedures and troubleshooting techniques for laptops and portable devices

OBJECTIVES	CHAPTERS	PAGE NUMBERS
Use procedures and techniques to diagnose power conditions, video, keyboard, pointer and wireless card issues for example:		
◢ Verify AC power (e.g. LEDs, swap AC adapter)	11	1060–565
◢ Verify DC power	11	1060–565
◢ Remove unneeded peripherals	11	1060–565
◢ Plug in external monitor	8, 11	366–374/1060–565
◢ Toggle Fn keys	8, 11	366–374/1060–565
◢ Check LCD cutoff switch	8, 11	366–374/1060–565
◢ Verify backlight functionality and pixilation	8, 11	366–374/1060–565
◢ Stylus issues (e.g. digitizer problems)	8, 11	366–374/1060–565
◢ Unique laptop keypad issues	8, 11	366–374/560–561
◢ Antenna wires	10, 11	481–491/556–558

DOMAIN 3 OPERATING SYSTEMS—UNLESS OTHERWISE NOTED, OPERATING SYSTEMS REFERRED WITH WITHIN INCLUDE MICROSOFT WINDOWS 2000, XP PROFESSIONAL, XP HOME AND MEDIA CENTER.

3.1   Identify the fundamental principles of operating systems

OBJECTIVES	CHAPTERS	PAGE NUMBERS
Use command-line functions and utilities to manage operating systems, including proper syntax and switches for example:		
◢ CMD		See *A+ Guide to Software*
◢ HELP		See *A+ Guide to Software*
◢ DIR		See *A+ Guide to Software*
◢ ATTRIB		See *A+ Guide to Software*
◢ EDIT		See *A+ Guide to Software*
◢ COPY		See *A+ Guide to Software*
◢ XCOPY		See *A+ Guide to Software*
◢ FORMAT		See *A+ Guide to Software*
◢ IPCONFIG	10	497–501 More content in *A+ Guide to Software*
◢ PING	10	497–501 More content in *A+ Guide to Software*
◢ MD / CD / RD		See *A+ Guide to Software*
Identify concepts and procedures for creating, viewing and managing disks, directories and files on operating systems		
◢ Disks (e.g. active, primary, extended and logical partitions and file systems including FAT32 and NTFS)		See *A+ Guide to Software*
◢ Directory structures (e.g. create folders, navigate directory structures)		See *A+ Guide to Software*
◢ Files (e.g. creation, attributes, permissions)		See *A+ Guide to Software*
Locate and use operating system utilities and available switches for example:		
◢ Disk Management Tools (e.g. DEGRAG, NTBACKUP, CHKDSK, Format)		See *A+ Guide to Software*
◢ System management tools		
• Device and Task Manager		See *A+ Guide to Software*
• MSCONFIG.EXE		See *A+ Guide to Software*
• REGEDIT.EXE		See *A+ Guide to Software*
• REGEDT32.EXE		See *A+ Guide to Software*
• CMD		See *A+ Guide to Software*
• Event Viewer		See *A+ Guide to Software*
• System Restore		See *A+ Guide to Software*
• Remote Desktop		See *A+ Guide to Software*
◢ File management tools (e.g. Windows Explorer, ATTRIB.EXE)		See *A+ Guide to Software*

3.2   Install, configure, optimize and upgrade operating systems—references to upgrading from Windows 95 and NT may be made

OBJECTIVES	CHAPTERS	PAGE NUMBERS
Identify procedures and utilities used to optimize operating systems for example:		
◢ Virtual memory		See *A+ Guide to Software*
◢ Hard drives (e.g. disk defragmentation)		See *A+ Guide to Software*
◢ Temporary files		See *A+ Guide to Software*

◢ Services   *See A+ Guide to Software*

◢ Startup   *See A+ Guide to Software*

◢ Application   *See A+ Guide to Software*

3.3 Identify tools, diagnostic procedures and troubleshooting techniques for operating systems

OBJECTIVES	CHAPTERS	PAGE NUMBERS
Demonstrate the ability to recover operating systems (e.g. boot methods, recovery console, ASR, ERD)		*See A+ Guide to Software*
Recognize and resolve common operational problems for example:		
◢ Windows specific printing problems (e.g. print spool stalled, incorrect/incompatible driver form print)	12	601–606, 617–623
◢ Auto-restart errors		*See A+ Guide to Software*
◢ Bluescreen error		*See A+ Guide to Software*
◢ System lock-up		*See A+ Guide to Software*
◢ Device drivers failure (input/output devices)	8, 12	349–354/601–606, 617–623 More content in *A+ Guide to Software*
◢ Application install, start or load failure		*See A+ Guide to Software*
Recognize and resolve common error messages and codes for example:		
◢ Boot (e.g. invalid boot disk, inaccessible boot drive, missing NTLDR)	7	303–304 More content in *A+ Guide to Software*
◢ Startup (e.g. device/service has failed to start, device/program in registry not found)		*See A+ Guide to Software*
◢ Event viewer		*See A+ Guide to Software*
◢ Registry		*See A+ Guide to Software*
◢ Windows reporting		*See A+ Guide to Software*
Use diagnostic utilities and tools to resolve operational problems for example:		
◢ Bootable media	11	513–517 More content in *A+ Guide to Software*
◢ Startup modes (e.g. safe mode, safe mode with command prompt or networking, step-by-step/single step mode)		*See A+ Guide to Software*
◢ Documentation resources (e.g. user/installation manuals, internet/web based, training materials)	11	513–517 More content in *A+ Guide to Software*
◢ Task and Device Manager	8	349–354 More content in *A+ Guide to Software*
◢ Event Viewer		*See A+ Guide to Software*
◢ MSCONFIG		*See A+ Guide to Software*
◢ Recover CD/Recovery partition	2, 11	37–38/513–517 More content in *A+ Guide to Software*
◢ Remote Desktop Connection and Assistance		*See A+ Guide to Software*
◢ System File Checker (SFC)		*See A+ Guide to Software*

3.4 Perform preventative maintenance for operating systems

OBJECTIVES	CHAPTERS	PAGE NUMBERS
Demonstrate the ability to perform preventative maintenance on operating systems including software and Windows updates (e.g. service packs), scheduled backups/restore, restore points		*See A+ Guide to Software*

DOMAIN 4 PRINTERS AND SCANNERS

4.1   Identify the fundamental principles of using printers and scanners

OBJECTIVES	CHAPTERS	PAGE NUMBERS
Describe processes used by printers and scanners including laser, ink dispersion, thermal, solid ink and impact printers and scanners	12	578–589

4.2   Install, configure, optimize and upgrade printers and scanners

OBJECTIVES	CHAPTERS	PAGE NUMBERS
Install and configure printers and scanners		
◢ Power and connect the device using local or network port	12	590–606
◢ Install and update device driver and calibrate the device	12	590–606
◢ Configure options and default settings	12	590–606
◢ Install and configure print drivers (e.g. PCL™, Postscript™, GDI)	12	590–606
◢ Validate compatibility with operating system and applications	12	590–606
◢ Educate user about basic functionality	12	590–606
Install and configure printer upgrades including memory and firmware	12	590–606
Optimize scanner performance including resolution, file format and default settings	12	590–606

4.3   Identify tools and diagnostic procedures to troubleshooting printers and scanners

OBJECTIVES	CHAPTERS	PAGE NUMBERS
Gather information about printer/scanner problems	12	606–629
Review and analyze collected data	12	606–629
Isolate and resolve identified printer/scanner problem including defining the cause, applying the fix and verifying functionality	12	606–629
Identify appropriate tools used for troubleshooting and repairing printer/scanner problems		
◢ Multi-meter	12	606–629
◢ Screw drivers	12	606–629
◢ Cleaning solutions	12	606–629
◢ Extension magnet	12	606–629
◢ Test patterns	12	606–629

4.4   Perform preventative maintenance of printers and scanners

OBJECTIVES	CHAPTERS	PAGE NUMBERS
Perform scheduled maintenance according to vendor guidelines (e.g., install maintenance kits, reset page counts)	12	606–629
Ensure a suitable environment	12	606–629
Use recommended supplies	2, 12	46–47/606–629

DOMAIN 5 NETWORKS

5.1   Identify the fundamental principles of networks

OBJECTIVES	CHAPTERS	PAGE NUMBERS
Identify names, purposes and characteristics of basic network protocols and terminologies for example:		
◢ ISP		See *A+ Guide to Software*
◢ TCP/IP (e.g. gateway, subnet mask, DNS, WINS, static and automatic address assignment)	10	466–472 More content in *A+ Guide to Software*

5.3   Identify tools and diagnostic procedures to troubleshoot network problems

OBJECTIVES	CHAPTERS	PAGE NUMBERS
Identify names, purposes and characteristics of tools for example:		
◢ Commands line tools (e.g. IPCONFIG.EXE, PING.EXE, TRACERT.EXE, NSLOOKUP.EXE)	10	497–501 More content in *A+ Guide to Software*
◢ Cable testing device	10	448–456
Diagnose and troubleshoot basic network issue for example:		
◢ Driver/network interface	10	497–501
◢ Protocol configuration	10	497–501 More content in *A+ Guide to Software*
• TCP/IP (e.g. gateway, subnet mask, DNS, WINS, static and automatic address assignment)	10	497–501 More content in *A+ Guide to Software*
• IPX/SPX (NWLink)	10	471–478
◢ Permissions		See *A+ Guide to Software*
◢ Firewall configuration		See *A+ Guide to Software*
◢ Electrical interference	10	497–501 More content in *A+ Guide to Software*

5.4   Perform preventative maintenance of networks including securing and protecting network cabling

OBJECTIVES	CHAPTERS	PAGE NUMBERS
	10	497–501

DOMAIN 6 SECURITY

6.1   Identify the fundamental principles of security

OBJECTIVES	CHAPTERS	PAGE NUMBERS
Identify the purposes and characteristics of access control for example:		
◢ Access to operating system (e.g. accounts such as user, admin and guest, groups, permission actions, types and levels), components, restricted spaces		See *A+ Guide to Software*
Identify the purposes and characteristics of auditing and event logging		See *A+ Guide to Software*

6.2   Install, configure, upgrade and optimize security

OBJECTIVES	CHAPTERS	PAGE NUMBERS
Install and configure software, wireless and data security for example:		
◢ Authentication technologies	8	319–322 More content in *A+ Guide to Software*
◢ Software firewalls		See *A+ Guide to Software*
◢ Auditing and event logging (enable/disable only)		See *A+ Guide to Software*
◢ Wireless client configuration	10	457–460, 481–491, 492–497 More content in *A+ Guide to Software* 481–491, 492–497
◢ Unused wireless connections	10	457–460, 481–491 492–497

⊿ Data access (e.g. permissions, basic local security policy)	See A+ *Guide to Software*
⊿ File systems (converting from FAT 32 to NTFS only)	See A+ *Guide to Software*

6.3 **Identify tools, diagnostic procedures and troubleshooting techniques for security**

OBJECTIVES	CHAPTERS	PAGE NUMBERS
Diagnose and troubleshoot software and data security issues for example:		
⊿ Software firewall issues		See A+ *Guide to Software*
⊿ Wireless client configuration issues	10	457–460, 481–491, 492–497
⊿ Data access issues (e.g. permissions, security policies)		See A+ *Guide to Software*
⊿ Encryption and encryption technology issues	10, 11	457–460, 481–491, 492–497/518–520 More content in A+ *Guide to Software*

6.4 **Perform preventative maintenance for security**

OBJECTIVES	CHAPTERS	PAGE NUMBERS
Recognize social engineering and address social engineering situations		See A+ *Guide to Software*

DOMAIN 7 SAFETY & ENVIRONMENTAL ISSUES

7.1 **Identify potential hazards and proper safety procedures including power supply, display devices and environment (e.g. trip, liquid, situational, atmospheric hazards and high-voltage and moving equipment)** — 2, 11 — 38–54/517–518

DOMAIN 8 PROFESSIONALISM AND COMMUNICATION

8.1 **Use good communication skills including listening and tact/discretion, when communicating with customers and colleagues**

OBJECTIVES	CHAPTERS	PAGE NUMBERS
Use clear, concise and direct statements		See A+ *Guide to Software*
Allow the customer to complete statements—avoid interrupting		See A+ *Guide to Software*
Clarify customer statements—ask pertinent questions		See A+ *Guide to Software*
Avoid using jargon, abbreviations and acronyms		See A+ *Guide to Software*
Listen to customers		See A+ *Guide to Software*

8.2 **Use job-related professional behavior including notation of privacy, confidentiality and respect for the customer and customers' property**

OBJECTIVES	CHAPTERS	PAGE NUMBERS
Behavior		
⊿ Maintain a positive attitude and tone of voice		See A+ *Guide to Software*
⊿ Avoid arguing with customers and/or becoming defensive		See A+ *Guide to Software*
⊿ Do not minimize customers' problems		See A+ *Guide to Software*
⊿ Avoid being judgmental and/or insulting or calling the customer names		See A+ *Guide to Software*
⊿ Avoid distractions and/or interruptions when talking with customers		See A+ *Guide to Software*
Property		
⊿ Telephone, laptop, desktop computer, printer, monitor, etc.		See A+ *Guide to Software*

CompTIA A+ 220-603
2006 Examination Objectives

DOMAIN 1 PERSONAL COMPUTER COMPONENTS

1.1   Install, configure, optimize, and upgrade personal computer components

OBJECTIVES	CHAPTERS	PAGE NUMBERS
Add, remove, and configure display devices and adapter cards including basic input and multimedia devices	8, 9, 10	310–322, 331–341, 357–366/382–393/497–501

1.2   Identify tools, diagnostic procedures, and troubleshooting techniques for personal computer components

OBJECTIVES	CHAPTERS	PAGE NUMBERS
Identify and apply basic diagnostic procedures and troubleshooting techniques, for example:	2, 5, 8, 11, 12	72–83/212–213/366–374/539–542, 558–565/617–629
▲ Identify and analyze the problem/potential problem	2, 3, 4, 5, 6, 7, 8, 9, 10, 11, 12	72–83/115–122/167–169/210–213/243–244/294–304/366–373/432–436/497–501/558–565 617–629
▲ Test related components and evaluate results	2, 3, 4, 5, 6, 8, 9, 10, 11, 12	72–83/115–122/167–169/210–213/243–244/366–373/432–436/497–501/558–565/617–629
▲ Identify additional steps to be taken if/when necessary	2, 3, 4, 5, 6, 8, 9, 10, 11	72–83/115–122/167–169/210–213/243–244/366–373/432–436/497–501/558–565
▲ Document activities and outcomes		See A+ Guide to Software
Recognize and isolate issues with display, peripheral, multimedia, specialty input device and storage	2, 3, 4, 5, 6, 7, 8, 9, 10, 11, 12	72–83/115–122/167–169/210–213/243–244/294–304/366–373/432–436/497–501/558–565/617–629
Apply steps in troubleshooting techniques to identify problems (e.g. physical environment, functionality and software/driver settings) with components including display, input devices and adapter cards	2, 3, 4, 5, 6, 8, 9, 10, 11, 12	72–83/115–122/167–169/210–213/243–244/366–373/432–436/497–501/558–565/617–629

1.3   Perform preventative maintenance on personal computer components

OBJECTIVES	CHAPTERS	PAGE NUMBERS
Identify and apply common preventative maintenance techniques for storage devices, for example:	2, 8, 11, 12	40–48/366–368/509–518/606–613, 616–617
▲ Software tools (e.g., Defrag, CHKDSK)		See A+ Guide to Software
▲ Cleaning (e.g., optics, tape heads)	2, 8, 9, 11, 12	36–40/314, 317/417–418, 424/509–518/606–613, 616–617

DOMAIN 2 OPERATING SYSTEMS—UNLESS OTHERWISE NOTED, OPERATING SYSTEMS REFERRED TO WITHIN INCLUDE MICROSOFT WINDOWS 2000, XP PROFESSIONAL, XP HOME AND MEDIA CENTER.

2.1   Identify the fundamental principles of using operating systems

OBJECTIVES	CHAPTERS	PAGE NUMBERS
Use command-line functions and utilities to manage Windows 2000, XP Professional and XP Home, including proper syntax and switches, for example:		
◢ CMD		See *A+ Guide to Software*
◢ HELP		See *A+ Guide to Software*
◢ DIR		See *A+ Guide to Software*
◢ ATTRIB		See *A+ Guide to Software*
◢ EDIT		See *A+ Guide to Software*
◢ COPY		See *A+ Guide to Software*
◢ XCOPY		See *A+ Guide to Software*
◢ FORMAT		See *A+ Guide to Software*
◢ IPCONFIG	10	497–501 More content in *A+ Guide to Software*
◢ PING	10	497–501 More content in *A+ Guide to Software*
◢ MD/CD/RD		See *A+ Guide to Software*
Identify concepts and procedures for creating, viewing, managing disks, directories and files in Windows 2000, XP Professional and XP Home, for example:		
◢ Disks (e.g. active, primary extended and logical partitions)		See *A+ Guide to Software*
◢ File systems (e.g. FAT 32, NTFS)		See *A+ Guide to Software*
◢ Directory structures (e.g. create folders, navigate directory structures)		See *A+ Guide to Software*
◢ Files (e.g. creation, extensions, attributes, permissions)		See *A+ Guide to Software*
Locate and use Windows 2000, XP Professional and XP Home utilities and available switches		
◢ Disk Management Tools (e.g. DEFRAG, NTBACKUP, CHKDSK, Format)		See *A+ Guide to Software*
◢ System Management Tools		
• Device and Task Manager		See *A+ Guide to Software*
• MSCONFIG.EXE		See *A+ Guide to Software*
• REGEDIT.EXE		See *A+ Guide to Software*
• REGEDT32.EXE		See *A+ Guide to Software*
• CMD		See *A+ Guide to Software*
• Event Viewer		See *A+ Guide to Software*
• System Restore		See *A+ Guide to Software*
• Remote Desktop		See *A+ Guide to Software*
◢ File Management Tools (e.g. Windows Explorer, ATTRIB.EXE)		See *A+ Guide to Software*

2.2   Install, configure, optimize and upgrade operating systems

OBJECTIVES	CHAPTERS	PAGE NUMBERS
Identify procedures and utilities used to optimize the performance of Windows 2000, XP Professional and XP Home, for example:		
◢ Virtual memory		See *A+ Guide to Software*
◢ Hard drives (i.e. disk defragmentation)		See *A+ Guide to Software*

◢ Temporary files | See *A+ Guide to Software*

◢ Services | See *A+ Guide to Software*

◢ Startup | See *A+ Guide to Software*

◢ Applications | See *A+ Guide to Software*

2.3 Identify tools, diagnostic procedures and troubleshooting techniques for operating systems

OBJECTIVES	CHAPTERS	PAGE NUMBERS
Recognize and resolve common operational problems, for example:		
◢ Windows-specific printing problems (e.g. print spool stalled, incorrect/incompatible driver form print)	12	601–606, 617–623
◢ Auto-restart errors		See *A+ Guide to Software*
◢ Bluescreen error		See *A+ Guide to Software*
◢ System lock-up		See *A+ Guide to Software*
◢ Device drivers failure (input/output devices)	8, 12	349–354/601–606, 617–623 More content in *A+ Guide to Software*
◢ Application install, start or load failure		See *A+ Guide to Software*
Recognize and resolve common error messages and codes, for example:		
◢ Boot (e.g. invalid boot disk, inaccessible boot device, missing NTLDR)	7	303–304 More content in *A+ Guide to Software*
◢ Startup (e.g. device/service has failed to start, device/program references in registry not found)		See *A+ Guide to Software*
◢ Event viewer		See *A+ Guide to Software*
◢ Registry		See *A+ Guide to Software*
◢ Windows		See *A+ Guide to Software*
Use diagnostic utilities and tools to resolve operational problems, for example:		
◢ Bootable media	11	513–517 More content in *A+ Guide to Software*
◢ Startup Modes (e.g. safe mode, safe mode with command prompt or networking, step-by-step/ single step mode)		See *A+ Guide to Software*
◢ Documentation resources (e.g. user/installation manuals, internet/web-based, training materials)	11	513–517 More content in *A+ Guide to Software*
◢ Task and Device Manager	8	349–354 More content in *A+ Guide to Software*
◢ Event Viewer		See *A+ Guide to Software*
◢ MSCONFIG		See *A+ Guide to Software*
◢ Recovery CD/Recovery partition	2, 11	37–38/513–517 More content in *A+ Guide to Software*
◢ Remote Desktop Connection and Assistance		See *A+ Guide to Software*
◢ System File Checker (SFC)		See *A+ Guide to Software*

2.4 Perform preventative maintenance for operating systems.

OBJECTIVES	CHAPTERS	PAGE NUMBERS
Perform preventative maintenance on Windows 2000, XP Professional and XP Home including software and Windows updates (e.g. service packs)		See *A+ Guide to Software*

DOMAIN 3 PRINTERS AND SCANNERS

3.1   Identify the fundamental principles of using printers and scanners

OBJECTIVES	CHAPTERS	PAGE NUMBERS
Describe processes used by printers and scanners including laser, ink dispersion, impact, solid ink and thermal printers.	12	578–589

3.2   **Install, configure, optimize and upgrade printers and scanners.**

OBJECTIVES	CHAPTERS	PAGE NUMBERS
Install and configure printers and scanners		
◢ Power and connect the device using network or local port	12	590–606
◢ Install/update the device driver and calibrate the devicei	12	590–606
◢ Configure options and default settings	12	590–606
◢ Install and configure print drivers (e.g. PCL™, Postscript™, and GDI)	12	590–606
◢ Validate compatibility with OS and applications	12	590–606
◢ Educate user about basic functionality	12	590–606
Optimize scanner performance for example: resolution, file format and default settings	12	590–606

3.3   **Identify tools, diagnostic procedures and troubleshooting techniques for printers and scanners**

OBJECTIVES	CHAPTERS	PAGE NUMBERS
Gather information required to troubleshoot printer/scanner problems	12	606–629
Troubleshoot a print failure (e.g. lack of paper, clear queue, restart print spooler, recycle power on printer, inspect for jams, check for visual indicators)	12	606–629

DOMAIN 4 NETWORKS

4.1   Identify the fundamental principles of networks

OBJECTIVES	CHAPTERS	PAGE NUMBERS
Identify names, purposes, and characteristics of the basic network protocols and terminologies, for example:		
◢ ISP		See *A+ Guide to Software*
◢ TCP/IP (e.g. Gateway, Subnet mask, DNS, WINS, Static and automatic address assignment)	10	466–472 More content in *A+ Guide to Software*
◢ IPX/SPX (NWLink)	10	466–472
◢ NETBEUI/NETBIOS	10	466–472
◢ SMTP		See *A+ Guide to Software*
◢ IMAP		See *A+ Guide to Software*
◢ HTML		See *A+ Guide to Software*
◢ HTTP		See *A+ Guide to Software*
◢ HTTPS		See *A+ Guide to Software*
◢ SSL		See *A+ Guide to Software*
◢ Telnet		See *A+ Guide to Software*
◢ FTP		See *A+ Guide to Software*
◢ DNS	10	466–472

Identify names, purposes, and characteristics of technologies for establishing connectivity, for example:		
◢ Dial-up networking	8	358–366 More content in *A+ Guide to Software*
◢ Broadband (e.g. DSL, cable, satellite)	10	444–464 More content in *A+ Guide to Software*
◢ ISDN Networking	10	444–464 More content in *A+ Guide to Software*
◢ Wireless	10	444–464 More content in *A+ Guide to Software*
◢ LAN/WAN	10	444–464 More content in *A+ Guide to Software*

4.2 Install, configure, optimize and upgrade networks

OBJECTIVES	CHAPTERS	PAGE NUMBERS
Establish network connectivity and share network resources	10, 11	471–478, 481–489/536–539 More content in *A+ Guide to Software*

4.3 Identify tools, diagnostic procedures and troubleshooting techniques for networks

OBJECTIVES	CHAPTERS	PAGE NUMBERS
Identify the names, purposes, and characteristics of command line tools, for example:		
◢ IPCONFIG.EXE	10	497–501 More content in *A+ Guide to Software*
◢ PING.EXE	10	497–501 More content in *A+ Guide to Software*
◢ TRACERT.EXE	10	497–501 More content in *A+ Guide to Software*
◢ NSLOOKUP.EXE	10	497–501 More content in *A+ Guide to Software*
Diagnose and troubleshoot basic network issues, for example:		
◢ Driver/network interface	10	497–501
◢ Protocol configuration	10	497–501 More content in *A+ Guide to Software*
• TCP/IP (e.g. Gateway, Subnet mask, DNS, WINS, static and automatic address assignment)	10	497–501 More content in *A+ Guide to Software*
• IPX/SPX (NWLink)		See *A+ Guide to Software*
◢ Permissions		See *A+ Guide to Software*
◢ Firewall configuration		See *A+ Guide to Software*
◢ Electrical interference	10	497–501 More content in *A+ Guide to Software*

DOMAIN 5 SECURITY

5.1 Identify the fundamental principles of security

OBJECTIVES	CHAPTERS	PAGE NUMBERS
Identify the names, purposes, and characteristics of access control and permissions		
◢ Accounts including user, admin and guest		See *A+ Guide to Software*
◢ Groups		See *A+ Guide to Software*
◢ Permission levels, types (e.g. file systems and shared) and actions (e.g. read, write, change and execute)		See *A+ Guide to Software*

5.2 Install, configure, optimizing and upgrade security

OBJECTIVES	CHAPTERS	PAGE NUMBERS
Install and configure hardware, software, wireless and data security, for example:		
◢ Smart card readers		See *A+ Guide to Software*
◢ Key fobs		See *A+ Guide to Software*
◢ Biometric devices	8	319–322 More content in *A+ Guide to Software*
◢ Authentication technologies	8, 11	319–322/518–520 More content in *A+ Guide to Software*
◢ Software firewalls	2	42–44 More content in *A+ Guide to Software*
◢ Auditing and event logging (enable/disable only)		See *A+ Guide to Software*
◢ Wireless client configuration	10	457–460, 481–491, 492–497 More content in *A+ Guide to Software*
◢ Unused wireless connections	10	457–460, 481–491, 492–497
◢ Data access (e.g. permissions, security policies)		See *A+ Guide to Software*
◢ Encryption and encryption technologies	10, 11	457–460, 481–491, 492–497/518–520 More content in *A+ Guide to Software*

5.3 Identify tools, diagnostic procedures and troubleshooting techniques for security issues

OBJECTIVES	CHAPTERS	PAGE NUMBERS
Diagnose and troubleshoot software and data security issues, for example:		
◢ Software firewall issues		See *A+ Guide to Software*
◢ Wireless client configuration issues	10	457–460, 481–491, 492–497
◢ Data access issues (e.g. permissions, security policies)		See *A+ Guide to Software*
◢ Encryption and encryption technologies issues	10, 11	457–460, 481–491, 492–497/518–520 More content in *A+ Guide to Software*

5.4 Perform preventative maintenance for security.

OBJECTIVES	CHAPTERS	PAGE NUMBERS
Recognize social engineering and address social engineering situations		See *A+ Guide to Software*

DOMAIN 6 PROFESSIONALISM AND COMMUNICATION

6.1   Use good communication skills, including listening and tact/discretion, when communicating with customers and colleagues

OBJECTIVES	CHAPTERS	PAGE NUMBERS
Use clear, concise and direct statements		See A+ *Guide to Software*
Allow the customer to complete statements— avoid interrupting		See A+ *Guide to Software*
Clarify customer statements—ask pertinent questions		See A+ *Guide to Software*
Avoid using jargon, abbreviations and acronyms		See A+ *Guide to Software*
Listen to customers		See A+ *Guide to Software*

6.2   Use job-related professional behavior including notation of privacy, confidentiality and respect for the customer and customers' property

	CHAPTERS	PAGE NUMBERS
		See A+ *Guide to Software*

CompTIA A+ 220-604
2006 Examination Objectives

DOMAIN 1 PERSONAL COMPUTER COMPONENTS

1.1   Install, configure, optimize and upgrade personal computer components.

OBJECTIVES	CHAPTERS	PAGE NUMBERS
Add, remove and configure internal storage devices, motherboards, power supplies, processor/CPUs, memory and adapter cards, including:		
◢ Drive preparation	7, 9, 11	290–291/428–432/546–549 More content in *A+ Guide to Software*
◢ Jumper configuration	7	255–257, 276–293
◢ Storage device power and cabling	7, 9	255–257, 276–293/ 406–432
◢ Selection and installation of appropriate motherboard	5	199–210
◢ BIOS set-up and configuration	5	188–202
◢ Selection and installation of appropriate CPU	4	130–131, 157–169
◢ Selection and installation of appropriate memory	6	231–243
◢ Installation of adapter cards including hardware and software/drivers	8, 9, 10	331–341, 357–366/ 382–393/497–501
◢ Configuration and optimization of adapter cards including adjusting hardware settings and obtaining network card connection	8, 9, 10	331–341, 357–366/ 382–393/497–501
Add, remove and configure cooling systems	3, 4	118–121/157–169

1.2   Identify tools, diagnostic procedures and troubleshooting techniques for personal computer components.

OBJECTIVES	CHAPTERS	PAGE NUMBERS
Identify and apply diagnostic procedures and troubleshooting techniques, for example:	2, 5, 8, 9, 11, 12	72–83/212–213/366–374/ 432–436/558–565/ 617–629
◢ Identify and isolate the problem using visual and audible inspection of components and minimum configuration	2, 5, 8, 9, 11, 12	72–83/212–213/366–374/ 432–436/558–565/ 617–629
Identify the steps used to troubleshoot components (e.g. check proper seating, installation, appropriate component, settings, current driver), for example:		
◢ Power supply	2, 3, 11	72–83/115–122/558–565
◢ Processor/CPUs and motherboards	2, 4, 7, 11	72–83/167–169/210–213/ 558–565
◢ Memory	2, 6, 11	72–83/243–244/ 558–565
◢ Adapter cards	2, 8, 9, 10, 11	72–83/366–374/432–436/ 497–501/558–565
Recognize names, purposes, characteristics and appropriate application of tools, for example:		
◢ Multi-meter	11	559–560
◢ Anti-static pad and wrist strap	2, 11	49–54/549–550
◢ Specialty hardware/tools	2, 11	36–40/549–550
◢ Loop back plugs	2	38
◢ Cleaning products (e.g. vacuum, cleaning pads)	2, 8, 9, 11, 12	36–40/314, 317, 366–368/ 417–418, 424/517–518/ 606–613

1.3 **Perform preventative maintenance of personal computer components.**

OBJECTIVES	CHAPTERS	PAGE NUMBERS
Identify and apply common preventive maintenance techniques, for example:		
◢ Thermally sensitive devices (e.g. motherboards CPUs, adapter cards, memory)	2, 3, 4, 5, 11	44–48/115–122/153–156, 167–169/210–213/ 517–518
• Cleaning	2, 8, 9, 11, 12	36–40/314, 317, 366–368/417–418, 424/ 517–518/606–613
• Air flow (e.g. slot covers, cable routing)	2, 3, 4, 7, 11	44–48/115–122/153–156, 167–169/210–213/ 517–518
◢ Adapter cards (e.g. driver/firmware updates)	2, 8, 9, 10, 11	44–48, 72–83/366–374/ 432–436/497–501/ 517–518, 558–565

DOMAIN 2 LAPTOPS AND PORTABLE DEVICES

2.1 **Identify the fundamental principles of using laptops and portable devices.**

OBJECTIVES	CHAPTERS	PAGE NUMBERS
Identify appropriate applications for laptop-specific communication connections, for example:		
◢ Bluetooth	8, 10, 11	346–347/448–464/ 536–539
◢ Infrared devices	8, 10, 11	346–347/448–464/ 536–539
◢ Cellular WAN	8, 10, 11	346–347/448–464/ 536–539
◢ Ethernet	8, 10, 11	346–347/448–464/ 536–539
Identify appropriate laptop-specific power and electrical input devices, for example: ◢ Output performance requirements for amperage and voltage	11	558–565
Identify the major components of the LCD (e.g. inverter, screen, video card)	8, 11	322–328/549

2.2 **Install, configure, optimize and upgrade laptops and portable devices.**

OBJECTIVES	CHAPTERS	PAGE NUMBERS
Demonstrate the safe removal of laptop-specific hardware including peripherals, hot-swappable and non hot-swappable devices	8, 11	349–358/527–536
Identify the affect of video sharing on memory upgrades	11	542–544

2.3 **Identify tools, diagnostic procedures and troubleshooting techniques for laptops and portable devices.**

OBJECTIVES	CHAPTERS	PAGE NUMBERS
Use procedures and techniques to diagnose power conditions, video issues, keyboard and pointer issues and wireless card issues, for example:		
◢ Verify AC power (e.g. LEDs, swap AC adapter)	11	558–565
◢ Verify DC power	11	558–565

DOMAIN 3 PRINTERS AND SCANNERS

3.1   Identify the fundamental principles of using printers and scanners.

3.2   Install, configure, optimize and upgrade printers and scanners.

3.3   Identify tools, diagnostic methods and troubleshooting procedures for printers and scanners.

3.4   Perform preventative maintenance of printer and scanner problems.

DOMAIN 4 SECURITY

4.1   Identify the names, purposes and characteristics of physical security devices and processes.

OBJECTIVES	CHAPTERS	PAGE NUMBERS
Control access to PCs, servers, laptops and restricted spaces		
⊿ Hardware		See *A+ Guide to Software*
⊿ Operating systems		See *A+ Guide to Software*

4.2   **Install hardware security**

OBJECTIVES	CHAPTERS	PAGE NUMBERS
Smart card readers		See *A+ Guide to Software*
Key fobs		See *A+ Guide to Software*
Biometric devices	8, 11	319–322/518–520 More content in *A+ Guide to Software*

DOMAIN 5 SAFETY AND ENVIRONMENTAL ISSUES

5.1   Identify potential hazards & proper safety procedures including power supply, display devices and environment (e.g. trip, liquid, situational, atmospheric hazards, high-voltage and moving equipment).

	CHAPTERS	PAGE NUMBERS
	2, 11	38–39, 44–46/ 517–518, 549–550 More content in *A+ Guide to Software*

Introduction CompTIA A+

A+ Guide to Hardware, Fourth Edition, was written to be the very best tool on the market today to prepare you to support personal computer hardware. Updated to include the most current technologies with expanded content on troubleshooting and PC repair fundamentals and a new chapter on processors and chipsets, this book takes you from the just-a-user level to the I-can-fix-this level for PC hardware matters. This book achieves its goals with an unusually effective combination of tools that powerfully reinforce both concepts and hands-on, real-world experiences. In combination with its companion book, *A+ Guide to Software, Fourth Edition,* these two books provide thorough preparation for the new 2006 CompTIA A+ Certification exams and the older (but still alive) CompTIA's 2003 A+ Certification exams. Competency in using a computer is a pre-requisite to using this book. No background knowledge of electronics is assumed. An appropriate pre-requisite course for this book would be a general course in microcomputer applications.

This book includes:

▲ **Comprehensive review and practice end-of-chapter material,** including a chapter summary, key terms, review questions, critical thinking questions, hands-on projects, and real-world problems to solve.

▲ **Step-by-step instructions** on installation, maintenance, optimization of system performance, and troubleshooting.

▲ **Video clips** featuring Jean Andrews illustrating key points from the text to aid your understanding of the material.

▲ **A wide array of photos, drawings, and screen shots** support the text, displaying in detail the exact hardware and software features you will need to understand to manage and maintain your PC.

▲ **Several in-depth, hands-on projects** at the end of each chapter designed to make certain that you not only understand the material, but also execute procedures and make decisions on your own.

In addition, the carefully structured, clearly written text is accompanied by graphics that provide the visual input essential to learning. For instructors using the book in a classroom, a special CD-ROM is available that includes an Instructor's Manual, an Online Testing system, and a PowerPoint presentation.

Coverage is balanced—while focusing on new hardware and software, the text also covers the real work of PC repair, where some older technology remains in widespread use and still needs support. For example, the book covers all the PCI and PCI Express expansion slot technologies, but also addresses using AGP and ISA expansion slots because many systems with AGP and ISA slots are still in use.

This book together with its companion book, *A+ Guide to Software,* provide thorough preparation for CompTIA's A+ 2006 and 2003 Certification examinations and the two books in tandem map completely to these new and older exam objectives. This certification credential's popularity among employers is growing exponentially, and obtaining certifi-cation increases your ability to gain employment and improve your salary. To get more information on A+ certification and its sponsoring organization, the Computing Technology Industry Association, see their Web site at *www.comptia.org.*

FEATURES

To ensure a successful learning experience, this book includes the following pedagogical features:

- ◢ **Learning Objectives:** Every chapter opens with a list of learning objectives that sets the stage for you to absorb the lessons of the text.
- ◢ **Comprehensive Step-by-Step Troubleshooting Guidance:** Troubleshooting guidelines are included in almost every chapter. In addition, Chapter 2 gives insights into general approaches to troubleshooting that help apply the specifics detailed in each chapter for different hardware problems.
- ◢ **Step-by-Step Procedures:** The book is chock-full of step-by-step procedures covering subjects from hardware installation and maintenance to troubleshooting hardware subsystems.
- ◢ **Art Program:** Numerous detailed photographs, three-dimensional art, and screenshots support the text, displaying hardware features exactly as you will see them in your work.
- ◢ **CompTIA A+ Table of Contents:** This table of contents indicates every page that relates to each certification objective. You'll find mapping grids for both the 2006 and 2003 objectives. This is a valuable tool for quick reference. (CompTIA has announced that the 2003 exams will stay live until June, 2007, and the 2006 exams are expected to go live by the time this book is in print.). The mapping grids for all of the CompTIA A+ 2006 objectives (CompTIA A+ Essentials, CompTIA A+ 220-602, CompTIA A+ 220-603, and CompTIA A+ 220-604) are placed here in the front of the book. The mapping grids for the CompTIA A+ 2003 objectives are placed on the accompanying CD.
- ◢ **Applying Concepts:** These sections offer practical applications for the material being discussed. Whether outlining a task, developing a scenario, or providing pointers, the Applying Concepts sections give you a chance to apply what you've learned to a typical PC problem.

 **Notes:** Note icons highlight additional helpful information related to the subject being discussed.

 **A+ Icons:** All of the content that relates to CompTIA's A+ 2006 Essentials and 220-602 Certification exams, whether it's a page or a sentence, is highlighted with an A+ icon. The icon notes the exam name and the objective number. This unique feature highlights the relevant content at a glance, so you can pay extra attention to the material.

 **A+ Exam Tip Boxes:** These boxes highlight additional insights and tips to remember if you are planning to take the CompTIA A+ Exams.

 **Caution Icons:** These icons highlight critical safety information. Follow these instructions carefully to protect the PC and its data and to ensure your own safety.

 **Video Clips:** Short video passages reinforce concepts and techniques discussed in the text, and offer insight into the life of a PC repair technician.

 End-of-Chapter Material: Each chapter closes with the following features, which reinforce the material covered in the chapter and provide real-world, hands-on testing:

 Chapter Summary: This bulleted list of concise statements summarizes all major points of the chapter.

 Key Terms: The content of each chapter is further reinforced by an end-of-chapter key-term list. The definitions of all terms are included at the end of the book in a full-length glossary.

Review Questions: You can test your understanding of each chapter with a comprehensive set of review questions. The "Reviewing the Basics" questions check your understanding of fundamental concepts, while the "Thinking Critically" questions help you synthesize and apply what you've learned.

 Hands-On Projects: You get to test your real-world understanding with hands-on projects involving a full range of software and hardware problems. Each hands-on activity in this book is preceded by the Hands-On icon and a description of the exercise that follows.

 Real World, Real Problems: Each comprehensive problem allows you to find out if you can apply what you've learned in the chapter to a real-life situation.

CD Resource Pak: The CD placed in the book includes video clips which features Jean Andrews illustrating key concepts in the text and providing advice on the real world of PC repair. Other helpful tools on the CD include mapping grids to the CompTIA A+ 2003 exams, Frequently Asked Questions, Sample Reports, Troubleshooting Flowcharts, and an electronic Glossary.

 Web Site: For additional content and updates to this book and information about our complete line of CompTIA A+ and PC Repair topics, please visit our Web site at *www.course.com/pcrepair.*

INSTRUCTOR RESOURCES

The following supplemental materials are available when this book is used in a classroom setting. All of the supplements available with this book are provided to the instructor on a single CD-ROM.

Electronic Instructor's Manual: The Instructor's Manual that accompanies this textbook includes additional instructional material to assist in class preparation, including suggestions for classroom activities, discussion topics, and additional projects.

Solutions: Answers to the end-of-chapter material are provided. These include the answers to the Review Questions and to the Hands-On Projects (when applicable).

ExamView®: This textbook is accompanied by ExamView, a powerful testing software package that allows instructors to create and administer printed, computer (LAN-based), and Internet exams. ExamView includes hundreds of questions that correspond to the topics covered in this text, enabling students to generate detailed study guides that include page references for further review. The computer-based and Internet testing components allow students to take exams at their computers, and also save the instructor time by grading each exam automatically.

PowerPoint Presentations: This book comes with Microsoft PowerPoint slides for each chapter. These are included as a teaching aid for classroom presentation, to make available to students on the network for chapter review, or to be printed for classroom distribution. Instructors, please feel at liberty to add your own slides for additional topics you introduce to the class.

Figure Files: All of the figures in the book are reproduced on the Instructor Resource CD, in bit-mapped format. Similar to the PowerPoint presentations, these are included as a teaching aid for classroom presentation, to make available to students for review, or to be printed for classroom distribution.

Daily Lesson Planner: This free teaching tool enables instructors to use our CompTIA A+ products with even greater ease. It includes detailed lecture notes and teaching instructions that incorporate all of the components of the CompTIA A+ Total Solutions. A user name and password are required for download. The Daily Lesson Planner is available on the Instructor's CD and online at *www.course.com/pcrepair*.

ACKNOWLEDGMENTS

Thank you to the wonderful people at Thomson Course Technology who continue to provide support, warm encouragement, patience, and guidance: Nick Lombardi, Michelle Ruelos Cannistraci, and Summer Hughes. You've truly helped make this fourth edition fun! Thank you, Jill Batistick, Developmental Editor, for your careful attention to detail and your genuine friendship, and to Karen Annett, our excellent copy editor. Thank you, Susan Whalen and Serge Palladino, for your careful attention to the technical accuracy of the book. Thank you Abigail Reip for your research efforts.

Thank you to all the people who took the time to voluntarily send encouragement and suggestions for improvements to the previous editions. Your input and help is very much appreciated. The reviewers all provided invaluable insights and showed a genuine interest in the book's success. Thank you to:

Paul J. Bartoszewicz, Hudson Valley Community College, Troy, NY
Steve Belville, Bryant & Stratton, Milwaukee, MI
Keith Conn, Cleveland Institute of Electronics, Cleveland, OH
Kevin Crawford, Community College of Rhode Island
Chuck Lund, Central Lakes College, Brainerd, MN
Erik Schmid, The Chubb Institute, Cherry Hill, NJ

Thank you to Joy Dark who was here with me making this book happen. I'm very grateful.

This book is dedicated to the covenant of God with man on earth.

Jean Andrews, Ph.D.

PHOTO CREDITS

Figure 1-16	Courtesy of Seagate Technologies LLC
Figure 2-3	Courtesy of Smith Micro Software, Inc.
Figure 2-6	Courtesy of postcodemaster.com
Figure 3-10	Courtesy of Acqutek Corporation
Figure 3-11	Courtesy of Acqutek Corporation
Figure 3-21	Courtesy of Tripp Lite
Figure 4-7	Courtesy of Intel Corporation
Figure 4-9	Courtesy of Intel Corporation
Figure 4-10	Courtesy of AMD
Figure 4-11	Courtesy of VIA Technologies, Inc.
Figure 4-12	Courtesy of Intel Corporation
Figure 4-20	Courtesy of Thermaltake
Figure 5-4	Courtesy of Intel Corporation
Figure 7-7	Courtesy of Y-E Data Inc
Figure 7-19	Courtesy of Addonics
Figure 7-27	Courtesy of Belkin Corporation
Figure 7-31	Courtesy of SmartDisk Corporation

Figure 8-1	Courtesy of Microsoft Corporation
Figure 8-2	Steve Kahn Photography
Figure 8-6a	Courtesy of Microsoft Corporation
Figure 8-6b	Courtesy of Microsoft Corporation
Figure 8-6c	Courtesy of Acer America Inc.
Figure 8-11	Courtesy of Symbol Technologies, Inc.
Figure 8-12	Courtesy of Panasonic
Figure 8-13a	Courtesy of Microsoft Corporation
Figure 8-13b	Courtesy of Microsoft Corporation
Figure 8-21	Courtesy of Panasonic
Figure 8-22	Courtesy of ATI Technologies, Inc.
Figure 8-25	Courtesy of Belkin Corporation
Figure 8-28	MSI Computer Corporation
Figure 8-29	Courtesy of Vantec Thermal Technologies
Figure 8-40	Courtesy of Belkin Corporation
Figure 8-51	Courtesy of ADS Technology
Figure 8-55	Courtesy of Zoom Technologies
Table 9-3a	Courtesy of SanDisk Corporation
Table 9-3b	Courtesy of SanDisk Corporation
Table 9-3c	Courtesy of SanDisk Corporation
Table 9-3d	Courtesy of SanDisk Corporation
Table 9-3e	Courtesy of SanDisk Corporation
Table 9-3f	Courtesy of Hitachi Global Storage Technologies
Table 9-3g	Courtesy of SanDisk Corporation
Table 9-3h	Courtesy of SanDisk Corporation
Table 9-3i	Courtesy of SanDisk Corporation
Table 9-3j	Courtesy of SanDisk Corporation
Figure 9-18	PRNewsFoto/XM Satellite Radio
Figure 9-20	Courtesy of Turtle Beach/ Courtesy of Hosa Technology, Inc. www.hosatech.com
Figure 9-21	Courtesy of Yamaha Corporation of America
Figure 9-24	Courtesy of AVerMedia Technologies, Inc. USA
Figure 9-25	Courtesy of Hauppauge Computer Works, Inc.
Figure 9-36	Courtesy of Plextor Corporation
Figure 9-40	Courtesy of Quantum Corporation
Figure 9-43	Courtesy of Maxell Corporation of America
Figure 9-44	Courtesy of Quantum Corporation
Figure 9-45	Courtesy of Hewlett-Packard Company
Figure 9-49	Courtesy of Iomega
Table 10-2a	Courtesy of Cables4Computer.com
Table 10-2b	Courtesy of Black Box Corporation
Table 10-2c	Courtesy of Tyco Electronics
Table 10-2d	Courtesy of Black Box Corporation
Figure 10-5a	Courtesy of Fiber Communications, Inc. (www.fiberc.com)
Figure 10-5b	Courtesy of Fiber Communications, Inc. (www.fiberc.com)
Figure 10-5c	Courtesy of Fiber Communications, Inc. (www.fiberc.com)
Figure 10-5d	Courtesy of Fiber Communications, Inc. (www.fiberc.com)
Figure 10-18	Courtesy of Tekkeon, Inc.
Figure 10-23	Courtesy of 3Com
Figure 10-24	Courtesy of 3Com
Figure 10-61	Courtesy of D-Link Corporation

Most of the other photos are courtesy of Joy Dark and Jennifer Dark.

READ THIS BEFORE YOU BEGIN

The following hardware, software, and other equipment are needed to do the Hands-on Projects in each chapter:

- ◢ You need a working PC that can be taken apart and reassembled. Use a Pentium or equivalent computer.
- ◢ Troubleshooting skills can better be practiced with an assortment of nonworking expansion cards that can be used to simulate problems.
- ◢ Equipment required to work on hardware includes a grounding mat and grounding strap and flat-head and Phillips-head screwdrivers. A multimeter is needed for Appendix B projects.
- ◢ Before undertaking any of the lab exercises, starting with Chapter 2, please review the safety guidelines in the next section.

 This icon highlights critical safety information. Follow these instructions carefully for your own safety.

PROTECT YOURSELF, YOUR HARDWARE, AND YOUR SOFTWARE

When you work on a computer, it is possible to harm both the computer and yourself. The most common accident that happens when attempting to fix a computer problem is erasing software or data. Experimenting without knowing what you are doing can cause damage. To prevent these sorts of accidents, as well as the physically dangerous ones, take a few safety precautions. The text below describes the potential sources of damage and danger and how to protect against them.

POWER TO THE COMPUTER

To protect both yourself and the equipment when working inside a computer, turn off the power, unplug the computer, and always use a grounding bracelet as described in Chapter 3. Consider the monitor and the power supply to be "black boxes." Never remove the cover or put your hands inside this equipment unless you know about the hazards of charged capacitors. Both the power supply and the monitor can hold a dangerous level of electricity even after they are turned off and disconnected from a power source.

PROTECT AGAINST ESD

To protect the computer against electrostatic discharge (ESD), commonly known as static electricity, always ground yourself before touching electronic components, including the hard drive, motherboard, expansion cards, processors, and memory modules. Ground yourself and the computer parts, using one or more of the following static control devices or methods:

- ◢ **Ground bracelet or static strap:** A ground bracelet is a strap you wear around your wrist. To protect components against ESD, the other end is attached to a grounded conductor such as the computer case or a ground mat.

◢ **Ground mats:** Ground mats can come equipped with a cord to plug into a wall outlet to provide a grounded surface on which to work. Remember, if you lift the component off the mat, it is no longer grounded and is susceptible to ESD.

◢ **Static shielding bags:** New components come shipped in static shielding bags. Save the bags to store other devices that are not currently installed in a PC.

The best solution to protect against ESD is to use a ground bracelet together with a ground mat. Consider a ground bracelet to be essential equipment when working on a computer. However, if you find yourself in a situation without one, touch the computer case before you touch a component. When passing a chip to another person, touch the other person first so that ESD is discharged between you and the other person before you pass the chip. Leave components inside their protective bags until ready to use. Work on hard floors, not carpet, or use antistatic spray on the carpets. Generally, don't work on a computer if you or the computer have just come inside from the cold.

When working inside older computers using the AT form factor, you can turn off the computer and leave the computer plugged in. However, for today's computers using the ATX or BTX form factor, it is best to unplug the computer from the wall outlet before you open the case.

There is an exception to the ground-yourself rule. Inside a monitor case, there is substantial danger posed by the electricity stored in capacitors. When working inside a monitor, you *don't* want to be grounded, as you would provide a conduit for the voltage to discharge through your body. In this situation, be careful *not* to ground yourself.

When handling motherboards and expansion cards, don't touch the chips on the boards. Don't stack boards on top of each other, which could accidentally dislodge a chip. Hold cards by the edges, but don't touch the edge connections on the card.

Don't touch a chip with a magnetized screwdriver. When using a multimeter to measure electricity, be careful not to touch a chip with the probes. When changing DIP switches, don't use a graphite pencil, because graphite conducts electricity; a very small screwdriver works very well.

After you unpack a new device or software that has been wrapped in cellophane, remove the cellophane from the work area quickly. Don't allow anyone who is not properly grounded to touch components. Do not store expansion cards within one foot of a monitor, because the monitor can discharge as much as 29,000 volts of ESD onto the screen.

Hold an expansion card by the edges. Don't touch any of the soldered components on a card. If you need to put an electronic device down, place it on a grounded mat, inside a static shielding bag, or on a flat, hard surface. Keep components away from your hair and clothing.

PROTECT HARD DRIVES AND DISKS

Always turn off a computer before moving it, to protect the hard drive, which is always spinning when the computer is turned on (unless the drive has a sleep mode). Never jar a computer while the hard disk is running. Avoid placing a PC on the floor, where the user can accidentally kick it.

Follow the usual precautions to protect CD and DVD discs and floppy disks. Keep CDs and DVDs away from heat, direct sunlight, and extreme cold, and protect them from scratches. Protect floppy disks from magnetic fields. Don't open the floppy shuttle window or touch the surface of the disk inside the housing. Treat disks with care and they'll generally last for years.

COMPTIA AUTHORIZED CURRICULUM PROGRAM

The logo of the CompTIA Authorized Curriculum Program and the status of this or other training material as "Authorized" under the CompTIA Authorized Curriculum Program signifies that, in CompTIA's opinion, such training material covers the content of the CompTIA's related certification exam. CompTIA has not reviewed or approved the accuracy of the contents of this training material and specifically disclaims any warranties of merchantability or fitness for a particular purpose. CompTIA makes no guarantee concerning the success of persons using any such "Authorized" or other training material in order to prepare for any CompTIA certification exam.

The contents of this training material were created for the CompTIA A+ 2006 certification exams.

STATE OF THE INFORMATION TECHNOLOGY (IT) FIELD

Most organizations today depend on computers and information technology to improve business processes, productivity, and efficiency. Opportunities to become global organizations and reach customers, businesses, and suppliers are a direct result of the widespread use of the Internet. Changing technology further changes how companies do business. This fundamental change in business practices has increased the need for skilled and certified IT workers across industries. This transformation has moved many IT workers out of traditional IT businesses and into various IT-dependent industries such as banking, government, insurance, and healthcare.

In the year 2004, the U.S. Department of Labor, Bureau of Labor Statistics, reported that there were 1.1 million computer and data processing services jobs within organizations and an additional 132,000 self-employed workers.

In any industry, the workforce is important to continuously drive business. Having correctly skilled workers in IT is a struggle with the ever-changing technologies. It has been estimated that technologies change approximately every 2 years. With such a quick product life cycle, IT workers must strive to keep up with these changes to continue to bring value to their employer.

CERTIFICATIONS

Different levels of education are required for the many jobs in the IT industry. Additionally, the level of education and type of training required varies from employer to employer, but the need for qualified technicians remains constant. As technology changes and advances in the industry continue to rapidly evolve, many employers consistently look for employees that possess the skills necessary to implement these new technologies. Traditional degrees and diplomas do not identify the skills that a job applicant has. With the growth of the IT industry, companies increasingly rely on technical certifications to identify the skills a particular job applicant possesses. Technical certifications are a way for employers to ensure the quality and skill qualifications of their computer professionals, and they can offer job seekers a competitive edge. According to Thomas Regional Industrial Market Trends, one of the 15 trends that will transform the workplace over the next decade is a severe labor and skill shortage, specifically in technical fields, which are struggling to locate skilled and educated workers.

There are two types of certifications, vendor neutral and vendor specific. Vendor neutral certifications are those that test for the skills and knowledge required in specific industry job roles and do not subscribe to a specific vendor's technology solution. Vendor neutral certifications include all of the Computing Technology Industry Association's (CompTIA) certifications, Project Management Institute's certifications, and Security Certified Program certifications. Vendor specific certifications validate the skills and knowledge necessary to be successful by utilizing a specific vendor's technology solution. Some examples of vendor specific certifications include those offered by Microsoft, IBM, Novell, and Cisco.

As employers struggle to fill open IT positions with qualified candidates, certifications are a means of validating the skill sets necessary to be successful within an organization. In most careers, salary and compensation are determined by experience and education, but in IT, the number and type of certifications an employee earns also factors into salary and wage increases. The Department of Labor, Bureau of Labor Statistics, reported that the computer and data processing industry is expected to grow about 40% by the year 2014, compared to a 14% increase in the entire economy.

Certifications provide job applicants with more than just a competitive edge over their non-certified counterparts who apply for the same IT positions. Some institutions of higher education grant college credit to students who successfully pass certification exams, moving them further along in their degree programs. Certifications also give individuals who are interested in careers in the military the ability to move into higher positions more quickly. And many advanced certification programs accept, and sometimes require, entry-level certifications as part of their exams. For example, Cisco and Microsoft accept some CompTIA certifications as prerequisites for their certification programs.

CAREER PLANNING

Finding a career that fits a person's personality, skill set, and lifestyle is challenging and fulfilling, but can often be difficult. What are the steps individuals should take to find that dream career? Is IT interesting to you? Chances are that if you are reading this book, this question has been answered. What about IT do you like? The world of work in the IT industry is vast. Some questions to ask include the following: Are you a person who likes to work alone, or do you like to work in a group? Do you like speaking directly with customers or do you prefer to stay behind the scenes? Is your lifestyle conducive to a lot of travel, or do you need to stay in one location? All of these factors influence your decision when faced with choosing the right job. Inventory assessments are a good first step to learning more about your interests, work values, and abilities. There are a variety of Web sites that offer assistance with career planning and assessments.

The Computing Technology Industry Association (CompTIA) hosts an informational Web site called the TechCareer Compass™ (TCC) that defines careers in the IT industry. The TCC is located at *tcc.comptia.org*. This Web site was created by the industry and outlines over 100 industry jobs. Each defined job includes a job description, alternate job titles, critical work functions, activities and performance indicators, and skills and knowledge required by the job. In other words, it shows exactly what the job entails so that you can find one that best fits your interests and abilities. Additionally, the TCC maps over 750 technical certifications to the skills required by each specific job, allowing you to research and plan your certification training. The Web site also includes a resource section, which is updated regularly with articles and links to other career Web sites. The TechCareer Compass is the one-stop location for IT career information.

In addition to CompTIA's TechCareer Compass, there are many other Web sites that cover components of IT careers and career planning. Many of these sites can also be found in the TCC Resources section. Some of these other career planning sites include *YourITFuture.com*, *ITCompass.net*, and *About.com*.

CITATION

Bureau of Labor Statistics, U.S. Department of Labor. *Career Guide to Industries, 2006-7 Edition, Computer and Data Processing Services.* On the Internet at http://www.bls.gov/oco/cg/cgs033.htm (visited September 6, 2006).

Bureau of Labor Statistics, U.S. Department of Labor, *Occupational Outlook Handbook, 2006-7 Edition, Computer Support Specialists and System Administrators.* On the internet at http://www.bls.gov/oco/home.htm (visited September 3, 2006).

Thomas Regional Industrial Market Trends. July 8, 2003 Newsletter: *15 Trends that Will Transform the Workforce.* On the Internet at http://www.thomasregional.com/ newsarchive2.html?us=3f61ed4162269&to=5&from=0&id=1057266649 (visited September 3, 2006).

WHAT'S NEW WITH COMPTIA A+ CERTIFICATION

In June 2006, CompTIA *(www.comptia.org)* published the objectives for the 2006 CompTIA A+ Certification exams. These exams go live in September 2006. However, you can still become CompTIA A+ certified by passing the older 2003 exams that are to remain live until the end of 2006 and, in some educational environments, until June 2007. The 2003 exams consist of two exams: the CompTIA A+ Core Hardware Service Technician exam and the CompTIA A+ Operating System Technologies exam. You must past both exams to become CompTIA A+ certified. Content on hardware and operating systems on these two hardware and OS exams does not overlap, except for a few instances. Most students have found it convenient to study for one exam and pass it before preparing for the other exam.

The format of the 2006 exams is new. Here are the key facts regarding these exams:

- Currently, there are four 2006 exams. Everyone must pass the CompTIA A+ Essentials exam. You must also pass one of three advanced exams, which are named the CompTIA A+ 220-602 exam, the CompTIA A+ 220-603 exam, and the CompTIA A+ 220-604 exam.
- All four exams cover the same content, which includes both hardware and software. The advanced exams cover the content in a greater depth than does the CompTIA A+ Essentials exam.
- The CompTIA A+ 220-602 exam is the most comprehensive of the three advanced exams. Basically, the CompTIA A+ 220-603 and CompTIA A+ 220-604 exams are subsets of the CompTIA A+ 220-602 exam.
- The type of CompTIA A+ Certification you receive depends on which of the three advanced exams you pass, as diagrammed in Figure 1.
- By passing the CompTIA A+ 220-602 and CompTIA A+ Essentials exams, you are awarded the CompTIA A+ Certification for IT Technician. This certification targets those who intend to work in a "mobile or corporate technical environment with a high level of face-to-face client interaction." Job roles include IT administrator, enterprise technician, field service technician, and PC support technician.
- By passing the CompTIA A+ 220-603 and CompTIA A+ Essentials exams, you are awarded the CompTIA A+ Certification for Remote Support Technician. This certification targets those who intend to work "in a remote-based work environment where client interaction, client training, operating system and connectivity issues are emphasized." Job roles include help desk technician, remote support technician, and call center technician.

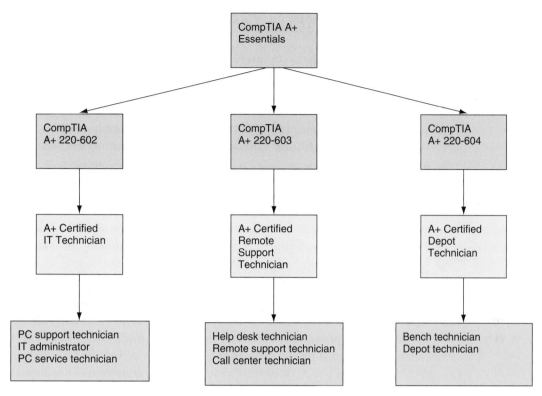

Figure 1 Paths to CompTIA A+ Certification and job roles

◢ By passing the CompTIA A+ 220-604 and CompTIA A+ Essentials exams, you are awarded the CompTIA A+ Certification for Depot Technician. This certification targets those who intend to work in settings where hardware is emphasized. Job roles include bench technician and depot technician.

All of the four 2006 A+ exams contain content on both hardware and software. Basically, the hardware content for all four exams is contained in this book and the software content for all four exams is contained in the companion book, *A+ Guide to Software*. Here is a breakdown of the domains covered on each of the four exams:

Domain	CompTIA A+ Essentials	CompTIA A+ 220-602	CompTIA A+ 220-603	CompTIA A+ 220-604
1.0 Personal Computer Components	21%	18%	15%	45%
2.0 Laptop and Portable Devices	11%	9%	0	20%
3.0 Operating Systems	21%	20%	29%	0
4.0 Printers and Scanners	9%	14%	10%	20%
5.0 Networks	12%	11%	11%	0
6.0 Security	11%	8%	15%	5%
7.0 Safety and Environmental Issues	10%	5%	0	10%
8.0 Communication and Professionalism	5%	15%	20%	0

HOW TO BECOME COMPTIA CERTIFIED

This training material can help you prepare for and pass a related CompTIA certification exam or exams. In order to achieve CompTIA certification, you must register for and pass a CompTIA certification exam or exams. In order to become CompTIA certified, you must:

1. Select a certification exam provider. For more information please visit the following Web site: *www.comptia.org/certification/general_information/test_locations.asp*.

2. Register for and schedule a time to take the CompTIA certification exam(s) at a convenient location.

3. Read and sign the Candidate Agreement, which will be presented at the time of the exam(s). The text of the Candidate Agreement can be found at the following Web site: *www.comptia.org/certification/general_information/candidate_agreement.asp*.

4. Take and pass the CompTIA certification exam(s).

For more information about CompTIA's certifications, such as their industry acceptance, benefits, or program news, please visit *www.comptia.org/certification/default.asp*.

CompTIA is a non-profit information technology (IT) trade association. CompTIA's certifications are designed by subject matter experts from across the IT industry. Each CompTIA certification is vendor-neutral, covers multiple technologies, and requires demonstration of skills and knowledge widely sought after by the IT industry.

To contact CompTIA with any questions or comments, call + 1 630 678 8300 or send an email to *questions@comptia.org*.

Hardware Needs Software to Work

In this chapter, you will learn:

- That a computer requires both hardware and software to work
- About the many different hardware components inside of and connected to a computer

Like millions of other computer users, you have probably used your desktop or notebook computer to play games, surf the Web, write papers, or build spreadsheets. You can use all these applications without understanding exactly what goes on inside your computer case or notebook. But if you are curious to learn more about personal computers, and if you want to graduate from simply being the end user of your computer to becoming the master of your machine, then this book is for you. It is written for anyone who wants to understand what is happening inside the machine, in order to install new hardware and software, diagnose and solve both hardware and software problems, and make decisions about purchasing new hardware and operating systems. The only assumption made here is that you are a computer user—that is, you can turn on your machine, load a software package, and use that software to accomplish a task. No experience in electronics is assumed.

In addition, this book prepares you to pass the hardware-related content of the A+ Essentials exam and any one of the advanced exams (the A+ 220-602, the A+ 220-603, or the A+ 220-604) required by CompTIA (*www.comptia.org*) for A+ Certification. At the time this book went to print, the older 2003 A+ exams were still live; therefore, the book also includes the content on the 2003 A+ Core Hardware Service Technician exam. Its companion book, *A+ Guide to Software: Managing, Maintaining, and Troubleshooting Software* (Course Technology 0-619-21760-x), prepares you for the software-related content of the four exams for A+ Certification, as well as the older 2003 A+ Operating System Technology exam.

HARDWARE NEEDS SOFTWARE TO WORK

In the world of computers, the term hardware refers to the computer's physical components, such as the monitor, keyboard, memory chips, and hard drive. The term software refers to the set of instructions that directs the hardware to accomplish a task. To perform a computing task, software uses hardware for four basic functions: input, processing, storage, and output (see Figure 1-1). Also, hardware components must communicate both data and instructions among themselves, which requires an electrical system to provide power, because these components are electrical. In this chapter, we introduce the hardware components of a computer system and help you see how they work.

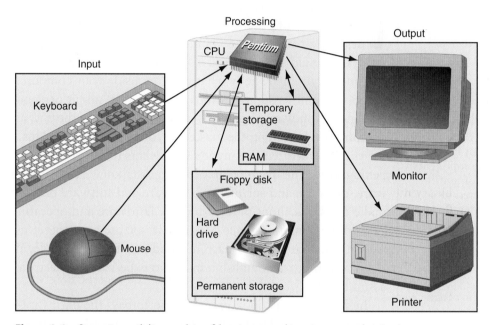

Figure 1-1   Computer activity consists of input, processing, storage, and output

A computer user must interact with a computer in a way that both the user and the software understand, such as with entries made by way of a keyboard or a mouse (see Figure 1-2). However, software must convert that instruction into a form that hardware can "understand." As incredible as it might sound, every communication between hardware and software, or between software and other software, is reduced to a simple yes or no, which is represented inside the computer by two simple states: on and off.

It was not always so. For almost half a century, people attempted to invent an electronic computational device that could store all 10 digits in our decimal number system and even some of our alphabet. Scientists were attempting to store a charge in a vacuum tube, which is similar to a light bulb. The charge would later be "read" to determine what had been stored there. Each digit in our number system, one through nine, was stored with increasing degrees of charge, similar to a light bulb varying in power from dim all the way up to bright. However, the degree of "dimness" or "brightness" was difficult to measure, and it would change because the voltage in the equipment could not be accurately regulated. For example, an eight would be stored with a partially bright charge, but later it would be read as a seven or nine as the voltage on the vacuum tube fluctuated slightly.

Then, in the 1940s, John Atanasoff came up with the brilliant idea to store and read only two values, on and off. Either there was a charge or there was not a charge, and this was easy to write and read, just as it's easy to determine if a light bulb is on or off.

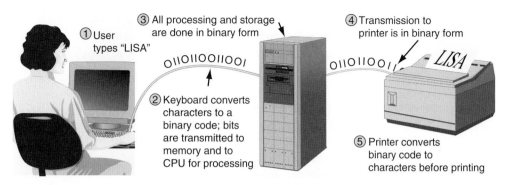

Figure 1-2 All communication, storage, and processing of data inside a computer are in binary form until presented as output to the user

This technology of storing and reading only two states is called binary, and the number system that only uses two digits, 0 and 1, is called the binary number system. A 1 or 0 in this system is called a bit, or binary digit. Because of the way the number system is organized, grouping is often done in groups of eight bits, each of which is called a byte. (Guess what four bits are called? A nibble!)

In a computer, all counting and calculations use the binary number system. Counting in binary goes like this: 0, 1, 10, 11, 100, 101, and so forth. For example, in binary code the number 25 is 0001 1001 (see Figure 1-3). When text is stored in a computer, every letter or other character is first converted to a code using only zeros and ones. The most common coding method for text is ASCII (American Standard Code for Information Interchange). For example, the uppercase letter A in ASCII code is 0100 0001(see Figure 1-3).

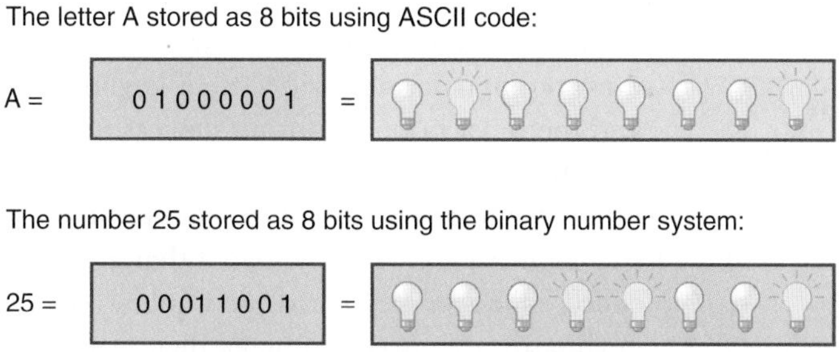

> **Notes**
>
> To learn more about binary and computer terminology related to the binary and hexadecimal number system, ask your instructor about the online content "The Hexadecimal Number System and Memory Addressing" that accompanies this book.

The letter A stored as 8 bits using ASCII code:

A =   0 1 0 0 0 0 0 1

The number 25 stored as 8 bits using the binary number system:

25 =   0 0 0 1 1 0 0 1

Figure 1-3 All letters and numbers are stored in a computer as a series of bits, each represented in the computer as on or off

PC HARDWARE COMPONENTS

In this section, we cover the major hardware components of a microcomputer system used for input, output, processing, storage, electrical supply, and communication. Most input and output devices are outside the computer case. Most processing and storage components are contained inside the case. The most important component in the case is the central processing unit (CPU), also called the processor or microprocessor. As its name implies, this device is central to all processing done by the computer. Data received by input devices is read by the CPU, and output from the CPU is written to output devices. The CPU writes data and instructions in storage devices and performs calculations and other data processing. Whether inside or outside the case, and regardless of the function the device performs, each hardware input, output, or storage device requires these elements to operate:

▲ *A method for the CPU to communicate with the device*. The device must send data to and/or receive data from the CPU. The CPU might need to control the device by passing instructions to it, or the device might need to request service from the CPU.

▲ *Software to instruct and control the device*. A device is useless without software to control it. The software must know how to communicate with the device at the detailed level of that specific device, and the CPU must have access to this software in order to interact with the device. Each device responds to a specific set of instructions based on the device's functions. The software must have an instruction for each possible action you expect the device to accomplish.

▲ *Electricity to power the device*. Electronic devices require electricity to operate. Devices can receive power from the power supply inside the computer case, or they can have their own power supplied by a power cable connected to an electrical outlet.

In the next few pages, we take a sightseeing tour of computer hardware, first looking outside and then inside the case. I've tried to keep the terminology and concepts to a minimum in these sections, because in future chapters, everything is covered in much more detail.

HARDWARE USED FOR INPUT AND OUTPUT

A+ ESS
1.1

Most input/output devices are outside the computer case. These devices communicate with components inside the computer case through a wireless connection or through cables attached to the case at a connection called a port. Most computer ports are located on the back of the case (see Figure 1-4), but some cases have ports on the front for easy access.

For wireless connections, a wireless device communicates with the system using a radio wave or infrared port. The most popular input devices are a keyboard and a mouse, and the most popular output devices are a monitor and a printer.

A+ Exam Tip

The A+ Essentials exam expects you to know many computer terms, and lots of them are found in this chapter. Pay close attention to all key terms.

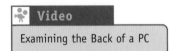
Video
Examining the Back of a PC

The keyboard is the primary input device of a computer (see Figure 1-5). The keyboards that are standard today are called enhanced keyboards and hold 104 keys. Ergonomic keyboards are curved to make them more comfortable for the hands and wrists. In addition, some keyboards come equipped with a mouse port used to attach a mouse to the keyboard, although it is more common for the mouse port to be on the computer case. Electricity to run the keyboard comes from inside the computer case and is provided by wires in the keyboard cable.

A mouse is a pointing device used to move a pointer on the screen and to make selections. The bottom of a mouse has a rotating ball or an optical sensor that tracks movement and controls the location of the pointer. The one, two, or three buttons on the top of the mouse serve different purposes for different software. For example, Windows XP uses the left mouse button to execute a command and the right mouse button to display related shortcut information.

1

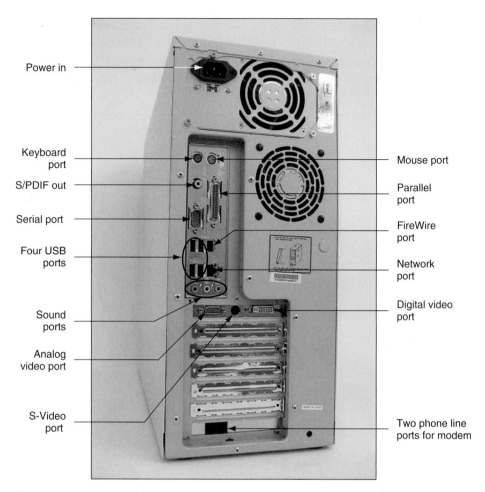

Power in

Keyboard port

S/PDIF out

Serial port

Four USB ports

Sound ports

Analog video port

S-Video port

Mouse port

Parallel port

FireWire port

Network port

Digital video port

Two phone line ports for modem

Figure 1-4   Input/output devices connect to the computer case by ports usually found on the back of the case

6-pin keyboard and mouse connectors

Figure 1-5   The keyboard and the mouse are the two most popular input devices

The monitor and the printer are the two most popular output devices (see Figure 1-6). The monitor is the visual device that displays the primary output of the computer. Hardware manufacturers typically rate a monitor according to the diagonal size of its screen (in inches) and by the monitor's resolution, which is a function of the number of dots on the screen used for display.

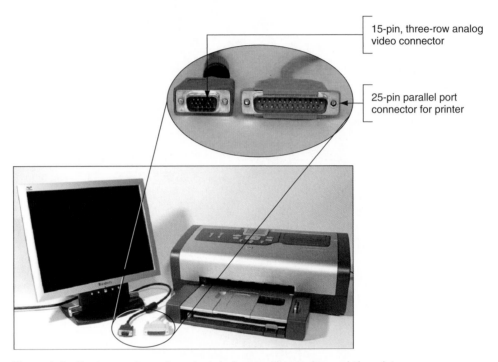

15-pin, three-row analog
video connector

25-pin parallel port
connector for printer

Figure 1-6 The two most popular output devices are the monitor and the printer

A very important output device is the printer, which produces output on paper, often called hard copy. The most popular printers available today are ink-jet, laser, thermal, solid ink, and dot-matrix printers. The monitor and the printer need separate power supplies. Their electrical power cords connect to electrical outlets. Sometimes, the computer case provides an electrical outlet for the monitor's power cord, to eliminate the need for one more power outlet.

Figure 1-6 showed the most common connectors used for a monitor and a printer: a 15-pin analog video connector and a 25-pin parallel connector. Note that in addition, a digital monitor can use a digital video connector and a printer sometimes uses a universal serial bus (USB) connector (see Figure 1-7).

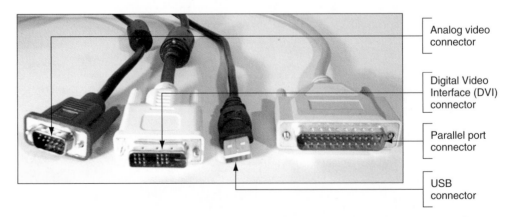

Analog video
connector

Digital Video
Interface (DVI)
connector

Parallel port
connector

USB
connector

Figure 1-7 Two video connectors and two connectors used by a printer

HARDWARE INSIDE THE COMPUTER CASE

Most storage and all processing of data and instructions are done inside the computer case, so before we look at components used for storage and processing, let's look at what you see when you first open the computer case. Most computers contain these devices inside the case (see Figure 1-8):

▲ A motherboard containing the CPU, memory, and other components
▲ A floppy drive, hard drive, and CD drive used for permanent storage
▲ A power supply with power cords supplying electricity to all devices inside the case
▲ Circuit boards used by the CPU to communicate with devices inside and outside the case
▲ Cables connecting devices to circuit boards and the motherboard

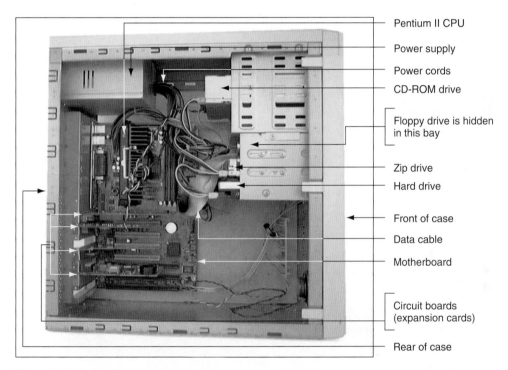

Pentium II CPU
Power supply
Power cords
CD-ROM drive
Floppy drive is hidden in this bay
Zip drive
Hard drive
Front of case
Data cable
Motherboard
Circuit boards (expansion cards)
Rear of case

Figure 1-8 Inside the computer case

Some of the first things you'll notice when you look inside a computer case are circuit boards. A circuit board is a board that holds microchips, or integrated circuits (ICs), and the circuitry that connects these chips. Some circuit boards, called expansion cards, are installed in long narrow expansion slots on the motherboard. All circuit boards contain microchips, which are most often manufactured using (CMOS) complementary metal-oxide semiconductor technology. CMOS chips require less electricity and produce less heat than chips manufactured using earlier technologies such as TTL (transistor-transistor logic). The other major components inside the case look like small boxes, including the power supply, hard drive, CD drive, and floppy drive.

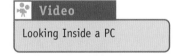

Video

Looking Inside a PC

There are two types of cables inside the case: data cables, which connect devices to one another, and power cables or power cords, which supply power. Most often, you can distinguish between the two by the shape of the cable. Data cables are flat and wide, and power cords are round and small. There are some exceptions to this rule, so the best way to identify a cable is to trace its source and destination.

THE MOTHERBOARD

The largest and most important circuit board in the computer is the motherboard, also called the main board or system board (see Figure 1-9), which contains the CPU, the component in which most processing takes place. The motherboard is the most complicated piece of equipment inside the case, and Chapter 5 covers it in detail. Because all devices must communicate with the CPU on the motherboard, all devices in a computer are either installed directly on the motherboard, directly linked to it by a cable connected to a port on the motherboard, or indirectly linked to it by expansion cards. A device that is not installed directly on the motherboard is called a peripheral device. Some ports on the motherboard stick outside the case to accommodate external devices such as a keyboard, and some ports provide a connection for a device inside the case, such as a floppy disk drive.

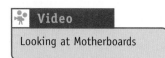

Video

Looking at Motherboards

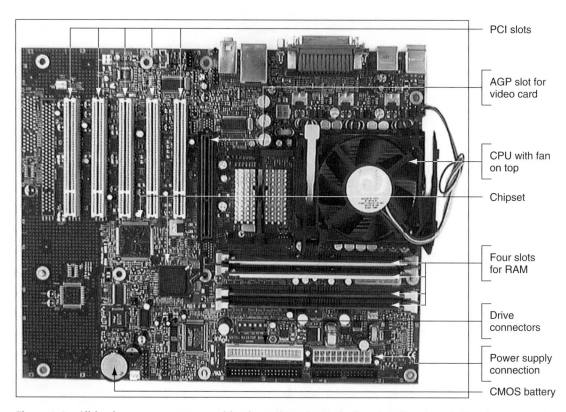

Figure 1-9 All hardware components are either located on the motherboard or directly or indirectly connected to it because they must all communicate with the CPU

Figure 1-10 shows the ports coming directly off a motherboard to the outside of the case: a keyboard port, a mouse port, a parallel port, two S/PDIF ports (for optical or coaxial cable), a FireWire port, a network port, four USB ports, six sound ports, and a wireless LAN antenna port. A parallel port transmits data in parallel and is most often used by a printer. A S/PDIF (Sony-Philips Digital Interface) sound port connects to an external home theater audio system, providing digital output and the best signal quality. A FireWire port (also called a 1394 port) is used for high-speed multimedia devices such as digital camcorders. A universal serial bus (USB) port can be used by many different input/output devices, such as keyboards, printers, scanners, and digital cameras.

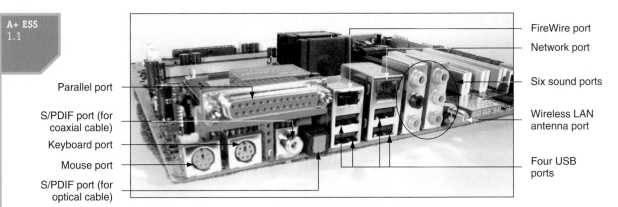

Parallel port

S/PDIF port (for coaxial cable)

Keyboard port

Mouse port

S/PDIF port (for optical cable)

FireWire port

Network port

Six sound ports

Wireless LAN antenna port

Four USB ports

Figure 1-10 A motherboard provides ports for common I/O devices

In addition to these ports, some older motherboards provide a serial port that transmits data serially (one bit follows the next); it is often used for an external modem or a serial mouse (a mouse that uses a serial port). A serial port looks like a parallel port, but is not as wide. You will learn more about ports in Chapter 8.

Listed next are the major components found on all motherboards; some of them are labeled in Figure 1-9. In the sections that follow, we discuss these components in detail. Components used primarily for processing:

▲ Processor or CPU (central processing unit), the computer's most important chip
▲ Chipset that supports the processor by controlling many motherboard activities

Components used for temporary storage:

▲ RAM (random access memory) used to hold data and instructions as they are processed
▲ Cache memory to speed up memory access (optional, depending on the type of processor)

Components that allow the processor to communicate with other devices:

▲ Traces, or wires, on the motherboard used for communication
▲ Expansion slots to connect expansion cards to the motherboard
▲ The system clock that keeps communication in sync
▲ Connections for data cables to devices inside the case
▲ Ports for devices outside the case

Electrical system:

▲ Power supply connections to provide electricity to the motherboard and expansion cards

Programming and setup data stored on the motherboard:

▲ Flash ROM, a memory chip used to permanently store instructions that control basic hardware functions (explained in more detail later in the chapter)
▲ CMOS RAM and CMOS setup chip that holds configuration data

THE PROCESSOR AND THE CHIPSET

The processor or CPU is the chip inside the computer that performs most of the actual data processing (see Figure 1-11). The processor could not do its job without the assistance of the chipset, a group of microchips on the motherboard that control the flow of data and instructions to and from the processor, providing careful timing of activities (see Figure 1-12).

CPU fan

Motherboard

Heat sink

Figure 1-11 The processor is hidden underneath the fan and the heat sink, which keep it cool

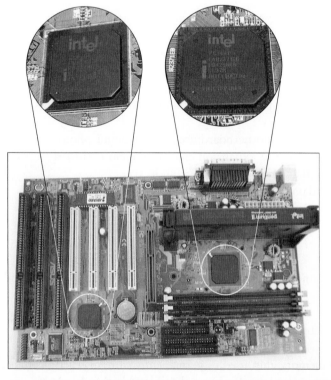

Figure 1-12 This motherboard uses two chips in its chipset (notice the bus lines coming from each chip used for communication)

A+ ESS
1.1

In this book, we discuss various types of computers, but we focus on the most common personal computers (PCs), referred to as IBM-compatible. These are built around microprocessors and chipsets manufactured by Intel Corporation, AMD, VIA, SiS, Cyrix, and other manufacturers. The Macintosh family of computers, manufactured by Apple Computer, Inc., has been built around a family of microprocessors, the PowerPC by IBM, although Apple is currently moving toward Intel processors. You will learn more about processors and chipsets in Chapter 4.

STORAGE DEVICES

In Figure 1-1, you saw two kinds of storage: temporary and permanent. The processor uses temporary storage, called **primary storage** or **memory**, to temporarily hold both data and instructions while it is processing them. Primary storage is much faster to access than permanent storage. However, when data and instructions are not being used, they must be kept in permanent storage, sometimes called **secondary storage**, such as a hard drive, CD, or floppy disk. Figure 1-13 shows an analogy to help you understand the concept of primary and secondary storage.

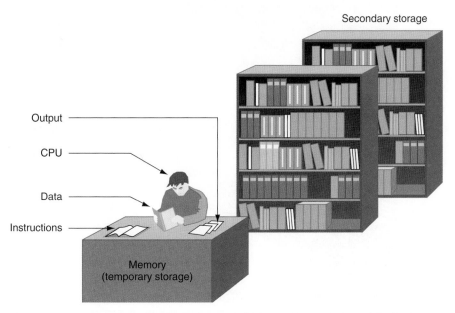

Figure 1-13 Memory is a temporary place to hold instructions and data while the CPU processes both

In our analogy, suppose you must do some research at the library. You go to the stacks, pull out several books, carry them over to a study table, and sit down with your notepad and pencil to take notes and do some calculations. When you're done, you leave with your notepad full of information and calculations, but you don't take the books with you. In this example, the stacks are permanent storage, and the books (data and instructions) are permanently kept there. The table is temporary storage, a place for you to keep data and instructions as you work with them. The notepad is your output from all that work, and you are the CPU, doing the work of reading the books and writing down information.

You kept a book on the table until you knew you were finished with it. As you worked, it would not make sense to go back and forth with a book, returning and retrieving it to and from the stacks. Similarly, the CPU uses primary storage, or memory, to temporarily hold data and instructions as long as it needs them for processing. Memory (your table) gives fast but temporary access, while secondary storage (the stacks) give slow but permanent access.

PRIMARY STORAGE

Primary storage is provided by devices called memory or RAM (random access memory), located on the motherboard and on other circuit boards. RAM chips can be installed individually directly on the motherboard or in banks of several chips on a small board that plugs into the motherboard (see Figure 1-14). These small RAM boards are called memory modules. There are three general types of modules: a DIMM (dual inline memory module), which is the most common type, a RIMM designed by Rambus, Inc., and an older, outdated type called a SIMM (single inline memory module). Each type module comes in several sizes and features, and generally you must match the module size and type to that which the motherboard supports.

> 🖐 **A+ Exam Tip**
>
> The A+ Essentials exam expects you to know about DIMMs and RIMMs.

DIMM

Three
empty
DIMM
slots

Figure 1-14 A SIMM, DIMM, or RIMM holds RAM and is mounted directly on a motherboard

Whatever information is stored in RAM is lost when the computer is turned off, because RAM chips need a continuous supply of electrical power to hold data or software stored in them. This kind of memory is called volatile because it is temporary in nature. By contrast, another kind of memory holds its data permanently, even when the power is turned off. This type of memory is nonvolatile and is called ROM (read-only memory). You will see examples of ROM chips later in the chapter and examples of RAM modules in Chapter 6.

APPLYING **CONCEPTS** Using Windows XP, you can see what type of CPU you have and how much memory you have installed. Click **Start**, right-click **My Computer**, and then select **Properties** on the shortcut menu. Then click the

General tab (see Figure 1-15). You can also see which version of Windows you are using. Using Windows 9x or Windows 2000, right-click the **My Computer** icon on your desktop, select **Properties** on the shortcut menu, and click the **General** tab.

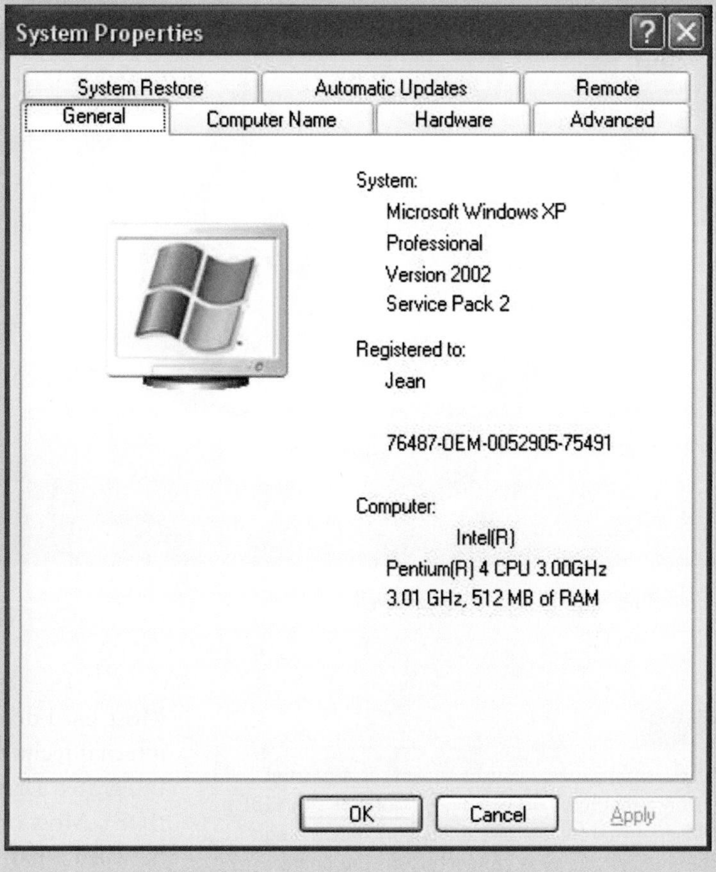

System Properties

| System Restore | Automatic Updates | Remote |
| General | Computer Name | Hardware | Advanced |

System:
Microsoft Windows XP
Professional
Version 2002
Service Pack 2

Registered to:
Jean

76487-OEM-0052905-75491

Computer:
Intel(R)
Pentium(R) 4 CPU 3.00GHz
3.01 GHz, 512 MB of RAM

OK   Cancel   Apply

Figure 1-15 System Properties gives useful information about your computer and OS

SECONDARY STORAGE

As you remember, the RAM on the motherboard is called primary storage. Primary storage temporarily holds both data and instructions as the CPU processes them. These data and instructions are also permanently stored on devices such as CDs, hard drives, and floppy disks, in locations that are remote from the CPU. Data and instructions cannot be processed by the CPU from this remote storage (called secondary storage), but must first be copied into primary storage (RAM) for processing. The most important difference between primary and secondary storage is that secondary storage is permanent. When you turn off your computer, the information in secondary storage remains intact. The most popular secondary storage devices are hard disks, CDs, DVDs, USB flash drives, and floppy disks.

A **hard drive** is a sealed case containing platters or disks that rotate at a high speed (see Figure 1-16). As the platters rotate, an arm with a sensitive read/write head reaches across the platters, both writing new data to them and reading existing data from them.

 Notes

Don't forget that primary storage, or RAM, is temporary; as soon as you turn off the computer, any information there is lost. That's why you should always save your work frequently into secondary storage.

A+ ESS
1.1

Figure 1-16   Hard drive with sealed cover removed

A+ Exam Tip

The A+ Essentials exam expects you to know that a parallel ATA connector on a motherboard can support one or two EIDE devices, and a serial ATA connector can support only a single hard drive. The number and type connectors on the board determine the total number of drives the board can support.

Notes

Confusion with industry standards can result when different manufacturers call a standard by a different name, which happens all too often with computer parts. The industry uses the terms ATA, IDE, and EIDE almost interchangeably even though technically they have different meanings. Used correctly, ATA refers to drive interface standards as published by ANSI. Used correctly, IDE refers to the technology used internally by a hard drive, and EIDE is commonly used by manufacturers to refer to the parallel ATA interface that CD drives, DVD drives, Zip drives, tape drives, and IDE hard drives can use to connect to a motherboard. The term IDE is most often used, when in fact EIDE is actually the more accurate name for the interface standards. To be consistent with manufacturer documentation, in this book, we loosely use the term IDE to mean IDE, EIDE, and parallel ATA. For instance, look closely at Figure 1-17 where the motherboard connectors are labeled Primary IDE and Secondary IDE, when technically they really should be labeled Primary EIDE and Secondary EIDE.

Most hard drives today use an internal technology called Integrated Drive Electronics (IDE). Most often, the interface between a hard drive and the motherboard is done according to an ATA (AT Attachment) standard as published by the American National Standards Institute (ANSI, see *www.ansi.org*).

The two major ATA standards for a drive interface are serial ATA (the newer standard) and parallel ATA (the older standard). Parallel ATA, sometimes called the EIDE (Enhanced IDE) standard or the IDE standard, allows for two connectors on a motherboard for two data cables (see Figure 1-17). Each IDE ribbon cable has a connection at the other end for an IDE device and a connection in the middle of the cable for a second IDE device. Using this interface, a

A+ ESS
1.1

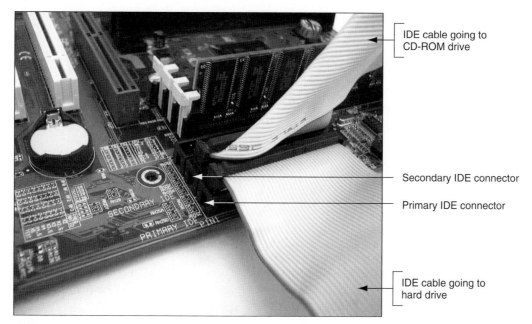

IDE cable going to
CD-ROM drive

Secondary IDE connector

Primary IDE connector

IDE cable going to
hard drive

Figure 1-17 Using a parallel ATA interface, a motherboard has two IDE connectors, each of which can accommodate two devices; a hard drive usually connects to the motherboard using the primary IDE connector

motherboard can accommodate up to four IDE devices in one system. Hard drives, Zip drives, CD drives, DVD drives, and tape drives, among other devices, can use these four IDE connections, which are controlled by the chipset. A typical system has one hard drive connected to one IDE connector and a CD drive connected to the other (see Figure 1-18).

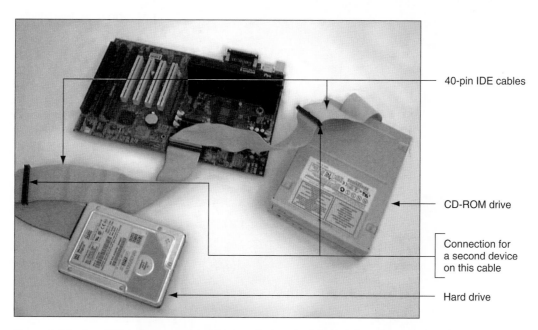

40-pin IDE cables

CD-ROM drive

Connection for
a second device
on this cable

Hard drive

Figure 1-18 Two IDE devices connected to a motherboard using both IDE connections and two cables

The serial ATA standard allows for more than four drives installed in a system and applies only to hard drives and not to other drives. So, a motherboard that uses serial ATA for hard drives will also have parallel ATA connectors for other type drives. Figure 1-19 shows a serial ATA drive interface.

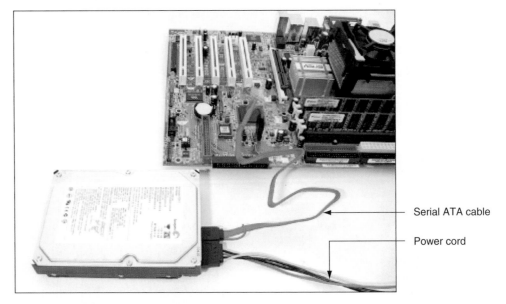

Figure 1-19 A hard drive subsystem using the new serial ATA data cable

Figure 1-20 shows the inside of a computer case with three IDE devices. The CD-ROM drive and the Zip drive share an IDE cable, and the hard drive uses the other cable.

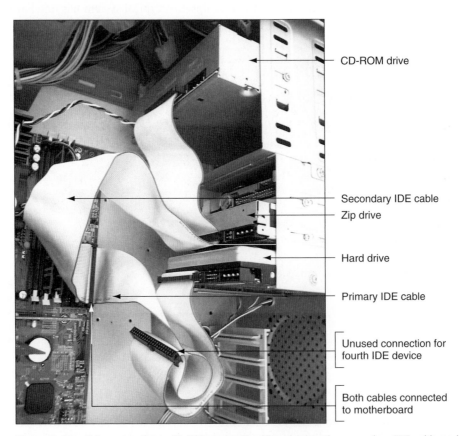

Figure 1-20 This system has a CD-ROM and a Zip drive sharing the secondary IDE cable and a hard drive using the primary IDE cable

A+ ESS
1.1

Both cables connect to the motherboard at the two IDE connections. (You will learn more about IDE, EIDE, and ATA in Chapter 7.)

A hard drive receives its power from the power supply by way of a power cord (see Figure 1-21). Looking back at Figure 1-20, you can see the power connections to the right of the cable connections on each drive (the power cords are not connected to make it easier to see the data cable connections). Chapter 7 covers how a hard drive works and how to install one.

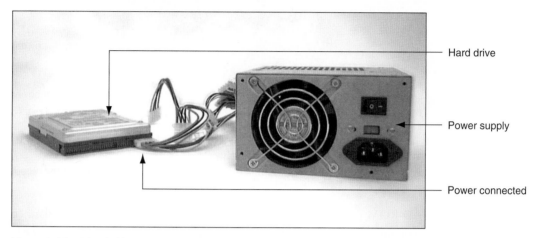

Hard drive

Power supply

Power connected

Figure 1-21   A hard drive receives power from the power supply by way of a power cord connected to the drive

Another secondary storage device sometimes found inside the case is a floppy drive that can hold 3.5-inch disks containing up to 1.44 MB of data. Most motherboards provide a connection for a floppy drive cable (see Figure 1-22).

Floppy drive connector

Secondary IDE connector

Primary IDE connector

Figure 1-22   A motherboard usually provides a connection for a floppy drive cable

The floppy drive cable can accommodate one or two drives (see Figure 1-23). The drive at the end of the cable is drive A. If another drive were connected to the middle of the cable, it would be drive B in a computer system. Electricity to a floppy drive is provided by a power cord from the power supply that connects to a power port at the back of the drive.

Floppy drives are not as necessary as they once were because the industry is moving toward storage media that can hold more data, such as CDs, DVDs, and flash drives. For years, every PC and notebook computer had a floppy drive, but many newer notebook computers don't, and manufacturers often offer floppy drives on desktop systems as add-on options only.

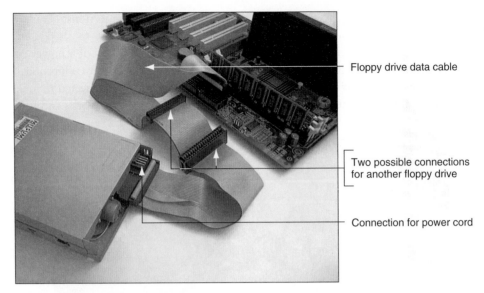

Floppy drive data cable

Two possible connections
for another floppy drive

Connection for power cord

Figure 1-23 One floppy drive connection on a motherboard can support one or two floppy drives

A CD-ROM (compact disc read-only memory) drive is considered standard equipment on most computer systems today because most software is distributed on CDs. Figure 1-24 shows the rear of a CD-ROM drive with the IDE data cable and power cord connected. Don't let the name of the CD-ROM drive confuse you. It's really not memory but secondary storage, because when you turn off the power, the data stored on a CD remains intact. Chapter 9 discusses different CD technologies and drives, some of which can both read and write data to the disc.

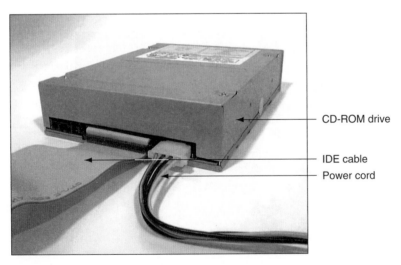

CD-ROM drive

IDE cable
Power cord

Figure 1-24 Most CD drives are EIDE devices and connect to the motherboard by way of an IDE data cable

MOTHERBOARD COMPONENTS USED FOR COMMUNICATION AMONG DEVICES

When you look carefully at a motherboard, you see many fine lines on both the top and the bottom of the board's surface (see Figure 1-25). These lines, sometimes called traces, are circuits or paths that enable data, instructions, and power to move from component to component on the board. This system of pathways used for communication and the protocol and methods used for transmission are collectively called the bus.

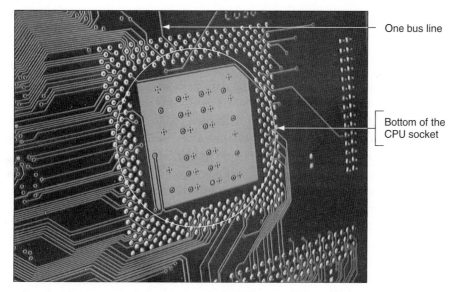

One bus line

Bottom of the
CPU socket

Figure 1-25 On the bottom of the motherboard, you can see bus lines terminating at the CPU socket

(A **protocol** is a set of rules and standards that any two entities use for communication.)
The parts of the bus that we are most familiar with are the lines of the bus that are used
for data, called the data bus.

Binary data is put on a line of a bus by placing voltage on that line. We can visualize that
bits are "traveling" down the bus in parallel, but in reality, the voltage placed on each line is
not "traveling," but rather is all over the line. When one component at one end of the line
wants to write data to another component, the two components get in sync for the write
operation. Then, the first component places voltage on several lines of the bus, and the other
component immediately reads the voltage on these lines.

The CPU or other devices interpret the voltage, or lack of voltage, on each line on
the bus as binary digits (0s or 1s). Some buses have data paths that are 8, 16, 32, 64, or
128 bits wide. For example, a bus that has eight wires, or lines, to transmit data is
called an 8-bit bus. Figure 1-26 shows an 8-bit bus between the CPU and memory that
is transmitting the letter A (binary 0100 0001). All bits of a byte are placed on their
lines of the bus at the same time. Remember there are only two states inside a
computer: on and off, which represent zero and one. On a bus, these two states are
no voltage for a zero and voltage for a one. So, the bus in Figure 1-26 has voltage on
two lines and no voltage on the other six lines, in order to pass the letter A on the bus.

0 = No voltage
1 = Voltage

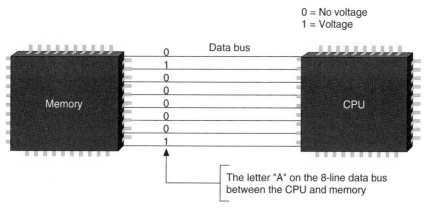

The letter "A" on the 8-line data bus
between the CPU and memory

Figure 1-26 A data bus has traces or lines that carry voltage interpreted by the CPU and other devices as bits

This bus is only 8 bits wide, but most buses today are much wider: 16, 32, 64, or 128 bits wide. Also, most buses today use a ninth bit for error checking. Adding a check bit for each byte allows the component reading the data to verify that it is the same data written to the bus.

The width of a data bus is called the data path size. A motherboard can have more than one bus, each using a different protocol, speed, data path size, and so on. The main bus on the motherboard that communicates with the CPU, memory, and the chipset goes by several names: system bus, front side bus (FSB), memory bus, host bus, local bus, or external bus. In our discussions, we'll use the term system bus or memory bus because they are more descriptive, but know that motherboard ads typically use the term front side bus. The data portion of most system buses on today's motherboards is 64 bits wide with or without additional lines for error checking.

One of the most interesting lines, or circuits, on a bus is the system clock or system timer, which is dedicated to timing the activities of the chips on the motherboard. A crystal on the motherboard (Figure 1-27), similar to that found in watches, generates the oscillation that produces the continuous pulses of the system clock. Traces carry these pulses over the motherboard to chips and expansion slots to ensure that all activities are synchronized.

Motherboard crystal generates the system clock

Figure 1-27 The system clock is a pulsating electrical signal sent out by this component that works much like a crystal in a wristwatch (one line, or circuit, on the motherboard bus is dedicated to carrying this pulse)

Remember that everything in a computer is binary, and this includes the activities themselves. Instead of continuously working to perform commands or move data, the CPU, bus, and other devices work in a binary fashion. Do something, stop, do something, stop, and so forth. Each device works on a clock cycle or beat of the clock. Some devices, such as the CPU, do two or more operations on one beat of the clock, and others do one operation for each beat. Some devices might even do something on every other beat, but all work according to beats or cycles. You can think of this as similar to children jumping rope. The system clock (child turning the rope) provides the beats or cycles, while devices (children jumping) work in a binary fashion (jump, don't jump). In the analogy, some children jump two or more times for each rope pass.

How fast does the clock beat? The beats, called the clock speed, are measured in hertz (Hz), which is one cycle per second; megahertz (MHz), which is one million cycles per second; and gigahertz (GHz), which is one billion cycles per second. Common ratings for motherboard buses today are 1066 MHz, 800 MHz, 533 MHz, or 400 MHz, although you still see some motherboards rated at 200 MHz, 133 MHz, or slower. In other words, data or instructions can

A+ ESS
1.1

be put on the system bus at the rate of 800 million every second. A CPU operates from 166 MHz to almost 4 GHz. In other words, the CPU can put data or instructions on its internal bus at this much higher rate. Although we often refer to the speed of the CPU and the motherboard bus, talking about the frequency

Notes

Motherboard buses are most often measured in frequencies such as 800 MHz, but sometimes you see a motherboard bus measured in performance such as the A8V motherboard by Asus built to support a high-end AMD processor (see *www.asus.com* and *www.amd.com*). This motherboard bus is rated at 2000 MT/s. One MT/s is one megatransfer per second or one million bytes per second transferred over the bus.

of these devices is more accurate, because the term "speed" implies a continuous flow, while the term "frequency" implies a digital or binary flow: on and off, on and off.

The lines of a bus, including data, instruction, and power lines, often extend to the expansion slots (see Figure 1-28). The size and shape of an expansion slot depend on the kind of bus it uses. Therefore, one way to determine the kind of bus you have is to examine the expansion slots on the motherboard.

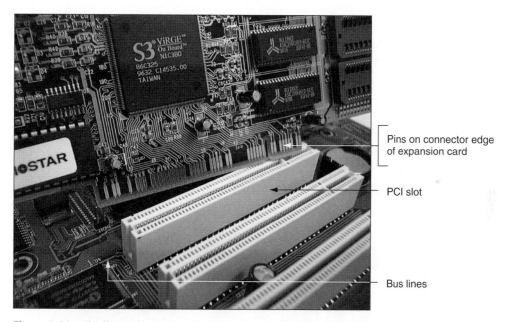

Pins on connector edge of expansion card

PCI slot

Bus lines

Figure 1-28 The lines of a bus terminate at an expansion slot where they connect to pins that connect to lines on the expansion card inserted in the slot

Figure 1-29 shows an older motherboard with three types of expansion slots, and Figure 1-30 shows a newer motherboard that also has three types of expansion slots. The types of slots shown on both boards include:

▲ PCI (Peripheral Component Interconnect) expansion slot used for input/output devices
▲ PCI Express slots that come in several lengths and are used by high-speed input/output devices
▲ AGP (Accelerated Graphics Port) expansion slot used for a video card
▲ ISA (Industry Standard Architecture) expansion slot is outdated and seldom seen today

Notice in Figures 1-29 and 1-30 the white PCI slots are used on both the older and newer boards. A motherboard will have one slot intended for use by a video card. The older board uses an AGP slot for that purpose, and the newer board uses a long PCI Express x16 slot for video.

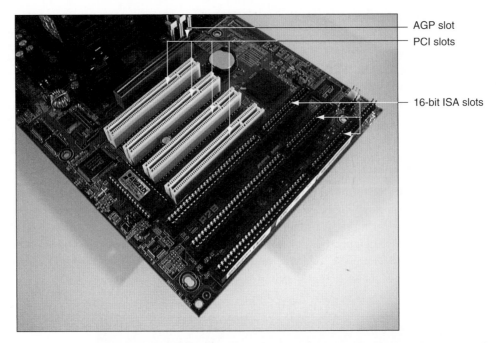

Figure 1-29 PCI bus expansion slots are shorter than ISA slots and offset farther; the one AGP slot is set farther from the edge of the board

PCI Express currently comes in four different slot sizes; the longest size (PCI Express x16) and the shortest size (PCI Express x1) are shown in Figure 1-30.

With a little practice, you can identify expansion slots by their length, by the position of the breaks in the slots, and by the distance from the edge of the motherboard to a slot's position.

Figure 1-30 This motherboard has three PCI Express slots and three slower and older PCI slots

A+ ESS
1.1

In Chapter 5, you'll learn that each expansion slot communicates with the CPU by way of its own bus. There can be a PCI Express bus, a PCI bus, an AGP bus, and, for older systems, an ISA bus, each running at different speeds and providing different features to accommodate the expansion cards that use these different slots. But all these buses connect to the main bus or system bus, which connects to the CPU.

INTERFACE (EXPANSION) CARDS

Circuit boards other than the motherboard inside the computer are sometimes called circuit cards, adapter boards, expansion cards, interface cards, or simply cards, and are mounted in expansion slots on the motherboard (see Figure 1-31).

Modem card

PCI slot

Motherboard
Phone line ports

Figure 1-31 This circuit board is a modem card and is mounted in a PCI slot on the motherboard

Figure 1-32 shows the motherboard and expansion cards installed inside a computer case. By studying this figure carefully, you can see the video card installed in the one AGP slot, a sound card and a network card installed in two PCI slots (the other two PCI slots are not used), and a modem card installed in an ISA slot (two ISA slots are not used). Figure 1-32 also shows the ports these cards provide at the rear of the PC case.

Video

Identifying Expansion Cards

You can see a full view of a video card in Figure 1-33. These cards all enable the CPU to connect to an external device or, in the case of the network card, to a network. The video card provides a port for the monitor. The sound card provides ports for speakers and microphones. The network card provides a port for a network cable to connect the PC to a network, and the modem card provides ports for phone lines. The technology to access these devices is embedded on the card itself, and the card also has the technology to communicate with the slot it is in, the motherboard, and the CPU.

The easiest way to determine the function of a particular expansion card (short of seeing its name written on the card, which doesn't happen very often) is to look at the end of the card that fits against the back of the computer case. A network card, for example, has a port designed to fit the network cable. An internal modem has one, or usually two, telephone jacks as its ports. You'll get lots of practice in this book identifying ports on expansion cards. However, as you examine the ports on the back of your PC, remember that sometimes the motherboard provides ports of its own.

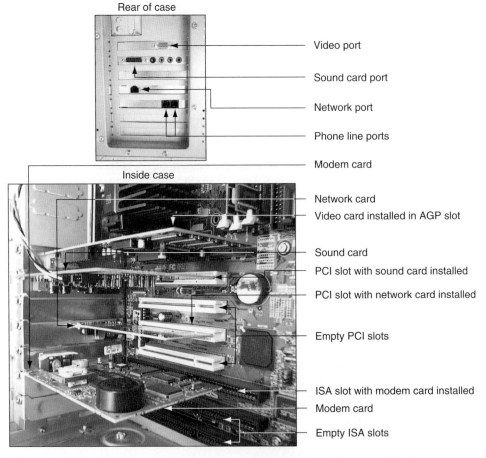

Rear of case

Video port

Sound card port

Network port

Phone line ports

Modem card

Inside case

Network card
Video card installed in AGP slot

Sound card
PCI slot with sound card installed
PCI slot with network card installed

Empty PCI slots

ISA slot with modem card installed
Modem card
Empty ISA slots

Figure 1-32   Four cards installed on a motherboard, providing ports for several devices

15-pin, 3-row
video port

Figure 1-33   The easiest way to identify this video card is to look at the port on the end of the card

THE ELECTRICAL SYSTEM

The most important component of the computer's electrical system is the power supply, which is usually near the rear of the case (see Figure 1-34). This power supply does not actually generate electricity but converts and reduces it to a voltage that the computer can handle. A power supply receives 110–120 volts of AC power from a wall outlet and converts it to a much lower

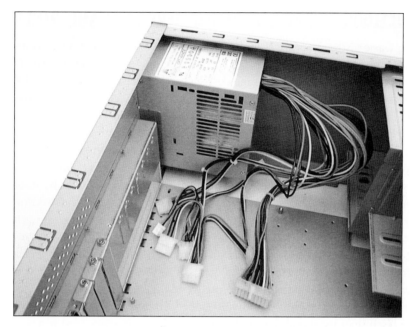

Figure 1-34 Power supply with connections

DC voltage. Older power supplies had power cables that provided either 5 or 12 volts DC. Newer power supplies provide 3.3, 5, and 12 volts DC. In addition to providing power for the computer, the power supply runs a fan directly from the electrical output voltage to help cool the inside of the computer case. Temperatures over 185 degrees Fahrenheit (85 degrees Celsius) can cause components to fail. When a computer is running, this and other fans inside the case and the spinning of the hard drive and CD drive are the primary noisemakers.

Every motherboard has one or more connections to receive power from the power supply (see Figure 1-35). This power is used by the motherboard, the CPU, and other components that receive their power from ports and expansion slots coming off the motherboard. In addition, there might be other power connectors on the motherboard to power a small fan that cools the CPU, or to power the CPU itself.

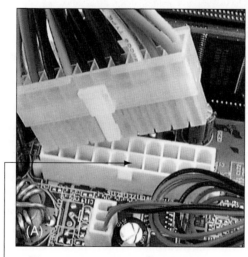

(A)
└─ P1 power connector on a motherboard

(B)
└─ Power connectors on a motherboard

Figure 1-35 The motherboard receives its power from the power supply by way of one or more connections located near the edge of the board or near the processor

INSTRUCTIONS STORED ON THE MOTHERBOARD AND OTHER BOARDS

Some very basic instructions are stored on the motherboard—just enough to start the computer, use some simple hardware devices such as a floppy disk and keyboard, and search for an operating system stored on a storage device such as a hard drive or CD. These data and instructions are stored on special ROM (read-only memory) chips on the board and are called the BIOS (basic input/output system). Sometimes other circuit boards, such as a video card, also have ROM BIOS chips. In the case of ROM chips, the distinction between hardware and software becomes vague. Most of the time, it's easy to distinguish between hardware and software. For example, a floppy disk is hardware, but a file on the disk containing a set of instructions is software. This software file, sometimes called a program, might be stored on the disk today, but you can erase that file tomorrow and write a new one to the disk. In this case, it is clear that a floppy disk is a permanent physical entity, whereas the program is not. Sometimes, however, hardware and software are not so easy to distinguish. For instance, a ROM chip on a circuit board inside your computer has software instructions permanently etched into it during fabrication. This software is actually a part of the hardware and is not easily changed. In this case, hardware and software are closely tied together, and it's difficult to separate the two, either physically or logically. Software embedded into hardware is often referred to as firmware because of its hybrid nature. Figure 1-36 shows an embedded firmware chip on a motherboard that contains the ROM BIOS programs.

Figure 1-36 This firmware chip contains flash ROM and CMOS RAM; CMOS RAM is powered by the coin battery located near the chip

The motherboard ROM BIOS serves three purposes: The BIOS that is sometimes used to manage simple devices is called system BIOS, the BIOS that is used to start the computer is called startup BIOS, and the BIOS that is used to change some settings on the motherboard is called CMOS setup.

These motherboard settings are stored in a small amount of RAM located on the firmware chip and called CMOS RAM or just CMOS. Settings stored in CMOS RAM include such things as the current date and time, which hard drives and floppy drives are present, and how the serial and parallel ports are configured. When the computer is first turned on, it looks to settings in CMOS RAM to find out what hardware it should expect to find. CMOS RAM is powered by a trickle of electricity from a small battery located on the motherboard or computer case, usually close to the firmware chip (refer back to Figure 1-36), so that when the computer is turned off, CMOS RAM still retains its data.

A+ ESS
1.1

Motherboard manufacturers often publish updates for the ROM BIOS on their motherboards; if a board is giving you problems or you want to use a new feature just released, you might want to upgrade the BIOS. In the past, this meant buying new ROM chips and exchanging them on the motherboard. However, ROM chips on motherboards today can be reprogrammed. Called flash ROM, the software stored on these chips can be overwritten by new software that remains on the chip until it is overwritten. (You will learn how to do this in Chapter 5; the process is called flashing ROM.)

Important technologies the motherboard BIOS might support are Advanced Configuration and Power Interface (ACPI), Advanced Power Management (APM), and Plug and Play (PnP).

ADVANCED CONFIGURATION AND POWER INTERFACE

Most motherboard BIOSs and operating systems support a power-saving feature using standards developed by Intel, Microsoft, and Toshiba, called the Advanced Configuration and Power Interface (ACPI) standards. Using ACPI, a system can be powered up by an external device such as a keyboard. Windows 2000/XP and Windows 9x support ACPI. Microsoft calls an ACPI-compliant BIOS a "good" BIOS.

An older BIOS power management standard is Advanced Power Management (APM), which is also supported by Windows 2000/XP and Windows 9x. APM is used only for power management on legacy notebook computers that don't support ACPI.

PLUG AND PLAY

Another feature of both the BIOS and the OS is Plug and Play (PnP), a standard designed to make the installation of new hardware devices easier. If the BIOS is a PnP BIOS, it will begin the process of configuring hardware devices in the system. It gathers information about the devices and then passes that information to the operating system. If the operating system is also PnP-compliant, it will use that information to complete the hardware configuration.

ESCD (extended system configuration data) Plug and Play BIOS is an enhanced version of PnP. It creates a list of all the things you have done manually to the configuration that PnP does not do on its own. This ESCD list is written to the BIOS chip so that the next time you boot, the startup BIOS can faithfully relay that information to Windows. Windows 9x benefits from this information, but it is not important to Windows 2000/XP. The BIOS chip for ESCD BIOS is a special RAM chip called Permanent RAM, or PRAM, that can hold data written to it without the benefit of a battery, which the CMOS setup chip requires.

>> CHAPTER SUMMARY

- ◢ A computer requires both hardware and software to work.

- ◢ The four basic functions of the microcomputer are input, output, processing, and storage of data.

- ◢ Data and instructions are stored in a computer in binary form, which uses only two states for data—on and off, or 1 and 0—which are called bits. Eight bits equal one byte.

- ◢ The four most popular input/output devices are the printer, monitor, mouse, and keyboard.

- ◢ The most important component inside the computer case is the motherboard, also called the main board or system board. It contains the most important microchip inside the case, the central processing unit (CPU), a microprocessor or processor, as well as access to other circuit boards and peripheral devices. All communications between the CPU and other devices must pass through the motherboard.

⊿ A ROM BIOS or firmware microchip is a hybrid of hardware and software containing programming embedded into the chip.

⊿ Most microchips are manufactured using CMOS (complementary metal-oxide semiconductor) technology.

⊿ Each hardware device needs a method to communicate with the CPU, software to control it, and electricity to power it.

⊿ Devices outside the computer case connect to the motherboard through ports on the case. Common ports are network, FireWire, sound, serial, parallel, USB, game, keyboard, and mouse ports.

⊿ A circuit board inserted in an expansion slot on the motherboard can provide an interface between the motherboard and a peripheral device, or can itself be a peripheral. (An example is an internal modem.)

⊿ The chipset on a motherboard controls most activities on the motherboard and includes several device controllers, including the USB controller, memory controller, IDE controller, and so forth.

⊿ Primary storage, called memory or RAM, is temporary storage the CPU uses to hold data and instructions while it is processing both.

⊿ RAM is stored on single chips, SIMMs, DIMMs, and RIMMs.

⊿ Secondary storage is slower than primary storage, but it is permanent storage. Some examples of secondary storage devices are hard drives, CD drives, DVD drives, flash drives, Zip drives, and floppy drives.

⊿ Most hard drives, CD drives, and DVD drives use an ATA interface standard commonly called EIDE (Enhanced Integrated Drive Electronics) technology, which can accommodate up to four EIDE or IDE devices on one system. Newer hard drives are the serial ATA interface standard.

⊿ The system clock is used to synchronize activity on the motherboard. The clock sends continuous pulses over the bus that different components use to control the pace of activity.

⊿ A motherboard can have several buses, including the system bus, the PCI Express bus, the PCI bus, the AGP bus, and the outdated ISA bus.

⊿ The frequency of activity on a motherboard is measured in megahertz (MHz), or one million cycles per second. The processor operates at a much higher frequency than other components in the system, and its activity is measured in gigahertz (GHz), or one billion cycles per second.

⊿ The power supply inside the computer case supplies electricity to components both inside and outside the case. Some components external to the case get power from their own electrical cables.

⊿ ROM BIOS on a motherboard holds the basic software needed to start a PC and begin the process of loading an operating system. Most ROM chips are flash ROM, meaning that these programs can be updated without exchanging the chip.

⊿ The CMOS setup program is part of ROM BIOS stored on the firmware chip. This program is used to change motherboard settings or configuration information. When power to the PC is turned off, a battery on the motherboard supplies power to CMOS RAM that holds these settings.

>> KEY TERMS

For explanations of key terms, see the Glossary near the end of the book.

Advanced Configuration and
  Power Interface (ACPI)
Advanced Power Management
  (APM)
binary number system
BIOS (basic input/output system)
bit
bus
byte
cards
central processing unit (CPU)
chipset
circuit board
clock speed
CMOS (complementary metal-
  oxide semiconductor)
CMOS RAM
CMOS setup
data bus
data path size
DIMM (dual inline memory
  module)
expansion cards
expansion slots

firmware
flash ROM
front side bus (FSB)
gigahertz (GHz)
hard copy
hard drive
hardware
hertz (Hz)
host bus
keyboard
main board
megahertz (MHz)
memory
microprocessor
monitor
motherboard
mouse
nonvolatile
parallel port
peripheral device
Plug and Play (PnP)
port
power supply
primary storage

printer
processor
program
protocol
RAM (random access memory)
RIMM
ROM (read-only memory)
S/PDIF (Sony-Philips Digital
  Interface) sound port
secondary storage
serial port
SIMM (single inline memory
  module)
software
startup BIOS
system BIOS
system board
system bus
system clock
traces
USB (universal serial bus) port
video card
volatile

>> REVIEWING THE BASICS

1. Why is all data stored in a computer in binary form?

2. What are the four primary functions of hardware?

3. What are the two main input devices and two main output devices?

4. What three things do electronic hardware devices need in order to function?

5. How many bits are in a byte?

6. What is the purpose of an expansion slot on a motherboard?

7. Which component on the motherboard is used primarily for processing?

8. Name three CPU manufacturers.

9. What technology is most often used today to manufacture microchips?

10. What are two other names for the system bus?

11. What are two other names for the motherboard?

12. What are the two basic types of cables found inside a computer case and what are their basic functions?

13. List three types of ports that are often found coming directly off the motherboard to be used by external devices.

14. What is the purpose of the S/PDIF port?

15. List three kinds of memory modules.

16. What is the difference between volatile and nonvolatile memory?

17. Of the two types of storage in a system, which type is generally faster and holds data and instructions while the data is being processed? Which type of storage is generally slower, but more permanent?

18. What technology standard provides for up to four devices on a system, including the hard drive as one of those devices? What are two common industry names loosely used to describe this standard?

19. What is the size of the data path on most system buses today?

20. What is the measurement of frequency of a system bus and CPU? Which is faster, the system bus or the CPU?

21. Name four types of buses that might be on a motherboard today.

22. A power supply receives 120 volts of _____ power from a wall outlet and converts it to 3.3, 5, and 12 volts of _____ power.

23. ROM BIOS or firmware chips that can be upgraded without replacing the chips are called _____.

24. CMOS setup allows a technician to change configuration settings on a motherboard stored in _____.

25. Name three examples of secondary storage devices.

26. A hertz is _____ cycles per second; a megahertz is _____ cycles per second, and a gigahertz is _____ cycles per second.

27. An AGP slot is normally used for a(n) _____ expansion card.

28. How many sizes of PCI Express slots are currently manufactured for personal computers?

29. Name the three purposes the motherboard ROM BIOS serves.

30. From where does CMOS RAM receive its power?

>> THINKING CRITICALLY

1. When selecting secondary storage devices for a new desktop PC, which is more important, a CD-ROM drive or a floppy drive? Why?

2. Based on what you have learned in this chapter, when working on a Microsoft Word document, why is it important to save your work often? Explain your answer using the two terms, primary storage and secondary storage.

3. Most buses are 16, 32, 64, or 128 bits wide. Why do you think these bus widths are multiples of eight?

4. Why would it be difficult to install four hard drives, one CD-ROM drive, and one DVD drive in a single low-end system?

5. In this chapter, a light bulb is used to demonstrate the binary concept used for computer storage and communication. Give another example in everyday life to explain this binary concept. Get creative.

6. If the CMOS battery inside your computer system died, when you first turn on your system, will you expect the system to boot up normally to the operating system level?

What information do you think the system would not have available for a successful boot?

7. Why is it more accurate to describe the CPU and motherboard bus using the term frequency rather than speed? Explain your answer.

>> HANDS-ON PROJECTS

PROJECT 1-1:   Identifying Ports on Your Computer

Look at the back of your home or lab computer and make a diagram showing the ports. Label all the ports in the diagram and note which ones are used and which ones are not used.

PROJECT 1-2:   Researching on the Internet

The Internet is an incredibly rich source of information about computer hardware and software. Answer these questions, using the Internet as your source:

1. What is the frequency of the fastest CPU for a desktop computer that you can find advertised on the Web? Print the Web page showing the CPU and its frequency.

2. Print a Web page advertising a motherboard. What is the frequency of the system bus? What is the system bus called?

3. Print a Web page advertising computer memory. How much RAM is on one module?

4. Print the Web page of any hardware device that uses a USB port.

PROJECT 1-3:   Identifying Motherboard Components

Copy the diagram in Figure 1-37 and label as many of the components on the diagram as you can, using the photographs in Figures 1-9, 1-12, 1-30, and other photographs in the chapter. This exercise is very important for visual recognition of motherboard components and for helping you identify these components in motherboard documentation.

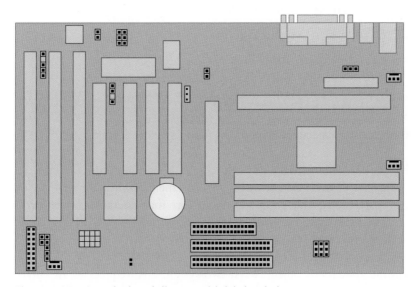

Figure 1-37   A motherboard diagram with labels missing

A+ Exam Tip

The A+ Essentials exam expects you to be able to recognize components on a motherboard diagram similar to the one in Figure 1-37.

Notes

You can capture just the active window, instead of the entire screen, by pressing Alt+PrintScrn instead of PrintScrn.

PROJECT 1-4: Examining Your Computer

What type of CPU does your computer have, and how much memory is installed? To answer these questions, using Windows XP, click **Start**, right-click **My Computer**, and select **Properties** on the shortcut menu. The System Properties dialog box opens. Click the **General** tab. (Using Windows 2000 or Windows 98, right-click the **My Computer** icon on your desktop and select **Properties** on the shortcut menu.) The CPU information is listed in this dialog box. Print a screen shot of this dialog box. One quick and easy way to get a hard copy of a screen is to use Paint. Follow these directions to print the screen:

1. Press the **PrintScrn** (print screen) key. This puts the screen capture on your Windows Clipboard.

2. Open Paint. Click **Start, All Programs, Accessories, Paint**.

3. Click **Edit, Paste** to put the contents of the Clipboard into Paint. If necessary, click **Yes** to the dialog box that pops up to confirm the paste.

4. To print the page, click **File, Print**.

PROJECT 1-5: Learning to Think in Binary and Hex

Use the online content, "The Hexadecimal Number System and Memory Addressing" and "ASCII Character Set and Ansi.sys" that accompanies this book to answer these questions:

1. What is the ASCII code in binary and in decimal for a lowercase z?

2. What is the ASCII code in binary and in decimal for a period?

3. Write the binary numbers from 1 to 20.

4. What is the largest decimal number that can be stored using 8 bits, or 1 byte?

5. Write the hex numbers from 1 to 20.

6. Convert 43 to binary. Convert 43 to hex.

7. What is 1101 1001 in decimal? In hex?

>> REAL PROBLEMS, REAL SOLUTIONS

REAL PROBLEM 1-1: Reading a Technical Ad for a Computer System

Computer ads can sometimes be difficult to read, especially those targeting tech-savvy computer buyers. Figure 1-38 shows an advertisement published by GIM Computer Corp (*www.gimcomputers.com*), a computer parts store that assembles systems from parts and sells them as a single unit price with a one-year warranty on all parts. Answer the following questions about this ad:

1. What is the system bus called? What two system bus frequencies are offered?

2. In the ad, what do you think P4 means?

3. What are the four choices of frequencies for the processor?

4. What is the brand of the processor?

5. How much RAM is on the motherboard? What is the cost of doubling that amount of RAM?

6. What type of expansion slot is used for the video card?

7. What terms describe the hard drive in the system?

8. List the terms in the ad that you do not understand (many are not covered in this chapter) and save this list. You will need it in future chapters.

GIM 13. Intel SK775 P4 Business System

SK775 330 Celeron 2.66G 533FSB retail box w/fan-**$399.99**/414.12

SK 775 340 Celeron 2.93G 533FSB retail box w/fan-**$428.99**/437.58

P4-530-3.0G (**1M** /800FSB, Hyper Threading, retail box w/fan)-**$499.99**/ 520.2

P4-540-3.2G (1M/800FSB, Hyper Threading, retail box w/fan)-**$545.99**/ 556.92

all above cpu chips are retail boxed, 3 years Intel warranty.

ASUS P5DG1-VM Intel 915P, SK775, 4 SATA, 8 USB 2.0, ATX MB

512MB DDR400 PC3200 (+ $50 to add 1 more 512MB for Dual DDR400)

80GB SATA ATA150 8M buffer 7200RPM **ATA100 UIDE HDD (+ $38 to upgrade to 160GB)**

Integrated Intel Graphics Media Accelerator 900 w/16x PCI Express port// **1.44 FDD**

52x32x52x16x **IDE CDRW & DVD Combo w/Nero** (+ $20 to upgrade to 16x DVDRW)

3D Sound 6 Channel // 10-100 **Network**

Super Mid-tower case w/2 fans & 2 USB front (retail @ $50)

*** Add $10 to upgrade to P5GD1-VM-S w/gigabit lan & 1394; or + $12 Ug to ASUS P5GD1 Raid, PCI-X MB, also +$ 59 for

ATI Radeon x300se 128MB 16X PCI-X video. *** Add $85.99 for Windows XP Home; 0r + $138.99 for Windows XP Pro. w/CD & Manual.

Figure 1-38 GIM Computer sells preassembled systems to tech-savvy customers

CHAPTER 2

PC Repair Fundamentals

In the last chapter, you were introduced to hardware. In this chapter, you will learn about your job as a PC support technician and the tools and techniques you'll use. The best support technicians are good at preventing a problem from happening in the first place, so in this chapter, you'll learn how to develop a preventive maintenance plan and use it. You'll also learn how to work inside a computer case and about what happens when you first turn on a PC.

Next in the chapter, you'll learn about some common-sense guidelines to solving computer problems. You'll learn how to interview the user, how to isolate a problem into one that either happens before or after the boot, and how to troubleshoot and solve a problem with a failed boot. This chapter is the first of several chapters that take you one step at a time into diagnosing and solving PC problems.

This chapter lays a strong foundation for troubleshooting that we will build on in later chapters. Much of what is covered in this chapter is introductory in nature; in later chapters, we'll dig into the many details of troubleshooting each subsystem introduced in this chapter.

PC SUPPORT TECHNICIAN TOOLS

A+ ESS
1.4
7.1

A+
220-602
1.2

Several hardware and software tools can help you maintain a computer and diagnose and repair computer problems. The tools you choose depend on the amount of money you can spend and the level of PC support you expect to provide.

Essential tools for PC troubleshooting are listed here, and several of them are shown in Figure 2-1. You can purchase some of these tools in a PC toolkit, although most PC tool kits contain items you really can do without.

Cable ties

Network cable testers

AC ground tester

Multimeter

Figure 2-1 PC support technician tools

Here is a list of essential tools:

- Ground bracelet, ground mat, or ground gloves to use when working inside the computer case. How to use them is covered later in the chapter.
- Flat-head screwdriver
- Phillips-head or cross-head screwdriver
- Torx screwdriver set, particularly size T15
- Tweezers, preferably insulated ones, for picking pieces of paper out of printers or dropped screws out of tight places
- Extractor, a spring-loaded device that looks like a hypodermic needle (When you push down on the top, three wire prongs come out that can be used to pick up a screw that has fallen into a place where hands and fingers can't reach.)
- Recovery CD, DVD, or floppy disk for any OS you might work on (You might need several, depending on the OSs you support.)

The following tools might not be essential, but they are very convenient:

- Cans of compressed air or anti-static vacuum cleaner to clean dust from inside a computer case
- Cleaning solutions and pads such as contact cleaner, monitor wipes, cleaning solutions for CDs, DVDs, and tapes and drives
- Multimeter to check the power supply output (see Appendix B)
- Needle-nose pliers for removing jumpers and for holding objects in place while you screw them in (especially those pesky nuts on cable connectors)
- Cable ties to tie cables up and out of the way inside a computer case
- Flashlight to see inside the PC case

2

A+ ESS
1.4
7.1

A+
220-602
1.2

- ▲ AC outlet ground tester
- ▲ Network cable tester
- ▲ Loop-back plugs to test ports
- ▲ Small cups or bags to help keep screws organized as you work
- ▲ Antistatic bags (a type of Farady Cage) to store unused parts
- ▲ Chip extractor to remove chips (to pry up the chip; a simple screwdriver is usually more effective, however)
- ▲ Pen and paper for taking notes
- ▲ Diagnostic cards
- ▲ Utility software, virus detection software, and diagnostic software on floppy disks or CD

Keep your tools in a toolbox designated for PC troubleshooting. If you put disks and hardware tools in the same box, be sure to keep the disks inside a hard plastic case to protect them from scratches and dents. In addition, make sure the diagnostic and utility software you use is recommended for the hardware and software you are troubleshooting.

Now let's turn our attention to the details of several support technician tools, including recovery CDs, loop-back plugs, cleaning pads and solutions, and POST diagnostic cards.

RECOVERY CDs

A+
220-602
1.2
3.3

A recovery CD can be used to boot a system and repair or reinstall the Windows operating system. This recovery CD should be the Windows Setup CD that was used to originally install Windows. However, in a pinch, you can use another Windows Setup CD as long as it is for the version of Windows you are using.

If you have a notebook computer or a brand-name computer such as a Dell, IBM, or Gateway, use the recovery CD provided by the manufacturer instead of a regular Windows Setup CD. This recovery CD, as shown in Figure 2-2, has drivers specific to your system, and the Windows build that is on the recovery CD might be different from the one provided by an off-the-shelf Windows Setup CD. For example, a Windows XP Home Edition installation on a notebook computer might have been built with all kinds of changes made to it by the notebook manufacturer. These changes will make it different from a Windows XP Home Edition installation that was sourced from a package bought in a retail store. When you purchase a

Figure 2-2 Windows Setup CD and Windows Recovery CDs for a notebook computer

A+ ESS
1.4
7.1

brand-name computer, the recovery CD is sometimes included in the package. If it is not included, you can order it from the manufacturer. To order it, go to the manufacturer's Web site support section and find the recovery CD specific to your desktop or notebook computer.

A+
220-602
1.2
3.3

For some brand-name computers, the hard drive contains a hidden recovery partition that can be used to reinstall Windows. Sometimes this hidden partition contains a utility that can be used to create a recovery CD. However, know that the CD must have already been created if it is to be there to help you in the event the entire hard drive fails. To access the utilities on the hidden partition, press a key during startup. Which key to press is displayed on the screen early in the boot before the OS is loaded. For example, one Gateway computer displays the message "Press F11 to start recovery." When you press F11, a menu is displayed giving you the opportunity to reinstall Windows from setup files kept in the hidden partition.

LOOP-BACK PLUGS

A+
220-602
1.2

A loop-back plug is used to test a serial, parallel, USB, network, or other port. To use one to test a port, you plug in the loop-back plug and then run the software that comes with the plug to test the port. Figure 2-3 shows loop-back plugs that come with CheckIt diagnostic software from SmithMicro Software (*www.smithmicro.com*).

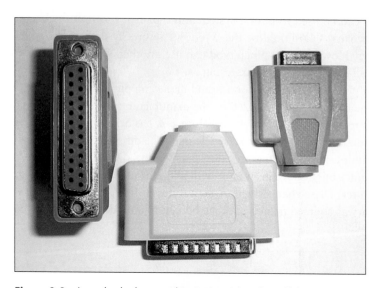

Figure 2-3   Loop-back plugs used to test serial and parallel ports

CLEANING PADS AND SOLUTIONS

A+ ESS
1.4
6.1
7.1

As a PC technician, you'll find yourself collecting different cleaning solutions and cleaning pads to clean a variety of devices, including the mouse and keyboard, CDs and DVDs and their drives, tapes and tape drives, and CRT and LCD monitors. Figure 2-4 shows a few of these products. The contact cleaner in the figure is used to clean the contacts on expansion cards, which might solve a problem with a faulty connection. You'll learn how and when to use these products later in this chapter and in other chapters in the book.

A+
220-602
1.2
1.3
7.1

Most of these cleaning solutions contain flammable and poisonous materials. Take care when using them that they don't get on your skin or in your eyes. To find out what to do if you accidentally get exposed to a dangerous solution, look on the instructions printed on the can or check out the material safety data sheet (see Figure 2-5). A material safety data sheet (MSDS) explains how to properly handle substances such as chemical solvents.

A+ ESS
1.4
6.1
7.1

A+
220-602
1.2
1.3
7.1

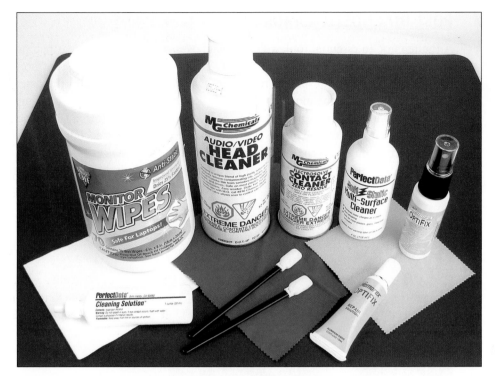

Figure 2-4 Cleaning solutions and pads

Figure 2-5 Each chemical you use should have available a material safety data sheet

An MSDS includes information such as physical data, toxicity, health effects, first aid, storage, shipping, disposal, and spill procedures. It comes packaged with the chemical, or you can order one from the manufacturer, or find one on the Internet (see *www.ilpi.com/msds*).

If you have an accident with these or other dangerous products, your company or organization might require you to report the accident to your company and/or fill out an accident report. Check with your organization to find out how to handle reporting these types of incidents.

A+ ESS
1.4
7.1

A+
220-602
1.2
7.1

POST DIAGNOSTIC CARDS

Although not an essential tool, a POST diagnostic card can be of great help to discover and report computer errors and conflicts at POST. If you have a problem that prevents the PC from booting that you suspect is related to hardware, you can install the diagnostic card in an expansion slot on the motherboard and then attempt to boot. The card monitors the boot process and reports errors, usually as coded numbers on a small LED panel on the card. You then look up the number in the documentation that accompanies the card to get more information about the error and its source.

Examples of these cards are listed below. The Post Code Master card is shown in Figure 2-6:

Figure 2-6   Post Code Master diagnostic card by MSD, Inc.

◢ PCI Error Testing/Debug Card by Winic Corporation (*www.winic.com*)
◢ POSTcard V3 by Unicore Software, Inc. (*www.unicore.com*)
◢ Post Code Master by MSD, Inc. (*www.postcodemaster.com*)

Before purchasing these or any other diagnostic tools or software, read the documentation about what they can and cannot do, and, if possible, read some product reviews. The Internet is a good source of information.

PERSONAL COMPUTER PREVENTIVE MAINTENANCE

A+ ESS
1.4
2.4

A+
220-602
7.1

Much in this chapter is about troubleshooting, but it is much better to know how to take some steps to prevent certain computer problems from occurring in the first place. The more preventive maintenance work you do initially, the fewer problems you are likely to have later, and the less troubleshooting and repair you will have to do.

If you are responsible for the PCs in an organization, make and implement a preventive maintenance plan to help prevent failures and reduce repair costs and downtime. In addition, you need a disaster recovery plan to manage failures when they occur. PC failures are caused by many different environmental and human factors, including heat, dust, magnetism, power supply problems, static electricity, human error (such as spilled liquids or an accidental change of setup and software configurations), and viruses. The goals of preventive maintenance are to reduce the likelihood that the events that cause PC failures will occur and to lessen the damage if they do.

2

A+ ESS
1.4
2.4

A+
220-602
7.1

This section focuses on several preventive maintenance tasks including what to do when a computer becomes your permanent responsibility, how to create a preventive maintenance plan, how to deal with dust, how to prepare a computer for shipping, and how to dispose of used equipment.

WHEN A PC IS YOUR PERMANENT RESPONSIBILITY

When you are the person responsible for a PC, either as the user or as the ongoing support person for the PC and the user, you need to prepare for future troubleshooting situations. This section describes tasks and procedures for doing this.

KEEP GOOD BACKUPS OF DATA AND SYSTEM FILES

Suppose the hard drive on your computer stopped working. It's totally dead and everything on it is lost. How would that affect you? What would be lost and what would that cost you in time, stress, and money? You need to keep good backups of data, including your data files, e-mail address list, and e-mail attachments. You also need backups of Windows system files including the registry.

DOCUMENT ALL SETUP CHANGES, PROBLEMS, AND SOLUTIONS

When you first set up a new computer, start a record book about this computer, using either a file on disk or a notebook dedicated to this machine. In this notebook or file, record any changes in setup data as well as any problems you experience or maintenance that you do on this computer. Be diligent in keeping this notebook up to date, because it will be invaluable in

Notes

In most situations, you don't need to back up installed applications. If the application gets corrupted, you can install it again using the setup CDs. It's extremely important that you have the original setup CDs handy when a hard drive fails—without these CDs, you won't be able to reinstall the software. If you like, you can also make one backup copy of a setup CD. According to copyright laws, you have the right to make a backup of the installation CD or floppy disks in case the CD or disks fail. You can keep your copy in a safe place in the event that something happens to the original. Users that you support also need to understand that you cannot reinstall software installed on their systems if the software has been pirated and the CDs are no longer available.

diagnosing problems and upgrading equipment. Keep a printed or handwritten record of all changes to setup data for this machine, and store the record with the hardware and software documentation. This record needs to include changes to BIOS and jumper settings on the motherboard, which you'll learn how to do later in the chapter.

If you are not the primary user of the computer, you might want to keep the hardware documentation separate from the computer itself. Label the documentation so that you can easily identify that it belongs to this computer. Some support people tape a large envelope inside the computer case, containing

Notes

You can also keep a record of all troubleshooting you do on a computer in a word-processing document that lists all the problems you have encountered and the solutions you used. This will help you save time in troubleshooting problems you have encountered before. Store the document file on a flash drive or floppy disk that you keep with the computer's documentation. You might want to make a new printout each time the document changes.

important documentation and records specific to that computer. On the other hand, if you're also responsible for software reference manuals, know that these manuals need to be kept in a location that is convenient for users.

A+ ESS
1.4
2.4
6.1
6.3

A+
220-602
7.1

PROTECT THE SYSTEM AGAINST VIRUSES AND OTHER ATTACKS

In today's world, most people have Internet access and the Internet is full of viruses, worms, and other malicious software looking for a way into your system. To protect your system, use the following tips:

Always Use a Firewall

A firewall is hardware or software that prevents hackers or malicious software from getting into your computer without your knowledge. For Windows XP, you can use Windows Firewall. (Windows 2000 and Windows 9x/Me do not offer a firewall. For these OSs, you need to use third-party software.) Within Windows XP, you can change firewall settings by clicking **Start** and right-clicking **My Network Places**. Then, select **Properties** from the shortcut menu. The Network Connections window opens, as shown in Figure 2-7.

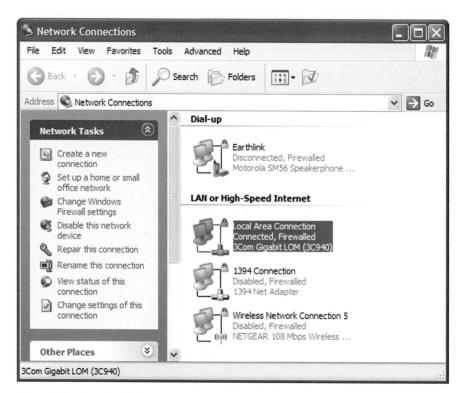

Figure 2-7   Use the Windows XP Network Connections window to change firewall settings

Select your network connection (in the figure, the Local Area Connection is selected), and click **Change Windows Firewall settings**. The Windows Firewall window opens, as shown in Figure 2-8. Make sure **On (recommended)** is selected and click **OK** to apply the change. You'll learn more about this and other firewalls in Chapter 10.

Install and Run Antivirus Software

Install and run antivirus (AV) software and keep it current. Configure the AV software so that it automatically downloads updates to the software and runs in the background. To be effective, AV software must be kept current and must be turned on. Set the AV software to automatically scan e-mail attachments (see Figure 2-9).

A+ ESS
1.4
2.4
6.1
6.3

A+
220-602
7.1

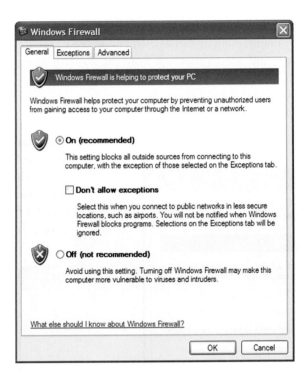

Figure 2-8   Turn on Windows Firewall to protect your system

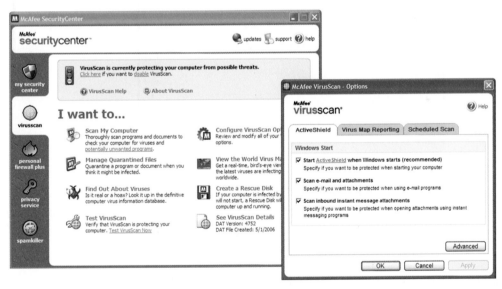

Figure 2-9   Configure antivirus software to scan e-mail and instant message attachments and to download updates automatically

Keep Windows Updates Current

Microsoft is continually releasing new patches, fixes, and updates for Windows XP, and, to a limited degree, for Windows 2000. For these OSs, you need to keep your installation of Windows current with all the latest updates. Many of these updates are to fix bugs in the system and to plug up security leaks.

Windows XP offers a way to automatically download and install updates. To verify that Windows XP is automatically maintaining updates when connected to the Internet, click **Start**, right click **My Computer**, and select **Properties** from the shortcut menu. The System Properties dialog box opens. Click **Automatic Updates**, as shown in Figure 2-10. For best results, select **Automatic (recommended)** and chose the day and time to download and install updates. Click **OK** to apply your changes.

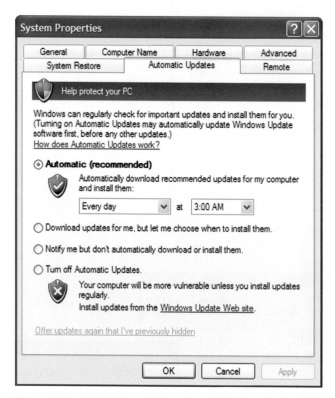

Figure 2-10   Set Windows XP to automatically download and install updates

Windows 2000 does not offer automatic updates. For this OS, you need to periodically go to the Microsoft Web site (*update.microsoft.com*) and manually download and install updates. Currently, Microsoft only updates Windows 2000 to solve problems with security. There are no more updates for Windows 9x/Me.

PHYSICALLY PROTECT YOUR EQUIPMENT

There are some things you can do to physically protect your computer equipment. Here is my list of do's and don't's. You can probably add your own tips to the list:

▲ *Don't move or jar your computer when it's turned on.* Before you move the computer case even a foot or so, power it down. Don't put the computer case under your desk where it might get bumped or kicked. Although modern hard drives are sealed and much less resistant to vibration than earlier models, it's still possible to crash a drive by banging into it while it's reading or writing data.

▲ *Don't smoke around your computer.* Tar from cigarettes can accumulate on fans, causing them to jam and the system to overheat. For older hard drives that are not adequately sealed, smoke particles can get inside and crash a drive.

A+ ESS
1.4
2.4
7.1
7.2

A+
220-602
1.3
7.1

▲ *Don't leave the PC turned off for weeks or months at a time.* Once my daughter left her PC turned off for an entire summer. At the beginning of the new school term, the PC would not boot. We discovered that the boot record at the beginning of the hard drive had become corrupted. PCs, like old cars, can give problems after long spans of inactivity.

▲ *Don't block air vents on the front and rear of the computer case or on the monitor.* Proper air circulation is essential to keeping a system cool. Also, for optimum air flow, put covers on expansion slot openings on the rear of the case and put faceplates over empty bays on the front of the case (see Figure 2-11).

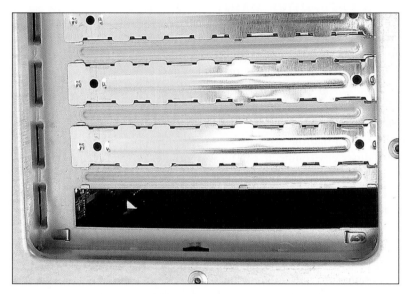

Figure 2-11   For optimum airflow, don't leave empty expansion slots and bays uncovered

▲ *Use keyboard covers for dirty environments.* You can purchase plastic keyboard covers to protect the keyboard in a dirty or extremely dusty environment.

▲ *High humidity can be dangerous for hard drives.* I once worked in a basement with PCs, and hard drives failed much too often. After we installed dehumidifiers, the hard drives became more reliable.

▲ *In CMOS setup, disable the ability to write to the boot sector of the hard drive.* This alone can keep boot viruses at bay. However, before you upgrade your OS, such as when you upgrade Windows XP to Windows Vista, be sure to enable writing to the boot sector, which the OS setup will want to do. How to make changes to BIOS settings using the CMOS setup utility is covered later in the chapter.

▲ *If your data is really private, keep it under lock and key.* You can use all kinds of security methods to encrypt, password protect, and hide data, but if it really is that important, one obvious thing you can do is store the data on a removable storage device such as a flash drive and, when you're not using the data, put the flash drive in a fire-proof safe. And, of course, keep two copies. Sounds simple, but it works.

▲ *Protect your CDs, DVDs, and other storage media.* To protect discs, keep them away from direct sunlight, heat, and extreme cold. Don't allow the bottom of a CD or DVD to be scratched. Don't open the shuttle window on a floppy disk or touch the disk's surface. Keep floppy disks and hard drives away from magnetic fields. In Chapter 9, you'll learn how to clean CDs and DVDs.

▲ *Keep magnets away from your computer.* Don't work inside the computer case with magnetized screwdrivers and or sit magnets on top of the computer case.

◢ *Don't unpack and turn on a computer that has just come in from the cold.* If your new laptop has just arrived and sat on your doorstep in freezing weather, don't bring it in and immediately unpack it and turn it on. Wait until a computer has had time to reach room temperature to prevent damage from condensation and static electricity. In addition, when unpacking hardware or software, to help protect against static electricity, remove the packing tape and cellophane from the work area as soon as possible.

 A+ Exam Tip

The A+ 220-602 exam expects you to know how to keep computers and monitors well ventilated and clean and to use protective covers for input devices such as the keyboard.

CREATING A PREVENTIVE MAINTENANCE PLAN

It is important to develop an overall preventive maintenance plan. If your company has established written guidelines for PC preventive maintenance, read them and follow the procedures necessary to make them work. If your company has no established plan, make your own.

A preventive maintenance plan tends to evolve from a history or pattern of malfunctions within an organization. For example, dusty environments can mean more maintenance, whereas a clean environment can mean less maintenance. Table 2-1 lists some guidelines for developing a preventive maintenance plan that may work for you.

A+ Exam Tip

The A+ Essentials exam expects you to know how to clean internal and external components and use appropriate cleaning materials as part of a regular preventive maintenance plan.

The general idea of preventive maintenance is to do what you can to make a PC last longer and cause as little trouble as possible. You may also be responsible for ensuring that data is secure and backed up, that software copyrights are not violated, and that users are supported. As with any plan, when designing your preventive maintenance plan, first define your overall goals, and then design the plan accordingly. The guidelines listed in Table 2-1 primarily address the problems that prevent a PC from lasting long and from performing well.

Component	Maintenance	How Often
Inside the case	◢ Make sure air vents are clear. ◢ Use compressed air to blow the dust out of the case, or use a vacuum to clean vents, power supply, and fan. ◢ Ensure that chips and expansion cards are firmly seated.	Yearly
CMOS setup	◢ Keep a written record of any changes you make to CMOS setup, or you can back up CMOS using third-party software such as Norton Utilities by Symantec (*www.symantec.com*).	Whenever changes are made to CMOS setup
Floppy drive	◢ Clean the floppy drive only when the drive does not work.	When the drive does not work
Hard drive	◢ Perform regular backups.	At least weekly
	◢ Delete temporary files and empty the Recycle Bin.	Monthly

Table 2-1 Guidelines for developing a PC preventive maintenance plan

A+ ESS
1.4
2.4

A+
220-602
1.3
4.4
7.1

Component	Maintenance	How Often
	◢ Defragment the drive and scan the drive for errors.	Monthly
	◢ Using third-party utility software such as Norton Utilities, back up the partition table to floppy disk.	Whenever changes are made
Keyboard	◢ Clean the keyboard (covered in Chapter 8).	Monthly
Mouse	◢ Clean the mouse rollers and ball (covered in Chapter 8).	Monthly
Monitor	◢ Clean the screen with a soft cloth.	At least monthly
Printers	◢ Clean out the dust and bits of paper, using compressed air and a vacuum. Small pieces of paper can be removed with tweezers, preferably insulated ones. ◢ Clean the paper and ribbon paths with a soft, lint-free cloth. ◢ Don't re-ink ribbons or use recharged toner cartridges. ◢ If the printer uses an ozone filter, replace it as recommended by the manufacturer. ◢ Replace other components as recommended by the manufacturer. You can purchase maintenance kits from the printer manufacturer, which include a scheduled maintenance plan for the printer.	At least monthly or as recommended by the manufacturer
UPS/Surge Suppressors	◢ Run weak battery test. ◢ Run diagnostic test.	As recommended by manufacturer
Software	◢ If directed by your employer, check that only authorized software is present.	At least monthly
Written records	◢ Keep a record of all software, including version numbers and the OS installed on the PC. ◢ Keep a record of all hardware components installed, including hardware settings. ◢ Record when and what preventive maintenance is performed. ◢ Record any repairs done to the PC.	Whenever changes are made

Table 2-1 Guidelines for developing a PC preventive maintenance plan (continued)

DEALING WITH DUST

A+
220-602
1.3
7.1

📹 Video

Preventative Maintenance

Dust is not good for a PC because it insulates PC parts like a blanket, which can cause them to overheat. Dust inside fans can jam fans; fans not working can cause a system to overheat (see Figure 2-12). Therefore, ridding the PC of dust is an important part of preventive maintenance. Some PC technicians don't like to use a vacuum inside a PC because they're concerned that the vacuum might produce ESD. However, inside the PC case, it's safe to use a special antistatic vacuum designed to be used around sensitive equipment. If you don't have one of these vacuums, you can use compressed air to blow the dust out of the chassis, power supply, and fans. The dust will get all over everything; you can then use a regular vacuum to clean up the mess. While you're cleaning up dust, you can also blow or vacuum out the keyboard.

A+ ESS
1.4
2.4

A+
220-602
1.3
7.1

Figure 2-12 This dust-jammed fan caused a system to overheat

A+ ESS
2.4

A+
220-602
7.1

PREPARING A COMPUTER FOR SHIPPING

When shipping a desktop or notebook computer, remember that rough handling can cause damage, as can exposure to water, heat, and cold. The computer can also be misplaced, lost, or stolen. When you are preparing a computer for shipping, take extra precautions to protect it and its data. Follow these general guidelines when preparing to ship a computer:

- Back up the hard drive onto a tape cartridge or other backup medium separate from your computer. If you don't have access to a medium that can back up the entire drive, at the least, back up important Windows system files and all data to another media. Whatever you do, don't ship a computer that has the only copy of important data on the hard drive, or data that should be secured from unauthorized access.
- Remove any removable disks, tape cartridges, or CDs from the drives. Make sure that the tapes or disks holding the backup data are secured and protected during transit. Consider shipping them separately.
- Turn off power to the computer and all other devices.
- Disconnect power cords from the electrical outlet and the devices. Disconnect all external devices from the computer. For notebook computers, remove the battery.
- If you think someone might have trouble later identifying which cord or cable belongs to which device or connection, label the cable connections with white tape or white labels.
- Coil all external cords and secure them with plastic ties or rubber bands.
- Pack the computer, monitor, and all devices in their original shipping cartons or similar boxes with enough packing material to protect them. Each device needs to be wrapped or secured separately so devices will not bump against each other.
- Purchase insurance on the shipment. Postal insurance is not expensive and can save you a lot of money if materials are damaged in transit.

A+ ESS
6.1
7.3

A+
220-602
7.1

DISPOSING OF USED EQUIPMENT

As a PC technician, it will often be your responsibility to dispose of used equipment and con-sumables, including batteries, printer toner cartridges, hard drives, and monitors. Table 2-2 lists such items and how to dispose of them. Manufacturer documentation and local environ-mental regulators can also provide disposal instructions or guidance.

Part	How to Dispose
Alkaline batteries including AAA, AA, A, C, D, and 9 volt	Dispose of these batteries in the regular trash. First check to see if there are recycling facilities in your area.
Button batteries used in digital cameras, Flash Path, and other small equipment; battery packs used in notebooks	These batteries can contain silver oxide, mercury, lithium, or cadmium and are considered hazardous waste. Dispose of them by returning them to the original dealer or by taking them to a recycling center. To recycle, pack them separately from other items. If you don't have a recycling center nearby, contact your county for local regulations for disposal.
Laser printer toner cartridges	Return these to the manufacturer or dealer to be recycled.
Ink-jet printer cartridges Computer cases, power supplies, and other computer parts Monitors Chemical solvents and cans	Check with local county or environmental officials for laws and regulations in your area for proper disposal of these items. The county might have a recycling center that will receive them. Discharge a monitor before disposing of it.
Storage media such as hard drives, CDs, and DVDs	Do physical damage to the device so it is not possible for sensitive data to be stolen. Then the device can be put in the trash.

Table 2-2 Computer parts and how to dispose of them

Monitors and power supplies can contain a charge even after the devices are unplugged. Most CRT monitors today are designed to discharge if allowed to sit unplugged for 60 minutes or more. To manually discharge a monitor, a high-voltage probe is used with the monitor case opened. Ask a technician trained to fix monitors to do this for you.

Don't throw out a hard drive that might have personal or corporate data on it unless you know the data can't be stolen off the drive. To assure yourself there's no way someone is going to read from the drive, you can take a hammer and nail and punch the drive housing, forcing the nail straight through to the other side so that all drive disks are damaged. To dis-pose of CDs, floppy disks, DVDs and other storage media, do similar damage, such as breaking a CD in half.

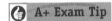 **A+ Exam Tip**

The A+ Essentials exam expects you to know how to follow environmental guide-lines to dispose of batteries, CRTs, chemical solvents, and cans. If you're not certain how to dispose of a product, see its MSDS document.

A+ ESS
7.2

HOW TO WORK INSIDE A COMPUTER CASE

A+
220-602
1.2
7.1

In this section, you'll learn how to take a computer apart and put it back together. When working inside a computer, note that you can damage both the computer and yourself. Here are some important safety precautions that will help keep you and

A+ ESS
7.2

A+
220-602
1.2
7.1

your equipment safe as you go through the process of taking it apart and putting it back together:

▲ Make notes as you work so that you can backtrack later if necessary. (When you're first learning to take a computer apart, it's really easy to forget where everything fits when it's time to put it back together. Also, in troubleshooting, you want to avoid repeating or overlooking things to try.)

▲ To stay organized and not lose small parts, keep screws and spacers orderly and in one place, such as a cup or tray.

▲ Don't stack boards on top of each other: You could accidentally dislodge a chip this way.

▲ When handling motherboards and expansion cards, don't touch the chips on the boards. Hold expansion cards by the edges. Don't touch any soldered components on a card, and don't touch chips or edge connectors unless it's absolutely necessary. All this helps prevent damage from static electricity.

▲ To protect the chip, don't touch it with a magnetized screwdriver.

▲ Don't use a graphite pencil to change DIP (dual inline package) switch settings, because graphite is a conductor of electricity, and the graphite can lodge in the switch.

▲ In a classroom environment, after you have reassembled everything, have your instructor check your work before you put the cover back on and power up.

▲ To protect both yourself and the equipment when working inside a computer, turn off the power, unplug the computer, and always use a ground bracelet (which you will learn more about later).

▲ Never ever touch the inside of a computer that is turned on.

▲ Consider the monitor and the power supply to be "black boxes." Never remove the cover or put your hands inside this equipment unless you know about the hazards of charged capacitors and have been trained to deal with them. Both the power supply and the monitor can hold a dangerous level of electricity even after you turn them off and disconnect them from a power source. The power supply and monitor contain enough power to kill you, even when they are unplugged.

▲ When unpacking hardware or software, to help protect against static electricity, remove the packing tape and cellophane from the work area as soon as possible.

▲ To protect against static electricity, keep components away from your hair and clothing.

The last two bullets in this list are about static electricity. This topic is so important that it warrants its own subsection. That section comes up next; afterward, you'll read about how to take a computer apart and put it back together.

STATIC ELECTRICITY

Suppose you come indoors on a cold day, pick up a comb, and touch your hair. Sparks fly! What happened? Static electricity caused the sparks. Electrostatic discharge (ESD), commonly known as static electricity, is an electrical charge at rest. When you came indoors, this charge built up on your hair and had no place to go. An ungrounded conductor (such as wire that is not touching another wire) or a nonconductive surface (such as your hair) holds a charge until the charge is released. When two objects with dissimilar electrical charges touch, electricity passes between them until the dissimilar charges become equal.

To see static charges equalizing, turn off the lights in a room, scuff your feet on the carpet, and touch another person. Occasionally, you can see and feel the charge in your fingers. If you can feel the charge, you discharged at least 1,500 volts of static electricity. If you hear the discharge, you released at least 6,000 volts. If you see the discharge, you released at least

A+ ESS
7.2

A+
220-602
1.2
7.1

8,000 volts of ESD. A charge of only 10 volts can damage electronic components! You can touch a chip on an expansion card or motherboard, damage the chip with ESD, and never feel, hear, or see the discharge.

ESD can cause two types of damage in an electronic component: catastrophic failure and upset failure. A catastrophic failure destroys the component beyond use. An upset failure damages the component so that it does not perform well, even though it may still function to some degree. Upset failures are more difficult to detect because they are not as easily observed. Both types of failures permanently affect the device.

To protect the computer against ESD, always ground yourself before touching electronic components, including the hard drive, motherboard, expansion cards, processors, and memory modules. You can ground yourself and the computer parts by using one or more of the following static control devices or methods:

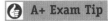

A+ Exam Tip

The A+ Essentials exam emphasizes that you should know how to protect computer equipment as you work on it.

Caution

A monitor can also damage components with ESD. Do not place or store expansion cards on top of or next to a monitor, which can discharge as much as 29,000 volts onto the screen.

▲ *Ground bracelet.* A ground bracelet, also called an antistatic strap or ESD bracelet, is a strap you wear around your wrist. One end attaches to a grounded conductor such as the computer case or a ground mat, or plugs into a wall outlet. (Only the ground prong makes a connection!) The bracelet also contains a resistor that prevents electricity from harming you. Figure 2-13 shows a ground bracelet.

Figure 2-13 A ground bracelet, which protects computer components from ESD, can clip to the side of the computer case and eliminate ESD between you and the case

A+ ESS
7.2

A+
220-602
1.2
7.1

▲ *Ground mats.* Ground mats dissipate ESD and are commonly used by bench technicians (also called depot technicians) who assemble and repair computers at their workbenches or in an assembly line. Ground mats have a connector in one corner that you can use to connect the mat to ground (see Figure 2-14). If you lift a component off the mat, it is no longer grounded and is susceptible to ESD, so it's important to use a ground bracelet with a ground mat.

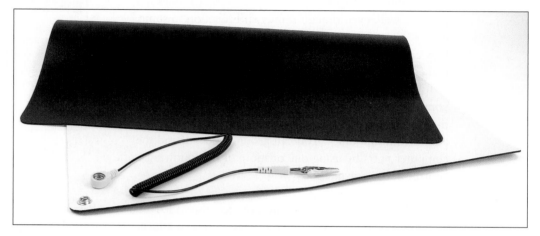

Figure 2-14 A ground mat dissipates ESD and should be connected to ground

▲ *Static shielding bags.* New components come shipped in static shielding bags, also called antistatic bags. These bags are a type of Faraday Cage, named after Michael Faraday, who built the first cage in 1836. A Faraday Cage is any device that protects against an electromagnetic field. Save the bags to store other devices that are not currently installed in a PC. As you work on a computer, know that a device is not protected from ESD if you place it on top of the bag; the protection is inside the bag (see Figure 2-15).

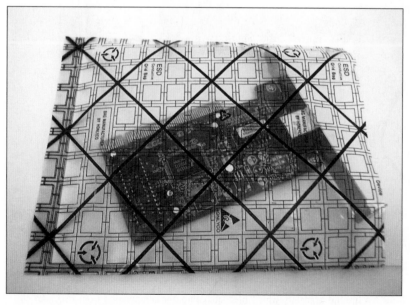

Figure 2-15 Static shielding bags help protect components from ESD

A+ ESS
7.2

A+
220-602
1.2
7.1

◢ *Antistatic gloves.* You can purchase antistatic gloves designed to prevent an ESD discharge between you and a device as you pick it up and handle it (see Figure 2-16). The gloves can be substituted for an antistatic bracelet and are good for moving, packing, or unpacking sensitive equipment. However, they tend to get in the way when working inside computer cases.

Figure 2-16 Use antistatic gloves to prevent static discharge between you and the equipment you are handling

The best way to guard against ESD is to use a ground bracelet together with a ground mat. Consider a ground bracelet essential equipment when working on a computer. However, if you are in a situation in which you must work without one, touch the computer case or the power supply before you touch a component. When passing a circuit board, memory module, or other sensitive component to another person, ground yourself and then touch the other person before you pass the component. Leave components inside their protective bags until you are ready to use them. Work on hard floors, not carpet, or use antistatic spray on the carpets. Generally, don't work on a computer if you or the computer have just come in from the cold, because there is more danger of ESD when the atmosphere is cold and dry.

There are exceptions to the rule of always being grounded when you work with PCs. You *don't* want to be grounded when working inside a monitor, inside a power supply, or inside high-voltage equipment such as a laser printer. These devices maintain high electrical charges, even

> 🖉 **Notes**
>
> When working inside the older AT cases, it was safe enough to leave the power cord plugged into the power outlet if the power switch was turned off. Leaving the power cord plugged in helped to ground the case. However, with newer ATX and BTX cases, residual power is still on even when the power switch on the rear of the case is turned off. Some motherboards even have a small light inside the case to remind you of this fact and to warn you that power is still getting to the system. For this reason, when working on newer ATX and BTX systems, be certain to unplug the power cord before working inside these cases.

A+ ESS
7.2

A+
220-602
1.2
7.1

A+ ESS
1.2

when the power is turned off. Inside a monitor case, the electricity stored in capacitors can be dangerous. When working inside a monitor, laser printer, or power supply, you don't want to be grounded, because you would provide a conduit for the voltage to discharge through your body. In this situation, be careful not to ground yourself. *Don't* wear a ground bracelet when working inside these devices, because you don't want to be the ground for these charges!

STEPS TO TAKE APART A COMPUTER

A PC technician needs to be comfortable with taking apart a computer and putting it back together. In most situations, the essential tools you'll need for the job are a ground bracelet, a Phillips-head screwdriver, a flat-head screwdriver, paper, and pen. As you work inside a computer, be sure to use a ground bracelet, the safety precautions in the chapter, and the guidelines in the following list:

1. If you are starting with a working computer, enter CMOS setup and write down any customized settings you have made so that, in the event you must return CMOS to its default settings, you can restore the customized settings. Back up any important data on the hard drive.

2. Power down the system and unplug it. Unplug the monitor, mouse, keyboard, and any other peripherals or cables attached and move them out of your way.

3. Put the computer on a table with plenty of room. Have a plastic bag or cup handy to hold screws. When you reassemble the PC, you will need to insert the same screws in the same holes. This is especially important with the hard drive, because screws that are too long can puncture the hard drive housing.

4. Sometimes I think figuring out how to open a computer case is the most difficult part of disassembling. To remove the cover of your PC, do the following:

   - Many newer cases require you to remove the faceplate on the front of the case first. Other cases require you to remove a side panel first, and really older cases require you to first remove the entire sides and top as a single unit. Study your case for the correct approach.

   - If you find screws on the rear of the case along the edges such as those in Figure 2-17, start with removing these screws.

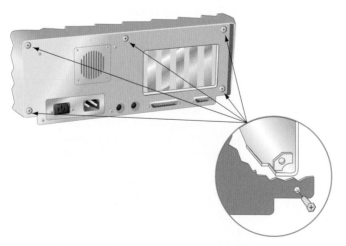

Figure 2-17   Locate the screws that hold the cover in place

- For a desktop case or tower case, locate and remove the screws on the back of the case. For a desktop case, like the one in Figure 2-17, look for the screws in each corner and one in the top. Be careful not to unscrew any screws besides these. The other screws probably are holding the power supply in place (see Figure 2-18).

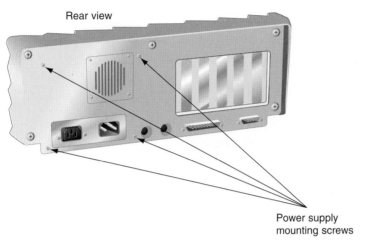

Rear view

Power supply
mounting screws

Figure 2-18 Power supply mounting screws

- After you remove the cover screws, slide the cover forward and up to remove it from the case, as shown in Figure 2-19.

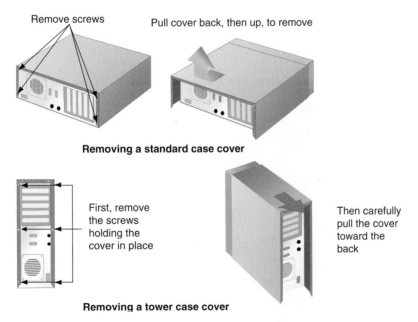

Remove screws

Pull cover back, then up, to remove

Removing a standard case cover

First, remove the screws holding the cover in place

Then carefully pull the cover toward the back

Removing a tower case cover

Figure 2-19 Removing the cover

- Older tower cases also have the screws on the back. Look for screws in all four corners and down the sides (see Figure 2-19). Remove the screws and then slide the cover back slightly before lifting it up

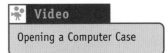

Video

Opening a Computer Case

to remove it. Some tower cases have panels on either side of the case, held in place with screws on the back of the case (see Figure 2-20). Remove the screws and slide each panel toward the rear, then lift it off the case.

Figure 2-20   Slide a side panel to the rear and then lift it off the case

- Newer cases require you to pop the front panel off the case before removing the side panels. Look for a lever on the bottom of the panel and hinges at the top. Squeeze the lever to release the front panel and lift it off the case (see Figure 2-21). Then remove a single screw (see Figure 2-22) and slide the side panel to the front and then off the case. Also, know that some case panels don't use screws; these side panels simply pop up and out with a little prying and pulling.

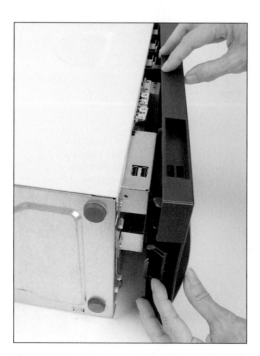

Figure 2-21   Newer cases require you remove the front panel before removing the side panels of a computer case

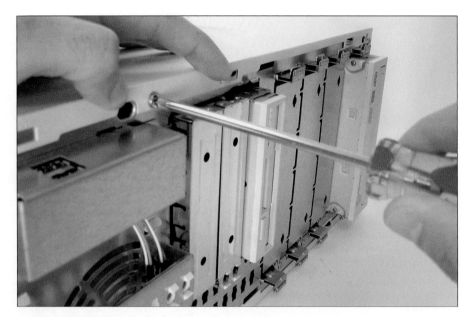

Figure 2-22 One screw holds the side panel in place

5. If you're working on a tower case, lay it on its side so the motherboard is on the bottom. If you plan to remove several components, draw a diagram of all cable connections, DIP switch settings, and jumper settings. You might need the cable connection diagram to help you reassemble. If you want, use a felt-tip marker to make a mark across components, to indicate a cable connection, board placement, motherboard orientation, speaker connection, brackets, and so on, so that you can simply line up the marks when you reassemble.

6. Drives are connected to the motherboard with ribbon cables or thinner serial ATA cables. Before removing any ribbon cables, look for a red color or stripe down one side of each cable. This edge color marks this side of the cable as pin 1. Look on the board or drive that the cable is attached to. You should see that pin 1 or pin 2 is clearly marked, as shown in Figure 2-23. However, some boards mark pin 34 or pin 40. For these boards, pin 1 is on the other side of the connector. Also know that some boards and drives don't mark the pins, but rather have a notch in the connector so that a notched ribbon cable can only be inserted in one direction (see Figure 2-24).

Figure 2-23 Pin 1 for this IDE connection is clearly marked

Figure 2-24 The notch on the side of this floppy drive connector allows the floppy drive cable to connect in only one direction

Verify that the edge color is aligned with pin 1. Serial ATA cables can only connect to serial ATA connectors in one direction (see Figure 2-25).

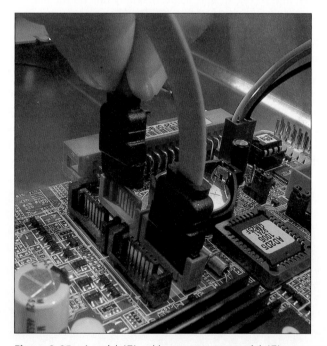

Figure 2-25 A serial ATA cable connects to a serial ATA connector in only one direction

7. A system might have up to three types of ribbon cables. A floppy drive cable has 34 pins and a twist in the cable. IDE cables have 40 pins. A CD or DVD drive can use the 40-conductor IDE cable, but most hard drives today use the higher quality 80-conductor IDE cable. See Figure 2-26 for a comparison of these three cables.

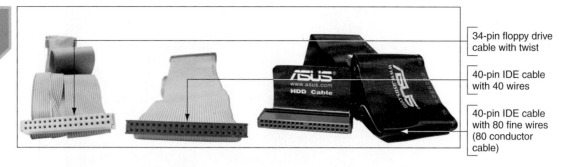

34-pin floppy drive
cable with twist

40-pin IDE cable
with 40 wires

40-pin IDE cable
with 80 fine wires
(80 conductor
cable)

Figure 2-26 A system might have up to three types of ribbon cables

Remove the cables to all drives. Remove the power supply cords from the drives. Notice as you disconnect the power cord, the Molex connector is shaped so it only connects in one direction (see Figure 2-27).

> **Video**
>
> Replacing an Expansion Card

Figure 2-27 Molex power connector to a drive orients in only one direction

8. Do the following to remove the expansion cards:

- Remove any wire or cable connected to the card.

- Remove the screw holding the card to the case (see Figure 2-28).

- Grasp the card with both hands and remove it by lifting straight up. If you have trouble removing it from the expansion slot, you can *very slightly* rock the card from end to end (*not* side to side). Rocking the card from side to side might spread the slot opening and weaken the connection.

> **Notes**
>
> Some video cards use a latch that helps to hold the card securely in the slot. To remove these cards, use one finger to hold the latch back from the slot, as shown in Figure 2-29, as you pull the card up and out of the slot.

Figure 2-28   Remove the screw holding an expansion card to the case

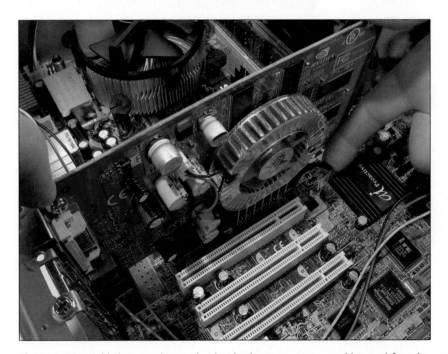

Figure 2-29   Hold the retention mechanism back as you remove a video card from its expansion slot

- As you remove the card, don't put your fingers on the edge connectors or touch a chip, and don't stack the cards on top of one another. Lay each card aside on a flat surface.

9. Depending on the system, you might need to remove the motherboard next or remove the drives next. My choice is to first remove the motherboard. It and the processor are the most expensive and easily damaged parts in the system. I like to get them out of harm's way before working with the drives. However, in some cases, you must remove

the drives or the power supply before you can get to the motherboard. Study your situation and decide which to do first. To remove the motherboard, do the following:

- Unplug the power supply lines to the motherboard. You'll find a main power line, and maybe one auxiliary power line from the power supply to the motherboard. There might also be an audio wire from the CD drive to the motherboard. Disconnect it from the motherboard.

>
> **Notes**
>
> Older AT power supplies and motherboards use two main power lines that plug in side-by-side on the motherboard and are labeled P8 and P9. You will want to be certain that you don't switch these two lines when reconnecting them, because this would cause the wrong voltage to flow in the circuits on the motherboard and could destroy the board. Fortunately, most connections today only allow you to place the lines in the correct order, which is always black leads on P8 next to black leads on P9. For these older boards, remember, "black to black."

- The next step is to disconnect wires leading from the front of the computer case to the motherboard. If you don't have the motherboard manual handy, be very careful to diagram how these wires connect because they are never labeled well on a motherboard. Make a careful diagram and then disconnect the wires. Figure 2-30 shows five leads and the pins on the motherboard that receive these leads. The pins are color-coded and cryptically labeled on the board. You'll learn more about matching these wires to their connectors in Chapter 5.

Figure 2-30   Five leads from the front panel connect to two rows of pins on the motherboard

- You're now ready to remove the screws that hold the motherboard to the case. For an older motherboard, instead of screws you'll see spacers that keep the board from resting directly on the bottom of the computer case. Carefully pop off these spacers and/or remove the screws (up to nine) that hold the board to the case (see Figure 2-31) and

A+ ESS
1.2

Figure 2-31   Remove up to nine screws that hold the motherboard to the case

then remove the board. Set it aside in a safe place. Figure 2-32 shows a motherboard sitting to the side of these spacers. One spacer is in place and the other is lying beside its case holes. Also notice in the photo the two holes in the motherboard where screws are used to connect the board to the spacers.

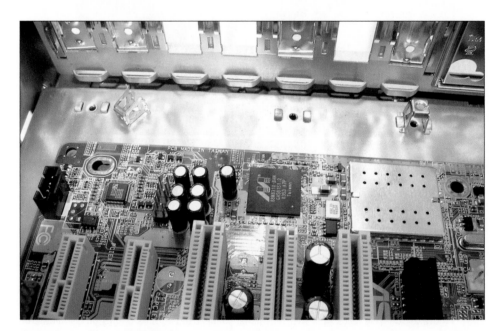

Figure 2-32   This motherboard connects to a case using screws and spacers that keep the board from touching the case

- The motherboard should now be free and you can carefully remove it from the case as shown in Figure 2-33.

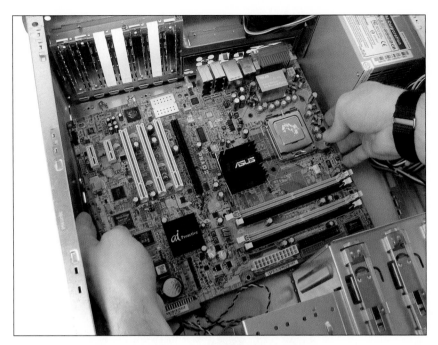

Figure 2-33 Remove the motherboard from the case

10. To remove the power supply from the case, look for screws that attach the power supply to the computer case, as shown in Figure 2-34. Be careful not to remove

> **Caution**
>
> Some processors have heavy cooling assemblies installed on top of them. For these systems, it is best to remove the cooler before you take the motherboard out of the case because the motherboard is not designed to support this heavy cooler when the motherboard is not securely seated in the case. How to remove this cooler is covered in Chapter 4.

Figure 2-34 Removing the power supply mounting screws

any screws that hold the power supply housing together. You do not want to take the housing apart. After you have removed the screws, the power supply still might not be free. Sometimes, it is attached to the case on the underside by recessed slots. Turn the case over and look on the bottom for these slots. If they are present, determine in which direction you need to slide the power supply to free it from the case.

11. Remove each drive next, handling the drives with care. Here are some tips:

   • Some drives have one or two screws on each side of the drive attaching the drive to the drive bay. After you remove the screws, the drive slides to the front or to the rear and then out of the case.

   • Sometimes, there is a catch underneath the drive that you must lift up as you slide the drive forward.

   • Some drive bays have a clipping mechanism to hold the drive in the bay. First release the clip and then pull the drive forward and out of the bay (see Figure 2-35). Handle the drives with care.

Figure 2-35   To remove this CD drive, first pull the clip forward to release the drive from the bay

   • Some cases have a removable bay for small drives (see Figure 2-36). These bays can hold narrow drives such as hard drives, floppy drives, and Zip drives. The bay is removed first and then the drives are removed from the bay. To remove the bay, first remove the screws or release the clip holding the bay in place and then slide the bay out of the case. The drives are usually installed in the bay with two screws on each side of each drive. Remove the screws and then the drives (see Figure 2-37).

Video

Replacing a Power Supply

STEPS TO PUT A COMPUTER BACK TOGETHER

To reassemble a computer, reverse the process of disassembling. Do the following:

1. Install the power supply, drives, motherboard, and cards in the case. When installing drives, know that for some systems, it's easier to connect data cables to the drives and then slide the drives into the bay.

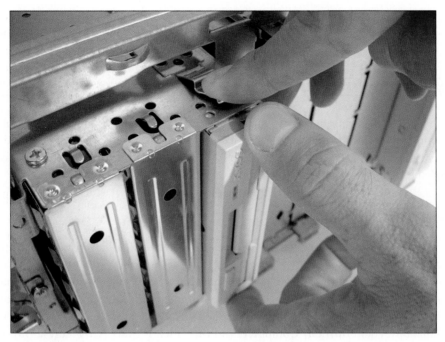

Figure 2-36 Push down on the clip and then slide the removable bay forward and out of the case

Figure 2-37 Drives in this removable bay are held in place with screws on each side of the bay

2. Connect all data and power cables. Before you replace the cover, take a few minutes to double-check each connection to make sure it is correct and snug.

3. Plug in the keyboard, monitor, and mouse.

4. In a classroom environment, have the instructor check your work before you power up.

5. Turn on the power and check that the PC is working properly. If the PC does not work, most likely the problem is a loose connection. Just turn off the power and go

back and check each cable connection and each expansion card. You probably have not solidly seated a card in the slot. After you have double-checked, try again.

UNDERSTANDING THE BOOT PROCESS

Another skill you need as a PC support technician is to know how to fix a problem with booting the PC. The first steps in learning that skill are to know how to boot a PC and to understand what happens when you first turn on a PC and it begins the process of loading an operating system. That's the subject of this section of the chapter.

BOOTING A COMPUTER

The term booting comes from the phrase "lifting yourself up by your bootstraps" and refers to the computer bringing itself up to a working state without the user having to do anything but press the on button. This boot can be a "hard boot" or a "soft boot." A hard boot, or cold boot, involves turning on the power with the on/off switch. A soft boot, or warm boot, involves using the operating system to reboot. For Windows XP, one way to soft boot is to click **Start**, click **Turn Off Computer**, and then click **Restart** (see Figure 2-38). For Windows NT/2000 and Windows 9x/Me, click **Start**, click **Shut Down**, and then select **Restart** and click **OK**. For DOS, pressing the keys **Ctrl**, **Alt**, and **Del** (or Delete) at the same time performs a soft boot. (You will often see this key combination written as **Ctrl+Alt+Del**.)

Figure 2-38   Windows XP Turn off computer dialog box

CHOOSING BETWEEN A HARD BOOT AND A SOFT BOOT

A hard boot is more stressful on your machine than a soft boot because of the initial power surge through the equipment that occurs when you press the power switch. Thus, whenever possible, use a soft boot. Also, a soft boot is faster because the initial steps of a hard boot don't happen.

To save time, you should always use the soft boot to restart unless soft booting doesn't work. If you cannot soft boot, look for power or reset buttons on the front or rear of the case. My newest computer has three power switches: a power button and a reset button on the front of the case and a power switch on the rear of the case (see Figure 2-39). The power button in front is a "soft" power button, causing a normal Windows shutdown and restart, and the reset button is a "hard" power switch, abruptly turning off power and then restarting. The switch on the rear of the case simply turns off the power abruptly and is a "hard" power button. Know, however, that some systems only have a single power switch on the front of the case.

Soft power button does a normal Windows shutdown

Hard power switch on rear of case

Hard power button abruptly reboots

Figure 2-39 This computer case has two power buttons on the front and one power switch on the rear of the case

THE STARTUP BIOS CONTROLS THE BEGINNING OF THE BOOT

The startup BIOS is programming contained on the firmware chip on the motherboard that is responsible for getting a system up and going and finding an OS to load. A successful boot depends on the hardware, the BIOS, and the operating system all performing without errors. If errors occur, they might or might not stall or lock up the boot. Errors are communicated as beeps or as messages onscreen. Some of these error messages and beep codes are listed in Table 2-4 at the end of this chapter.

The functions performed during the boot can be divided into four parts, as shown in the following numbered list. The first two items in the list are covered in detail in this section. (The last two steps depend on the OS being used and are not covered in this book.)

Video

Beep Codes

1. *The startup BIOS runs the POST and assigns system resources.* The POST (power-on self test) is a series of tests performed by the startup BIOS to determine if it can communicate correctly with essential hardware components required for a successful boot. The startup BIOS surveys hardware resources and needs, and assigns system resources to meet those needs (see Figure 2-40). The startup BIOS begins the startup process by reading configuration information stored primarily in CMOS RAM, and then comparing that information to the hardware—the processor, video slot, PCI slots, hard drive, and so on. (Recall that CMOS RAM is a small amount of memory on the motherboard that holds information about installed hardware.)

2. *The startup BIOS program searches for and loads an OS.* Most often the OS is loaded from logical drive C on the hard drive. Configuration information stored in CMOS RAM tells startup BIOS where to look for the OS. Most new BIOSs support loading the OS from the hard drive, a floppy disk, a CD, a DVD, or a USB device. The BIOS turns to the specified device, reads the beginning files of the OS, copies them into memory, and then turns control over to the OS. This part of the loading process works the same for any operating system; only the OS files being loaded change.

Notes

The four system resources on a motherboard that the OS and processor use to interact with hardware are IRQ lines, I/O addresses, memory addresses, and DMA channels, all defined in Table 2-3. Older systems using DOS and Windows 9x/Me required a technician to make decisions about managing these resources when installing hardware devices, but newer systems generally manage these resources without our involvement. For an explanation of how each resource works, see Appendix A.

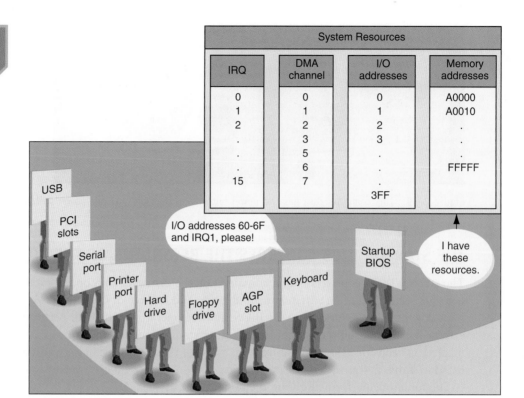

Figure 2-40   Boot Step 1: The ROM BIOS startup program surveys hardware resources and needs and assigns system resources to satisfy those needs

System Resource	Definition
IRQ numbers	A line of a motherboard bus that a hardware device or expansion slot can use to signal the CPU that the device needs attention. Some lines have a higher priority for attention than others. Each IRQ line is assigned a number (0 to 15) to identify it.
I/O addresses	Numbers assigned to hardware devices that software uses to send a command to a device. Each device "listens" for these numbers and responds to the ones assigned to it. I/O addresses are communicated on the address bus.
Memory addresses	Numbers assigned to physical memory located either in RAM or ROM chips. Software can access this memory by using these addresses. Memory addresses are communicated on the address bus.
DMA channels	A number designating a channel on which the device can pass data to memory without involving the CPU. Think of a DMA channel as a shortcut for data moving to and from the device and memory.

Table 2-3   System resources used by software and hardware

3. *The OS configures the system and completes its own loading.* The OS checks some of the same settings and devices that startup BIOS checked, such as available memory and whether that memory is reliable. Then the OS loads the core components necessary to access the files and folders on the hard drive and to use memory, the expansion buses on the motherboard, and the cards installed in these expansion slots. The OS also loads the software to control installed devices, such as the mouse, the video card,

2

the DVD drive, or the scanner. These devices generally have device drivers stored on the hard drive. The Windows desktop is then loaded.

4. *Application software is loaded and executed.* Sometimes an OS is configured to automatically launch application software as part of the boot. After this, the user is in control. When the user tells the OS to execute an application, the OS first must find the application software on the hard drive, CD, or other secondary storage device, copy the software into memory, and then turn control over to it. Finally, the user can command the application software, which makes requests to the OS, which, in turn, uses the system resources, system BIOS, and device drivers to interface with and control the hardware.

POST AND ASSIGNMENT OF SYSTEM RESOURCES

When you turn on the power to a PC, the processor begins the boot by initializing itself and then turning to startup BIOS for instructions. The startup BIOS first performs POST. The following list contains the key steps in this process:

1. When the power is first turned on, the system clock begins to generate clock pulses.

2. The processor begins working and initializes itself (resetting its internal values).

3. The processor turns to memory address FFFF0h, which is the memory address always assigned to the first instruction in the ROM BIOS startup program.

4. This instruction directs the processor to run POST.

5. POST first checks the BIOS program operating it and then tests CMOS RAM.

6. A test determines that there has been no battery failure.

7. Hardware interrupts are disabled. (This means that pressing a key on the keyboard or using another input device at this point does not affect anything.)

8. Tests are run on the processor, and it is initialized further.

9. A check determines if this is a cold boot. If so, the first 16 KB of RAM is tested.

10. Hardware devices installed on the computer are inventoried and compared to configuration information.

11. The video card is tested and configured. During POST, before the processor has checked the video system, beeps sometimes communicate errors. Short and long beeps indicate an error; the coding for the beeps depends on the BIOS. After POST checks and verifies the video controller card (note that POST does not check to see if a monitor is present or working), POST can use video to display its progress.

12. POST checks RAM by writing and reading data. The monitor displays a running count of RAM during this phase.

13. Next, the keyboard is checked, and if you press and hold any keys at this point, an error occurs with some BIOSs. Secondary storage—including floppy disk drives and hard drives—ports, and other hardware devices are tested and configured. The hardware that POST finds is checked against the data stored in the CMOS chip, jumpers, and/or DIP switches to determine if they agree. IRQ, I/O addresses, and DMA assignments are made; the OS completes this process later. Some hardware devices have BIOSs of their own that request resources from startup BIOS, which attempts to assign these system resources as requested.

14. Some devices are set up to go into "sleep mode" to conserve electricity.

15. The DMA and interrupt controllers are checked.

16. CMOS setup is run if requested.

17. BIOS begins its search for an OS.

STARTUP BIOS FINDS AND LOADS THE OS

After POST and the first pass at assignment of resources are complete, the next step is to load an OS. The startup BIOS looks to CMOS setup to find out which device is set to be the boot device. Most often the OS is loaded from logical drive C on the hard drive. The minimum information required on the hard drive to load an OS is shown in the following list. You can see some of these items labeled in Figure 2-41.

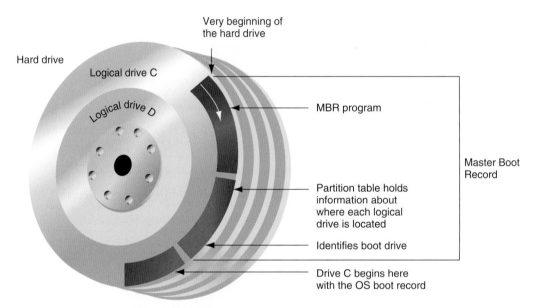

Figure 2-41   For a successful boot, a hard drive must contain a healthy Master Boot Record (MBR) and a healthy OS boot record

◢ Even though a hard drive is a circular affair, it must begin somewhere. On the outermost track, one sector (512 bytes) is designated the "beginning" of the hard drive. This sector, called the Master Boot Record (MBR), contains two items. The first item is the master boot program, which is needed to locate the beginning of the OS on the drive.

◢ The second item in the MBR is a table, called the partition table, which contains a map to the partitions on the hard drive. This table tells BIOS how many partitions the drive has and how each partition is divided into one or more logical drives, which partition contains the drive to be used for booting (called the **active partition**), and where each logical drive begins and ends.

◢ At the beginning of the boot drive (usually drive C) is the OS boot record, which loads the first program file of the OS. (A program file contains a list of instructions stored in a file.) For Windows NT/2000/XP, that program is Ntldr, and for Windows 9x/Me, that program is Io.sys.

◢ The boot loader program for the OS (Ntldr or Io.sys) begins the process of loading the OS into memory. For Windows NT/2000/XP, Ntbootdd.sys is optional and used next (if the hard drive uses SCSI technology, which is discussed in Chapter 7), followed by

A+ ESS
1.3

Boot.ini. For Windows 9x/Me, Msdos.sys is required next, followed by Command.com. These two files, plus Io.sys, are the core components of the real-mode portion of Windows 9x/Me. In addition to the files introduced here, Windows NT/2000/XP requires several more startup files.

 Notes

Program files can be a part of the OS or applications and have a .com, .sys, .bat, or .exe file extension. Ntldr is an exception to that rule because it has no file extension.

A+ ESS
1.1
1.3

CHANGING THE BOOT SEQUENCE

The BIOS looks to CMOS RAM settings to find out which secondary storage device should have the OS (see Figure 2-42). CMOS might contain the setting for BIOS to look first to drive C, and, if it finds no OS there, then try drive A, or the setting might be first A then C. The order of drives that the BIOS follows when looking for an OS is called the boot sequence. You can change the boot sequence on your PC by using CMOS setup unless another technician responsible for the system has password protected it.

A+ ESS
1.3

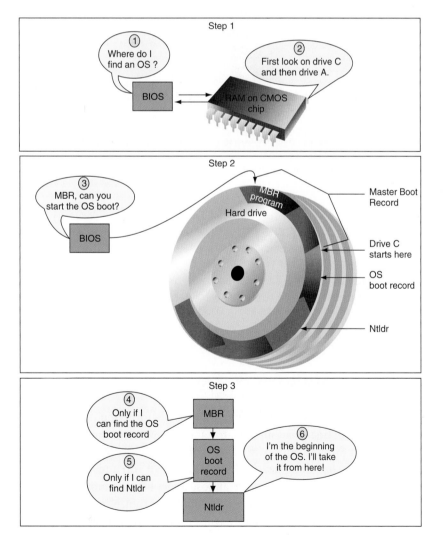

Figure 2-42 Numbered steps show how BIOS searches for and begins to load an operating system (in this example, Windows NT/2000/XP is the OS)

CMOS setup is accessed when you first turn on a computer. The keystrokes to enter CMOS setup are displayed somewhere on the screen during startup in a statement such as "Press the Del key to enter setup" or "Press F8 for setup." Different BIOSs use different keystrokes. The CMOS setup does not normally need to be changed except, for example, when there is a problem with hardware, a new floppy drive is installed, or a power-saving feature needs to be disabled or enabled. The CMOS setup can also hold one or two power-on passwords to help secure a system. Know that these passwords are not the same password that can be required by a Windows OS at startup. Figure 2-43 shows a CMOS setup screen that shows the boot sequence to be: (1) CD/DVD drive, (2) floppy drive, and (3) hard drive.

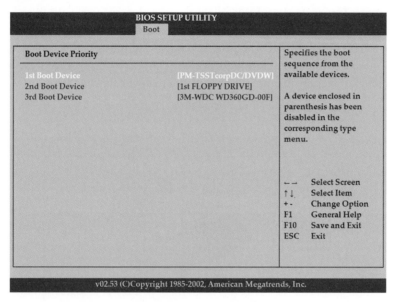

Figure 2-43 CMOS Setup Boot menu

APPLYING CONCEPTS Reboot your PC and look for the message on the first or second display screen that tells you how to enter CMOS setup. Press that key. What version of BIOS are you using? Explore the CMOS setup menus until you find the boot sequence. What is the order of storage media that startup BIOS uses to find an OS? What keystrokes do you use to change that order? Exit setup without making any changes. The system should reboot to the Windows desktop.

HOW TO TROUBLESHOOT A PC PROBLEM

When a computer doesn't work and you're responsible for fixing it, you should generally approach the problem first as an investigator and discoverer, always being careful not to compound the problem through your own actions. If the problem seems difficult, see it as an opportunity to learn something new. Ask questions until you understand the source of the problem. Once you understand it, you're almost done, because most likely the solution will be evident. Take the attitude that you can understand the problem and solve it, no matter how deeply you have to dig, and you probably will. In this section, you'll learn some fundamental rules useful when troubleshooting, and you'll also learn how to approach a troubleshooting problem, including how to interact with the user and how to handle an emergency.

A+ ESS
1.3

A+
220-602
1.2

STEPS TO SOLVING A PC PROBLEM

Generally, when troubleshooting a PC problem (or any problem for that matter), you begin by asking a question and finding its answer (see Figure 2-44). Based on the answer, you then take appropriate action and evaluate the result. Always keep in mind that you don't want to make things worse, so you should use the least destructive solution. If you want to be an expert troubleshooter, there's one last, very important step: Document what you learned so you can carry it forward into the next troubleshooting situation.

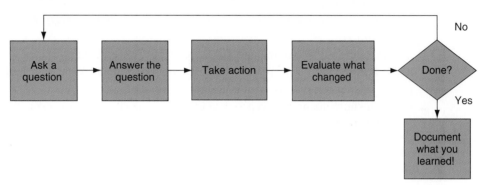

Figure 2-44 General approach to troubleshooting

When facing a problem with a PC, follow this four-step process:

A+ Exam Tip

The A+ Essentials and A+ 220-602 exams expect you to know about all the aspects of troubleshooting theory and strategy and how to apply the troubleshooting procedures and techniques described in this section.

1. Interview the user. You need to know what happened when the problem occurred, if valuable data is not backed up, and what you must do to reproduce the problem.

2. Take appropriate action to protect any valuable data on the computer that is not backed up.

3. Analyze the problem, make an initial determination of the problem, and begin testing, evaluating, and researching until the problem is solved.

4. If you think the problem is fixed, test the fix and the system. Make sure all is working before you stop. Then document activities, outcomes, and what you learned.

STEP 1: INTERVIEW THE USER

A+ ESS
1.3
8.1

Begin by asking the user questions like these to learn as much as you can about the problem and its root cause:

 Please describe the problem. What error messages, unusual displays, or failures did you see? (Possible answer: I see this blue screen with a funny looking message on it that makes no sense to me.)

 When did the problem start? (Possible answer: When I first booted after loading this neat little screen saver I downloaded from the Web.)

 What was the situation when the problem occurred? (Possible answers: I was trying to start up my PC. I was opening a document in MS Word. I was researching a project on the Internet.)

A+ ESS
1.3
8.1

A+
220-602
1.2

A+ ESS
1.3

◢ What programs or software were you using? (Possible answer: I was using Internet Explorer.)

◢ Did you move your computer system recently? (Possible answer: Well, yes. Yesterday I moved the computer case across the room.)

◢ Has there been a recent thunderstorm or electrical problem? (Possible answer: Yes, last night. Then when I tried to turn on my PC this morning, nothing happened.)

◢ Have you made any hardware, software, or configuration changes? (Possible answer: No, but I think my sister might have.)

◢ Has someone else used your computer recently? (Possible answer: Sure, my son uses it all the time.)

◢ Is there some valuable data on your system that is not backed up that I should know about before I start working on the problem? (Possible answer: Yes! Yes! My term paper! It's not backed up! You gotta get me that!)

◢ Can you show me how to reproduce the problem? (Possible answers: Yes, let me show you what to do.)

> **👍 A+ Exam Tip**
>
> The A+ Essentials exam expects you to know how to interact with a user and know what questions to ask given a troubleshooting scenario.

> **👍 A+ Exam Tip**
>
> The A+ Essentials exam expects you to know the importance of making back-ups before you make changes to a system.

A good PC support technician knows how to interact with a user so that the user gains confidence in your skills and does not feel talked down to or belittled.

STEP 2: BACK UP DATA

After you have talked with the user, be sure to back up any important data that is not currently backed up before you begin work on the PC. If valuable data is at stake and you have not yet backed it up, don't do anything to jeopardize it. Back it up as soon as possible. If you must take a risk with the data, let it be the user's decision to do so, not yours.

If the PC is working well enough to boot to the Windows desktop, you can use Windows Explorer to copy data to a flash drive, floppy disk, or other storage media. If you are about to change Windows configuration or install hardware or software, back up Windows system files as appropriate.

STEP 3: SOLVE THE PROBLEM

You are now ready to solve the problem. It's impossible to give a step-by-step plan that will solve any PC problem; therefore, in this section, you'll learn about the fundamental principles that you can apply to solve any computer problem. Then, later in this chapter and in other chapters in the book, you'll learn the step-by-step procedures you can use to solve problems with each major subsystem and component in a computer. In this section, you'll learn about several troubleshooting principles. The first is to establish your priorities.

Establish Your Priorities

This rule can help make for a satisfied customer. Decide what your first priority is. For example, it might be to recover lost data, or to get the PC back up and running as soon as possible. Ask the user or customer for advice when practical.

Know Your Starting Point

Find out what works and doesn't work before you take anything apart or try some possible fix. Suppose, for example, you decide the power supply is bad and exchange it. After you make the exchange, you discover the CD-ROM drive doesn't work. You don't know if you broke the drive while working on the system or it was already broken before you started. As much as possible, find out what works or doesn't work before you attempt a fix. For example, you can reboot the computer and read a file from CD or use an application to print a file on the network.

To help you solve the problem, gather as much information as you can about the problem by examining the computer. Find out the answers to these questions:

- ◢ What operating system is installed?
- ◢ What physical components are installed? What processor, expansion cards, drives, and peripheral devices are installed? Is the PC connected to a network?
- ◢ What is the nature of the problem? Does the problem occur before or after the boot? Does an error message appear? Does the system hang at certain times? Start from a cold boot, and do whatever you must do to cause the problem to occur. What specific steps did you take to duplicate the problem?
- ◢ Can you duplicate the problem? Does the problem occur every time you do the above steps, or is the problem intermittent? Intermittent problems are generally more difficult to solve than problems that occur consistently.

Approach the Problem Systematically

When trying to solve the problem, start at the beginning and walk through the situation in a thorough, careful way. This one rule is invaluable. Remember it and apply it every time. If you don't find the explanation to the problem after one systematic walkthrough, then repeat the entire process. Check and double-check to find the step you overlooked the first time. Most problems with computers are simple, such as a loose cable or circuit board. Computers are logical through and through. Whatever the problem, it's also very logical. First, try to reproduce the problem, and then try to figure out whether it is a hardware or software problem. Determine if the problem occurs during or after the boot.

MAKE NO ASSUMPTIONS

This rule is the hardest to follow, because there is a tendency to trust anything in writing and assume that people are telling you exactly what happened. But documentation is sometimes wrong, and people don't always describe events as they occurred, so do your own investigating. For example, if the user tells you that the system boots up with no error messages, but that the software still doesn't work, boot for yourself. You never know what the user might have overlooked.

Analyze the Problem and Make an Initial Determination

Given what you've learned by interviewing the user, examining the computer, and duplicating the problem, consider what might be the source of the problem, which might or might not be obvious at this point. For example, if a user complains that his Word documents are getting corrupted, possible sources of the problem might be that the user does not know how to save documents properly, the software or the OS might be corrupted, the PC might have a virus, or the hard drive might be intermittently failing. Then, based on what you have initially discovered, decide if the problem is caused by software, hardware, or the user.

Check Simple Things First

Most problems are so simple that we overlook them because we expect the problem to be difficult. Don't let the complexity of computers fool you. Most problems are easy to fix.

Really, they are! To save time, check the simple things first such as whether a power switch is not turned on or a cable is loose. Here are some practical examples of applying this principle:

▲ When a Word document gets corrupted, the most obvious or simplest source of the problem is that the user is not saving documents properly. Eliminate that possibility as the source of the problem before you look at the software or the hard drive.

▲ When a CD-ROM drive doesn't work, the problem might be that the CD is scratched or cracked. Check that first.

▲ If the video does not work, the problem might be with the monitor or the video card. When faced with the decision of which one to exchange first, choose the easy route: Exchange the monitor before the video card.

Beware of User Error

Remember that many problems stem from user error. Watch what the user is doing and ask questions.

Divide and Conquer

This rule is the most powerful. Isolate the problem. In the overall system, remove one hardware or software component after another, until the problem is isolated to a small part of the whole system. As you divide a large problem into smaller components, you can analyze each component separately. You can use one or more of the following to help you divide and conquer on your own system:

▲ In Windows, stop all non-essential services running in the background to eliminate them as the problem.

▲ Boot from a bootable CD or floppy disk to eliminate the OS and startup files on the hard drive as the problem.

▲ Remove any unnecessary hardware devices, such as a scanner card, internal modem, CD drive, and even the hard drive. Once down to the essentials, start exchanging components you know are good for those you suspect are bad, until the problem goes away. You don't need to physically remove the CD drive or hard drive from the bays inside the case. Simply disconnect the data cable and the power cable. Remember that the problem might be a resource conflict. If the network card worked well until the CD drive was reconnected and now neither works, try the CD drive without the network card. If the CD drive works, you most likely have a resource conflict.

Trade Known Good for Suspected Bad

When diagnosing hardware problems, this method works well if you can draw from a group of parts that you know work correctly. Suppose the monitor does not work; it appears dead. The parts of the video subsystem are the video card, the power cord to the monitor, the cord from the monitor to the PC case, and the monitor itself. Also, don't forget that the video card is inserted into an expansion slot on the motherboard, and the monitor depends on electrical power. Suspect each of these five components to be bad; try them one at a time. Trade the monitor for one that you know works. Trade the power cord, trade the cord to the PC video port, move the video card to a new slot, and trade the video card. When you're trading a good component for a suspected bad one, work methodically by eliminating one component at a time. Don't trade the video card and the monitor and then turn on the PC to determine if they work. It's possible that both the card and the monitor are bad, but assume that only one component is bad before you consider whether multiple components need trading.

In this situation, suppose you keep trading components in the video subsystem until you have no more variations. Next, take the entire subsystem—video card, cords, and monitor—to a PC that you know works, and plug each of them in. If they work, you have isolated the problem to the PC, not the video. Now turn your attention back to the PC: the motherboard, the software settings within the OS, the video driver, and other devices. Knowing that the video subsystem works on the good PC gives you a valuable tool. Compare the video driver on the good PC to the one on the bad PC. Make certain the CMOS settings, software settings, and other settings are the same.

Trade Suspected Bad for Known Good

An alternate approach works well in certain situations. If you have a working PC that is configured similarly to the one you are troubleshooting (a common situation in many corporate or educational environments), rather than trading good for suspected bad, you can trade suspected bad for good. Take each component that you suspect is bad and install it in the working PC. If the component works on the good PC, then you have eliminated it as a suspect. If the working PC breaks down, then you have probably identified the bad component.

Become a Researcher

Following this rule is the most fun. When a computer problem arises that you can't easily solve, be as tenacious as a bulldog. Read, make phone calls, ask questions, then read more, make more calls, and ask more questions. Take advantage of every available resource, including online help, the Internet, documentation, technical support, and books such as this one. Learn to use a good search engine on the Web, such as *www.google.com*. What you learn will be yours to take to the next problem. This is the real joy of computer troubleshooting. If you're good at it, you're always learning something new.

Write Things Down

Keep good notes as you're working. They'll help you think more clearly. Draw diagrams. Make lists. Clearly and precisely write down what you're learning. Later, when the entire problem gets "cold," these notes will be invaluable.

Keep Your Cool and Don't Rush

In an emergency, protect the data and software by carefully considering your options before acting and by taking practical precautions to protect software and OS files. When a computer stops working, if unsaved data is still in memory or if data or software on the hard drive has not been backed up, look and think carefully before you leap! A wrong move can be costly. The best advice is not to hurry. Carefully plan your moves. Read the documentation if you're not sure what to do, and don't hesitate to ask for help. Don't simply try something, hoping it will work, unless you've run out of more intelligent alternatives!

Don't Assume the Worst

When it's an emergency and your only copy of data is on a hard drive that is not working, don't assume that the data is lost. Much can be done to recover data. If you want to recover lost data on a hard drive, don't write anything to the drive; you might write on top of lost data, eliminating all chances of recovery.

Reboot and Start Over

This is an important rule. Fresh starts are good for us and uncover events or steps that we might have overlooked. Take a break; get away from the problem. Begin again.

A+ ESS
1.3

A+
220-602
1.2

STEP 4: VERIFY THE FIX AND DOCUMENT THE SOLUTION

If you think you have solved the problem, reboot the system and make sure everything is working before you stop. Ask the user to verify all is working. Then document what happened so you can take what you learned into the next troubleshooting situation. Write down the initial symptoms, the source of the problem, and what you did to fix it.

APPLYING CONCEPTS Intermittent problems can make troubleshooting challenging. The trick in diagnosing problems that come and go is to look for patterns or clues as to when the problems occur. If you or the user can't reproduce the problem at will, ask the user to keep a log of when the problems occur and exactly what messages appear. Tell the user that intermittent problems are the hardest to solve and might take some time, but that you won't give up. Show the user how to get a printed screen of the error messages when they appear. Here's one method to print a screen shot:

1. Press the **Print Screen** key to copy the displayed screen to the Windows Clipboard.

2. Launch the Paint software accessory program and paste the contents of the Clipboard into the document. You might need to use the Zoom Out command on the document first. You can then print the document with the displayed screen, using Paint. You can also paste the contents of the Clipboard into a document created by a word-processing application such as Word.

TROUBLESHOOTING A FAILED BOOT

A+ ESS
1.3
2.3

It's really hard to learn to troubleshoot a PC in one fell swoop, so we're going to ease into it slowly. This section is your first introduction to troubleshooting, and we'll only cover simple problems, which, in this case, prevent the computer from booting correctly and don't involve loading the Windows desktop. Solutions in this section are limited to things that you can do that are quite simple.

MY COMPUTER WON'T BOOT

It's been a long day; you've worked late, and now you sit down in front of your home PC to have a little relaxing fun surfing the Web, chatting with friends in foreign places, and updating your blog. You turn on your PC, and this big problem smacks you in the face; you just want to cry. Been there? I have.

What do you do first? First thing to remember is don't panic. Most PC problems are simple and can be simply solved, but you do need a game plan. That's what Figure 2-45 gives you. As we work our way through it, you're eliminating one major computer subsystem after another until you zero in on the problem. After you've discovered the problem, many times the solution is obvious.

Does the PC boot properly? If not, then ask, "Is the screen blank?" If it is blank and you cannot hear any spinning fans or drives and see no lights, then assume the problem has to do with the power system and begin troubleshooting there. If the screen is blank

A+ ESS
1.3
3.3

A+
220-602
1.2

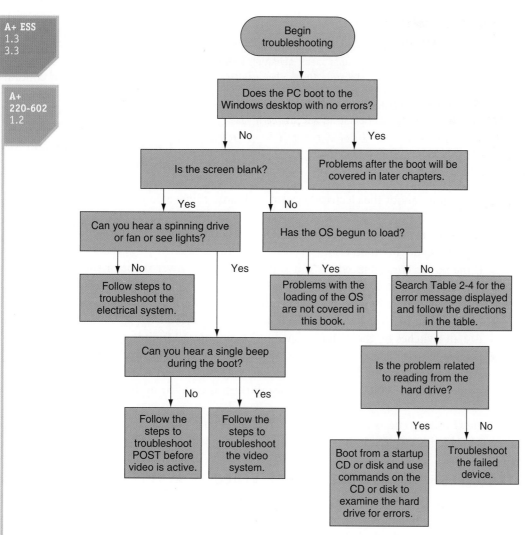

Figure 2-45 Use this flowchart when first facing a computer problem

and you heard a single beep, then the BIOS has signaled that POST completed successfully and you can assume the problem must be with the video system. Thus, you should then begin troubleshooting video. If you see

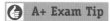 **A+ Exam Tip**

The A+ Essentials and A+ 220-602 exams expect you to be able to recognize and isolate problems during the boot caused by video, power, overheating, the keyboard, the hard drive, and memory. You also need to know how to deal with an error at POST.

an error message onscreen, but Windows has not started to load, then use the error message to help you identify the problem.

TROUBLESHOOTING MAJOR SUBSYSTEMS USED FOR BOOTING

The remainder of this section is divided into the major categories of troubleshooting steps laid out in Figure 2-45. We'll look at problems with the electrical subsystem, problems with essential hardware devices such as the motherboard, memory, and the processor, problems with video, and problems with reading from the hard drive.

A+ ESS
1.3
3.3

A+
220-602
1.2

> **✎ Notes**
>
> Because we're still early in the book, we have not covered problems that occur when a new component, operating system, or application has just been installed or some other major modification to the system has just been made. In such cases, you would assume that the problem was related to these changes. These types of problems are covered in later chapters.

TROUBLESHOOTING THE ELECTRICAL SYSTEM

Without opening the computer case, the following list contains some questions you can ask and things you can do to solve a problem with the electrical system. The rule of thumb is "try the simple things first." In the next chapter, you will learn much more about the electrical system and more things you can try.

- ◢ Are there any burnt parts or odors? (Definitely not a good sign!) Read Chapter 3 before you do anything else!
- ◢ Is the power cord plugged in? If it is plugged into a power stripe or surge suppressor, is the device turned on and also plugged in?
- ◢ Is the power outlet controlled by a wall switch? If so, is the switch turned on?
- ◢ Is the circuit breaker blown? Is the house circuit overloaded?
- ◢ Are all switches on the system turned on? Computer? Monitor?
- ◢ Is there a possibility the system has overheated? If so, wait awhile and try again. If the system comes on, but later turns itself off, you might need additional cooling fans inside the unit. Where and how to install them is covered in the next chapter.

The next thing to do is to open the case and begin checking electrical components inside the case, which is covered in the next chapter.

TROUBLESHOOTING POST BEFORE VIDEO IS ACTIVE

If the electrical system is working, one of the first things startup BIOS does is check the essential hardware components on the motherboard it must have to boot. If it sees a problem with a device it checks before it has access to video, BIOS communicates that problem as a beep code.

If you observe that power is getting to the system (you see lights and hear fans or beeps) but the screen is blank, turn off the system and turn it back on and carefully listen to any beep codes. Each BIOS manufacturer has its own beep codes, but Table 2-4 lists the more common meanings. For specific beep codes for your motherboard, see the Web site of the motherboard or BIOS manufacturer. Look in the motherboard documentation for the name of the BIOS manufacturer. If you can't find the name, then know that in Chapter 5 you'll learn how to identify the BIOS and motherboard.

Here is a list of the Web sites for the most common BIOS manufacturers:

- ◢ AMI BIOS: *www.ami.com*
- ◢ Award BIOS and Phoenix BIOS: *www.phoenix.com*
- ◢ Compaq or HP: *thenew.hp.com*
- ◢ Dell: *www.dell.com*
- ◢ IBM: *www.ibm.com*
- ◢ Gateway: *www.gateway.com*

If no beeps are heard, even after you reboot a couple of times, then assume the problem is with the processor, the BIOS, or the motherboard. All these problems are covered in Chapters 4 and 5

A+ ESS
1.3
3.3

A+
220-602
1.2

Beeps During POST	Description
One beep followed by three, four, or five beeps	Motherboard problems, possibly with DMA, CMOS setup chip, timer, or system bus. Most likely the motherboard will need replacing. How to do this is covered in Chapter 5.
Two beeps	The POST numeric code is displayed on the monitor. See the list of numeric codes later in this section.
Two beeps followed by three, four, or five beeps	First 64K of RAM has errors. The solution is to replace RAM, which is covered in Chapter 6.
Three beeps followed by three, four, or five beeps	Keyboard controller failed or video controller failed. Most likely these are embedded components on the motherboard. How to deal with these motherboard problems is covered in Chapter 5.
Four beeps followed by two, three, or four beeps	Problem with serial or parallel ports, system timer, or time of day, which probably means the motherboard must be replaced.
Continuous beeps	Problem with power supply. The power supply might need replacing; see Chapter 3.

Table 2-4 Beep codes and their meanings

TROUBLESHOOTING VIDEO

If you hear one beep during the boot and you see a blank screen, then BIOS has successfully completed POST, which includes a test of the video card. You can then assume the problem must be with the monitor or the monitor cable. Ask these questions and try these things:

1. Is the monitor electrical cable plugged in?

2. Is the monitor turned on? Try pushing the power button on the front of the monitor. It should turn yellow or green, indicating the monitor has power.

3. Is the monitor cable plugged into the video port at the back of the PC and the connector on the rear of the monitor?

4. Try a different monitor and a different monitor cable that you know are working.

More things to do and try concerning the video system are covered in Chapter 8.

TROUBLESHOOTING ERROR MESSAGES DURING THE BOOT

If video and the electrical systems are working, then most boot problems show up as an error message displayed onscreen. These error messages can have several sources:

▲ After video is active, a hardware device such as the keyboard, hard drive, or CD drive failed POST.

▲ After POST, when startup BIOS turned to the hard drive to find an OS, it could not read from the drive. Recall that it must be able to read the Master Boot Record containing the master boot program and partition table, the OS boot record, and the first OS boot program (Ntldr or Io.sys).

▲ After Ntldr or Io.sys are in control, they could not find the OS files they use to load the OS.

Now let's look at some possible error messages listed in Table 2-5, along with their meanings. For other error messages, look in your motherboard or computer documentation or use a good search engine to search for the error message on the Internet.

A+ ESS
1.3
3.3

A+
220-602
1.2

Error Message	Meaning of the Error Message
Numeric codes during POST	Sometimes numeric codes are used to communicate errors at POST. Some examples for IBM XT/AT error codes include:
Code in the 100 range	Motherboard errors. Troubleshooting the motherboard is covered in Chapter 5.
Code in the 200 range	RAM errors. Troubleshooting RAM is covered in Chapter 6.
Code in the 300 range	Keyboard errors. Verify the keyboard is plugged in or try a known good keyboard.
Code in the 500 range	Video controller errors. The video card might need replacing. This is covered in Chapter 8.
Code in the 600 or 7300 range	Floppy drive errors. Verify CMOS setup has the floppy drive configured correctly.
Code in the 900 range	Parallel port errors
Code in the 1300 range	Game controller or joystick errors
Code in the 1700 range	Hard drive errors
Code in the 6000 range	SCSI device or network card errors
Configuration/CMOS error	Setup information does not agree with the actual hardware the computer found during boot. May be caused by a bad or weak battery or by changing hardware without changing setup. Check setup for errors.
Hard drive not found Fixed disk error	The BIOS cannot locate the hard drive, or the controller card is not responding. How to solve hard drive problems is covered in Chapter 7.
Invalid drive specification	The BIOS is unable to find a hard drive or a floppy drive that setup tells it to expect. Look for errors in CMOS setup. For Windows 2000/XP, you can use the Diskpart command in the Recovery Console to examine the partition table for errors. For Windows 9x/Me, use the Fdisk command to examine the partition table.
No boot device available	The hard drive is not formatted, or the format is corrupted, and there is no disk in drive A. Use Diskpart or Fdisk to examine the partition table on the hard drive.
Invalid partition table Error loading operating system Missing operating system Missing NTLDR Invalid boot disk Inaccessible boot device	The Master Boot program at the beginning of the hard drive displays these messages when it cannot find the active partition on the hard drive or the boot record on that partition. Use Diskpart or Fdisk to examine the drive for errors.
Error in Config.sys line xx	In a Windows 9x/Me environment, an entry in Config.sys is incorrect or is referencing a 16-bit program that is missing or corrupted.
Nonsystem disk or disk error Bad or missing Command.com No operating system found Can't find NTLDR	The disk in drive A is not bootable. Remove the disk in drive A and boot from the hard drive. If you still get the error, use Diskpart or Fdisk to examine the partition table on the hard drive. If you can access drive C, look for missing system files on the drive. For Windows 9x or DOS, use the Sys command to restore system files.

Table 2-5 Error messages and their meanings

Error Message	Meaning of the Error Message
Not ready reading drive A: Abort, Retry, Fail? General failure reading drive A:; Abort, Retry, Fail?	The disk in drive A is missing, is not formatted, or is corrupted. Try another disk or remove the disk to boot from the hard drive.
Missing operating system, error loading operating system	The MBR is unable to locate or read the OS boot sector on the active partition, or there is a translation problem on large drives. Boot from a bootable floppy or CD and examine the hard drive file system for corruption.
Device or service has failed to start An error message about a reference to a device or service in the registry	These errors occur late in the boot when the OS is loading services and device drivers.
While Windows 2000/XP is loading, an unknown error message on a blue background displays and the system halts.	These errors are called stop errors or blue screen errors and are usually caused by viruses, errors in the file system, a corrupted hard drive, a corrupted system file, or a hardware problem.

Table 2-5 Error messages and their meanings (continued)

Notice in the table that several problems pertain to BIOS not being able to read from the hard drive, and the suggested next step is to try booting from another media, which can be either a CD or floppy disk.

Each OS provides one or more methods and media to use if booting from the hard drive fails. Windows XP uses the setup CD or a floppy disk for this purpose, Windows 2000 uses the setup CD or a set of four rescue disks, and Windows 9x/Me uses a single rescue disk. In later chapters you'll learn to use all these methods for each OS.

>> CHAPTER SUMMARY

▲ Tools used by a PC support technician might include screwdrivers, tweezers, recovery CDs, cans of compressed air, cleaning solutions, needle-nose pliers, multimeter, cable ties, flashlight, AC outlet ground tester, loop-back plugs, POST diagnostic cards, and utility software.

▲ To protect against ESD, a support technician can use a ground bracelet, ground mat, anti-static bags, and antistatic gloves.

▲ The goals of preventive maintenance are to make PCs last longer and work better, protect data and software, and reduce repair costs.

▲ When a PC is your permanent responsibility, keep good backups of data and system files, document all setup changes, problems, and solutions, and take precautions to protect the system against viruses and other attacks.

▲ To protect a system against attack, use a firewall, install and run antivirus software, and keep Windows updates current.

▲ A PC preventive maintenance plan includes blowing dust from the inside of the computer case, keeping a record of setup data, backing up the hard drive, and cleaning the mouse, monitor, and keyboard.

◢ Protecting software and hardware documentation is an important preventive maintenance chore.

◢ Never ship a PC when the only copy of important data is on its hard drive.

◢ CMOS setup holds most of the motherboard configuration information. In addition, some motherboards use jumpers or DIP switches for a few settings.

◢ The boot process can be divided into four parts: POST, loading the OS, the OS initializing itself, and loading and executing an application.

◢ The startup BIOS is in control when the boot process begins. Then the startup BIOS turns control over to the OS.

◢ During the boot, the ROM BIOS startup program performs a power-on self test (POST) and assigns system resources to devices. It then searches secondary storage for an OS.

◢ When the OS loads from a hard drive, the BIOS first executes the Master Boot Record (MBR) program, which turns to the partition table to find the OS boot record. The program in the OS boot record attempts to find a boot loader program for the OS, which for Windows NT/2000/XP is Ntldr. For Windows 9x/Me, the program is Io.sys.

◢ When troubleshooting a failed boot, the subsystems to check are the electrical system, the major components on the motherboard and other hardware required to boot, the video system, and errors that occur when BIOS tries to read from the hard drive.

>> KEY TERMS

For explanations of key terms, see the Glossary near the end of the book.

boot record	hard boot	partition table
booting	Io.sys	POST (power-on self test)
cold boot	loop-back plug	program file
Command.com	Master Boot Record (MBR)	soft boot
diagnostic card	material safety data sheet	startup BIOS
DIP (dual inline package) switch	(MSDS)	static electricity
electrostatic discharge (ESD)	Msdos.sys	warm boot
ground bracelet	Ntldr	

>> REVIEWING THE BASICS

1. What is the difference between a hard boot and a soft boot?

2. What are the four main parts of the boot process?

3. What memory address is always assigned to the first instruction in the ROM BIOS startup program?

4. How does startup BIOS communicate errors during POST if video is not yet available?

5. Name the program that is needed to locate the beginning of the OS on a drive.

6. List three types of information contained in a hard drive's partition table.

7. What is the name of the Windows NT/2000/XP boot loader program?

8. How many startup disks are needed to boot Windows 2000 from floppy disks?

9. When troubleshooting a failed boot, if you don't see any lights or hear any noises, what hardware system do you first assume is at fault?

10. When booting your computer and you see a blank screen, but hear a single beep, what can you assume worked with no errors?

11. When booting your computer and you see a blank screen, but hear a single beep, what component should you check first?

12. Using the rule "trade good for suspected bad," describe how to easily troubleshoot a video problem.

13. Give five possible questions that should be asked of a user who is experiencing computer problems.

14. What is the best way to document intermittent problems?

15. Using Windows, list the steps to print a screen that shows an error message.

16. What preventive maintenance measures need to be done inside the case at least once a year?

17. List at least three tasks you should complete before moving or shipping a computer.

18. How do you properly dispose of a battery pack from a notebook computer? A broken monitor? A toner cartridge from a laser printer?

19. If you are unsure how to properly dispose of a can of contact cleaner, how can you find out the acceptable method of disposal?

20. What two tools can be used to remove dust from inside a computer case?

21. What are three types of ribbon cables you might find inside a PC?

22. Why is it important to *not* rock an expansion card from side to side as you remove it from its slot?

23. What type of expansion card can have a retention mechanism at the bottom of the card to help stabilize it in the slot?

24. Name three tools that you can use to protect a system against ESD as you work on it.

25. If you suspect that a USB port is faulty, what tool can you use to test the port?

>> THINKING CRITICALLY

1. As a help-desk technician, list some good detective questions to ask if the user calls to say, "My PC won't boot."

2. Starting with the easiest procedures, list five things to check if your PC does not boot.

3. Someone calls saying he has attempted to install a modem, but the modem does not work. List the first four questions you would ask.

4. If a PC boots first to the hard drive before checking the floppy disk for an OS, how do you change this boot sequence so that it first looks on the floppy disk for an OS?

>> HANDS-ON PROJECTS

PROJECT 2-1:   Observing the Boot Process

If your computer has a reset button, press it and then watch what happens. If your computer does not have a reset button, turn it off, wait a few seconds, and then turn it back on. Try to note every beep, every light that goes on or off, and every message you see on the screen. Compare your notes to those of others to verify that you did not overlook something. Then, answer these questions from observing the boot:

1. What type of video card are you using?

2. Who is the BIOS vendor, and what version of the BIOS are you using?

3. As the computer boots, memory is counted. Observe the memory count and record the amount of memory detected. What number system is used to count this memory?

4. Unplug the keyboard and reboot the computer. What is different about the boot? Write down your observations. (Some systems report a missing keyboard and some do not.)

5. Plug in the keyboard again, unplug the monitor, and reboot. After you reboot, plug in the monitor. Did the computer know the monitor was missing?

6. Put a floppy disk that is not bootable in drive A, and reboot. Write down what you observe. If the PC booted to the desktop as usual, why didn't it look to the floppy disk to load the OS?

PROJECT 2-2:   Developing Help-Desk Skills

Work with a partner who will play the role of the user and a third person who will create a problem. Sit with your back to the partner/user, who is in front of the PC. Troubleshoot the problem and talk the user through to a solution. Abide by these rules:

1. A third person created an error so that the PC does not boot successfully. Neither you nor your partner knows what the third person did.

2. The user does not have technical insight but is good at following directions and is willing to answer any nontechnical questions.

3. You can't turn around to look at the screen.

4. You have to practice professional mannerisms and speech.

5. As you work, you have to keep a log of the "phone call to the help desk," recording in the log the major steps toward diagnosing and correcting the problem.

When the problem is resolved, have the third person create a different problem that causes the PC not to boot correctly, and exchange roles with your partner.

PROJECT 2-3:   Saving CMOS Setup Using Freeware

Research the Internet for freeware to save CMOS setup data on a floppy disk. Print the Web page of the product. Download the program and use it to save the setup data to disk. When you run the software, print the main menu of the software. Try these Web sites when looking for software: *www.zdnet.com*, *www.cnet.com* and *www.download.com*.

2

PROJECT 2-4:   Researching Disposal Rules

Research the laws and regulations in your community concerning the disposal of batteries and old computer parts. Answer these questions regarding your community:

1. How do you properly dispose of a monitor?

2. How do you properly dispose of a battery pack used by a notebook computer?

3. How do you properly dispose of a large box of assorted computer parts, including hard drives, floppy drives, computer cases, and circuit boards?

>> REAL PROBLEMS, REAL SOLUTIONS

REAL PROBLEM 2-1:   Taking Apart a Computer and Putting It Back Together

A PC technician needs to be comfortable with taking apart a computer and putting it back together. To learn the most from this project, do it using more than one system. Be sure to use a ground bracelet as you work, and follow the other safety precautions in the chapter. You'll also need a Phillips-head screwdriver, flat-head screwdriver, paper, and pen. Do the following:

1. Following the instructions in the chapter, begin to take apart the PC. When you get the case cover removed, identify the following major components. (Drawings in this and the last chapter should help.)

   ◢ Expansion cards

   ◢ Power supply

   ◢ Floppy disk drive

   ◢ CD drive

   ◢ Hard drive

   ◢ Motherboard

2. Remove the expansion cards, drives, power supply, and motherboard. As you work, don't force anything. If you find yourself needing to force something, ask your instructor for help.

3. You are ready to reassemble. Reverse the preceding disassembling activities. Install the power supply, drives, motherboard, and cards in the case. Connect all internal cables and cords.

4. Before you replace the case cover, ask your instructor to check your work.

5. Replace the case cover and plug in the keyboard, monitor, and mouse.

6. Turn on the power and check that the PC is working properly. If the PC does not work, don't panic! Just turn off the power and go back and check each cable connection and each expansion card. You probably have not solidly seated a card in the slot. After you have double-checked, try again.

Form Factors and Power Supplies

This chapter focuses on the power supply, which provides power to all other components inside the computer case. Several types of power supplies are available. The form factor of the computer case and motherboard drive which type of power supply can be installed in a system. Therefore, we begin the chapter discussing the form factors of computer cases, motherboards, and power supplies. To troubleshoot problems with the power system of a PC, you need a basic understanding of electricity. You'll learn about the measurements of electricity and the form in which it comes to you as house current. The chapter then covers how to protect a computer system from damage caused by electrical problems. Next, we discuss Energy Star devices that save energy. Finally, we talk about ways to detect and correct problems with the PC's electrical system, including how to change a defective power supply.

COMPUTER CASE, MOTHERBOARD, AND POWER SUPPLY FORM FACTORS

This chapter is all about a computer's electrical system and power supply, such as the one shown in Figure 3-1. However, because motherboards, power supplies, and computer cases are often sold together and must be compatible with each other, we begin by looking at these three components as an interconnecting system. When you put together a new system, or replace components in an existing system, the form factors of the motherboard, power supply, and case must all match. The form factor describes the size, shape, and major features of a hardware component.

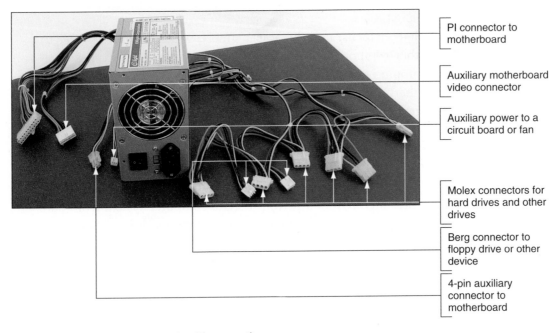

PI connector to motherboard

Auxiliary motherboard video connector

Auxiliary power to a circuit board or fan

Molex connectors for hard drives and other drives

Berg connector to floppy drive or other device

4-pin auxiliary connector to motherboard

Figure 3-1 Computer power supply with connections

When you are deciding which form factor to use, the motherboard drives the decision because it determines what the system can do. After you've decided to use a certain form factor for the motherboard, you must use the same form factor for the case and power supply. Using a matching form factor for the motherboard, power supply, and case assures you that:

> **Notes**
>
> A computer case is also known as a chassis.

▲ The motherboard fits in the case.
▲ The power supply cords to the motherboard provide the correct voltage, and the connectors match the connections on the board.
▲ The holes in the motherboard align with the holes in the case for anchoring the board to the case.
▲ Holes in the case align with ports coming off the motherboard.
▲ For some form factors, wires for switches and lights on the front of the case match up with connections on the motherboard.

When selecting a computer case, motherboard, and power supply, choose a design that fits its intended use. You might need a high-end tower system, a rack-mounted server, or a low-profile desktop. First decide which form factor you will use, which will apply to the case, motherboard, and power supply. Each type of form factor is discussed next, followed by a discussion of the different sizes and shapes of computer cases.

TYPES OF FORM FACTORS

A+ ESS 1.1

Different form factors apply to power supplies, cases, and motherboards: the BTX, ATX, LPX, NLX, backplane systems, and the outdated AT form factor. Each of these form factors has several variations. The most common form factors used on personal computers today are the ATX, MicroATX, BTX, and NLX. The most popular form factor is the ATX, but the latest is the BTX. These form factors and other less common and up-and-coming form factors are discussed next.

> **A+ Exam Tip**
>
> The A+ Essentials exam expects you to recognize and know the more important features of the ATX, BTX, MicroATX, and NLX motherboards.

AT FORM FACTOR

Of historical significance is the AT form factor, sometimes called full AT, that measure 12" x 13.8". These boards are no longer produced and you seldom see them around. The form factor uses the full-size AT cases that the original IBM AT (Advanced Technology) personal computer used

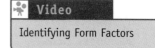

in the 1980s. A smaller, more convenient version of AT called the Baby AT came later.

AT motherboards were difficult to install, service, and upgrade. Another problem with the AT form factor is that the CPU was placed on the motherboard in front of the expansion slots; long cards might not fit in these slots because they will bump into the CPU. You can visualize this problem by looking at the AT motherboard in Figure 3-2.

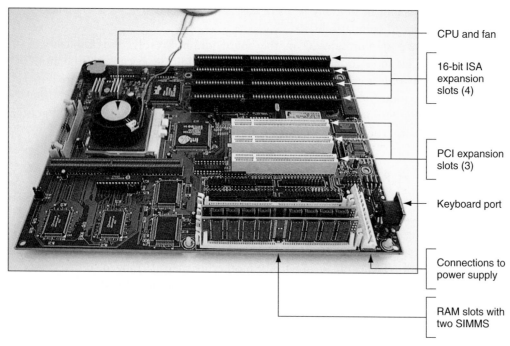

Figure 3-2 The CPU on the AT motherboard sits in front of the expansion slots

Power supplies for AT systems supply +5, -5, +12, and -12 volts to the motherboard and other components. The AT board uses two power connections, the **P8 connector** and the **P9 connector** (see Figure 3-3).

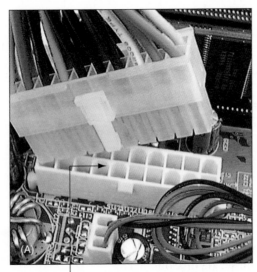

P1 on an ATX motherboard

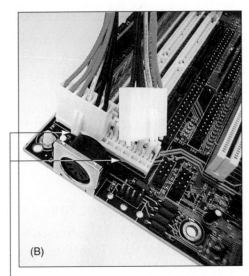

P8 and P9 on an AT motherboard

Figure 3-3   ATX uses a single P1 power connector (A), but AT-type motherboards use P8 and P9 power connectors (B)

BABY AT FORM FACTOR

The **Baby AT** form factor provided more flexibility than full AT. Baby AT was the industry standard form factor from about 1993 to 1997. Power supplies designed for the Baby AT form factor blow air out of the computer case, rather than pull air into it as does the AT case fan. At 13" x 8.7", Baby AT motherboards are smaller than full AT motherboards and fit in many types of cases, including newer ATX cases designed to provide backward compatibility.

The design of Baby AT motherboards did not resolve the problem with the position of the CPU in relation to expansion slots. In addition, because of the motherboard's configuration and orientation within the case, drives and other devices are not positioned close to their connections on the motherboard. This means that cables might have to reach across the motherboard and not be long enough or might get in the way of good air flow. Baby AT motherboards are no longer produced, but occasionally you still see one in use.

ATX FORM FACTOR

ATX is the most commonly used form factor today. It is an open, nonproprietary industry specification originally developed by Intel in 1995. ATX improved upon AT by making adding and removing components easier, providing greater support for I/O devices and processor technology, and lowering costs.

With ATX, components on the motherboard are arranged so that they don't interfere with each other and for better position inside the case. In addition, the position of the power supply and drives inside the case makes connecting them to the motherboard easier and makes it possible to reduce cable lengths, which can help reduce the potential for EMI and corrupted data. EMI (electromagnetic interference) is explained later in the chapter. Connecting the switches and lights on the front of the case to components inside the case requires fewer wires, making installation simpler and reducing the potential for mistakes.

An ATX motherboard measures 12" x 9.6", so it's smaller than a full AT motherboard. On an ATX motherboard, the CPU and memory slots are rotated 90 degrees from the position on the AT motherboard. Instead of sitting in front of the expansion slots, the CPU and memory slots sit beside them, preventing interference with full-length expansion cards (see Figure 3-4). ATX is an evolution of the Baby AT form factor and blows air out of the case, as did Baby AT.

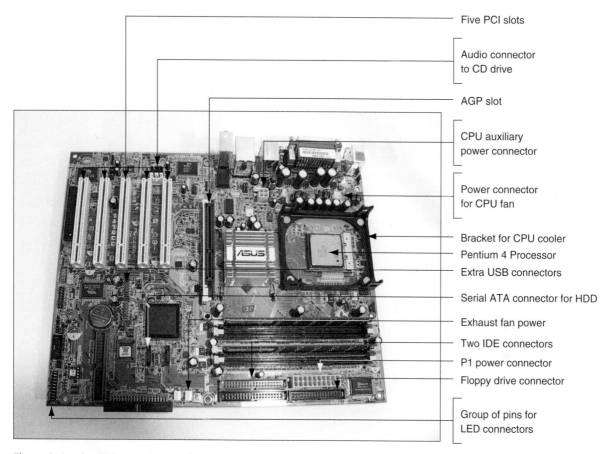

Five PCI slots

Audio connector to CD drive

AGP slot

CPU auxiliary power connector

Power connector for CPU fan

Bracket for CPU cooler
Pentium 4 Processor
Extra USB connectors

Serial ATA connector for HDD

Exhaust fan power

Two IDE connectors

P1 power connector

Floppy drive connector

Group of pins for LED connectors

Figure 3-4 The CPU on an ATX motherboard sits opposite the expansion slots and does not block the room needed for long expansion cards

The first ATX power supplies and motherboards use a single power connector called the **P1 connector** that includes, in addition to the voltages provided by AT, a +3.3-volt circuit for a low-voltage CPU (refer to Figure 3-3). The first ATX P1 connector has 20 pins.

The electrical requirements for motherboards change over time as new technologies make additional demands for power. When processors began to require more power, the ATX Version 2.1 specifications added a 4-pin auxiliary connector near the processor socket to provide an additional 12 V of power (see Figure 3-5). A power supply that provides this 4-pin 12-volt power cord is called an **ATX12V** power supply.

Later, when PCI Express slots were added to motherboards, more power was required and a new ATX specification (ATX Version 2.2) allowed for a 24-pin P1 connector. The extra 4 pins on the P1 connector provide 12V, 5V, and 3.3V pins and with this newer connector, the 4-pin auxiliary connector is no longer needed. Motherboards that support PCI Express and have the 24-pin P1 connector are sometimes called Enhanced ATX boards. Figure 3-6 shows a 20-pin P1 power cord from the power supply and a 24-pin P1 connector on a motherboard.

Figure 3-5 The 4-pin 12V auxiliary power connector on a motherboard

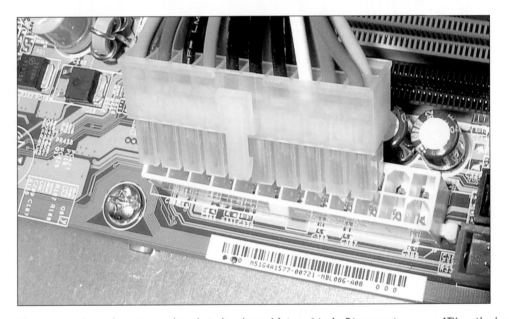

Figure 3-6 A 20-pin power cord ready to be plugged into a 24-pin P1 connector on an ATX motherboard

> **Notes**
>
> For more information about all the form factors discussed in this chapter, check out the form factor Web site sponsored by Intel at *www.formfactors.org*.

Figure 3-7 shows the power connectors used by a motherboard, floppy drive, and parallel ATA and serial ATA drives as defined in the ATX specifications.

Another feature of an ATX motherboard not found on AT boards is a soft switch, sometimes called the soft power feature. Using this feature, an OS, such as Windows 2000/XP or Windows 98, can turn off the power to a system after the shutdown procedure is done. In addition, CMOS can be configured to cause a keystroke or network activity to power up the system (wake on LAN). If a case has a soft switch and the installed operating system supports the feature, when a user presses the power switch on the front of the case while the computer is on, the OS goes through a normal shutdown procedure before powering off. There are several variations of ATX. The Mini-ATX, a smaller ATX motherboard (11.2" x 8.2"), can be used with ATX cases and power supplies. FlexATX allows for maximum flexibility in the design of system cases and boards and therefore can be a good choice for custom systems. FlexATX is used in slimline and all-in-one cases.

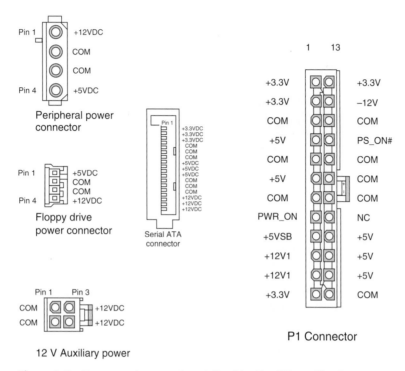

Figure 3-7 Power supply connectors defined by the ATX specifications

MICROATX FORM FACTOR

The MicroATX form factor is a major variation of ATX and addresses some technologies that have emerged since the original development of ATX. MicroATX reduces the total cost of a system by reducing the number of I/O slots on the motherboard, reducing the power supplied to the board, and allowing for a smaller case size. MicroATX motherboards can be used in an ATX 2.1 computer case with minor modifications.

ATX is still the most popular motherboard form factor, and it remains to be seen if ATX will be replaced by BTX, the latest form factor.

BTX FORM FACTOR

The BTX (Balanced Technology Extended) form factor was designed by Intel for flexibility and can be used by everything from large tower systems to those ultrasmall systems that sit under a monitor. BTX was designed to take full advantage of serial ATA, USB 2.0, and PCI Express technologies. The BTX form factor design focuses on reducing heat with better airflow and improved fans and coolers. It also gives better structural support for the motherboard than does ATX. BTX motherboards use a 24-pin power connector that has the same pinout arrangement as the ATX 24-pin P1 connector and can also use one or more auxiliary power connectors for the processor, fans, and lighting inside the case (for really cool-looking systems). Because the 24-pin connectors are the same, a BTX motherboard can use an ATX power supply.

In the case configuration shown in Figure 3-8, notice how the processor is sitting immediately in front of the intake fan installed on the front of the case. This intake fan together with the exhaust fan on the rear of the case produce a strong wind tunnel effect over the processor, making it unnecessary to have a fan on top of the processor itself. Also notice in Figure 3-8 that memory modules and expansion cards fit into the slots parallel to airflow rather than blocking airflow as they sometimes do with ATX and AT form factors. Airflow in a BTX system is also designed to flow underneath the BTX motherboard.

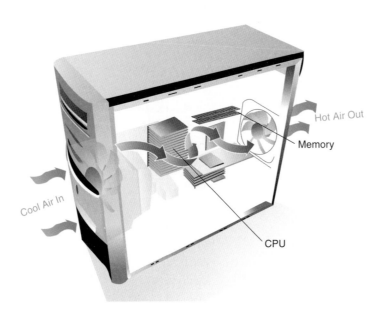

Figure 3-8 Improved airflow in a BTX case and motherboard makes it unnecessary to have a fan on top of the processor

LPX AND MINI-LPX FORM FACTORS

LPX and Mini-LPX form factors were originally developed by Western Digital for low-end personal computer motherboards and are used with low-profile cases. In these systems, the motherboard has only one expansion slot, in which a **riser card** (also called a **bus riser** or **daughter card**), is mounted. Expansion cards are mounted on the riser card, and the card also contains connectors for the floppy and hard drives. Difficult to upgrade, they cannot handle the size and operating temperature of today's faster processors. In addition, a manufacturer often makes proprietary changes to the standard LPX motherboard design, forcing you to use only the manufacturer's power supply. LPX and Mini-LPX use small cases called low-profile cases and slimline cases.

NLX FORM FACTOR

The **NLX** form factor for low-end personal computer motherboards was developed by Intel in 1998 to improve on the older LPX form factor. The riser card (sometimes called a daughter board or daughter card) on an NLX motherboard is on the edge of the board, which differs from the LPX motherboard that has the riser card near the center of the board. The NLX form factor allowed for larger DIMM modules, support for AGP, and the ability to remove the motherboard without using tools. The NLX standard applies only to motherboards; NLX motherboards are designed to use ATX power supplies. An example of an NLX system is shown in Figure 3-9.

 **A+ Exam Tip**

The A+ Essentials exam expects you to know the purpose of the riser card or daughter board used with the NLX form factor.

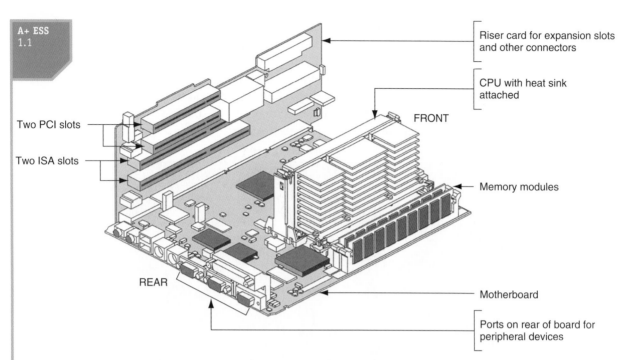

Riser card for expansion slots and other connectors

CPU with heat sink attached

FRONT

Two PCI slots

Two ISA slots

Memory modules

REAR

Motherboard

Ports on rear of board for peripheral devices

Figure 3-9 The NLX form factor uses a riser card that connects to the motherboard; the riser card provides expansion slots for the expansion cards

BACKPLANE SYSTEMS

Backplane systems do not use a true motherboard; instead, they use backplanes such as the one shown in Figure 3-10. A backplane is a board that normally sits against the back of a proprietary case with slots on it for other cards. Active backplanes contain no circuits other

Figure 3-10 A 16-slot passive backplane board by Acqutek (*www.acqu.com*)

than bus connectors and some buffer and driver circuits. Passive backplanes contain no circuitry at all; the circuits are all on a mothercard, also called a CPU card. The mothercard is a circuit board that plugs into the backplane and contains a processor (see Figure 3-11). These systems are generally not used in personal computers. Passive backplanes are sometimes used for industrial rack-mounted systems and high-end file servers. A rack-mounted system is not designed for personal use, and often several of these systems are mounted in cases stacked on a rack for easy access by technicians.

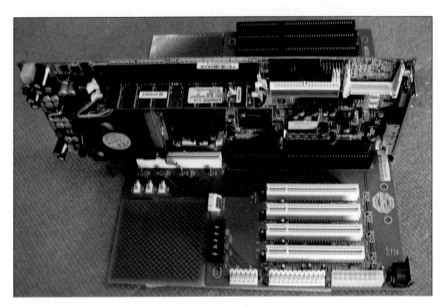

Figure 3-11   This CPU card by Acqutek (*www.acqu.com*) plugs into a passive backplane board and contains socket 478 with a Pentium 4 processor installed

TYPES OF CASES

Several types and sizes of cases are on the market for each form factor. The computer case, sometimes called the chassis, houses the power supply, motherboard, expansion cards, and drives. The case has lights and switches on the front panel that can be used to control and monitor the PC. Generally, the larger the case, the larger the power supply and the more amps it carries. These large cases allow for the extra space and power needed for a larger number of devices, such as multiple hard drives needed in a server.

Cases for personal computers and notebooks fall into three major categories: desktop cases, tower cases, and notebook cases. The following sections discuss each in turn.

DESKTOP CASES

The classic case with four drive bays and around six expansion slots that sits on your desktop doing double duty as a monitor stand is called a desktop case. The motherboard sits on the bottom of a desktop case, and the power supply is near the back. Because of the space a desktop case takes, it has fallen out of favor in recent years and is being replaced by smaller and more space-efficient cases.

For low-end desktop systems, compact cases, sometimes called low-profile cases or slimline cases, follow either the NLX, LPX, or Mini-LPX form factor. Likely to have fewer drive bays, they generally still provide for some expansion. You can see the rear of a compact case in Figure 3-12. An LPX motherboard that uses this case has a riser card for expansion cards, which is why the expansion card slots in the figure run parallel to the motherboard sitting on the bottom of the case.

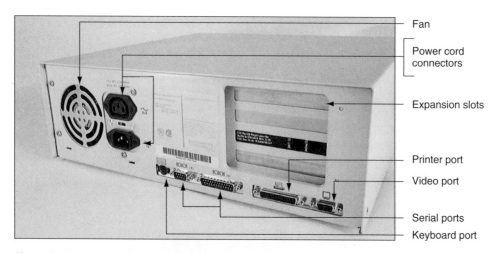

Fan

Power cord
connectors

Expansion slots

Printer port

Video port

Serial ports

Keyboard port

Figure 3-12 Because the expansion slots are running parallel to the motherboard on the bottom
of this desktop case, you know that a riser card is being used

TOWER CASES

A tower case can be as high as two feet and has room for several drives. Often used for
servers, this type of case is also good for PC users who anticipate upgrading, because tower
cases provide maximum space for working inside a computer and moving components
around. Figure 3-13 shows examples of each of the three main tower sizes, as well as two
desktop cases.

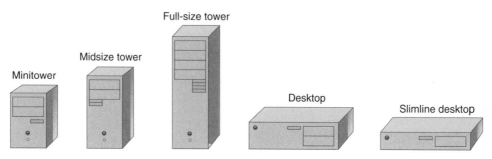

Full-size tower

Midsize tower

Minitower

Desktop

Slimline desktop

Figure 3-13 Tower and desktop cases

The variations in cases are as follows:

◢ Midsize towers, also called miditowers, are the most popular. They are midrange in size
and generally have around six expansion slots and four drive bays, providing moderate
potential for expansion. They are used for ATX, Mini-ATX, and BTX systems.

◢ The minitower, also called a microtower, is the smallest type of tower case and does
not provide room for expansion.

◢ Full-size towers are used for high-end personal computers and servers. They
are usually built to accommodate ATX, Mini-ATX, and BTX systems (see
Figure 3-14).

◢ Desktop cases are losing popularity because they take up too much space on our desks
unless you place your monitor on top of it. If you have a desktop case, don't place it
on its end because the CD or DVD drive will not work properly. Desktop cases are
built to accommodate all form factors for personal computers.

◢ Slimline desktop cases are gaining in popularity for low-end personal computers
because they come in cool colors and do double duty as a monitor stand.

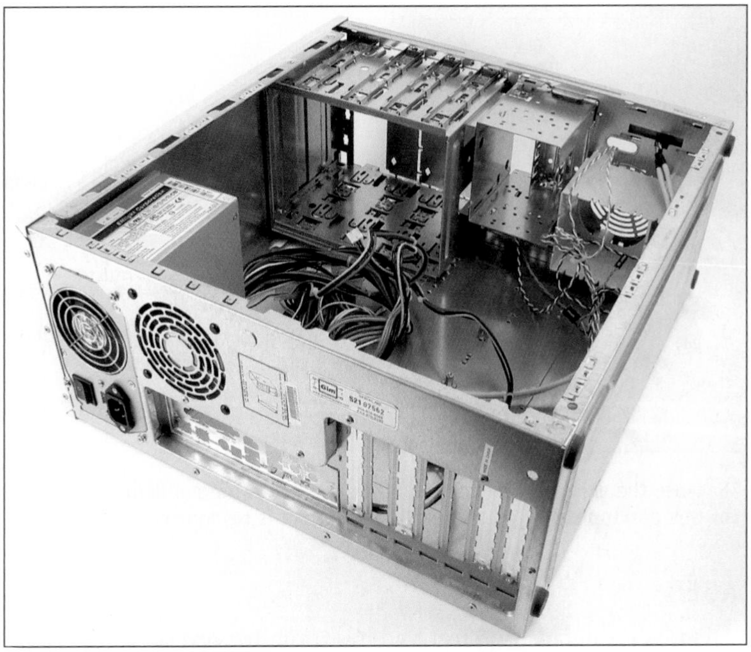

Figure 3-14   Full-size tower case for an ATX motherboard

NOTEBOOK CASES

Notebook cases are used for portable computers that have all the components of a desktop computer. The cost and power of notebook systems vary widely. As with other small systems, notebooks can present difficulties in expansion. The smallest notebook cases are called subnotebooks. Notebook designs are often highly proprietary, but are generally designed to conserve space, allow portability, use less power, and produce less heat. The case fan in a notebook usually attaches to a thermometer and runs only when temperature needs to be lowered. In addition, the transformer and rectifier functions of the power supply are often moved to an AC adapter on the power cable.

Table 3-1 lists a few case and power supply vendors.

Manufacturer	Web Site
Asus	*www.asus.com*
Axxion Group Corporation	*www.axxion.com*
Enlight Corporation	*www.enlightcorp.com*
Maxpoint Computers	*www.enermaxusa.com*
MGE Company	*www.mgecompany.com*
PC Power and Cooling	*www.pcpowerandcooling.com*
PCI Case Group	*www.pcicase.co.uk*
Sunus Suntek	*www.suntekgroup.com*

Table 3-1   Manufacturers of cases and power supplies for personal computers

Toward our goal of learning about power supplies and the electrical current they provide, let's turn our attention to understanding how electricity is measured and about some of its properties.

MEASURES AND PROPERTIES OF ELECTRICITY

In our modern world, we take electricity for granted, and we miss it terribly when it's cut off. Nearly everyone depends on it, but few really understand it. But to become a successful PC technician (that is, no fried motherboards, smoking monitors, or frizzed hair), you need to understand electricity, know how to use it, how it's measured, and how to protect computer equipment from its damaging power. So let's start with the basics. To most people, volts, ohms, watts, and amps are vague terms that simply mean electricity. All these terms can be used to measure some characteristic of electricity, as listed in Table 3-2.

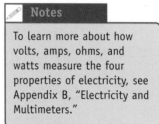

Notes

To learn more about how volts, amps, ohms, and watts measure the four properties of electricity, see Appendix B, "Electricity and Multimeters."

Unit	Definition	Computer Example
Volt (for example, 110 V)	A measure of electrical "pressure" differential. Volts are measured by finding the potential difference between the pressures on either side of an electrical device in a circuit. The symbol for volts is V.	An AT power supply provides four separate voltages: +12 V, -12 V, +5 V, and -5 V. An ATX power supply provides these voltages and +3.3 V as well. The BTX power supply provides +12 V, -12 V, +5 V, and +3.3 V.
Amp or ampere (for example, 1.5 A)	A measure of electrical current. Amps are measured by placing an ammeter in the flow of current. The symbol for Amps is A.	A 17-inch monitor requires less than 2 A to operate. A small laser printer uses about 2 A. A CD-ROM drive uses about 1 A.
Ohm (for example, 20 Ω)	A measure of resistance to electricity. Devices are rated according to how much resistance they offer to electrical current. The ohm rating of a resistor or other electrical device is often written somewhere on the device. The symbol for ohm is Ω.	Current can flow in typical computer cables and wires with a resistance of near zero Ω (ohm).
Watt (for example, 20 W)	A measure of electrical power. Whereas volts and amps are measured to determine their value, watts are calculated by multiplying volts by amps. Watts measure the total electrical power needed to operate a device. The symbol for watts is W.	A computer power supply is rated at 200 to 600 W.

Table 3-2 Measures of electricity

Now let's look at how electricity gets from one place to another and how it is used in house circuits and computers.

AC AND DC

Electricity can be either AC, alternating current, or DC, direct current. **Alternating current (AC)** goes back and forth, or oscillates, rather than traveling in only one direction. House current in the United States oscillates 60 times in one second (60 hertz). Voltage in the system is constantly alternating from positive to negative, which causes the electricity to flow first in one direction and then in the other. Voltage alternates from +110 V to -110 V. AC is the most economical way to transmit electricity to our homes and workplaces. By decreasing current and increasing voltage, we can force alternating current to travel great distances. When alternating current reaches its destination, it is made more suitable for driving our electrical devices by decreasing voltage and increasing current.

Direct current (DC) travels in only one direction and is the type of current that most electronic devices require, including computers. A rectifier is a device that converts alternating current to direct current. A transformer is a device that changes the ratio of current to voltage. Large transformers reduce the high voltage on power lines coming to your neighborhood to a lower voltage before the current enters your home. The transformer does not change the amount of power in this closed system; if it decreases voltage, it increases current. The overall power stays constant, but the ratio of voltage to current changes is illustrated in Figure 3-15.

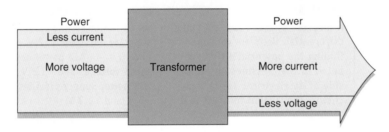

Figure 3-15   A transformer keeps power constant but changes the ratio of current to voltage

A computer power supply changes and conditions the house electrical current in several ways, functioning as both a transformer and a rectifier. It steps down the voltage from the 110-volt house current to 3.3, 5, and 12 volts, or to 5 and 12 volts, and changes incoming alternating current to direct current, which the computer and its peripherals require. The monitor, however, receives the full 110 volts of AC voltage, converting that current to DC.

Direct current flows in only one direction. Think of electrical current like a current of water that flows from a state of high pressure to a state of low pressure or rest. Electrical current flows from a high pressure state (called hot) to a state of rest (called ground or neutral). For a PC, a line may be either +5 or -5 volts in one circuit, or +12 or -12 volts in another circuit. The positive or negative value is determined by how the circuit is oriented, either on one side of the power output or the other. Several circuits coming from the power supply accommodate different devices with different power requirements.

HOT, NEUTRAL, AND GROUND

When AC comes from the power source at the power station to your house, it travels on a hot line and completes the circuit from your house back to the power source on a neutral line, as shown in Figure 3-16.

When the two lines reach your house and enter an electrical device, such as a lamp, electricity flows through the device to complete the circuit between the hot line and the neutral line. The device contains resistors and other electrical components that control the flow of electricity between the hot and neutral lines. In a controlled environment, the hot source then seeks and finds a state of rest by returning to the power station on the neutral line.

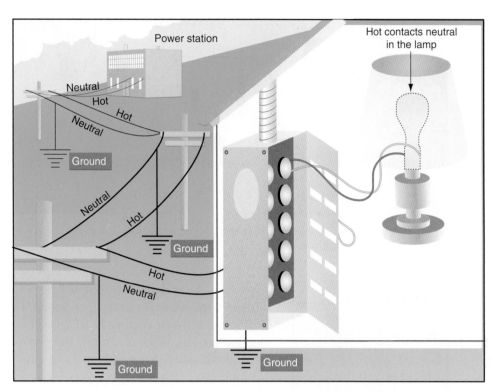

Figure 3-16 Normally, electricity flows from hot to neutral to make a closed circuit in the controlled environment of an electrical device such as a lamp

A short circuit, or a short, occurs when uncontrolled electricity flows from the hot line to the neutral line or from the hot line to ground. Electricity naturally finds the easiest route to a state of rest. Normally that path is through some device that controls the current flow and then back through the neutral line. If an easier path (one with less resistance) is available, the electricity follows that path. This can cause a short, a sudden increase in flow that can also create a sudden increase in temperature—enough to start a fire and injure both people and equipment. Never put yourself in a position where you are the path of least resistance between the hot line and ground!

A fuse is a component included in a circuit and designed to prevent too much current from flowing through the circuit. A fuse is commonly a wire inside a protective case, which is rated in amps. If too much current begins to flow, the wire gets hot and eventually melts, breaking the circuit, as an open switch would, and stopping the current flow. Many devices have fuses, which can be easily replaced when damaged.

To prevent uncontrolled electricity from continuing to flow indefinitely, which can happen because of a short, the neutral line is grounded. Grounding a line means that the line is connected directly to the earth, so that, in the event of a short, the electricity flows into the earth and not back to the power station. Grounding serves as an escape route for out-of-control electricity. The earth is at no particular state of charge and so is always capable of accepting a flow of current.

The neutral line to your house is grounded many times along its way (in fact, at each electrical pole) and is also grounded at the breaker box where the electricity enters your house. You can look at a three-prong plug and see the three lines: hot, neutral, and ground (see Figure 3-17).

 Caution

Beware of the different uses of black wire. In PCs and in DC circuits, black is used for ground, but in home wiring and in AC circuits, black is used for hot!

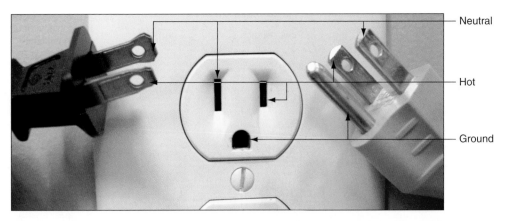

Figure 3-17   A polarized plug showing hot and neutral, and a three-prong plug showing hot, neutral, and ground

> **Notes**
>
> House AC voltage in the United States is about 110 V, but know that in other countries, this is not always the case. In many countries, the standard is 220 V. Outlet styles also vary from one country to the next.

Generally, electricians use green or bare wire for the ground wire, white for neutral, and black for hot in home wiring for 110-volt circuits. In a 220-volt circuit, black and red are hot, white is neutral, and green or bare is ground. To verify that a wall outlet is wired correctly, use a simple receptacle tester, as shown in Figure 3-18. Even though you might have a three-prong outlet in your home, the ground plug might not be properly grounded. To know for sure, always test the outlet with a receptacle tester.

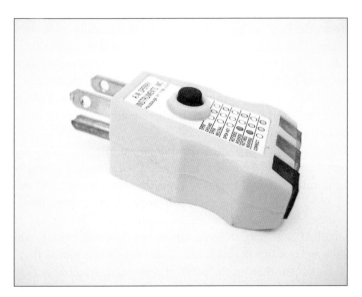

Figure 3-18   Use a receptacle tester to verify that hot, neutral, and ground are wired correctly

SOME COMMON ELECTRONIC COMPONENTS

It's important you understand what basic electronic components make up a PC and how they work. Basic electronic components in a PC include transistors, capacitors, diodes, ground, and resistors (each of which we will discuss in detail in a moment). Figure 3-19 shows the symbols for these components.

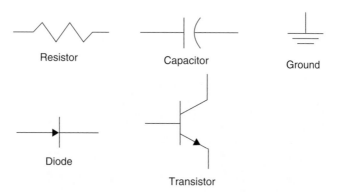

Figure 3-19 Symbols for some electronic components and for ground

To understand how these components are constructed, it helps to know that all the materials used to make the components fall into one of these three categories:

▲ *Conductors*. Material, such as gold or copper, that easily conducts electricity

▲ *Insulators*. Material, such as glass or ceramic, that resists the flow of electricity

▲ *Semiconductors*. Material, such as silicon, whose ability to conduct electricity, when a charge is applied, falls between that of a conductor and an insulator

TRANSISTOR

A transistor is an electronic device that can serve as a gate or switch for an electrical signal and can amplify the flow of electricity. Invented in 1947, the transistor is made of three layers of semiconductor material.

A charge (either positive or negative, depending on the transistor's design) placed on the center layer can cause the two outer layers of the transistor to complete a circuit to create an "on" state. An opposite charge placed on the center layer can make the reverse happen, causing the transistor to create an "off" state. Manipulating these charges to the transistor allows it to hold a logic state of either on or off. The on state represents binary 1 and the off state represents binary 0 when used to hold data in a computer.

When the transistor maintains this state, it requires almost no electrical power. Because the initial charge sent to the transistor is not as great as the resulting current that the transistor creates, a transistor sometimes is used as a small amplifier. For instance, transistors are used to amplify the tiny dots or pixels on an LCD monitor screen used to create a sharper image. The transistor is also used as the basic building block of an integrated circuit (IC), which is used to build a microchip.

CAPACITOR

A **capacitor** is an electronic device that can hold an electrical charge for a period of time and can smooth the uneven flow of electricity through a circuit. Capacitors inside a PC power supply create the even flow of current the PC needs. Capacitors maintain their charge long after current is no longer present, which is why the inside of a power supply can be dangerous even when it is unplugged. You can see many capacitors on mother-boards, video cards, and other circuit boards (see Figure 3-20).

Crosshatch on top of capacitor

Figure 3-20   Capacitors on a motherboard or other circuit board often have embedded crossed lines on top

DIODE

A diode is a semiconductor device that allows electricity to flow in only one direction. (A transistor contains two diodes.) One to four diodes used in various configurations can be used to convert AC to DC. Singularly or collectively, depending on the configuration, these diodes are called a rectifier.

RESISTOR

A resistor is an electronic device that limits the amount of current that can flow through it. In a circuit, a resistor is used to protect a circuit from overload or to control the current. Resistors are color-coded to indicate the degree of resistance measured in ohms.

PROTECTING YOUR COMPUTER SYSTEM

Now that you have learned some basic information about how electricity is measured and managed, let's look at ways to protect your computer system from the danger of electricity. Electricity can be a dangerous enemy to your computer when it comes in the form of static electricity, electromagnetic interference, and power surges. In the following sections, you'll learn about these dangers and what you can do to protect your computer against them.

STATIC ELECTRICITY

In the last chapter, you learned that static electricity (also called ESD) is a dangerous enemy when you're working inside a computer case. If you touch a sensitive computer component when there is a static charge on your body different from the static charge on the component, there is a resulting discharge as your body and the component reach equal charges. This sudden discharge can damage the component even when it is so slight you don't feel the spark. ESD is especially a problem in dry and cold climates. Recall from Chapter 2 to protect components against ESD, use a ground bracelet or ESD gloves. If you don't have this equipment available, be careful to touch the computer case before you touch a component so any charge between you and the case is dissipated before you touch a component.

Also remember from Chapter 2 to unplug the power cord from the computer case before working inside the case. Even when the power switch on the rear of the case is turned off, residual power is still on and can damage a system or give you a shock if you touch a live wire. Some motherboards even have a small light inside the case to remind you of this fact and to warn you that power is still getting to the system. For this reason, be certain to unplug the power cord before working inside it.

> **A+ Exam Tip**
>
> The A+ Essentials exam emphasizes that you should know how to protect computer equipment as you work on it.

EMI (ELECTROMAGNETIC INTERFERENCE)

Another phenomenon that can cause electrical problems with computers is electromagnetic interference (EMI). EMI is caused by the magnetic field produced as a side effect when electricity flows. EMI in the radio frequency range, which is called radio frequency interference (RFI), can cause problems with radio and TV reception. Data in data cables that cross an electromagnetic field can become corrupted, causing crosstalk. Crosstalk can be partially controlled by using data cables covered with a protective material; these cables are called shielded cables. Power supplies are also shielded to prevent them from emitting EMI.

If mysterious, intermittent errors persist on a PC, one thing to suspect is EMI. Try moving the PC to a new location. If the problem continues, try moving it to a location that uses an entirely different electric circuit. A simple way to detect EMI is to use an inexpensive AM radio. Turn the tuning dial away from a station and all the way down into a low-frequency range. With the radio on, you can hear the static that EMI produces. Try putting the radio next to several electronic devices to detect the EMI they emit.

If EMI in the electrical circuits coming to the PC causes a significant problem, you can use a line conditioner to filter the electrical noise that causes the EMI. Line conditioners are discussed later in the chapter.

> **Notes**
>
> PCs can emit EMI to other nearby PCs, which is one reason a computer needs to be inside a case. To help cut down on EMI between PCs, always install face plates in empty drive bays or slot covers over empty expansion slots.

> **Video**
>
> Testing for EMI

> **Notes**
>
> After you remove the source of EMI, the problem it is causing goes away. In contrast, the problems caused by ESD permanently damage a component.

A+
220-602
1.3

SURGE PROTECTION AND BATTERY BACKUP

The power supplies in most computers can operate over a wide range of electrical voltage input; however, operating the computer under these conditions for extended periods of time can shorten not only the power supply's life, but also the computer's. Also, electrical storms can end a computer's life quite suddenly. To prevent such things from happening, consider installing a device to filter AC input.

A wide range of devices on the market condition the AC input to computers and their peripherals to eliminate highs and lows and provide backup power when the AC fails. These devices, installed between the house current and the computer, fall into three general categories: surge suppressors, power conditioners, and uninterruptible power supplies (UPSs). All these devices should have the UL (Underwriters Laboratory) logo, which says that the laboratory, a provider of product safety certification, has tested the device. The UL standard that applies to surge suppressors is UL 1449, first published in 1985 and revised in 1998.

SURGE SUPPRESSORS

A surge suppressor, also called a surge protector, protects equipment against sudden changes in power level, such as spikes from lightning strikes. The device, such as the one shown in Figure 3-21, typically provides a row of power outlets, an on/off switch, and a protection light that indicates the device is protecting equipment from overvoltages (also called transient voltages) on AC power lines and telephone lines. Surge suppressors can come as power strips (note that not all power strips have surge protection), wall-mounted units that plug into AC outlets, or consoles designed to sit beneath the monitor on a desktop. Some provide RJ-11 telephone jacks to protect modems and fax machines from spikes.

Figure 3-21 This surge suppressor has six electrical outlets, two phone jacks, and a power protection light

A surge suppressor might be a shunt type that absorbs the surge, a series type that blocks the surge from flowing, or a combination of the two. A suppressor is rated in joules, which is a measure of work or energy. One joule (pronounced "jewel") is the work or energy required to produce one watt of power in one second, and a suppressor is rated as to the amount of joules it can expend before it no longer can work to protect the circuit from the power surge. Suppressors are commonly rated from 250 joules to several thousand joules—the higher the better.

Some suppressors are also rated by clamping voltage (also called let-through voltage), which is the voltage point at which a suppressor begins to absorb or block voltage. Normally, house current is rated at 120 V, so you would think the clamping voltage should be close to this number such as around 130 V. However, the clamping voltage value is best not set this low. House current regularly spikes past 200 V, and a PC power supply is

A+
220-602
1.3

designed to handle these types of quick spikes. If the surge suppressor kicks in to work on these spikes, not only is it unnecessary, but the suppressor is likely to wear out prematurely. A clamping voltage of 330 V or higher is appropriate.

The circuitry inside the suppressor that handles a surge can burn out if a surge is too high or lasts too long. In this case, most suppressors continue to work just like a normal extension cord, providing no surge protection. Because of this fact, it's important a surge suppressor has a light indicator that says the suppressor part of the device is still working. Otherwise, you might not have protection, but not know it.

A data line protector serves the same function for your telephone line to your modem that a surge suppressor does for the electrical lines. Telephone lines carry a small current of electricity and need protection against spikes, just as electrical lines do.

Notes

Whenever a power outage occurs, unless you have a reliable power conditioner or UPS installed, unplug all power cords to the PC, printers, monitors, and the like. Sometimes when the power returns, sudden spikes are accompanied by another brief outage. You don't want to subject your equipment to these surges. When buying a surge suppressor, look for those that guarantee against damage from lightning and that reimburse for equipment destroyed while the surge suppressor is in use.

When shopping for a surge protector, look for these features:

- Joules rating (more than 600 joules) and the time it takes for the protection to start working (less than 2 nanoseconds is good)
- Warranty for connected equipment and UL seal of approval
- A light that indicates the surge protection is working and phone line protection
- Let-through voltage rating and line noise filtering

When you plug in a surge protector, know that if the protector is not grounded using a three-prong outlet, the protector cannot do its job. One more thing to consider: You can purchase a whole-house surge protection system that is installed by an electrician at your breaker box. It's more expensive, but your entire house or office building is protected.

POWER CONDITIONERS

In addition to providing protection against spikes, power conditioners also regulate, or condition, the power, providing continuous voltage during brownouts. These voltage regulators, sometimes called line conditioners, can come as small desktop units. They provide a degree of protection against swells or spikes (temporary voltage surges) and raise the voltage when it drops during brownouts or sags (temporary voltage reductions). Power conditioners are measured by the load they support in watts, volt-amperes (VA), or kilovolt-amperes (kVA).

To determine the VA required to support your system, multiply the amperage of each component by 120 volts and then add up the VA for all components. For example, a 17-inch monitor has "1.9 A" written on its back, which means 1.9 amps. Multiply that value by 120 volts, and you see that the monitor requires 228 VA or 228 watts. A Pentium PC with a 17-inch monitor and tape backup system requires about 500 VA or 500 watts of support.

Power conditioners are a good investment if the AC in your community suffers excessive spikes and brownouts. However, a device rated under 1 kVA will probably provide corrections only for brownouts, not for spikes. Line conditioners, like surge suppressors, provide no protection against a total blackout (complete loss of power).

UNINTERRUPTIBLE POWER SUPPLY

A+
220-602
1.3

Unlike a power conditioner, the **uninterruptible power supply (UPS)** provides backup power in the event that the AC fails completely. The UPS also provides some filtering of the AC. A UPS offers these benefits:

⬛ Conditions the line to account for both brownouts and spikes
⬛ Provides backup power during a blackout
⬛ Protects against very high spikes that could damage equipment

A UPS device that is suitably priced for personal computer systems is designed as a standby device (battery-powered circuit is used when AC input fails), an inline device (battery-powered circuit is used continually), or a line-interactive device (which combines features of the first two). Several variations of these three types of UPS devices are on the market at widely varying prices.

A common UPS device is a rather heavy box that plugs into an AC outlet and provides one or more outlets for the computer and its peripherals (see Figure 3-22). It has an on/off switch, requires no maintenance, and is very simple to install.

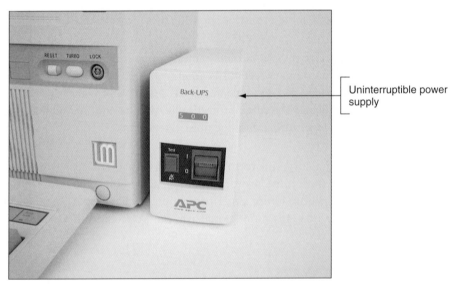

    Uninterruptible power
    supply

Figure 3-22 Uninterruptible power supply (UPS)

The Smart UPS

When you look through ads of UPS devices, some of them are labeled as a smart UPS. A smart UPS (also called an **intelligent UPS**) can be controlled by software from a computer. For example, from the front panel of some UPSs you can check for a weak battery, but with a smart UPS, you can perform the same function from utility software installed on your computer. To accommodate this feature, a UPS must have a serial port or USB connection to the PC and a microprocessor on board.

Some activities this utility software and a smart UPS can do include the following:

⬛ Diagnose the UPS.
⬛ Check for a weak battery.
⬛ Monitor the quality of electricity received.
⬛ Monitor the percentage of load the UPS is carrying during a blackout.

A+
220-602
1.3

⬧ Automatically schedule the weak-battery test or UPS diagnostic test.

⬧ Send an alarm to workstations on a network to prepare for a shutdown.

⬧ Close down all servers protected by the UPS during a blackout.

⬧ Provide pager notification to a facilities manager if the power goes out.

⬧ After a shutdown, allow for startup from a remote location over phone lines.

What to Consider When Buying a UPS

When you purchase a UPS, do not buy a UPS that runs at full capacity. This is especially important for an inline UPS because this type of UPS is constantly recharging the battery. If this battery charger is operating at full capacity, it is producing a lot of heat, which can reduce the battery's life. The UPS rating should exceed your total VA or wattage output by at least 25 percent.

You should also be aware of the degree of line conditioning that the UPS provides. Consider the warranty and service policies as well as the guarantee the UPS manufacturer gives for the equipment that the UPS protects. For example, one standby UPS by Tripp Lite that costs less than $90 claims to support up to 750 VA or 450 watts power requirements for up to 35 minutes during a complete power failure. This smart UPS has a USB connector to a computer, and carries a guarantee on connected equipment of $100,000. Table 3-3 lists some UPS manufacturers.

Manufacturer	Web Site
American Power Conversion Corp. (APC)	www.apcc.com
Circuit Components, Inc.	www.surgecontrol.com
CyberPower	www.cyberpowersystems.com
MGE UPS Systems	www.mgeups.com
Tripp Lite	www.tripplite.com
Belkin Corporation	www.belkin.com
Eaton Corporation	www.powerware.com
Liebert Corporation	www.liebert.com
Para Systems, Inc.	www.minuteman-ups.com
Toshiba International Corp.	www.tic.toshiba.com

Table 3-3 UPS manufacturers

ENERGY STAR SYSTEMS (THE GREEN STAR)

A+ ESS
2.2

As you build or maintain a computer, one very important power consideration is energy efficiency and conservation. Toward that end, you should know that Energy Star systems and peripherals have the U.S. Green Star, indicating that they satisfy certain energy-conserving standards of the U.S. Environmental Protection Agency (EPA). Devices that can carry the Green Star are computers, monitors, printers, copiers, and fax machines.

Energy Star standards are designed to decrease overall

> **Notes**
>
> Office equipment is among the fastest growing source of electricity consumption in industrialized nations. Much of this electricity is wasted because people often leave computers and other equipment on overnight. Because Energy Star devices go into sleep mode when they are unused, they create overall energy savings of about 50 percent.

A+ ESS
2.2

electricity consumption in the United States to protect and preserve natural resources. These standards, sometimes called the Green Standards, generally mean that the computer or the device has a standby program that switches the device to sleep mode when it is not in use. In addition, during sleep mode, the device must use no more than 30 watts of power.

POWER-MANAGEMENT METHODS AND FEATURES

Computer systems implement Energy Star standards in several ways. All these methods of power management are intended to conserve energy. Some of the more significant ones are listed below:

- ◢ Advanced Configuration and Power Interface (ACPI), used with Windows 2000/XP and Windows 98/Me and supported by the system BIOS, is a set of standards so that BIOS can communicate with the OS about what hardware is present and what energy-saving features are present and how they can be used.
- ◢ The older Advanced Power Management (APM) specifications championed by Intel and Microsoft were used by older notebook computers and allow BIOS to control power management.
- ◢ AT Attachment (ATA) for hard drives and other type drives allows drives to stop spinning when not in use.
- ◢ Display Power Management Signaling (DPMS) standards for monitors and video cards

Notes

To see if your system is ACPI-compliant, open Device Manager and then open the Computer item in the list of devices (see Figure 3-23). Look for ACPI in the detail line.

ACPI is the current standard used by most desktop and notebook computers. Using this standard, there are four modes, S1 through S4, used to indicate different levels of power-saving functions. They are listed below from the least to the greatest energy-saving level:

- ◢ In S1 mode, the hard drive and monitor is turned off and everything else runs normally. Some manufacturers call this mode the sleep mode or standby mode.

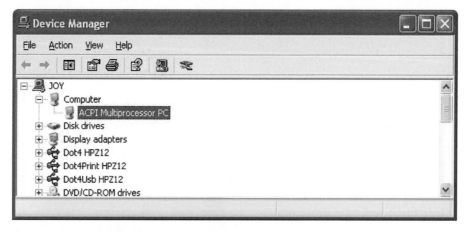

Figure 3-23 Use Device Manager to quickly see if a system is ACPI-compliant

- ◢ In S2 mode, the hard drive, monitor, and processor are turned off. This mode is also called standby or sleep mode.
- ◢ In S3 mode, everything is shut down except RAM and enough of the system to respond to a wake-up call such as pressing the keyboard or moving the mouse.

This mode is sometimes called sleep mode, suspend mode, standby mode, or suspend to RAM.

⊿ S4 mode is called hibernation. In hibernation, everything in RAM is copied to a file on the hard drive and then the system shuts down. Later, when a power button is pressed, the system does not have to go through the slow boot process, but can quickly read contents of the hibernation file and restore the system to its state before S4 mode was enabled.

Some ACPI power-management features can be controlled from Windows and others can be controlled from BIOS. In many situations, Windows and BIOS share the control of a power-management feature, which can often cause conflicts and confusion. The trend is to manage power using Windows. For example, hibernation settings can be controlled from Windows, but hibernation in BIOS must be enabled before it will work. To manage power features in Windows, go to Control Panel and open the Power Options applet. The Power Options Properties window opens. How to use this window is covered in Chapter 11.

To control power using the BIOS, go to CMOS setup and access the Power menu. Options on this menu depend on the BIOS. For example, in Figure 3-24, you see the Power screen for an Asus Pentium 4 motherboard BIOS (*www.asus.com*). The options on the left of the screen allow you to control the power-management features, and the right side of the screen gives not-too-helpful information about these options.

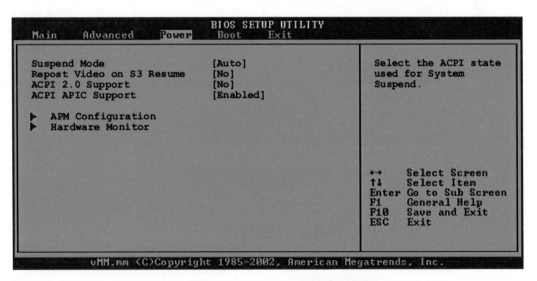

Figure 3-24 A power management BIOS setup screen showing power-management features

The following list describes each option shown in Figure 3-24:

⊿ *Suspend Mode.* Choices are S1 Only, S3 Only, or Auto. Auto is the default choice, which can send everything except memory to sleep incrementally depending on how long the system remains inactive.

⊿ *Repost Video on S3 Resume.* Choices are Yes or No. The default is No. For Windows 9x/Me, set it to Yes so that VGA BIOS POST is run after video comes out of an S3 sleep state.

⊿ *ACPI 2.0 Support.* Choices are Yes or No. The default is No. ACPI stores information that it needs to pass on to the OS in a series of tables. The master table is the Root System Description Table (RSDT). Originally, this table was designed to use 32-bit addresses. By saying Yes to this choice, you can use additional 64-bit tables if you have a 64-bit processor such as the Itanium.

▲ *ACPI APIC Support.* Choices are Enabled or Disabled. The default choice is Enabled, which means the APIC (Advanced Programmable Interrupt Controller) information is included in ACPI information. This controller can sometimes solve problems with devices not coming out of a sleep state correctly.

▲ *APM Configuration.* When you select this choice, you are taken to a submenu where you can configure the legacy APM configuration. Normally, you wouldn't want to.

▲ *Hardware Monitor.* When you select this choice, you can configure how you want to monitor and (to some degree) control hardware devices, including the CPU temperature, fan speeds, and voltage output from the motherboard.

ENERGY STAR MONITORS

Most computers and monitors sold today are Energy Star–compliant; you know they are compliant because they display the green Energy Star logo onscreen when the PC is booting. Most monitors that follow the Energy Star standards adhere to the Display Power Management Signaling (DPMS) specifications developed by Video Electronics Standards Association (VESA), which allow for the video card and monitor to go into sleep mode simultaneously.

> **Notes**
>
> For a monitor's power-saving feature to function, the video card or computer must also support this function.

> **Notes**
>
> For a Windows 9x/Me system, problems might occur if the system BIOS is turning off the monitor because of power-management settings, and Windows is also turning off the monitor. If the system hangs when you try to get the monitor going again, try disabling one or the other setting. It is best to use the OS or BIOS for power management, but not both.

To view and change energy settings of an Energy Star monitor using Windows 2000/XP, right-click the desktop and select Properties. The Display Properties dialog box opens. Click the Screen Saver tab. If your monitor is Energy Star–compliant, you will see the Energy Star logo at the bottom. When you click the Power button, the Power Options Properties dialog box opens, and you can change your power options (see Figure 3-25). Your power options might differ depending on the power-management features your BIOS supports.

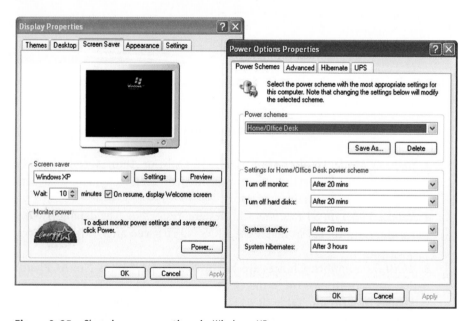

Figure 3-25 Changing power options in Windows XP

TROUBLESHOOTING THE ELECTRICAL SYSTEM

A+ ESS
1.3

A+
220-602
1.2

Electrical problems can occur before or after the boot and can be consistent or intermittent. Many times PC repair technicians don't recognize the cause of a problem to be electrical because of the intermittent nature of some electrical problems. In these situations, the hard drive, memory, the OS, or even user error might be suspected as the source of the problem and then systematically eliminated before the electrical system is suspected. This section will help you to be aware of symptoms of electrical problems so that you can zero in on the source of an electrical problem as quickly as possible.

APPLYING CONCEPTS

Your friend Sharon calls to ask your help with a computer problem. Her system has been working fine for over a year, but now strange things are happening. Sometimes, the system powers down while she is working for no apparent reason, and sometimes Windows locks up. As you read this section, look for clues as to what the problem might be. Also, as you read, think of questions to ask your friend that will help you.

Possible symptoms of a problem with the electrical system are:

- The PC appears "dead"—no lights, no spinning drive or fan.
- The PC sometimes halts during booting. After several tries, it boots successfully.
- Error codes or beeps occur during booting, but they come and go.
- You smell burnt parts or odors. (Definitely not a good sign!)

Check the simple things first. Most PC problems have simple solutions. Try these things:

- Is everything connected and turned on? Are any cable connections loose? Is the computer plugged in?
- Are all the switches turned on? Computer? Monitor? Surge protector? Uninterruptible power supply? Separate circuit breaker? Is the wall outlet (or surge protector) in working condition?
- If the fan is not running, turn off the computer, open the case, and check the connections to the power supply. Are they secure? Are all cards securely seated?
- If you smell burnt parts, turn off the system and carefully search for the source of the problem. Look for shorts and frayed and burnt wires. Disassemble the parts until you find the one that is damaged.

As you read through the rest of this section on troubleshooting, you'll see other possible solutions to electrical problems during the boot such as loose internal connections.

PROBLEMS WITH EXTERNAL POWER

A brownout (reduced current) of the house current might cause symptoms of electrical power problems. If you suspect the house current could be low, check other devices that are using the same circuit. A copy machine, laser printer, or other heavy equipment might be drawing too much power. Remove the other devices from the same house circuit.

A line conditioner might solve the problem of intermittent errors caused by noise in the power line to the PC. Try installing a line conditioner to monitor and condition voltage to the PC.

PROBLEMS WITH LOOSE INTERNAL CONNECTIONS

A+ ESS
1.3

A+
220-602
1.1
1.2

Loose connections inside the computer case can cause a system to appear dead or reboot itself. For most of the ATX and BTX power supplies, a wire runs from the power switch on the front of the case to the motherboard. This wire must be connected to the pins on the motherboard and the switch turned on before power comes up. Check that the wire is connected correctly to the motherboard. Figure 3-26 shows a wire, which is labeled "REMOTE SW," connected to pins on the motherboard labeled "PWR.SW." If you are not sure of the correct connection on the motherboard, see the motherboard documentation. While inside the case, check all power connections from the power supply to the motherboard and drives. Also, some cases require the case's front panel be in place before the power-on button will work.

> **Notes**
>
> Remember from earlier in the chapter that strong magnetic or electrical interference can affect how a power system functions. Sometimes an old monitor emits too much static and EMI (electromagnetic interference) and brings a whole system down. When you troubleshoot power problems, remember to check for sources of electrical or magnetic interference such as an old monitor or electric fan sitting near the computer case.

Remote SW

Figure 3-26 For an ATX or BTX power supply, the remote switch wire must be connected to the motherboard before power will come on

PROBLEMS THAT COME AND GO

If a system boots successfully to the Windows desktop, you still might have a power system problem. Some problems are intermittent, that is, they come and go. Here are some symptoms that might indicate an intermittent problem with the electrical system after the boot:

- The computer stops or hangs for no reason. Sometimes it might even reboot itself.
- Memory errors appear intermittently.
- Data is written incorrectly to the hard drive.
- The keyboard stops working at odd times.
- The motherboard fails or is damaged.
- The power supply overheats and becomes hot to the touch.
- The power supply fan becomes very noisy or stops.

3

A+ ESS
1.1
1.3

A+
220-602
1.1
1.2

Generally, intermittent problems (those that come and go) are more difficult to solve than a dead system. There can be many causes of intermittent problems, such as an inadequate power supply, overheating, and devices and components damaged by ESD. Each of these sources of intermittent problems are covered in this section.

PROBLEMS WITH AN INADEQUATE POWER SUPPLY

If you have just installed a new device such as a second hard drive or a DVD drive and are concerned that the power supply is not adequate, you might test it after you finish the installation.

Make all the devices in your system work at the same time. For instance, you can make both the new drive and the floppy drive work at the same time by copying files from one to the other. If the new drive and the floppy drive each work independently, but data errors occur when both work at the same time, suspect a shortage of electrical power.

If you prefer a more technical approach, you can estimate how much total wattage your system needs by calculating the watts required for each device and adding them together. (Calculate watts by multiplying volts in the circuit by amps required for each device.) However, in most cases, the computer's power supply is more than adequate if you add only one or two new devices.

Power supplies for microcomputers range from 200 watts for a small desktop computer system to 600 watts for a tower floor model that uses many multimedia or other power-hungry devices. If you suspect your power supply is inadequate for newly installed devices, upgrade to one with a higher wattage rating.

PROBLEMS WITH THE POWER SUPPLY, BOARDS, OR DRIVES

The power supply might be faulty or not be adequate for power needs, or components drawing power might be bad. These problems can cause the system to hang, reboot, give intermittent errors, or not boot at all. Expansion boards or drives might be defective and drawing too much power. Remove all nonessential expansion cards (modem, sound card, mouse) one at a time. This verifies that they are not drawing too much power and pulling the system down.

A system with a standard power supply of about 250 watts that has multiple hard drives, multiple CD drives, and several expansion cards is most likely operating above the rated capacity of the power supply, which can cause the system to unexpectedly reboot or give intermittent, otherwise unexplained errors. Upgrade the power supply as needed to accommodate an overloaded power system.

If these suggestions don't correct the problem, check the power supply by exchanging it for one you know is good.

You can use a multimeter to measure the voltage output of a power supply and determine if it is supplying correct voltages, but know that a power supply that gives correct voltages when you measure it might still be the source of problems, because power problems can be intermittent. See Appendix B, "Electricity and Multimeters," to learn more about how to use a multimeter to measure voltage output from a power supply.

Video

Using a Multimeter

PROBLEMS WITH THE POWER SUPPLY FAN

An improperly working fan sometimes causes power supply problems. Usually just before a fan stops working, it hums or whines, especially when the PC is first turned on. If this has just happened, replace the fan if you are trained to service the power supply. If not, replace the entire power supply. If you replace the power supply or fan and the fan still does not

A+ ESS
1.1
1.3

A+
220-602
1.1
1.2

work, the problem might not be the fan. A short somewhere else in the system drawing too much power might cause the problem. Don't operate the PC if the fan does not work. Computers without cooling fans can quickly overheat and damage chips.

To troubleshoot a nonfunctional fan, which might be a symptom of another problem and not a problem of the fan itself, follow these steps:

1. Turn off the power and remove all power cord connections to all components, including the connections to the motherboard, and all power cords to drives. Turn the power back on. If the fan works, the problem is with one of the systems you disconnected, not with the power supply or its fan.

2. Turn off the power and reconnect the power cords to the drives. If the fan comes on, you can eliminate the drives as the problem. If the fan does not come on, try one drive after another until you identify the drive with the short.

3. If the drives are not the problem, suspect the motherboard subsystem. With the power off, reconnect all power cords to the drives.

4. Turn off the power and remove the power to the motherboard by disconnecting P1 or P8 and P9. Turn the power back on.

5. If the fan works, the problem is probably not the power supply but a short in one of the components powered by the power cords to the motherboard. The power to the motherboard also powers expansion cards.

6. Remove all expansion cards and reconnect plugs to the motherboard.

7. If the fan still works, the problem is one of the expansion cards. If the fan does not work, the problem is the motherboard or something still connected to it.

POWER PROBLEMS WITH THE MOTHERBOARD

A+
220-602
1.1
1.2
1.3

The motherboard, like all other components inside the computer case, should be grounded to the chassis. Look for a metal screw that grounds the board to the computer case. However, a short might be the problem with the electrical system if some component on the board makes improper contact with the chassis. This short can seriously damage the motherboard. Check for missing standoffs (small plastic or metal spacers that hold the motherboard a short distance away from the chassis). A missing standoff most often causes these improper connections. Also check for extra standoffs not used by the motherboard that might be touching a wire on the bottom of the board and causing a short.

Shorts in the circuits on the motherboard might also cause problems. Look for damage on the bottom of the motherboard. These circuits are coated with plastic, and quite often damage is difficult to spot. Also look for burned-out capacitors that are spotted brown or corroded.

Frayed wires on cable connections can also cause shorts. Disconnect hard drive cables connected directly to the motherboard. Power up with P1 or P8 and P9 connected but all cables disconnected from the motherboard. If the fan works, the problem is with one of the systems you disconnected.

 Caution

Never replace a damaged motherboard with a good one without first testing or replacing the power supply. You don't want to subject another good board to possible damage.

PROBLEMS WITH OVERHEATING

An overheated system can cause intermittent problems or cause the system to reboot or refuse to boot. In fact, the temperature inside the case should never exceed 100 degrees F (38 degrees C).

A+ ESS
1.1
1.3

A+
220-602
1.1
1.2
1.3

Here are some simple things you can do to solve an over-heating problem:

> **A+ Exam Tip**
>
> The A+ Essentials and IT 220-602 exams expect you to recognize that a given symptom is possibly power or heat related.

▲ Verify the cooler is connected properly to the processor. If it doesn't fit well, the system might not boot and certainly the processor will overheat.

▲ Use compressed air or an antistatic vacuum to remove dust from the power supply, the vents over the entire computer, and the processor heat sink. Excessive dust insulates components and causes them to overheat. Use an ESD-safe service vacuum or a can of compressed air—both can be purchased from electronic tools suppliers.

▲ Check airflow inside the case. Are all fans running? Are cables in the way of airflow? You might need to replace a fan or tie up cables so they don't obstruct airflow. A case is generally designed for optimal airflow when slot openings on the front and rear of the case are covered. To improve airflow, replace missing faceplates over empty drive bays and replace missing slot covers over empty expansion slots.

▲ After you close the case, leave your system off for a few hours. When you power up the computer again, let it run for 10 minutes, go into CMOS setup, check the temperature readings, and reboot. Next, let your system run until it shuts down. Power it up again and check the temperature in setup again. A significant difference in this reading and the first one you took after running the computer for 10 minutes indicates an overheating problem.

▲ Use tie wraps to secure cables and cords so that they don't block airflow across the processor.

If you try the preceding list of things to do and still have an overheating problem, it's time to move on to more drastic solutions. The problem might be caused by poor air circulation inside the case. The power supply fan in ATX cases blows air out of the case, pulling outside air from the vents in the front of the case across the processor to help keep it cool. Another exhaust fan is usually installed on the back of the case to help the power supply fan pull air through the case (see Figure 3-27).

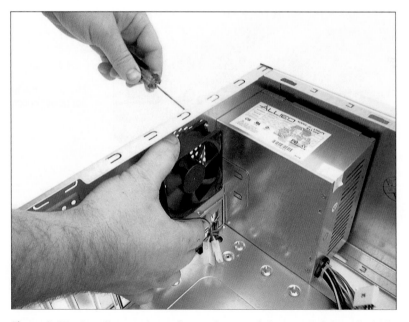

Figure 3-27 Install one exhaust fan on the rear of the case to help pull air through the case

In addition, most processors require a cooler with a fan installed on top of the processor. Figure 3-28 shows a good arrangement of vents and fans for proper airflow and a poor arrangement.

Good arrangement for proper airflow

Poor arrangement for proper airflow

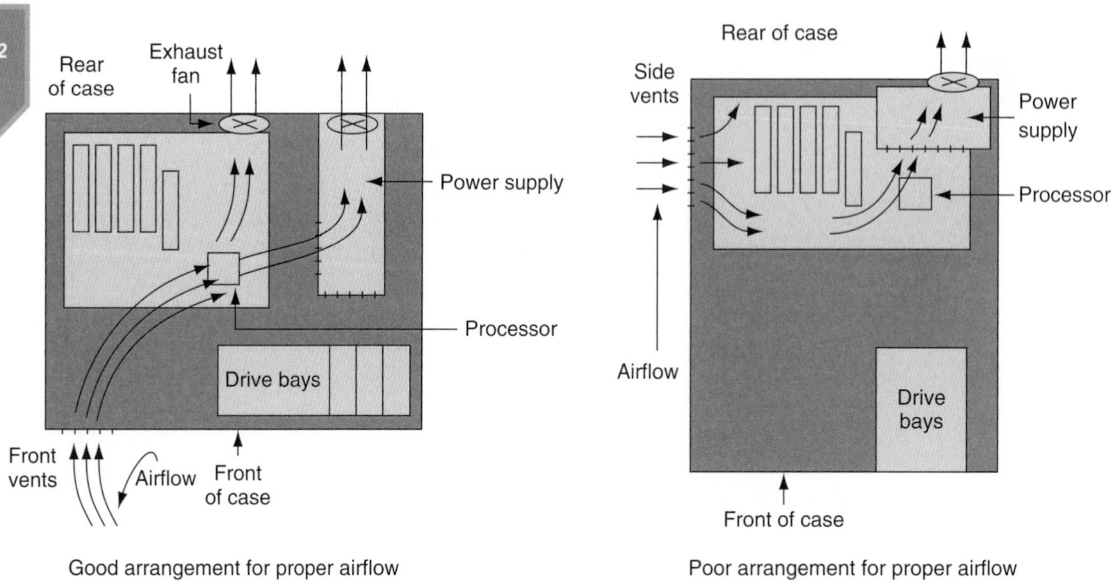

Figure 3-28 Vents and fans need to be arranged for best airflow

For better ventilation, use a power supply that has vents on the bottom and front of the power supply. Note in Figure 3-28 airflow is coming into the bottom of the power supply because of these bottom vents. The power supply in Figure 3-27 has vents only on the front and not on the bottom. Compare that to the power supply in Figure 3-29, which has vents on both the front and bottom.

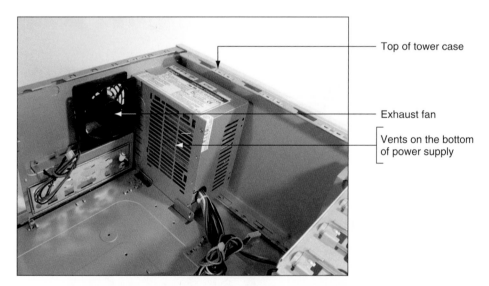

Figure 3-29 This power supply has vents on the bottom to provide better airflow inside the case

An intake fan on the front of the case might help pull air into the case. Intel recommends you use a front intake fan for high-end systems, but AMD says a front fan for ATX systems is not necessary. Check with the processor manufacturer for specific instructions as to the

A+ ESS
1.1
1.3

A+
220-602
1.1
1.2
1.3

placement of fans and what type of fan and heat sink to use. You will see some examples of processor fans in Chapter 4.

When all else fails, you can try the following to solve stubborn overheating problems:

⊿ Check that your system vents and at least one exhaust fan are in the right position so that air flows across the processor without expansion cards or ribbon cables obstructing the flow.
⊿ Check with the processor manufacturer Web site that you are using the right size processor fan and heat sink and the right thermal compound recommended for the specific processor.
⊿ Check that your power supply has vents on the bottom.
⊿ An AGP video card generates a lot of heat. Make sure that you leave the PCI slot next to the AGP slot open to better ventilate the AGP card. Also, you can purchase a fan that installs in the empty expansion slot next to the video card to help keep it cool.
⊿ Install hard drives in large bays using a bay kit to make the small drive fit in the large bay, thus improving airflow around the drive.
⊿ Monitor the temperature inside the case using a temperature sensor that sounds an alarm when a high temperature is reached or uses software to alert you of a problem.

Be careful when trying to solve an overheating problem. Excessive heat itself may damage the CPU and the motherboard, and the hard reboots necessary when your system hangs may damage the hard drive. If you suspect damaged components, try substituting comparable components that you know are good.

APPLYING CONCEPTS

Back to Sharon's computer problem. Here are some questions that will help you identify the source of the problem:

⊿ Have you added new devices to your system? (These new devices might be drawing too much power from an overworked power supply.)
⊿ Have you moved your computer recently? (It might be sitting beside a heat vent or electrical equipment.)
⊿ Does the system power down or hang after you have been working for some time?
⊿ Are case vents free so that air can flow? (The case might be close to a curtain covering the vents.)

Intermittent problems like the one Sharon described are often heat related. If the system only hangs but does not power off, the problem might be caused by faulty memory or bad software, but because it actually powers down, you can assume the problem is related to power or heat.

If Sharon tells you that the system powers down after she's been working for several hours, you can probably assume overheating. Check that first. If that's not the problem, the next thing to do is replace the power supply.

REPLACING THE POWER SUPPLY

The easiest way to fix a power supply you suspect is faulty is to replace it. A power supply is considered a field replaceable unit (FRU) for a PC support technician. When selecting a replacement power supply, be sure the new power supply uses the correct form factor, is adequately

 A+ Exam Tip

The A+ IT 220-602 exam expects you to know how to select and install a power supply.

Caution

Remember from Chapter 2 that you need to consider the monitor and the power supply to be "black boxes." Never remove the cover or put your hands inside this equipment unless you know about the hazards of charged capacitors and have been trained to deal with them. Both the power supply and the monitor can hold a dangerous level of electricity even after you turn them off and disconnect them from a power source. The power supply and monitor contain enough power to kill you, even when they are unplugged.

rated for power in watts, and has all the power connectors needed by your system. To determine if the power supply really is the problem, turn off the PC, open the computer case, and set the new power supply on top of the old one. Disconnect the old power supply's cords and plug the PC devices into the new power supply. Turn on the PC and verify that the new power supply solves your problem before installing it.

Follow these steps to replace a power supply:

1. Turn off the power to the computer.

2. Remove all external cables from the computer case including the power cable.

3. Remove the computer case cover.

4. Inside the case, disconnect all power cords from the power supply to other devices.

5. Determine which components must be removed before the power supply can be safely removed from the case. You might need to remove the hard drive, several cards, or the CD drive. In some cases, you may even need to remove the motherboard.

6. Remove all the components necessary to get to the power supply. Remember to protect the components from static electricity as you work.

7. Unscrew the screws on the back of the computer case that hold the power supply to the case.

8. Look on the bottom or back of the case for slots that hold the power supply in position. Often the power supply must be shifted in one direction to free it from the slots.

9. Remove the power supply.

10. Place the new power supply in position, sliding it into the slots the old power supply used.

11. Replace the power supply screws.

12. Replace all other components.

13. Before replacing the case cover, connect the power cords, turn on the PC, and verify that all is working.

14. Turn off the PC, replace the cover, and connect all external cables.

15. Turn on the PC and verify all is working.

>> CHAPTER SUMMARY

▲ A form factor is a set of specifications for the size and configuration of hardware components, such as cases, power supplies, and motherboards.

▲ The most common form factor today is ATX. There is an ATX variation called Mini-ATX. ATX superseded the earlier AT and Baby AT form factors. BTX is the lastest form factor.

- Other form factors include LPX and NLX, in which expansion cards are mounted on a riser card that plugs into the motherboard.

- Case types include desktop, low-profile or slimline desktops, minitower, miditower, full-size tower, and notebook. The most popular case type in use today is the miditower.

- Electrical voltage is a measure of the potential difference in an electrical system.

- Electrical current is measured in amps, and electrical resistance is measured in ohms.

- Wattage is a measure of electrical power. Wattage is calculated by multiplying volts by amps in a system.

- Microcomputers require direct current (DC), which is converted from alternating current (AC) by the PC's power supply inside the computer case.

- A PC power supply is actually a transformer and rectifier, rather than a supplier of power.

- Materials used to make electrical components include conductors, insulators, and semiconductors.

- A transistor is a gate or switch for an electrical signal, a capacitor holds an electrical charge, a diode allows electricity to flow in one direction, and a resistor limits electrical current.

- To protect a computer system against ESD, use a ground bracelet, ground mat, and static shielding bags.

- Protect a computer system against EMI by covering expansion slots (which also reduces dust inside the case and improves airflow), by not placing the system close to or on the same circuit as high-powered electrical equipment, and by using line conditioners.

- Devices that control the electricity to a computer include surge suppressors, line conditioners, and UPSs.

- A surge suppressor protects a computer against damaging spikes in electrical voltage.

- Line conditioners level the AC to reduce brownouts and spikes.

- A UPS provides enough power to perform an orderly shutdown during a blackout.

- There are two kinds of UPSs: the true UPS (called the inline UPS) and the standby UPS.

- The inline UPS is more expensive because it provides continuous power. The standby UPS must switch from one circuit to another when a blackout begins.

- Utility software at a remote computer or a computer connected to the UPS through a USB or serial cable can control and manage a smart UPS.

- Data line protectors are small surge suppressors designed to protect modems from spikes on telephone lines.

- A faulty power supply can cause memory errors, data errors, system hangs, or reboots; it can damage a motherboard or other components.

- To reduce energy consumption, the U.S. Environmental Protection Agency has established Energy Star standards for electronic devices.

- Devices that are Energy Star–compliant go into sleep mode, in which they use less than 30 watts of power.

- PCs that are Energy Star–compliant often have CMOS settings that affect the Energy Star options available on the PC.

- When troubleshooting the electrical system, consider the problem might be caused by loose connections, bad components drawing too much power, the power supply, or overheating.

>> KEY TERMS

For explanations of key terms, see the Glossary near the end of the book.

active backplane
alternating current (AC)
amp
ampere
AT
ATX
ATX12V power supply
Baby AT
backplane system
brownouts
BTX (Balanced Technology
  Extended)
bus riser
capacitor
clamping voltage
compact case
data line protector
daughter card
desktop case
diode
direct current (DC)
Display Power Management
  Signaling (DPMS)

electromagnetic interference
  (EMI)
Energy Star
field replaceable unit (FRU)
FlexATX
form factor
full AT
Green Standards
intelligent UPS
joule
line conditioner
line-interactive
low-profile case
LPX
MicroATX
Mini-ATX
Mini-LPX
NLX
notebook case
ohm
P1 connector
P8 connector
P9 connector

passive backplanes
power conditioners
rectifier
resistor
riser card
sags
sleep mode
slimline case
smart UPS
soft power
soft switch
spikes
surge protector
surge suppressor
swells
tower case
transformer
transistor
uninterruptible power supply
  (UPS)
volt
watt

>> REVIEWING THE BASICS

1. Volts are a measure of what characteristic of electricity?

2. What is the normal voltage of house electricity in the United States?

3. Hot wires in home wiring are normally colored _____ and ground wires in computers are normally colored _____.

4. What is the difference between a transformer and a rectifier? Which are found in a PC power supply?

5. What are the five voltages produced by an ATX or BTX power supply?

6. What is the purpose of the 4-pin auxiliary connector on a motherboard?

7. How many pins does the main power connector on a BTX board have?

8. What form factor for the case and power supply does a NLX motherboard use?

9. Describe the purpose of the ground line in a house circuit. What is the electrical symbol for ground?

10. What is the basic electronic building block of an integrated circuit?

11. Why is a power supply dangerous even after the power is disconnected?

12. What is the symbol for a diode?

13. What is a simple way to detect EMI?

14. What is an unintended, high-current, closed connection between two points in a circuit called?

15. Which form factor uses a riser card on the edge of the motherboard?

16. List four types of computer case form factors. What is the most popular type of form factor for PCs today?

17. List three advantages an ATX system has over a Baby AT system.

18. List four computer symptoms that indicate a faulty power supply.

19. According to ACPI standards, the S1 mode causes what two devices to stop using power?

20. What is another name for the ACPI standard S4 mode?

21. What power management standard is older than ACPI and has mostly been replaced by ACPI?

22. How can you easily tell if a computer is designed to comply with Green Standards?

23. What unit of measure is used to describe the amount of work a surge suppressor can do before it stops protecting the circuit from an electrical surge?

24. Why is it important to have an indicate light on a surge suppressor?

25. What are the two main types of uninterruptible power supplies?

26. How does a smart UPS differ from one that is not smart?

27. If you are asked to identify the form factor of a motherboard, what are two criteria you can use to help you identify the board?

28. What are three motherboard form factors that can be used with a compact case?

29. What is one thing you can regularly do to prevent a computer system from overheating?

30. Which type of case form factor is best designed to keep a system cool?

>> THINKING CRITICALLY

1. How much power is consumed by a load drawing 5 A with 120 V across it?

2. You suspect that a power supply is faulty, but you use a multimeter to measure its voltage output and find it to be acceptable. Why is it still possible that the power supply may be faulty?

3. Someone asks you for help with a computer that hangs at odd times. You turn it on and work for about 15 minutes, and then the computer freezes and powers down. What do you do first?

   ◢ Replace the surge protector.

   ◢ Replace the power supply.

   ◢ Turn the PC back on, go into CMOS setup, and check the temperature reading.

   ◢ Install an additional fan.

4. When working on a computer, which of the following best protects against ESD? Why?

   ◢ Always touch the computer case before touching a circuit board inside the case.

   ◢ Always wear an antistatic bracelet clipped to the side of the case.

   ◢ Always sit a computer on an antistatic mat when working on it.

>> HANDS-ON PROJECTS

PROJECT 3-1:   Exploring Energy Star Features on a PC

To investigate and test the power-management features on your computer, do the following:

1. Enter CMOS setup and write down each Energy Star feature that can be enabled or disabled through CMOS.

2. Using either CMOS or the OS, set hibernation to begin after 10 minutes of inactivity. List the steps you took to do this.

3. Open Paint and draw a figure. Wait 10 minutes. Did the computer go into hibernation?

4. Press the power button to wake up the computer from hibernation. Did the computer wake up?

5. Is Paint still open on your desktop with your drawing in progress? Why or why not?

PROJECT 3-2:   Making Price and Value Comparisons

Using Web sites or a local computer store, find out the following about products discussed in the chapter:

1. Compare the prices and ratings of two different surge suppressors. Write down your findings.

2. Compare the prices and ratings of two different UPS devices. Compare a smart UPS to one that does not interface with a PC, but otherwise has similar ratings.

PROJECT 3-3:   Finding PC Power Supply Facts

Remove the cover from your home or lab PC, and answer the following questions:

1. How many watts are supplied by your power supply? (The number is usually printed on the label on the top of the power supply.)

2. How many cables are supplied by your power supply?

3. Where does each cable lead?

4. Does the back of the power supply have a switch that can be set for 220 volts (Europe) or 110 volts (U.S.)?

PROJECT 3-4:   Building a Circuit to Turn On a Light

1. From the following components, build a circuit to turn on a light:

   ▲ An AC light bulb or LED (*Note*: An LED has polarity—it must be connected with the negative and positive terminals in the correct positions.)

   ▲ A double-A battery (*Note*: A 9-volt battery can burn out some bulbs.)

   ▲ A switch (A knife switch or even a DIP switch will work.)

   ▲ Three pieces of wire to connect the light, the switch, and the battery

2. Add a second battery to the circuit, and record the results.

3. Add a resistor to the circuit, and record the results.

4. Place an extra wire in the middle of the circuit running from the battery to the switch (thus making a short), and record the results.

PROJECT 3-5:   Researching the Market for a UPS for Your Computer System

For a computer system you can access, determine how much wattage output a UPS should have in the event of a total blackout, and estimate how long the UPS should sustain power. Research the market and report on the features and prices of a standby UPS and an inline UPS. Include the following information in your report:

- ◢ Wattage supported
- ◢ Length of time the power is sustained during total blackout
- ◢ Line-conditioning features
- ◢ AC backup present or not present for the inline UPS
- ◢ Surge suppressor present or not present
- ◢ Number of power outlets on the box, and other features
- ◢ Written guarantees
- ◢ Brand name, model, vendor, and price of the device

PROJECT 3-6:   Detecting EMI

Use a small, inexpensive AM radio. Turn the dial to a low frequency, away from a station. Put the radio next to several electronic devices. List the devices in order, from the one producing the most static to the one producing the least static. Listen to the devices when they are idle and in use.

PROJECT 3-7:   Calculating Wattage Used by Your Drives

Fill in the following table, and then calculate the total wattage requirements of all drives in your system. (Your computer might not have all the drives listed in the table.) Look for a wattage rating printed somewhere on the device. Note that some devices might not have the information written on it; in that case, write "Not Found" in the table.

Component	Wattage
Hard drive	
Floppy drive	
CD drive	
DVD drive	
Zip drive	
Other drive	

Total wattage requirements for all drives:_____

<u>**PROJECT 3-8:**</u>   Exploring Computer System Form Factors

You will need to open your computer case to answer these questions about your computer system:

◢ What type of case do you have?

◢ What are the dimensions of your motherboard in inches?

◢ What form factor does your motherboard use?

◢ What is the power rating of your power supply?

>> *REAL PROBLEMS, REAL SOLUTIONS*

<u>**REAL PROBLEM 3-1:**</u>   Replacing a Power Supply

Suppose you turn on a system and everything is dead—no lights, nothing on the monitor screen, and no spinning fan or hard drive. You verify the power to the system works, all power connections and power cords are securely connected, and all pertinent switches are turned on. You can assume the power supply has gone bad. It's time to replace it. Simulate this activity by exchanging power supplies with another student in your lab.

Processors and Chipsets

In the last chapter, you learned about the different form factors used for motherboards. In this chapter, you'll learn about the most important components on the motherboard, the processor, and the chipset. You'll learn how a processor works and about the many different types and brands of processors and chipsets and how to make wise purchasing decisions. A processor must be kept cool, so this chapter covers the various cooling systems used for processors. Although the chipset is embedded on a motherboard, the processor is considered a field replaceable unit. And so you'll learn how to install and upgrade a processor.

PROCESSORS

A+ ESS
1.1

A+
220-602
1.1

The processor installed on a motherboard and the chipset embedded on the board primarily determine the power and features of the system (see Figure 4-1). In this chapter, you'll learn about processors and chipsets and in the next chapter you'll learn about motherboards.

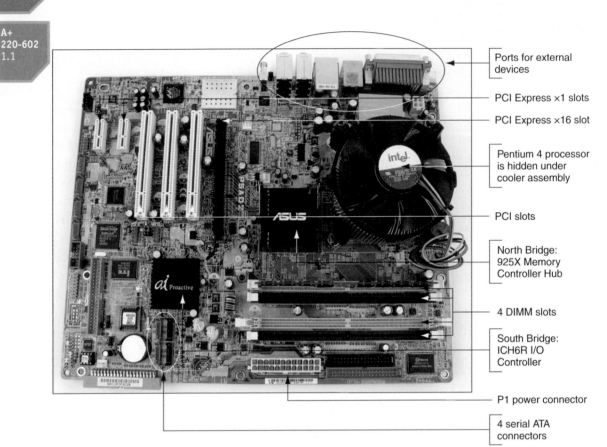

Ports for external devices
PCI Express ×1 slots
PCI Express ×16 slot
Pentium 4 processor is hidden under cooler assembly
PCI slots
North Bridge: 925X Memory Controller Hub
4 DIMM slots
South Bridge: ICH6R I/O Controller
P1 power connector
4 serial ATA connectors

Figure 4-1 This Asus P5AD2 motherboard uses an Intel 925X chipset with a North Bridge and a South Bridge, and the motherboard has a Pentium 4 processor installed

Most IBM and IBM-compatible computers manufactured today use processors made by Intel (*www.intel.com*) or AMD (*www.amd.com*), or to a lesser degree by Cyrix, which is currently owned by VIA Technologies (*www.via.com.tw*). Processors are rated based on several factors that affect performance and the motherboards that can support them. These factors are listed here:

▲ The system bus speeds the processor supports. Today's front-side buses run at 1066, 800, 533, or 400 MHz. System buses and motherboards are covered in the next chapter.

▲ Processor core frequency measured in gigahertz, such as 3.2 GHz.

▲ Word size, either 32 bits or 64 bits, which is the number of bits a processor can process at one time.

▲ Data path for most computers today, which is 64 bits or 128 bits and is the number of bits a processor can receive at one time.

▲ Multiprocessing ability, which is the ability of a system to do more than one thing at a time. This is accomplished by several means, including two processing units installed on the same die (used by Pentium processors), a motherboard using two processor

4

sockets (supported by Xeon processors), and two processors installed in the same processor housing (called dual-core processing).

◢ The amount of memory included with the processor. Today's processors all have some memory on the processor chip (called a die). Some processors have memory off the die but inside the processor housing, and some processors have memory embedded on the motherboard.

◢ Efficiency and special functionality of programming code. Examples of technologies used by a processor to improve efficiency of executing programming code are Intel's Hyper-Threading and AMD's HyperTransport.

◢ The type of RAM, motherboard, and chipset the processor supports. RAM comes in a variety of modules, speeds, and features, which are all discussed in Chapter 6. The processor must work with the chipset that is embedded on the motherboard. Chipsets are discussed later in this chapter. The processor and the chipset determine what type and how much RAM you can use in the system. And each processor is designed to fit a particular socket or slot on a motherboard.

HOW A PROCESSOR WORKS

A processor contains three basic components: an input/output (I/O) unit, a control unit, and one or more arithmetic logic units (ALUs), as shown in Figure 4-2. The I/O unit manages data and instructions entering and leaving the processor. The control unit manages all activities inside the processor itself. The ALU does all comparisons and calculations.

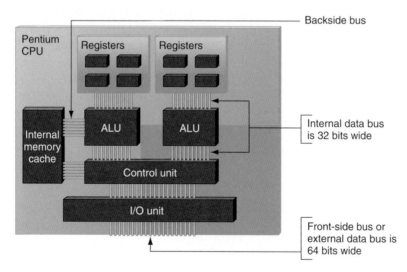

Figure 4-2 Since the Pentium processor was first released in 1993, the standard has been for a processor to have two arithmetic logic units so that it can process two instructions at once

Registers are small holding areas on the processor chip that work much as RAM does outside the processor. Registers hold counters, data, instructions, and addresses that the ALU is currently processing. In addition to registers, the processor has its own internal memory cache that holds data and instructions waiting to be processed by the ALU. Also notice in Figure 4-2 the existence of the external bus, where data, instructions, addresses, and control signals are sent into and out of the processor. The data portion of the external bus is 64 bits wide. This bus is sometimes called the front-side bus (FSB) because it connects to the front side of the processor that faces the outside world. Inside the processor housing, data, instructions, addresses, and control signals travel on the internal bus. The data portion of that bus, called the internal data bus, is 32 bits wide. In Figure 4-2, you can see this internal data bus

A+ ESS
1.1

connects to each of the ALUs. The portion of the internal bus that connects the processor to the internal memory cache is called the back-side bus (BSB). The processor's internal bus operates at a much higher frequency than the external bus (system bus).

Let's now turn our attention to the details of several characteristics of processors, including system bus speed, processor speed, data path size, multiprocessing abilities, memory cache, and instruction sets.

SYSTEM BUS FREQUENCY OR SPEED

Recall that bus frequency is the frequency or speed at which data is placed on a bus. Remember also that a motherboard has several buses. Each bus runs at a certain frequency, some faster than others.

Although the motherboard has several buses, only the fastest bus connects directly to the processor. This bus has many names. It's called the front-side bus, the external bus, the motherboard bus, or the system bus. In the past, the more popular term was system bus, although the current trend is to call it the front-side bus; you see it written in computer ads as the FSB. In this book, we'll call it the system bus or the front-side bus.

Common speeds for the system bus are 1066 MHz, 800 MHz, 533 MHz, 400 MHz, 200 MHz, 133 MHz, and 100 MHz, although the bus can operate at several other speeds, depending on the processor and how the motherboard is configured.

> **Notes**
>
> When you read that Intel supports a motherboard speed of 533 MHz or 800 MHz, the speed refers to the system bus speed. Other slower buses connect to the system bus, which serves as the go-between for other buses and the processor.

PROCESSOR FREQUENCY OR SPEED

Processor frequency is the speed at which the processor operates internally. The first processor used in an IBM PC was the 8088, which worked at about 4.77 MHz, or 4,770,000 clock beats per second. An average speed for a new processor today is about 3.2 GHz, or 3,200,000,000 beats per second. In less than one second, this processor "beats" more times than a human heart beats in a lifetime!

If the processor operates at 3.2 GHz internally but 800 MHz externally, the processor frequency is 3.2 GHz, and the system bus frequency is 800 MHz. In this case, the processor operates at four times the system bus frequency. This factor is called the multiplier. If you multiply the system bus frequency by the multiplier, you get the processor frequency:

$$\text{System bus frequency} \times \text{multiplier} = \text{processor frequency}$$

On some motherboards, you must know the value of the multiplier in order to configure the frequency of the processor and system bus. On other motherboards, the frequencies are automatically set by CMOS setup without your intervention. Older boards used jumpers on the motherboard or CMOS setup to set the system bus frequency and multiplier, which then determine the processor frequency. For these older boards, common multipliers were 1.5, 2, 2.5, 3, 3.5, and 4. You must know the documented processor speed in order to set the correct system bus frequency and multiplier, so that the processor runs at the speed for which it is designed.

> **Notes**
>
> Processor frequencies or speeds are rated at the factory and included with the processor documentation. However, sometimes the actual speed of the processor might be slightly higher or lower than the advertised speed.

Newer boards automatically detect the processor speed and adjust the system bus speed accordingly. Your only responsibility is to make sure you install a processor that runs at a speed the motherboard can support.

Overclocking

For newer motherboards and processors, you can override the default frequencies by changing a setting in CMOS setup. For example, one CMOS setup screen allows you to set the processor frequency at 5%, 10%, 15%, 20%, or 30% higher than the default frequency. Running a motherboard or processor at a higher speed than the manufacturer suggests is called overclocking and is not recommended because the speed is not guaranteed to be stable. Also, know that running a processor at a higher-than-recommended speed can result in overheating, which can damage the processor.

Throttling

Most motherboards and processors offer some protection against overheating so that, if the system overheats, it will throttle down or shut down to prevent the processor from being damaged permanently. If you plan to overclock a system, check CMOS setup for the option to enable automatic throttling. Turn it on so that the processor frequency will automatically decrease if overheating occurs. Also, some processors will throttle back when they begin to overheat in order to protect themselves from damage.

DATA PATH SIZE AND WORD SIZE

The data path, sometimes called the external data path size, is that portion of the system bus that transports data into the processor. The data path in Figure 4-2 is 64 bits wide. The word size, sometimes called the internal data path size, is the largest number of bits the processor can process in one operation. Word size of today's processors is 32 bits (4 bytes) or 64 bits (8 bytes). The word size need not be as large as the data path size; some processors can receive more bits than they can process at one time, as in the case of the Pentium in Figure 4-2.

Earlier processors always operated in real mode, using a 16-bit word size and data path on the system bus. Later, protected mode was introduced, which uses a 32-bit word size. Most applications written today use 32-bit protected mode, because the most popular processors today for desktop and notebook computers are the Pentiums, which use a 32-bit word size. But this is expected to soon change because Intel and AMD both have 64-bit processors that are currently used in the server market, and AMD has 64-bit processors for the desktop and notebook market.

> **Notes**
>
> To take full advantage of a 64-bit processor, such as the Intel Itanium or the AMD Athlon, software developers must recompile their applications to use 64-bit processing and write operating systems that use 64-bit data transfers. Microsoft provides a 64-bit version of Windows XP that works with the 64-bit processors.

MULTIPROCESSING, MULTIPLE PROCESSORS, AND DUAL-CORE PROCESSING

CPU designers have come up with several creative ways of doing more than one thing at a time to improve performance. Three methods are popular: multiprocessing, dual processors, and dual-core processing. Multiprocessing is accomplished when a processor contains more than one ALU. Older processors had only a single ALU. Pentiums, and those processors coming after them, have at least two ALUs. With two ALUs, processors can process two instructions at once and, therefore, are true multiprocessing processors.

> **Notes**
>
> Recall that Intel has 64-bit processors, called Itaniums, that have a 128-bit front-side bus, and AMD has the Opteron, the Athlon 64, and the Turion 64, all of which are 64-bit processors.

Because Pentiums have two ALUs, the front-side data bus is 64 bits wide, and the back-side data bus is only 32 bits wide. Because each ALU processes only 32 bits at a time, the industry calls the Pentium a 32-bit processor even though it uses a 64-bit bus externally.

A second method of improving performance is installing more than one processor on a motherboard, creating a multiprocessor platform. A motherboard must be designed to support more than one processor by providing more than one processor socket. For example, some motherboards designed for servers have two processor sockets on the board for a dual-processor configuration. The processors installed on these boards must be rated to work in a multiprocessor platform. Some Xeon processors are designed to be used this way. You can install a single Xeon processor in one of the processor sockets, but for improved performance, a second Xeon can be installed in the second socket. In computer ads, a Xeon processor rated to run on a multiprocessor platform is listed as a Xeon MP processor (MP stands for multiprocessor).

The latest advancement in multiple processing is dual-core processing. Using this technology, the processor housing contains two processors that operate at the same frequency, but independently of each other. They share the front-side bus, but have independent internal caches. Figure 4-3 shows how dual-core processing is implemented by AMD, which is similar to Intel's configuration used by the Pentium D and Celeron D processors (D stands for dual-core). (For Pentium and Celeron dual-core processors, each of the two processors in the processor housing still use two ALUs.)

(a) Single-core processing

(b) Dual-core processing

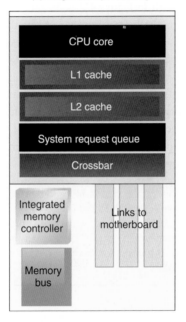
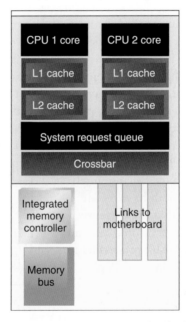

Figure 4-3 AMD dual-core processing using two Opteron processors in the single processor housing

MEMORY CACHE

A memory cache is a small amount of RAM (referred to as static RAM [SRAM]) that is much faster than the rest of RAM, which is called dynamic RAM (DRAM). SRAM is faster than DRAM because SRAM does not need refreshing and can hold its data as long as power is available. (DRAM loses data rapidly and must be refreshed often.) The processor can process instructions and data faster if they are temporarily stored in SRAM cache. The cache size a processor can support is a measure of its performance, especially during memory-intensive calculations.

To take advantage of the little SRAM available, when the processor requests data or programming code, the memory controller anticipates what the processor will request next and copies that data or programming code to SRAM (see Figure 4-4). Then, if the controller guessed correctly, it can satisfy the processor request from SRAM without accessing the slower DRAM. Under normal conditions, the controller guesses right more than 90 percent of the time and caching is an effective way of speeding up memory access.

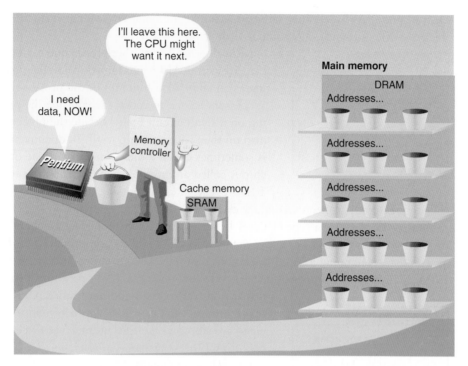

Figure 4-4 Cache memory (SRAM) is used to temporarily hold data in expectation of what the processor will request next

In the past, SRAM was contained on the motherboards, and upgrading SRAM could be accomplished by adding SRAM to slots on the board. SRAM on a motherboard was contained in individual chips or on a memory module called a cache on a stick (COAST). Figure 4-5 shows an older motherboard supporting the Classic Pentium with 256 K of SRAM installed on the board in two single chips. A COAST slot is available to hold an additional 256 K.

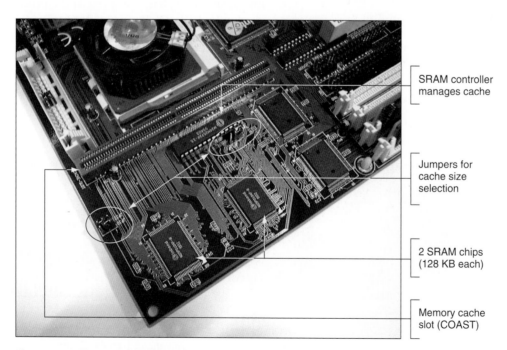

Figure 4-5 SRAM on this older motherboard is stored in individual chips, and the board also has a COAST slot

Historically, SRAM used these different technologies: burst SRAM, pipelined SRAM, pipelined burst SRAM, and synchronous and asynchronous SRAM.

> **Notes**
>
> When making purchasing decisions about processors, consider that the more L1 or L2 cache the processor contains, generally the better the processor performs.

Most present-day motherboards don't contain SRAM—rather most SRAM is contained inside the processor housing as an embedded function of the processor itself. Processors have a memory cache inside the processor housing on a small circuit board beside the processor chip and also on the processor chip itself. In documentation, the chip is sometimes called a die. A memory cache on the processor chip is called an internal cache, a primary cache, or a Level 1 (L1) cache. A cache outside the processor microchip is called an external cache, a secondary cache, or a Level 2 (L2) cache.

Some processors use a type of Level 1 cache called Execution Trace Cache. For example, the Pentium 4 has 8 K of Level 1 cache used for data and an additional 12 K of Execution Trace Cache containing a list of operations that have been decoded and are waiting to be executed. Many times, a processor decides to follow one branch of operations in a program of instructions rather than another branch. Only branches of operations that the processor has determined will be executed are stored in the Execution Trace Cache, making the execution process faster.

> **Notes**
>
> When SRAM was contained on the motherboard, there was usually room to upgrade SRAM to improve performance. Because SRAM is now inside the processor housing, for today's systems, upgrading SRAM is not normally an option.

L2 caches are usually 128 K, 256 K, 512 K, 1 MB, or 2 MB in size. In the past, all L2 cache was contained on the motherboard, but beginning with the Pentium Pro, some L2 cache has been included inside the processor housing. Figure 4-6 shows two methods in which Intel implements L2 cache inside the processor housing. Using one method, a Pentium has L2 cache stored on a separate microchip within the processor housing, which is called discrete L2 cache or On-Package L2 cache. The back-side bus servicing this cache runs at half the speed of the processor, which is why Intel advertises this cache as "half speed On-Package L2 cache." Using another method, some Pentiums contain L2 cache directly on the same die as the processor core, making it difficult to distinguish between L1 and L2 cache;

> **A+ Exam Tip**
>
> The A+ Essentials exam expects you to know the purpose and characteristics of external cache memory.

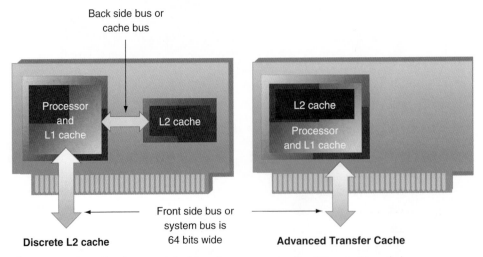

Figure 4-6 Some Pentiums contain L2 cache on separate dies (discrete L2 cache), and some contain L2 cache on the same die (Advanced Transfer Cache)

4

this is called Advanced Transfer Cache (ATC). ATC makes it possible for the Pentium to fit on a smaller and less expensive form factor. The ATC bus is 256 bits wide and runs at the same speed as the processor.

If there is L2 cache in the processor housing and additional cache on the motherboard, the cache on the motherboard is called Level 3 (L3) cache. In addition, some advanced processors manufactured by AMD have L1, L2, and L3 cache inside the processor housing. In this case, the L3 cache is further removed from the processor than the L2 cache, even though both are inside the processor housing. Table 4-1 summarizes the locations for memory caches.

Memory Cache	Location
L1 cache	On the processor die. All processors today have L1 cache.
L2 cache	Inside the processor housing of newer processors, but not as close to the processor as L1 cache. The first processor to contain L2 was the Intel Pentium Pro.
L2 cache	On the motherboard of older systems.
L3 cache	Inside the processor housing, farther away from the processor than the L2 cache. The Intel Itanium housing contains L3 cache.
L3 cache	On the motherboard when there is L2 cache in the processor housing. L3 is used with some AMD processors.

Table 4-1 The locations of memory caches in a system

INSTRUCTION SET AND MICROCODE

Groups of instructions that accomplish fundamental operations, such as comparing or adding two numbers, are permanently built into the processor chip. Less efficient processors require more steps to perform these simple instructions than do more efficient processors.

These instructions are called microcode and the groups of instructions are collectively called the instruction set. Earlier processors use an instruction set called reduced instruction set computing (RISC), and many later processors use a more complex instruction set called complex instruction set computing (CISC).

The Intel Itaniums use a new instruction set called explicitly parallel instruction computing (EPIC). With EPIC, the processor receives a bundle of commands at one time. The bundle also contains instructions for how the processor can execute two commands at the same time (in parallel), using the processor's multiprocessing abilities.

Intel has made several improvements to its instruction sets with multimedia applications in mind. These applications typically perform many repetitive operations, using the same command for a long stream of data. For these applications, MMX (Multimedia Extensions) is used by the Pentium MMX and Pentium II; SSE (Streaming SIMD Extension) is used by the Pentium III; and SSE2, SSE3, and Hyper-Threading for the Pentium 4. SIMD, which stands for "single instruction, multiple data," is a process that allows the CPU to receive a single instruction and then execute it on multiple pieces of data rather than receiving the same instruction each time each piece of data is received.

The Pentium 4 can use MMX, SSE, SSE2, SSE3, and Hyper-Threading. MMX and SSE help with repetitive looping, which happens a lot when the CPU is managing audio and graphics data. SSE also improves on 3D graphics.

 **A+ Exam Tip**

The A+ Essentials exam expects you to be familiar with the characteristics of the different processors. Know the purposes and characteristics of Hyper-Threading, dual-core processing, throttling, and overclocking.

A+ ESS
1.1

> **Notes**
>
> Some instruction sets are tailored for specific functions, such as the Xeons' and Pentiums' Hyper-Threading Technology designed to improve multitasking performance whereby two threads of a process run in parallel.

AMD, a favorite CPU manufacturer for gamers and hobbyists, uses 3DNow!, a processor instruction set designed to improve performance with 3D graphics and other multimedia data. In addition, AMD uses HyperTransport! to increase bandwidth and PowerNow! to improve a processor's performance and lower power requirements.

THE INTEL PROCESSORS

Early CPUs by Intel were identified by model numbers: 8088, 8086, 80286, 386, and 486. The model numbers were written with or without the 80 prefix and were sometimes preceded with an *i*, as in 80486, 486, or i486. After the 486, Intel introduced the Pentium processor, and several Intel processors that followed included Pentium in their names. Pentiums are sometimes identified simply with a *P*, as in P4 for Pentium 4.

More recently, Intel began using three-digit processor numbers to aid in identifying its processors. The Pentium processors use *5xx* to *8xx* (for example, Pentium Extreme Edition 840); the Celeron processors use *3xx* (for example, Celeron D Processor 340); and the Pentium M processors use *7xx* (for example, the Pentium M Processor 735). The numbering system along with the processor family name uniquely identify the processor, making it easier to compare processor benefits and features when making purchasing decisions. Generally, the higher the last two digits of the processor number within the processor family, the better the processor, considering the processor speed, system bus speed, architectural features, and cache size.

OVERVIEW OF THE PENTIUM FAMILY OF PROCESSORS

A Pentium has two ALUs, so it can perform two calculations at once; it is, therefore, a true multiprocessor. Pentiums have a 64-bit external path size and two 32-bit internal paths, one for each ALU. Each ALU uses a 32-bit word size. Because the Celeron and the older Xeon processors have a 32-bit word size and 64-bit path size, they are also included in this discussion as belonging to the Pentium family. However, recent Xeon processors use a 64-bit word size, so they technically don't belong to the Pentium family, but are still included in our discussion.

Table 4-2 lists the eight types of Pentium processors: Classic Pentium, Pentium MMX, Pentium Pro, Pentium II, Xeon, Celeron, Pentium III, and Pentium 4. Within each type, there are several variations of processors. Earlier variations of the Pentium II processor included the Celeron and Xeon. At first, Intel produced a family of processors called the Pentium Xeon, but now the Xeon is considered by Intel to be a separate group of processors. The Xeon processors are intended to be used in high-end workstations and servers.

> **Notes**
>
> The Pentium 4 processors use full-speed Advanced Transfer Cache. The Pentium III processors use either ATC or half-speed On-Package cache. The Pentium II processors use half-speed On-Package cache.

OLDER PENTIUMS NO LONGER SOLD BY INTEL

You need to be familiar with the older Pentiums that are no longer sold by Intel because many are still in use. The first Pentium to be manufactured by Intel was the Classic Pentium. Occasionally, you see a 166-MHz Classic Pentium system still supported in a corporation setting because it works just fine and runs a legacy application.

4

Processor	Processor Speeds (MHz or GHz)	System Bus Speeds (MHz)	Description
Classic Pentium	60 to 200 MHz	60, 66	16K L1 cache
Pentium MMX	133 to 300 MHz	66	32K L1 cache
Pentium Pro	150 to 200 MHz	60, 66	16K L1 and 256K, 512K, or 1 MB L2 cache
Pentium II	233 to 450 MHz	66, 100	32K L1 and 256K or 512K L2 cache
Pentium II Xeon	400 or 450 MHz	100	32K or 512K, 1MB, or 2MB L2 cache
Pentium III	450 MHz to 1.33 GHz	100, 133	32K L1 and 512K unified, nonblocking L2 cache or 256K L2 Advanced Transfer Cache
Pentium III Xeon	600 MHz to 1 GHz	100 or 133	32K L1 and 256K, 1 MB, or 2 MB L2 Advanced Transfer Cache
Celeron	850 MHz to 2.9 GHz	400, 533	32K Execution Trace Cache (ETC) and 128K or 256K Advanced Transfer L2 cache. Uses FC-PGA2 package. Installs in an mPGA478 socket.
Pentium 4	1.4 GHz to 3.06 GHz	400, 533	ETC L1 and 256K, 512K, or 1 MB L2 Advanced Transfer Cache, uses FC-PGA4, mPGA478, FC-PGA2, PPGA INT3, or PPGA INT2 packages, and DDR, Dual Channel DDR, or RDRAM memory. Installs in a 423-pin or 478-pin socket.
Xeon	1.8 GHz to 3.2 GHz	400, 533, 800	ETC L1 and 512K to 2 MB L2 cache and none, 1MB, or 2 MB L3 cache. Uses Quad Channel DDR or DDR2 RAM. Can use dual-core processing. Uses FC-mPGA or int-microPGA package in a 603-pin or 604-pin socket. Newer Xeons are 64-bit processors.
Xeon MP	1.4 GHz to 3.66 GHz	400, 667	ETC L1 and 256K, 512K, or 1 MB L2 cache and 512K to 8 MB L3 cache. Can use dual-core processing. Uses Quad Channel DDR or DDR2 RAM or Dual Channel DDR RAM. Uses FC-mPGA4 or int-microPGA package in a 603-pin or 604-pin socket. Some are 64-bit processors.
Celeron D 320 to 351	2.4 GHz to 3.2 GHz	533	ETC L1 and 256K L2 cache. Uses an FC-LGA, FC-PGA478, FC-PGA4, or FC-LGA4 package. Installs in an LGA775 land socket or mPGA478 pin socket.
Pentium 4 with HT Technology, 520 to 670	2.4 GHz to 3.8 GHz	800	ETC L1 and 512K to 2 MB L2 cache. Uses an FC-PGA2, FC-PGA4, or FC-LGA package, and installs in an LGA775 land socket. Uses DDR, Dual Channel DDR, or Dual Channel DDR2 RAM.
Pentium D, 820, 830, 840, 920, 930, 940, 950	2.8 GHz to 3.4 GHz	800	2 MB or 4MB L2 cache. Dual-core processor uses an FC-LGA package and installs in an LGA775 socket. Uses Dual Channel DDR2 RAM.

Table 4-2   The Intel desktop Pentium and Xeon family of processors

A+ ESS
1.1

Processor	Processor Speeds (MHz or GHz)	System Bus Speeds (MHz)	Description
Pentium Extreme Edition, 840, 955	3.2 GHz to 3.46 GHz	800, 1066	2 MB or 4 MB L2 cache. Dual-core processor uses an FC-LGA package and 955x or 975x chipset. Uses Dual Channel DDR2 RAM and installs in a LGA775 socket.
Pentium 4 Extreme Edition with HT	3.2 GHz to 3.73 GHz	800, 1066	ETC L1 and 512K or 2 MB L2 and 2 MB L3 cache. Uses an FC-LGA, mPGA478, or FC-PGA2 package. Installs in a 775-land or 478-pin socket. Uses Dual Channel DDR and Dual Channel DDR2 RAM.

Table 4-2 The Intel desktop Pentium and Xeon family of processors (continued)

The Pentium MMX (Multimedia Extension) targeted the home game and multimedia market, and the Pentium Pro and Pentium II targeted the computing-intensive workstation and server market. The Pentium II was the first processor to use a slot (slot 1) instead of a socket to connect to the motherboard (processor sockets and slots are covered later in the chapter). Intel patented slot 1, thus attempting to force its competitors to stay with the slower socket technology as they developed equivalent processors.

The Pentium III (see Figure 4-7) uses either a slot or a socket and runs with the 100-MHz or 133-MHz system bus with a processor speed up to 1.33 GHz. The Pentium III introduced Intel's performance enhancement called SSE, for Streaming SIMD Extensions. (SIMD stands for single instruction, multiple data, and is a method MMX uses to speed up multimedia processing.) SSE is an instruction set designed to provide better multimedia processing than MMX.

Figure 4-7 This Pentium III is contained in a SECC cartridge that stands on its end in slot 1 on a motherboard

The Pentium III Xeon is a high-end Pentium III processor that runs on the 100-MHz system bus. It was designed for midrange servers and high-end workstations. It uses a 330-pin slot called the SC330 (slot connector 330), sometimes called slot 2, and is contained within a cartridge called a Single Edge Contact Cartridge (SECC).

CELERON

The Celeron processor is a low-end Pentium processor that targets the low-end PC multimedia and home market segments. Celerons use a 478-pin socket or a 775-land socket. You'll see examples of these sockets later in the chapter. Celerons use Level 2 cache within the processor housing and work well with the most common Windows applications. The more recent Celeron D processor uses dual-core processing.

PENTIUM 4

The Pentium 4 processor (see Figure 4-8) currently runs at up to 3.8 GHz and has undergone several improvements since it was first introduced. The earlier Pentium 4 processors use a 423-pin or 478-pin socket, and later Pentium 4 processors use Socket 775.

Figure 4-8   The Pentiums are sometimes sold boxed with a cooler assembly

The first Pentium 4 processors increased performance for multimedia applications such as digital video, as well as for new Web technologies, using a processor architecture Intel calls NetBurst. Later Pentium 4 processors use Hyper-Threading Technology. The motherboard and the operating system must both support HT Technology for it to be effective. Windows XP supports HT Technology, but Windows 2000 and Windows 9x/Me do not.

One of the latest Intel releases in the Pentium family is the Pentium 4 Extreme Edition with HT Technology, which is designed for high performance and can run on a 1066 MHz front-side bus. Dual-core processing is used by the Pentium D and Pentium 4

 Notes

When first setting up a system using a Pentium 4 with HT Technology and Windows XP, check CMOS setup to verify that the motherboard support for HT Technology is enabled. If you use a Pentium 4 with HT Technology and an operating system other than Windows XP, use CMOS setup to disable HT Technology to avoid an unstable system. Remember that you can access CMOS setup by pressing a key at startup.

Extreme Edition. The latest Pentium processors all use the latest memory module type, DDR2. DDR2 is covered in Chapter 6.

MOBILE PENTIUM PROCESSORS

Processors currently sold by Intel designed for mobility are the Pentium M, Mobile Pentium 4 with Hyper-Threading Technology, Mobile Pentium 4, Mobile Pentium 4 Processor-M, Celeron M, and Mobile Celeron. A Pentium M processor is the processor component of the Intel Centrino technology, which is an integrated component that includes the processor, chipset, and wireless LAN all bundled together for a notebook system. The Pentium M processor runs at up to 2.26 GHz, using a 533- or 400-MHz system bus. The Mobile Pentium 4 processor runs at up to 3.46 GHz, using a 533-MHz system bus. Both processors support low-voltage technologies designed to produce less heat, run on less power, and be housed in smaller and lighter notebooks.

XEON PROCESSORS

Originally, the Xeon (pronounced "Zee-on") processors were 32-bit Pentium processors, but more recently, Intel is producing 64-bit Xeon processors that are no longer considered part of the Pentium family of processors. Xeons use Hyper-Threading Technology and dual-core processing and are designed to be used on servers and high-end workstations in a corporate environment. The Xeon can be used with dual-processor motherboards, and the Xeon MP (multiprocessing) can be used in a server that contains more than two processors. The 64-bit Xeon processors are more powerful than the Pentiums, but are not as robust as the Itaniums.

THE ITANIUMS

Intel's first 64-bit processors for microcomputers are the Itaniums. The newest version of the Itanium, the Itanium 2, is shown in Figure 4-9. When installed, the processor fits inside a protective package called the PAC 611. Itaniums provide backward compatibility with older 32-bit applications, although the older applications are not able to take full advantage of the Itanium's capabilities. The Itaniums don't use Hyper-Threading, but do use EPIC, a newer instruction set than CISC used by the Pentium family of processors.

Table 4-3 shows the specifications for the two Itanium processors. The Itanium uses an L1 cache on the processor die and L2 and L3 caches on the processor board. The L2 cache is closer to the processor than the L3 cache. Even though the system bus speeds seem slow, know that the data path is 128 bits, which makes for a high-performance bus.

Figure 4-9 The Itanium 2

AMD PROCESSORS

Processors by Advanced Micro Devices, Inc., or AMD (*www.amd.com*), are popular in the game and hobbyist markets, and are generally less expensive than comparable Intel processors. Whereas Intel has chosen to stick with 32-bit Pentium

Processor	Current Processor Speeds	L1 Cache	L2 Cache	L3 Cache	System Bus Speed
Itanium	733 and 800 MHz	32K	96K	2 MB or 4 MB	266 MHz
Itanium 2	900 MHz to 1.66 GHz	32K	256K	1.5 MB to 9 MB	400 or 533 MHz

Table 4-3 The Intel Itanium processors

processors for the desktop and notebook market, AMD has concentrated on the 64-bit desktop and mobile processor market since it was first to market with the first 64-bit processor for the desktop, the Athlon 64. Older and newer AMD processors are discussed next.

OLDER AMD PROCESSORS

Table 4-4 lists AMD desktop processors (*www.amd.com*) no longer sold by AMD. However, you need to be aware of them because many are still in use. AMD processors use different sockets and slots than do Intel processors, so the motherboard must be designed for one manufacturer's processor or the other, but not both. Many motherboard manufacturers offer two comparable motherboards—one for an Intel processor and one for an AMD processor. Earlier AMD processors used a 321-pin socket called Super Socket 7, which supports an AGP video slot and 100-MHz system bus. The AMD Athlon can use a 242-pin slot called Slot A, which looks like the Intel slot 1 and has 242 pins. Also, the AMD Athlon and the AMD Duron use a 462-pin socket called Socket A.

Processor	Latest Clock Speeds (MHz or GHz)	Compares to	System Bus Speed (MHz)	Package Type	Socket or Slot
AMD-K6-2	166 to 500 MHz	Pentium II, Celeron	66, 95, 100	CPGA	Socket 7 or Super Socket 7
AMD-K6-III	350 to 450 MHz	Pentium II	100	CPGA	Super Socket 7
Duron	1 GHz to 1.3 GHz	Celeron	200	CPGA or OPGA	Socket A
Athlon	Up to 1.9 GHz	Pentium III	200	Card	Slot A
Athlon Model 4	Up to 1.4 GHz	Pentium III	266	CPGA	Socket A

Table 4-4 Older AMD processors

CURRENT AMD PROCESSORS

AMD processors currently sold by AMD are listed next:

◢ Processors designed for desktops include the Athlon 64 X2 Dual-Core (uses 939-pin socket), the Athlon 64 FX (uses a 939-pin or 940-pin socket), the Athlon 64 (uses a 754-pin or 939-pin socket), the Athlon XP (uses Socket A), and the 32-bit Sempron processor. The Sempron is comparable to the Celeron and uses Socket A or a 754-pin socket.

▲ Two processors designed for high-end workstations or servers are the Athlon MP, which uses Socket A, and the Opteron, which uses dual-core processing and Socket 940.

▲ Processors designed for notebooks include the Turion 64 Mobile, Mobile Athlon 64, Athlon 64 for Notebooks, Mobile Athlon XP-M, and Mobile Sempron.

AMD claims that the Athlon 64 X2 Dual-Core processor (see Figure 4-10) outperforms other AMD processors by about 30% because of its dual-core processing feature.

Figure 4-10 AMD Athlon 64 X2 Dual-Core processor

VIA AND CYRIX PROCESSORS

Table 4-5 shows the performance ratings of older VIA and Cyrix processors. When VIA *(www.via.com.tw)* purchased Cyrix, it introduced a new processor, the VIA C3, which is similar to, but faster than, the Cyrix III processor (see Figure 4-11). The Cyrix and VIA processors use the same sockets as earlier Pentium processors. The VIA C3 also comes in a small EBGA package and even smaller nanoBGA package intended for use in personal electronic devices.

Processor	Latest Clock Speeds (MHz)	Compares to	System Bus Speed (MHz)	Socket or Slot
Cyrix M II	300, 333, 350	Pentium II, Celeron	66, 75, 83, 95, 100	Socket 7
Cyrix III	433 to 533	Celeron, Pentium III	66, 100, 133	Socket 370
VIA C3	Up to 1.4 GHz	Celeron	100, 133, 200	Socket 370

Table 4-5 VIA and Cyrix processors

VIA is now concentrating on developing processors for personal electronics and the embedded device market. Current VIA processors include the following:

▲ The VIA C7 processor uses the nanoBGA2 package and is designed for personal electronic devices, home theater equipment, and desktop computers.

▲ The VIA C7-M uses the nanoBGA2 package and is designed for ultrasmall notebook computers.

Figure 4-11 VIA C3 processor

PROCESSOR PACKAGES

In the computer industry, the processor's housing is called the processor package. A processor package can be thin and lay flat in a socket such as the Pentium package shown in Figure 4-8, or the package can be a thicker cartridge type package such as the one shown in Figure 4-7. The cartridge package can have edge connectors similar to an expansion card and stand up on its end in a slot or it can lay flat in a socket. There are many variations of both kinds of packages used for desktop PCs and high-end workstations. In this section, you'll learn about these flat and thin packages and cartridge packages.

FLAT AND THIN PROCESSOR PACKAGES

Most processor packages are flat and thin and can be square or rectangular. The package lays flat in a socket on the motherboard. The connectors on the bottom of the package can be pins or lands. You can see lands embedded on the bottom of the processor in Figure 4-11. Compare these lands to the pins on the bottom of the processor shown in Figure 4-12. The lands are the newer and preferred method of contact because pins can sometimes be bent when installing the processor. The processor package must fit the socket it is intended for.

Figure 4-12 This Intel Celeron processor is housed in the PPGA form factor, which has pins on the underside that insert into Socket 370

Flat and thin processor packages used by Intel are listed below:

◢ *PPGA (Plastic Pin Grid Array)*. The processor is housed in a square box designed to fit flat into Socket 370 (see Figure 4-12). Pins are on the underside of the flat housing, and heat sinks or fans can be attached to the top of the housing by using a thermal plate or heat spreader. The early Celeron processors used this package with 370 pins.

◢ *PPGA INT2 and PPGA INT3.* These packages are used by Pentium 4s and have 423 pins.

◢ *PGA (Pin Grid Array).* Pins on the bottom of this package are staggered and can be inserted only one way into the socket. It is used by the Xeon with 603 pins. When used by the Pentium 4, it has 423 pins and is called the PGA 423 package.

◢ *int-microPGA 603.* This package has 603 pins and is used by the Xeon processors. It uses a zero-insertion force (ZIF) socket.

◢ *FC-mPGA and FC-mPGA4.* This package has 604 pins and is used by the Xeon processors.

◢ *OOI or OLGA (Organic Land Grid Array).* Used by some Pentium 4s, this 423-pin package is similar to the PGA package, but is designed to dissipate heat faster.

◢ *FC-PGA (Flip Chip Pin Grid Array).* This package looks like the PPGA package and uses 370 pins in Socket 370. It is called a flip chip package because the processor is turned upside down so that the CPU die itself is on top of the processor housing, making it possible to apply a thermal solution directly to the die. Pins on the bottom of the package are staggered. Some Pentium III and Celeron processors use this package.

◢ *FC-PGA2 (Flip Chip Pin Grid Array 2).* This package is similar to the FC-PGA package, but has an integrated heat sink. When used by a Pentium III or Celeron processor, it has 370 pins. When used by the Pentium 4, it has 478 pins.

◢ *mPGA 478.* This package has 478 pins and is used by the Celeron and Pentium 4.

◢ *FC-LGA775 (Flip-Chip Land Grid Array), FC-LGA, or FC-LGA4.* This is the newest Pentium package used by the Pentium 4s and Celerons. It uses 775 lands rather than pins.

AMD has its own processor packages different from Intel. These flat and thin packages are listed next:

◢ *CPGA (Ceramic Pin Grid Array).* This is a flat package with pins on the underside used by several AMD processors, including the Duron, AMD-K6-2, and AMD-K6-III. Number of pins varies among processors.

◢ *OPGA (Organic Pin Grid Array).* This package is used by the AMD Athlon MP and Athlon XP and some models of the AMD Duron.

◢ *µPGA (Micro Pin Grid Array).* This package is used by the AMD 64-bit processors, including the AMD Opteron, Athlon 64 X2 Dual Core, Athlon 64, and Athlon 64 FX.

CARTRIDGE PROCESSOR PACKAGES

Cartridge processor packages can stand up on their end and install in a slot on the motherboard or lay flat in a socket. Figure 4-13 shows a Pentium II with a heat sink and fan attached to it. In the figure, slot 1 on the motherboard has the arms of the slot in the upright position ready to receive the processor.

The following cartridge packages used by Intel stand on their end in a slot:

◢ *SECC (Single Edge Contact Cartridge).* The processor housing stands up on its end and inserts in a slot on the motherboard. The processor is completely covered with a black plastic housing, and a heat sink and fan are attached to the housing. You can't see the circuit board or edge connector in a SECC package. The Pentium II and Pentium III use a SECC package in slot 1 with 242 contacts. The Pentium II Xeon and Pentium III Xeon use a SECC with 330 contacts. You can see the SECC in Figure 4-7.

◢ *SECC2 (Single Edge Contact Cartridge, version 2).* This is similar to the SECC, but it does not have the heat sink thermal plate. Also, the edge connector on the processor

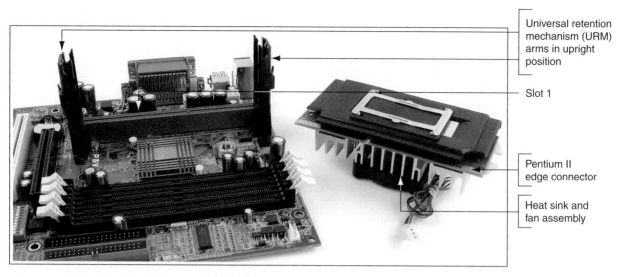

Figure 4-13 Pentium II with heat sink and fan attached goes in slot 1 on this motherboard

circuit board is visible at the bottom of the housing. The Pentium II and Pentium III use the SECC2 package with 242 contacts.

◢ *SEP (Single Edge Processor)*. This package is similar to the SECC package, but the black plastic housing does not completely cover the processor, making the circuit board visible at the bottom of the housing. The first Celeron processors used the SEP package in slot 1. It has 242 contacts.

A cartridge package for a processor that lays flat in a socket on the motherboard is called a flat cartridge package. There is only one entry in this category:

◢ *PAC (Pin Array Cartridge)*. The Itaniums use this flat cartridge, which is about the size of an index card (see Figure 4-14). The Itanium uses the PAC418 socket, which has 418 pins, and the Itanium2 uses the PAC611 socket, which has 611 pins.

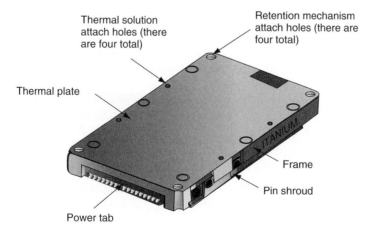

Figure 4-14 418-pin PAC processor package used by the Itanium

Every Intel processor has a specification number called a spec number printed somewhere on the processor. If you can find and read the number (sometimes difficult), you can use the Intel Web site (*processorfinder.intel.com*) to identify the exact processor. For example, suppose you read SL7KM on the processor. Figure 4-15 shows the results of searching the Intel site for this processor information.

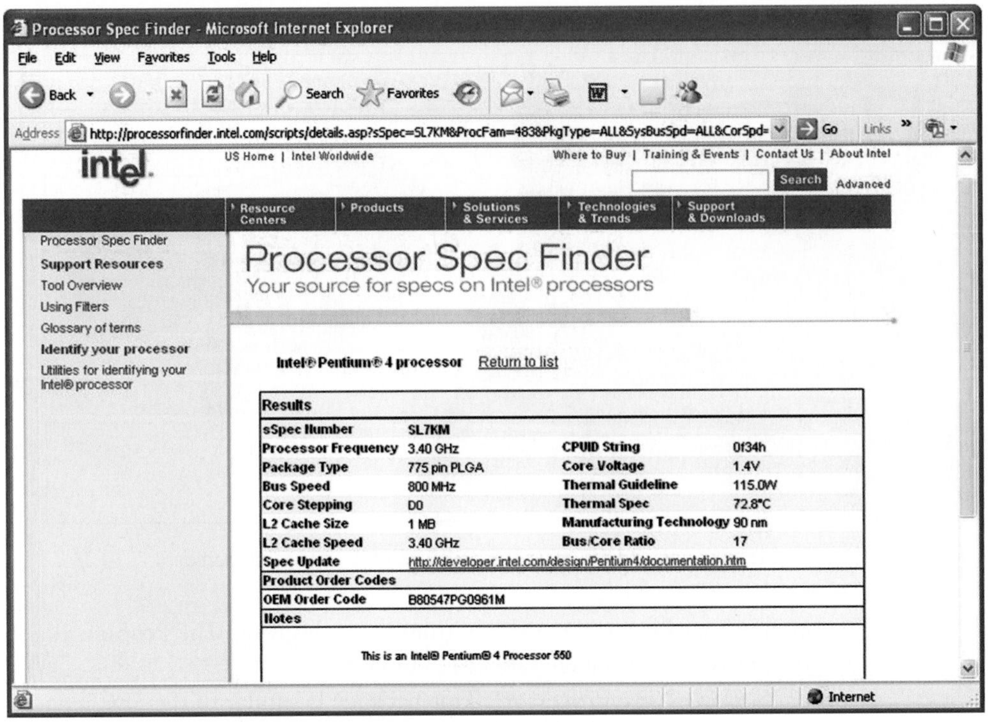

Figure 4-15 Processor Spec Finder using the Intel Web site

A+ ESS 1.1

PROCESSOR SOCKETS AND SLOTS

A processor connects to the motherboard by way of a socket (shown in Figure 4-1 with processor installed) or a slot (shown in Figure 4-13). The type of socket or slot supplied by the motherboard for the processor must match that required by the processor. Most processors today come in more than one package, so it is important to match the processor package to the motherboard that has the right socket or slot. Table 4-6 lists several types of sockets and slots used by Intel, AMD, and VIA processors. Early processors from different manufacturers used the same sockets, but later processors require proprietary sockets and slots.

TYPES OF SOCKETS

Earlier Pentiums used a **pin grid array (PGA)** socket, with pins aligned in uniform rows around the socket. Later sockets use a **staggered pin grid array (SPGA)**, with pins staggered

Connector Name	Used by Processor	Description
Socket 4	Classic Pentium 60/66	273 pins, 21 x 21 PGA grid supplies 5 V
Socket 5	Classic Pentium 75/90/ 100/120/133	320 pins, 37 x 37 SPGA grid supplies 3.3 V
Socket 7	Pentium MMX, Fast Classic Pentium, AMD KS, AMD KS, Cyrix M	321 pins, 37 x 37 SPGA grid supplies 2.5 V to 3.3 V
Super Socket 7	AMD KS-2, AMD KS-III	321 pins, 37 x 37 SPGA grid supplies 2.5 V to 3.3 V
Socket 8	Pentium Pro	387 pins 24 x 26 SPGA grid supplies 3.3 V

Table 4-6 Processor sockets and slots for desktop computers

A+ ESS
1.1

Connector Name	Used by Processor	Description
Socket 370 or PGA370 Socket	Pentium III FC-PGA, Celeron PPGA, Cyrix III	370 pins in a 37 x 37 SPGA grid supplies 1.5 V or 2 V
Slot 1 or SC242	Pentium II, Pentium III	242 pins in 2 rows, rectangular shape supplies 2.8 V and 3.3 V
Slot A	AMD Athlon	242 pins in 2 rows, rectangular shape supplies 1.3 V to 2.05 V
Socket A or Socket 462	AMD Athlon and Duron	462 pins, SPGA grid, rectangular shape supplies 1.5 V to 1.85 V
Slot 2 or SC330	Pentium II Xeon, Pentium III Xeon	330 pins in 2 rows, rectangular shape supplies 1.5 V to 3.5 V
Socket 423	Pentium 4	423 pins, 39 x 39 SPGA grid supplies 1.7 V and 1.75 V
Socket 478	Pentium 4, Celeron	478 pins in a dense micro PGA (mPGA) supplies 1.7 V and 1.75 V
Socket PAC418	Itanium	418 pins supplies 3.3 V
Socket PAC611	Itanium 2	611 pins supplies 3.3 V
Socket 603 and 604	Xeon, Xeon DP, and Xeon MP	603 pins or 604 pins supply 1.5 and 1.7 V
Sockets 754, 939, and 940	Athlon 64, Sempron, Opteron, and Athlon 64 FX	754, 939, or 940 pins; Socket 754 is the most current socket
Socket LGA775	Pentium 4, Celeron	775 lands, not pins, and supplies 1.5 to 1.6 V

Table 4-6 Processor sockets and slots for desktop computers (continued)

over the socket to squeeze more pins into a small space. The latest Intel socket uses a land grid array (LGA) that uses lands rather than pins. This socket is called the LGA775 socket. It has 775 lands and is shown with the socket lever and top open in Figure 4-16.

PGA, SPGA, and LGA sockets are all square or nearly square. Earlier processor sockets, called dual inline package (DIP) sockets, were rectangular with two rows of pins down each side. DIP and some PGA sockets, called low insertion force (LIF) sockets, were somewhat troublesome to install because it was difficult to apply even force when inserting the processor in the socket. Current processor sockets, called zero insertion force (ZIF) sockets, have a small lever on the side that lifts the processor up and out of the socket. Push the lever down and the processor moves into its pin or land connectors with equal force over the entire housing. With this method, you can more easily remove and replace the processor if necessary.

A+ Exam Tip

The A+ Essentials exam expects you to be familiar with the processor sockets in use today.

TYPES OF SLOTS

Slots were used a few years back with some cartridge packages by Intel and AMD, but all processors sold today use sockets. Slot 1, Slot A, and slot 2 are all designed to accommodate processors using SEP or SECC housings that stand on end much like an expansion card. Clips on each side of the slot secure the processor in the slot. You can attach a heat sink or cooling fan to the side of the processor case.

A+ ESS
1.1

Plastic cover protects the socket when it's not in use

Figure 4-16 Socket LGA775 is the latest Intel socket

Note that some motherboards with a slot 1 can accommodate processors that use flat packages, such as the Celeron housed in a PPGA package, by using a riser processor card (see Figure 4-17). The riser card inserts into slot 1, and the Celeron processor inserts into Socket 370 on the riser card. This feature, sometimes called a slocket, allows you to upgrade an older Pentium II system to the faster Celeron. Always consult the motherboard documentation to learn which processors the board can support.

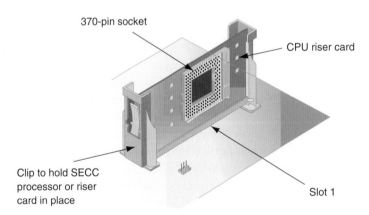

370-pin socket

CPU riser card

Clip to hold SECC processor or riser card in place

Slot 1

Figure 4-17 A riser card can be used to install a Celeron processor into a motherboard with slot 1

Later in the chapter, you'll learn to install a processor on the motherboard, using both a socket and a slot. We now turn our attention to the chipset.

THE CHIPSET

Recall from Chapter 1 that a chipset is a set of chips on the motherboard that collectively controls the memory cache, external buses, and some peripherals. Intel makes the most popular chipsets; Table 4-7 lists the currently available Intel chipsets.

A+ ESS
1.1

Common Name	Model Number	Processors Supported	System Bus Speed Supported	Memory Supported
"E" chipset family	E8870	Up to four Itanium 2 processors	400 MHz	DDR
	E8500	Up to four Xeon MP processors	667 MHz	DDR 266/333 or DDR2 400
	E7525, E7520	Dual 64-bit Xeon, Xeon	800 MHz	DDR 333 and Dual Channel DDR2-400, DDR 266
	E7505, E7501, E7500	Dual Xeon processors	400 MHz or 533 MHz	Dual Channel DDR 266
	E7320	Dual 64-bit Xeon, Xeon	800 MHz	Dual Channel DDR2-400 and Dual Channel DDR 266
	E7230	Pentium 4 with HT, Pentium D	1066 MHz or 800 MHz	Unbuffered Dual-Channel DDR2-667, 533, 400
	E7221, E7210	Pentium 4, Pentium 4 with HT	800 MHz or 533 MHz	Unbuffered Dual-Channel DDR2-533, DDR2-400, DDR-400, DDR333/266
	E7205	Pentium 4, Pentium 4 with HT	533 MHz or 400 MHz	Dual-Channel DDR 266
i900 Express Series	955X	Pentium Extreme Edition, Pentium D, Pentium 4 Extreme Edition with HT, Pentium 4 with HT	1066 MHz or 800 MHz	Dual-Channel DDR2
	945G, 945P	Pentium D, Pentium 4 with HT, and all other System Bus Pentium processors	1066 MHz, 800 MHz, or 533 MHz	Dual-Channel DDR2
	925XE	Pentium 4	1066 MHz or 800 MHz	Dual-Channel DDR2 533/400
	925X	Pentium 4, Pentium 4 Extreme Edition	800 MHz	Dual-Channel DDR2 533/400
	915P, 915G, 915GV	Pentium 4	800 MHz, 533 MHz	Dual-Channel DDR2 533/400, DDR 400/333
	915GL, 915PL	Pentium 4 or Celeron D	800 MHz or 533 MHz	Dual-Channel DDR 400/333, DDR 400/333

Table 4-7   Intel chipsets

Common Name	Model Number	Processors Supported	System Bus Speed Supported	Memory Supported
	910GL	Pentium 4, Celeron, Celeron D	533 MHz	Dual-Channel DDR 400/333
i800 Series	875P	Pentium 4	800 MHz or 533 MHz	Dual-Channel DDR 400/333/266
	865G, 865PE, or 865GV, 865P, 848P	Pentium 4, Celeron, or Celeron D	800 MHz, 533 MHz, or 400 MHz	Dual-Channel DDR 400/333/266 or DDR 400/333/266
	860	Dual Xeon DP processors	400 MHz	PC800/600 RDRAM
	850E, 850	Pentium 4	533 MHz or 400 MHz	PC1066/800/600 RDRAM
	845, 845E, 845G, 845GL, 845PE, 845GE, 845GV	Pentium 4 or Celeron	533 MHz or 400 MHz	DDR 333/266/200, PC133 SDRAM
	840	Dual Pentium III or Pentium III Xeon	133 MHz or 100 MHz	PC800/600 RDRAM
	820, 820E	Dual Pentium III or Pentium II	133 MHz or 100 MHz	PC800/700/600 RDRAM
	815, 815E, 815EP, or 815P, 815EG, 815G	Celeron or Pentium III	133 MHz, 100 MHz, or 66 MHz	PC133/100/66 SDRAM
	810E2, 810E, 810	Celeron or Pentium III	133 MHz, 100 MHz, or 66 MHz	PC100/66 SDRAM

Table 4-7   Intel chipsets (continued)

The types of memory listed in the table that are supported by these chipsets are explained in detail in Chapter 6.

Beginning with the Intel i800 series of chipsets, the interconnection between buses is done using a hub interface architecture, in which all I/O buses connect to a hub, which connects to the system bus. This hub is called the hub interface, and the architecture is called Accelerated Hub Architecture (see Figure 4-18). The fast end of the hub, which contains the graphics and memory controller, connects to the system bus and is called the hub's **North Bridge**. The slower end of the hub, called the **South Bridge**, contains the I/O controller hub. All I/O devices, except display and memory, connect to the hub by using the slower South Bridge. On a motherboard, when you see two major chips for the chipset, one is controlling the North Bridge and the other is controlling the South Bridge (refer to Figure 4-1).

Table 4-8 lists manufacturers of chipsets. Currently, Intel dominates the chipset market for several reasons: It knows more about its own Intel processors than other manufacturers do, and it produces the chipsets most compatible with the Pentium family of processors. Intel's investment in research and development also led to the creation of the PCI bus, the universal serial bus, the AGP, and more recently, the Accelerated Hub Architecture.

A+ ESS
1.1

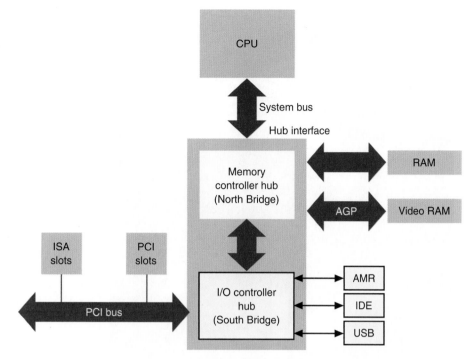

Figure 4-18 Using Intel 800 series Accelerated Hub Architecture, a hub interface is used to connect slower I/O buses to the system bus

Company	URL
ALi, Inc.	*www.ali.com.tw*
AMD	*www.amd.com*
Intel Corporation	*www.intel.com*
NVIDIA Corporation	*www.nvidia.com*
Silicon Integrated Systems Corp. (known as SiS)	*www.sis.com*
QuickLogic Corporation	*www.quicklogic.com*
Texas Instruments	*www.ti.com*
VIA Technologies, Inc.	*www.via.com.tw*

Table 4-8 Chipset manufacturers

Chipsets generate heat, but not as much heat as a processor generates. Most chipsets today have a heat sink installed on top that is appropriate to keep the chipset cool. These heat sinks are considered part of the motherboard and you should never have to replace or install one. However, when you install a processor, you must also install whatever cooler is necessary to keep the processor cool. We now turn our attention to heat sinks and cooling fans used for processors.

HEAT SINKS AND COOLING FANS

A+
220-602
1.3

Because a processor generates so much heat, computer systems use a cooling assembly to keep temperatures below the Intel maximum limit of 185 degrees Fahrenheit/85 degrees Celsius (see Figure 4-19).

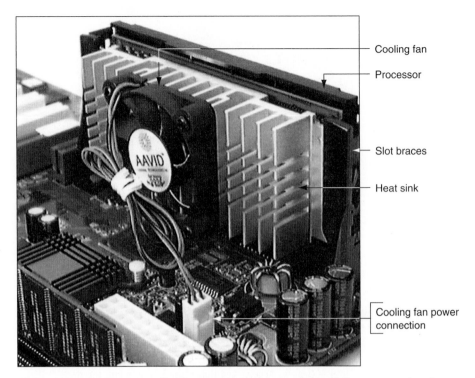

Cooling fan

Processor

Slot braces

Heat sink

Cooling fan power connection

Figure 4-19   A processor cooling fan mounts on the top or side of the processor housing and is powered by an electrical connection to the motherboard

Good processor cooling fans maintain a temperature of 90–110 degrees F (32–43 degrees C). At one time, processor cooling fans were optional equipment used to prevent system errors and to prolong the life of the processor. Today's power-intensive processors installed on ATX motherboards require one or more cooling fans to maintain a temperature that will not damage the processor. High-end systems can have as many as seven or eight fans mounted inside the computer case. Using the BTX form factor, fewer fans are required and the processor might only have a heat sink sitting on top of it. Ball-bearing cooling fans last longer than other kinds.

The cooling fan usually fits on top of the processor with a wire or plastic clip. Sometimes a creamlike thermal compound is placed between the fan and the processor. This compound eliminates air pockets between the heat sink and processor, helping to draw heat off the processor. The thermal compound transmits heat better than air and makes an airtight connection between the fan and the processor. The fan is equipped with a power connector that connects to one of the power cables coming from the power supply or to a connector on the motherboard.

A processor might use a heat sink in addition to a cooling fan. A **heat sink** is a clip-on device that mounts on top of the processor; fingers or fins at its base pull the heat away from the processor. Today most cooling fans designed to mount on the processor housing also have a heat sink attached, as shown in Figure 4-19. The combination heat sink and cooling fan is sometimes called a **cooler**. A cooler is made of aluminum or copper. Copper is more expensive, but does a better job. For example, the Volcano 11+ by Thermaltake (*www.thermaltake.com*) is a copper cooler that can be set to run continuously or you can use a temperature-controlled fan speed (see Figure 4-20). The temperature sensor connects to the heat sink.

Heat sinks sometimes mount on top of other chips to keep them cool. For example, in Figure 4-21 you can see a heat sink mounted on top of a chipset sitting behind the Pentium 4 processor. Also notice in Figure 4-21 the frame to hold the cooler for the Pentium 4.

4

Figure 4-20   Volcano 11+ by Thermaltake is a copper PC cooler

CPU

Frame to hold cooler

Socket 478

Figure 4-21   A Pentium 4 installed in Socket 478

When purchasing a cooler, one factor to consider is the weight of the cooler; don't exceed Intel or AMD recommendations for the weight the processor can handle. Other factors to consider are the noise level and ease of installation of the cooler and the guarantee made by the cooler manufacturer.

APPLYING CONCEPTS   Before installing a cooling fan, read the directions carefully. Clips that hold the fan and heat sink to the processor frame or housing are sometimes difficult to install, and you must be very careful to use the right amount of thermal compound. If you use too much compound, it can slide off the housing and damage circuits on the motherboard.

When processors and coolers are purchased boxed together, the cooler might have thermal compound already stuck to the bottom (see Figure 4-22). For these installations, you install the processor and then install the cooler on top, causing the thermal compound to make contact with the processor.

A+ ESS
1.1

A+
220-602
1.3

Keeping a system cool is important; if the system overheats, components can be damaged. In addition to using a cooling fan, you can also install an alarm that sounds if a system overheats. Because the fan is a mechanical device, it is more likely to fail than the electronic devices inside the case. To protect the expensive processor, you can purchase a temperature sensor for a few dollars. The sensor plugs into a power connection coming from the power supply and mounts on the side of the case or the inside of a faceplate. The sensor sounds an alarm when the inside of the case becomes too hot.

Preapplied thermal compound

Figure 4-22 Thermal compound is already stuck to the bottom of this cooler that was purchased boxed with the processor

In addition to using fans and heat sinks to keep a processor cool, there are more exotic options such as refrigeration, peltiers, and water coolers. These solutions are described in the following list; for the most part, they are used by hobbyists attempting to overclock a processor to the max. These cooling systems might include a PCI card that has a power supply, temperature sensor, and processor to control the cooler.

- A peltier is a heat sink carrying an electrical charge that causes it to act as an electrical thermal transfer device. The peltier's top surface can be as hot as 500 degrees F while the bottom surface next to the processor can be as cool as 45 degrees. The major disadvantage of a peltier is that this drastic difference in temperature can cause condensation inside the case when the PC is turned off.
- Refrigeration can also be used to cool a processor. These units contain a small refrigerator compressor that sits inside the case and can reduce temperatures to below zero.
- The most popular method of cooling overclocked processors is a water cooler unit. A small water pump sits inside the computer case, and tubes move distilled water up and over the processor to keep it cool.

Some manufacturers of these types of cooling systems are AquaStealth (*www.aquastealth.com*), asetek (*www.vapochill.com*), Thermaltake (*www.thermaltake.com*), and Frozenprocessor (*www.frozencpu.com*). Remember, overclocking is not a recommended best practice.

INSTALLING A PROCESSOR

A+
220-602
1.1

A PC repair technician is sometimes called on to assemble a PC from parts, exchange a processor that is faulty, add a second processor to a dual-processor system, or upgrade an existing processor to improve performance. When selecting a processor to install in a particular motherboard, select a processor the board supports. Check the motherboard documentation for a list of processors that can be installed. You'll need to take into account the socket or slot the processor uses, its core frequency, the system bus speeds the processor supports, and features that will affect its performance. These features include multiprocessing abilities and features that affect efficiency of operation, such as Hyper-Threading by Intel or HyperTransport by AMD. After you have selected the processor, study its installation guide to find out what type of cooler to install, or you can purchase the cooler and processor boxed together. You'll also need some thermal compound if it is not included in the boxed processor and cooler. One important thing to consider when installing a processor is the voltage requirements of the processor, so we begin there.

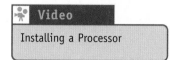

You're now ready to install the processor in a socket or slot. Both of these types of installations are covered in this section.

A+ ESS
1.1

VOLTAGE TO THE PROCESSOR

Earlier processors received all their electrical power from the traces or wires on the system bus that carry power. But many newer processors require additional power. For this reason, some motherboards include a new power connector, called the ATX12V (see Figure 4-23). For example, the Pentium 4 receives voltage from the +12-volt power line to the motherboard, rather than the lower-voltage lines that previous Pentiums used. Always read the motherboard and processor documentation to know how to use these auxiliary power connections.

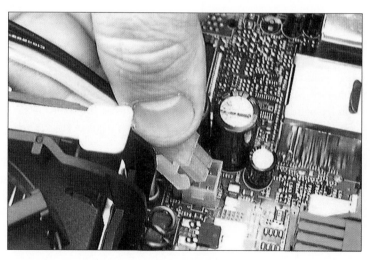

Figure 4-23   Auxiliary 4-pin power cord from the power supply connects to the ATX12V connector on the motherboard to provide power to the Pentium 4

A+ ESS
1.1

A+
220-602
1.1

For today's processors, when a processor is installed in a socket it is designed to use, the motherboard regulates the voltage to this socket that is needed by the processor. There is nothing more for you to do to regulate the voltage other than connect up the auxiliary power line. However, this is not the case with older processors because several older processors with different voltage requirements could use the same socket. You can see this for yourself by looking back at Table 4-5. Several older processors had different voltage requirements, yet used the same socket.

For example, the Celeron processor that uses 2.00 volts can be installed in Socket 370, but the Pentium III FC-PGA that uses either 1.60 or 1.65 volts can also be installed in Socket 370. A motherboard might have a Socket 370 built to support only the Celeron and another motherboard might have a Socket 370 built to support only the Pentium III FC-PGA. If you install a Pentium III FC-PGA in a socket designed only for the Celeron, the processor might physically fit in the socket, but the overvoltage can damage the Pentium III. For older processors, because sockets are more universal than for newer processors, its very important to use only a processor and processor package that the motherboard documentation claims the board can support.

Also be aware that some processors require one voltage for external operations and another for internal operations. Those that require two different voltages are called dual-voltage processors. Other processors are single-voltage processors.

CPU VOLTAGE REGULATOR

Some older motherboards could accommodate more than one type of processor in a socket if you configure the voltage requirements of the processor during installation. For example, a motherboard might require that you set jumpers to configure the voltage to the processor. The motherboard might use a voltage regulator module (VRM) installed on the board to control the amount of voltage to the processor. A VRM can be embedded in the motherboard or can be added later when you upgrade the processor.

A+ Exam Tip

The A+ Essentials exam expects you to understand the purpose of a VRM.

APPLYING CONCEPTS   As an example of having to configure the voltage requirements of an older processor, suppose you want to upgrade a Classic Pentium to the Pentium MMX on a motherboard that supports either processor. The Classic Pentium used only a single voltage (2.8 volts), but the Pentium MMX uses a core voltage of 2.8 volts and an I/O voltage of 3.3 volts. If you upgrade a system from the Classic Pentium to the Pentium MMX, you can use the motherboard's embedded VRM to regulate the 2.8 volts and install another VRM to regulate the 3.3 volts.

Figure 4-24 shows sample documentation of jumper settings to use for various processor voltage selections on an older motherboard. Notice that the two jumpers called JP16, located near Socket 7 on the board, select the voltage. For single voltage, on a Pentium, Cyrix 6 x 86, or AMD K5, both jumpers are open. Dual voltage, used by the Pentium MMX, Cyrix M2, and AMD K6, is selected by opening or closing the two jumpers according to the diagram. Follow the recommendations for your processor when selecting the voltages from documentation.

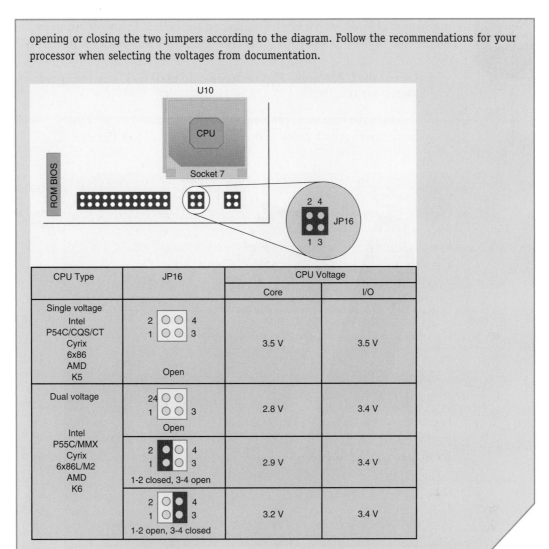

CPU Type	JP16	CPU Voltage	
		Core	I/O
Single voltage Intel P54C/CQS/CT Cyrix 6x86 AMD K5	2 ○○ 4 1 ○○ 3 Open	3.5 V	3.5 V
Dual voltage Intel P55C/MMX Cyrix 6x86L/M2 AMD K6	24 ○○ 1 ○○ 3 Open	2.8 V	3.4 V
	2 ●○ 4 1 ●○ 3 1-2 closed, 3-4 open	2.9 V	3.4 V
	2 ○● 4 1 ○● 3 1-2 open, 3-4 closed	3.2 V	3.4 V

Figure 4-24 For older motherboards, a processor voltage regulator can be configured using jumpers on the motherboard to apply the correct voltage to the processor

When assembling a system from parts, sometimes it works best to install the processor and cooler on the motherboard before the board goes in the case. But for very heavy cooler assemblies, to protect the motherboard, first install the motherboard in the case and then install the processor and cooler. For the best order of installation, see the motherboard documentation. Also, for older motherboards, jumpers are sometimes set on the board to set the frequency or speed of the processor and system bus. How to set these jumpers and how to install motherboards are covered in the next chapter.

We'll look at three examples of installing a processor: a Pentium II installed in slot 1, a Pentium 4 installed in Socket 478, and a Pentium 4 installed in Socket 775.

INSTALLING A PENTIUM II IN SLOT 1

When installing a processor, be careful to protect the processor and the motherboard against ESD as you work. Wear an antistatic bracelet and use other precautions you learned about in Chapter 2. For slot 1, used by the Pentium II, the motherboard uses a universal retention mechanism (URM), which is preinstalled on the board. Follow these steps to install the fan on the side of the processor first, and then install the processor on the motherboard:

1. Unfold the URM arms. Flip both arms up until they lock into position (refer to Figure 4-13).

2. Examine the heat sink, fan assembly, and processor to see how the cooling assembly brace lines up with holes in the side of the SECC (see Figure 4-25).

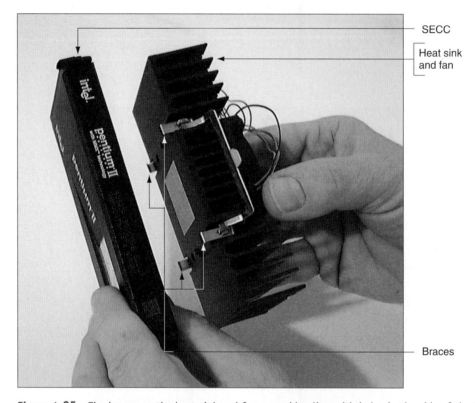

SECC

Heat sink and fan

Braces

Figure 4-25 The braces on the heat sink and fan assembly align with holes in the side of the SECC

3. Place the heat sink on the side of the SECC. The two should fit tightly together, with absolutely no space between them.

4. After you fit the heat sink and SECC together, place the SECC on a table and push the clamp on the fan down and into place to secure the cooling assembly to the SECC (see Figure 4-26).

5. Insert the cooling assembly and SECC into the supporting arms (see Figure 4-27). The SECC should fit snugly into slot 1, similar to the way an expansion card settles into an expansion slot. The arms should snap into position when the SECC is fully seated. Be certain you have a good fit.

6. Lock the SECC into position by pulling the SECC locks outward until they lock into the supporting arm lock holes.

A+
220-602
1.1

Push clamp down

Figure 4-26 Push the clamp on the fan down until it locks in place, locking the heat sink and fan to the SECC

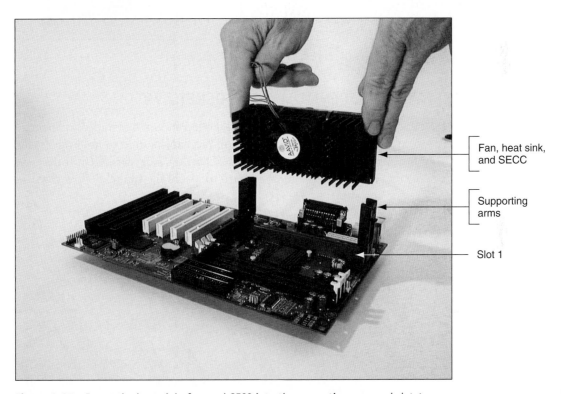

Fan, heat sink, and SECC

Supporting arms

Slot 1

Figure 4-27 Insert the heat sink, fan, and SECC into the supporting arms and slot 1

7. Connect the power cord coming from the fan to the power connection on the mother-board (see Figure 4-28). Look for the power connection near slot 1. If you have trouble finding it, see the motherboard documentation.

A+
220-602
1.1

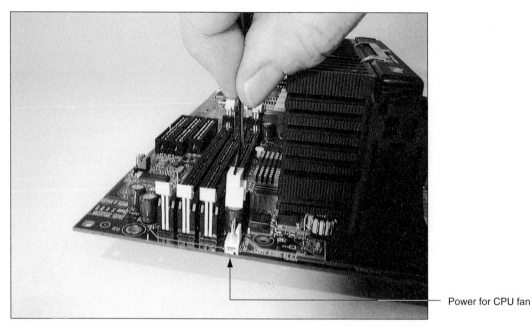

Power for CPU fan

Figure 4-28 Connect the fan power cord to the motherboard

INSTALLING A PENTIUM 4 IN SOCKET 478

If you look back at Figure 4-21, you can see the Pentium 4 installed in Socket 478 on a motherboard. Notice the frame or retention mechanism used to hold the cooler in place. This frame might come separately from the board or be preinstalled. If necessary, follow the directions that come with the motherboard to install the frame. Follow these steps to install the processor and cooler:

1. Lift the ZIF socket lever, as shown in Figure 4-29.

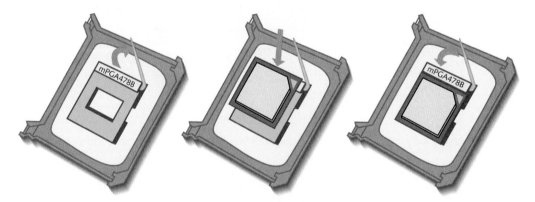

Figure 4-29 Install the processor in the mPGA478B socket

2. Place the processor on the socket so that the corner marked with a triangle is aligned with the connection of the lever to the socket. After the processor is in place, lower the lever to insert the processor firmly into the socket. As you work, be very careful not to force the processor in at an offset or disoriented position.

3. Before installing the processor cooling assembly over the processor, place a small amount of thermal compound on top of the processor. This greaselike substance helps

4

A+
220-602
1.1

transfer heat from the processor to the heat sink. Do not use too much; if you do, it may squish out the sides and interfere with other components.

4. Carefully examine the clip assembly that surrounds the fan and heat sink. Line up the clip assembly with the retention mechanism already installed on the motherboard, and press lightly on all four corners to attach it (see Figure 4-30).

Figure 4-30   Carefully push the cooler assembly clips into the retention mechanism on the motherboard until they snap into position

5. After the cooling assembly is in place, push down the two clip levers on top of the processor fan (see Figure 4-31). Different coolers use different types of clipping mechanisms, so follow the directions that come with the cooler. Sometimes the clipping mechanism is difficult to clip onto the processor, and the plastic levers and housing are flimsy, so work carefully.

Figure 4-31   The clip levers attach the cooling assembly to the retention mechanism around the processor

6. Connect the power cord from the processor fan to the power connection on the mother-board next to the cooler (see Figure 4-32).

Figure 4-32 Connect the processor fan power cord to the motherboard power connector

INSTALLING A PENTIUM 4 IN SOCKET 775

The Pentium 4 we're installing in Socket 775 is shown in Figure 4-8 along with the cooler assembly. Because this cooler is so heavy, it is best to install it after the mother-board is securely seated in the case. Socket 775 has a lever and a socket cover. Figure 4-33 shows the socket with the lever and cover open, together with the processor (laying upside down) and the cooler.

> **Tip**
>
> The A+ IT 220-602 exam expects you to know how to install a processor.

Figure 4-33 Pentium 4, cooler, and open socket 775

A+
220-602
1.1

Do the following to install the processor and cooler using socket 775:

1. Push down on the lever and gently push it away from the socket to lift it (see Figure 4-34).

Figure 4-34 Release the lever from the socket

2. Lift the socket cover (see Figure 4-35).

Figure 4-35 Lift the socket cover

3. Orient the processor so that the notches on the two edges of the processor line up with the two notches on the socket (see Figure 4-36). Gently place the processor in the socket.

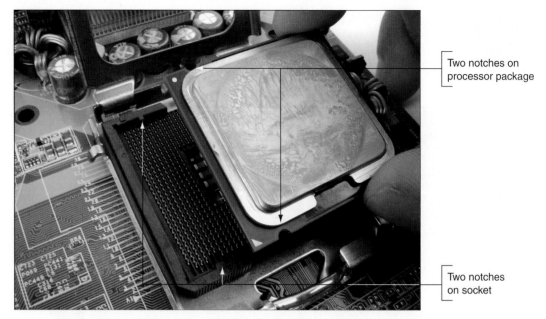

Two notches on processor package

Two notches on socket

Figure 4-36 Place the processor in the socket orienting the notches on two sides

4. Close the socket cover. Push down on the lever and gently return it to its locked position (see Figure 4-37).

Thermal compound

Figure 4-37 Force is applied to the processor when the lever is pushed into position

Figure 4-38 shows how the cooler is aligned over the processor so that all four spacers fit into the four holes on the motherboard and the fan power cord connects to the power connector on the motherboard. First install the motherboard in the case (how to do this is covered in the next chapter). Then place the cooler over the four holes and push down on each fastener until you hear it pop into the hole (see Figure 4-39). (Later, if you need to remove the cooler, use a flathead screwdriver to turn each fastener counterclockwise to release it from the hole.)

A+
220-602
1.1

Four holes for
cooler fasteners

Cooler power
connector

Figure 4-38 The cooler is installed on the motherboard using four holes in the motherboard

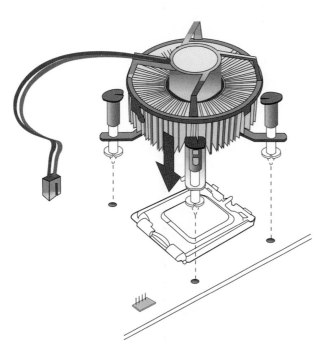

Figure 4-39 Four spacers on the cooler pop into each hole on the motherboard

A+ ESS
1.3

5. Connect the power cord from the cooler fan to the motherboard power connector near the processor, as shown in Figure 4-40.

A+
220-602
1.2

After the processor and cooler are installed, you can plug back up the system, turn it on, and verify all is working. If the power comes on (you hear the fan spinning and see lights), but the system fails to work, most likely the processor is not seated solidly in the socket or slot. Turn everything off and recheck your installation. If the system comes up and begins the boot process, but suddenly turns off before the boot is complete, most likely the processor is

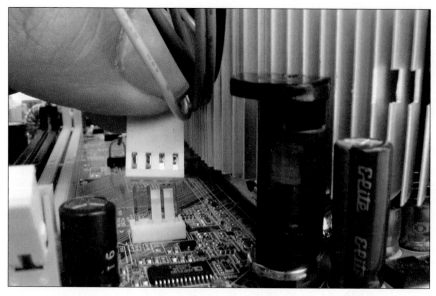

Figure 4-40   Connect the cooler fan power cord to the motherboard connector

> **Notes**
>
> Notice in Figure 4-37 that the processor has thermal compound already on it. If the compound seems light or has hardened, you can remove this compound using a soft cloth and add more thermal compound to the bottom of the cooler. Figure 4-41 shows new thermal compound added to the bottom of the cooler. Be careful to not apply too much compound that might ooze off onto the processor connectors.

overheating because the cooler is not installed correctly. Turn everything off and verify the cooler is securely seated and connected. After the system is up and running, you can check the CPU and motherboard temperatures by entering CMOS setup. Then, under the Power menu, look for a Hardware Monitor window similar to the one shown in Figure 4-42. Other troubleshooting tips for processors are covered at the end of the next chapter.

Figure 4-41   When reinstalling a processor and cooler, you can add new thermal compound to the bottom of the cooler

4

A+ ESS
1.3

A+
220-602
1.2

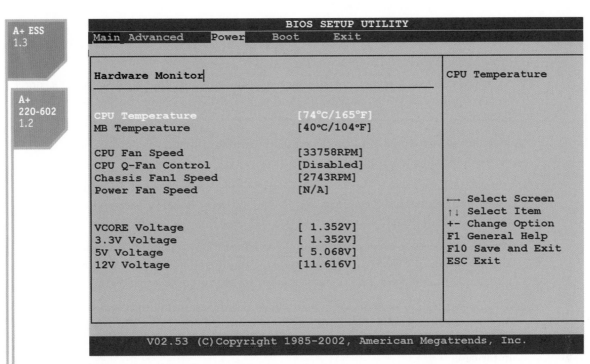

```
                         BIOS SETUP UTILITY
  Main  Advanced    Power    Boot    Exit

  Hardware Monitor                              CPU Temperature


  CPU Temperature          [74°C/165°F]
  MB Temperature           [40°C/104°F]

  CPU Fan Speed            [33758RPM]
  CPU Q-Fan Control        [Disabled]
  Chassis Fan1 Speed       [2743RPM]
  Power Fan Speed          [N/A]
                                          ←→  Select Screen
                                          ↑↓  Select Item
  VCORE Voltage            [ 1.352V]      +-  Change Option
  3.3V Voltage             [ 1.352V]      F1  General Help
  5V Voltage               [ 5.068V]      F10 Save and Exit
  12V Voltage              [11.616V]      ESC Exit



      V02.53 (C)Copyright 1985-2002, American Megatrends, Inc.
```

Figure 4-42 The CPU and motherboard temperature is monitored by CMOS setup

>> CHAPTER SUMMARY

◢ The most important component on the motherboard is the processor, or central processing unit. The processor is rated according to its speed, efficiency of programming code, word size, data path size, size of internal cache, multiprocessing abilities, and special functions.

◢ Processor performance can be improved by using multiprocessing, multiple processors installed in a system, and dual-core processing.

◢ SRAM (static RAM) is fast and is used as a memory cache, which speeds overall computer performance by temporarily holding data and programming that the CPU may use in the near future.

◢ L1 cache is contained on the processor microchip, and L2 and L3 cache are external to this microchip. L2 and L3 can be on the motherboard or in the processor housing. If a processor has L2 cache, cache on the motherboard is called L3 cache.

◢ Older motherboards sometimes provided an extra COAST slot to upgrade SRAM, but most systems today come with an optimum amount of SRAM inside the CPU housing or on the motherboard.

◢ The Intel Pentium processor family includes the Classic Pentium, Pentium MMX, Pentium Pro, Pentium II, Celeron, Xeon, Pentium III, and Pentium 4.

◢ The Itanium, Intel's 64-bit processor family, has L1, L2, and L3 cache.

◢ AMD is Intel's chief competitor for the processor market. AMD produces the Athlon 64 X2 Dual-Core, Athlon 64 FX, Duron, Athlon, Athlon MP, Athlon XP, Opteron, Sempron, Turion, and Athlon 64 processors.

◢ Newer processors require extra cooling, which you can accomplish by installing a processor heat sink and cooling fan on top of or near the processor.

◢ Processor packages can be flat and thin or of the cartridge variety. Flat and thin packages are installed in sockets that use either pins or lands. Cartridges can be installed on their end in a slot or flat in a socket.

◢ Some processor sockets and slots are Socket 7, Socket 370, Socket 423, Socket 478, slot 1, Slot A, slot 2, Socket 603, Socket 775, Socket 754, Socket 939, and Socket 940. A slot looks like an expansion slot.

◢ A chipset is a group of chips on the motherboard that supports the processor. Intel is the most popular manufacturer of chipsets.

◢ A modern chipset uses a hub with two ends. The fast end of the hub is called the North Bridge and connects to the system bus, RAM, and processor. The slow end of the hub, called the South Bridge, connects to slower I/O buses.

◢ Because some legacy processors require one voltage for internal core operations and another voltage for external I/O operations, when upgrading a processor, you might have to upgrade or add a voltage regulator module to control these voltages.

◢ When installing a processor, for lighter cooler assemblies, install the processor and cooler on the motherboard and then install the motherboard in the case. When the cooling assembly is heavy and bulky, it is best to install it after the motherboard is securely seated in the case.

>> KEY TERMS

For explanations of key terms, see the Glossary near the end of the book.

Advanced Transfer Cache (ATC)	front-side bus (FSB)	On-Package L2 cache
back-side bus (BSB)	heat sink	overclocking
bus frequency	internal bus	pin grid array (PGA)
complex instruction set computing (CISC)	internal cache	primary cache
	land grid array (LGA)	processor frequency
cooler	Level 1 (L1) cache	reduced instruction set computing (RISC)
data path	Level 2 (L2) cache	
discrete L2 cache	Level 3 (L3) cache	single-voltage processors
dual inline package (DIP)	low insertion force (LIF) sockets	South Bridge
dual-core processing	memory cache	staggered pin grid array (SPGA)
dual-voltage processors	microcode	static RAM (SRAM)
Execution Trace Cache	motherboard bus	system bus
explicitly parallel instruction computing (EPIC)	multiplier	voltage regulator module (VRM)
	multiprocessor platform	word size
external cache	North Bridge	zero insertion force (ZIF) sockets

>> REVIEWING THE BASICS

1. If a motherboard has a slot 1, what processor(s) is it designed to support?

2. What was the first Intel processor to contain external cache?

3. When is it appropriate to use a Celeron rather than a Pentium 4 in a computer system?

4. Which is more powerful, the current Celeron or the current Xeon processor?

5. Who is the major competitor of Intel in the processor market?

6. Why did the competitors of the Intel Pentium II choose to stay with Socket 7 rather than use slot 1 for their competing processors?

7. What components inside a computer case keep a processor cool?

8. Describe the difference between a PGA socket and an SPGA socket.

9. Name a processor that requires dual voltage. How are the two voltages used?

10. Name a processor that uses Socket A.

11. What are the four speeds of the most popular motherboards currently available on the market that support Intel processors?

12. Name three manufacturers of motherboard chipsets.

13. Beginning with the Intel i800 chipsets, what are the two main chips of the chipset called?

14. What is the name for the bus that connects L2 cache to the processor inside the Pentium II processor housing?

15. What is the word size of the Pentium family of processors?

16. What is the data path size of the front-side bus of the Pentium family of processors?

17. If a Pentium 4 Extreme Edition uses two ALU units inside the processor housing, how many ALU units does the Pentium D have?

18. Why is a land socket preferred to a pin socket?

19. Explain the difference between the locations of discrete L2 cache and Advanced Transfer Cache.

20. Which instruction set is used by the Itanium processors?

21. Which group of Intel processors use a 32-bit word size and a 64-bit word size?

22. Which Windows personal computing operating system(s) support Intel Hyper-Threading Technology?

23. Name an AMD processor that uses dual-core processing.

24. What processor manufacturer once targeted the desktop processor market, but is now more focused on processors used for personal electronics?

25. What is the latest socket used by Intel desktop processors?

>> THINKING CRITICALLY

1. When overclocking a system, what two problems are most likely to occur?

   a. "Low memory" errors

   b. An unstable system that causes intermittent errors

   c. Loss of hard drive space used by the overclocking virtual memory file

   d. Overheating

2. What must software developers do to take advantage of a 64-bit processor such as the Itanium?

3. You upgrade a Windows 98 system by upgrading a Pentium 4 processor to a Pentium4 Extreme Edition with HT. Now users complain to you that Windows hangs a lot and gives errors. What do you do first?

   a. Reinstall Windows 98.

   b. Upgrade Windows 98 to Windows XP.

   c. Check CMOS setup to verify that Hyper-Threading is disabled.

   d. Check CMOS setup to verify that Hyper-Threading is enabled.

>> HANDS-ON PROJECTS

PROJECT 4-1: Recognizing Processors

Using your home or lab computer, open the computer case and examine the processor and cooler assembly. Answer these questions:

1. What processor is installed?

2. What slot or socket is the processor using?

3. Describe the cooler assembly. Does it contain a heat sink and fan?

PROJECT 4-2: Understanding Processor Configuration

Using your home or lab computer, use CMOS setup and Windows to answer these questions:

1. What is the processor frequency? How did you find your answer?

2. In CMOS setup, list the settings that apply to the processor and the current configuration of each setting.

PROJECT 4-3: Understanding Dual-Processing Motherboards

Print the Web page of a picture of a motherboard that supports dual processors. Use one of these Web sites to find the picture:

◢ Asus at *www.asus.com*

◢ Intel at *www.intel.com*

◢ Abit at *www.abit.com.tw*

Answer these questions about the motherboard:

1. What is the manufacturer and model number of the motherboard?

2. What is the frequency of the motherboard FSB?

3. What operating systems does the board support?

4. What processors does the board support?

PROJECT 4-4:   Inserting and Removing a Processor

In this project, you remove and install a processor. As you work, be very careful to not bend pins on the processor socket and protect the processor against ESD. Do the following:

1. Verify the computer is working. Turn off the system, unplug it, and open the computer case. Remove the cooler assembly and processor.

2. You are now ready to reinstall the processor and cooler. But first have your instructor check the thermal compound. You might need to install a small amount of compound to account for compound lost when you removed the cooler.

3. Reinstall the processor and cooler. Power up the system and verify all is working.

PROJECT 4-5:   Using the Internet for Research

Search the Web sites of Intel and AMD (*www.intel.com* and *www.amd.com*), and print information on the following:

◢ The most recent processor for the desktop offered by each company

◢ The most recent processor for a server offered by each company

PROJECT 4-6:   Researching the Intel Web Site

Research the Intel Web site (*www.intel.com*), and do the following:

1. Print a photograph of a motherboard that supports two processors (dual processors).

2. Print the information that tells which chipset this motherboard uses.

3. List the processor packages that these processors currently use:

   ◢ Celeron

   ◢ Pentium 4 Extreme Edition

   ◢ Itanium

   ◢ Itanium 2

>> REAL PROBLEMS, REAL SOLUTIONS

REAL PROBLEM 4-1:   Troubleshooting a Hung System

A user complains to you that her system hangs for no known reason. After asking her a few questions, you identify these symptoms:

1. The system hangs after about 15–20 minutes of operation.

2. When the system hangs, it doesn't matter what application is open or how many applications are open.

3. When the system hangs, it appears as though power is turned off: no lights, spinning drives, or other evidence of power.

You suspect overheating might be the problem. To test your theory, you decide to do the following:

1. You want to verify that the user has not overclocked the system. How do you do that?

2. You decide to check for overheating by examining the temperature of the system immediately after the system is powered up and then again immediately after the system hangs. Describe the steps you take to do this.

3. After doing the first two steps and you decide overheating is the cause of the problem, what do you do to fix it?

Motherboards

In the last chapter, we looked at the two most important components on the motherboard: the processor and chipset. In this chapter, we turn our attention to the motherboard itself. You'll learn about the buses and expansion slots on the motherboard and how to configure these and other components on the board. The motherboard is considered a field replaceable unit. So, in this chapter, you'll learn to troubleshoot problems with the motherboard and how to install and replace one.

SELECTING A MOTHERBOARD

A+ ESS
1.1

When selecting a motherboard, the first consideration is the form factor of the board. A motherboard form factor determines the size of the board and its features that make it compatible with power supplies, cases, processors, and expansion cards. The most popular motherboard form factor is the ATX. ATX motherboards have been around for a long time and have seen many improvements. A recent ATX motherboard designed for a Pentium 4 or Celeron processor is shown in Figure 5-1,

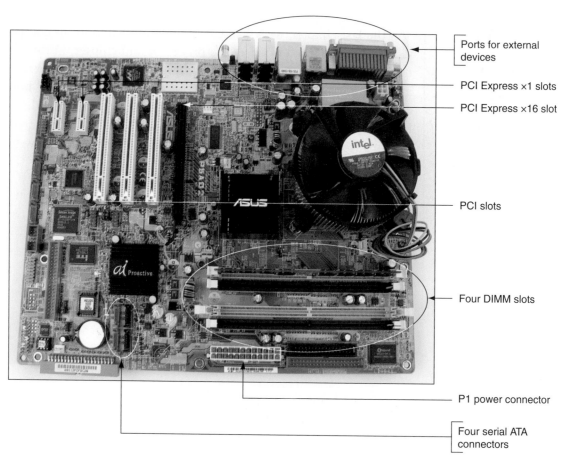

Ports for external devices

PCI Express ×1 slots

PCI Express ×16 slot

PCI slots

Four DIMM slots

P1 power connector

Four serial ATA connectors

Figure 5-1   An ATX motherboard with PCI Express and Socket 775

A+ ESS
1.1

and an older ATX motherboard designed for a Pentium III is shown in Figure 5-2. An older motherboard form factor is the AT (see Figure 5-3).

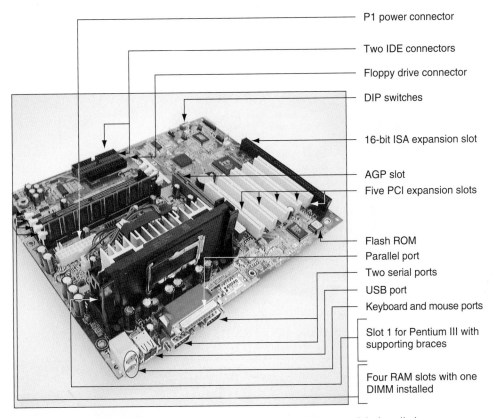

P1 power connector

Two IDE connectors

Floppy drive connector

DIP switches

16-bit ISA expansion slot

AGP slot
Five PCI expansion slots

Flash ROM
Parallel port
Two serial ports
USB port
Keyboard and mouse ports

Slot 1 for Pentium III with supporting braces

Four RAM slots with one DIMM installed

Figure 5-2 An ATX motherboard with a Pentium III and one DIMM module installed

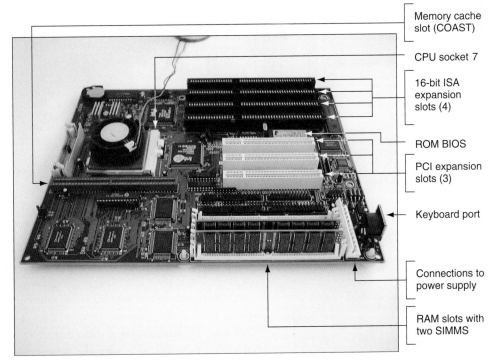

Memory cache slot (COAST)

CPU socket 7

16-bit ISA expansion slots (4)

ROM BIOS

PCI expansion slots (3)

Keyboard port

Connections to power supply

RAM slots with two SIMMS

Figure 5-3 An older AT motherboard with memory cache and socket 7 for the Intel Classic Pentium processor. The processor with a fan on top is installed, as well as two SIMM memory modules.

The latest motherboard form factor is the BTX. Figure 5-4 shows a BTX motherboard, and Figure 5-5 shows a BTX case with a BTX motherboard installed. This BTX case has fans on the front and rear to force air over the processor heat sink. Notice in the figure the green encasement that directs airflow over the heat sink. Also notice the vents on the front case panel to help with airflow.

Socket 775

Figure 5-4   A BTX motherboard with an LGA 775 land socket

Front panel

Air vents

Rear exhaust fan

Heat sink over processor

Encasement to direct airflow over heat sink

Front intake fan is behind this grid

Figure 5-5   A BTX system is designed for optimum airflow

🔲 **A+ Exam Tip**

The A+ Essentials exam expects you to know about the ATX, BTX, microATX, and NLX form factors.

Each form factor has several sizes, which are listed in Table 5-1.

Because the motherboard determines so many of your computer's features, selecting the motherboard is a very important decision when you purchase a computer or assemble one from parts. Depending on which

A+ ESS 1.1	Type of Motherboard	Description
	ATX	▲ Developed by Intel for Pentium systems ▲ Includes a power-on switch that can be software-enabled and extra power connections for extra fans and processor voltage needs ▲ Uses a single 20-pin P1 power connector with optional 4-pin auxiliary power connector ▲ Measures 30.5 cm x 24.4 cm (12 inches x 9.6 inches)
	Enhanced ATX	▲ Improved ATX, specified in ATX version 2.2 ▲ Uses a 24-pin P1 power connector ▲ Supports PCI Express
	MiniATX	▲ An ATX board with a more compact design ▲ Measures 28.4 cm x 20.8 cm (11.2 inches x 8.2 inches)
	MicroATX	▲ A smaller ATX design intended to reduce overall system cost ▲ Measures 24.4 cm x 24.4 cm (9.6 inches x 9.6 inches) ▲ A smaller power supply and an ATX 2.1 case can be used
	FlexATA	▲ Smaller variation of microATX ▲ Measures 22.9 cm x 19.1 cm (9.0 inches x 7.5 inches) ▲ Uses same mounting holes as microATX
	BTX	▲ Has up to seven expansion slots ▲ Can be up to 325.12 mm wide ▲ Layouts of BTX motherboards include a tower, desktop, and small form factor layout ▲ BTX boards have a 24-pin power connector and can use an ATX 2.2 power supply with a 4-pin auxiliary connector
	MicroBTX	▲ Has up to four expansion slots ▲ Can be up to 264.16 mm wide
	NanoBTX	▲ Has up to two expansion slots ▲ Can be up to 223.52 mm wide
	PicoBTX	▲ None or one expansion slot ▲ Can be up to 203.20 mm wide
	NLX	▲ Improvement over earlier LPX design ▲ Uses a riser card (daughter board) near the edge of the board ▲ Sizes include 8.0 inches x 10.0 inches up to 9.0 inches x 13.6 inches
	AT	▲ Oldest type of motherboard, still used in some systems ▲ Uses P8 and P9 power connections ▲ Measures 30.5 cm x 33 cm (12 inches x 13 inches)
	Baby AT	▲ Smaller version of AT and is compatible with ATX cases ▲ Uses P8 and P9 power connections ▲ Measures 33 cm x 22 cm (12 inches x 8.7 inches)

Table 5-1 Types of motherboards

applications and peripheral devices you plan to use with the computer, you can take one of three approaches to selecting a motherboard. The first approach is to select the board that provides the most room for expansion, so you can upgrade and exchange components and add devices easily. A second approach is to select the board that best suits the needs of the computer's current configuration, knowing that when you need to upgrade, you will likely switch to new technology and a new motherboard. The third approach is to select a motherboard that meets your present needs with moderate room for expansion.

Ask the following questions when selecting a motherboard:

- What form factor does the motherboard use?
- Does the motherboard support the number and type of processor you plan to use (for example, Socket LGA 775 for the Intel Pentium 4 up to 3.3 GHz)?
- What are the supported frequencies of the system bus (for example, 1066/800/ 533 MHz)?
- What chipset does the board use?
- What type of memory does the board support (DDR or DDR2), and how much memory can the board hold?
- What type and how many expansion slots are on the board (for example, PCI, PCI Express, and AGP)?
- What hard drive controllers and connectors are on the board (for example, IDE, serial ATA, RAID, and SCSI)?
- What are the embedded devices on the board and what internal slots or connections does the board have? (For example, the board might provide a network port, wireless antenna port, FireWire port, two or more USB ports, modem port, and so forth.)
- What type of BIOS does the motherboard use?
- Does the board fit the case you plan to use?
- What is the warranty on the board?
- How extensive and user-friendly is the documentation?
- How much support does the manufacturer supply for the board?

Sometimes a motherboard contains a component more commonly offered as a separate device. A component on the board is called an embedded component or an on-board component. One example is support for video. The video port might be on the motherboard or might require a video card. The cost of a motherboard with an embedded component is usually less than the combined cost of a motherboard with no embedded component and an expansion card. If you plan to expand, be cautious about choosing a proprietary board that has many embedded components. Often such boards do not easily accept add-on devices from other manufacturers. For example, if you plan to add a more powerful video card, you might not want to choose a motherboard that contains an embedded video controller. Even though you can often use a jumper or CMOS setup to disable the proprietary video controller, there is little advantage to paying the extra money for it.

Table 5-2 lists some manufacturers of motherboards and their Web addresses.

Tip

If you have an embedded component, make sure you can disable it so you can use another external component if needed.

Notes

A motherboard is configured through jumpers or DIP switches on the board or through CMOS setup. Embedded components are almost always configured through CMOS setup.

Manufacturer	Web Address
Abit	*www.abit.com.tw*
American Megatrends, Inc. (AMI)	*www.megatrends.com* or *www.ami.com*
ASUS	*www.asus.com*
BIOSTAR Group	*www.biostar.com.tw*
Dell	*www.dell.com*
First International Computer of America, Inc.	*www.fica.com*
Gateway	*www.gateway.com*
Gigabyte Technology Co., Ltd.	*us.giga-byte.com*
IBM	*www.ibm.com*
Intel Corporation	*www.intel.com*
Iwill Corporation	*www.iwill.net*
MicroStar International	*www.msicomputer.com*
Motherboards.com	*www.motherboards.com*
Supermicro Computer, Inc.	*www.supermicro.com*
Tyan Computer Corporation	*www.tyan.com*

Table 5-2 Major manufacturers of motherboards

CONFIGURING AND SUPPORTING A MOTHERBOARD

The components on the motherboard that you must know how to configure and support are the expansion slots and other internal and external connectors. In this section, you'll learn about the expansion slots and the buses that support them, and then you'll learn how to configure these expansion slots and other components and connectors on the board. In later chapters, you'll learn more about the other connectors on the board, including memory module slots, and the various drive, USB, FireWire, serial, and parallel connectors.

BUSES AND EXPANSION SLOTS

A+ ESS
1.1

As cities grow, so do their transportation systems. Small villages have only simple, two-lane roads, but large cities have one-way streets, four-lane roads, and major freeways, each with their own set of traffic laws, including minimum and maximum speeds, access methods, and protocols. As microcomputer systems have evolved, so too have their "transportation" systems. The earliest PC had only a single simple bus. Today's PCs have four or five buses, each with different speeds, access methods, and protocols. As you have seen in previous chapters, backward compatibility dictates that older buses be supported on a motherboard, even when faster, better buses exist. All this makes for a maze of buses on a motherboard.

WHAT A BUS DOES

Look on the bottom of the motherboard, and you see a maze of circuits that make up a bus. These embedded wires carry four kinds of cargo:

▲ *Electrical power.* Chips on the motherboard require power to function. These chips tap into a bus's power lines and draw what they need.

A+ ESS
1.1

▲ *Control signals.* Some wires on a bus carry control signals that coordinate all the activity.

▲ *Memory addresses.* Components pass memory addresses to one another, telling each other where to access data or instructions. The number of wires that make up the memory address lines of the bus determines how many bits can be used for a memory address. The number of wires thus limits the amount of memory the bus can address.

▲ *Data.* Data passes over a bus in a group of wires, just as memory addresses do. The number of lines in the bus used to pass data determines how much data can be passed in parallel at one time. The number of lines depends on the type of processor and determines the number of bits in the data path. (Remember that a data path is the part of the bus on which the data is placed; it can be 8, 16, 32, 64, or more bits wide.)

BUS EVOLUTION

Just as a city's road system improves to increase the speed and number of lanes of traffic, buses have evolved around similar issues, data path and speed. Cars on a freeway generally travel at a continuous speed, but traffic on a computer's processor or bus is digital (on and off), rather than analog (continuous). The system clock keeps the beat for components. If a component on the motherboard works by the beat, or clock cycle, then it is synchronized, or in sync, with the processor. For example, the back-side bus of the Pentium works at half the speed of the processor. This means that the processor does something on each clock cycle, but the back-side bus is doing something on every other clock cycle.

Some components don't attempt to keep in sync with the processor, even to work at one-half or one-third of clock cycles. These components work asynchronously with the processor. They might work at a rate determined by the system clock or by another crystal on or off the motherboard. Either way, the frequency is much slower than the processor's and not in sync with it. If the processor requests something from one of these devices and the device is not ready, the device issues a **wait state**, which is a command to the processor to wait for slower devices to catch up.

The first expansion slots on early PCs were **Industry Standard Architecture (ISA)** slots. These slots had an 8-bit data path and ran at 4.77 MHz. Later, the 16-bit ISA slots were added that ran at 8.33 MHz. The 16-bit slots were backward-compatible with 8-bit cards; an 8-bit card used only a portion of the 16-bit slot. These 16-bit ISA slots are still in use on some older motherboards. To know how to support these legacy slots and cards, see Appendix C, "Supporting Legacy Devices."

Table 5-3 lists the various buses, in order of throughput speed from fastest to slowest. The evolution of buses includes earlier proprietary designs and the outdated ISA, EISA, MCA, and VESA buses. In Figure 5-6, you can see the shape of each of these bus connectors. Current buses include the USB bus, the IEEE 1394 (FireWire) bus, the original PCI bus, the AGP bus (for video only), the PCI-X, and the newer PCI Express bus. The USB, FireWire, and AGP buses are discussed in Chapter 8.

Looking at the second column of Table 5-3, you can see that a bus is called an expansion bus, local bus, local I/O bus, or local video bus. A bus that does not run in sync with the system clock is called an expansion bus and always connects to the slow end of the chipset, the South Bridge. Most buses today are local buses, meaning they run in sync with the system clock. If a local bus connects to the slower I/O controller hub or South Bridge of the chipset, it is called a local I/O bus. Because the video card needs to run at a faster rate than other expansion cards, this one slot always connects to the faster end of the chipset, the North Bridge. This video slot can be either an AGP slot or a PCI Express x16 slot, and the bus is called a local video bus. Several PCI buses are covered next.

A+ ESS
1.1

Bus	Bus Type	Data Path in Bits	Address Lines	Bus Speed in MHz	Throughput
System bus	Local	64	32	Up to 1600	Up to 3.2 GB/sec
Newer Bus Standards					
PCI Express x16	Local video and local I/O	Up to 16 lanes	Up to 16 lanes	2.5 GHz to 40 GHz	Up to 4 GB/sec
PCI-X	Local I/O	64	32	66, 133, 266, 533, 1066	Up to 8.5 GB/sec
AGP	Local video	32	NA	66, 75, 100 . . .	Up to 528 MB/sec
PCI	Local I/O	32 or 64	32	33, 66	133, 266, or 532 MB/sec
FireWire	Local I/O or expansion	1	Serial	NA	Up to 3.2 Gb/sec (gigabits)
USB	Expansion	1	Serial	3	12 to 480 Mbps (megabits)
Older Bus Standards					
VESA or VL Bus	Local video or expansion	32	32	Up to 33	Up to 250 MB/sec
MCA	Expansion	32	32	12	Up to 40 MB/sec
EISA	Expansion	32	32	12	Up to 32 MB/sec
16-bit ISA	Expansion	16	24	8.33	8 MB/sec
8-bit ISA	Expansion	8	20	4.77	1 MB/sec

Table 5-3 Buses listed by throughput

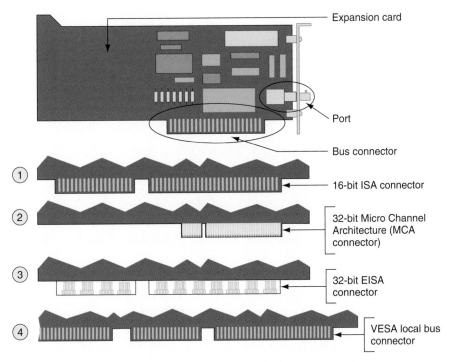

Figure 5-6 Four outdated bus connections on expansion cards

A+ ESS
1.1

THE PCI BUSES

The original PCI bus was introduced by Intel in 1991, intended to replace the 16-bit ISA bus. For many years, most motherboards had both ISA and PCI slots. You can see an example of one of these boards in Chapter 1, Figure 1-12, which has three black 16-bit ISA slots, four white PCI slots, and an early version of an AGP slot. PCI has been improved several times; there are currently three major categories and within each category, several variations of PCI. In the following sections, we discuss each category in turn.

Conventional PCI

The first PCI bus had a 32-bit data path, supplied 5 V of power to an expansion card, and operated at 33 MHz. It was the first bus that allowed expansion cards to run in sync with the CPU. PCI Version 2.x introduced the 64-bit, 3.3-V PCI slot, doubling data throughput of the bus. Because a card can be damaged if installed in the wrong voltage slot, a notch in a PCI slot distinguishes between a 5-V slot and a 3.3-V slot. A Universal PCI card can use either a 3.3-V or 5-V slot and contains both notches (see Figure 5-7).

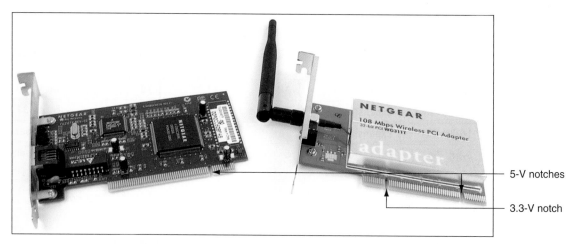

Figure 5-7 A 32-bit, 5-V PCI network card and a 32-bit, universal PCI wireless card show the difference in PCI notches set to distinguish voltages in a PCI slot

Conventional PCI now has four types of slots and six possible PCI card configurations to use these slots (see Figure 5-8).

PCI-X

The next evolution of PCI is PCI-X, which has had three major revisions; the latest is PCI-X 3.0. All PCI-X revisions are backward-compatible with conventional PCI cards and slots, except 5-V PCI cards are no longer supported. PCI-X is focused on technologies that increase bandwidth and data integrity and target the server market, and PCI-X revisions are generally keeping up with system bus speeds. Motherboards that use PCI-X tend to have several different PCI slots with some 32-bit or 64-bit slots running at different speeds.

PCI Express

PCI Express (PCIe) uses an altogether different architectural design than conventional PCI and PCI-X and is not backward compatible with either. PCI Express is intended to ultimately replace both these buses as well as the AGP bus, although it is expected PCI Express will coexist with these buses for some time to come (see Figure 5-9). Whereas PCI uses a 32-bit or 64-bit parallel bus, PCI Express uses a serial bus, which is faster than a parallel bus because it transmits data in packets similar to how an Ethernet network, USB, and FireWire transmit data.

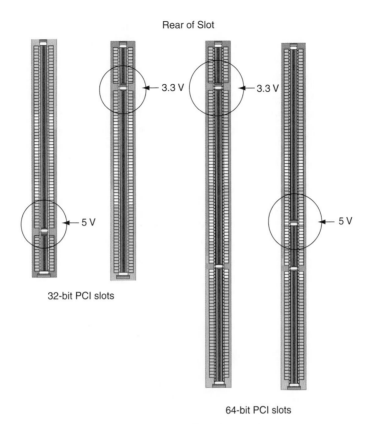

Rear of Slot

3.3 V

3.3 V

5 V

5 V

32-bit PCI slots

64-bit PCI slots

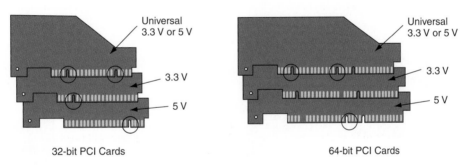

Universal
3.3 V or 5 V

Universal
3.3 V or 5 V

3.3 V

3.3 V

5 V

5 V

32-bit PCI Cards

64-bit PCI Cards

Figure 5-8   With PCI Version 2.x, there are four possible types of expansion slots
and six differently configured PCI expansion cards to use these slots

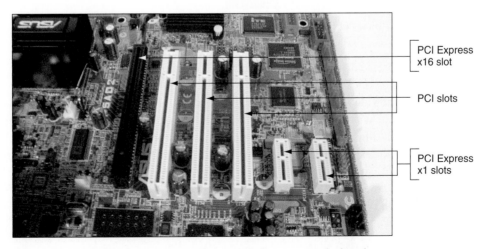

PCI Express
x16 slot

PCI slots

PCI Express
x1 slots

Figure 5-9   Three PCI Express slots and three PCI slots on a motherboard

Another difference in PCI Express is how it connects to the processor. Looking back in Chapter 4 at Figure 4-18, you can see that PCI cards all connect to the processor by way of a single PCI bus, which connects to the I/O controller hub or South Bridge. Compare this configuration to the one for PCI Express shown in Figure 5-10. With PCI Express, each PCI Express slot for a PCIe card has its own link or bus to the South Bridge, and one PCI Express slot has a direct link to the faster memory controller hub or North Bridge. This last PCI Express slot is intended to be used for a PCIe video card, thus replacing the slower AGP video slot. A motherboard will have either an AGP slot for the video card or a PCI Express x16 slot, but not both.

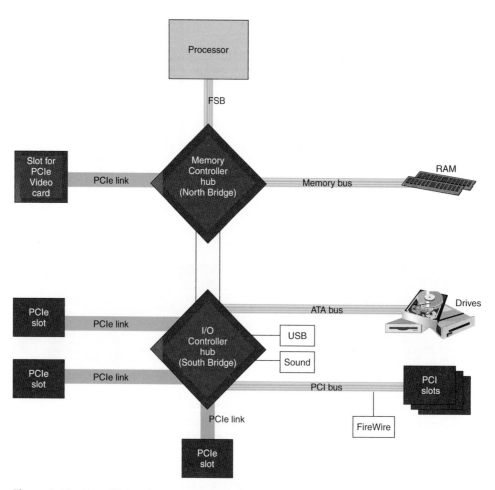

Figure 5-10 How PCI Express connects to the chipset and processor

PCI Express currently comes in four different slot sizes called PCI Express x1 (pronounced "by one"), x4, x8, and x16 (see Figure 5-11). PCI Express x16 is the fastest and is used for the video card slot. A PCI Express x1 slot contains a single lane for data, which is actually four wires. One pair of wires is used to send data and the other pair receives data, one bit at a time. The x16 slot contains 16 lanes, each lane timed independently of other lanes. A shorter PCI Express card (such as a x1 card) can be installed in a longer PCI Express slot (such as a x4 slot).

ON-BOARD PORTS, CONNECTORS, AND RISER SLOTS

In addition to expansion slots, a motherboard might also have several on-board ports, internal connectors, and riser slots.

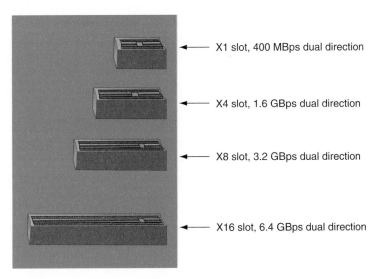

Figure 5-11   Current PCI Express slots

Ports coming directly off the motherboard are called **on-board ports** or integrated components. Almost all motherboards have a keyboard port, mouse port, parallel printer port, and one or more USB ports, and an older motherboard might have a serial port. In addition, the board might have a video port, sound ports, network port, modem port, 1394 (FireWire) port, and a port for a wireless antenna.

A motherboard might have several internal connectors, including parallel ATA connectors (also called EIDE connectors), a floppy drive connector, serial ATA connectors, SCSI connectors, or a 1394 connector.

To reduce the total cost of a computer system, some older motherboards might have a small expansion slot, about the length of a PCI Express x1 slot, called an **audio/modem riser (AMR)** slot (see Figure 5-12) or a **communication and networking riser (CNR)** slot.

Video

PCI Express and On-Board Wireless

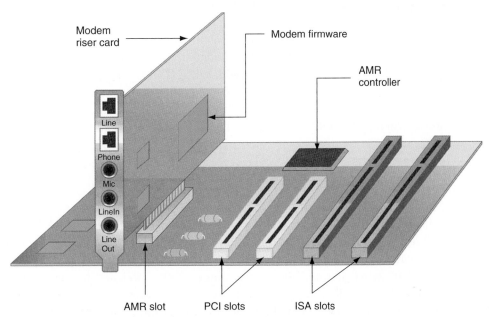

Figure 5-12   An audio/modem riser slot can accommodate an inexpensive modem riser card

**A+ ESS
1.1**

These small slots accommodate small, inexpensive expansion cards called **riser cards**, such as a modem riser card, audio riser card, or network riser card. Part of a riser card's audio, modem, or networking logic is on the card, and part is on a controller on the motherboard.

> **🔘 A+ Exam Tip**
>
> The A+ Essentials exam expects you to be familiar with an AMR slot, CNR slot, and riser card, also called a daughter board.

Some motherboards come with connector modules that provide additional ports off the rear of the case. For example, Figure 5-13 shows three modules that came bundled with one motherboard. To use the ports on a module, you connect its cable to a connector on the motherboard and install the module in the place of a faceplate at the rear of the case.

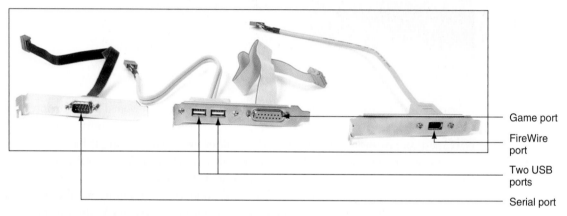

Game port

FireWire port

Two USB ports

Serial port

Figure 5-13   These modules provide additional ports off the rear of a computer case

> **✏️ Notes**
>
> You don't have to replace an entire motherboard if one port fails. Most ports on a motherboard can be disabled through CMOS setup. On older motherboards, look for jumpers or DIP switches to disable a port. Then use an expansion card for the port instead.

HARDWARE CONFIGURATION

You can configure the motherboard in three different ways: DIP switches, jumpers, and CMOS RAM. Storing configuration information by physically setting DIP switches or jumpers on the motherboard or peripheral devices is inconvenient, because it often requires you to open the computer case to make a change. A more convenient method is to hold configuration information in CMOS RAM. A program in BIOS, called CMOS setup, can then be used to easily make changes to the setup values stored in CMOS RAM. In this section, you will learn more about each method of storing configuration information. We'll also look at some examples of CMOS setup screens.

SETUP DATA STORED BY DIP SWITCHES

Many older motherboards and expansion cards and a few newer ones store setup data using a **dual inline package (DIP) switch**, as shown in Figure 5-14. A DIP switch has an ON position and an OFF position. ON represents binary 1 and OFF represents binary 0. If you add or remove equipment, you can communicate that to the computer by changing a DIP switch setting. When you change a DIP switch setting, use a pointed instrument such as a ballpoint pen to push the switch. Don't use a graphite pencil because graphite conducts electricity. In addition, pieces of graphite dropped into the switch can damage it.

A+ ESS
1.1

Figure 5-14   DIP switches are sometimes used to store setup data on motherboards

SETUP DATA STORED BY JUMPERS

A motherboard can also retain setup or installation information in different settings of jumpers on the board. **Jumpers** are considered open or closed based on whether a jumper cover is present on two small posts or metal pins that stick up off the motherboard (see Figure 5-15). A group of jumpers is sometimes used to tell the system at what speed the CPU is running, or to turn a power-saving feature on or off.

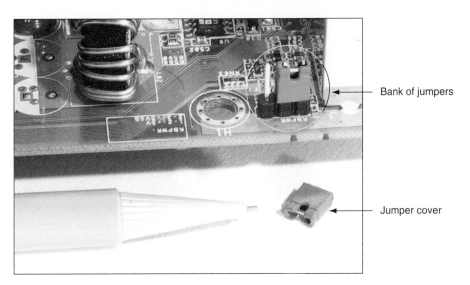

Bank of jumpers

Jumper cover

Figure 5-15   Setup information about the motherboard can be stored by setting a jumper on (closed) or off (open). A jumper is closed if the cover is in place, connecting the two pins that make up the jumper; a jumper is open if the cover is not in place.

Most motherboards use at least one set of jumpers, such as the set in Figure 5-16. Look at the jumper cover in Figure 5-16b that is "parked," meaning it is hanging on a single pin for safekeeping, but is not being used to turn a jumper setting on.

A typical setting that uses jumpers is enabling or disabling keyboard power-up. (With this feature enabled, you can press a key to power up the system.)

a   b   c

Figure 5-16 A 6-pin jumper group on a circuit board (a) has no jumpers set to on, (b) has a cover parked on one pin, and (c) is configured with one jumper setting turned on

You change the jumper setting by removing the computer case, finding the correct jumper, and then either placing a metal cover over the jumper or removing the cover already there. Figure 5-17 shows a diagram of a motherboard with the keyboard power-up jumper. For older motherboards, typical uses of jumpers were to indicate the presence of cache memory or to communicate the type and speed of the CPU present.

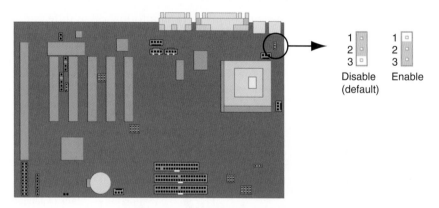

1
2   1
3   2
3

Disable   Enable
(default)

Figure 5-17 The keyboard power-up jumper allows you to use your keyboard to power up the computer

SETUP DATA STORED IN CMOS RAM

Computers today store most configuration information in CMOS RAM, also called the real-time clock/nonvolatile RAM (RTC/NVRAM) chip, which retains the data even when the computer is turned off. (There are actually many CMOS chips on a motherboard, used for various purposes.) On older computers (mostly IBM 286 PCs built in the 1980s), changes are made to the CMOS setup data using a setup program stored on a floppy disk. You booted from the disk to launch the setup program, which allowed you to make changes to CMOS RAM stored on the motherboard. One major disadvantage of this method, besides the chance that you might lose or misplace the disk, is that the floppy disk drive must be working before you can change the setup. An advantage of this method is that you cannot unintentionally change the setup. If you have an older computer and you do not have the floppy disk with the setup program, check the Web site of the motherboard manufacturer or the BIOS manufacturer for a replacement disk.

> **Notes**
>
> Even though a computer has many CMOS chips, the term "CMOS chip" has come to mean the one chip on the motherboard that holds the configuration or setup information. If you hear someone ask: "What does CMOS say?" or "Let's change CMOS," the person is talking about the configuration or setup information stored on this one CMOS chip.

A+ ESS
1.1

Changing CMOS Using the Setup Program

The CMOS setup does not normally need to be changed except, for example, when there is a problem with hardware, a new floppy drive is installed, or a power-saving feature needs to be disabled or enabled. The CMOS setup can also hold one or two power-on passwords to help secure a system. Know that these passwords are not the same password that can be required by a Windows OS at startup.

On newer computers, you usually change the data stored in CMOS by accessing the setup program stored in ROM BIOS. You access the program by pressing a key or combination of keys during the boot process. The exact way to enter setup varies from one motherboard manufacturer to another. Table 5-4 lists the keystrokes needed to access CMOS setup for some common BIOS types.

BIOS	Key to Press During POST to Access Setup
AMI BIOS	Del
Award BIOS	Del
Older Phoenix BIOS	Ctrl+Alt+Esc or Ctrl+Alt+s
Newer Phoenix BIOS	F2 or F1
Dell computers using Phoenix BIOS	Ctrl+Alt+Enter
Older Compaq computers such as the Deskpro 286 or 386	Place the diagnostics disk in the disk drive, reboot your system, and choose Computer Setup from the menu
Newer Compaq computers such as the ProLinea, Deskpro, Deskpro XL, Deskpro XE, or Presario	Press the F10 key while the cursor is in the upper-right corner of the screen, which happens just after the two beeps during booting*
All other older computers	Use a setup program on the disk that came with the PC

*For Compaq computers, the CMOS setup program is stored on the hard drive in a small, non-DOS partition of about 3 MB. If this partition becomes corrupted, you must run setup from a bootable CD or floppy disk that comes with the system. If you cannot run setup by pressing F10 at startup, suspect a damaged partition or a virus taking up space in conventional memory.

Table 5-4 How to access CMOS setup

For the exact method you need to use to enter setup, see the documentation for your motherboard. A message such as the following usually appears on the screen near the beginning of the boot:

```
Press DEL to change Setup
```

or

```
Press F8 for Setup
```

When you press the appropriate key or keys, a setup screen appears with menus and Help features that are often very user-friendly. Although the exact menus depend on the maker and version of components you are working with, the sample screens that follow will help you become familiar with the general contents of CMOS setup screens. Figure 5-18 shows a main menu for setup. On this menu, you can change the system date and time, the keyboard language, and other system features.

Recall the discussion of power management from Chapter 3. The power menu in CMOS setup allows you to configure automatic power-saving features for your system, such as suspend mode. Figure 5-19 shows a sample power menu.

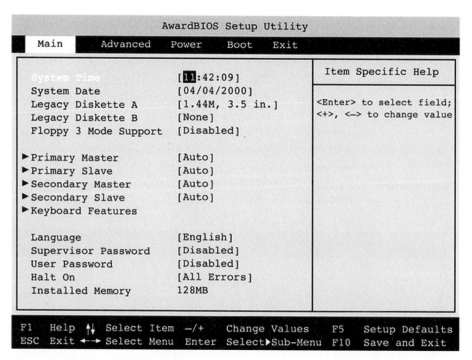

Figure 5-18 CMOS Setup Main menu

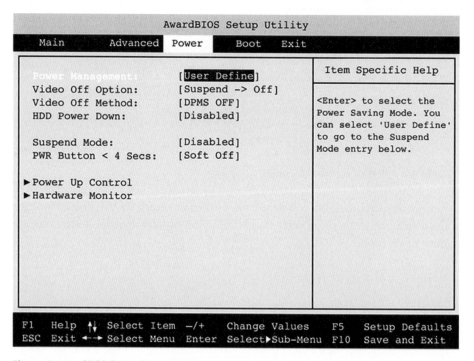

Figure 5-19 CMOS Setup Power menu

Figure 5-20 shows a sample Boot menu in CMOS setup. Here, you can set the order in which the system tries to boot from certain devices (called the boot sequence). Most likely when you first install a hard drive or an operating system, you will want to have the BIOS attempt to first boot from a CD and, if no CD is present, turn to the hard drive. After the OS is installed, to prevent accidental boots from a CD or other media, change CMOS setup to boot first from the hard drive. You will learn more about this in the installation procedures at the end of this chapter, as well as in later chapters.

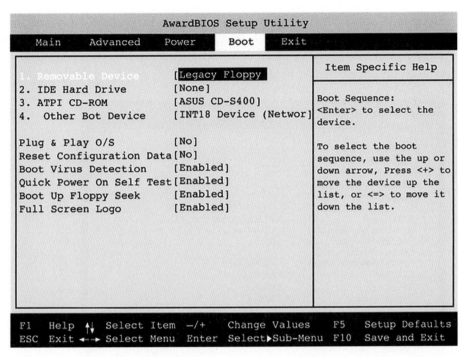

Figure 5-20 CMOS Setup Boot menu

Depending on the specific BIOS you are working with, an Advanced menu in the setup program or on other menus might contain other configuration options. When you finish, an exit screen such as the one shown in Figure 5-21 gives you various options, such as saving or discarding changes and then exiting the program, restoring default settings, or saving changes and remaining in the program.

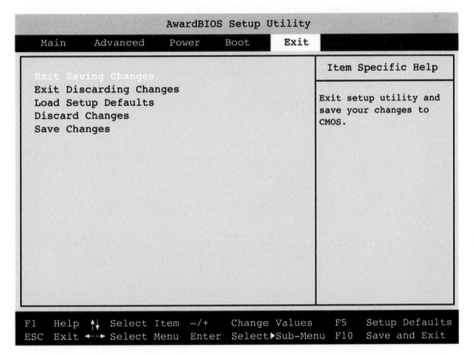

Figure 5-21 CMOS Setup Exit menu

Changing CMOS Setup for Brand-Name Computers

Many brand-name computer manufacturers, such as IBM, Dell, and Gateway, use their own custom-designed setup screens. These screens differ from the ones just shown. For example,

A+ ESS
1.1

Figure 5-22 shows the IBM BIOS Setup main menu for an IBM Thinkpad notebook computer. Under the Config option on the screen, you can configure the network port, serial port, parallel port, PCI bus, USB port, floppy drive, keyboard, display settings, power settings, power alarm, and memory settings.

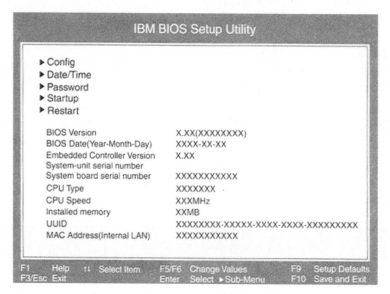

Figure 5-22 CMOS setup main menu for an IBM computer

Compare this CMOS main menu to the one shown in Figure 5-23 for a Gateway desktop computer. For all these different brand-name computers, what you can configure is similar, but the setup screens are likely to be organized differently.

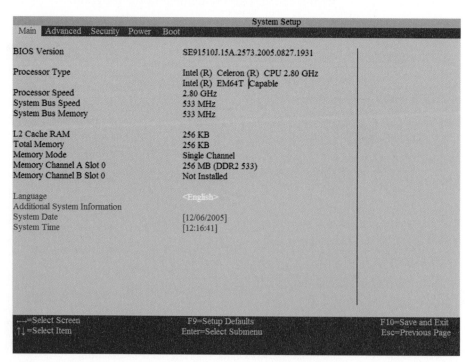

Figure 5-23 CMOS setup main menu for a Gateway computer

Battery Power to CMOS RAM

A small trickle of electricity from a nearby battery enables CMOS RAM to hold configuration data even while the main power to the computer is off. If the battery is disconnected

A+ ESS
1.1

or fails, setup information is lost. An indication that the battery is getting weak is that the system date and time are incorrect after the PC has been turned off and turned back on.

Several types of CMOS batteries are available:

◢ A 3.6-V lithium battery with a four-pin connector; connects with a Velcro strip
◢ A 4.5-V alkaline battery with a four-pin connector; connects with a Velcro strip
◢ A 3.6-V barrel-style battery with a two-pin connector; soldered on
◢ A 3-V lithium coin-cell battery

Figure 5-24 shows the coin cell, the most common type of CMOS battery.

Coin cell battery

Figure 5-24   The coin cell is the most common type of CMOS battery

A+ ESS
1.1
6.3

Setting Startup Passwords in CMOS

Access to a computer can be controlled using a **startup password**, sometimes called a **user password** or **power-on password**. If the password has been enabled and set in CMOS setup, the startup BIOS asks for the password during the boot just before the BIOS begins searching for an OS. If the password is entered incorrectly, the boot process terminates. The password is stored in CMOS RAM and is changed by accessing the setup screen. (This password is not the same as the OS password.) Many computers also provide a jumper near the chip holding CMOS RAM; when the jumper is set to on, the computer "forgets" any changes made to default settings stored in CMOS. By jumping these pins, you can disable a forgotten password.

> **⬆ A+ Exam Tip**
>
> The A+ IT 220-602 exam expects you to be able to configure a motherboard. You need to know how and when to use CMOS setup to make appropriate changes. And to help secure a computer, you need to know how to set startup passwords.

Lists of CMOS Settings

Motherboard manuals should contain a list of all CMOS settings, an explanation of their meanings, and their recommended values. When you purchase a motherboard or a computer, be sure the manual is included. If you don't have the manual, you can sometimes go to the motherboard manufacturer's Web site and download the information you need to understand the specific CMOS settings of your computer. Table 5-5 lists some CMOS settings. Several of these are discussed in future chapters.

> **✎ Notes**
>
> In documentation, a.k.a. stands for "also known as."

A+ ESS
1.1
6.3

Category	Setting	Description
Standard	Date and time	Sets the system date and time (called the CMOS setup real-time clock).
	Keyboard	Tells the system if the keyboard is installed or not; useful if the computer is used as a print or file server and you don't want someone changing settings.
	Hard disk type	Records the size and mapping of the drive or sets to automatically detect the HDD (discussed in Chapter 7).
	Floppy disk type	Sets the floppy disk type; choices are usually $3\frac{1}{2}$-inch and $5\frac{1}{4}$-inch.
BIOS Features Menu	Quick boot	Enable/disable. Enable to cause POST to skip some tests and speed up booting. Disable this feature when installing or testing a motherboard to get a thorough POST.
	Above 1 MB memory test	Disables POST check of this memory to speed up booting; the OS checks this memory anyway.
	Memory parity error check	For older motherboards, enables parity checking to ensure that memory is correct.
	System boot sequence	Establishes the drive the system turns to first to look for an OS; normally the hard drive (drive C) and then CD or floppy drive (drive A).
	External cache memory	Enables L2 cache. A frequent error in setup is to have cache but not use it because it's disabled here. Used on older motherboards that have on-board cache memory.
	Password checking option	Establishes a startup password. Use this only if you need to prevent someone untrustworthy from using your PC. Sometimes there are two passwords, each with different levels of security.
	Video ROM Shadow C000, 16K	For DOS and Windows 9x, shadowing video ROM is recommended because ROM runs slower than RAM.
	System ROM Shadow F000, 64K	Enabling shadow system ROM is recommended.
	IDE multiblock mode	Enables a hard drive to read or write several sectors at a time; depends on the kind of hard drive you have.
	Plug and Play (PnP)	Enable/disable. Enable for Windows 9x, which uses PnP data from BIOS. Disable for Windows 2000/XP, which does all the PnP configuration.
	Boot sector virus protection	Gives a warning when something is being written to the boot sector of the hard drive. Can be a nuisance if your software is designed to write to the boot sector regularly. When installing or upgrading an operating system, disable this protection so the OS install process can alter the boot sector without interruption.
Advanced Chipset Setup	AT cycle wait state	Sets the number of wait states the processor must endure while it interfaces with a device on the ISA or EISA bus. Increase this if an old and slow ISA card is not working well.

Table 5-5   CMOS settings and their purpose

A+ ESS
1.1
6.3

Category	Setting	Description
	AGP capability	Switches between AGP 1x, AGP 2x, AGP 4x, and AGP 8x versions to accommodate different AGP video cards.
	AGP aperture size	Adjusts the amount of system memory AGP can address.
	AGP voltage	Sets AGP operating voltage according to video card requirements.
	VGA BIOS sequence	Determines the order in which PCI/AGP is initialized; important mainly with dual monitors.
	Processor serial number	Allows processor ID# to be switched off for privacy (Pentium III only).
	Serial port	Sets beginning I/O address and IRQ; sometimes you can enable/disable the port.
	Parallel port mode	ECP or EPP (differences are discussed in Chapter 8).
	Infrared	Enable/disable (sometimes enabling infrared disables the second serial port, which uses the same resources).
Power Management Menu	Power management	Disables or enables all power management features; these features are designed to conserve electricity.
	Video off method	Sets which way video to the monitor will be suspended.
	HDD power down	Disables or enables the feature to shut down the hard drive after a period of inactivity.
	Wake on LAN	Allows your PC to be booted from another computer on the same network; it requires an ATX or BTX power supply that supports the feature.
	Wake on keyboard	Allows you to power up your PC by pressing a certain key combination.
Hard Drive Settings	IDE HDD autodetect	Detects HDDs installed on either IDE channel; allows you to specify Normal, Large, or LBA mode, but Autodetect is recommended.
	Serial ATA	Configure to IDE or RAID.
	SMART monitoring	Monitors the HDD for failure.
Hardware Device Settings	Processor operating speed	Sets the appropriate speed for your processor; used for throttling and overclocking.
	External clock	Sets the system bus speed.
	I/O voltage	Sets the appropriate I/O voltage for the processor.
	Core voltage	Sets the appropriate core voltage for the processor.

Note: The titles, locations, and inclusion or exclusion of BIOS categories and settings depend on the manufacturer, BIOS version, or both. For instance, Plug and Play might be a group of settings sharing a category with other settings in one version of BIOS, whereas Plug and Play might be its own category in another BIOS version.

Table 5-5 CMOS settings and their purpose (continued)

A+ ESS
1.1
6.3

PROTECTING DOCUMENTATION AND CONFIGURATION SETTINGS

If the battery goes bad or is disconnected, you can lose the settings saved in CMOS RAM. If you are using default settings, reboot with a good battery and instruct setup to restore the default settings. Setup has to autodetect the hard drive present, and you need to set the date and time, but you can easily recover from the problem. However, if you have customized some CMOS settings, you need to restore them. The most reliable way to restore settings is to keep a written record of all the changes you make to CMOS.

If you are permanently responsible for a computer, you should consider keeping a written record of what you have done to maintain it. Use a small notebook or similar document to record CMOS settings that are not the default settings, hardware and software installed, network settings, and similar information. Suppose someone decides to tinker with a PC for which you are responsible, changes a jumper on the motherboard, and cannot remember which jumper she changed. The computer no longer works, and the documentation for the board is now invaluable. Lost or misplaced documentation greatly complicates the otherwise simple job of reading the settings for each jumper and checking them on the board. Keep the documentation well labeled in a safe place. If you have several computers to maintain, you might consider a filing system for each computer.

APPLYING | CONCEPTS *Saving and Restoring CMOS Settings Using Third-Party Utility Software*

If you lose CMOS settings, another way to restore them is to use a backup of the settings that you have previously saved on a floppy disk. One third-party utility that allows you to save CMOS settings is Norton Utilities by Symantec (*www.symantec.com*). Sometimes the support CD that comes with a motherboard has a utility on it to save CMOS settings to a floppy disk.

You can also download a shareware utility to record CMOS settings. One example follows, but know that the files might change with new releases of the software.

1. Access the Internet and use a search engine to find a site offering Cmos.zip. Two current locations are: *www.programmersheaven.com/zone24/cat31/4174.htm* and *www.computerhope.com/downlod.htm*.

2. Select and download Cmos.zip. You can then exit the Internet.

3. Unzip the compressed file and print the contents of the documentation file.

4. Double-click the **Cmos.exe** file you unzipped. The program shows the current contents of CMOS memory in a DOS box.

5. Enter **S** (for Save) at the command line. Enter the drive letter of your floppy drive and a filename to save the current CMOS settings to floppy disk. A sample path and filename might be **A:MYCMOS**.

6. Enter **Q** to quit the program.

 Notes

When you want to retrieve the contents of the file from the floppy disk, run the Cmos.exe program again, and enter L (for Load) at the command line, specifying the name of the file you saved on the floppy disk.

A+ ESS
1.1
1.4

A+
220-602
1.1

Another method is to carefully tape a cardboard folder to the inside top or side of the computer case and safely tuck the hardware documentation there. This works well if you are responsible for several computers spread over a wide area.

Regardless of the method you use, it's important that you keep your written record up to date and stored with the hardware documentation in a safe place. Leaving it in the care of users who might not realize its value is probably not a good idea. The notebook and documentation will be invaluable as you solve future problems with this PC.

FLASHING ROM BIOS

Recall that ROM BIOS includes the CMOS setup program, the startup BIOS that manages the startup process, and the system BIOS that manages basic I/O functions of the system.

APPLYING CONCEPTS

When flashing ROM, the first step is to accurately identify the BIOS version currently installed. You can identify your motherboard and BIOS in several different ways:

- ◢ Look on the CMOS setup main screen for the BIOS manufacturer and version number.
- ◢ Look on the motherboard for the brand and model imprinted on the board (see Figure 5-25). If you download the BIOS upgrade from the motherboard manufacturer Web site, this information might be all you need to select the correct BIOS upgrade.

Model

Brand

Figure 5-25 The motherboard brand and model are imprinted somewhere on the board

- ◢ Use third-party software (such as BIOS Agent at *www.unicore.com*) or an OS utility (such as Windows System Information) to determine the BIOS information.
- ◢ Stop the boot process and look for the BIOS information reported early in the boot process.

To stop the boot process early so you can read the BIOS information, first try the following:

1. Turn off the system power and then turn it back on.

2. While memory is counting on the screen, hold down the Pause/Break key to stop the startup process.

3. Look for the long string of numbers in the lower-left corner of your screen that identifies the motherboard.

4. Look for the BIOS manufacturer and version number somewhere near the top of the screen.

If the above list doesn't work, try turning off the PC, unplugging the keyboard, and then turning on the PC. For older systems, the resulting keyboard error stops the boot process.

To flash ROM, carefully read the motherboard documentation, as different motherboards use different methods. If you can't find the documentation, check the motherboard manufacturer's Web site, and check the directions that came with the upgrade software. Generally, you perform these tasks:

1. Download the BIOS upgrade from the motherboard manufacturer Web site. If you can't find an upgrade on this site, try the BIOS manufacturer Web site or a third-party site. Most often you are instructed to save this upgrade to a bootable floppy disk.

2. Set a jumper on the motherboard, or change a setting in CMOS setup to tell BIOS to expect an upgrade.

3. Boot from the floppy disk and follow the menu options to upgrade BIOS. If the menu gives you the option to save the old BIOS to disk, do so in case you need to revert to the old BIOS.

4. Set the jumper back to its original setting, reboot the system, and verify that all is working.

 Notes

After flashing BIOS, if the motherboard gives problems, you need to consider that the chipset drivers might also need updating. To update the chipset drivers, go to the Web site of the motherboard manufacturer and download the chipset driver files for the OS you are using. Then follow the manufacturer's instructions to perform the update.

Makers of BIOS code are likely to change BIOS frequently because providing the upgrade on the Internet is so easy for them. You can get upgraded BIOS code from manufacturers' Web sites or disks, or from third-party BIOS resellers' Web sites or disks. Generally, however, follow the principle that "if it's not broke, don't fix it"; update your BIOS only if you're having a problem with your motherboard or there's a new BIOS feature you want to use.

Caution

Be *very careful* that you upgrade BIOS with the correct upgrade and that you follow the manufacturer's instructions correctly. Upgrading with the wrong file could make your system BIOS useless. If you're not sure that you're using the correct upgrade, *don't guess*. Check with the technical support for your BIOS before moving forward. Before you call technical support, have the information that identifies your BIOS and motherboard available.

A+ ESS
1.1
1.4

A+
220-602
1.1

All these programs are considered firmware and are stored on a chip on the motherboard, called the ROM BIOS chip or firmware chip. If a motherboard becomes unstable (such as when the system hangs at odd times), some functions are lost (such as a USB port stops working), or you want to incorporate some new feature or component on the board (such as when you upgrade the processor), you might need to upgrade the programming stored on the ROM BIOS chip. The process of upgrading or refreshing the ROM BIOS chip is called flashing ROM.

Figure 5-26 shows a sample Web site for flash ROM BIOS upgrades for Intel motherboards. If you can't find an upgrade on your motherboard or BIOS manufacturer Web site, try the BIOS Upgrades Web site by eSupport.com, Inc. at *www.esupport.com*. Table 5-6 lists BIOS manufacturers. A list of motherboard manufacturers is given in Table 5-2 earlier in the chapter.

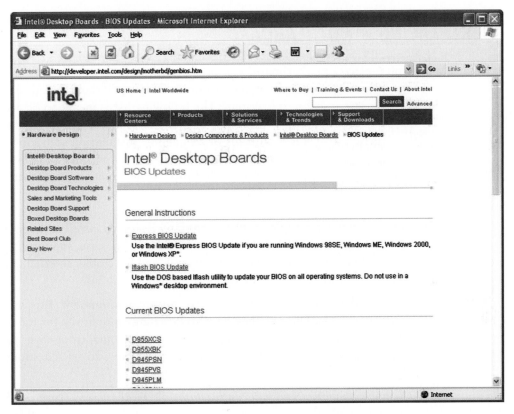

Figure 5-26 Intel displays a list of motherboard model numbers that have a Flash BIOS upgrade available

Company	URL
American Megatrends, Inc. (AMI)	*www.megatrends.com* or *www.ami.com*
Compaq and Hewlett-Packard	*thenew.hp.com*
Dell	*www.dell.com*
eSupport.com (BIOS upgrades)	*www.esupport.com*
Gateway	*www.gateway.com*
IBM	*www.ibm.com/support*
Phoenix Technologies (First BIOS, Phoenix, and Award)	*www.phoenix.com*
Wim's BIOS	*www.wimsbios.com*

Table 5-6 BIOS manufacturers

MOTHERBOARD DRIVERS

A motherboard comes bundled with a CD that contains drivers for all the onboard components. Most likely Windows can use its own internal drivers for these components, but if you have trouble with an onboard component or want to use a feature that is not working, use the motherboard CD to install the manufacturer drivers into Windows. Also, the motherboard manufacturer updates motherboard drivers from time to time. For an unstable motherboard, you can try downloading and installing updated chipset drivers and other drivers for onboard components.

The motherboard CD might also contain useful utilities such as a utility that you can install under Windows to monitor the CPU temperature and alert you if overheating occurs.

REPLACING A MOTHERBOARD

When you replace a motherboard, you pretty much have to disassemble an entire computer, install the new motherboard, and reassemble the system. The following list is meant to be a general overview of the process and is not meant to include the details of all possible installation scenarios, which can vary according to the components and OS you are using. The general process for replacing a motherboard is as follows:

 A+ Exam Tip

The A+ IT 220-602 exam expects you to know how to select and install a motherboard.

1. *Verify that you have selected the right motherboard to install in the system.* The new motherboard should have the same form factor as the case, support the RAM modules and processor you want to install on it, and have other internal and external connectors you need for your system.

2. *Determine proper configuration settings for the motherboard.* Especially important are any jumpers, DIP switches, or CMOS settings specifically for the processor, and RAM speeds and timing. Read the motherboard manual from cover to cover. You can also check the manufacturer Web site for answers to any questions you might have.

3. *Remove components so you can reach the old motherboard.* Turn off the system and disconnect all cables and cords. Open the case cover and remove all internal cables and cords connected to the motherboard. Remove all expansion cards. To safely remove the old motherboard, you might have to remove drives.

4. *Set any jumpers or switches on the new motherboard.* This is much easier to do before you put the board in the case.

5. *Install the processor and processor cooler.* The processor comes already installed on some motherboards, in which case you just need to install the cooler. You might need to add thermal compound. Also, if you are working with a heavy cooling assembly, some manufacturers suggest you install the motherboard in the case before installing the cooler. Follow motherboard and processor installation instructions. Processor instructions take precedent over motherboard instructions.

6. *Install RAM into the appropriate slots on the motherboard.*

7. *Install the motherboard.* Place the motherboard into the case and, using spacers or screws, securely fasten the board to the case.

A+
220-602
1.1

8. *Attach cabling that goes from the case switches to the motherboard, and from the power supply and drives to the motherboard.* Pay attention to how cables are labeled and to any information in the documentation about where to attach them. Position and tie cables neatly together to make sure they don't obstruct the fans and the air flow.

9. *Install the video card on the motherboard.* Usually this card goes into the AGP slot or PCI Express x16 slot.

10. *Plug the computer into a power source, and attach the monitor and keyboard.* Note that you do not attach the mouse now, for the initial setup. Although the mouse generally does not cause problems during setup, initially install only the things you absolutely need.

11. *Boot the system and enter CMOS setup.* As you learned earlier in the chapter, you can do this using several methods, depending on what type of system you have.

12. *Make sure settings are set to the default.* If the motherboard comes new from the manufacturer, it will already be at default settings. If you are salvaging a motherboard from another system, you might need to reset settings to the default. Generally a jumper or switch sets all CMOS settings to default settings. You will need to do the following while you are in CMOS:

   ▲ Check the time and date.
   ▲ Check the floppy drive type.
   ▲ Make sure abbreviated POST is disabled. While you're installing a motherboard, you generally want it to do as many tests as possible. After you know the system is working, you can choose to abbreviate POST.
   ▲ Set the boot order to the hard drive, then a CD, if you will be booting the OS from the hard drive.
   ▲ Make sure "autodetect hard disk" is set so that the system automatically looks for drives.
   ▲ Leave everything else at their defaults unless you know that particular settings should be otherwise.
   ▲ Save and exit.

13. *Observe POST and verify that no errors occur.*

14. *Check for conflicts with system resources.* For Windows, use Device Manager to verify that the OS recognizes all devices and that no conflicts are reported.

15. *Install the motherboard drives.* If your motherboard comes with a CD that contains some motherboard drivers, install them now.

16. *Install any other expansion cards and drives.* Install each device and its drivers, one device at a time, rebooting and checking for conflicts after each installation.

17. *Verify that everything is operating properly, and make any final OS and CMOS adjustments, such as power management settings.*

Now let's look at the details of installing the motherboard into the computer case.

 Notes

Whenever you install or uninstall software or hardware, keep a notebook with details about the components you are working on, configuration settings, manufacturer specifications, and other relevant information. This helps if you need to back-track later, and can also help you document and troubleshoot your computer system. Keep all hardware documentation for this system together with the notebook in an envelope in a safe place.

A+
220-602
1.1

Caution

As with any installation, remember the importance of using a ground strap (ground bracelet) to ground yourself when working inside a computer case to protect components against ESD.

Video

Preparing a Motherboard for Installation

PREPARING THE MOTHERBOARD TO GO INTO THE CASE

Before you begin preparing the motherboard, read the manual that comes with it from beginning to end. The steps listed in this section are general, and you will need to know information specific to your motherboard. Visually familiarize yourself with the configuration of the case and the motherboard.

SETTING THE JUMPERS

The first step in preparing the motherboard to go in the case is to set the jumpers or DIP switches. When doing an installation, read the motherboard documentation carefully, looking for explanations of how jumpers and DIP switches on the board are used. This information differs from one motherboard to another. For older boards, a jumper group might control the system bus frequency and another group might control the CPU frequency multiplier. Set the jumpers and DIP switches according to the hardware you will be installing.

For example, Figure 5-27 shows the documentation for one motherboard that uses three jumpers to configure the BIOS; the jumper group is shown in Figure 5-28. Set the jumper group to the normal setting so that BIOS uses the current configuration for booting. Once set, the jumpers should be changed only if you are trying to recover when the power-up password is lost or flashing BIOS has failed. Figure 5-28 shows the jumper cap in the normal position.

Jumper Position	Mode	Description
1 • 3	Normal (default)	The current BIOS configuration is used for booting.
1 • 3	Configure	After POST, the BIOS displays a menu in CMOS setup that can be used to clear the user and supervisor power-on passwords.
1 • 3	Recovery	Recovery is used to recover from a failed BIOS update. Details can be found on the motherboard CD.

Figure 5-27   BIOS configuration jumper settings

Jumpers set for normal boot

Figure 5-28   BIOS setup configuration jumpers

5

ADDING THE PROCESSOR, FAN, HEAT SINK, AND MEMORY MODULES

Now that you have set the jumpers on the motherboard, you are ready to add the processor itself. Check out Chapter 4 for information on how to install a processor and cooler assembly. You then need to install RAM in the memory slots. Chapter 6 covers how to buy and install RAM for a specific motherboard.

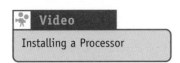

Video

Installing a Processor

INSTALLING THE MOTHERBOARD IN THE CASE

Here are the general steps for installing the motherboard in the case:

1. Install the faceplate. The faceplate or I/O shield is a metal plate that comes with the computer case and fits over the ports to create a well-fitting enclosure for them. A case might have several faceplates designed for several types of motherboards. Select the correct one and discard the others (see Figure 5-29). Insert the faceplate in the hole at the back of the case (see Figure 5-30).

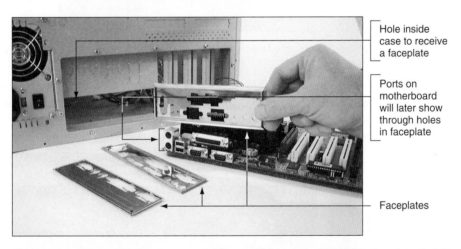

Hole inside case to receive a faceplate

Ports on motherboard will later show through holes in faceplate

Faceplates

Figure 5-29 The computer case comes with several faceplates. Select the faceplate that fits over the ports that come off the motherboard. The other plates can be discarded.

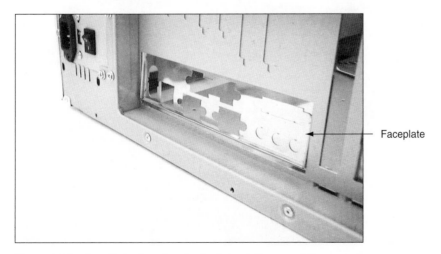

Faceplate

Figure 5-30 Install the faceplate in the hole at the rear of the computer case

A+
220-602
1.1

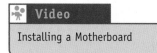
Video

Installing a Motherboard

2. Install the standoffs. **Standoffs**, also called **spacers**, are round plastic or metal pegs that separate the motherboard from the case, so that components on the back of the motherboard do not touch the case. Make sure the locations of the standoffs match the screw holes on the motherboard (see Figure 5-31). If you need to remove a standoff to move it to a new slot, needle-nose pliers work well to unscrew or unplug the standoff. The case will have more holes than you need to support several types of motherboards.

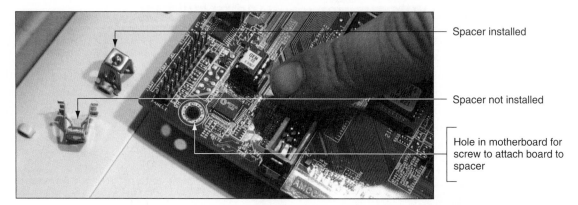

Spacer installed

Spacer not installed

Hole in motherboard for screw to attach board to spacer

Figure 5-31 The spacers line up with the holes on the motherboard and keep it from touching the case

3. Place the motherboard inside the case (see Figure 5-32), and use screws to attach it to the case. Figure 5-33 shows how you must align the standoffs to the holes on the motherboard. The screws fit into the standoffs you installed earlier. There should be at least six standoff/screw sets, and there might be as many as nine. Use as many as there are holes in the motherboard.

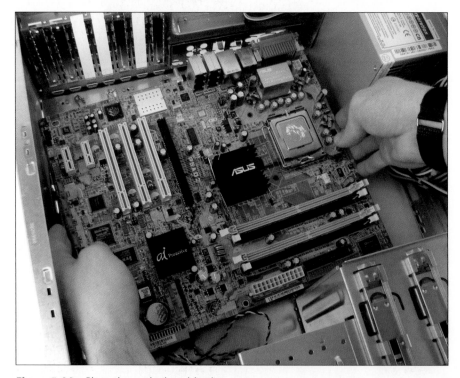

Figure 5-32 Place the motherboard in the case

A+
220-602
1.1

Figure 5-33 Use screws to attach the motherboard to the case via the spacers

4. Connect the power cord from the power supply to the P1 power connection on the motherboard. (If you are using an AT motherboard, you have two power connections, P8 and P9, which are connected using the black-to-black rule.) See Figure 5-34.

Figure 5-34 The 20-pin connector supplies power to the motherboard

5. Connect the 4-pin auxiliary power cord coming from the power supply to the motherboard, as shown in Figure 5-35. This cord supplies the supplemental power required for a Pentium 4 processor.

A+
220-602
1.1

Figure 5-35 The auxiliary 4-pin power cord provides power to the Pentium 4 processor

6. Connect the wire leads from the front panel of the case to the motherboard. These are the wires for the switches and lights on the front of the computer. Because your case and your motherboard might not have been made by the same manufacturer, you need to pay close attention to the source of the wires to determine where they connect on the motherboard. For example, Figure 5-36 shows a computer case that has five wires from the front panel that connect to the motherboard.

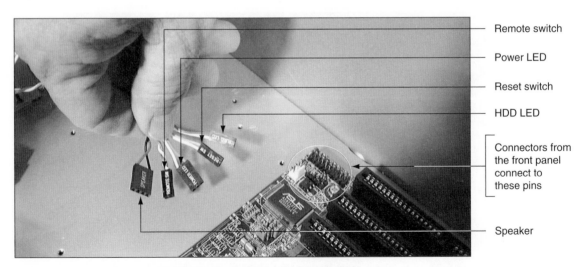

Remote switch

Power LED

Reset switch

HDD LED

Connectors from the front panel connect to these pins

Speaker

Figure 5-36 Five wires from the front panel connect to the motherboard

The five wires showing in the figure are labeled as follows:

▲ *Remote switch*. Controls power to the motherboard; must be connected for the PC to power up
▲ *Power LED*. Light indicating that power is on
▲ *Reset switch*. Used to reboot the computer

5

A+
220-602
1.1

▲ *HDD LED*. Controls a light on the front panel that lights up when any IDE device is in use. (LED stands for light-emitting diode; an LED is a light on the front panel.)

▲ *Speaker*. Controls the speaker.

7. To know which wire connects to which pins, see the motherboard documentation or look for cryptic labels imprinted on the motherboard near the banks of pins. Sometimes the motherboard documentation is not clear, but guessing is okay when connecting a wire to a connection. If it doesn't work, no harm is done.

> **Notes**
>
> To help orient the connector on the motherboard pins, look for a small triangle embedded on the connector that marks one of the outside wires as pin 1 (see Figure 5-37). Look for pin 1 to be labeled on the motherboard as a small 1 embedded to either the right or the left of the group of pins. Also, sometimes the documentation marks pin 1 as a square pin in the diagram, rather than round like the other pins. The diagram in Figure 5-38 shows what you can expect from motherboard documentation where the leads connect to the pins in Panel 1.

Figure 5-37 Look for the small triangle embedded on the wire lead connectors to orient the connector correctly to the motherboard connector pins

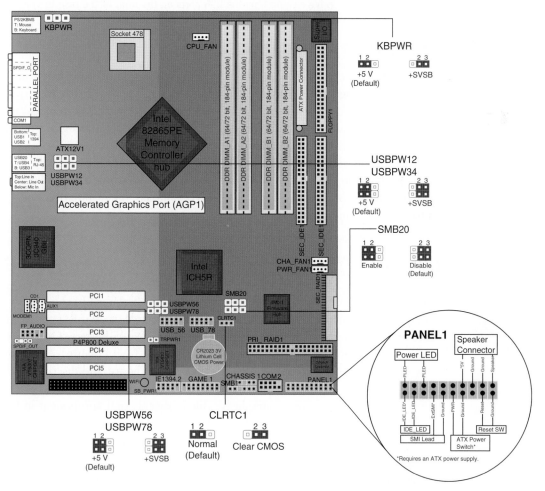

Figure 5-38 Connector group for front-panel leads

A+
220-602
1.1

8. Depending on your motherboard, there might be a cable to connect an internal USB connection to USB ports on the front of the case. Connect the cable, as shown in Figure 5-39.

Two USB ports on the front of the case

Figure 5-39 Connect the cable coming from the USB ports on the front of the case to one of the two USB connectors on the motherboard

COMPLETING THE INSTALLATION

After you install the motherboard and connect all cables and cords, next you install the video card and plug in the keyboard and monitor. You are now ready to turn on the system and observe POST occurs with no errors. After the Windows desktop loads, insert the CD that came bundled with the motherboard and execute any setup program on the CD. Follow the steps onscreen to install any drivers, which might include drivers for onboard devices and ports such as video, network, audio, USB, RAID, or the chipset.

Look back at the general list of steps to replace a motherboard at the beginning of this section for the list of things to check and do to complete the installation and return the system to good working order.

TROUBLESHOOTING THE MOTHERBOARD AND PROCESSOR

A+ ESS
1.3

A+
220-602
1.2

Items that can be exchanged without returning the motherboard to the factory are called field replaceable units (FRUs). On older AT motherboards, these FRU components were the processor, RAM, RAM cache, ROM BIOS chip, and CMOS battery. On newer motherboards, FRU components are the processor, RAM, and CMOS battery. Also, the motherboard itself is an FRU. As you troubleshoot the motherboard and discover that some component is not working, such as a network port, you might be able to disable that component in CMOS setup and install a card to take its place.

When troubleshooting the motherboard, use whatever clues POST can give you. Recall that, before it checks video, POST reports any error messages as beep codes. When a PC boots, one beep indicates that all is well after POST.

 A+ Exam Tip

The A+ Essentials and IT 220-602 exams expect you to know how to troubleshoot problems with motherboards and processors.

A+ ESS
1.3

A+
220-602
1.2

If you hear more than one beep, look up the beep code in Chapter 2. Error messages on the screen indicate that video is working. If the beep code or error message is not in Chapter 2, try the Web site of the ROM BIOS or motherboard manufacturer for information. Figure 5-40 shows the Web site for AMI with explanations of beep codes produced by its startup BIOS.

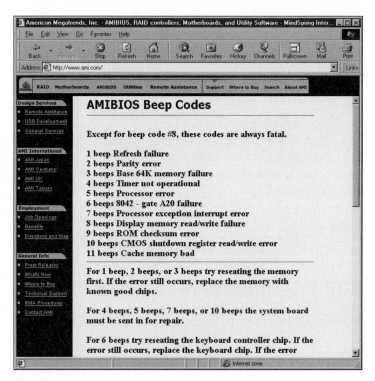

Figure 5-40 The ROM BIOS manufacturer's Web site is a good source of information about beep codes

Remember that you can try substituting good hardware components for those you suspect are bad. Be cautious here. A friend once had a computer that would not boot. He replaced the hard drive, with no change. He replaced the motherboard next. The computer booted up with no problem; he was delighted, until it failed again. Later he discovered that a faulty power supply had damaged his original motherboard. When he traded the bad one for a good one, the new motherboard also got zapped! If you suspect problems with the power supply, check the voltage coming from the power supply before putting in a new motherboard! (Instructions on troubleshooting the power supply are in Chapter 3.)

The following sections contain descriptions of some common problems and what to do about them.

PROBLEMS WITH INSTALLATIONS

If you have just installed a new processor on a working motherboard and the system does not boot, do the following:

1. Open the case and check these things:

   ◢ Did you install thermal paste (thermal compound) between the processor and the heat sink?
   ◢ Is the cooler securely fastened to the frame on the motherboard? If the cooler and thermal paste are not installed correctly, the CPU can overheat during the boot, causing BIOS to immediately power down the system.
   ◢ Remove the processor from its socket and look for bent or damaged pins or lands on the socket and processor.

A+ ESS
1.3

A+
220-602
1.2

2. Reinstall the processor and try the boot again.

3. Reinstall the old processor, flash BIOS, and then try the new processor again.

If you have just installed a new motherboard that is not working, check the following:

- Have you installed the front cover on the case? Sometimes a system refuses to power up until this cover is in place.
- Is there a power switch on the back of the case that is not turned on?
- Study the documentation and verify all connections are correct. Most likely this is the problem. Remember the Power Switch lead from the front of the case must be connected to the panel on the motherboard.
- Verify the processor, thermal compound, and cooler are all installed correctly.
- Remove RAM and reinstall the modules.
- Verify a standoff that is not being used by the motherboard is not under the motherboard and causing a short.
- If the system can boot into Windows, install all motherboard drivers on the CD that came bundled with the board.
- Check the motherboard Web site for other things you can check or try.

PROBLEMS WITH THE MOTHERBOARD AND PROCESSOR

Symptoms that a motherboard or processor is failing can appear as:

- The system begins to boot but then powers down.
- An error message displays during the boot. Investigate this message.
- The system becomes unstable, hangs, or freezes at odd times.
- Intermittent Windows or hard drive errors occur.
- Components on the motherboard or devices connected to it don't work.

The motherboard might have come bundled with a support CD. Look on it for drivers of board components that are not working. For example, if the USB ports are not working, try updating the USB drivers with those stored on the support CD. Load the CD and follow directions onscreen.

If this doesn't resolve the problem, try the following:

- A power-saving feature might be the source of the problem. Ask yourself, "Is the system in a doze or sleep mode?" Many "green," or environmentally friendly, systems can be programmed through CMOS to suspend the monitor or even the drive if the keyboard or processor has been inactive for a few minutes. Pressing any key usually causes operations to resume exactly where the user left off.
- If the fan is running, reseat or replace the processor, BIOS, or RAM. Try installing a DIMM in a different slot. A POST code diagnostic card is a great help at this point. These cards are discussed in Chapter 2.
- Sometimes a dead computer can be fixed by simply disassembling it and reseating cables, adapter cards, socketed chips, and SIMMs, DIMMs, or RIMMs. Bad connections and corrosion are common problems.
- Check jumpers, DIP switches, and CMOS settings.
- Look for physical damage on the motherboard. Look for frayed traces on the bottom of the board or brown or burnt capacitors on the board.
- Check CMOS for a temperature reading that indicates overheating.

A+ ESS
1.3

A+
220-602
1.2

▲ Flash BIOS.

▲ A dead or dying battery may cause problems. Sometimes, after a long holiday, a weak battery causes the CMOS to forget its configuration.

▲ Try using the CD that came with the motherboard, which most likely has diagnostic tests on it that might identify the problem with the motherboard.

▲ Reduce the system to essentials. Remove any unnecessary hardware, such as expansion cards, and then try to boot again.

▲ Exchange the processor.

▲ If an onboard component isn't working but the motherboard is stable, go into CMOS setup and disable the component. Then install a replacement component using a port or expansion slot.

▲ Exchange the motherboard, but before you do, measure the voltage output of the power supply or simply replace it, in case it is producing too much power and has damaged the board.

APPLYING CONCEPTS

Jessica complained to Wally, her PC support technician, that Windows was occasionally giving errors, data would get corrupted, or an application would not work as it should. At first Wally suspected Jessica might need a little more training in how to open and close an application or save a file, but he discovered user error was not the problem. He tried reinstalling the application software Jessica most often used, and even reinstalled Windows, but the problems persisted.

Then he began to suspect a hardware problem. Carefully examining the motherboard revealed the source of the problem: failing capacitors. Look carefully at Figure 5-41 and you can see five bad capacitors with bulging and discolored heads. (Know that sometimes a leaking capacitor can also show crusty corrosion at the base of the capacitor.) When Wally replaced the motherboard, the problems went away.

Notes

Catastrophic errors (errors that cause the system to not boot or a device to not work) are much easier to resolve than intermittent errors (errors that come and go).

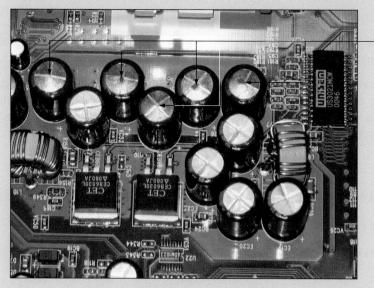

Bad capacitors

Figure 5-41 These five bad capacitors have bulging and discolored heads

>> CHAPTER SUMMARY

▲ The motherboard is the most complicated of all components inside the computer. It contains the processor and accompanying chipset, real-time clock, ROM BIOS, CMOS configuration chip, RAM, RAM cache, system bus, expansion slots, jumpers, ports, and power supply connections. The motherboard you select determines both the capabilities and limitations of your system.

▲ Some components can be built in to the motherboard, in which case they are called on-board components. Other components can be attached to the system in some other way, such as on an expansion card.

▲ A bus is a path on the motherboard that carries electrical power, control signals, memory addresses, and data to different components on the board.

▲ A bus can be 16, 32, 64, or more bits wide. The first ISA bus had an 8-bit data path. The second ISA slot had a 16-bit data path.

▲ Some outdated buses are the 16-bit ISA, 32-bit MCA and EISA buses, and VESA bus. Current buses are the PCI bus, AGP bus, and PCI Express. A local bus runs in sync with the system clock and is designed to allow fast devices quicker and more direct access to the processor than other buses. In addition, if the bus connects to the North Bridge of the chipset, it has more direct and faster access to the processor than if it attaches to the slower South Bridge. A bus slot used for a PCI Express x16 or AGP video card connects to the North Bridge.

▲ The most common method of configuring components on a motherboard is CMOS setup. Some motherboards also use jumpers or DIP switches to contain configuration settings.

▲ Jumpers on older motherboards can be used to set the motherboard speed and the processor frequency multiplier, which determines the processor speed. For newer boards, these settings are autodetected without the use of jumpers.

▲ ROM chips contain the programming code to manage POST and the system BIOS and to change CMOS settings. The setup or CMOS chip holds configuration information.

▲ Sometimes ROM BIOS programming stored on the firmware chip needs updating or refreshing. This process is called flashing BIOS.

▲ When installing a motherboard, first study the motherboard and set jumpers and DIP switches on the board. Sometimes the processor and cooler are best installed before installing the motherboard in the case. When the cooling assembly is heavy and bulky, it is best to install it after the motherboard is securely seated in the case.

>> KEY TERMS

For explanations of key terms, see the Glossary near the end of the book.

audio/modem riser (AMR)	jumper	startup password
communication and networking riser (CNR)	on-board ports	user password
	power-on password	wait state
dual inline package (DIP) switch	riser card	
Industry Standard Architecture (ISA) slot	spacers	
	standoffs	

>> REVIEWING THE BASICS

1. What are three main categories of form factors used for motherboards?

2. How many power cords connect to a Baby AT motherboard?

3. On the Enhanced ATX motherboard that supports PCI Express, how many pins does the P1 power connector have?

4. What are the names of the two power connectors used on the AT motherboard form factors?

5. What is the name of the one power connector on the ATX motherboard form factor?

6. How many pins does the regular ATX power connector to the motherboard have? How many pins does the Enhanced ATX power connector to the motherboard have?

7. What are the three versions of the BTX form factor for motherboards?

8. Name 10 components that are contained on a motherboard.

9. What are two data bus widths used by the conventional PCI bus?

10. When people speak of bus size, to what are they specifically referring?

11. What are the four speeds of the most popular motherboards currently available on the market that support Intel processors?

12. Name the three most popular manufacturers of the system BIOS programs.

13. Which is faster, a PCI Express x16 bus or the latest AGP bus?

14. What is one reason to flash BIOS?

15. What is the easiest way to obtain the latest software to upgrade BIOS?

16. When examining a PCI expansion card, how can you tell what voltage(s) the card can use?

17. What are the four categories of cargo that are carried over a bus?

18. What bus is expected to replace AGP to support the video card in a system?

19. What is the name of the BIOS program that edits the values in CMOS RAM?

20. Describe how you can access the CMOS setup program.

>> THINKING CRITICALLY

1. Why does a motherboard sometimes support more than one system bus speed?

2. Why don't all buses on a motherboard operate at the same speed?

3. When you turn off a computer at night, it loses the date, and you must reenter it each morning. What is the problem and how do you solve it?

4. Why do you think the trend is to store configuration information on a motherboard in CMOS setup rather than by using jumpers or switches?

5. When troubleshooting a motherboard, you discover the modem port no longer works. What is the best and least expensive solution to this problem?

    a. Replace the motherboard.

    b. Disable the modem port and install a modem card in an expansion slot.

   c. Use an external modem that connects to the serial or USB port.

   d. Return the motherboard to the factory for repair.

6. A computer freezes at odd times. At first you suspect the power supply or overheating, but you have eliminated overheating and replaced the power supply without solving the problem. What do you do next?

   a. Replace the processor.

   b. Replace the motherboard.

   c. Reinstall Windows.

   d. Replace the memory modules.

   e. Flash BIOS.

>> HANDS-ON PROJECTS

PROJECT 5-1: Recognizing Motherboard Components

Obtain the manual for a motherboard. If you don't have a printed manual, use the Internet to search for a motherboard Web site, then download and print a manual. For example, try ASUS at *www.asus.com* or Abit at *www.abit.com.tw*. Look for a diagram of the motherboard components. Identify as many components from your diagram as you can. Copy the diagram and circle the components you recognize.

PROJECT 5-2: Examining the Motherboard in Detail

1. Look at the back of your computer. Without opening the case, list the ports that you believe come directly from the motherboard.

2. Remove the cover of the case, which you learned to do in Chapter 2. List the different circuit boards in the expansion slots. Was your guess correct about which ports come from the motherboard?

3. To expose the motherboard so you can identify its parts, remove all the expansion boards, as discussed in Chapter 2.

4. Draw a diagram of the motherboard and label these parts:

   ▲ Processor (include the prominent label on the processor housing)
   ▲ RAM (SIMMs, DIMMs, or RIMMs)
   ▲ CMOS battery
   ▲ Expansion slots (identify the slots as PCI, PCIe, AGP, ISA, EISA, MCA)
   ▲ Each port coming directly from the motherboard
   ▲ Power supply connections
   ▲ Hard drive data connectors and floppy drive connector

5. Draw a rectangle on the diagram to represent each bank of jumpers on the board.

6. You can complete the following activity only if you have the documentation for the motherboard: Locate the jumper on the board that erases CMOS and/or the startup password, and label this jumper on your diagram. It is often found near the battery. Some boards might have more than one, and some have none.

7. Reassemble the computer, as you learned to do in Chapter 2.

PROJECT 5-3: Saving and Restoring CMOS Settings

Save your CMOS settings on a disk, using either Norton Utilities or the shareware program contained in Cmos.zip that you can download from the Web. This chapter includes instructions in the section "Saving and Restoring CMOS Settings Using Third-Party Utility Software."

PROJECT 5-4: Inserting and Removing Motherboards

Using old or defective expansion cards and motherboards, practice inserting and removing expansion cards and motherboards.

PROJECT 5-5: Understanding Hardware Documentation

Obtain the manual for the motherboard for your PC. (If you cannot find the manual, try downloading it from the motherboard manufacturer's Web site.) List at least three functions of jumpers on the board as well as the corresponding jumper settings. List the processors that the board supports.

PROJECT 5-6: Using the Internet for Research

In this project, you will learn how useful the Internet can be for a PC support technician.

1. Using your own or a lab computer, pretend that the motherboard manual is not available and you need to know the settings for the jumpers on the motherboard. Identify the manufacturer and model of the motherboard by looking for the manufacturer name and model number stamped on the board. Research the Web site for that manufacturer. Print the jumper settings for the motherboard from the Web site.

2. Research the Web site for your motherboard and print the instructions for flashing BIOS.

3. Research the Abit Web site (*www.abit.com.tw*) and print a photograph of a motherboard that has a riser slot. Also print the photograph of the riser card that fits this slot. What is the function of the riser card?

PROJECT 5-7: Exchanging the CMOS Battery

To practice the steps for exchanging a CMOS battery, do the following:

1. Locate the CMOS battery on your computer's motherboard. What is written on top of the battery?

2. Using the Internet, find a replacement for this battery. Print the Web page showing the battery. How much does the new battery cost?

3. Enter CMOS setup on your computer. Write down any CMOS settings that are not default settings. You'll need these settings later when you reinstall the battery.

4. Turn off the PC, remove the battery, and boot the PC. What error messages appear? What is the system date and time?

5. Power down the PC, replace the battery, and boot the PC. Return CMOS settings to the way you found them.

PROJECT 5-8:   Labeling the Motherboard

Figure 5-42 shows a blank diagram of an ATX motherboard. Using what you learned in this chapter and in previous chapters, label as many components as you can.

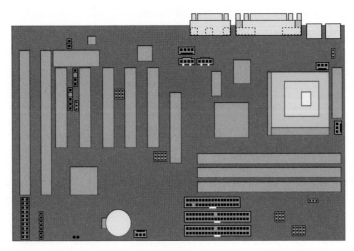

Figure 5-42   Label the motherboard

>> REAL PROBLEMS, REAL SOLUTIONS

REAL PROBLEM 5-1:   Troubleshooting an Unstable Motherboard

Mary is responsible for all the PCs used by herself and her 10 coworkers in a small real estate firm. When a problem gets too complicated for her, she packs up the PC and sends it off to a local computer store for repair. For the last couple of weeks, Adriana's computer has been hanging at odd times. Last week, Mary reinstalled Windows XP, but the problem has not gone away, so now Mary suspects a hardware problem. The next thing she wants to do is reinstall the drivers for the motherboard. To practice this skill, locate the CD that came with your motherboard and explore what's on the CD. Then install all the drivers stored on the CD that pertain to your system. Answer these questions:

1. What is the brand and model of the motherboard?

2. What chipset does this board use?

3. What troubleshooting utilities are found on the CD that came bundled with the board?

4. What manuals (most likely in PDF format) are found on the CD?

5. What drivers are stored on the CD?

6. Which of these drivers did you install on your system?

Assume you can't find the CD that came bundled with the board. Go to the Web site of the motherboard manufacturer and locate the support pages for this board. List all the utilities, documentation, and drivers for this board found on the Web site.

REAL PROBLEM 5-2: Selecting a Replacement Motherboard

When a motherboard fails, you can select and buy a new board to replace it. Suppose the motherboard used in Real Problem 5-1 has failed and you want to buy a replacement and keep your repair costs to a minimum. Try to find a replacement motherboard on the Internet that can use the same case, power supply, processor, memory, and expansion cards as your current system. If you cannot find a good match, what other components might have to be replaced (for example, the processor or memory)? What is the total cost of the repair? Print Web pages showing what you need to purchase.

Upgrading Memory

In earlier chapters, we talked about several important hardware components, how they work, and how to support them. In this chapter, we look at another component, memory, and examine the different memory technologies and how to upgrade memory. Memory technologies have evolved over the years. When you support an assortment of desktop and notebook computers, you'll be amazed at all the different variations of memory modules used in newer computers and older computers still in use. A simple problem of replacing a bad memory module can become a complex research project if you don't have a good grasp of current and past memory technologies. The first part of the chapter is devoted to studying all these technologies. Then we look at how to upgrade memory. Adding more memory to a system can sometimes greatly improve performance. Finally, you'll learn how to deal with problems with memory.

RAM TECHNOLOGIES

A+ ESS
1.1

Recall that memory temporarily holds data and instructions as the CPU processes them and that computer memory is divided into two categories, ROM (read-only memory) and RAM (random access memory). ROM retains its data when the PCI is turned off, but RAM loses all its data. In Chapter 4, you learned about static RAM (SRAM) contained within the processor housing and sometimes embedded on the motherboard. In Chapter 5, you learned about ROM that is contained in the firmware chip on the motherboard where it holds the ROM BIOS. In this chapter, we focus on dynamic RAM (DRAM). Let's begin by summarizing what has already been covered in earlier chapters about SRAM and DRAM:

◢ In Chapter 1, you learned that most RAM is stored on the motherboard in modules called DIMMs, RIMMs, or SIMMs. An example of a DIMM is shown in Figure 6-1.

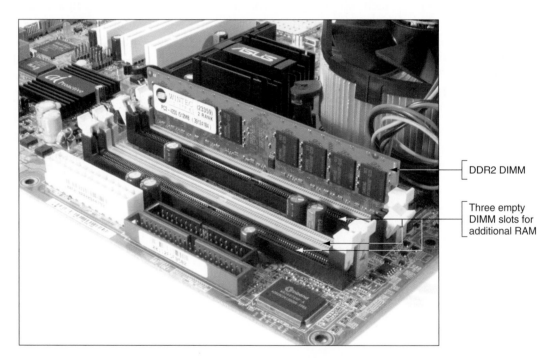

DDR2 DIMM

Three empty DIMM slots for additional RAM

Figure 6-1   DRAM on most motherboards today is stored on DIMMs

◢ In Chapter 4, it was explained there can be two types of RAM: dynamic RAM (DRAM) and static RAM (SRAM). SRAM is faster than DRAM because SRAM does not lose its data as quickly as does DRAM and does not have to be refreshed as often.

◢ In Chapter 4, you learned that most processors today contain a memory cache inside the processor housing used to speed up memory access. This cache is made of SRAM because SRAM is faster than DRAM. Some motherboards have a small SRAM cache embedded on the motherboard separate from the cache inside the processor housing.

In earlier PCs, main memory was stored on the motherboard as single, socketed chips, but today DRAM is always stored in either DIMM, RIMM, or SIMM modules, which plug directly into the motherboard. The major differences among these modules are the width of the data path that each type of module accommodates and the way data moves from the system bus to the module. Figure 6-2 shows some examples of memory modules.

> **Notes**
>
> You might be interested in knowing why SRAM doesn't have to be refreshed the way DRAM does. SRAM and DRAM are both made of transistors, which are switches, and a transistor switch can stay in place as long as it has voltage available. However, DRAM transistor switches are charged by capacitors, which must be recharged, and SRAM transistors don't use capacitors. SRAM is more expensive than DRAM; therefore, most computers have a little SRAM and a lot of DRAM.

Description of Module	Example
240-pin DDR2 DIMM is currently the fastest memory. Can support dual channels or be installed as a single DIMM. Has one notch near the center of the edge connector.	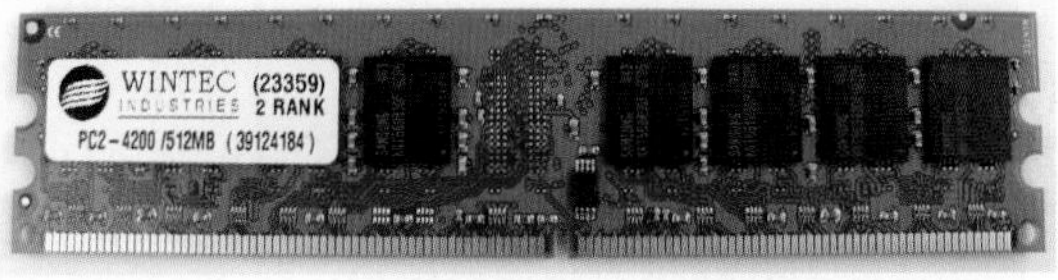
184-pin DDR DIMM can support dual channeling or be installed as single DIMMs. Has one offset notch.	
168-pin SDR DIMM has two notches that are positioned on the edge connector to indicate buffered, registered, unbuffered, and voltage requirements.	
RIMM has 184 pins and two notches near the center of the edge connector.	
72-pin SIMM must be installed two modules to a bank of memory.	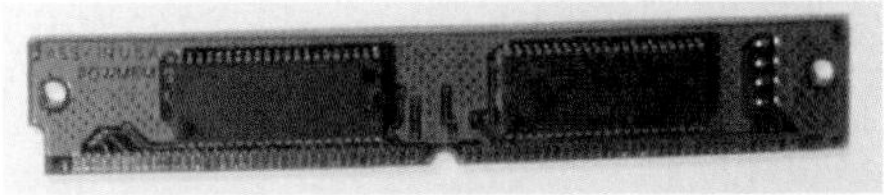
30-pin SIMM must be installed four modules to a bank of memory.	

Figure 6-2 Types of memory modules

Older DRAM memory technologies operated asynchronously with the system bus, but newer DRAM memory types operate synchronously. To understand the difference between asynchronous and synchronous memory, consider this analogy: Children are jumping rope with a long rope, and one child on each end is turning the rope. A child who cannot keep in step with the turning rope can only run through on a single pass and must come back around to make another pass. A child who can keep in step with the rope can run into the center and jump awhile, until he is tired and runs out. Which child performs the most rope-jumping cycles in a given amount of time? The one who keeps in step with the rope. Similarly, synchronous memory retrieves data faster than asynchronous memory, because it keeps time with the system clock.

Table 6-1 summarizes DRAM technologies, old and new. How these DRAM technologies are used with SIMMs, DIMMs, and RIMMs is discussed in more detail in the following sections.

Technology	Description	Used with
Old Technologies		
Conventional	Used with earlier PCs but currently not available.	◢ 30-pin SIMM
Fast page memory (FPM)	Improved access time over conventional memory. FPM is seldom seen today.	◢ 30-pin or 72-pin SIMM ◢ 168-pin DIMM
Extended data out (EDO)	Refined version of FPM that speeds up access time. Might still see it on older motherboards.	◢ 72-pin SIMM ◢ 168-pin DIMM
Burst EDO (BEDO)	Refined version of EDO that significantly improved access time over EDO. Seldom seen today because Intel chose not to support it.	◢ 72-pin SIMM ◢ 168-pin DIMM
Synchronous DRAM (SDRAM)	SDRAM runs in sync with the system clock and is rated by clock speed, whereas earlier types of memory run independently of (and slower than) the system clock.	◢ 66/100/133/150 MHz, 168-pin DIMM ◢ 66/100/133 MHz, 144-pin SO-DIMM
Current Technologies		
DDR (Double-Data Rate) SDRAM	A faster version of SDRAM.	◢ 184-pin DIMM, up to 500 MHz ◢ 200-pin SO-DIMM, up to 400 MHz
Rambus DRAM (RDRAM)	RDRAM is housed on a RIMM, uses a faster system bus (800 MHz or 1066 MHz), and can use a 16- or 32-bit data path.	◢ 184-pin or 168-pin RIMM with 16-bit single channel ◢ 232-pin RIMM with 32-bit dual channel
DDR2	Faster than DDR and uses less power.	◢ 240-pin DIMM up to 2 GB size ◢ 214-pin SO-DIMM up to 1 GB size ◢ 244-pin Mini-DIMM
Dual Channeling	A technique whereby the memory controller interleaves access to DIMM pairs.	◢ Used by DDR and DDR2 DIMMs

Table 6-1 DRAM memory technologies

A+ ESS
1.1

The goal of each new technology is increasing overall throughput while retaining accuracy. The older the motherboard, the older the memory technology it can use, so as a PC technician, you must be familiar with older technologies even though the boards sold today only use the latest memory technology.

> **Notes**
>
> Smaller versions of DIMMs and RIMMs, called SO-DIMMs and SO-RIMMs, are used in notebook computers. (SO stands for "small outline.") MicroDIMMs are used on subnotebook computers and are smaller than SO-DIMMs. You'll learn more about these memory modules and how to upgrade memory in notebooks in Chapter 11.

SIMM TECHNOLOGIES

SIMMs have a 32-bit data path and are rated by speed, measured in nanoseconds (ns). Common SIMM speeds are 60, 70, or 80 ns. This speed is a measure of access time, which is the time it takes for the processor to access the data stored on a SIMM. The access time includes the time it takes for the processor to request the data, for the memory controller to locate the data on the SIMM and place the data on the memory bus, for the processor to read the data off the bus, and for the memory controller to refresh the memory chip on the SIMM. Note that an access time of 60 ns is faster than an access time of 70 ns. Therefore, the smaller the speed rating is, the faster the chip.

> **Notes**
>
> **EDO (extended data out)** was used on 72-pin SIMMs on motherboards rated at about 33 to 75 MHz. EDO was also used on earlier DIMMs and video memory and often provides on-board RAM on various expansion boards.

DIMM TECHNOLOGIES

A+ ESS
1.1

Next came DIMM technologies, which have a 64-bit data path. (Some early DIMMs had a 128-bit data path, but they're now obsolete.) A DIMM (dual inline memory module) is called that because it has independent pins on opposite sides of the module. SIMMs have pins on both sides of the module, too, but with a SIMM, each pin pair is tied together into a single contact. A DIMM can have memory chips on one side (single-sided) or both sides (double-sided) of the module.

DIMMs are rated by speed and the amount of memory they hold. DIMMs have 168, 184, or 240 pins on the edge connector of the board and hold from 8 MB to 2 GB of RAM. The early DIMMs used EDO (168 pins) or burst EDO (BEDO), which is a refined version of EDO. BEDO was faster than EDO, but never gained a market share because Intel chose not to support it. BEDO and EDO DIMMs have two notches on the edge connector and run at constant speeds independent of the system bus speed.

> **A+ Exam Tip**
>
> The A+ Essentials exam expects you to know the purposes and characteristics of the following memory technologies: DRAM, SRAM, SDRAM, DDR, DDR2, and Rambus.

The first DIMM to run synchronized with the system clock is synchronous DRAM (SDRAM), which has two notches, and uses 168 pins. An early version of SDRAM is SyncLink SDRAM (SLDRAM), which was never embraced by the industry.

DIMMs have undergone several improvements. Next, we'll look at these DIMM technologies used to improve the performance and reliability of DIMMs. They include DDR, DDR2, buffered, registered, and dual channel DIMMs.

DDR AND DDR2 DIMMS

Current DIMM technologies are DDR and DDR2. Double Data Rate SDRAM (DDR SDRAM or SDRAM II) is an improved version of SDRAM. When DDR first came out, it was called DDR SDRAM or SDRAM II. DDR runs twice as fast as regular SDRAM, has one notch, and uses 184 pins. Instead of processing data for each beat of the system clock, as regular SDRAM does, it processes data when the beat rises and again when it falls, doubling the data rate of memory. If a motherboard runs at 200 MHz, DDR memory runs at 400 MHz. A consortium of 20 major computer manufacturers supports DDR. It is an open standard, meaning that its users pay no royalties.

After DDR SDRAM was introduced, regular SDRAM became known as Single Data Rate SDRAM (SDR SDRAM). The latest SDRAM is DDR2 SDRAM, which is faster than DDR, uses less power, and has a 240-pin DIMM and a 64-bit data path.

BUFFERED AND REGISTERED DIMMS

Buffers and registers hold data and amplify a signal just before the data is written to the module. Some DIMMs use buffers, some use registers, and some use neither. If a DIMM uses buffers, it's called a buffered DIMM; if it uses registers, it's called a registered DIMM. If a memory module doesn't support registers or buffers, it's always referred to as an unbuffered DIMM.

Older EDO and FPM modules used buffers, which did not degrade performance. SDRAM modules use registers, which do reduce performance somewhat but make it possible for the motherboard to support a larger number of modules. A fully buffered DIMM (FB-DIMM) uses an advanced buffering technique that makes it possible for servers to support a large number of DIMMs.

Notches on memory modules are positioned to identify the technologies that the module supports. In Figure 6-3, the position of the notch on the left identifies the module as registered (RFU), buffered, or unbuffered memory. The notch on the right identifies the voltage used by the module. The position of each notch not only helps identify the type of module, but also prevents the wrong kind of module from being used on a motherboard.

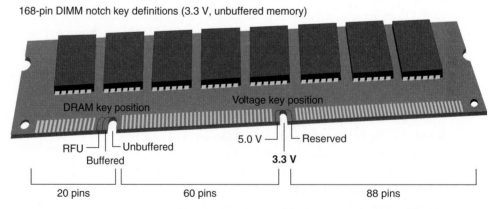

Figure 6-3   The positions of two notches on a SDRAM DIMM identify the type of DIMM and the voltage requirement and also prevent the wrong type from being installed on the motherboard

DUAL CHANNELING

To improve overall memory performance, a motherboard can use dual channels with either DDR or DDR2 DIMMs. With dual channels, the memory controller can communicate with two DIMMs at the same time, effectively doubling the speed of memory access.

Figure 6-4 shows how dual channeling works on a motherboard with four DIMM slots. The board has two channels, Channel A and Channel B. Each channel can implement dual channeling. With dual channeling, the two DIMMs installed in the two slots labeled Channel A can be accessed at the same time. If two more DIMMs are installed in Channel B slots, they can be accessed at the same time. Two memory buses connect to DIMM slots, and each bus uses the normal 64-bit data path of the system bus, making an effective data path of 128 bits.

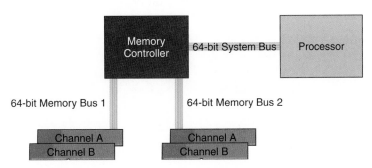

Figure 6-4 Using dual channels, the memory controller can read from two DIMMs at the same time

For dual channeling to work, the pair of DIMMs in a channel must be equally matched in size, speed, and features, and it is recommended they come from the same manufacturer. Suppose two matching DIMMs are installed in Channel A slots. The memory controller reads from both DIMMs at the same time using the two 64-bit memory buses. The controller then places data on the 64-bit system bus to the processor, interleaving between the two buses of Channel A.

A motherboard using dual channeling configuration is shown in Figure 6-1. The two DIMM slots for Channel A are yellow, and the two Channel B slots are black. To accomplish dual channeling, matching DIMMs must be installed in the yellow slots, and, if either of the black slots are used, they, too, must have a matching pair of two DIMMs, although this pair does not have to match the first pair. That's because Channel A runs independently of Channel B. If the two DIMM slots of a channel are not populated with matching pairs of DIMMs, then the motherboard reverts to single channeling. You'll see an example of motherboard documentation using dual channeling later in the chapter.

RIMM TECHNOLOGIES

Direct Rambus DRAM (sometimes called RDRAM or Direct RDRAM or simply Rambus) is named after Rambus, Inc., the company that developed it. RDRAM uses RIMM memory modules. A few years back, it was thought that RIMM memory modules might replace or at least compete with the DIMM market, but this has not been the case. RIMMs are expensive and now slower than current DIMMs. Thus, they are quickly becoming a legacy memory (no pun intended).

> **Tip**
>
> RDRAM data can travel on a 16- or 32-bit data path. RDRAM works like a packeted network, not a traditional system bus, and can run at internal speeds of 800 MHz to 1600 MHz.

With RIMMs, each memory slot on the motherboard must be filled to maintain continuity throughout all slots. If a slot does not hold a RIMM, it must hold a placeholder module called a **C-RIMM** (Continuity RIMM) to ensure continuity throughout all slots. The C-RIMM contains no memory chips (see Figure 6-5).

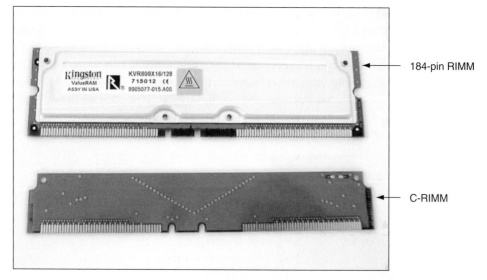

184-pin RIMM

C-RIMM

Figure 6-5 A C-RIMM or RIMM must be installed in every RIMM slot on a motherboard

Concurrent RDRAM, an earlier version of Rambus memory, is not as fast as Direct RDRAM. Rambus designed the RDRAM technology but does not actually manufacture RIMMs: It licenses the technology to memory manufacturers. Because these manufacturers must pay licensing fees to use RDRAM, the industry did not embrace RIMMs and turned to improving and advancing DIMM technologies.

ERROR CHECKING AND PARITY

In older machines, RAM existed as individual chips socketed to the motherboard in banks or rows of nine chips each. A **bank** is an area on the motherboard that holds the minimum number of memory chips or memory modules that must work together as a unit. Because the data path of earlier memory buses was eight bits, eight memory chips were required for the data path. Each bank held one byte by storing one bit in each chip, with the ninth chip holding a parity bit (see Figure 6-6). On older PCs, the parity chip was separated slightly from the other eight chips. **Parity** refers to an error-checking procedure in which either every byte has an even number of ones or every byte has an odd number of ones. The use of a parity bit means that every byte occupies nine rather than eight bits.

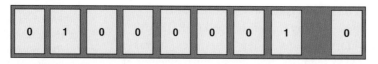

| 0 | 1 | 0 | 0 | 0 | 0 | 0 | 1 | 0 |

Figure 6-6 Eight chips and a parity chip hold nine bits that represent the letter A in ASCII with even parity

Notes

For more information on 8-bit ASCII binary codes assigned to letters, see "ASCII Character Set and Ansi.sys," in the online content. For more information about the binary number system, see "The Hexadecimal Number System and Memory Addressing."

**A+ ESS
1.1**

Parity is a method of testing the integrity of the bits stored in RAM or some secondary medium, or testing the integrity of bits sent over a communications device. When data is written to RAM, the computer calculates how many ON bits (binary 1) are in the eight bits of a byte. If the computer uses odd parity, it makes the ninth or parity bit either a 1 or a 0, to make the number of ones in the nine bits odd. If it uses even parity, the computer makes the parity bit a 1 or a 0 to make the number of ones in the nine bits even.

Later, when the byte is read back, the computer checks the odd or even state. If the number of bits is not an odd number for odd parity or an even number for even parity, a parity error occurs. A parity error always causes the system to halt. On the screen, you see the error message "Parity Error 1" or "Parity Error 2" or a similar error message about parity. Parity Error 1 is a parity error on the motherboard; Parity Error 2 is a parity error on an expansion board.

Older DRAM memory used parity checking, but today's memory uses an altogether new method of error checking called **ECC (error-correcting code)** that can detect and correct an error in a single bit. Memory modules today are either ECC or non-ECC, and there are some improvements in ECC that ECC memory might use. The first ECC method can detect and correct an error in one bit of the byte. Newer ECC methods can detect an error in two bits but cannot correct these double-bit errors.

Some SDRAM, DDR, DDR2, and RIMM memory modules support ECC. DIMMs that support ECC have an odd number of chips on the module (the odd chip is the ECC chip), whereas a DIMM normally has only an even number of chips. A DIMM is normally a 64-bit module, but ECC makes it a 71- or 72-bit module; the extra 7 or 8 bits are used to verify the integrity of every 8 bits stored on the module and to correct any error, when possible. ECC memory costs more than non-ECC memory, but it is more reliable and is generally used on servers.

As with most other memory technologies discussed in this chapter, when buying memory to add to a motherboard, match the type of memory to the type the board supports. To see if your motherboard supports parity or ECC memory, look for the ability to enable or disable the feature in CMOS setup, or check the motherboard documentation.

> **A+ Exam Tip**
>
> The A+ Essentials exam expects you to know that parity memory uses 9 bits (8 bits for data and 1 bit for parity). You also need to be familiar with ECC and non-ECC memory technologies.

> **Notes**
>
> RAM chips that have become undependable and cannot hold data reliably can cause parity errors. Sometimes this happens when chips overheat or power falters.

> **Tip**
>
> Some older motherboards support parity memory, and some use only nonparity memory. If a SIMM has an odd number of chips, it is likely **parity memory**; an even number of chips usually indicates **nonparity memory**.

CAS LATENCY AND RAS LATENCY

Two other memory features are **CAS Latency** (CAS stands for "column access strobe") and **RAS Latency** (RAS stands for "row access strobe"), which are two ways of measuring speed. Both features refer to the number of clock cycles it takes to write or read a column or row of data off a memory module. Times to read or write data are two or three clock cycles.

> **Notes**
>
> In memory ads, CAS Latency is sometimes written as CL, and RAS Latency might be written as RL.

Tip

When selecting memory, use the memory type that the motherboard manufacturer recommends.

CAS Latency is used more than RAS Latency. CL2 (CAS Latency 2) is a little faster than CL3 (CAS Latency 3). Ads for memory modules sometimes give the CAS Latency value within a series of timing numbers, such as 5-5-5-15. The first value is CAS Latency, which means the module is CL5. The second value is RAS Latency.

TIN OR GOLD LEADS

On a motherboard, the connectors inside the memory slots are made of tin or gold, as are the edge connectors on the memory modules. It used to be that all memory sockets were made of gold, but now most are made of tin to reduce cost. You should match tin leads to tin connectors and gold leads to gold connectors to prevent a chemical reaction between the two metals, which can cause corrosion. Corrosion can create intermittent memory errors and even make the PC unable to boot.

MEMORY SPEEDS

Several factors contribute to how fast memory runs, and speeds are measured in different ways. Measurements of speed include nanoseconds, MHz, PC rating, CAS Latency, and RAS Latency. Technologies that might affect speed include ECC, parity memory, dual channeling, and buffering. Recall that a SIMM's speed is measured in nanoseconds.

SDRAM, DDR, DDR2, and RIMM are measured in MHz. A DDR module is often described with its speed in the name, such as DDR266 for a DDR running at 266 MHz, or DDR333 for a DDR running at 333 MHz. Sometimes a DIMM or RIMM speed is measured in a PC rating. A PC rating is a measure of the total bandwidth of data moving between the module and the CPU. To understand PC ratings, let's take an example of a DDR DIMM module that runs at 266 MHz (DDR266). The module has a 64-bit (8 bytes) data path. Therefore, the transfer rate is 8 bytes multiplied by 266 MHz, which yields 2128 MB/second. This value equates to the PC rating of PC2100 for a DDR266 DIMM. For DDR2 memory, the PC rating is sometimes written as PC2. Current PC ratings are PC1600 (200 MHz), PC2100 (266 MHz), PC2700 (333 MHz), PC3200 (400 MHz), PC 4000 (500 MHz), PC 4200 (533 MHz), PC 5300 (667 MHz), and PC 6400 (800 MHz).

Factors to consider when looking at the overall speed of memory are listed below:

▲ *How much RAM is installed.* The more memory there is, the faster the system. Generally use as much memory in a system as it can support and you can afford.

▲ *The memory technology used.* DDR2 is faster than DDR, and DDR is faster than SDR SDRAM. Where required by the motherboard, buffered or registered memory can improve performance. For all these technologies, use what the board supports.

▲ *The speed of memory in ns, MHz, or PC rating.* Use the fastest memory the motherboard supports. If you install modules of different speeds in the same system, the system will run at the slowest speed or might become unstable. Know that most computer ads today give speeds in MHz or PC rating, but some ads give both values.

▲ *ECC/parity or non-ECC/nonparity.* Non-ECC or nonparity is faster and less expensive. Use what the board supports.

A+ ESS
1.1

▲ *CL or RL rating.* The lower the better. Use what the board supports, although most boards don't specify a particular CL rating.

▲ *Dual channeling.* To use this motherboard feature, install matching pairs of DIMMs from the same manufacturer in each pair of channel slots.

HOW TO UPGRADE MEMORY

A+
220-602
1.1

To upgrade memory means to add more RAM to a computer. Adding more RAM might solve a problem with slow performance, applications refusing to load, or an unstable system. When Windows does not have adequate memory to perform an operation, it gives an "Insufficient memory" error.

When first purchased, many computers have empty slots on the motherboard, allowing you to add DIMMs or RIMMs to increase the amount of RAM, and sometimes memory goes bad and must be replaced. In this section, we talk about how to select, purchase, and install memory.

HOW MUCH AND WHAT KIND OF MEMORY TO BUY

When you add more memory to your computer, ask yourself these questions:

▲ How much memory do I need?
▲ How much RAM is currently installed in my system?
▲ How many and what kind of memory modules are currently installed on my motherboard?
▲ How much and what kind of memory can I fit on my motherboard?
▲ How do I select and purchase the right memory for my upgrade?

All these questions are answered in the following sections.

HOW MUCH MEMORY DO I NEED?

With the demands today's software places on memory, the answer is probably, "All you can get." The minimum requirement for Windows 2000/XP is 64 MB of RAM to install (not necessarily run) the OS. Windows 95 and Windows 98 require 16 MB to 32 MB of memory. But for adequate performance, install 128 MB into a Windows 9x/Me system and 256 MB or more into a Windows 2000/XP system. I have 512 MB of RAM installed on my Windows XP desktop PC, which gives me good performance.

APPLYING | CONCEPTS   HOW MUCH MEMORY IS CURRENTLY INSTALLED?

To determine how much memory your Windows system has, you can use the Properties window of My Computer or you can use the System Information window, which gives more useful information. To use System Information, in the Run dialog box, type **Msinfo32** and press **Enter**. The System Information window shown in Figure 6-7 reports the total and available amounts of physical and virtual memory. (Virtual memory is space on the hard drive that the OS can use as overflow memory.)

If the amounts of available physical and virtual memory are low and your system is sluggish, it's a good indication you need to upgrade memory.

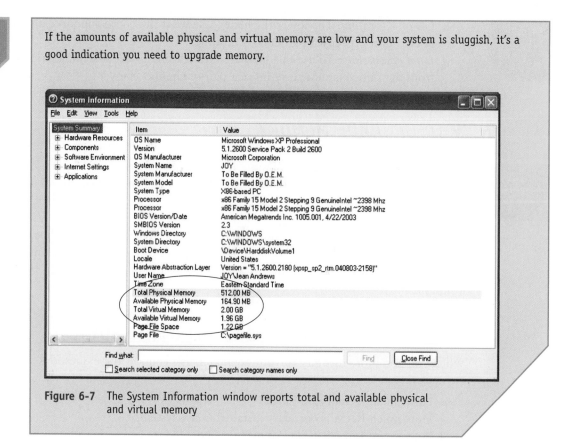

Figure 6-7   The System Information window reports total and available physical and virtual memory

HOW MANY AND WHAT KIND OF MEMORY MODULES ARE CURRENTLY INSTALLED?

The next step to upgrading memory is to determine what type of memory the motherboard is currently using and how many memory slots are used. In this section, we also take into consideration you might be dealing with a motherboard that has no memory currently installed. If the board already has memory installed, you want to do your best to match the new memory with whatever is already installed. To learn what memory is already installed, do the following:

- ◢ Open the case and look at the memory slots. How many slots do you have? How many are filled? Remove each module from its slot and look on it for imprinted type, size, and speed. For example, a module might say "PC2-4200/512MB." The PC2 tells you the memory is DDR2, the 4200 is the PC rating and tells you the speed, and the 512MB is the size. This is not enough information to know exactly what memory to purchase, but it's a start.
- ◢ Examine the module for the physical size and position of the notches. Compare the notch positions to those in Figures 6-2 and 6-3.
- ◢ Read your motherboard documentation. If the documentation is not clear (and some are not) or you don't have the documentation, look on the motherboard for the imprinted manufacturer and model (see Figure 6-8). With this information, you can search a good memory Web site such as Kingston (*www.kingston.com*) or Crucial (*www.crucial.com*), which can tell you what memory this board supports.
- ◢ If you still have not identified the memory type, you can take the motherboard and the old memory modules to a good computer parts store and they should be able to match it for you.

A+
220-602
1.1

— Model

— Manufacturer

Figure 6-8 Look for the manufacturer and model of a motherboard imprinted somewhere on the board

HOW MUCH AND WHAT KIND OF MEMORY CAN FIT ON MY MOTHERBOARD?

Now that you know what memory is already installed, you're ready to decide how much and what kind of memory modules you can add to the board. Keep in mind that if all memory slots are full, sometimes you can take out small-capacity modules and replace them with larger-capacity modules, but you can only use the type, size, and speed of modules that the board is designed to support. Also, if you must discard existing modules, the price of the upgrade increases.

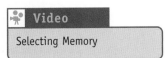

To know how much memory your motherboard can physically hold, read the documentation that comes with the board. Not all sizes of memory modules fit on any one computer. You need to use the right number of SIMMs, DIMMs, or RIMMs with the right amount of memory on each module to fit the memory banks on your motherboard. Next, let's look at what to consider when deciding how many and what kind of SIMMs, DIMMs, or RIMMs to add to a system.

30-Pin SIMMs

On older motherboards, 30-pin SIMMs are installed in groups of four. SIMMs in each group or bank must be the same type and size. See the motherboard documentation for the exact combination of SIMMs in each bank that the board can support.

72-Pin SIMMs

To accommodate a 64-bit system bus data path, 72-pin SIMMs have a 32-bit data path and are installed in groups or banks of two. Most older motherboards that use these SIMMs have one to three banks that can be filled with two, four, or six SIMMs. The two SIMMs in each bank must match in size and speed. See the motherboard documentation for the sizes and type of SIMMs the board supports.

RIMM Modules

**A+
220-602
1.1**

When you purchase a system using RIMMs, all RIMM slots will be filled with either RIMMs or C-RIMMs. When you upgrade, you replace one or more C-RIMMs with RIMMs. Match the new RIMMs with those already on the motherboard, following the recommendations of the motherboard documentation.

Let's look at one example of a RIMM configuration. The current system has 256 MB installed RAM. The motherboard is an Intel D850MV board, and it's shown in Figure 1-9 of Chapter 1. If you look carefully at that photo, you can see there are four RIMM slots. The first two slots are populated with RIMMs and the second two slots hold C-RIMMs. The label on one of the RIMMs is shown in Figure 6-9. Before we interpret this rather cryptic label, let's examine the motherboard documentation concerning upgrading RAM.

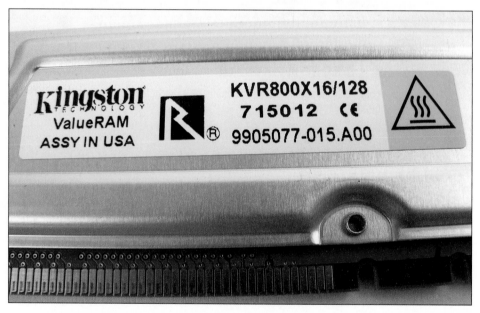

Figure 6-9   Use the label on this RIMM to identify its features

Table 6-2 shows the table found in the motherboard manual to be used to decide how to upgrade RAM. The column headings in the table are not as clear as they need to be, but I've written them as they are written in the motherboard documentation so you can learn to understand this kind of cryptic documentation. In the table, a chip on a RIMM module is called a component (sometimes it's also called a device). The first column tells us the amount of memory stored on one component (one chip). This value is called the density of the RIMM, which is 128 Mb (megabits) or 256 Mb (megabits). If you multiply the density times the number of components on a RIMM, you get the total amount of memory on one RIMM. The remaining columns in the table list the number of components per RIMM supported by this board, which are 4, 6, 8, 12, or 16 components per RIMM.

A+
220-602
1.1

Rambus Technology	Capacity with 4 DRAM Components per RIMM	Capacity with 6 DRAM Components per RIMM	Capacity with 8 DRAM Components per RIMM	Capacity with 12 DRAM Components per RIMM	Capacity with 16 DRAM Components per RIMM
128/144 Mb	64 MB	96 MB	128 MB	192 MB	256 MB
256/288 Mb	128 MB	192 MB	256 MB	384 MB	512 MB

Table 6-2 One motherboard's memory configurations using RIMMs

Let's look at one sample calculation from the table. Look in the first row of the first column and read the value 128 Mb. The second column shows the amount of memory for RIMMs with four devices. To get that amount, multiply 128 Mb by 4, which yields 512 Mb (megabits). Divide that number by 8 to convert the value to megabytes, which gives 64 MB of RAM on this RIMM.

One last item in the table needs explaining. This board supports ECC or non-ECC memory, so that's why there are two values in the first column. For example, in the first row the density is stated as 128/144 Mb. The second number, 144 Mb, applies to the ECC version of a non-ECC 128-Mb chip. In the second row, the 288-Mb RIMM is the ECC version of the 256-Mb RIMM. The extra bits are used for error correcting. A data path on a RIMM is 16 bits without ECC and 18 bits with ECC. The extra 2 bits are used for error correcting. For a 128 Mb component, an additional 16 Mb are required for error correcting.

This motherboard has two memory banks with two slots in each bank. The board requires that the RIMMs in a bank must match in size and density. As for speed, the board supports PC600 or PC800 RDRAM, which for a RIMM refers to the speeds of 600 MHz or 800 MHz. All RIMMs installed must run at the same speed. For ECC to work, all RIMMs installed must support ECC.

With this information in hand, let's look back at Figure 6-9 and interpret the label on this RIMM. The important information for us is "800X16/128." The value 128 is the size of the RIMM, 128 MB. The value 800 is the speed, 800 MHz. The value X16 tells us this RIMM is a non-ECC RIMM. (If it had been ECC compliant, the value would have been X18.)

Now we know exactly what kind of RIMM to buy for our upgrade. The RIMMs in the second bank don't have to match in size or density with the RIMMs in the first bank, but they do need to match in speed. To upgrade this system to 512 MB, we'll need to purchase two non-ECC, 800 MHz RIMMs that each contain 128 MB of RAM. It's also best to match the manufacturer and buy Kingston modules.

DIMM Modules

A+ ESS
1.1

Today's DIMMs have a 64-bit data path and can thus be installed as a single module rather than in pairs. Pentium motherboards that use single-sided DIMM modules use only one socket to a bank, because the DIMM module accommodates a data path of 64 bits. Single-sided DIMMs come in sizes of 8, 16, 32, 64, and 128 MB, and double-sided DIMMs come in sizes of 32, 64, 128, 256, and 512 MB, 1 GB, and 2 GB. Single-sided DIMMs contain one 64-bit bank, and double-sided DIMMs contain two 64-bit banks, one on each side of the DIMM. A DIMM slot can therefore hold two banks, one on each side of a double-sided DIMM.

Let's look at an example of a board that supports single-sided DIMMs. The Pentium motherboard uses 168-pin DIMM modules, and the documentation says to use unbuffered,

> **A+ Exam Tip**
>
> The A+ Essentials exam expects you to know how to upgrade a system using DIMMs or RIMMs. SIMMs are not covered on the exam.

3.3-V, PC100 DIMM SDRAM modules. The PC100 means that the modules should be rated to work with a motherboard that runs at 100 MHz. You can choose to use ECC modules. If you choose not to, CMOS setup should show the feature disabled. Three DIMM sockets are on the board, and each socket represents one bank. Figure 6-10 shows the possible combinations of DIMMs that can be installed in these sockets.

DIMM Location	168-Pin DIMM		Total Memory
Socket 1 (Rows 0 & 1)	SDRAM 8, 16, 32, 64, 128, 256 MB	×1	
Socket 2 (Rows 2 & 3)	SDRAM 8, 16, 32, 64, 128, 256 MB	×1	
Socket 3 (Rows 4 & 5)	SDRAM 8, 16, 32, 64, 128, 256 MB	×1	
	Total System Memory (Max 768 MB)	=	

Figure 6-10 This table is part of the motherboard documentation and is used to show possible DIMM sizes and calculate total memory on the motherboard

Let's look at another example of a DIMM installation. The motherboard is the Asus P4P800 shown in Chapter 4, Figure 4-30. The board allows you to use three different speeds of DDR DIMMs in one to four sockets on the board. The board supports dual channeling. Looking carefully at the photo in Figure 5-30, you can see two blue memory sockets and two black sockets. The two blue sockets use one channel and the two black sockets use a different channel. For dual channeling to work, matching DIMMs must be installed in the two blue sockets. If two DIMMs are installed in the two black sockets, they must match each other.

This board supports up to 4 GB of unbuffered 184-pin non-ECC memory running at PC3200, PC2700, or PC2100. The documentation says the system bus can run at 800 MHz, 533 MHz, or 400 MHz, depending on the speed of the processor installed. Therefore, the speed of the processor determines the system bus speed, which determines the speed of memory modules you can install.

Figure 6-11 outlines the possible configurations of these DIMM modules, showing that you can install one, two, or four DIMMs and which sockets should hold these DIMMs. To take advantage of dual channeling on this motherboard, you must populate the sockets according to Figure 6-11, so that identical DIMM pairs are working together in DIMM_A1 and DIMM_B1 sockets (the blue sockets), and another pair can work together in DIMM_A2 and DIMM_B2 sockets (the black sockets).

Mode		Sockets			
		DIMM_A1	DIMM_A2	DIMM_B1	DIMM_B2
Single-channel	(1)	Populated	—	—	—
	(2)	—	Populated	—	—
	(3)	—	—	Populated	—
	(4)	—	—	—	Populated
Dual-channel*	(1)	Populated	—	Populated	—
	(2)	—	Populated	—	Populated
	(3)	Populated	Populated	Populated	Populated

Figure 6-11 Motherboard documentation shows that one, two, or four DIMMs can be installed

This motherboard has two installed DDR DIMMs. The label on one of these DIMMs is shown in Figure 6-12. The important items on this label are the size (256 MB), the speed (400 MHz or 3200 PC rating), and the CAS Latency (CL3). With this information and

A+ ESS
1.1

A+
220-602
1.1

knowledge about what the board can support, we are now ready to select and buy the memory for the upgrade. For example, if you decide to upgrade the system to 1 GB of memory, you would buy two DDR, 400 MHz, CL3 DIMMs that support dual channeling. For best results, you need to also match the manufacturer and buy Elixir memory.

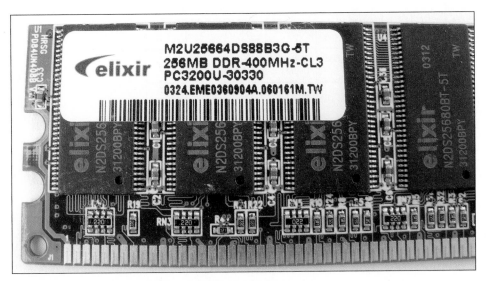

Figure 6-12 Use the label on this DIMM to identify its features

Let's look at two examples of boards that use a combination of single-sided and double-sided DIMMs. The Intel CC820 motherboard has two DIMM slots that can use two single-sided DIMMs, two double-sided DIMMs, or one single-sided and one double-sided DIMM. In the last case, the single-sided DIMM must be in the first slot. Figure 6-13 shows part of the board's documentation explaining how these DIMMs can be installed.

Types of DIMMs to be installed	Slot 0	Slot 1
One DIMM	DIMM	Empty
Two DIMMs - Same size, same number of sides (both single-sided or both double-sided)	Either DIMM	Either DIMM
Two DIMMs - Different sizes	Larger DIMM	Smaller DIMM
Two DIMMs - Same size, one is single-sided and one is double-sided	Single-sided DIMM	Double-sided DIMM

Figure 6-13 The Intel CC820 motherboard can use a combination of single-sided and double-sided DIMMs

This next example is a little more complicated. The Abit ZM6 board has three DIMM slots, and the chipset can support up to four 64-bit banks. Using three slots to fill four banks is accomplished by installing a combination of single-sided and double-sided DIMMs. Figure 6-14 shows how this can be done, considering that a single-sided DIMM uses only one bank, but a double-sided DIMM uses two banks of the four available.

As you can see, the motherboard documentation is essential when selecting memory. If you can't find the motherboard manual, look on the motherboard manufacturer's Web site.

Bank 1	Bank 2	Bank 3	Bank 4	Slots used
Single-sided DIMM				1
Double-sided DIMM				1
Single-sided DIMM	Single-sided DIMM			2
Single-sided DIMM	Single-sided DIMM	Single-sided DIMM		3
Double-sided DIMM		Single-sided DIMM		2
Double-sided DIMM		Double-sided DIMM		2
Double-sided DIMM		Single-sided DIMM	Single-sided DIMM	3

Figure 6-14 How three DIMM slots can use four 64-bit memory banks supported by a motherboard chipset

HOW DO I SELECT AND PURCHASE THE RIGHT MEMORY?

You're now ready to make the purchase. As you select your memory, you might find it difficult to find an exact match to SIMMs, DIMMs, or RIMMs already installed on the board. If necessary, here are some compromises you can make:

◢ When matching memory, for best results, also match the module manufacturer. But in a pinch, you can try using memory from two different manufacturers.

◢ Because SIMMs are so outdated, your choices will be slim. When buying SIMMs, you should match speed; although if you have to buy a different speed, know that all SIMMs installed will run at the speed of the slowest SIMM. Always put the slower SIMMs in the first bank.

Now let's look at how to select top-quality memory and how to use a Web site or other computer ad to search for the right memory.

Buying High-Quality Memory

Before you buy, you need to be aware that chips embedded on a memory module can be high-grade, low-grade, remanufactured, or used. Poor-quality memory chips can cause frequent errors in Windows or cause the system to be unstable, so it pays to know the quality and type of memory you are buying.

Stamped on each chip of a RAM module is a chip ID that identifies the date the chip was manufactured. Look for the date in the YYWW format, where YY is the year the chip was made, and WW is the week of that year. For example, 0510 indicates a chip made in the tenth week of 2005. Date stamps on a chip that are older than one year indicate that the chip is probably used memory. If some chips are old, but some are new, the module is probably remanufactured. When buying memory modules, look for ones with dates on all chips that are relatively close together and less than one year old.

New chips have a protective coating that gives them a polished, reflective surface. If the chip's surface is dull or matted, or you can scratch off the markings with a fingernail or knife, suspect that the chip has been re-marked. Re-marked chips have been used, returned to the factory, marked again, and then resold. For best results, buy memory from a reputable source that sells only new components.

A+
220-602
1.1

Using a Web Site to Research Your Purchase

When purchasing memory from a Web site such as Crucial Technology's site (*www.crucial.com*) or Kingston Technology's site (*www.kingston.com*), look for a search utility that will match memory modules to your motherboard (see Figure 6-15). These utilities are easy to use and help you confirm you have made the right decisions about type, size, and speed to buy. They can also help if motherboard documentation is inadequate, and you're not exactly sure what memory to buy.

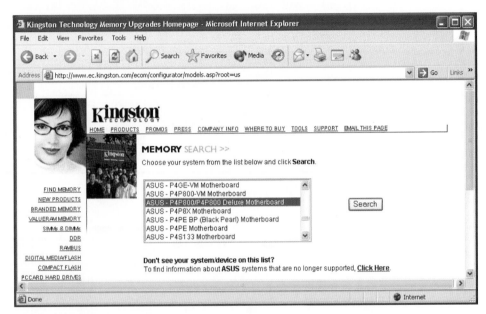

Figure 6-15 Web sites used to purchase memory, such as this Kingston site, often provide search utilities to help you select the right memory modules for your motherboard

Let's look at one example on the Crucial site. Suppose we're looking for DDR, 400 MHz, CL3, unbuffered DIMMs for a dual channeled motherboard. We want to install 256 MB of RAM, so we need two 128 MB modules. Figure 6-16 shows the Crucial Web site where I found that match. It's the last item in the list.

Reading Ads About Memory Modules

Sometimes Web sites or printed material present memory ads as cryptic tables that can be difficult to read if you're not familiar with the shorthand used. This is especially true when you're buying older memory technologies for an old system. Figure 6-17 shows a typical memory module ad listing various types of DIMMs and RIMMs.

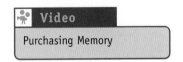

Let's take a closer look at this ad. For each memory module, the ad lists the amount of memory, density, speed, and price. For DIMMs, the ad lists the density of the module, which tells us the width of the data bus, whether the module supports error checking, and the size of the module. Here's how it works. The density is written as two numbers separated by an x, such as 16 x 64, and is read "16 by 64." Let's start with the second number, which is 64 or 72. If it's 64, then it's the width of the data bus in bits, grouped as eight bits to a byte. If the number is 72, then it's the width of the data bus plus an extra bit for each byte, used for error checking and correction (for ECC memory).

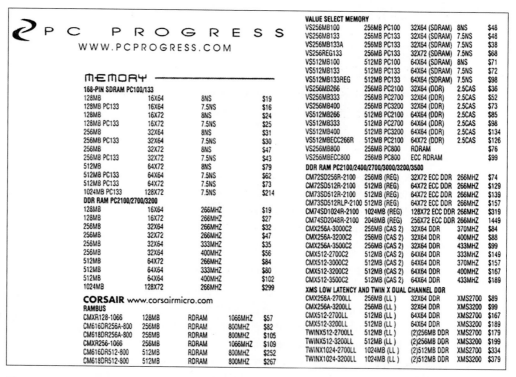

Figure 6-16 Selecting memory off the Crucial Web site

Figure 6-17 Typical memory ad

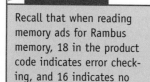

Recall that when reading memory ads for Rambus memory, 18 in the product code indicates error checking, and 16 indicates no error checking.

When calculating the module's size, ignore the ninth bit and use only the value 64 to calculate. Convert this number to bytes by dividing it by 8, and then multiply that value (number of bytes) by the number on the left in the density listing, to determine the size of the module. For example, if the density is 16 x 64, the size of the module is 16 x (64/8) = 16x 8 = 128 MB.

A+
220-602
1.1

INSTALLING MEMORY

When installing RAM modules, remember to protect the chips against static electricity, as you learned in Chapter 2. Follow these precautions:

- Always use a ground bracelet as you work.
- Turn off the power, unplug the power cord, and remove the cover to the case.
- Handle memory modules with care.
- Don't stack cards or modules because you can loosen a chip.
- Usually modules pop into place easily and are secured by spring catches on both ends. Make sure that you look for the notches on one side or in the middle of the module that orient the module in the slot.

Let's now look at the details of installing a SIMM, a RIMM, and a DIMM.

INSTALLING SIMMS

For most SIMMs, the module slides into the slot at an angle, as shown in Figure 6-18. (Check your documentation for any instructions specific to your modules.) As you install each SIMM, make sure each module is securely placed in its slot. Then turn on the PC and watch POST count the amount of memory during the boot process. If the memory count is not what you expect, power off the system, then carefully remove and reseat each module. To remove a module, release the latches on both sides of the module and gently rotate it out of the socket at a 45-degree angle.

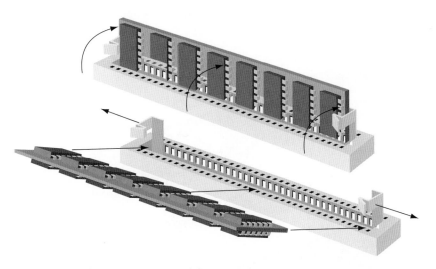

Figure 6-18 Installing a SIMM module

A+
220-602
1.1

INSTALLING RIMMS

For RIMM modules, install the RIMMs beginning with bank 0, followed by bank 1. If a C-RIMM is already in the slot, remove the C-RIMM by pulling the supporting arms on the sides of the socket outward and pulling straight up on the C-RIMM. When installing the RIMM, notches on the edge of the RIMM module will help you orient it correctly in the socket. Insert the module straight down in the socket (see Figure 6-19). When it is fully inserted, the supporting arms should pop back into place.

RIMM supporting arms
in outward position

Figure 6-19   Install RIMM modules in banks beginning with bank 0

INSTALLING DIMMS

For DIMM modules, small latches on each side of the slot hold the module in place, as shown in Figure 6-20. To install a DIMM, first pull the supporting arms on the sides of the slot outward. Look on the DIMM edge connector for the notches, which help you orient the DIMM correctly over the slot, and insert the DIMM straight down into the slot. When the DIMM is fully inserted, the supporting arms should pop back into place. Figure 6-21 shows a DIMM being inserted into a slot on a motherboard.

Most often, placing memory on the motherboard is all that is necessary for installation. When the computer powers up, it counts the memory present without any further instruction and senses the features that the modules support, such as parity or ECC.

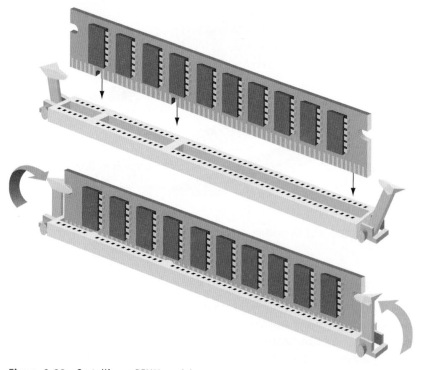

Figure 6-20   Installing a DIMM module

A+
220-602
1.1

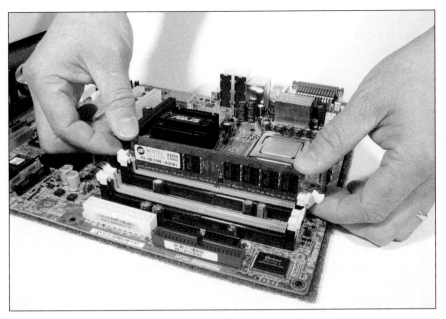

Figure 6-21 Insert the DIMM into the slot by pressing down until the support arms lock into position

For some older computers, you must tell CMOS setup the amount of memory present. Read the motherboard documentation to determine what yours requires. If the new memory is not recognized, power down the system and reseat the module. Most likely it's not installed solidly in the slot.

TROUBLESHOOTING MEMORY

A+ ESS
1.1

A+
220-602
1.2

Issues with memory modules can cause a variety of problems, including boot failure; errors that cause the system to hang, freeze, or become unstable; and intermittent application errors. In Windows, memory errors can cause frequent **General Protection Fault (GPF)** errors. We now look at things that can go wrong with memory and what to do about them.

 A+ Exam Tip

The A+ 220-602 exam expects you to know how to troubleshoot problems with memory.

UPGRADE PROBLEMS

When upgrading memory, if the computer does not recognize new SIMMs, DIMMs, or RIMMs, or if memory error messages appear, do the following:

▲ Remove and reinstall the module. Make sure it sits in the socket at the same height as other modules, and clips on each side of the slot are in latched positions.
▲ Check that you have the right memory modules supported by your motherboard. Verify that CMOS setup recognizes the memory features correctly.
▲ Check that you have installed the right module size, as stated in the motherboard documentation. Verify each module that was already installed or newly installed.
▲ Remove the newly installed memory and check whether the error message disappears. Try the memory in different sockets. Try installing the new memory without the old installed. If the new memory works without the old, the problem is that the modules are not compatible.

◢ Clean the module edge connectors with a soft cloth or contact cleaner. Blow or vacuum dust from the memory sockets.

◢ Try flashing BIOS. Perhaps BIOS has problems with the new memory that a BIOS upgrade can solve.

RECURRING PROBLEMS

Recurring errors during normal operations can mean unreliable memory. If the system locks up or you regularly receive error messages about illegal operations and General Protection Faults occur during normal operation, and you have not just upgraded memory, do the following:

◢ Run a current version of antivirus software to check for viruses.

◢ Run diagnostic software such as PC Technician (*www.windsortech.com*) to test memory.

◢ Are the memory modules properly seated? Remove and reinstall each one. For a DIMM module, try a different memory slot.

◢ Replace memory modules one at a time. For example, if the system only recognizes six out of eight megabytes of RAM, swap the last two SIMM modules. Did the amount of recognized RAM change? You might be able to solve the problem just by reseating the modules.

◢ Sometimes a problem can result from a bad socket or a broken trace (a fine-printed wire or circuit) on the motherboard. If so, you might have to replace the entire motherboard.

◢ The problem might be with the OS or applications. Download the latest patch for the software from the manufacturer's Web site. Make sure Windows has all the latest patches and service packs applied.

◢ If you have just installed new hardware, the hardware device might be causing an error, which the OS interprets as a memory error. Try uninstalling the new hardware.

◢ A Windows error that occurs randomly and generates an error message with "exception fault 0E at >>0137:BFF9z5d0" or similar text is probably a memory error. Test, reseat, or replace RAM.

◢ Excessive hard drive use and a sluggish system might indicate excessive paging. Check virtual memory settings.

> **✎ Notes**
>
> Other than PC Technician, Memtest86 is a utility to test installed memory modules. Check the site *www.memtest86.com* to download this program.

A sluggish system that occasionally gives "Insufficient memory" errors probably needs more RAM. Try the following:

◢ Scan the system for viruses and other malicious software. Use OS utilities such as Defrag and Chkdsk to reorganize and clean up the hard drive and repair file system errors.

◢ Using the System Properties window, find out how much RAM is installed and compare that to the recommended amounts. Consider adding more RAM.

◢ Use the System Properties window in the OS to verify that virtual memory settings are optimized for your system. (How to manage virtual memory is beyond the scope of this chapter.)

◢ Don't open too many applications at the same time. Look for running background services that are not necessary and using up valuable memory resources.

>> CHAPTER SUMMARY

▲ DRAM (dynamic RAM) is slower than SRAM because it needs constant refreshing.

▲ DRAM is stored on three kinds of modules: SIMM, DIMM, and RIMM modules.

▲ SIMM memory modules must be installed in pairs, and are considered outdated technology for today's computers.

▲ DIMM technology has been improved several times and is currently the most popular type of memory.

▲ Direct Rambus DRAM, Double Data Rate SDRAM (DDR SDRAM), and DDR2 are the three current memory technologies.

▲ Synchronous DRAM (which moves in sync with the system bus) is a faster kind of memory than the less expensive asynchronous DRAM (which does not move in sync with the system bus) found on SIMMs.

▲ When upgrading memory, use the type, size, and speed the motherboard supports and match new modules to those already installed. Features to match include buffered, registered, unbuffered, single-sided, double-sided, CL rating, tin or gold connectors, support for dual channeling, ECC, non-ECC, parity, nonparity, speed in ns, MHz, or PC rating, DDR, DDR2, and size in MB or GB. Using memory made by the same manufacturer is recommended.

▲ When buying memory, beware of remanufactured and re-marked memory chips, because they have been either refurbished or re-marked before resale.

▲ When troubleshooting Windows memory errors, know the problems might be caused by a virus, Windows corruption, application corruption, failing hardware device, memory modules not seated properly, or failing memory modules.

>> KEY TERMS

For explanations of key terms, see the Glossary near the end of the book.

bank	dual channel	RDRAM
burst EDO (BEDO)	dynamic RAM (DRAM)	refresh
cache on a stick (COAST)	ECC (error-correcting code)	re-marked chips
CAS Latency	EDO (extended data out)	SDRAM II
C-RIMM (Continuity RIMM)	General Protection Fault (GPF)	synchronous DRAM (SDRAM)
DDR2 SDRAM	nonparity memory	SyncLink DRAM (SLDRAM)
Direct Rambus DRAM	parity	
Direct RDRAM	parity error	
Double Data Rate SDRAM	parity memory	
(DDR SDRAM)	RAS Latency	

>> REVIEWING THE BASICS

1. Name two ways that a SIMM and a DIMM are alike. Name two ways they are different.

2. How many pins are on a SDRAM DIMM? On a DDR DIMM? On a SIMM? On a RIMM?

3. Which is likely to be more expensive, a 512-MB DIMM or a 512-MB RIMM? Why?

4. How many notches are on a DDR SDRAM module?

5. What prevents a DDR DIMM from being installed in a DDR2 DIMM slot on a motherboard?

6. What component must be installed in every empty memory slot on a motherboard using Rambus technology?

7. What types of memory can be used on a 100-MHz motherboard?

8. Looking at an SDRAM DIMM, how can you know for certain the voltage needed by the module?

9. How many 30-pin SIMMs are installed in one bank?

10. How many 72-pin SIMMs are installed in one bank?

11. What are the two speeds of RIMMs?

12. List at least four things you can do if you receive memory errors during a memory upgrade.

13. What might be a symptom in Windows of unreliable memory on a motherboard?

14. List at least four things you can do if you receive memory errors during normal operation when you have not recently upgraded memory.

15. If your motherboard calls for 60-ns memory, can you substitute 70-ns memory? Why or why not?

16. When buying memory, what can you look for that might indicate that the memory is remanufactured?

17. Which memory module standard (RIMM or DIMM) is an open standard? Which standard is a copyrighted standard?

18. What is the data path size of a SIMM? A current DIMM?

19. What are the two current data path sizes of RIMMs?

20. What improvements did DDR make over regular SDRAM?

21. When a DIMM has chips on both sides of the module, do the pins on one side of the module work independently or are they dependent on pins on the other side of the module?

22. Which is faster, CL3 memory or CL5 memory?

23. You are looking to purchase two DIMMs running at 400 MHz. You find DIMMs advertised at PC4000 and PC3200. Which do you purchase?

24. You need to find out how much RAM is installed in a system. What command do you enter in the Run dialog box to launch the System Information utility?

25. Although ECC memory costs more than non-ECC memory, why would you chose to use it?

>> THINKING CRITICALLY

1. If your motherboard supports DIMM memory, will RIMM memory still work on the board?

2. If your motherboard supports ECC SDRAM memory, can you substitute SDRAM memory that does not support ECC? If your motherboard supports buffered SDRAM memory, can you substitute unbuffered SDRAM modules?

3. You have just upgraded memory on a computer from 64 MB to 128 MB by adding one DIMM. When you first turn on the PC, the memory count shows only 64 MB. Which of the following is most likely the source of the problem? What can you do to fix it?

   a. Windows is giving an error because it likely became corrupted while the PC was disassembled.

   b. The new DIMM you installed is faulty.

   c. The new DIMM is not properly seated.

   d. The DIMM is installed in the wrong slot.

4. Your motherboard supports dual channeling and you currently have two slots used in Channel A on the board. You want to install an additional 512 MB of RAM. Will your system run faster if you install two 256 MB DIMMs or one 512 MB DIMM? Explain your answer.

>> HANDS-ON PROJECTS

PROJECT 6-1:   Help Desk Support

1. A friend calls while sitting at his computer and asks you to help him determine how much RAM he has on his motherboard. Step him through the process. List at least two ways to find the answer. He is using Windows XP.

2. Answer Question 1, but assume that your friend is using Windows 2000.

3. Your friend has discovered he has 128 MB of RAM and wants to upgrade to 256 MB. He is using DIMMs and his motherboard is running at 133 MHz. Looking at Figure 6-17, what is the estimated cost of the upgrade?

PROJECT 6-2:   Planning and Pricing Memory

You need the documentation for your motherboard for this project. If you don't have it, download it from the Web site of the motherboard manufacturer. Use this documentation and the motherboard to answer the following:

1. What is the maximum amount of memory the banks on your motherboard can accommodate?

2. What type of memory does the board support?

3. How many modules are installed, and how much memory does each hold?

4. Look in a computer catalog, such as *Computer Shopper*, or use a retail Web site such as Kingston Technology (*www.kingston.com*) or Crucial Technology (*www.crucial.com*) to determine how much it will cost to fill the banks to full capacity. Don't forget to match the speed of the modules already installed, and plan to use only the size modules your computer can accommodate. How much will the upgrade cost?

PROJECT 6-3:   Upgrading Memory

To practice installing additional memory in a computer in a classroom environment, remove the SIMMs, DIMMs, or RIMMs from one computer and place them in another computer.

Boot the second computer and check that it counts the additional memory. When finished, return the borrowed modules to the original computer.

PROJECT 6-4:   Troubleshooting Memory

Follow the rules outlined in Chapter 2 to protect the PC against ESD as you work. Remove the memory module in the first memory slot on a motherboard, and boot the PC. Did you get an error? Why or why not?

>> REAL PROBLEMS, REAL SOLUTIONS

REAL PROBLEM 6-1:   Troubleshooting Memory

A friend has asked for your help in solving a problem with his desktop computer. The computer hangs at odd times and sometimes gives "Insufficient memory" errors. The Windows XP system has 512 MB of installed RAM, so you decide it really doesn't need a memory upgrade. You suspect one of the DIMM modules installed might be going bad. To test this theory, you download a memory testing utility from the Internet to test the modules. Do the following:

1. Find and download a memory testing utility. Use the utility to test the memory on your computer. What utility did you use? What were the results of the test?

2. If the test was successful, but the problem didn't go away, list the next five things you would suspect to be the source of the problem and describe what you would do to eliminate each possible source.

Hard Drives

The hard drive is the most important secondary storage device in a computer, and supporting hard drives is one of the more important tasks of a PC support technician. This chapter introduces the different kinds of hard drive technologies that have accounted for the continual upward increase in hard drive capacities and speeds over the past few years. The ways a computer interfaces with a hard drive have also changed several times over the years as both the computer and hard drives improve the technologies and techniques for communication. In this chapter, you will learn about past and present methods of communication between the computer and drive so that you can support both older and newer drives.

A hard drive is logically organized to hold data using methods similar to the ones used by floppy disks. We'll begin the chapter by discussing how data is organized on floppy disks and how to install a floppy disk. This information will help you understand the next sections of the chapter about hard drive organization and installation. Finally, you'll learn what to do when you have problems installing a drive and how to troubleshoot problems with hard drives after they are installed.

LEARNING FROM FLOPPY DRIVES

Floppy drives are an older technology mostly replaced by CD drives and USB flash memory. However, you still see them around and you need to know how to support them. More important, knowing how floppy drives work and are installed can be a great foundation for learning to support hard drives. In the following sections, you'll learn how floppy drives work and how to install and troubleshoot them.

HOW FLOPPY DRIVES WORK

Recall that memory is organized in two ways: physically (pertaining to hardware) and logically (pertaining to software). Similarly, data is stored physically and logically on a secondary storage device such as a floppy drive. Physical storage involves how data is written to and organized on the storage media, whereas logical storage involves how the OS and BIOS organize and view the stored data.

This section explains first how data is physically stored on a floppy disk and also how the OS logically views the data. Then you'll learn about what happens when a floppy disk is formatted for the first time. All the concepts learned here regarding physical and logical organization of data and how a disk is formatted also apply to hard drives.

HOW DATA IS PHYSICALLY STORED ON A FLOPPY DISK

Years ago, a **floppy disk drive (FDD)** came in two sizes to accommodate either a $5\frac{1}{4}$-inch or $3\frac{1}{2}$-inch floppy disk. The $3\frac{1}{2}$-inch disks were formatted as high density (1.44 MB), extra-high density (2.88 MB), and double density (720K). The only floppy drives you see in use today are the $3\frac{1}{2}$-inch, high-density drives that hold 1.44 MB of data.

Figure 7-1 shows the floppy drive subsystem, which consists of the floppy drive, its cable, and its connections. The data cable connects to a 34-pin floppy drive connector on the motherboard.

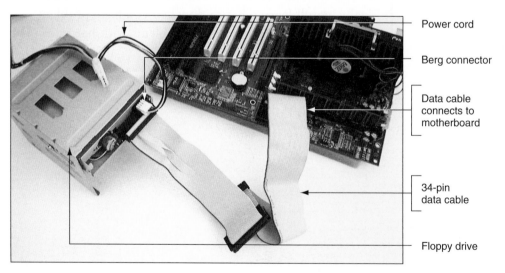

Figure 7-1 Floppy drive subsystem: floppy drive, data cable, and power connection

A floppy drive cable has 34 pins. Newer cables have a connector at each end and accommodate a single drive, but older cables, like the one in Figure 7-1, have an extra connector or two in the middle of the cable for a second floppy drive. For these systems, you can install two floppy drives on the same cable, and the drives will be identified by BIOS as drive A and drive B. Figure 7-2 shows an older floppy drive cable. Notice in the figure the twist in the cable. The drive that has the twist between it and the controller is drive A. The drive that does not have the twist between it and the controller is drive B. Also notice in the figure the edge color down one side of the cable, which identifies the pin-1 side of the 34-pin connector.

> **A+ Exam Tip**
>
> The A+ Essentials exam expects you to be familiar with a floppy disk drive (FDD).

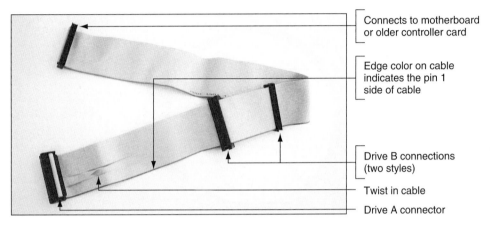

Connects to motherboard or older controller card

Edge color on cable indicates the pin 1 side of cable

Drive B connections (two styles)

Twist in cable

Drive A connector

Figure 7-2 Twist in cable determines which drive will be drive A

Floppy drives receive power from the power supply by way of a power cord, as shown in Figure 7-3. The power cord plugs into the back of the drive. Recall that most hard drives use the larger Molex connector, but floppy drives use the smaller Berg connector. The Berg connector has a small plastic latch that snaps in place when you connect it to the drive.

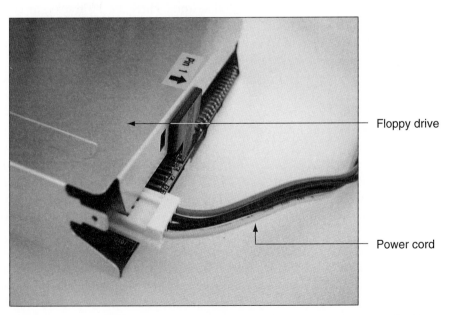

Floppy drive

Power cord

Figure 7-3 Power supply connection on the back of the drive (Note how well this drive manufacturer labeled pin 1 on the data connection.)

A+ ESS
1.1

When floppy disks are first manufactured, the disks have nothing on them; they are blank sheets of magnetically coated plastic. Disks are organized in tracks and sectors. Before data can be written to the disk, it must first be mapped in concentric circles called tracks, which are divided into segments called sectors (see Figure 7-4).

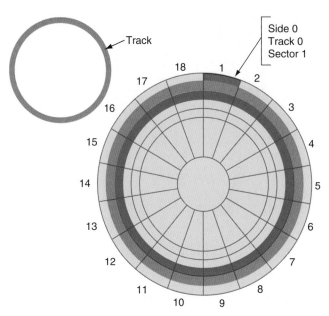

Figure 7-4   3 $\frac{1}{2}$-inch, high-density floppy disk showing tracks and sectors

The process of marking tracks and sectors to prepare the disk to receive data is called **formatting** the disk; you do this using the Format command at a command prompt or the Windows Explorer shortcut menu. Figure 7-4 shows how a 3 $\frac{1}{2}$-inch, high-density floppy disk is formatted into tracks and sectors. There are 80 tracks, or circles, on the top side of the disk and 80 more tracks on the bottom. The tracks are numbered 0 through 79. Each side of the disk has 18 sectors, numbered 1 through 18. Although the circles, or tracks, on the outside of the disk are larger than the circles closer to the center, all tracks store the same amount of data. Data is written to the tracks as bits, either 0s or 1s. Each bit is a magnetized, rectangular spot on the disk. Between the tracks and spots are spaces that are not magnetized. This spacing prevents one spot from affecting the magnetism of a nearby spot. The difference between a 0 spot and a 1 spot is the orientation of the spot's magnetization on the disk surface.

Data is written to and read from the disk via a magnetic **read/write head** mechanism in the floppy drive (see Figure 7-5). Two heads are attached at the end of an actuator arm that freely moves over the surface of the disk. The arm has one read/write head above the disk and another below the disk. Moving in unison back and forth across the disk, the two heads lightly touch the surface of the disk, which spins at 360 rpm (revolutions per minute). (Note that the read/write heads of a hard drive never touch the surface.) Data is written first to the bottom and then to the top (label side) of the disk, beginning at the outermost circle and moving in. In Figure 7-5, the floppy disk is shown bottom-side-up so that you can see the round metal pad on which the disk spins.

A+ ESS
1.1

Figure 7-5   Inside a floppy disk drive

HOW DATA IS LOGICALLY STORED ON A FLOPPY DISK

Under Windows 2000/XP, a hard drive can use either the NTFS or FAT file system, but under all Windows operating systems, a floppy drive is always formatted using the FAT12 file system. Using the FAT file system, a cluster, sometimes called a file allocation unit, is a group of sectors that is the smallest unit on a disk that the OS uses to hold a file or a portion of a file. "Sector" refers to the way data is physically stored on a disk, whereas "cluster" describes how data is logically organized. The BIOS manages the disk as physical sectors, but the OS considers the disk only a long list of clusters that can each hold a fixed amount of data, as shown in Figure 7-6. The OS keeps that list of clusters in the file allocation table (FAT).

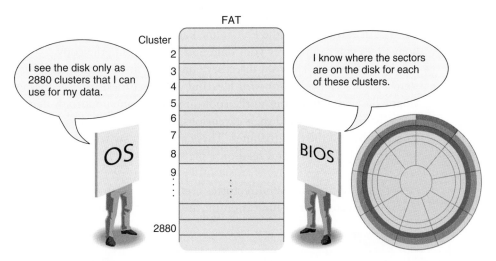

Figure 7-6   Clusters, or file allocation units, are managed by the OS in the file allocation table, but BIOS manages these clusters as one or two physical sectors on the disk

The 3$\frac{1}{2}$-inch, high-density floppy disk has 80 tracks x 18 sectors per track on each side, for a total of 1440 sectors on each side. The disk has only one sector per cluster, making 1440 x 2 sides, or 2880 clusters. Because each cluster holds 512 bytes (one sector) of data, a

$3\frac{1}{2}$-inch, high-density floppy disk has 2880 x 512 = 1,474,560 bytes of data. Divide this number by 1024 to convert bytes to kilobytes and you will find out that the storage capacity of this disk is 1440 kilobytes. You can then divide 1440 by 1000 to convert kilobytes to megabytes, and the storage is 1.44 MB.

HOW A FLOPPY DISK IS FORMATTED

Recall that before a floppy disk can be used, it must be formatted. Most floppy disks come already formatted, but occasionally you will need to format one. Whether you use the Format command or Windows Explorer to format a floppy disk, the following are created:

▲ *Tracks and sectors.* The tracks and sectors are created by writing tracks as a series of F6s in hex and, as necessary, writing the sector address mark to identify the beginning sector on a track

▲ *The boot record.* The first sector on the disk, called the boot sector or boot record, contains the information about the disk, including the total number of sectors, the number of sectors per cluster, the number of bits in each FAT entry, and the version of DOS or Windows used to format the disk. The boot record also includes the name of the program for which it searches to load an OS, either Io.sys or Ntldr. If one of these files is on the disk, this program searches for and loads the rest of the OS files needed on the disk to boot; then the disk is said to be bootable. The boot sector is always located at the beginning of the disk at track 0, sector 1 (bottom of the disk, outermost track). This uniform layout and content allows any version of DOS or Windows to read any floppy disk.

▲ *Two copies of the file allocation table (FAT).* Because the width of each entry in the FAT is 12 bits, the FAT on a floppy disk is called a 12-bit FAT, or FAT12. The FAT lists how each cluster (or file allocation unit) on the disk is currently used. A file is stored in one or more clusters that do not have to be contiguous on the disk. In the FAT, some clusters might be marked as bad (the 12 bits to mark a bad cluster are FF7h). An extra copy of the FAT immediately follows the first. If the first is damaged, sometimes you can recover your data and files by using the copy.

▲ *The root directory.* The root directory contains a fixed number of rows to accommodate a predetermined number of files and subdirectories. A $3\frac{1}{2}$-inch, high-density floppy disk has 224 entries in the root directory. Some important items in a directory are a list of filenames and their extensions, the time and date of creation or last update of each file, and the file attributes. These are on/off switches indicating the archive, system file, hidden file, and read-only file status of the file or directory.

The root directory and all subdirectories contain the same information about each file. Only the root directory has a limitation on the number of entries. Subdirectories can have as many entries as disk space allows. Because long filenames require more room in a directory than short filenames, assigning long filenames reduces the number of files that can be stored in the root directory.

HOW TO INSTALL A FLOPPY DRIVE

Many computers today come with a hard drive and CD-ROM drive, but don't include a floppy drive, although the motherboard most likely has a 34-pin floppy drive connector. Most computer cases also have one or more empty bays for a $3\frac{1}{2}$-inch floppy drive, Zip drive, or second hard drive.

If you have no extra bay and want to add a floppy drive, you can attach an external drive that comes in its own case and has its own power supply. Most external drives today connect to the main system using a USB port, such as the one in Figure 7-7.

Figure 7-7 An external floppy drive uses a USB connection

Floppy drives are now so inexpensive that repairing one is impractical. After you've determined that the drive itself has a problem, open the case, remove the drive, and replace it with a new one. This procedure takes no more than 30 minutes, assuming that you don't damage or loosen something in the process and create a new troubleshooting opportunity.

Here are the steps to add or replace a floppy drive. As described in Chapter 2, be sure to protect the computer against ESD as you work.

1. Turn off the computer, unplug the power cord, and remove the cover.

2. Unplug the power cable to the old floppy drive. Steady the drive with one hand while you dislodge the power cable with the other hand. Unplug the data cable from the old drive.

3. Unscrew and dismount the drive. Some drives have one or two screws on each side that attach the drive to the drive bay. After you remove the screws, the drive usually slides to the front and out of the case. Sometimes, you must lift a catch underneath the drive as you slide the drive forward. Sometimes, the drive is installed into a removable bay. For this type of case, first unscrew the screws securing the bay (most likely these screws are on the front of the case) and remove the bay. Then unscrew and remove the drive from the bay.

4. Slide the new drive into the bay. Screw the drive down with the same screws used on the old drive. Make sure the drive is anchored so that it cannot slide forward or backward, or up or down, even if a user turns the case on its side.

5. If you are adding (not replacing) a floppy drive, connect the floppy drive data cable to the motherboard. Align the edge color of the ribbon cable with pin 1 on the motherboard connectors. Some connectors only allow you to insert the cable in one direction. Be sure

A+
220-602
1.1

> **Notes**
>
> If your power supply doesn't have the smaller Berg connector for the floppy drive, you can buy a Molex-to-Berg converter to accommodate the floppy drive power connector.

the end of the cable with the twist connects to the drive and the other end to the motherboard.

6. Connect the data cable and power cord to the drive. Make sure that the data cable's colored edge is connected to the pin 1 side of the connection, as shown in Figure 7-8. With some newer floppy drives, pin 1 is marked as an arrow on the drive housing (see Figure 7-9).

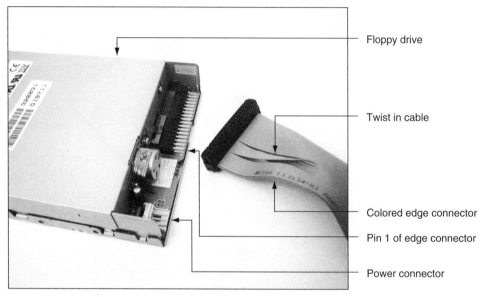

Floppy drive

Twist in cable

Colored edge connector

Pin 1 of edge connector

Power connector

Figure 7-8   Connect colored edge of cable to pin 1

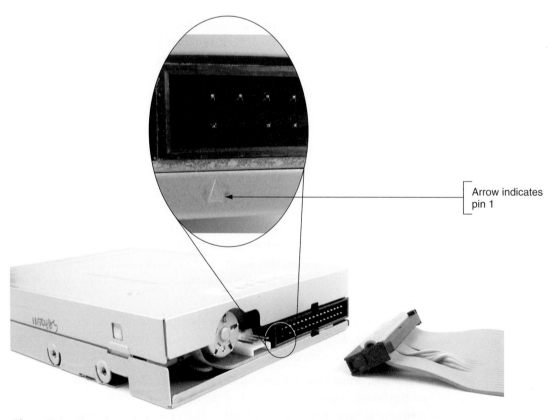

Arrow indicates pin 1

Figure 7-9   Pin 1 is marked on this floppy drive with an arrow on the drive housing

7

A+
220-602
1.1

Most connections on floppy drives are oriented the same way, so this one probably has the same orientation as the old drive. The power cable goes into the power connection in only one direction. Be careful not to offset the connection by one pin.

7. Replace the cover, turn on the computer, and enter CMOS setup to verify the drive is recognized with no errors. If you are adding (not replacing) a floppy drive, you must inform CMOS setup by accessing setup and changing the drive type. Boot to the Windows desktop and test the drive by formatting a disk or copying data to a disk.

In the troubleshooting section at the end of this chapter, you'll learn about problems with floppy drives and what you can do about them. Now let's turn our attention to hard drives. We'll begin by discussing how a hard drive works.

> **Notes**
>
> Note that you can turn on the PC and test the drive before you replace the computer case cover. If the drive doesn't work, having the cover off makes it easier to turn off the computer, check connections, and try again. Just make certain that you don't touch anything inside the case while the computer is on. Leaving the computer on while you disconnect and reconnect a cable is very dangerous for the PC and will probably damage something—including you!

HOW HARD DRIVES WORK

A+ ESS
1.1

A floppy disk has a single disk made of mylar inside the diskette plastic housing, but a hard drive has one, two, or more platters, or disks, that stack together and spin in unison inside a sealed metal housing that contains firmware to control reading and writing data to the drive and to communicate with the

motherboard. The top and bottom of each disk has a read/write head that moves across the disk surface as all the disks rotate on a spindle (see Figure 7-10). All the read/write heads are controlled by an actuator, which moves the read/write heads across the disk surfaces in unison. The disk surfaces are covered with a magnetic medium that can hold data as magnetized spots.

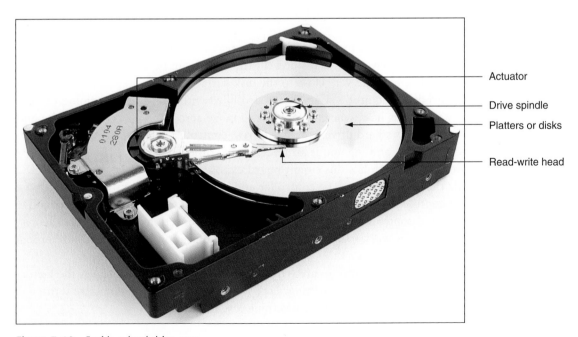

- Actuator
- Drive spindle
- Platters or disks
- Read-write head

Figure 7-10 Inside a hard drive case

Figure 7-11 shows a close-up of the hard drive in Figure 7-10. You can see that this drive has two platters. Both sides of each platter are used to store data. However, on some hard drives, the top side of the first platter holds only the information that is used to track data and manage the disk. Each side, or surface, of one hard drive platter is called a head. (Don't confuse this with the read/write mechanism that moves across a platter, which is called a read/write head.) Thus, the drive in Figure 7-11 has four heads because there are two platters, each having two heads.

Read/write head

Read/write heads between the platters (another is underneath the bottom platter)

Two disks have four tracks (one on each head) that make one cylinder

Figure 7-11 A hard drive with two platters

Recall that a track is a circle on a disk surface that is divided into segments called sectors. All the tracks that are the same distance from the center of the platters on a hard drive together make up one cylinder. For example, the hard drive in Figure 7-10 has four heads. The four tracks on these heads that are equidistant from the center of the platters make one cylinder. Suppose a disk has 300 tracks per head; it would then have 300 cylinders. As with floppy disks, data is written to a hard drive beginning at the outermost track. The entire first cylinder is filled before the read/write heads move inward and begin filling the second cylinder.

The drive fits into a bay inside the computer case where it is securely attached with clips or braces and screws. This helps prevent the drive from being jarred while the disk is spinning and the heads are very close to the disk surface.

A hard drive requires a controller board filled with ROM programming to instruct the read/write heads how, where, and when to move across the platters and write and read data. For today's hard drives, the hard drive controller is firmware on a circuit board on or inside the drive housing and is an integral part of it. Figure 7-12 shows the bottom side of a hard drive, which has this circuit board exposed. Most modern drives protect the board inside the drive housing. The controller and drive are permanently attached to one another. Don't confuse this controller with the ATA controller, which is part of the motherboard chipset and controls the parallel and serial ATA connections on the motherboard. These two controllers work together to manage communication between the motherboard and the hard drive.

Track and sector markings are written to a hard drive before it leaves the factory in a process called low-level formatting. Let's look at how these markings are written, and then we'll look at options you have concerning low-level formatting.

7

A+ ESS
1.1

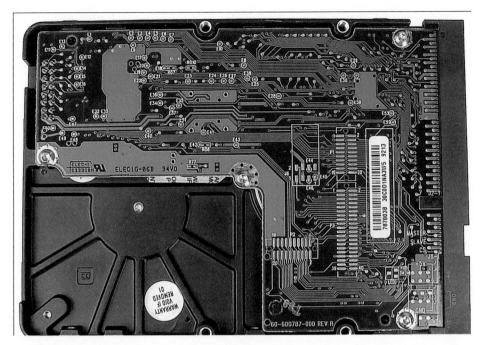

Figure 7-12 Bottom of a hard drive shows the circuit board that contains the drive controller

TRACKS AND SECTORS ON THE DRIVE

Older drives used a straightforward method of writing the tracks and sectors on the drive. They had either 17 or 26 sectors per track over the entire drive platter (see Figure 7-13). The centermost track determines the number of bytes that a track can hold and forces all other tracks to follow this restriction. Thus, the larger tracks near the outside of the platter end up containing the same number of bytes as the smaller tracks near the center of the platter. This arrangement makes formatting a drive and later accessing data simpler, but wastes drive space.

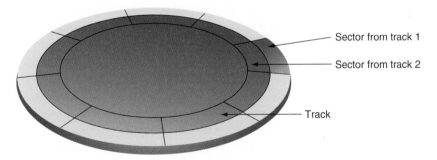

Figure 7-13 Floppy drives and older hard drives use a constant number of sectors per track

Today's drives eliminate this restriction. The number of sectors per track on a drive is not the same throughout the platter. In this new formatting system, called zone bit recording (see Figure 7-14), tracks near the center have the smallest number of sectors per track, and the number of sectors increases as the tracks grow larger. In other words, each track on an IDE drive is designed to have the optimum number of sectors appropriate to the size of the track. What makes this arrangement possible, however, is one fact that seldom changes: Every sector on the drive still has 512 bytes. Without this consistency, the OS needs a much more complex interface to the data on the drive.

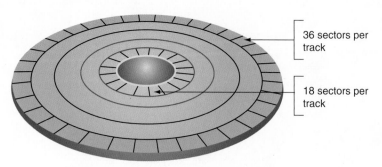

36 sectors per track

18 sectors per track

Figure 7-14 Zone bit recording can have more sectors per track as the tracks get larger

Because each track can have a different number of sectors, the OS cannot communicate with the hard drive controller (firmware on the hard drive) using sector and track coordinates, as it does with floppy disks and older hard drives. For current systems, the BIOS and the OS use a simple sequential numbering system called logical block addressing (LBA) to address all the sectors on the hard drive without regard to where these sectors are located.

LOW-LEVEL FORMATTING

Recall that when the OS formats a floppy disk, it writes sector and track markings on the disk. With IDE drives, because the track and sector markings don't follow a simple pattern, track and sector markings are written on the hard drive at the factory. This process is called low-level formatting. The OS still executes the remainder of the format process (creating a boot sector, file system, and root directory), which is called high-level formatting or operating system formatting.

With older drives, because the track and sector markings were written in a simple way as a constant number of sectors per track, technicians performed the low-level format when they installed the drive. Technicians would use a utility program to do the job. System BIOS, the OS, or utility software such as Norton Utilities or SpinRite could perform the low-level format. Because sector and track markings eventually fade, a hard drive eventually gives lots of bad sector errors. In the old days, the solution was to back up all the data on the drive and perform a low-level format to get a clean start. If a drive were periodically low-level formatted, it would last for years and years.

For today's drives, the track and sector markings on the drive created at the factory are normally expected to last for the life of the drive. For this reason, today's drives are considered more disposable than yesterday's drives. When track and sector markings fade, as they eventually do, and the drive gives many "Bad Sector or Sector Not

> **Notes**
>
> As computer parts become less expensive and labor becomes more expensive, the trend to replace rather than fix is becoming the acceptable best practice in the PC industry.

A+ ESS
1.1

Found" errors or becomes unusable, you salvage whatever data is still on the drive, throw the drive away, and buy a new one!

Manufacturers of today's hard drives advise to never do a low-level format. Using the wrong format program could permanently destroy the drive, unless the drive controller was smart enough to ignore the command. However, if you're about to throw out the drive anyway and you have the time to tinker, you might want to consider attempting a low-level format. Ask the manufacturer for a program to perform a low-level format of the drive. Note, however, that some manufacturers distribute these programs only to dealers, resellers, or certified service centers.

You should know another thing about low-level formatting. On the Web, you can download utilities from hard drive manufacturers and others that claim to be a low-level format utility but are actually a zero-fill utility. These programs work by checking each sector for errors (as does the Windows 2000/XP Chkdsk command) and filling each sector with zeroes. They're great for cleaning up a hard drive, but don't low-level format.

Now that you have an understanding of how data is physically written to a hard drive, let's turn our attention to how much data can be stored on the drive.

CALCULATING DRIVE CAPACITY ON OLDER DRIVES

In the early 1990s, hard drives used a constant number of sectors per track and measuring drive capacity was straightforward. Let's learn how to do that before we see how it's done today. All sectors in a track held 512 bytes regardless of the track's radius. If you knew the number of tracks, heads, and sectors per track, you could calculate the storage capacity of a drive, because all tracks had the same number of sectors. Software and operating systems were written to interface with the system BIOS, which managed a hard drive by assuming that for each hard drive there was a fixed relationship among the number of sectors, tracks, heads, and cylinders.

If you knew how many heads, cylinders (tracks), and sectors a drive had, you could calculate the capacity of the drive. This information was usually written on the top of the drive housing, as shown in Figure 7-15. For another older drive, if the drive parameters are 855 cylinders, 7 heads, and 17 sectors/track, the drive capacity would have been calculated as 855 cylinders x 7 heads x 17 sectors/track x 512 bytes/sector, which gives 52,093,440 bytes. If you divided this value by 1,024 to convert to KB and then divided by 1,024 again to convert to MB, you would end up with a drive capacity of 49.68 MB.

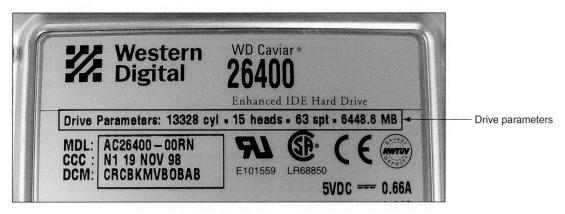

Figure 7-15 Older hard drives had the drive parameters written on the drive housing

> **Notes**
>
> When installing a hard drive, it was once necessary to tell CMOS setup the drive capacity by telling it how many heads, cylinders, and sectors the drive had. Today, most startup BIOSs offer autodetection, so the BIOS detects the new drive and automatically selects the correct drive capacity and configuration.

> **Notes**
>
> For today's drives, to know the capacity of the drive, look for it written on the drive label. As for the number of heads, cylinders, and sectors per track, only the hard drive controller knows and it's not telling.

DRIVE CAPACITY FOR TODAY'S DRIVES

After the drive is installed, you can use the operating system to report the capacity of a hard drive. Using Windows Explorer, right-click the drive letter and select **Properties** on the shortcut menu. Record the capacity of each logical drive on the hard drive, and then add them together to get the entire hard drive capacity, assuming all space on the hard drive is partitioned and format-ted. For Windows 2000/XP, use Disk Management, and for Windows 9x, use Fdisk to report the capacity of an entire hard drive regardless of whether the drive is fully partitioned and formatted.

> **Notes**
>
> In technical documentation, you might see a hard drive abbreviated as HDD (hard disk drive). However, this chapter uses the term hard drive.

> **Video**
>
> Examining Hard Drives

HARD DRIVE INTERFACE STANDARDS

One technology about hard drives that you need to under-stand is the different ways a hard drive interfaces with the computer. Several interface standards exist for hard drives and other drives and devices to connect to connectors and ports on a motherboard, including the several ATA stan-dards, SCSI, USB, FireWire (also called 1394), and Fibre Channel. All of these standards are discussed in this sec-tion. By far, the most popular standard is ATA, so we begin there.

THE ATA INTERFACE STANDARDS

The ATA (Advanced Technology Attachment) interface standards define how hard drives and other drives such as CD, DVD, tape, and Zip drives interface with a computer system. The standards define how the drive controller communicates with the BIOS, the chipset on the motherboard, and the OS. The standards also define the type of connectors used by the drive and the motherboard or expansion cards.

These ATA interface standards control data speeds and transfer methods and are devel-oped by Technical Committee T13 (*www.t13.org*) and published by ANSI (American National Standards Institute, *www.ansi.org.*) Figure 7-1 lists these standards. As these stan-dards developed, different drive manufacturers called them different names, which can be confusing when reading documentation or advertisements.

When selecting a hard drive standard, you should select the fastest standard your mother-board supports. Keep in mind that the OS, the system BIOS on the motherboard, and the firmware on the drive must all support your selected standard. If one of these three does not support the selected standard, the other two will probably revert to a slower standard that all three can use, or the drive will not work at all. You'll learn how to handle these incom-patibility issues later in the chapter.

A+ ESS
1.1

Standard (Can Have More Than One Name)	Speed	Description
ATA* IDE/ATA	Speeds range from 2.1 MB/sec to 8.3 MB/sec	The first T13 and ANSI standard for IDE hard drives. Limited to no more than 528 MB. Supports PIO modes 0-2.
ATA-2* ATAPI, Fast ATA, Parallel ATA (PATA), Enhanced IDE (EIDE)	Speeds up to 16.6 MB/sec	Broke the 528-MB barrier. Allows up to four IDE devices, defining the EIDE standard. Supports PIO modes 3-4 and DMA modes 1-2.
ATA-3*	Speeds up to 16.6 MB/sec (little speed increase)	Improved version of ATA-2 and introduced SMART.
ATA/ATAPI-4* Ultra ATA, Fast ATA-2, Ultra DMA Modes 0-2, DMA/33	Speeds up to 33.3 MB/sec	Defined Ultra DMA modes 0-2 and an 80-conductor cable to improve signal integrity.
ATA/ATAPI-5* Ultra ATA/66, Ultra DMA/66	Speeds up to 66.6 MB/sec	Ultra DMA modes 3-4.
ATA/ATAPI-6* Ultra ATA/100, Ultra DMA/100	Speeds up to 100 MB/sec	Requires the 80-conductor cable. Defined Ultra DMA mode 5, and supports drives larger than 137 GB.
ATA/ATAPI-7* Ultra ATA/133, Serial ATA (SATA), SAS STP	Parallel transfer speeds up to 133 MB/sec Serial transfer speeds up to 150 MB/sec	Can use the 80-conductor cable or serial ATA cable. Defines Ultra DMA mode 6, serial ATA (SATA), and Serial Attached SCSI (SAS) coexisting with SATA.
ATA/ATAPI-8 is currently being drafted.		

*Name assigned by the T13 Committee

Table 7-1 Summary of ATA interface standards for storage devices

Let's now turn our attention to several ATA standards that affect the cabling method used and the transfer rates. These standards include parallel and serial data transmission, DMA and PIO transfer modes, and independent device timing. We begin by looking at the two data transmission standards, parallel or serial. These two standards account for the two types of cables ATA connections can use: parallel ATA cables or serial ATA cables.

PARALLEL ATA OR EIDE CABLING

Parallel ATA, also called the EIDE (Enhanced IDE) standard or, more loosely, the IDE standard, allows for two connectors on a motherboard for two 40-pin data cables. These ribbon cables can accommodate one or two drives, as shown in Figure 7-16. All ATA standards since ATA-2 support this configuration. Parallel ATA or EIDE applies to other drives besides hard drives, including CD drives, Zip drives, tape drives, and so forth.

EIDE is named after IDE (Integrated Device Electronics) technology. Actually, IDE technology pertains to how the hard drive itself works, rather than to an interface standard. However, in the industry, IDE and EIDE are loosely used to talk about an interface standard. (That's not exactly correct, but it's what we do.) An EIDE drive such as a CD, DVD, tape, or

Zip drive must follow the ATAPI (Advanced Technology Attachment Packet Interface) standard in order to connect to a system using an EIDE connector. Using this standard, up to four parallel ATA devices can connect to a motherboard using two data cables.

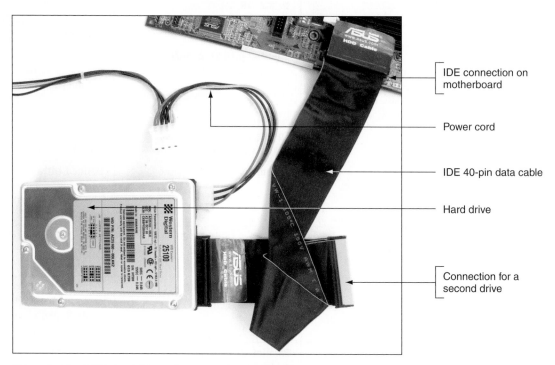

IDE connection on motherboard

Power cord

IDE 40-pin data cable

Hard drive

Connection for a second drive

Figure 7-16 A PC's hard drive subsystem using parallel ATA

Under parallel ATA, two types of ribbon cables are used. The **80-conductor IDE cable** has 40 pins and 80 wires. Forty wires are used for communication and data, and an additional 40 ground wires reduce crosstalk on the cable. An older 40-conductor cable has 40 wires and 40 pins. An 80-conductor IDE cable is required by ATA/100 and above. Figure 7-17 shows a comparison between the two parallel cables. The 80-conductor cable is color-coded with the blue connector always connected to the motherboard. The connectors on each cable otherwise look the same, and you can use an 80-conductor cable in place of a 40-conductor cable in a system. The maximum length of both cables is 18 inches.

> **Notes**
>
> Acronyms sometimes change over time. Years ago, we all knew IDE to mean Integrated Drive Electronics. As the term began to apply to other devices than hard drives, we renamed the acronym to become Integrated Device Electronics.

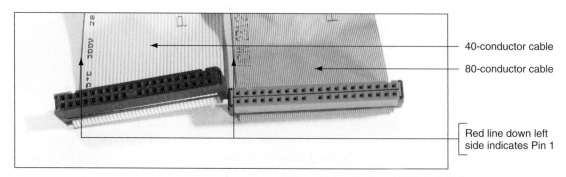

40-conductor cable

80-conductor cable

Red line down left side indicates Pin 1

Figure 7-17 In comparing the 80-conductor cable to the 40-conductor cable, note they are about the same width, but the 80-conductor cable has many more and finer wires

A+ ESS
1.1

SERIAL ATA CABLING

A consortium of manufacturers, called the Serial ATA International Organization (SATA-IO; see *www.sata-io.org*) and led by Intel, developed the serial ATA (SATA) standards. These standards use a serial data path rather than the traditional parallel data path. (Essentially, the difference between the two is that data is placed on a serial cable one bit following the next, but with parallel cabling, all data in a byte is placed on the cable at one time.) The T13 committee is clarifying and further defining serial ATA as it enhances the latest ATA/ATAPI-7 standard, which, as of this writing, is still a work in progress. Current transfer speed is 150 MB/sec, although standards are in the works that should up the speed to 300 or even 600 MB/sec.

Serial ATA drives use a serial ATA cable. Currently there are two types of serial ATA cables: an external serial ATA cable and an internal serial ATA cable.

The latest SATA standard allows for external drives (drives outside the case) and is called external SATA (eSATA). eSATA is up to six times faster than USB or FireWire. External SATA drives use a special external shielded serial ATA cable up to 2 meters long.

An internal serial ATA cable can be up to 1 meter in length, has 7 pins, and is much narrower compared to the 40-pin parallel IDE cable (see Figure 7-18). Serial ATA is a little faster than parallel ATA/133, but is currently more expensive because it is a relatively new technology. Serial ATA has been introduced into the industry not so much to handle the speeds of current drives, but to position the industry for the high-performance large drives expected to soon be inexpensive enough to fit into the desktop hard drive market. Another advantage of serial ATA is the thin cables don't hinder airflow inside a case as much as the wide parallel ATA cables do. One additional advantage is that serial ATA supports hot-swapping, also called hot-plugging. With hot-swapping, you can connect and disconnect a drive while the system is running.

If you have a parallel ATA drive and a serial ATA connector on the motherboard or you have a serial ATA drive and a parallel ATA connector on the motherboard, you can purchase

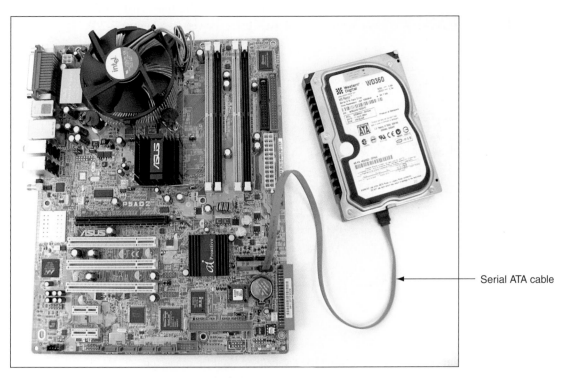

Serial ATA cable

Figure 7-18 A hard drive subsystem using the new serial ATA data cable

an adapter to make the hard drive connector fit your motherboard connector. Figure 7-19 shows a converter. For a motherboard that does not have a serial ATA connector or does not have enough of them, you can purchase an expansion card to provide both internal and external serial ATA connectors for drives.

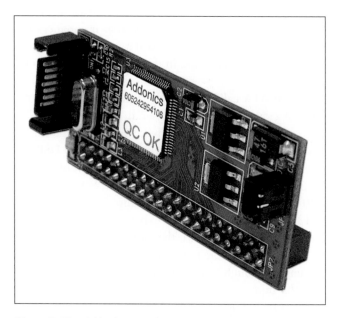

Figure 7-19   Addonics IDE Ultra ATA-100/133 parallel ATA to serial ATA converter

When serial ATA was first introduced into the market, only hard drives used it, but now all kinds of drives are using serial ATA, including CD, DVD, and tape drives. However, because PATA drives are still so commonplace, a motherboard needs at least one 40-pin parallel ATA connector for one or two EIDE drives (see Figure 7-20).

Figure 7-20   This motherboard has a variety of ATA drive connectors

A+ ESS
1.1

In Figure 7-20, the RAID (redundant array of independent disks) connectors are a hard drive interface method used with servers, which makes it possible to connect multiple hard drives together into a RAID array to improve performance and automatically recover from a failure. You'll learn more about RAID in Chapter 9.

DMA OR PIO TRANSFER MODES

A hard drive uses one of two methods to transfer data between the hard drive and memory: DMA (direct memory access) transfer mode or PIO (Programmed Input/Output) transfer mode. DMA transfers data directly from the drive to memory without involving the CPU. PIO mode involves the CPU and is slower than DMA mode, which does not involve the CPU.

There are different modes for PIO and DMA due to the fact that both standards have evolved over the last few years. There are five PIO modes, from the slowest (PIO mode 0) to the fastest (PIO mode 4), and seven DMA modes from the slowest (DMA mode 0) to the fastest (DMA mode 6).

Most often, when installing a drive, the startup BIOS autodetects the drive and selects the fastest mode that the drive and the BIOS support. After installation, you can go into CMOS setup and verify that setup recognized the drive correctly.

INDEPENDENT DEVICE TIMING

As you saw in Table 7-1, there are different hard drive standards, each running at different speeds. If two hard drives share the same parallel ATA cable but use different standards, both drives will run at the speed of the slower drive unless the motherboard chipset controlling the ATA connections supports a feature called Independent Device Timing. Most chipsets today support this feature and with it, the two drives can run at different speeds as long as the motherboard supports those speeds.

BREAKING THE 137 GB BARRIER

In 2002, the ATA/ATAPI-6 standard, also called the ATA/100 standard, was published and led the way to break a significant barrier with hard drive interfaces. Up until these standards were published, a hard drive could not have more than 137 GB of data. This limitation was caused by the fact that the hard drive, the system BIOS, and the OS used 28 bits to communicate addresses to the data on the drive (see Figure 7-21). The largest address that 28 bits could hold was 1111 1111 1111 1111 1111 1111 1111 in binary, which converts to 268,435,455 in decimal. Each address represented the location of one 512-byte sector on the drive so that the drive could have no more than 268,435,455 sectors. Therefore, the addressable space on the drive was 268,435,455 times 512, which yields 137,438,952,960 bytes, or about 137 GB. Understand the barrier limitation of 137 GB was not in how much data could be written to the drive, but how much data could be addressed by the interface to the drive. The newer ATA/ATAPI-6 allows 48 bits for the address, increasing the addressable space on a hard drive up to 144 petabytes (144,000,000,000,000,000 bytes). It's estimated that this limitation won't affect us for at least 50 years.

For your system to support drives larger than 137 GB, the OS, the system BIOS, the ATA controller (sometimes called the IDE controller in documentation), and the hard drive must all support the standard. Before investing in a drive larger than 137 GB, verify that your motherboard and the OS support it. If your motherboard does not support these drives, first check with the BIOS manufacturer for a possible update and flash BIOS. If an updated BIOS is not available, you can purchase an expansion card to provide the hard drive connectors that support the size drive you want to use. Note that Windows 9x does not support drives larger than 137 GB unless third-party software provided by the hard drive manufacturer is used. Windows 2000/XP support drives larger than 137 GB if service packs are applied.

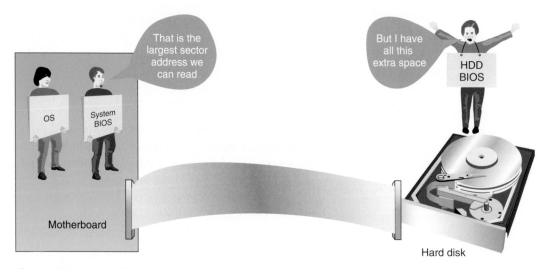

Figure 7-21 The 137-GB barrier existed because of the size of the numbers used to address a sector

CONFIGURING PARALLEL AND SERIAL ATA DRIVES IN A SYSTEM

Following the parallel ATA or EIDE standard, a motherboard can support up to four EIDE devices using either 80-conductor or 40-conductor cables. The motherboard offers two IDE connectors (see Figure 7-22). Each connector accommodates one IDE channel, and each channel can accommodate one or two IDE devices. One channel is called the primary channel and the other channel is called the secondary channel. Each IDE connector uses one 40-pin cable. The cable has two connectors on it: one connector in the middle of the cable and one at the far end for two EIDE devices. An EIDE device can be a hard drive, DVD drive, CD-ROM drive, Zip drive, or other type of drive. One device is configured to act as the master controlling the channel, and the other device on the channel is the slave. There are, therefore, four possible configurations for four EIDE devices in a system:

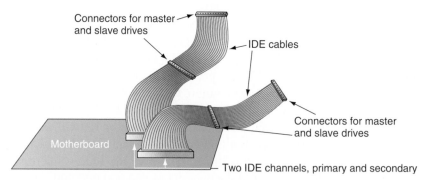

Figure 7-22 A motherboard has two IDE channels; each can support a master and slave drive using a single EIDE cable

- ▲ Primary IDE channel, master device
- ▲ Primary IDE channel, slave device
- ▲ Secondary IDE channel, master device
- ▲ Secondary IDE channel, slave device

The master or slave designations are made by setting jumpers or DIP switches on the devices or by using a special cable-select data cable. Documentation can be tricky.

7

A+ ESS
1.1

Some hard drive documentation labels the master drive setting as the Drive 0 setting and the slave drive setting as Drive 1 setting rather than using the terms master and slave. The connectors on a parallel ATA 80-conductor cable are color-coded (see Figure 7-23). Use the blue end to connect to the motherboard; use the black end to connect to the drive. If you only have one drive connected to the cable, put it on the black connector at the end of the cable, not the gray connector in the middle.

Notes

When installing a hard drive on the same channel with an ATAPI drive such as a CD-ROM drive, always make the hard drive, the master, and the ATAPI drive the slave. An even better solution is to install the hard drive on the primary channel and the CD drive and any other drive on the secondary channel.

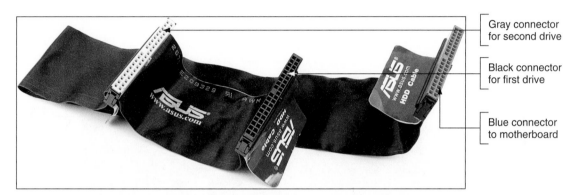

Gray connector for second drive

Black connector for first drive

Blue connector to motherboard

Figure 7-23   80-conductor cable connectors are color-coded

The motherboard might also be color-coded so that the primary channel connector is blue (see Figure 7-24). This color-coding is intended to ensure that the ATA/66/100/133 hard drive is installed on the primary IDE channel.

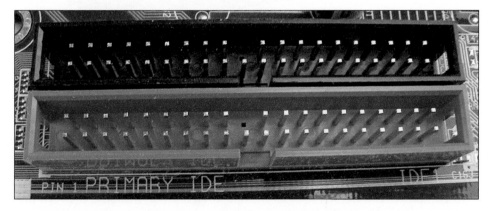

Figure 7-24   The primary IDE channel connector is often color-coded as blue

If a motherboard supports serial ATA, most likely it has two or four serial ATA connectors and one or two parallel ATA connectors. A serial ATA cable can accommodate only a single drive, so you don't have to use jumpers to set master or slave assignments. According to one motherboard documentation, when installing serial ATA drives

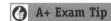 **A+ Exam Tip**

The A+ Essentials exam expects you to know how to configure PATA and SATA devices in a system.

using Windows 2000/XP, you can install up to six ATA devices in the system, including up to four parallel ATA devices and up to two serial ATA devices. Using Windows 9x/Me, you can install up to four devices using a combination of parallel ATA and serial ATA devices. You can have up to four parallel ATA devices and up to two serial ATA devices as long as the total number of devices in the Windows 9x/Me system does not exceed four.

In Figure 7-25, you can see the back of two hard drives; one uses a serial ATA interface and the other uses a parallel ATA interface. Notice the parallel ATA drive has a bank of jumpers and a 4-pin power connector. These jumpers are used to determine master or slave settings on the IDE channel. Because a serial data cable accommodates only a single drive, there is no need for jumpers on the drive for master or slave settings. However, a serial ATA drive might have jumpers used to set features such as the ability to power up from standby mode. Most likely, if jumpers are present on a serial ATA drive, the factory has set them as they should be and advises you not to change them.

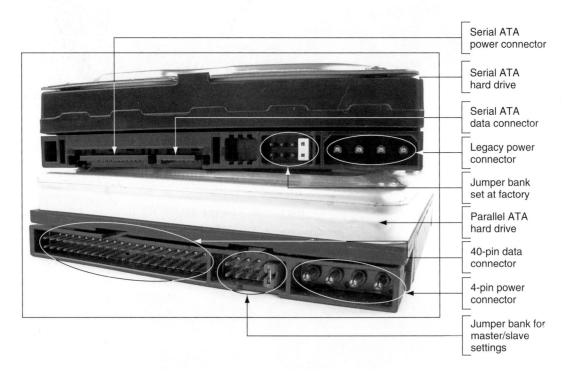

Figure 7-25 Rear of a serial ATA drive and a parallel ATA drive

The power connector for a serial ATA drive is different from a regular EIDE device. To accommodate the special power connector, a serial ATA drive often comes with its own special power adapter or power cord (see Figure 7-26). Some serial ATA drives have two power connectors, as does the one in Figure 7-25. Choose between the serial ATA power connector (which is the preferred connector) or the legacy 4-pin connector, but never install two power cords to the drive at the same time because this could damage the drive. You will see examples of parallel and serial ATA installations later in the chapter.

USING AN ATA CONTROLLER CARD

An ATA drive usually connects to the motherboard by way of a data cable from the drive to a parallel or serial ATA connection directly on the motherboard. However, you can use an ATA controller card to provide the ATA connectors when: (1) the motherboard IDE

7

A+ ESS
1.1

Serial ATA power
connector

Legacy 4-pin
power connector

Power connectors
from power supply

Figure 7-26 A serial ATA hard drive uses a special power cord to connect to a 4-pin power connector
coming from the power supply

connectors are not functioning; or (2) the motherboard does not support an ATA standard
you want to implement (such as a large-capacity drive). For example, suppose your older
motherboard supports ATA/100, but your hard drive uses ATA/133. You can purchase a
controller card such as the one by Belkin (*www.belkin.com*), shown in Figure 7-27. This
card uses a PCI slot, provides two 40-pin parallel IDE connections, and supports ATA/133
and previous ATA standards.

Figure 7-27 This Ultra ATA/133 controller card by Belkin, uses a PCI slot and has two 40-pin IDE
connections that can accommodate up to four EIDE devices

A+ ESS
1.1

Because a parallel ATA connector can accommodate one data cable for two drives, the card can support up to four drives. If you take into account the motherboard has two ATA/100 parallel ATA connectors that can support up to four drives, the entire system collectively can support up to eight parallel ATA drives when you use the card.

SCSI TECHNOLOGY

A+ ESS
1.1
4.1

Other than ATA, another interface standard for drives and other devices is SCSI, which provides better performance and greater expansion capabilities for many internal and external devices, including hard drives, CD-ROM drives, DVD drives, printers, and scanners. SCSI devices tend to be faster, more expensive, and more difficult to install than similar IDE devices. Because they are more expensive and more difficult to install, they are mostly used in corporate settings and are seldom seen in the small office or used on home PCs.

SCSI (pronounced "scuzzy") stands for Small Computer System Interface and is a standard for communication between a subsystem of peripheral devices and the system bus. The SCSI bus can support up to 7 or 15 devices, depending on the SCSI standard. The SCSI bus controller can be an expansion card called a host adapter or can be embedded on the motherboard. If it's embedded on the motherboard, the board will have one or more internal or external SCSI connectors.

THE SCSI SUBSYSTEM

If a motherboard does not have an embedded SCSI controller, the gateway from the SCSI bus to the system bus is the host adapter, a card inserted into an expansion slot on the motherboard. The adapter card, called the host adapter, is responsible for managing all devices on the SCSI bus. A host adapter can support both internal and external SCSI devices, using one connector on the card for a ribbon cable or round cable to connect to internal devices, and an external port that supports external devices (see Figure 7-28).

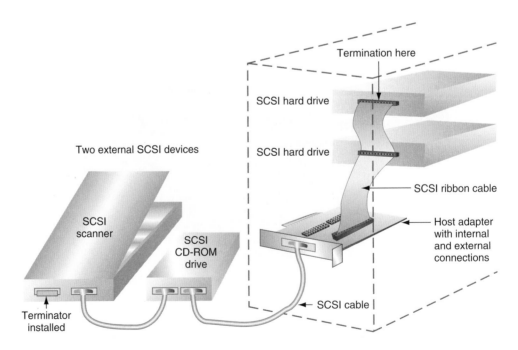

Figure 7-28 Using a SCSI bus, a SCSI host adapter can support internal and external SCSI devices

All the devices and the host adapter form a single daisy chain. In Figure 7-28, this daisy chain has two internal devices and two external devices, with the SCSI host adapter in the middle of the chain.

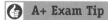

> **A+ Exam Tip**
>
> The A+ Essentials exam expects you to know that a motherboard might provide a SCSI controller and connector, or the SCSI host adapter can be a card installed in an expansion slot.

All devices go through the host adapter to communicate with the CPU or directly with each other without involving the CPU. Each device on the bus is assigned a number from 0 to 15 called the SCSI ID, by means of DIP switches, dials on the device, or software settings. The host adapter is generally assigned a number larger than all other devices, either 7 or 15. Cables connect the devices physically in a daisy chain, sometimes called a straight chain. The devices can be either internal or external, and the host adapter can be at either end of the chain or somewhere in the middle. The SCSI ID identifies the physical device, which can have several logical devices embedded in it. For example, a CD-ROM jukebox—a CD-ROM changer with trays for multiple CDs—might have seven trays. Each tray is considered a logical device and is assigned a Logical Unit Number (LUN) to identify it, such as 1 through 7 or 0 through 6. The ID and LUN are written as two numbers separated by a colon. For instance, if the SCSI ID is 5, the fourth tray in the jukebox is device 5:4.

> **Notes**
>
> During installation, when setting IDs for internal devices, older devices required that you set jumpers on the device. These devices use a binary code to set IDs, with three pin pairs for narrow SCSI and four pin pairs for wide SCSI. Figure 7-29 shows the jumper settings for wide SCSI IDs.

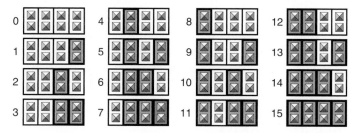

Figure 7-29 Wide SCSI ID binary jumper settings for internal devices

To reduce the amount of electrical "noise," or interference, on a SCSI cable, each end of the SCSI chain has a terminating resistor. The terminating resistor can be a hardware device plugged into the last device on each end of the chain (see Figure 7-30), or the chain can have software-controlled termination resistance, which makes installation simpler.

A+ ESS
1.1
4.1

Figure 7-30 External SCSI terminator

VARIOUS SCSI STANDARDS

Just as with IDE/ATA standards, SCSI standards have improved over the years and use different names. SCSI standards are developed by the SCSI T10 Technical Committee (*www.t10.org*) and sent to ANSI, which publishes and maintains the official versions of the standards. The SCSI Trade Association, which promotes SCSI devices and standards, can also be accessed at *www.t10.org*. In addition to varying standards, SCSI also uses different types of cabling and different bus widths. Because there are so many variations with SCSI, when setting up a SCSI subsystem, it's important to pay careful attention to compatibility and make sure all devices, the host adapter, cables, and connectors can work together.

The three major versions of SCSI are SCSI-1, SCSI-2, and SCSI-3, commonly known as Regular SCSI, Fast SCSI, and Ultra SCSI. The latest SCSI standard, serial SCSI, also called serial attached SCSI (SAS), allows for more than 15 devices on a single SCSI chain, uses smaller, longer, round cables, and uses smaller hard drive form factors that can support larger capacities than earlier versions of SCSI. Serial SCSI is compatible with serial ATA drives in the same system, and claims to be more reliable and better performing than serial ATA. For more information on serial SCSI, see the SCSI Trade Association's Web site at *www.serialattachedscsi.com*.

A+ ESS
1.1

OTHER INTERFACE STANDARDS

Other than ATA and SCSI, some other technologies used by hard drives are USB, FireWire (IEEE 1394), and Fibre Channel, which can all be used by external hard drives. Let's now look at USB, IEEE 1394, and Fibre Channel interfaces.

USB

USB (universal serial bus) is a popular way to connect many external peripheral devices to a system. The first USB standard, USB 1.0, is not fast enough to be used for a hard drive, but the latest standards, USB 1.1 and USB 2.0 (Hi-Speed USB) are fast enough. Most computers today have two or more USB ports, making USB an easy way to add a second external hard drive to a system. For example, Maxtor (*www.maxtor.com*) has a 120-GB external drive for under $200 that works with a USB 2.0 or USB 1.1 interface. Windows 98SE, Windows Me, and Windows 2000/XP support USB 1.1, and Windows XP supports USB 2.0 with a service pack applied. Before buying a USB hard drive, verify your OS and the motherboard USB connection support the same USB standard as the drive. Chapter 8 includes more information about USB.

IEEE 1394 OR FIREWIRE

IEEE 1394, also known as FireWire (named by Apple Computers) and i.Link (named by Sony Corporation), uses serial transmission of data and is popular for multimedia and home entertainment applications. IEEE refers to the Institute of Electrical and Electronics Engineers, which published standard 1394, more commonly known as FireWire. For more information, see *www.ieee.org*. For example, SmartDisk, Inc.(*www.smartdisk.com*), a manufacturer of multimedia devices, makes a hard drive designed for home entertainment electronics that uses FireWire or USB for the external hard drive interface (see Figure 7-31).

Figure 7-31   This CrossFire hard drive holds 160GB and uses a 1394a or USB 2.0 connection

A FireWire device connects to a PC through a FireWire external port or internal connector provided either directly on the motherboard or by way of a FireWire expansion card. For a computer system to use FireWire, the operating system must support it. Windows 98, Windows 2000, and Windows XP support FireWire, but Windows 95 and Windows NT do not. Chapter 8 includes more information about FireWire.

FIBRE CHANNEL

Fibre Channel is another type of interface that can support hard drives. Fibre Channel is designed for use in high-end systems that have multiple hard drives. To be precise, Fibre Channel is a type of SCSI technology, but in the industry, it is considered a rival of SCSI for high-end server solutions. One advantage Fibre Channel has over SCSI is that you can connect up to 126 devices together on a single Fibre Channel bus, as compared to 16 SCSI devices connected together on the same bus. Fibre Channel is faster than SCSI when

A+ ESS
1.1

more than five hard drives are strung together to provide massive secondary storage, but it is too expensive and has too much overhead to be a good solution for the average desktop PC or workstation.

SELECTING AND INSTALLING A HARD DRIVE

A+
220-602
1.1

This section of the chapter covers how to select a hard drive and then how to install it. You'll learn what to look for when selecting a drive and then how to install a drive in a system using either a parallel ATA drive and a serial ATA drive.

HOW TO SELECT A HARD DRIVE

When making purchasing decisions, you need to match the HDD technologies to the OS and the motherboard in a system. In most cases, when installing a drive, you don't need to know which ATA standard a hard drive supports, because the startup BIOS uses autodetection. With autodetection, the BIOS detects the new drive and automatically selects the correct drive capacity and configuration, including the best possible standard supported by both the hard drive and the motherboard.

One exception is when you install a new drive that the startup BIOS is not designed to support. The BIOS will either not recognize the drive at all or will detect the drive and report in CMOS setup that the drive has a smaller capacity or fewer features than it actually does. In this situation, your older BIOS or hard drive controller card does not support the newer ATA standard the drive is using. The solution is to flash BIOS, replace the controller card, or replace the motherboard.

APPLYING CONCEPTS   When purchasing a hard drive, consider the following factors that affect performance, use, and price:

▲ *The capacity of the drive.* Today's hard drives for desktop systems are in the range of 20 GB to more than 500 GB. The more gigabytes, the higher the price.

▲ *The spindle speed.* Hard drives for desktop systems run at 5400, 7200, or 10,000 RPM. The most common are 5400 and 7200 RPM. 7200 RPM drives are faster, make more noise, put off more heat, and are more expensive than 5400 RPM drives.

▲ *The technology standard.* Most likely, the hard drive technology standard you'll want to select is Ultra ATA/100, Ultra ATA/133, or Serial ATA 150, although you might choose SCSI or FireWire. As always, be sure your motherboard supports the standard you choose.

▲ *The cache or buffer size.* Look for a 2-MB or 8-MB cache (also called a buffer). The more the better, though the cost goes up as the size increases.

▲ *The average seek time (time to fetch data).* Look for 13 to 8.5 ms (milliseconds). The lower the number, the higher the drive performance and cost.

When selecting a drive, match the drive to what your motherboard supports. To find out what drive the motherboard supports, you can check the motherboard documentation or the CMOS setup screen

7

A+
220-602
1.1

for information. For example, the CMOS setup screens for one motherboard give these options:

- ▲ LBA Mode can be enabled or disabled.
- ▲ Multisector transfers (block mode) can be set to Disabled, 2, 4, 8, or 16 sectors.
- ▲ PIO Mode can be set to Auto, 0, 1, 2, 3, or 4.
- ▲ Ultra DMA Mode can be set to Disabled, 0, 1, 2, 3, 4, or 5.
- ▲ Cable detected displays the type of cable (40-conductor or 80-conductor).

Remember, when you install the drive, you won't have to set these values, because autodetection should do that for you. However, reading about the values allows you to know what the board supports and what drive you can purchase. After all, there's no point in buying an expensive hard drive with features your system cannot support.

> **Notes**
>
> Some BIOSs support a method of data transfer that allows multiple data transfers each time software requests data. This method is called **block mode** and should be used if your hard drive and BIOS support it. However, if you are having problems with hard drive errors, you can try disabling block mode. You can use CMOS setup to make this change.

After you know what drive your system can support, you then can select a drive that is appropriate for the price range and intended use of your system. For example, Seagate has two lines of IDE hard drives: The Barracuda is less expensive and intended for the desktop market, and the Cheetah is more expensive and targets the server market. When purchasing a drive, you can compare price and features by searching the Web sites of the drive manufacturers, some of which are listed in Table 7-2. The same manufacturers usually produce ATA drives and SCSI drives.

Manufacturer	Web Site
Fujitsu America, Inc.	*www.fujitsu.com*
IBM PC Company	*www.ibm.com*
Maxtor Corporation	*www.maxtor.com*
Quantum Corporation	*www.quantum.com*
Seagate Technology	*www.seagate.com*
Western Digital	*www.wdc.com*

Table 7-2 Hard drive manufacturers

Now let's turn our attention to the step-by-step process of installing an ATA hard drive. We begin by looking at special concerns that arise when installing a hard drive in a system that has an older BIOS that doesn't support the newer drive.

INSTALLATIONS USING LEGACY BIOS

Before installing a new hard drive, know the hard drive standards the BIOS on your motherboard supports. Here are the older standards that you might encounter with older motherboards:

- ▲ *CHS (cylinder, head, sector) mode or normal mode used for drives less than 528 MB.* System BIOS expects the hard drive controller to communicate the location of data on

A+
220-602
1.1

the drive using cylinder, head, and track coordinates. Using CHS mode, a drive can have no more than 1,024 cylinders, 16 heads, 63 sectors per track, and 512 bytes per sector. Therefore, the maximum amount of storage on a hard drive using CHS mode is 528 MB or 504 MB, depending on how the calculations are done (1K = 1,000 or 1K = 1,024). You'll probably never see one of the obsolete boards around, but, then again, you never know.

▲ *Large mode or ECHS mode used for drives between 504 MB and 8.4 GB.* System BIOS expects the hard drive controller to send cylinder, head, and track coordinates, but the BIOS communicates a different set of parameters to the OS and other software. This method is called translation, and system BIOS is said to be in large mode, or ECHS (extended CHS) mode.

▲ *33.8 GB limitation.* System BIOS on some systems does not recognize a drive larger than 33.8 GB, which can cause the system to lock up during POST, or to boot, but incorrectly report the size of the drive.

▲ *137 GB limitation.* System BIOS does not support the ATA/ATAPI-6 standard, which makes it unable to recognize drives larger than 137 GB.

If you want to install a drive in a system whose BIOS does not support it, you have the following choices:

▲ *Let the BIOS see the drive as a smaller drive.* For some systems, the BIOS assigns a drive capacity smaller than the actual capacity. You can use this method, although it wastes drive space. With other BIOSs, the system refuses to boot when it sees a drive it does not support.

▲ *Upgrade the BIOS.* The least expensive solution is to upgrade the BIOS. Be certain you use a BIOS upgrade compatible with your motherboard. It's also a good idea to update the chipset drivers at the same time you update the BIOS. You can download the BIOS upgrade and the chipset driver update from the motherboard manufacturer's Web site.

▲ *Replace the motherboard.* This is the most expensive solution.

▲ *Use software that interfaces between the older BIOS and the newer drive.* Most drive manufacturers provide software that performs the translation between an older BIOS and the newer drive. Examples of such translation or disk overlay software are Disk Manager by Ontrack Data International, Inc. (*www.ontrack.com*), SpeedStor by Storage Dimensions, EZ-Drive by Phoenix (*www.phoenix.com*), MaxBlast by Maxtor (*www.maxtor.com*), and DiscWizard by Seagate (*www.seagate.com*). You can find the software on a floppy disk with the drive or download it from the drive manufacturer's Web site. Boot from a floppy disk with the software installed, and follow directions onscreen. Before you decide to use this method, read the documentation on the hard drive manufacturer's Web site to understand how to handle problems that might later arise with the drive.

▲ *Use an ATA controller card to provide the ATA connector and firmware to substitute for motherboard BIOS.* You saw a photograph of one of these controller cards in Figure 7-27 earlier in the chapter.

STEPS TO INSTALL A PARALLEL ATA HARD DRIVE

We'll first look at how to install a parallel ATA hard drive and then look at the differences between that installation and one using a serial ATA drive.

To install a parallel ATA drive, you need the drive, an 80-conductor or 40-conductor data cable, and perhaps a kit to make the drive fit into a much larger bay. If the motherboard

7

A+
220-602
1.1

does not provide an IDE connection, you also need an adapter card.

To install a parallel ATA hard drive, do the following:

> **A+ Exam Tip**
>
> The A+ Essentials exam expects you to know how to install a device such as a hard drive. Given a list of steps for the installation, you should be able to order the steps correctly or identify an error in a step.

1. Prepare for the installation by preparing the existing computer system for a disassembly, reading the documentation, planning the drive configuration, and preparing your work area.

2. Set jumpers or DIP switches on the drive.

3. Physically install the drive inside the computer case, and attach the power cord and data cable.

4. Use CMOS setup to verify that autodetect correctly detected the drive.

5. If you are installing an OS on the drive, boot from the Windows setup CD. If the drive is not intended to hold an OS (it's a second drive in a two-drive system, for example), use the Windows 2000/XP Disk Management utility or the Windows 9x/Me Fdisk and Format commands to partition and format the drive.

> **Video**
>
> Installing a Hard Drive

Let's now look at each of the preceding steps in more detail.

STEP 1: PREPARE FOR THE INSTALLATION

Prepare for the installation by knowing your starting point, reading the documentation, planning the drive configuration, and preparing your work area.

Know Your Starting Point

As with installing any other devices, before you begin installing your hard drive, make sure you know where your starting point is. Do this by answering these questions: How is your system configured? Is everything working properly? Verify which of your system's devices are working before installing a new one. Later, if a device does not work, the information will help you isolate the problem. Remember from earlier chapters that keeping notes is a good idea whenever you install new hardware or software or make any other changes to your PC system. Write down what you know about the system that might be important later.

As always, just in case you lose setup information in the process, write down any variations in setup from the default settings. Two good places to record CMOS settings are the notebook you keep about this computer and the manual for the motherboard.

> **Notes**
>
> When installing hardware and software, don't install too many things at once. If something goes wrong, you won't know what's causing the problem. Install one device, start the system, and confirm that the new device is working before installing another.

Read Documentation

Before you take anything apart, carefully read all the documentation for the drive and controller card, and the part of your PC documentation that covers hard drive installation. Look for problems you have not considered, such as differing ATA standards. Check your motherboard documentation to verify the BIOS accommodates the size and type of hard drive you want to install. If you are not sure which ATA standards your motherboard supports, you can look for different options on the CMOS setup screens.

Plan the Drive Configuration

You must decide which IDE connector to use and if another drive will share the same IDE data cable with your new drive. Remember, when using parallel ATA, there are two IDE connectors on a motherboard, the primary and secondary IDE channels. Each channel can support up to two drives, a master and a slave, for a total of up to four EIDE drives in a system.

When possible, leave the hard drive as the single drive on one channel, so that it does not compete with another drive for access to the channel and possibly slow down performance. Use the primary channel before you use the secondary channel.

> **Notes**
>
> If you have three or fewer devices, allow the fastest hard drive to be your boot device and the only device on the primary channel.

Place the fastest devices on the primary channel and the slower devices on the secondary channel. This pairing helps keep a slow device from pulling down a faster device. As an example of this type of pairing, suppose you have a Zip drive, CD-ROM drive, and two hard drives. Because the two hard drives are faster than the Zip drive and CD-ROM drive, put the two hard drives on one channel and the Zip drive and CD-ROM drive on the other.

Make sure that you can visualize all the steps in the installation. If you have any questions, keep researching until you locate the answer. You can also call technical support or ask a knowledgeable friend for help. As you get your questions answered, you might discover that what you are installing will not work on your computer, but that is better than coping with hours of frustration and a disabled computer. You cannot always anticipate every problem, but at least you can know that you made your best effort to understand everything in advance. What you learn in thorough preparation pays off every time!

Prepare Your Work Area and Take Precautions

The next step is to prepare a large, well-lit place to work. Set out your tools, documentation, new hardware, and notebook. Remember the basic rules concerning static electricity, which you learned in Chapter 2. Be sure to protect against ESD by wearing a ground bracelet during the installation. You need to also avoid working on carpet in the winter when there's a lot of static electricity.

Some added precautions for working with hard drives are as follows:

- Handle the drive carefully.
- Do not touch any exposed circuitry or chips.
- Prevent other people from touching exposed microchips on the drive.
- When you first take the drive out of the static-protective package, touch the package containing the drive to a screw holding an expansion card or cover, or to a metal part of the computer case, for at least two seconds. This drains the static electricity from the package and from your body.
- If you must set down the drive outside the static-protective package, place it component-side-up on a flat surface.
- Do not place the drive on the computer case cover or on a metal table.

7

A+
220-602
1.1

So now you're ready to start work. Turn off the computer and unplug it. Unplug the monitor and move it to one side. Remove the computer case cover. Check that you have an available power cord from the power supply.

You need to decide which bay will hold which drive. To do that, examine the locations of the drive bays and the length of the data cables and power cords. Bays designed for hard drives do not have access to the outside of the case, unlike bays for Zip drives and other drives in which disks are inserted. Also, some bays are wider than others to accommodate wide drives such as CD-ROM drives and DVD drives (see Figure 7-32). Will the data cable reach the drives and the motherboard connector? If not, rearrange your plan for locating the drives in the bays, or purchase a custom-length data cable.

> **Notes**
>
> If there are not enough power cords from a power supply, you can purchase a Y connector that can add an additional power cord.

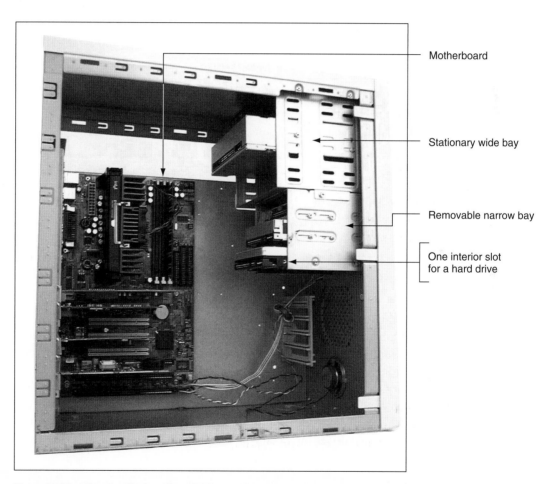

Motherboard

Stationary wide bay

Removable narrow bay

One interior slot for a hard drive

Figure 7-32 Plan for the location of drives within bays

STEP 2: SET JUMPERS

You normally configure a hard drive by setting jumpers on the drive housing. Often, diagrams of the jumper settings are printed on the top of the hard drive housing (see Figure 7-33). If they are not, see the documentation or visit the Web site of the drive manufacturer. (Hands-On Project 7-5 lets you practice this.)

A+
220-602
1.1

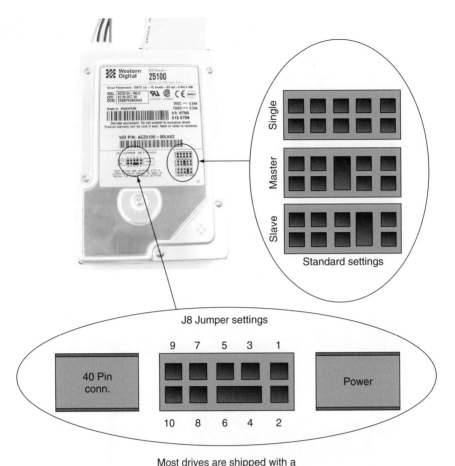

J8 Jumper settings

Most drives are shipped with a
jumper as shown above, no need to
remove for single drive setting

Figure 7-33 A parallel ATA drive most likely will have diagrams of jumper settings for master
and slave options printed on the drive housing

Table 7-3 lists the four choices for jumper settings, and Figure 7-34 shows a typical
jumper arrangement for a drive that uses three of these settings. In Figures 7-33 and 7-34,
note that a black square represents an empty pin and a black rectangle represents a pair of
pins with jumper in place. Know that your hard drive might not have the first configuration
as an option, but it should have a way of indicating if the drive will be the master device.
The factory default setting is usually correct for the drive to be the single drive on a system.
Before you change any settings, write down the original ones. If things go wrong, you can
revert to the original settings and begin again. If a drive is the only drive on a channel, set it
to single. For two drives on a controller, set one to master and the other to slave.

Configuration	Description
Single-drive configuration	**This is the only hard drive on this EIDE channel. (This is the standard setting.)**
Master-drive configuration	**This is the first of two drives; it most likely is the boot device.**
Slave-drive configuration	**This is the second drive using this channel or data cable.**
Cable-select configuration	**The cable-select data cable determines which of the two drives is the master and which is the slave.**

Table 7-3 Jumper settings on a parallel ATA hard drive

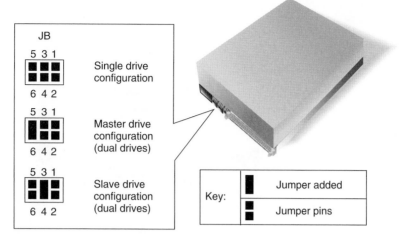

Figure 7-34 Jumper settings on a hard drive and their meanings

Some hard drives have a cable-select configuration option. If you choose this configuration, you must use a cable-select data cable. When you use one of these cables, the drive nearest the motherboard is the master, and the drive farthest from the motherboard is the slave. You can recognize a cable-select cable by a small hole somewhere in the data cable.

> **Notes**
>
> Know that some hard drive manufacturers label the master setting as Drive 0 and the slave setting as Drive 1.

STEP 3: MOUNT THE DRIVE IN THE BAY

Now that you've set the jumpers, your next step is to look at the drive bay that you will use for the drive. The bay can be stationary or removable. With a removable bay, you first remove the bay from the computer case and mount the drive in the bay. Then, you put the bay back into the computer case. In Figure 7-32, you can see a stationary, wide bay for large drives and a removable, narrow bay for small drives, including the hard drive.

In the following steps, you will see how the hard drive is installed in a computer case that has three other drives: a DVD drive, a Zip drive, and a floppy drive. Do the following to install the hard drive in the bay:

1. Remove the bay for the hard drive, and insert the hard drive in the bay. You can line up the drive in the bay with the front of the computer case (see Figure 7-35) to see how drives will line up in the bay. Put the hard drive in the bay flush with the front of the bay so it will butt up against the computer case once the bay is in position (see Figure 7-36). Line up other drives in the bay so they are flush with the front of the computer case. In Figure 7-36, a floppy drive and Zip drive are already in the bay.

2. You must be able to securely mount the drive in the bay; the drive should not move when it is screwed down. Line up the drive and bay screw holes, and make sure everything will fit. After checking the position of the drive and determining how screws are placed, install four screws (two on each side) to mount the drive in the bay.

> **Notes**
>
> Do not allow torque to stress the drive. For example, don't force a drive into a space that is too small for it. Also, placing two screws in diagonal positions across the drive can place pressure diagonally on the drive.

A+
220-602
1.1

Figure 7-35 Line up the floppy drive in the removable bay so it's flush with the front of the case

Figure 7-36 Position the hard drive flush with the end of the bay

3. Decide whether to connect the data cable to the drive before or after you insert the bay inside the computer case, depending on how accessible the connections are. In this example, the data cables are connected to the drives first and then the bay is installed inside the computer case. In the photograph in Figure 7-37, the data cables for all the drives in the bay are connected to the drives.

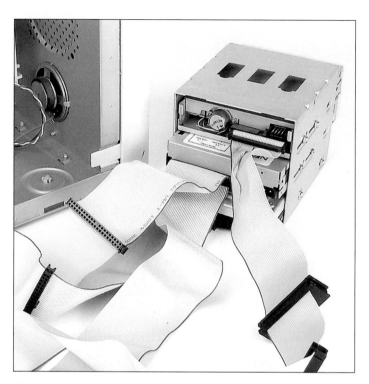

Figure 7-37 Connect the cables to all three drives

4. The next step is to place the bay back into position and secure the bay with the bay screw or screws (see Figure 7-38). Note that some bays are secured with clips. For example, for the bay shown in Figure 7-39, when you slide the bay into the case, you will hear the clipping mechanism pop into place when the bay is all the way in.

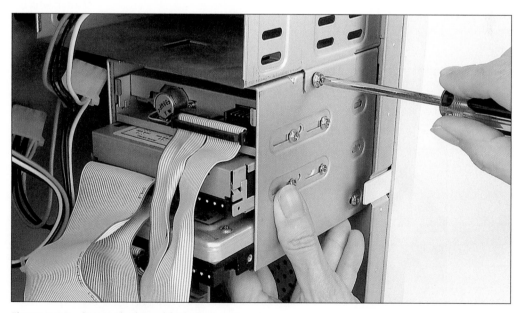

Figure 7-38 Secure the bay with the bay screw

A+
220-602
1.1

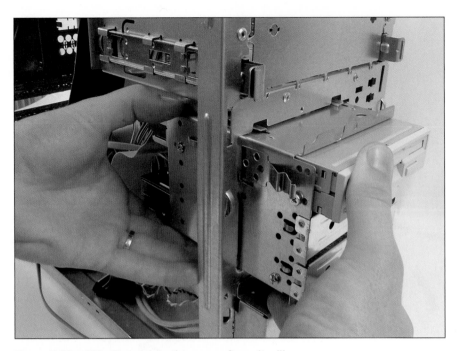

Figure 7-39 Slide the bay into the case as far as it will go

> ✎ **Notes**
>
> The previous steps to install a hard drive assume that you are using a removable bay. However, some computer cases use small, stationary bays like the one in Figure 7-40. For these installations, you need only slide the drive into the bay and secure it with four screws, two on each side of the bay.

5. You can now install a power connection to each drive (Figure 7-41). In Figure 7-41, the floppy drive uses the small Berg power connection, and the other drives use the large Molex ones. It doesn't matter which of the power cords you use, because they all produce the same voltage. Also, the cord only goes into the connection one way.

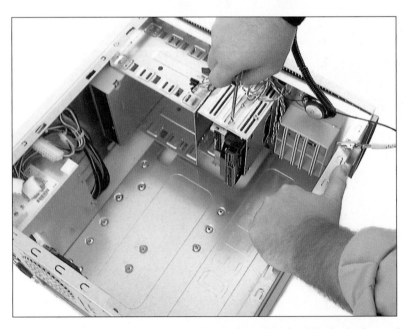

Figure 7-40 To install a drive in a stationary bay, slide the drive in the bay and secure it with four screws

7

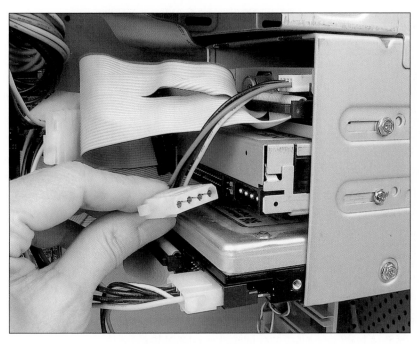

Figure 7-41   Connect a power cord to each drive

6. Next, connect the data cable to the IDE connector on the motherboard (see Figure 7-42). Make certain pin 1 and the edge color on the cable align correctly at both ends of the cable. Normally, pin 1 is closest to the power connection on the drive.

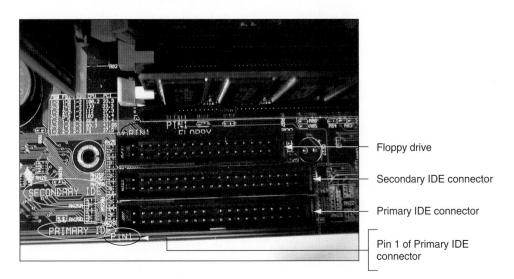

Floppy drive

Secondary IDE connector

Primary IDE connector

Pin 1 of Primary IDE connector

Figure 7-42   Floppy drive and two IDE connectors on the motherboard

7. If you are mounting a hard drive in an external bay, install a bay cover in the front of the case. Internal bays do not need this cover (see Figure 7-43).

8. When using a motherboard connection, if the wire connecting the motherboard to the hard drive light on the front of the case was not connected when the motherboard was installed, connect it now. If you reverse the polarity of the LED wire, the light will not work. Your motherboard manual should tell you the location of the LED wires on the motherboard.

A+
220-602
1.1

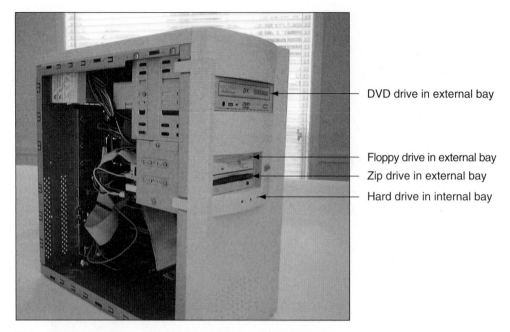

DVD drive in external bay

Floppy drive in external bay
Zip drive in external bay
Hard drive in internal bay

Figure 7-43 A tower case might have internal or external bays

 Caution

Be sure the screws are not too long. If they are, you can screw too far into the drive housing and damage the drive itself.

Notes

If the drive light does not work after you install a new drive, try reversing the LED wire on the motherboard pins.

9. Before you replace the case cover, plug in the monitor and turn on the computer. (On the other hand, some systems won't power up until the front panel is installed.) Verify that your system BIOS can find the drive before you replace the cover and that it recognizes the correct size of the drive. If you have problems, refer to the troubleshooting section at the end of this chapter.

STEP 4: USE CMOS SETUP TO VERIFY HARD DRIVE SETTINGS

When you first boot up after installing a hard drive, go to CMOS setup and verify that the drive has been recognized and that the settings are correct. Let's look at typical CMOS setup screens for an Award BIOS used on a motherboard with two parallel ATA connectors. The CMOS setup screens to view and change hard drive parameters are shown in Figures 7-44 through 7-47. Figure 7-44 shows the choice for IDE HDD Auto Detection in the third item in the second column. If Auto Detection is not enabled, enable it, and then save and exit setup. Later, after you have rebooted with the new drive detected, you can return to setup, view the selections that it made, and make appropriate changes.

It's interesting to see how this Award BIOS is designed to support older hard drives using legacy standards. Notice in Figure 7-45 the column labeled *mode*, referring to how the BIOS relates to the drive. Choices are normal, large, LBA, and auto. Most likely, when auto is the choice, setup automatically selects LBA, the current standard.

A+
220-602
1.1

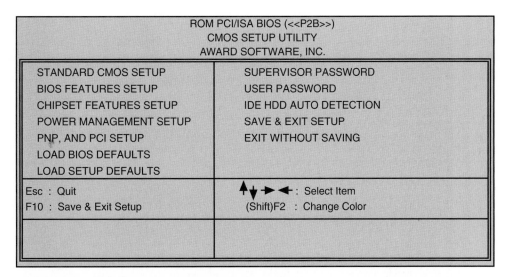

Figure 7-44 CMOS setup utility opening menu

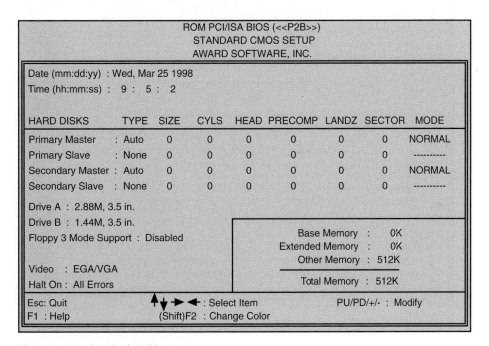

Figure 7-45 Standard CMOS setup

In Figure 7-46 (starting with the 10th item in the second column), you can see the hard drive features that the chipset on this motherboard supports. They are Ultra DMA, PIO, and DMA modes. Leave all these settings at Auto, and let the BIOS make the choice according to its detection of the features your hard drive supports.

In Figure 7-47, the 12th item in the first column indicates that the BIOS on this motherboard supports block mode. From this screen, you can also select the boot sequence (see ninth item in first column). Choices for this BIOS are A, C; A, CD Rom, C; CD Rom, C, A; D, A; F, A; C only; Zip, C; and C, A. Also notice on this screen (eighth item in the first column) that this BIOS supports booting from a SCSI drive even when an IDE drive is present. Booting from the IDE drive is the default setting.

A+ 220-602 1.1

ROM PCI/ISA BIOS (<<P2B>>)
CHIPSET FEATURES
AWARD SOFTWARE, INC.

SDRAM Configuration	: By SPD	Onboard FDC Controller	: Enabled
SDRAM CAS Latency	: 2T	Onboard FDC Swap A & B	: No Swap
SDRAM RAS to CAS Delay	: 3T	Onboard Serial Port	: 3F8H/IRQ4
SDRAM RAS Precharge Time	: 3T	Onboard Serial Port 2	: 2F8H/IRQ3
DRAM Idle Timer	: 16T	Onboard Parallel Port	: 378H/IRQ7
SDRAM MA Wait State	: Normal	Parallel Port Mode	: ECP+EPP
Snoop Ahead	: Enabled	ECP DMA Select	: 3
Host Bus Fast Data Ready	: Enabled	VART2 Use Infrared	: Disabled
16-bit I/O Recovery Time	: 1BUSCLK	Onboard PCI IDE Enable	: Both
8-bit I/O Recovery Time	: 1BUSCLK	IDE Ultra DMA Mode	: Auto
Graphics Aperture Size	: 64MB	IDE0 Master PIO/DMA Mode	: Auto
Video.Memory Cache Mode	: UC	IDE0 Slave PIO/DMA Mode	: Auto
PCI 2.1 Support	: Enabled	IDE1 Master PIO/DMA Mode	: Auto
Memory Hole At 15M-16M	: Disabled	IDE1 Slave PIO/DMA Mode	: Auto
DRAM are 64 (Not 72), bits wide			
Data Integrity Mode	: Non-ECC		

Esc : Quit ↑↓→← : Select Item
F1 : Help PU/PD/+/- : Modify
F5 : Old Values (Shift)F2 : Color
F6 : Load BIOS Defaults
F7 : Load Setup Defaults

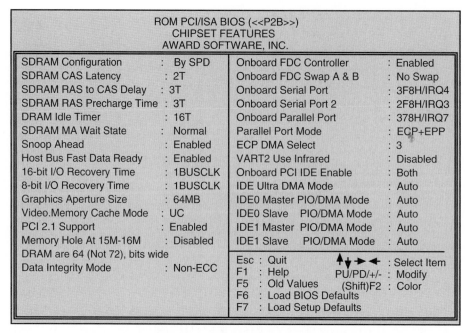

Figure 7-46 CMOS setup for chipset features

ROM PCI/ISA BIOS (<<P2B>>)
BIOS FEATURES SETUP
AWARD SOFTWARE, INC.

CPU Internal Core Speed	: 350Mhz	Video ROM BIOS Shadow	: Enabled
		C8000 - CBFFF Shadow	: Disabled
Boot Virus Detection	: Enabled	CC000 - CFFFF Shadow	: Disabled
CPU Level 1 Cache	: Enabled	D0000 - D3FFF Shadow	: Disabled
CPU Level 2 Cache	: Enabled	D4000 - D7FFF Shadow	: Disabled
CPU Level 2 Cache ECC Check	: Disabled	D8000 - DBFFF Shadow	: Disabled
BIOS Update	: Enabled	DC000 - DFFFF Shadow	: Disabled
Quick Power On Self Test	: Enabled		
HDD Sequence SCSI/IDE First	: IDE	Boot Up NumLock Status	: On
Boot Sequence	: A,C	Typematic Rate Setting	: Disabled
Boot Up Floppy Seek	: Disabled	Typematic Rate (Chars/Sec)	: 6
Floppy Disk Access Control	: R/W	Typematic Delay (Msec)	: 250
IDE HDD Block Mode Sectors	: HDD MAX		
Security Option	: System		
PS/2 Mouse Function Control	: Auto		
PCI/VGA Palette Snoop	: Disabled		
OS/2 Onboard Memory > 64M	: Disabled		

Esc : Quit ↑↓→← : Select Item
F1 : Help PU/PD/+/- : Modify
F5 : Old Values (Shift)F2 : Color
F6 : Load BIOS Defaults
F7 : Load Setup Defaults

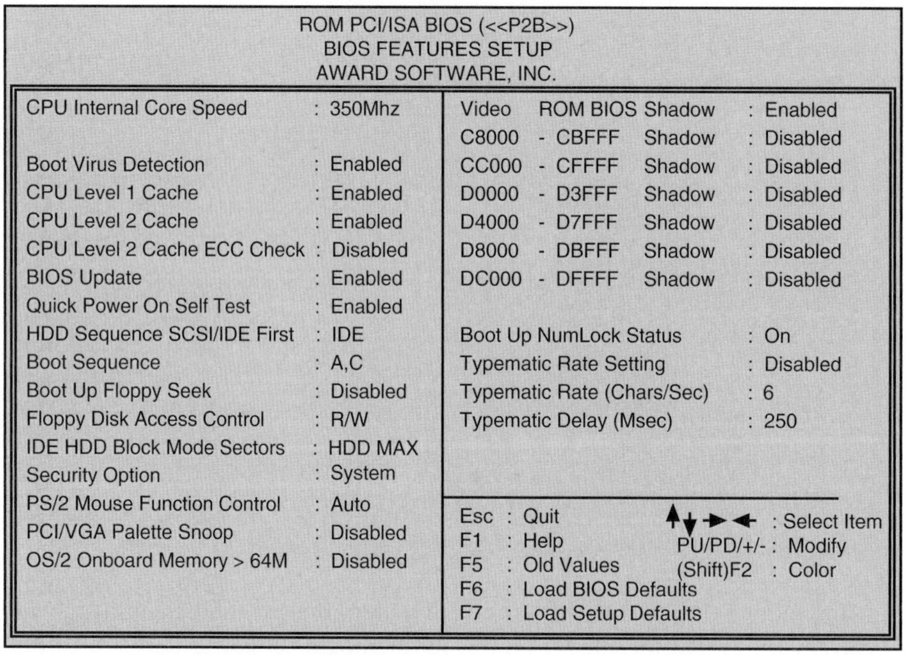

Figure 7-47 CMOS setup for BIOS features

After you confirm that your drive is recognized, the size of the drive is detected correctly, and supported features are set to be automatically detected, reboot the system. Then the next thing to do is to use an operating system to prepare the drive for first use.

A+ ESS 1.2

STEP 5: USE WINDOWS SETUP TO PARTITION AND FORMAT A NEW DRIVE

If you are installing a new hard drive in a system that is to be used for a new Windows installation, after you have physically installed the drive, boot from the Windows setup CD and

A+ ESS
1.1

A+
220-602
1.1

follow the directions on the screen to install Windows on the new drive. The setup process partitions and formats the new drive before it begins the Windows installation. If you are installing a second hard drive in a system that already has Windows 2000/XP installed on the first hard drive, use Windows to partition and format the second drive. After physically installing the second hard drive, boot into Windows as usual. Then use Disk Management to partition and format the new drive. For Windows 9x/Me, to partition and format the drive, use the Fdisk and Format commands.

SERIAL ATA HARD DRIVE INSTALLATIONS

Serial ATA hard drives are easier to install than parallel ATA drives because there are no jumpers to set on the drive and each serial ATA connector and cable is dedicated to a single drive. You install the drive in the bay the same as a parallel ATA drive. Next, connect a power cord to the drive. If your serial ATA drive has two power connectors, use only one.

Read the motherboard documentation to find out which serial ATA connectors on the board to use first. For example, the motherboard shown earlier in the chapter in Figure 7-18 has four serial ATA connectors and one parallel ATA connector. You can see a close-up of these four serial ATA connectors in Figure 7-48. The documentation says to use the two red connectors (labeled SATA1 and SATA2 on the board) before you use the black connectors (labeled SATA3 and SATA4). Connect the serial ATA data cable to the hard drive and to the red SATA1 connector. For both the drive and the motherboard, you can only plug the cable into the connector in one direction. Check all your connections and you're now ready to power up the system and verify the drive was recognized correctly.

Figure 7-48 This motherboard has four serial ATA connectors

Figures 7-49 and 7-50 show CMOS setup screens for this system when two hard drives are installed. A DVD drive is installed as the Primary IDE Master (using the parallel ATA connector) and the two serial ATA hard drives are installed as the Third IDE Master (using the first red serial ATA connector) and Fourth IDE Master (using the second red serial ATA connector).

A+
220-602
1.1

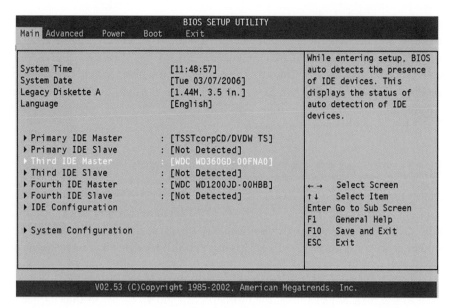

Figure 7-49 American Megatrends, Inc. CMOS setup screen shows installed drives

To see how the first hard drive is configured, highlight it and press Enter. The screen in Figure 7-50 appears showing the size of the drive, the hard drive standards the BIOS supports, and that most of these standards are automatically detected. In comparing the older BIOS screen shown earlier in Figure 7-45 to this newer BIOS screen, notice that the older BIOS gives cylinder, head, and sector information so that you can manually calculate the size of an installed drive, but the newer BIOS only gives the detected size of a drive.

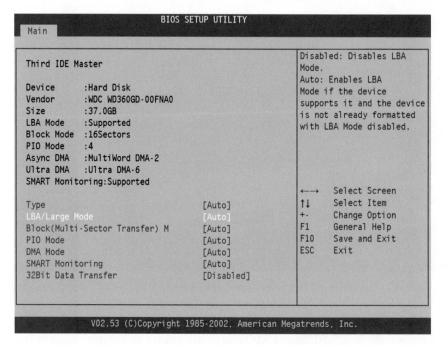

Figure 7-50 CMOS setup screen showing the size of the drive and supported standards

After you have verified the drive is detected correctly, reboot the system and move on to the next step of installing an operating system.

A+
220-602
1.1

INSTALLING A HARD DRIVE IN A WIDE BAY

If you are mounting a hard drive into a bay that is too large, a universal bay kit can help you securely fit the drive into the bay. These inexpensive kits should create a tailor-made fit. In Figure 7-51, you can see how the universal bay kit adapter works. The adapter spans the distance between the sides of the drive and the bay. Figure 7-52 shows the drive installed in a wide bay.

Side brackets connect to hard drive

Figure 7-51 Use the universal bay kit to make the drive fit the bay

Figure 7-52 Hard drive installed in a wide bay using a universal bay kit adapter

TROUBLESHOOTING HARD DRIVES

A+
220-602
1.2

In this part of the chapter, you'll learn to troubleshoot problems with hard drives and floppy drives. The following sections cover problems with hard drive installations and problems that occur after the installation with hard drives and floppy drives. Problems with hardware also are covered.

PROBLEMS WITH HARD DRIVE INSTALLATIONS

Sometimes, trouble crops up during an installation. Keeping a cool head, thinking things through carefully a second, third, and fourth time, and using all available resources will most likely get you out of any mess.

Installing a hard drive is not difficult unless you have an unusually complex situation. For example, your first hard drive installation should not involve the intricacies of installing a second SCSI drive in a system that has two SCSI host adapters. Nor should you install a second drive in a system that uses an IDE connection for one drive on the motherboard and an adapter card in an expansion slot for the other drive. If a complicated installation is necessary and you have never installed a hard drive, ask for expert help.

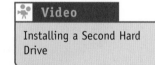

Video

Installing a Second Hard Drive

Here are some errors that cropped up during a few hard drive installations, their causes, and what was done about them. Everyone makes mistakes when learning something new, and you probably will too. You can then add your own experiences to this list.

- ◢ Shawn physically installed an IDE hard drive. He turned on the machine and accessed CMOS setup. The hard drive was not listed as an installed device. He checked and discovered that autodetection was not enabled. He enabled it and rebooted. Setup recognized the drive.
- ◢ When first turning on a previously working PC, John received the following error message: "Hard drive not found." He turned off the machine, checked all cables, and discovered that the data cable from the motherboard to the drive was loose. He reseated the cable and rebooted. POST found the drive.
- ◢ Lucia physically installed a new hard drive, replaced the cover on the computer case, and booted the PC with a bootable floppy disk in the drive. POST beeped three times and stopped. Recall that diagnostics during POST are often communicated by beeps if the tests take place before POST has checked video and made it available to display the messages. Three beeps on most computers signal a memory error. Lucia turned off the computer and checked the memory modules on the motherboard. A module positioned at the edge of the motherboard next to the cover had been bumped as she replaced the cover. She reseated the module and booted from a floppy disk again, this time with the cover still off. The error disappeared.
- ◢ Jason physically installed a new hard drive and turned on the computer. He received the following error: "No boot device available." He forgot to insert a bootable disk. He put the disk in the drive and rebooted the machine successfully.
- ◢ Stephen physically installed the hard drive, inserted a floppy disk in the disk drive, and rebooted. He received the following error message: "Configuration/CMOS error. Run setup." This error message is normal for an older BIOS that does not support autodetection. POST had found a hard drive it was not expecting. The next step is to run setup.

A+
220-602
1.2

▲ Larry physically installed the card and drive and tried to reboot from a floppy disk. Error message 601 appeared on the screen. Any error message in the 600 range refers to the floppy disk. Because the case cover was still off, he looked at the connections and discovered that the power cord to the floppy disk drive was not connected. (It had been disconnected earlier to expose the hard drive bay underneath.) Larry turned off the machine and plugged in the cable. The error disappeared.

▲ The hard drive did not physically fit into the bay. The screw holes did not line up. Juan got a bay kit, but it just didn't seem to work. He took a break, went to lunch, and came back to make a fresh start. Juan asked others to help view the brackets, holes, and screws from a fresh perspective. It didn't take long to discover the correct position for the brackets in the bay.

▲ Maria set the jumpers on a hard drive and physically installed the drive. She booted and received the following error message: "Hard drive not present." She rechecked all physical connections and found everything okay. After checking the jumper settings, she realized that she had set them as if this were the second drive of a two-drive system, when it was the only drive. She restored the jumpers to their original state. In this case, as in most cases, the jumpers were set at the factory to be correct when the drive is the only drive.

If CMOS setup does not recognize a newly installed hard drive, check the following:

▲ Does your system BIOS recognize large drives? Check CMOS setup.

▲ Has CMOS setup been correctly configured for autodetection?

▲ Are the jumpers on the drive set correctly?

▲ Have the power cord and data cable been properly connected? Verify that the parallel ATA data cable colored edge is connected to pin 1 on the edge connectors of both the motherboard and the drive.

▲ Check the Web site of the drive manufacturer for suggestions, if the above steps don't solve your problem. Look for diagnostic software that can be downloaded from the Web site and used to check the drive.

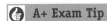 **A+ Exam Tip**

The A+ 220-602 exam might give you a symptom and expect you to select a probable source of a problem from a list of sources. These examples of what can go wrong can help you connect problem sources to symptoms.

 Caution

One last warning: When things are not going well, you can tense up and make mistakes more easily. Be certain to turn off the machine before doing anything inside! Not doing so can be a costly error. For example, a friend had been trying and retrying to boot for some time, and got frustrated and careless. He plugged the power cord into the drive without turning the PC off. The machine began to smoke and everything went dead. The next thing he learned was how to replace a power supply!

A+ ESS
1.3
3.3

HOW TO APPROACH A HARD DRIVE PROBLEM AFTER THE INSTALLATION

After the hard drive is working, later problems can arise, such as corrupted data files, a corrupted Windows installation, or a hardware problem that causes the system to refuse to boot. In this section, you'll learn about some tools you can use to solve hard drive problems and how to approach the problem and prioritize what to do first. Then, in later sections, we'll look at some specific error messages and symptoms and how to deal with them.

A+ ESS
1.3
3.3

A+
220-602
1.2

START WITH THE END USER

When an end user brings a problem to you, begin the troubleshooting process by interviewing the user. When you interview the user, you might want to include these questions:

◢ Can you describe the problem and show me how to reproduce it?
◢ Was the computer recently moved?
◢ Was any new hardware or software recently installed?
◢ Was any software recently reconfigured or upgraded?
◢ Did someone else use your computer recently?
◢ Does the computer have a history of similar problems?
◢ Is there important data on the drive that is not backed up?
◢ Can you show me how to reproduce the problem?

After you gather this basic information, you can prioritize what to do and begin diagnosing and addressing the hard drive problems.

PRIORITIZE WHAT YOU HAVE LEARNED

If a hard drive is not functioning and data is not accessible, setting priorities helps focus your work. For most users, data is the first priority unless they have a recent backup. Software can also be a priority if it is not backed up. Reloading software from the original installation disks or CD can be time-consuming, especially if the configuration is complex or you have written software macros or scripts but did not back them up.

If a system won't boot from the hard drive and your first priority is to recover data on the drive, before you try to solve the hardware or Windows problem that prevents booting, you need to consider removing the drive and installing it as a second drive in a working system. If the partition table on the problem drive is intact, you might be able to copy data from the drive to the primary drive in the working system. Then turn your attention to solving the original problem.

If you have good backups of both data and software, hardware might be your priority. It could be expensive to replace, but downtime can be costly, too. The point is, when trouble arises, determine your main priority and start by focusing on that.

BE AWARE OF AVAILABLE RESOURCES

Be aware of the resources available to help you resolve a problem:

◢ *Product documentation* often lists error messages and their meanings.
◢ *The Internet* can also help you diagnose hardware and software problems. Go to the Web site of the product manufacturer, and search for the FAQs (frequently asked questions) list or bulletin board. It's likely that others have encountered the same problem and posted the question and answer. If you search and cannot find your answer, you can post a new question.
◢ *Technical support* from the ROM BIOS, hardware, and software manufacturers can help you interpret an error message, or it can provide general support in diagnosing a problem. Most technical support is available during working hours by telephone. Check your documentation for telephone numbers. An experienced computer troubleshooter once said, "The people who solve computer problems do it by trying something and making phone calls, trying something else and making more phone calls, and so on, until the problem is solved."
◢ *Norton Utilities* by Symantec (*www.symantec.com*) offers several easy-to-use tools to prevent damage to a hard drive, recover data from a damaged hard drive, and

A+ ESS
1.3
3.3

A+
220-602
1.2

improve system performance. Many functions of these tools have been taken over and improved by utilities included with recent versions of Windows. The most commonly used Norton Utilities tools now are the recovery tools. Two examples are Norton Disk Doctor, which automatically repairs many hard drive and floppy disk problems, and UnErase Wizard, which allows you to retrieve accidentally deleted files. When using Norton Utilities, be certain you use the version of the software for the operating system you have installed. Using Norton with the wrong OS can do damage.

▲ *PartitionMagic* by Symantec (*www.symantec.com*) lets you manage partitions on a hard drive more quickly and easily than with Fdisk for Windows 9x/Me or Disk Management for Windows 2000/XP. You can create new partitions, change the size of partitions, and move partitions without losing data or moving the data to another hard drive while you work. You can switch file systems without disturbing your data, and you can hide and show partitions to secure your data.

> **Notes**
>
> Always check compatibility between utility software and the operating system with which you plan to use it. One place you can check for compatibility is the service and support section of the software manufacturer's Web site.

▲ *SpinRite* by Gibson Research (*www.grc.com*) is hard drive utility software that has been around for years. Still a DOS application without a sophisticated GUI interface, SpinRite has been updated to adjust to new drive technologies. It supports FAT32, NTFS, SCSI, Zip drives, and Jaz drives. You can boot your PC from a floppy disk and run SpinRite from a floppy, which means that it doesn't require much system overhead. Because it is written in a language closer to the binary code that the computer understands, it is more likely to detect underlying hard drive problems than software that uses Windows, which can stand as a masking layer between the software and the hard drive. SpinRite analyzes the entire hard drive surface, performing data recovery of corrupted files and file system information. Sometimes, SpinRite can recover data from a failing hard drive when other software fails.

▲ *GetDataBack* by Runtime Software (*www.runtime.org*) can recover data and program files even when Windows cannot recognize the drive. It can read FAT and NTFS file systems and can solve problems with a corrupted partition table, boot record, or root directory.

▲ *Hard drive manufacturer's diagnostic software* is available for download from the Web site of many hard drive manufacturers. For example, Maxtor's diagnostic software is PowerMax (*www.maxtor.com*). Download the software and use it to create a bootable diagnostic floppy disk. You can then boot from the floppy and use it to examine a Maxtor hard drive for errors and, if necessary, low-level format the drive.

> **Notes**
>
> Remember one last thing. After making a reasonable and diligent effort to resolve a problem, getting the problem fixed could become more important than resolving it yourself. There comes a time when you might need to turn the problem over to a more experienced technician.

> **A+ Exam Tip**
>
> The A+ Essentials exam expects you to know about diagnostic software to test hard drives.

HARD DRIVE HARDWARE PROBLEMS

In this section, we look at different problems with the hard drive that present themselves during the boot. These problems can be caused by the hard drive subsystem, by the partition table or file system on the drive, or by files required for the OS to boot. When trying to

A+ ESS
1.3
3.3

A+
220-602
1.2

solve a problem with the boot, you need to decide if the problem is caused by hardware or software. All the problems discussed in this section are caused by hardware. How to solve problems caused by software is not covered in this book.

PROBLEMS AT POST

Recall from Chapter 2 that the BIOS performs the POST at the beginning of the boot to verify that essential hardware devices are working. Hardware problems usually show up at POST, unless there is physical damage to an area of the hard drive that is not accessed during POST. Hardware problems often make the hard drive totally inaccessible. If BIOS cannot find a hard drive at POST, it displays an error message similar to this:

```
Hard drive not found

Fixed disk error

Invalid boot disk

Inaccessible boot device

Numeric error codes in the 1700s or 10400s
```

The reasons BIOS cannot access the drive can be caused by the drive, the data cable, the electrical system, the motherboard, the controller card (if one is present), or a loose connection. Here are some things to do and check:

- If BIOS displays numeric error codes during POST, check the Web site of the BIOS manufacturer for explanations of these numeric codes.
- Remove and reattach all drive cables. Check for correct pin 1 orientation.
- If you're using a controller card, remove and reseat it or place it in a different slot.
- Check the jumper settings on the drive.
- Inspect the drive for damage, such as bent pins on the connection for the cable.
- Determine if the hard drive is spinning by listening to it or lightly touching the metal drive (with power on).
- Check the cable for frayed edges or other damage.
- Check the installation manual for things you might have overlooked. Look for a section about system setup, and carefully follow all directions that apply.
- Be sure the power cable and drive data cable connections are good.
- Check CMOS setup for errors in the hard drive configuration. If you suspect an error, set CMOS to default settings, make sure autodetection is turned on, and reboot the system.
- Try booting from another media such as the Windows XP setup CD. If you can boot using another media, you have proven that the problem is isolated to the hard drive subsystem. The next thing to do is to use the Windows XP Recovery Console to try to access the drive. How to use the Recovery Console is not covered in this book.

A+ ESS
1.3
3.3

A+
220-602
1.2

◢ Check the drive manufacturer Web site for diagnostic software. You might be able to download the software to floppy disk or CD, boot from the disk or CD, and run the software to diagnose the drive. For example, you can download Data Lifeguard Diagnostic for DOS from the Western Digital Web site (*www.westerndigital.com*), burn the software to CD, and boot from the CD (see Figure 7-53). Using the software, you can do a quick test to check the drive for physical problems or an extended test to repair any correctable problems. You can also write zeroes to every sector on the drive to get a fresh start with the drive. Other hard drive manufacturers have similar programs. For example, Seagate offers SeaTools (see Figure 7-54) that can be downloaded and used to create a bootable CD or floppy that can be used to test and analyze most ATA and SCSI drives by Seagate and other manufacturers.

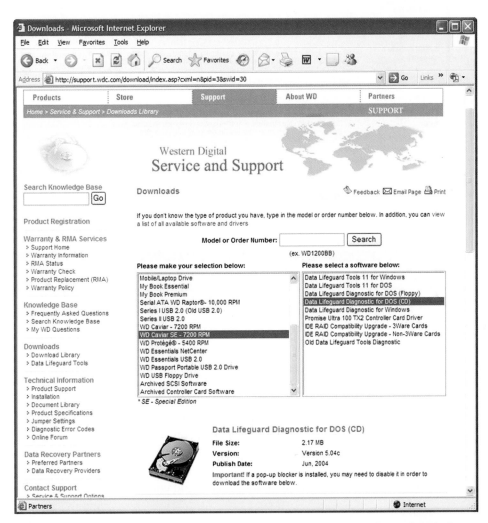

Figure 7-53 Download hard drive diagnostic software from the drive manufacturer's Web site

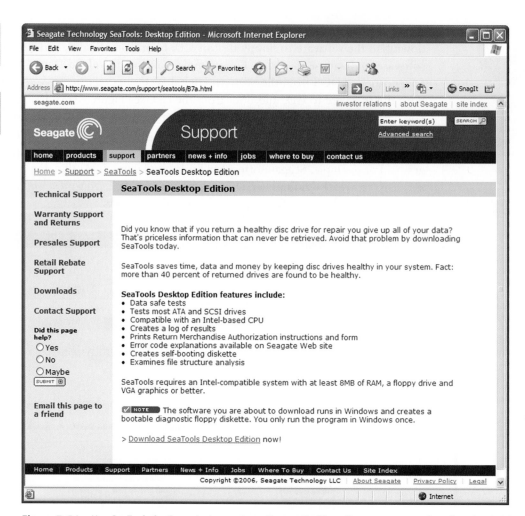

Figure 7-54 Use SeaTools by Seagate to create a diagnostic CD or floppy to test and analyze hard drives

◢ If it is not convenient to create a boot CD with hard drive diagnostic software installed, you can move the drive to a working computer and install it as a second drive in the system. Then you can use the diagnostic software installed on the primary hard drive to test the problem drive. While you have the drive installed in a working computer, be sure to find out if you can copy data from it to the good drive so that you can recover any data not backed up. Note that for these temporary tests, you don't have to physically install the drive in the working system. Open the computer case. Carefully lay the drive on the case and connect a power cord and data cable (see Figure 7-55). Then turn on the PC. While you have the PC turned on, be *very careful* to not touch the drive or touch inside the case. Also, while a tower case is lying on its side like the one in Figure 7-55, don't use the CD or DVD drive.

> **Notes**
>
> For less than $40, you can purchase a USB to IDE converter such as the one in Figure 7-56 to connect a failing parallel ATA hard drive to a working computer using a USB port. Some converters have ports for parallel ATA connections, serial ATA connections, and connections for hard drives used in notebook computers. These converters are really handy when troubleshooting problems with hard drives.

Figure 7-55 Temporarily connect a faulty hard drive to another system to diagnose the problem and try to recover data

▲ If the drive still does not boot, exchange the three field replaceable units—the data cable, the adapter card (optional), and the hard drive itself—for a hard drive subsystem. Do the following in order:

  ▲ Reconnect or swap the drive data cable.

  ▲ Reseat or exchange the drive adapter card, if one is present.

  ▲ Exchange the hard drive for a known good unit.

▲ If the hard drive refuses to work but its light stays on even after the system has fully booted, the problem might be a faulty controller on the hard drive or motherboard. Try replacing the hard drive. Next try an ATA controller card to substitute for the ATA connectors on the motherboard or replace the motherboard.

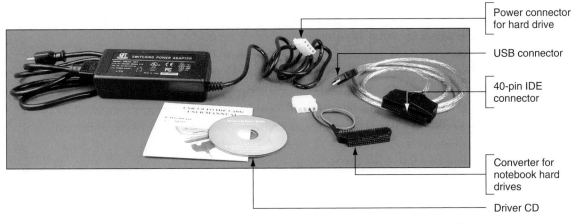

Power connector for hard drive

USB connector

40-pin IDE connector

Converter for notebook hard drives

Driver CD

Figure 7-56 Use a USB to IDE converter for diagnostic testing and to recover data from a failing hard drive

◢ Sometimes older drives refuse to spin at POST. Drives that have trouble spinning often whine at startup for several months before they finally refuse to spin altogether. If your drive whines loudly when you first turn on the computer, never turn off the computer. One of the worst things you can do for a drive that is having difficulty starting up is to leave the computer turned off for an extended period of time. Some drives, like old cars, refuse to start if they are unused for a long time.

A bad power supply or a bad motherboard also might cause a disk boot failure. If the problem is solved by exchanging one of the field replaceable units listed, you still must reinstall the old unit to verify that the problem was not caused by a bad connection.

BUMPS ARE BAD!

The read/write heads at the ends of the read/write arms on a hard drive get extremely close to the platters but do not actually touch them. This minute clearance between the heads and platters makes hard drives susceptible to destruction. Should a computer be bumped or moved while the hard drive is operating, a head can easily bump against the platter and scratch the surface. Such an accident causes a "hard drive crash," often making the hard drive unusable.

If the head mechanism is damaged, the drive and its data are probably total losses. If the first tracks that contain the partition table, boot record, FAT (for that file system), or root directory are damaged, the drive could be inaccessible, although the data might be unharmed.

Here's a trick that might work for a hard drive whose head mechanism is intact but whose first few tracks are damaged. First, find a working hard drive that has the same partition table information as the bad drive. Take the computer case off, place the good drive on top of the bad drive housing, and connect a spare power cord and the ATA data cable to the good drive. Leave a power cord connected to the bad drive. Boot from a bootable CD or floppy disk. No error message should show at POST. Access the good drive by entering C: at the command prompt. The C prompt should show on the monitor screen.

Without turning off the power, gently remove the data cable from the good drive and place it on the bad drive. Do not disturb the power cords on either drive or touch chips on the drive logic boards. Immediately copy the data you need from the bad drive to another media, using the Copy command. If the area of the drive where the data is stored, the FAT or MFT, and the directory are not damaged, this method should work.

Here's another trick for an older hard drive having trouble spinning when first turned on. Remove the drive from the case, hold it firmly in both hands, and give the drive a quick and sudden twist that forces the platters to turn inside the drive housing. Reinstall the drive. It might take several tries to get the drive spinning. After the drive is working, immediately make a backup and plan to replace the drive soon.

INVALID DRIVE OR DRIVE SPECIFICATION

If you get the error message "Invalid drive or drive specification," the system BIOS cannot read the partition table information. You'll need to boot from a recovery CD or bootable floppy disk to check the partition table using the Diskpart or Fdisk command.

BAD SECTOR ERRORS

Track and sector markings on a drive sometimes "fade" off the hard drive over time, which causes "bad sector" errors to crop up. These errors can also occur if an area of the drive has become damaged. Do not trust valuable data to a drive that has this kind of trouble. Plan to replace the drive soon. In the meantime, make frequent backups and leave the power on.

A+ ESS
1.3
3.3

A+
220-602
1.2
3.3

TROUBLESHOOTING FLOPPY DRIVES AND DISKS

Table 7-4 lists errors that occur during and after the boot with the floppy drive or disks.

Problem or Error Message	What to Do About It
During the boot, numeric error messages in the 600 range or text error messages about the floppy drive appear onscreen	◢ The floppy drive did not pass POST, which can be caused by problems with the drive, data cable, or motherboard. Check power and data cable connections. ◢ Try a different power cord. ◢ Check CMOS setup and reboot. ◢ Use a head-cleaning kit to clean the floppy drive heads. ◢ Replace the drive.
Cannot read from a floppy disk	◢ The disk is not formatted. Try a different disk or try formatting this disk. ◢ The shuttle window on the floppy disk cannot open fully. ◢ The command just issued has a mistake or is the wrong command. ◢ The disk is inserted incorrectly. ◢ Something is lodged inside the disk's plastic housing. Check the shuttle window. ◢ Does the drive light come on? CMOS setup might be wrong or the command you're using is wrong.
Non-system disk or disk error. Replace and strike any key when ready. No operating system found Missing NTLDR Invalid system disk Invalid boot disk	◢ You are trying to boot from a disk that is not bootable. Try a different disk or remove the disk and boot from the hard drive.
Not ready reading drive A:, Abort, Retry, Fail?	◢ The disk in drive A is not readable. Try formatting the disk.
General failure reading drive A:, Abort, Retry, Fail?	◢ The disk is badly corrupted or not yet formatted.
Track 0 bad, disk not usable	◢ The disk is bad or you or trying to format it using the wrong parameters on the Format command.
Write-protect error writing drive A:	◢ The disk is write-protected and the application is trying to write to it. Close the switch shown in Figure 7-57.
Bad sector or sector not found reading drive A, Abort, Retry, Ignore, Fail?	◢ Sector markings are corrupted or fading. Press I to ignore that sector and move on. Don't trust this disk with important data.

Table 7-4 Floppy drive and floppy disk errors that can occur during and after the boot

A+ ESS
1.3
3.3

A+
220-602
1.2
3.3

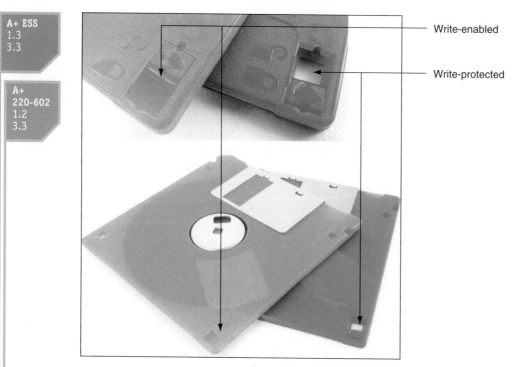

Write-enabled

Write-protected

Figure 7-57 For you to write to a disk, the write-protect notch must be closed

>> CHAPTER SUMMARY

▲ Today's floppy disks are $3\frac{1}{2}$-inch, high-density disks that hold 1.44 MB of data.

▲ A floppy drive data cable has 34 pins and can accommodate one or two floppy drives.

▲ Floppy disks are formatted into 80 tracks, each with 18 sectors of 512 bytes. Each cluster holds one sector. The boot record contains information about the organization of data on the disk and the name of the boot loader program (Ntldr or Io.sys) used to make the disk bootable.

▲ Most hard drives today use IDE technology, which has a complex method of organizing tracks and sectors on the disks.

▲ For current systems today, the BIOS and the OS use logical block addressing (LBA) to address all the sectors on a hard drive without regard to where these sectors are located.

▲ A hard drive is low-level formatted at the factory with tracks and sectors, and high-level formatted using an operating system. The high-level format creates a file system on the drive.

▲ Several ATA standards pertain to hard drives, including parallel ATA, EIDE, Fast ATA, Ultra ATA, Ultra ATA/66, Ultra ATA/100, Ultra ATA/133, and serial ATA.

▲ An EIDE device (also called a parallel ATA device) such as a hard drive or CD-ROM drive can be installed as a master drive, slave drive, or single drive on a system.

▲ The EIDE standards support two IDE connections on a motherboard, a primary and a secondary. Each connection can support up to two EIDE devices for a total of four devices on a system.

▲ Parallel ATA or EIDE standards apply to hard drives, CD-ROM drives, tape drives, Zip drives, and others.

- Serial ATA (SATA) supports a single serial ATA drive on a data cable connected to a serial ATA connector on a motherboard. External SATA (eSATA) can be used by an external drive.

- Most BIOSs today can autodetect the presence of a hard drive if the drive is designed to give this information to the BIOS.

- Installing a hard drive includes setting jumpers or DIP switches on the drive; physically installing the adapter card, cable, and drive; changing CMOS setup; and partitioning and formatting the drive.

- You can use an ATA controller card to provide additional ATA connectors in a system to add extra drives or to use newer standards the motherboard does not support.

- Drive interface standards include ATA, SCSI, USB, FireWire, and Fibre Channel.

- Protect the drive and the PC against static electricity during installation.

>> KEY TERMS

For explanations of key terms, see the Glossary near the end of the book.

80-conductor IDE cable	external SATA (eSATA)	parallel ATA
ANSI (American National Standards Institute)	FAT12	PIO (Programmed Input/Output) transfer mode
ATAPI (Advanced Technology Attachment Packet Interface)	file allocation unit	read/write head
	floppy disk drive (FDD)	SCSI (Small Computer System Interface)
autodetection	hard drive controller	
block mode	head	SCSI ID
boot record	high-level formatting	serial ATA (SATA)
boot sector	host adapter	serial ATA cable
cluster	IDE (Integrated Device Electronics)	terminating resistor
DMA (direct memory access) transfer mode	Logical Unit Number (LUN)	zone bit recording
EIDE (Enhanced IDE)	low-level formatting	
	operating system formatting	

>> REVIEWING THE BASICS

1. Name four ATA standards for interfacing with hard drives.

2. What are the two data transfer modes used by hard drives?

3. What are the two types of parallel ATA data cables used with hard drives?

4. What is the name of the ATA standard that uses a serial data cable?

5. What are the two most popular spindle speeds measured in RPMs currently used for hard drives?

6. How does serial ATA help keep a computer case cool better than parallel ATA?

7. If a hard drive has three platters, how many heads does it have?

8. Given that there are 512 bytes per sector, calculate the hard drive storage for the following: heads = 32, tracks (cylinders) = 1,024, sectors/track = 63.

9. What are three modes that system BIOS can use to relate to hard drives?

10. Which mode must be used for a 10 GB hard drive?

11. What is the ATA standard that changed the number of bits used to address data on a hard drive?

12. How does block mode give faster access to a hard drive? How can you disable block mode?

13. When installing a hard drive and a CD-ROM drive on the same IDE channel, which do you configure as the master and which as the slave?

14. What are three ATA hard drive interface standards that do not use a 40-conductor hard drive cable?

15. Generally, which transfer mode is faster, DMA or PIO?

16. When two drives are connected to the same data cable connected to an IDE channel, how does BIOS know which drive controls the channel?

17. If a motherboard has two parallel ATA connections, how many EIDE devices can the system support?

18. If a hard drive is too small to physically fit snugly into the drive bay, what can you do?

19. How can you tell which side of a hard drive's data cable connects to pin 1 on the drive?

20. If your BIOS does not support a large-capacity drive that you want to install, what five choices do you have?

21. Which ATA standard allows for serial ATA and Serial Attached SCSI to coexist in the same system?

22. What is the name of the power connector used with floppy drives?

23. How many pins does a floppy drive cable have?

24. What was the underlying cause that prevented hard drives from breaking the 137 GB size barrier until the ATA/ATAPI-6 standard was released?

25. Why does a serial ATA drive sometimes have two power connectors on the drive?

26. What is the name of the expansion card in a SCSI system that controls the SCSI bus?

27. Why is it not necessary to inform CMOS setup about the installation of a new hard drive?

28. Which has a faster interface to the system, an external serial ATA hard drive or an external FireWire hard drive?

29. On a floppy disk, how many bits are used for each entry in the FAT?

30. How can you tell if your motherboard chipset supports Ultra DMA mode?

>> THINKING CRITICALLY

1. You install a hard drive and then turn on the PC for the first time. You access CMOS setup and see that the drive is not recognized. Which of the following do you do next?

   a. Turn off the PC, open the case, and verify that memory modules on the motherboard have not become loose.

   b. Turn off the PC, open the case, and verify that the data cable and power cable are connected correctly and jumpers on the drive are set correctly.

   c. Verify that BIOS autodetection is enabled.

   d. Reboot the PC and enter CMOS setup again to see if it now recognizes the drive.

2. Every motherboard built today that includes serial ATA connectors has at least one parallel ATA connector on the board. What is the most important reason this parallel ATA is present?

   a. The hard drive used for booting the OS must use a parallel ATA connector.

   b. The IDE controller will not work without at least one parallel ATA connector.

c. The board can accommodate older drives using the parallel ATA connector.

d. The parallel ATA connector is needed for EIDE drives such as a CD or DVD drive.

3. You want to set up your desktop system to have a total hard drive space of 150 GB, but your system does not support drives larger than 132 GB. Which of the following do you do?

a. Buy a new motherboard that will support drives larger than 132 GB.

b. Use two hard drives in your system that together total 150 GB.

c. Flash BIOS so that your system will support a 150 GB drive.

d. Use a special IDE controller card that will support a 150 GB drive.

>> HANDS-ON PROJECTS

PROJECT 7-1:   Researching Floppy Drives on the Internet

Use the Internet to answer the following questions:

▲ What is the price of an internal floppy drive?

▲ What kind of connections do external floppy disk drives use? What is the price of an external drive?

▲ Why do you think external drives cost more than internal drives? What are the advantages of external drives? Internal drives?

PROJECT 7-2:   Examining the CMOS Setting for a Hard Drive

From the CMOS setup information on your computer, write down or print out all the CMOS settings that apply to your hard drive. Explain each setting that you can. What is the size of the installed drive?

PROJECT 7-3:   Selecting a Replacement Hard Drive

Suppose the 37 GB Western Digital hard drive installed as the first serial ATA hard drive in the Windows XP system shown in Figures 7-49 and 7-50 has failed. Search the Internet and find a replacement drive of about the same size. Print three Web pages showing the sizes, features, and prices of three possible replacements. Which drive would you recommend as the replacement drive and why?

PROJECT 7-4:   Preparing for Hard Drive Hardware Problems

1. Boot your PC and make certain that it works properly. Turn off your computer, remove the computer case, and disconnect the data cable to your hard drive. Turn on the computer again. Write down the message that you get.

2. Turn off the computer and reconnect the data cable. Reboot and make sure the system is working again.

3. Turn off the computer and disconnect the power supply cord to the hard drive. Turn on the computer. Write down the error that you get.

4. Turn off the computer, reconnect the power supply, and reboot the system. Verify the system is working again.

PROJECT 7-5:   Researching with the Internet

Suppose you plan to install a Maxtor Quantum Fireball Plus AS 20.5-GB hard drive as a second drive on a PC. You want the drive to be the slave drive, and you know that you must change the current jumper settings. The four jumpers on the drive are labeled *DS*, *CS*, *PK*, and *Rsvd*. The description of the jumpers doesn't tell you how to set the jumpers so the drive is the slave. The documentation is not available. What do you do?

The best solution is to use the Internet to access the drive manufacturer's Web site for this information. In this case, the site is *www.maxtor.com*. Use this example or some other example given by your instructor to determine the correct settings for the jumpers.

PROJECT 7-6:   Installing a Hard Drive

In a lab that has one hard drive per computer, you can practice installing a hard drive by removing a drive from one computer and installing it as a second drive in another computer. When you boot up the computer with two drives, verify that both drives are accessible in Windows Explorer. Then remove the second hard drive, and return it to its original computer. Verify that both computers and drives are working.

>> REAL PROBLEMS, REAL SOLUTIONS

REAL PROBLEM 7-1:   Data Recovery Problem

Your friend has a Windows XP desktop system that contains important data. He frantically calls you to say that when he turns on the computer, the lights on the front panel light up and he can hear the fan spin for a moment and then all goes dead. His most urgent problem is the data on his hard drive, which is not backed up. The data is located in several folders on the drive. What is the quickest and easiest way to solve the most urgent problem, recovering the data? Lists the major steps in that process.

REAL PROBLEM 7-2:   Salvaging Valuable Data on a Floppy Disk

On the job as a PC repair technician at a local university, a destraught student comes to you in a panic. Susan shows you the plastic housing of her floppy disk has been chipped and cracked so she can't insert it into a floppy disk drive. The problem is it holds her only copy of her term paper that is due tomorrow! She desperately needs your help.

You examine the floppy disk and confirm that, yes, the housing is completely destroyed. You ask her how that happened and she begins to turn red as she describes a very vindictive little brother. You begin to feel sorry for her and decide to take the time to help. You notice the disk inside the housing appears to be in good shape. Can you remove the disk from the floppy disk housing and carefully place it in a new housing so she can insert it in a floppy disk drive? Test your theory by removing a floppy disk that has data written to it from one housing, putting it into another housing, and then reading the data on the disk.

Installing and Supporting
I/O Devices

This chapter is packed full of details about the many I/O devices a PC support technician must be familiar with and must know how to install and support. We begin with the easiest-to-support devices (the keyboard and mouse) and move on to the more complicated devices, including video, peripheral devices, and expansion cards. At the end of the chapter, you'll learn how to troubleshoot problems with I/O devices. This chapter builds the foundation for Chapter 9, in which you will learn about multimedia devices.

BASIC PRINCIPLES TO SUPPORT I/O DEVICES

A+ ESS
1.1
3.2

A+
220-602
1.1

An I/O device can be either internal (installed inside the computer case) or external (installed outside the case). Internal devices include drives, such as hard drives, CD drives, DVD drives, Zip drives, and floppy drives. Internal devices can also be expansion cards inserted in expansion slots on the motherboard, such as a network card, modem card, video capture card, and video card. External devices include keyboards, monitors, mice, printers, scanners, digital cameras, and flash drives. You can connect an external device to the system using ports coming off the motherboard (serial, parallel, USB, IEEE 1394, and so forth), or a port can be provided by an expansion card.

In this chapter, you will learn a ton of information about these many I/O devices. However, for all these different devices, some basic principles apply to supporting each one of them. These principles are applied in numerous places throughout this chapter and are summarized here so you can get a first look at them. That being said, consider these fundamental principles and concepts used when supporting I/O devices:

▲ *Every I/O device is controlled by software.* When you install a new I/O device, such as a modem or printer, you must install both the device and the device drivers to control the device. These device drivers must be written for the OS you are using. Recall from earlier chapters that the exception to this principle is some simple devices, such as the floppy disk drive, that are controlled by the system BIOS or device drivers embedded in the OS. For the floppy drive, recall from Chapter 7 that when you install a floppy drive, you don't need to install a device driver; all you need to do is check CMOS setup to verify the drive is recognized.

▲ *When it comes to installing or supporting a device, the manufacturer knows best.* In this chapter, you will learn a lot of principles and procedures for installing and supporting a device, but when you're on the job installing a device or fixing a broken one, read the manufacturer documentation and follow those guidelines first. For example, for most installations, you install the device before you install the device driver. However, for some devices such as a digital camera and some modems, you install the device driver first. Check the device documentation to know which to do first.

▲ *Some devices need application software to use the device.* For example, after you install a scanner and its device drivers, you might also need to install Adobe Photoshop to use the scanner.

▲ *Problems with a device can sometimes be solved by updating the device drivers.* Device manufacturers often release updates to device drivers. Update the drivers to solve problems with the device or to add new features.

▲ *Learning about I/O devices is a moving target.* No matter how much information can be packed into this chapter, it won't be enough. I've done my best to make sure everything presented in this chapter is current, but I know that by the time this book is in print, some of the content will already be outdated. To stay abreast of all the latest technologies, an excellent source for information is the Internet. Use a good search engine to look up additional information about the I/O devices in this chapter and to learn about others.

We now turn our attention to the essential I/O devices for a PC: the keyboard, pointing devices, and video display.

WORKING WITH KEYBOARDS

A+ ESS
1.1

A+
220-602
1.1

Keyboards have either a traditional straight design or a newer ergonomic design, as shown in Figure 8-1. The word ergonomic means "designed for safe and comfortable interaction between human beings and machines." The ergonomically safer keyboard is designed to keep your wrists high and straight. Some users find it comfortable, and others do not.

Figure 8-1   An ergonomic keyboard

Keyboards differ in the feel of the keys as you type. Some people prefer more resistance than others, and some like more sound as the keys make contact. A keyboard might have a raised bar or circle on the F and J keys to help your fingers find the home keys as you type. Another feature is the depth of the ledge at the top of the keyboard that holds pencils, and so on. Some keyboards have a mouse port on the back, and specialized keyboards have trackballs or magnetic scanners for scanning credit cards in retail stores.

A danger from using keyboards too much is a type of repetitive stress injury (RSI) known as carpal tunnel syndrome (CTS). CTS is caused by keeping the wrists in an unnatural position and having to execute the same motions (such as pressing keys on a keyboard) over prolonged periods of time. You can help prevent CTS by keeping your elbows at about the same level as the keyboard and keeping your wrists straight and higher than your fingers. I've found that a keyboard drawer that slides out from under a desk surface is much more comfortable because the keyboard is low enough for me to keep the correct position. If I'm working at a desk with no keyboard drawer, I sometimes type with the keyboard in my lap to relieve the pressure on my arms and shoulders. Figure 8-2 shows a typist learning the correct position for her hands and arms at the keyboard.

Figure 8-2   Keep wrists level, straight, and supported while at the keyboard

HOW KEYBOARD KEYS WORK

Keyboards use one of two common technologies in the way the keys make contact: foil contact or metal contact. When you press a key on a foil-contact keyboard, two layers of foil make contact and close a circuit. A small spring just under the keycap raises the key again after it is released.

The more expensive and heavier metal-contact keyboards generally provide a different touch to the fingers than foil-contact keyboards. Made by IBM and AT&T, as well as other companies, the metal-contact keyboards add an extra feel of solid construction that is noticeable to most users, giving the keystroke a clear, definitive contact. When a key is pressed, two metal plates make contact, and again a spring raises the key when it is released.

KEYBOARD CONNECTORS

Keyboards connect to a PC by one of four methods: a DIN connector (mostly outdated now), a PS/2 connector (sometimes called a mini-DIN), a USB port, or the more recently available wireless connection.

The DIN connector (DIN is an acronym of the German words meaning "German industry standard") is round and has five pins. The most common keyboard and mouse connector is the smaller round PS/2 connector, which has six pins (see Figure 8-3).

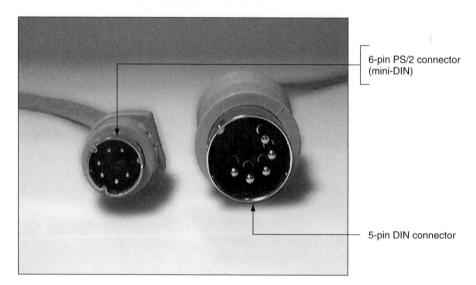

6-pin PS/2 connector
(mini-DIN)

5-pin DIN connector

Figure 8-3 Two common keyboard connectors are the PS/2 connector and the DIN connector

Table 8-1 shows the pinouts for the two connector types.

Description	5-Pin Connector (DIN)	6-Pin Connector (PS/2)
Keyboard data	2	1
Not used	3	2
Ground	4	3
Current (+5 volts)	5	4
Keyboard clock	1	5
Not used	—	6

Table 8-1 Pinouts for keyboard connectors

A+ ESS
1.1

A+
220-602
1.1

If the keyboard you use has a different connector from the keyboard port of your computer, use a keyboard connector adapter, like the one shown in Figure 8-4, to convert DIN to PS/2 or PS/2 to DIN.

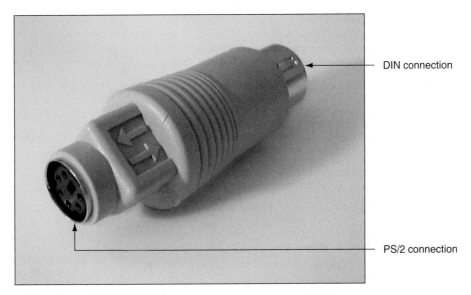

DIN connection

PS/2 connection

Figure 8-4 A keyboard adapter

Also, some keyboards are cordless, using radio frequency (RF) or, for older cordless devices, using infrared to communicate with a sensor connected to the keyboard port. For example, a cordless keyboard and mouse made by Logitech (*www.logitech.com*) use a receiver that plugs into a normal keyboard port (see Figure 8-5).

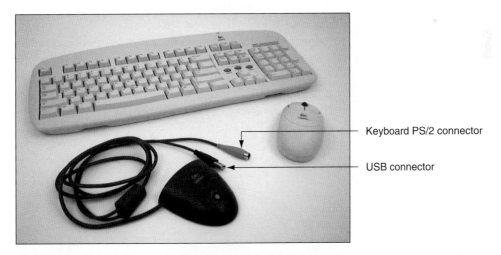

Keyboard PS/2 connector

USB connector

Figure 8-5 This wireless keyboard and mouse by Logitech use a receiver that connects to either a USB or keyboard port

Notes

Most computer cases have two PS/2 connectors: one for the mouse and the other for the keyboard. Physically, the mouse or keyboard connector fits into either port, but the mouse connector only works in the mouse port, and the keyboard connector only works in the keyboard port. This can make for a frustrating experience when setting up a computer. To help tell the two ports apart, know that a green PS/2 port is probably the mouse port and a purple port is most likely the keyboard port.

A+ ESS
1.2
1.4

A+
220-602
1.1
1.2

INSTALLING KEYBOARDS

Most often, installing a keyboard simply means plugging it in and turning on the PC. Because the system BIOS manages the keyboard, no keyboard drivers are necessary. The exception to this is a wireless keyboard that needs a driver to work. In this case, you must use a regular keyboard to install the software to use the wireless keyboard. Plug in the receiver, insert the CD or floppy disk, and run the setup program on the disk. You can then use the wireless keyboard.

CLEANING THE KEYBOARD

Heavily used input devices such as the mouse and keyboard need to be regularly cleaned to keep them working well. Food, dirt, and dust can accumulate under the keys and cause keys not to work. Routinely, you can use a damp cloth to clean a keyboard surface. (Note that "damp" is not the same thing as "wet"!) You can also turn the keyboard upside down and lightly bump multiple keys with your flat palm, which will help loosen and remove debris.

> **Notes**
>
> For a list of keyboard manu-
> facturers, see Table 8-2 later
> in this chapter, in a section
> titled, "Other Pointing
> Devices."

Use a can of compressed air to blow dust and debris out of the keyboard. If a few keys don't respond well to your touch, remove the caps on the bad keys with a chip extractor. Spray contact cleaner into the key well. Repeatedly depress the contact to clean it. Don't use rubbing alcohol to clean the key well, because it can leave a residue on the contact. If a keyboard is extremely dirty, you can clean all the keys using this method.

THE MOUSE AND OTHER POINTING DEVICES

A+ ESS
1.1
2.1

A+
220-602
1.1

A pointing device allows you to move a pointer on the screen and perform tasks such as executing (clicking) a command button. Common pointing devices are the mouse, the trackball, and the touch pad (see Figure 8-6). IBM and Lenovo ThinkPad notebooks use a unique and popular pointing device embedded in the keyboard (see Figure 8-7). Some mice, such as the one shown in Figure 8-8, are wireless and come with keypads, which are useful for working with notebook computers. The wireless connection is made through a receiver that plugs into a USB port.

Figure 8-6 The most common pointing devices: a mouse, a trackball, and a touch pad

Figure 8-7   An IBM ThinkPad pointing device

Figure 8-8   This wireless mouse and keypad use a USB wireless receiver

MOUSE TECHNOLOGIES

Mouse technologies include the wheel mouse and the optical mouse. Inside a wheel mouse is a ball that moves freely as you drag the mouse on a surface. As shown in Figure 8-9, two or more rollers on the sides of the ball housing turn as the ball rolls against them. Each roller turns a wheel. The turning of the wheel is sensed by a small light beam as the wheel "chops" the light beam when it turns. The chops in the light beams are interpreted as mouse movement and sent to the CPU. One of two rollers tracks the x-axis (horizontal) movement of the mouse, and a second roller tracks the y-axis (vertical) movement.

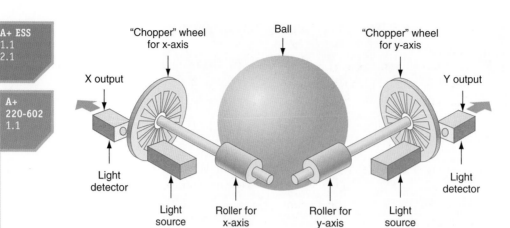

Figure 8-9   How a wheel mouse works

An optical mouse replaces the ball in a standard mouse with a microchip, miniature red light or laser light, and camera. The light illuminates the work surface, the camera takes 1500 snapshots every second, and the microchip reports the tiniest changes to the PC. An optical mouse works on most opaque surfaces and doesn't require a mouse pad. The bottom of an optical mouse has a tiny hole for the camera rather than a ball, and the light glows as you work.

A mouse can have two or three buttons or a scroll wheel. Software must be programmed to use these buttons. Almost all applications use the left button, and Windows uses the right button to display shortcut menus. You can use the scroll wheel between the two buttons to move through large documents onscreen.

A mouse can connect to the computer by several methods:

▲ By using a dedicated, round PS/2 mouse port coming directly from the motherboard (the mouse is then called a motherboard mouse or PS/2-compatible mouse)
▲ By using a mouse bus card that provides a PS/2 mouse port (the mouse is then called a bus mouse)
▲ By using the serial port (the mouse is then called a serial mouse)
▲ By using a USB port
▲ By using a Y-connection with the keyboard so that both the keyboard and the mouse can share the same port
▲ By using a cordless technology whereby the mouse sends signals to a sensor on the PC or to an access point connected to the PC

Except for the cordless mouse, all of these methods produce the same results (that is, the mouse port type is transparent to the user). Therefore, the advantages and disadvantages of each connection type are based mainly on the resources they require. The motherboard mouse is most users' first choice because the port on the motherboard does not take any resources that other devices might need. If you are buying a new mouse that you plan to plug into the motherboard port, don't buy a bus mouse unless the motherboard documentation states that you can use a bus mouse. The motherboard port and the bus port are identical, but a bus mouse might not work on the motherboard port.

If you have a motherboard mouse port, use it. If it becomes damaged, you can switch to a serial port or USB port. The motherboard mouse port most likely uses IRQ 12. If you are not using a mouse on this port, the motherboard might release IRQ 12 so that other devices

8

A+ ESS
1.1
2.1

A+
220-602
1.1

A+ ESS
1.4

A+
220-602
1.1
1.2

can use it. Check the documentation for your motherboard to determine how the unused IRQ is managed.

The serial mouse requires a serial port and an IRQ for that port. Most people prefer a USB or bus mouse to a serial port mouse so that the serial port remains available for another device. A bus mouse can use a bus card if the motherboard does not have a mouse port.

CLEANING A MOUSE

The rollers inside the wheel mouse housing collect dirt and dust and occasionally need cleaning. To clean a mouse, remove the cover of the mouse ball from the bottom of the mouse. The cover usually comes off with a simple press and shift or turn motion. Use compressed air to blow out dust. Clean the rollers with a cotton swab dipped in a very small amount of liquid soap. The sticky side of duct tape works well to clean the mouse ball.

You can purchase a cleaning kit for a mouse, trackball, and keyboard such as the one showing in Figure 8-10. However, using an expensive cleaning kit is not necessary for most maintenance needs.

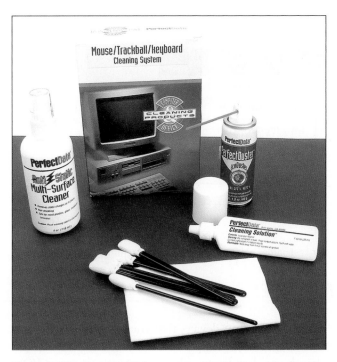

Figure 8-10   Cleaning kit for a mouse, trackball, and keyboard

A+ ESS
1.1
2.1

A+
220-602
1.1

TOUCH SCREENS

A **touch screen** is an input device that uses a monitor or LCD panel as the backdrop for input options. In other words, the touch screen is a grid that senses clicks and drags (similar to those created by a mouse) and sends these events to the computer by way of a serial or USB connection.

When someone is using a touch screen, the monitor displays user options and the user touches one of these options. The touch screen receives that touch in a way similar to how a mouse would receive a click. A touch screen can be embedded inside a monitor for a desktop system or an LCD panel in a notebook, or the touch screen can be installed on top of the monitor screen or LCD panel as an add-on device. As an add-on device, the touch screen has its own AC adapter to power it.

A+ ESS
1.1
2.1

A+
220-602
1.1

When installing a touch screen add-on device, follow the manufacturer's directions to attach the touch screen to the monitor or LCD panel, connect the USB or serial cable and the power cable, and then install the touch screen device drivers and management software. Then reboot the PC. You must then calibrate the touch screen to account for the monitor's resolution using the management software. If the resolution is later changed, the touch screen must be recalibrated. The screen can be cleaned with a damp cloth using a mild solution of alcohol and water.

OTHER POINTING DEVICES

Other pointing devices are trackballs and touch pads. A trackball is really an upside-down wheel mouse. You move the ball on top to turn rollers that turn a wheel sensed by a light beam. A touch pad allows you to duplicate the mouse function, moving the pointer by applying light pressure with one finger somewhere on a pad that senses the x, y movement. Some touch pads let you double-click by tapping their surfaces. Buttons on the touch pad serve the same function as mouse buttons. Use touch pads or trackballs where surface space is limited, because they remain stationary when you use them. Touch pads are popular on notebook computers.

Table 8-2 lists some of the manufacturers of keyboards, pointing devices, touch screens, and fingerprint readers.

Manufacturer	Web Site
BioStik	www.biostik.com
Mitsumi	www.mitsumi.com
Logitech	www.logitech.com
Microsoft	www.microsoft.com
Intel	www.intel.com
Belkin	www.belkin.com
Keytec, Inc.	www.magictouch.com

Table 8-2 Manufacturers of keyboards, pointing devices, and fingerprint readers

SPECIALTY INPUT DEVICES

A+ ESS
1.1

The keyboard and mouse are basic input devices that you need to know how to support. However, you also might be called on to support specialty devices such as a barcode reader, fingerprint reader, or other device. If you generally know how to support I/O devices, you will be able to figure out how to support a specialty device by carefully reading the documentation that comes with the device. This section helps you become familiar with some specialty devices, including barcode readers and biometric devices such as a fingerprint reader.

BARCODE READERS

A barcode reader is used to scan barcodes on products to maintain inventory or at the point of sale (POS). Barcode readers come in a variety of shapes, sizes and features, including a pen wand (simplest and least expensive), slot scanners (to scan ID cards as they are slid through a slot), a CCD scanner (Charge-Couple Device scanner is a gun-type scanner often used at check-out counters), an image scanner (includes a small video camera), and a laser scanner (most expensive and best type).

A barcode reader can interface with a PC using several methods. Some readers use a wireless connection, a serial port, a USB port, or a keyboard port. If the reader uses a keyboard

8

A+ ESS
1.1

A+
220-602
1.1

port, most likely it has a splitter (called a keyboard wedge) on it for the keyboard to use, and data read by the barcode reader is input into the system as though it were typed using the keyboard. Figure 8-11 shows a barcode reader by Symbol that is a laser scanner and can use a PC keyboard wedge or a USB port.

Figure 8-11 Handheld or hands-free barcode scanner by Symbol Technologies

When a barcode reader scans a barcode, it converts the code into numbers that are transferred to software on the computer. This software identifies two types of information from the numeric code: the company and the product. At point of sale, this information is then used to look up the price of the product in price tables accessed by the software.

FINGERPRINT READERS AND OTHER BIOMETRIC DEVICES

A+ ESS
1.1
6.1
6.2
6.3

A+
220-602
1.1
6.2

A biometric device is an input device that inputs biological data about a person, which can be input data to identify a person's fingerprints, handprints, face, voice, eye, and handwritten signatures. Figure 8-12 shows one biometric input device that scans your iris. Iris scanning is one of the most accurate ways to identify a person using biological data. The biometric data collected is then used to authenticate that person using some type of access control system.

Figure 8-12 An iris recognition camera by Panasonic (*www.panasonic.com/iris*)

Using a biometric device, a person presses his finger against a fingerprint reader or puts his face in front of a Web cam that has been programmed to scan facial features, and be authenticated into a computer or network using data that has previously been recorded about this person. For desktop and notebook computer users, the most common biometric device is a fingerprint reader.

Although using biometric devices is gaining in popularity, the disadvantages of using these devices still outweigh the advantages. The most important disadvantage to using biometric devices is the danger of false negatives or false positives. For organizations with high security needs, security personnel must decide the fault tolerance limit of the input data. If you set the fault tolerance limit too low (to make sure only the person's data is the only data authenticated) then you run the risk that the person will not be authenticated (false negative). If you set the fault tolerance level too high (to make sure this person gets authenticated), you run the risk that someone with similar biometric data can get access (false positive). Biometric devices are still to be considered in the pioneering stage of development. For best security, use a combination of two authentication techniques such as a smart card and a password.

> **Notes**
>
> For more information about biometric devices and how they can be used, see the Web site of the International Biometric Industry Association at *www.ibia.org.*

> **A+ Exam Tip**
>
> The A+ Essentials exam expects you to know about these input devices: mouse, keyboard, barcode reader, Web camera, digital camera, microphone, biometric devices, and touch screen. All these devices are covered in this chapter or the next.

For convenience, some people enjoy using a fingerprint reader to log onto their Windows desktop or a Web site rather than having to enter a password. These fingerprint readers are not to be considered as the only authentication to control access to sensitive data: for that, use a strong password. Fingerprint readers can look like a mouse and use a wireless or USB connection, such as the one shown in Figure 8-13. Or they can be embedded on the side of a keyboard or on the side of a flash drive. Some are embedded on cards that fit into PC Card slots for notebook computers. To use some fingerprint readers, you press your finger on the oval input surface, and for other readers, you slide your finger across a bar that scans your fingerprint as it goes by.

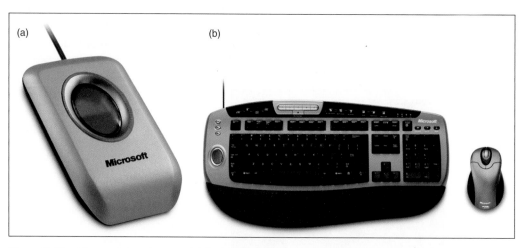

Figure 8-13 Fingerprint readers can (a) look like a mouse, but smaller, or (b) be embedded on a keyboard

Most fingerprint readers that are not embedded in other devices use a USB connection. For most USB devices, you install the software before you plug in the device. For example, using the fingerprint reader by Microsoft, shown in Figure 8-13a, do the following:

1. Insert the setup CD in the optical drive. The installation program on the CD launches. You must accept the license agreement. Figure 8-14 shows one window of the installation

A+ ESS
1.2
6.1
6.2
6.3

A+
220-602
1.1
6.2

process where you are reminded that a fingerprint reader is not to be used when security is required.

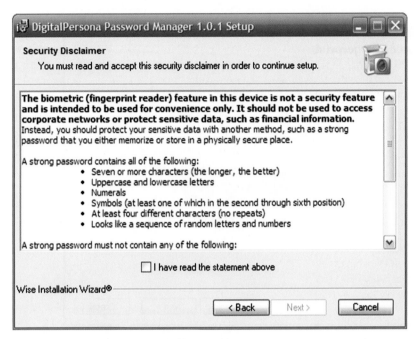

Figure 8-14 The setup program for this fingerprint reader warns to not rely on the reader to protect sensitive data

2. During the installation process, you are told to plug in the reader so it can be enabled. Do so when you are prompted.

3. Next, the Fingerprint Registration Wizard launches so that you can record your fingerprint (called registering your fingerprint). Figure 8-15 shows one screen in the wizard where you select which finger it is you are about to record.

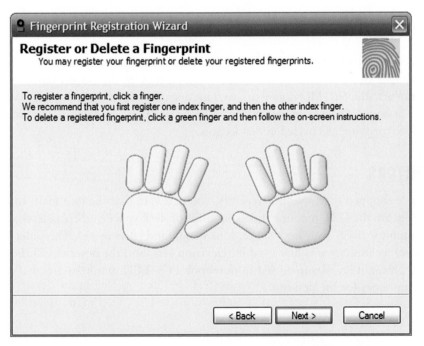

Figure 8-15 To register a fingerprint, select the finger you want to record

A+ ESS
1.2
6.1
6.2
6.3

A+
220-602
1.1
6.2

4. Then on the next screen, which is shown in Figure 8-16, press the reader four times to verify your fingerprint. You can then record more fingerprints or close the wizard.

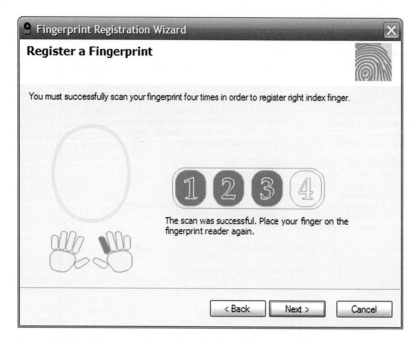

Figure 8-16   A fingerprint is registered after it is recorded four times

5. To use your fingerprints in the place of passwords, when you are logging onto Windows or onto a Web site, press your finger to the fingerprint reader.

Fingerprint readers that are used a lot can get dirty and refuse to read. To clean a fingerprint reader, use the sticky side of duct tape or clear tape, or clean it with a mild solution of glass cleaner containing ammonia. Don't use an alcohol solution to clean fingerprint readers.

MONITORS, PROJECTORS, AND VIDEO CARDS

A+ ESS
1.1
2.1

A+
220-602
1.1
2.1

The primary output device of a computer is the monitor. The two necessary components for video output are the monitor and the video card (also called the video controller, video adapter, and graphics adapter). Monitors work well for a single user or a small group of two or three users. For larger groups, a projector can connect to a second video port. Monitors, projectors, and video cards are all covered in this section.

MONITORS

If you've shopped for a monitor recently, you're aware that the two main categories of monitors are the CRT monitor (takes up a lot of desk space and costs less) and the LCD monitor (frees your desk space, looks cool, and costs more). The older CRT (cathode-ray tube) technology was first used in television sets, and the newer LCD (liquid crystal display) technology was first used in notebook PCs. LCD monitors are also called flat panel monitors for the desktop.

A+ ESS
1.1
2.1

A+
220-602
1.1
2.1

Let's now look at how CRT and LCD monitors work, and then we'll look at how to select one. Installing two or more monitors on a single computer is really a great help for some users, so you'll also learn how to do that.

HOW A CRT MONITOR WORKS

Many monitors use CRT technology, in which the filaments at the back of the cathode tube shoot a beam of electrons to the screen at the front of the tube, as illustrated in Figure 8-17. Plates on the top, bottom, and sides of the tube control the direction of the beam. The beam is directed by these plates to start at the top of the screen, move from left to right to make one line, and then move down to the next line, again moving from left to right. As the beam moves vertically down the screen, it builds the image. By turning the beam on and off and selecting the correct color combination, the grid in front of the filaments controls what goes on the screen when the beam hits that portion of the line or a single dot on the screen. When hit, special phosphors on the back of the monitor screen light up and produce colors. The grid controls which one of three electron guns fires, each gun targeting a different color (red, green, or blue) positioned on the back of the screen.

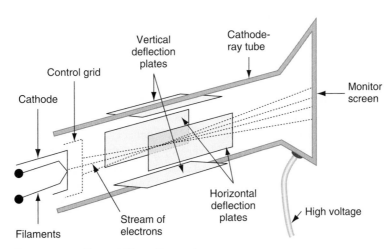

Figure 8-17   How a CRT monitor works

HOW AN LCD MONITOR WORKS

An LCD monitor produces an image using a liquid crystal material made of large, easily polarized molecules. Figure 8-18 shows the layers of the LCD panel that together create the image. At the center of the layers is the liquid crystal material. Next to it is the layer responsible for providing color to the image. These two layers are sandwiched between two grids of electrodes. One grid of electrodes is aligned in columns, and the other electrodes are aligned in rows. The two layers of electrodes make up the electrode matrix. Each intersection of a row electrode and a column electrode forms one pixel on the LCD panel. Software can manipulate each pixel by activating the electrodes that form it. The image is formed by scanning the column and row electrodes, much as the electronic beam scans a CRT monitor screen.

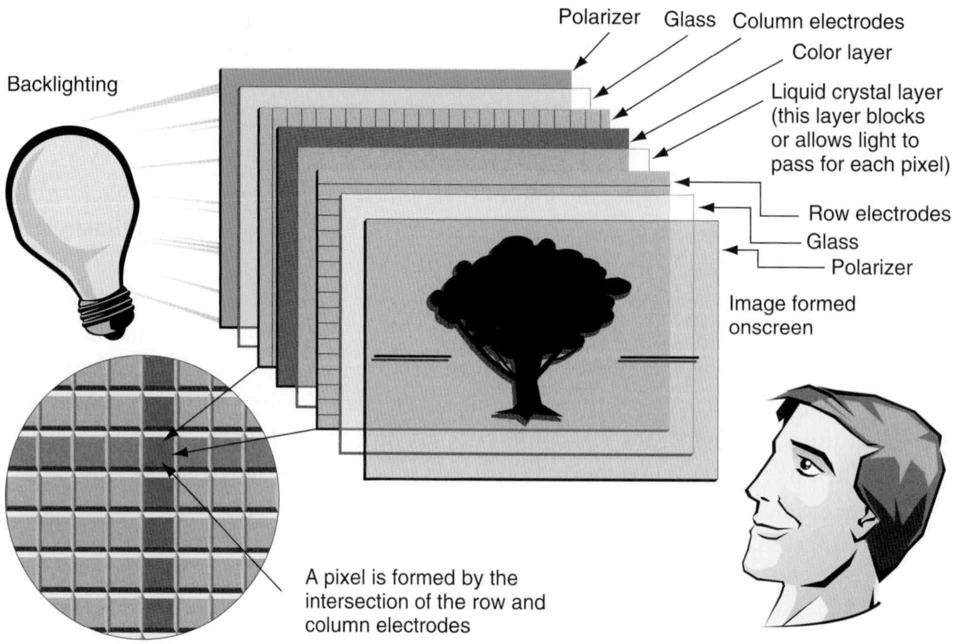

Figure 8-18 Layers of an LCD panel

The polarizer layers outside the glass layers in Figure 8-18 are responsible for preventing light from passing through the pixels when the electrodes are not activated. When the electrodes are activated, light on the backside of the LCD panel can pass through one pixel on the screen, picking up color from the color layer as it passes through the pixel.

Expect an LCD monitor you purchase today to use a technology called **TFT** (thin film transistor), which has almost completely replaced an older technology called **DSTN** (dual-scan twisted nematic). Using TFT technology, a transistor that amplifies the signal is placed at every intersection in the grid, which further enhances the pixel quality. A DSTN display is less expensive than a TFT display and provides a lower-quality image. With DSTN, two columns of electrodes are activated at the same time. TFT display is sometimes called active matrix display, and DSTN display is sometimes called passive matrix display.

Many LCD monitors are built to receive either an analog signal or a digital signal from the video card and have two ports to accommodate either signal. If the signal is analog, it must be converted to digital before the monitor can process it. LCD monitors are designed to receive an analog signal so that you can use a regular video card that works with a CRT monitor, thus reducing the price of upgrading from a CRT to an LCD monitor. Figure 8-19 shows the back of an LCD monitor.

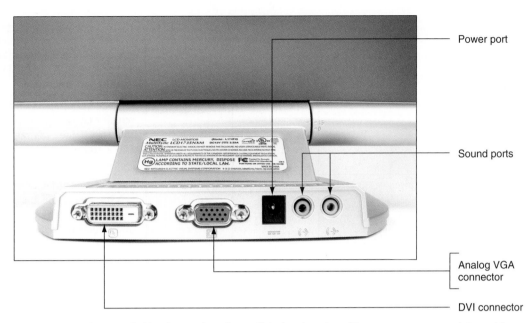

Figure 8-19 The rear of this LCD monitor shows digital and analog video ports to accommodate a video cable with either a 15-pin analog VGA connector or a digital DVI connector

CHOOSING BETWEEN A CRT MONITOR AND AN LCD MONITOR

When choosing between a CRT monitor and an LCD monitor, consider that an LCD monitor takes up much less desk space than a CRT monitor, is lighter, requires less electricity to operate, and is more expensive. Of course, there are other features that you need to compare as well. Table 8-3 summarizes these features; several of the more important ones are discussed in the following subsections.

Monitor Characteristic	CRT Monitor	LCD Monitor	Description
Screen size	X	X	Diagonal length of the screen surface. Common lengths are 14, 15, 17, 19, or 21 inches.
Refresh rate	X		The number of times an electronic beam fills a video screen with lines from top to bottom in one second, or the number of frames it can build in one second. Common refresh rates are 60, 70, and 75 Hz. A monitor rated at 75 Hz can build 75 frames per second. (For comparison, a movie displays 24 frames per second.)
Interlaced	X		The electronic beam draws every other line with each pass, which lessens the overall effect of a lower refresh rate.
Response time		X	The time it takes for an LCD monitor to build one screen. The lower the better. A monitor with a 12-ms response time can build 83 frames per second, and a 16-ms monitor can build 63 frames per second.

Table 8-3 Important features of a monitor

A+ ESS
1.1
2.1

A+
220-602
1.1
2.1

Monitor Characteristic	CRT Monitor	LCD Monitor	Description
Dot pitch	X		The distance between adjacent dots on the screen. An example of a dot pitch is .28 mm.
Resolution	X	X	The number of spots or pixels on a screen that can be addressed by software. Values can range from 640 x 480 up to 1920 x 1200 for high-end monitors.
Pixel pitch		X	Some LCD manufacturers call the monitor resolution the pixel pitch, and others call the distance between pixels the resolution.
Color quality	X	X	The number of bits used to store data about color for each pixel. Values are 8 bits, 16 bits, 24 bits, and 32 bits. Windows calls 24-bit and 32-bit color Truecolor.
Multiscan	X		CRT monitors that offer a variety of refresh rates so they can support several video cards.
Connectors	X	X	The most popular connectors are the 15-pin VGA connector for analog video (RGB video) and the digital video (DVI) connector. Both connectors are shown in Figure 8-19.
Contrast ratio		X	The contrast between true black and true white on the screen. The higher the contrast the better. 1000:1 is better than 700:1.
Viewing angle		X	The angle of view when an LCD monitor becomes difficult to see. A viewing angle of 170 degrees is better than 140 degrees.
Display type		X	For LCD monitors, TFT (active matrix) is better than DSTN (passive matrix).
Display type	X		For CRT monitors, flat screen monitors are high-end monitors that use a flat screen to help prevent glare.
Backlighting		X	For LCD monitors, some use better backlighting than others, which yields a brighter and clearer display.

Table 8-3   Important features of a monitor (continued)

Refresh Rate and Response Time

For CRT monitors, the refresh rate, or vertical scan rate, is the number of times in one second an electronic beam can fill the screen with lines from top to bottom. Refresh rates differ among monitors. The Video Electronics Standards Association (VESA) set a minimum refresh rate standard of 70 Hz, or 70 complete vertical refreshes per second, as one requirement of Super VGA monitors. (Many older VGA [Video Graphics Adapter] monitors are still in use, but most sold today meet the standards for Super VGA.) Slower refresh rates

A+ ESS
1.1
2.1

A+
220-602
1.1
2.1

make the image appear to flicker, whereas faster refresh rates make the image appear solid and stable. For LCD monitors, the response time is the time it takes for an LCD monitor to build all the pixels for one screen or frame, and is measured in ms (milliseconds). An LCD monitor with a response time of 16 ms yields about the same results as a CRT refresh rate of 60 Hz. LCD response times overall have been slightly less than CRT refresh rates.

> **Notes**
>
> The refresh rate and response time are set by using the Display applet in Control Panel.

> ⚡ **Caution**
>
> If you spend many hours in front of a computer, use a good monitor with a high refresh rate or response time. The lower rates that cause monitor flicker can tire and damage your eyes. Because the refresh rates of CRT monitors are generally higher than the response times of LCD monitors, people who spend hours and hours in front of a monitor often prefer a CRT monitor. Also, when you first install a monitor, set the rate at the highest value the monitor can support.

Interlaced or Noninterlaced

Interlaced CRT monitors draw a screen by making two passes. On the first pass, the electronic beam strikes only the even lines, and on the second pass, the beam strikes only the odd lines. The result is that a monitor can have a slow refresh rate with a less noticeable overall effect than there would be if the beam hit all lines for each pass. Interlaced monitors generally have slightly less flicker than noninterlaced monitors, which always draw the entire screen on each pass. Buy an interlaced monitor if you plan to spend long hours staring at the monitor. Your eyes will benefit.

Dot Pitch

Dot pitch is the distance between the spots, or dots, on a CRT screen that the electronic beam hits. Remember that three beams build the screen, one for each of three colors (red, green, and blue). Each composite location on the screen is really made up of three dots and is called a triad. The distance between a color dot in one triad and the same color dot in the next triad is the dot pitch. The smaller the pitch is, the sharper the image. Dot pitches of .28 mm or .25 mm give the best results and cost more. Although less expensive monitors can have a dot pitch of .35 mm or .38 mm, they can still create a fuzzy image, even with the best video cards.

Resolution and Pixel Pitch

For CRT monitors, resolution is a measure of how many spots on a CRT screen are addressable by software. Each addressable location is called a pixel (for picture element), which is composed of several triads. Because resolution depends on software, the video controller card must support the resolution, and the software you are using must make use of the monitor's resolution capabilities. The standard for most software packages is 800 x 600 pixels, although many monitors offer a resolution of 1024 x 768 pixels or higher. The resolution is set in Windows from the Display applet in Control Panel, and requires a driver specific for that resolution. Higher resolution usually requires more video RAM.

For LCD monitors, the number of pixels on the screen is sometimes called the resolution and sometimes called the pixel pitch. Whereas a CRT monitor is designed to use several resolutions, an LCD monitor uses only one resolution, called the native resolution, which is the actual (and fixed) number of pixels built into the monitor. When you change display settings to use a lower resolution than the monitor's native resolution, the LCD displayed area is reduced in size (creating a black area around the display) or video driver

A+ ESS
1.1
2.1

A+
220-602
1.1
2.1

> 🖰 **A+ Exam Tip**
>
> The A+ Essentials exam expects you to know about these resolutions used on LCD monitors: XGA, SXGA+, UXGA, and WUXGA. In addition, you need to be familiar with these terms: active and passive matrix, contrast ratio, and native resolution.

software builds each screen by mapping data using the chosen resolution onto the native resolution. This scaling process can slow down response time and/or cause an LCD monitor to appear fuzzy, which is why most serious gamers prefer CRT monitors to LCD monitors. For sharpest images when using an LCD monitor, use the highest resolution the monitor supports. If you do decide to use a different resolution than the native resolution, for the sharpest display, select a resolution that uses the same ratio of horizontal pixels to vertical pixels that the native resolution uses.

The different resolution standards are as follows:

 VGA (Video Graphics Array) supports up to 640 x 480, which is a 4:3 ratio between horizontal pixels and vertical pixels

 SVGA (Super VGA) supports up to 800 x 600

 XGA (eXtended Graphics Array) supports up to 1024 x 768

 SXGA (Super XGA) supports up to 1280 x 1024 and was first to use a 5:4 ratio between horizontal pixels and vertical pixels.

 SXGA + is a variation of SXGA and uses a resolution of 1400 x 1050

 WSXGA + (Wide SXGA +) uses a resolution of 1680 x 1050

 UXGA (Ultra XGA) supports up to 1600 x 1200

 WUXGA (Wide UXGA) supports up to 1920 x 1200

To convert the resolution to the number of pixels, multiply the horizontal pixels by vertical pixels. For example, SXGA supports up to 1280 x 1024 pixels or 1.3 million pixels.

> ✐ **Notes**
>
> There is some debate about the danger of monitors giving off ELF (extremely low frequency) emissions of electromagnetic fields. Standards to control ELF emissions are Sweden's MPR II standard and the TCO '95 standards. The TCO '95 standards also include guidelines for energy consumption, screen flicker, and luminance. Most monitors manufactured today comply with the MPR II standard, but very few comply with the more stringent TCO '95 or TCO '99 standards.

A+ ESS
1.2

A+
220-602
1.1

APPLYING | CONCEPTS   INSTALLING DUAL MONITORS

To increase the size of your Windows desktop, you can install more than one monitor for a single computer. Setting up dual monitors gives you more space for your Windows desktop as well as some redundancy if one goes down.

The following dual-monitor installation process assumes that you are using Windows XP and that you already have a monitor installed. To install dual monitors, you can use two video cards, one for each monitor, or you can use a video card that provides two video ports.

To install a second monitor and a dual-monitor setup using two video cards:

1. Verify that the original video card works properly, determine whether it is PCI Express or AGP, and decide whether it is to be the primary monitor.

8

2. Verify that the new PCI video card is compatible with Windows XP.

3. Boot the PC and enter CMOS setup. If CMOS has the option to select the order that video cards are initialized, verify that the currently installed card is configured to initialize first. If it does not initialize first, then, when you install the second card, video might not work at all when you first boot with two cards.

4. Install a second video card in the PCI slot nearest to the AGP or PCI Express slot, and attach the second monitor.

5. Boot the system. Windows recognizes the new hardware and might prompt you for the location of the drivers. If Windows does not recognize you have new hardware to install, go to Control Panel and select **Add Hardware** to manually install the drivers.

6. Now you are ready to configure the new monitor. Right-click the **desktop** and select **Display Properties** from the shortcut menu. The Display Properties dialog box shown in Figure 8-20 appears. Select the **Settings** tab.

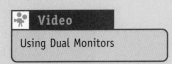
Video

Using Dual Monitors

Figure 8-20 You must choose to activate a second monitor before it will be used by Windows

7. Notice that there are two numbered blue boxes that represent your two monitors. When you click one of these blue boxes, the Display drop-down menu changes to show the selected monitor, and the Screen resolution and the Color quality display settings also follow the selected monitor. This lets you customize the settings for each monitor. If necessary, arrange the boxes so that they represent the physical arrangement of your monitors.

Notes

In Figure 8-20, if you arrange the two windows side by side, your extended desktop will extend left or right. If you arrange the two windows one on top of the other, your extended desktop will extend up and down.

8. On the Settings tab of the Display Properties dialog box, adjust your Screen resolution and the Color quality settings according to your preferences. Check **Extend my Windows desktop onto this monitor**. To save the settings, click **Apply**. Depending on the Advanced display settings in effect, you might be asked to restart your computer. The second monitor should initialize and show the extended desktop.

> 📝 Notes
>
> Settings for each video adapter that you add to your system must be saved and applied individually. Windows 2000/XP supports up to 10 separate monitors on a single system, and Windows 9x/Me supports up to nine monitors.

9. Close the Display Properties dialog box. From the **Start** menu, open an application and verify that you can use the second monitor by dragging the application over to the second monitor's desktop.

After you add a second monitor to your system, you can move from one monitor to another simply by moving your mouse. Switching from one monitor to the other does not require any special keystroke or menu option.

USING A PROJECTOR

A monitor gives excellent performance when only two or three people are viewing, but you may want to use a projector in addition to a monitor when larger groups of people are watching. Projectors are great in the classroom, for sales presentations, or for watching the Super Bowl with your friends. The prices of projectors have dropped significantly in the past few years, making them more of an option for business and pleasure. One portable projector, shown in Figure 8-21, has a native resolution of XGA 1024 x 768, and can connect to a desktop or notebook computer by way of a 15-pin video port or S-Video port.

Figure 8-21 Portable XGA projector by Panasonic

To use a projector, you'll need an extra video port. For desktop computers, you'll need to install a second video card or use a video card that has two video ports. Most notebook computers are designed to be used with projectors and provide the extra 15-pin video port. To use a projector, plug in the projector to the extra port and then turn it on. For a notebook computer, use a function key to activate the video port. For most notebooks, you can toggle the function key to: (1) use the LCD display and not use the port; (2) use both the LCD display and the port; or (3) use the port and don't use the LCD display. Also, when you first use the projector, it will show a mirrored image of exactly what you see on your LCD panel. If you want to make the projector an extension of the desktop, you can use the Display properties window. On that window, click the **Settings** tab, select the projector in the list of display devices, and then select **Extend my Windows desktop onto this monitor**. The projector now works as a dual monitor.

> ✎ **Notes**
>
> Many of us use PowerPoint by Microsoft for group presentations. If you configure your projector as a dual monitor, you can use PowerPoint to display a presentation to your audience on the projector at the same time you are using your LCD display to manage your computer. To do so, open PowerPoint in **Presenter View**, and then on the Slide Show menu, click **Set Up Show**. Next, under Multiple Monitors, check **Show Presenter View**. Then select the projector in the list, and click **Display slide show**.

VIDEO CARDS

Recall that the video controller card is the interface between the monitor and the computer. These cards are sometimes called graphic adapters, video boards, graphics cards, or display cards. Sometimes the video controller with a video port is integrated into the motherboard. If you are buying a motherboard with an integrated video controller, make sure that you can disable the controller on the motherboard if it gives you trouble. You can then install a video card and bypass the controller and port on the motherboard.

> 🎥 **Video**
>
> Installing a Video Card

A video card can pass data to a monitor or other display device in four ways. Each method uses a different type of video port on a video card. These five ports are used to connect to the monitor or television cable. Figure 8-22 shows a video card that has three of the five ports.

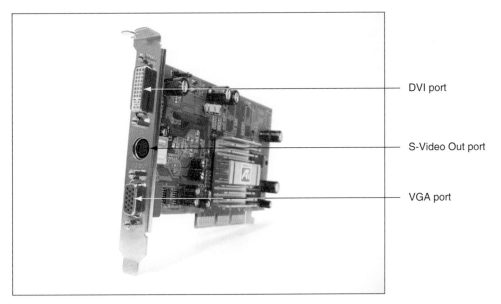

DVI port

S-Video Out port

VGA port

Figure 8-22 This ATI Radeon video card has three ports for video out: DVI, S-Video, and the regular VGA port

The five methods of data transfer are as follows:

▲ *RGB video using a VGA port.* This is the standard analog video method of passing three separate signals for red, green, and blue, which most video cards and CRT monitors use. This method uses a regular 15-pin Super-VGA port (commonly called a VGA port).

▲ *DVI (Digital Visual Interface).* This method is the digital interface standard used by digital monitors such as a digital LCD monitor and digital TVs (HDTV). For a video

A+ ESS
1.1

A+
220-602
1.1

card that only has a DVI port, you can purchase a VGA converter so you can connect a standard VGA video cable to use a regular analog monitor (see Figure 8-23).

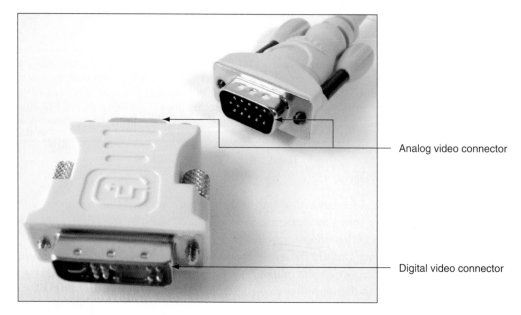

Analog video connector

Digital video connector

Figure 8-23   Digital to analog video port converter

◢ *Composite video.* Using this method, the red, green, and blue (RGB) are mixed together in the same signal. This is the method used by television, and can be used by a video card that is designed to send output to a TV. This method uses a Composite Out port, which is round and is the same size as the S-Video Out port shown in Figure 8-22, but has only a single pin in the center of the port. Composite video does not produce as sharp an image as RGB video or S-Video.

◢ *S-Video (Super-Video).* This method sends two signals over the cable, one for color and the other for brightness, and is used by some high-end TVs and video equipment. It uses a 4-pin round port. The television and the video card must support this method and you must use a special S-Video cable like the one shown in Figure 8-24. This standard is not as good as RGB for monitors, but is better than Composite video when output to a television.

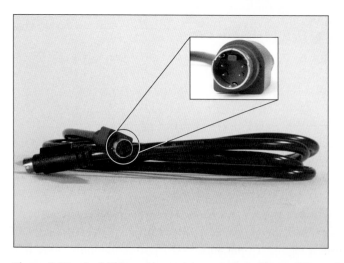

Figure 8-24   An S-Video cable used to connect a video card to an S-Video port on a television

8

A+ ESS
1.1

A+
220-602
1.1

▲ *HDMI (High-Definition Multimedia Interface)*. HDMI is the latest digital audio and video interface standard. It is not widely available on video cards or motherboards, but is expected to ultimately replace DVI. HDMI is currently used on televisions and other home theatre equipment. To connect a PC to this equipment that uses HDMI, you can purchase a HDMI to DVI cable such as the one shown in Figure 8-25.

Figure 8-25   An HDMI to DVI cable can be used to connect a PC that has a DVI port to home theatre equipment that uses an HDMI port

The quality of a video subsystem is rated by how it affects overall system performance, video quality (including resolution and color), power-saving features, and ease of use and installation. Because the video controller on the video card is separate from the core system functions, manufacturers can use a variety of techniques to improve performance without being overly concerned about compatibility with functions on the motherboard. An example of this flexibility is the many ways memory is managed on a video controller. Two main features to look for in a video card are the bus it uses and the amount and type of video RAM it has or can support. Also know that a motherboard might have its own on-board video controller and video port, but that this video subsystem is probably very basic and lacks many of the features you'll read about in this section.

THE BUSES USED BY VIDEO CARDS

Four buses have been used for video cards in the past 20 years or so. Listed in the order they were introduced, they are the VESA bus, the regular PCI bus, the AGP bus, and the newer PCI Express bus. The VESA and AGP buses were developed specifically for video cards, and the PCI buses are used for many types of cards, including a video card.

Video cards currently use the AGP bus or the PCI Express x16 bus. For most personal computer motherboards, if a second video card is installed for dual monitors, it uses a regular PCI slot. A motherboard will have a PCI Express x16 slot or an AGP slot, but not both. PCI Express x16 is much faster than AGP, but currently AGP is still the most popular slot for a video card.

AGP can share system memory with the CPU to do its calculations, and, therefore, does not always have to first copy data from system memory to video memory on the graphics card. This feature, known as direct memory execute (DIME), is probably the most powerful feature of AGP.

Different AGP Standards

AGP has evolved over the years, and the different AGP standards can be confusing. AGP standards include three major releases (AGP 1.0, AGP 2.0, and AGP 3.0), one major change in the AGP slot length standard (AGP Pro), four different speeds (1x, 2x, 4x, and 8x) yielding four different throughputs, three different voltages (3.3 V, 1.5 V, and 0.8 V), and six different expansion slots (AGP 3.3 V, AGP 1.5 V, AGP Universal, AGP Pro 3.3 V, APG Pro 1.5 V, and AGP Pro Universal). To help you make sense of all this, Table 8-4 sorts it all out.

Standard	Speeds (Cycles Per Clock Beat)	Maximum Throughput	Voltage	Slots Supported
AGP 1.0	1x	266 MB/sec	3.3 V	Slot keyed to 3.3 V
AGP 2.0	1x, 2x, or 4x	533 MB/sec or 1.06 GB/sec	3.3 V or 1.5 V	Slot keyed to 1.5 V Slot keyed to 3.3 V Universal slot (for either 1.5-V or 3.3-V cards)
AGP Pro	Applies to all speeds	NA	3.3 V or 1.5 V	AGP Pro 3.3 V keyed AGP Pro 1.5 V keyed AGP Pro Universal (for either 1.5-V or 3.3-V cards)
AGP 3.0	4x or 8x	2.12 GB/sec	1.5 V and 0.8 V	Universal AGP 3.0 (4x/8x) slot Slot keyed to 1.5 V AGP Pro 1.5-V keyed slot

Table 8-4 AGP standards summarized

As you can see from Table 8-4, there are several different AGP slots and matching card connectors that apply to the different standards. When matching video cards to AGP slots, be aware of these several variations. For instance, the first two slots in Figure 8-26 are used by cards that follow the AGP 1.0 or AGP 2.0 standards. These slots have key positions so that you cannot put an AGP 3.3-V card in an AGP 1.5-V slot or vice versa. The third slot is a universal slot that can accommodate 3.3-V or 1.5-V cards. All three slots are 2.9 inches wide and have 132 pins, although some pins are not used. Figure 8-27 shows a motherboard with an older AGP 3.3-V slot. Notice how the keyed 3.3-V break in the slot is near the back side of the motherboard where expansion cards are bracketed to the case.

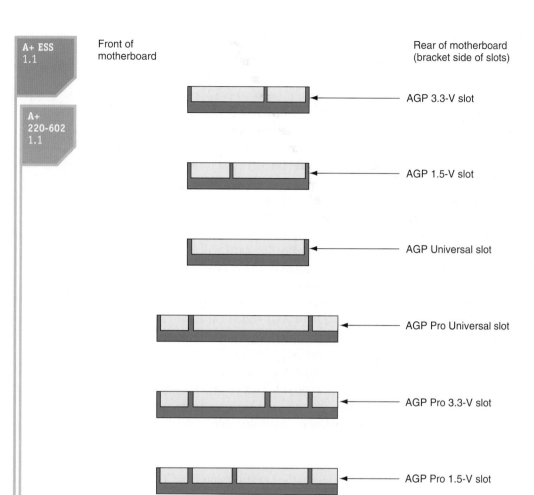

Front of motherboard

Rear of motherboard (bracket side of slots)

AGP 3.3-V slot

AGP 1.5-V slot

AGP Universal slot

AGP Pro Universal slot

AGP Pro 3.3-V slot

AGP Pro 1.5-V slot

Figure 8-26 Six types of AGP slots

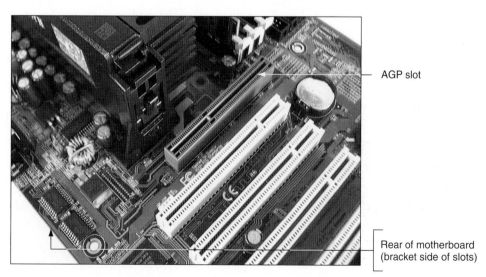

AGP slot

Rear of motherboard (bracket side of slots)

Figure 8-27 This motherboard uses an AGP 3.3-V slot, which accommodates an AGP 1.0 video card

Another AGP standard, called AGP Pro, has provisions for a longer slot. This 180-pin slot has extensions on both ends that contain an additional 20 pins on one end and 28 pins on the other end, to provide extra voltage for a high-end AGP video card that consumes more than 25 watts of power. These wider slots might be keyed to 3.3 V or 1.5 V or might be a Universal Pro slot that can hold either 3.3-V or 1.5-V cards. Also, when using an AGP Pro video card, leave the PCI slot next to it empty to improve ventilation and prevent overheating.

The latest AGP standard, AGP 3.0, runs at 8x or 4x speeds. APG 3.0 cards can be installed in an AGP 1.5-V slot, but signals are put on the data bus using 0.8 V. It's best to install an AGP 3.0 card in a slot that is designed to support AGP 3.0 cards. However, if you install an AGP 3.0 card in an older AGP 1.5-V slot, the card might or might not work, but the card will not be damaged.

> **Notes**
>
> If you're trying to buy an AGP video card to match a motherboard slot, you have to be really careful. When reading an AGP ad, it's hard to distinguish between AGP 3.3 V and AGP 3.0, but there's a big difference in these standards, and they are not interchangeable.

An AGP video card will be keyed to 1.5 V or 3.3 V or a universal AGP video card has both keys so that it can fit into either a 1.5-V keyed slot or a 3.3-V keyed slot. A universal AGP video card also fits into a universal AGP slot. If an AGP video card does not make use of the extra pins provided by the AGP Pro slot, it can still be inserted into the AGP Pro slot if it has a registration tab that fits into the end of the Pro slot near the center of the motherboard. Earlier in the chapter, Figure 8-22 showed a universal AGP video card with two notches on the edge connector and a registration tab that makes it possible to fit the card in an AGP Pro slot.

PCI Express

Recall from Chapter 5 that PCI Express is the latest version of PCI. PCI Express x16 is about twice as fast as AGP x8 and will ultimately replace AGP. Motherboards that support PCI Express x16 for the video card have a PCI Express x16 bus dedicated to video apart from the PCI Express bus used by the other PCI Express slots on the board. Figure 8-28 shows a PCI Express video card. Notice the tab next to the card's connectors that fits into a retention mechanism on the motherboard to help stabilize the card.

Cooling fan

Heat sink

Tab used to stabilize the card

PCI Express x16 connector

15-pin analog video port

TV-out connector

Digital video port

Figure 8-28 This PCX 5750 graphics card by MSI Computer Corporation uses the PCI Express x16 local bus

A+ ESS
1.1

A+
220-602
1.1

GRAPHICS ACCELERATORS

One of the more important advances made in video cards in recent years is the introduction of graphics accelerators. A graphics accelerator is a type of video card that has its own processor to boost performance. With the demands that graphics applications make in the multimedia environment, graphics accelerators have become not just enhancements, but common necessities, especially among the gaming crowd.

The processor on a graphics accelerator card is similar to a CPU but specifically designed to manage video and graphics. Some features included on a graphics accelerator are MPEG decoding, 3-D graphics, dual porting, color space conversion, interpolated scaling, EPA Green PC support, digital output to flat panel display monitors, and application support for popular, high-intensity graphics software such as Auto-CAD and Quark. All these features are designed to reduce the burden on the motherboard CPU and perform the video and graphics functions much faster than the motherboard CPU.

Notes

One problem high-end graphics cards have is overheating. One possible solution is a PCI fan card mounted next to the graphics card such as the one shown in Figure 8-29.

Notes

For serious game enthusiasts who have a motherboard with two PCI Express x16 slots, you can use two video cards designed to work in tandem using a technology called SLI (stands for "scalable link interface" or "scanline interleave mode"). The two video cards are installed side-by-side in the two slots and a bridging mechanism on top connects the two cards that together support a single monitor.

Figure 8-29 A PCI fan card by Vantec can be used next to a high-end graphics card to help keep it cool

VIDEO MEMORY

Older video cards had no memory, but today they need memory to handle the large volume of data generated by increased resolution and color. Video memory is stored on video cards as memory chips.

The amount of data a video card receives from the CPU for each frame (or screen) of data is determined by the screen resolution (measured in pixels), the number of colors (called color depth and measured in bits), and the enhancements to color information (called alpha blending). The more data required to generate a single screen of data, the more memory is required to hold that data. Memory on the video card that holds one frame of data before it is sent to the monitor is called a frame buffer.

Several factors affect the amount of memory required for the frame buffer, which can be as much as 8 MB. However, in addition to needing memory to hold each frame buffer, a graphics accelerator card might also need memory for other purposes. Software that builds 3-D graphics onscreen often uses textures and backgrounds, and sometimes a graphics card holds these backgrounds in memory to build future screens. Large amounts of video RAM keep the card from having to retrieve this data from the hard drive or system RAM multiple times.

A+ ESS
1.1

In addition, to improve performance, the graphics card might use buffering, in which the card holds not just the frame being built, but the next few frames. Because of backgrounds and buffering, a high-end card might need as much as 512 MB of RAM. See the graphics card documentation for information about memory recommendations for maximum performance.

The following list describes the different types of video memory:

A+
220-602
1.1

▲ VRAM (video RAM) is a type of dual-ported memory, which means that video memory can be accessed by both the input and output processes at the same time.

▲ SGRAM (synchronous graphics RAM) is similar to SDRAM and is discussed in Chapter 6. It is not dual-ported memory, but is faster than VRAM because it can synchronize itself with the CPU bus clock and uses other methods to increase overall performance for graphics-intensive processing.

▲ WRAM (window RAM) is dual ported and less expensive than VRAM. WRAM was named more for its ability to manage full-motion video than for its ability to speed up Microsoft Windows video processing. WRAM's increased speed is primarily due to its own internal bus on the chip, which has a data path that is 256 bits wide.

▲ MultiBank DRAM (MDRAM) is not dual ported, but is faster than VRAM or WRAM. It uses relatively small 32K blocks of memory that can be independently accessed.

▲ 3-D RAM was designed specifically to improve performance when simulating 3-D graphics. This chip can calculate which pixel of a 3-D graphic to display, depending on whether the pixel is behind other pixels, and, therefore, out of sight in a 3-D graphic. If the pixel is not to be visible, the chip writes it back to memory for use later.

▲ Direct RDRAM (DRDRAM), also discussed in Chapter 6, is used on video cards and game systems and is designed to work well with video streaming.

▲ Graphics DDR (GDDR), Graphics DDR2 (GDDR2), and Graphics DDR3 (GDDR3) are types of SDRAM specifically designed for video cards. Recall that DDR and DDR2 SDRAM are discussed in Chapter 6. DDR3 is an advanced version of DDR2. GDDR3 is considered the up-and-coming video memory that is expected to replace other types.

When upgrading memory on a video card, you must match the memory to the card. To do so, start by removing the card from the system and then installing the new memory chip. When you turn on the system, video memory counts up onscreen before system memory is counted. At this point, you can verify that the correct amount of video memory is installed.

Notes

When you match a monitor to a video card, a good rule of thumb is to match a low-end video card to a low-end monitor, a midrange video card to a midrange monitor, and a high-end video card to a high-end monitor, to get the best performance from both devices. However, you can compare the different features of the video card to those of the monitor, such as the resolutions and the refresh rates supported.

A+ ESS
1.2

APPLYING CONCEPTS   INSTALLING A VIDEO CARD

In general, when installing an expansion card, first read the documentation for the card and set any jumper switches or DIP switches on it. Like most cards today, the AGP 3.0 8x video card we are installing is Plug and Play–compatible and has no jumpers. The video card, shown in Figure 8-30, is a universal AGP card that is keyed for 3.3-V or 1.5-V slots and has a registration tab that allows it to also fit into an AGP Pro slot.

 A+ Exam Tip

The A+ Essentials exam expects you to know how to install a video card.

A+ ESS
1.2

A+
220-602
1.1

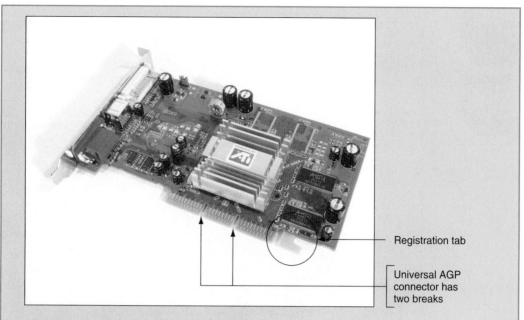

Registration tab

Universal AGP
connector has
two breaks

Figure 8-30 AGP 3.0 8x universal video card

To install the video card, do the following:

1. An AGP slot might require a retention mechanism around it that helps hold the card securely in the slot. Some motherboards require that you install this retention mechanism on the slot before you install the card, as shown in Figure 8-31. Check your motherboard documentation for specific instructions.

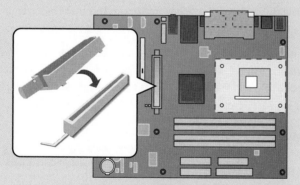

Figure 8-31 Some motherboard installations require you to install a retention mechanism around the AGP slot before installing the video card

2. Remove the faceplate for the slot from the computer case, and slide back the retention mechanism on the slot. Insert the card in the slot and slide the retention mechanism back in position. The retention mechanism slides over the registration tab at the end of the AGP slot to secure the card in the slot. Use a single screw to secure the card to the computer case (see Figure 8-32).

Figure 8-32 Secure the video card to the case with a single screw

3. Replace the computer case cover, plug in the video cable, and turn on the system. When Windows starts up, it will launch the Found New Hardware Wizard. Follow the onscreen instructions to install the drivers. Windows will most likely install its own generic video drivers.

4. To take full advantage of the features of your video card, rather than using Windows generic drivers, you need to use the video card drivers provided by the manufacturer. To do that, right-click anywhere on the desktop and select **Properties** on the shortcut menu. The Display Properties window opens, as shown in Figure 8-33.

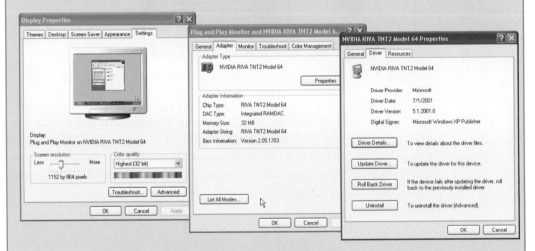

Figure 8-33 Updating the video card drivers in Windows XP

A+ ESS
1.2

A+
220-602
1.1

5. Select the **Settings** tab and click **Advanced**. On the next window, click the **Adapter** tab, also shown in Figure 8-33. The adapter's Properties window opens.

6. Insert the CD that came with the video card and click **Update Drivers**. Follow the onscreen directions to install the new drivers.

7. After the drivers are installed, use the Display Properties window to check the resolution and refresh rate for the monitor.

For more information about video cards, including graphics accelerators, see the Web sites of the manufacturers listed in Table 8-5.

Manufacturer	Web Site
ASUSTeK Computer, Inc.	www.asus.com
ATI Technologies, Inc.	www.ati.com
Creative Technology, Ltd.	www.creative.com
Gainward Co., Ltd.	www.gainward.com
Hercules Computer Technology	www.hercules.com
Matrox Graphics, Inc.	www.matrox.com
MSI Computer Corporation	www.msicomputer.com
nVidia	www.nvidia.com
VisionTek	www.visiontek.com

Table 8-5 Video card manufacturers

We now turn our attention to using standard ports for installing devices on a computer system. Then you will learn how to install expansion cards in expansion slots.

USING PORTS AND EXPANSION SLOTS FOR ADD-ON DEVICES

A+ ESS
1.1
4.1

Devices can plug into a port that comes directly off the motherboard, such as a serial, parallel, USB, FireWire (IEEE 1394), or network port. Or a port, such as serial ATA, video, or SCSI, can be provided by an expansion card. In this section, you'll learn how to use the serial, parallel, USB, and FireWire ports that come directly off a motherboard. Then you'll learn how to install expansion cards in expansion slots on the motherboard.

Figure 8-34 shows the ports on the rear of a computer case; some of them are provided by the motherboard and others are provided by an expansion card. When deciding what type of port a new device should use, the speed of the port is often a tiebreaker. Table 8-6 shows the speeds of various ports, from fastest to slowest.

A+ ESS
1.1
4.1

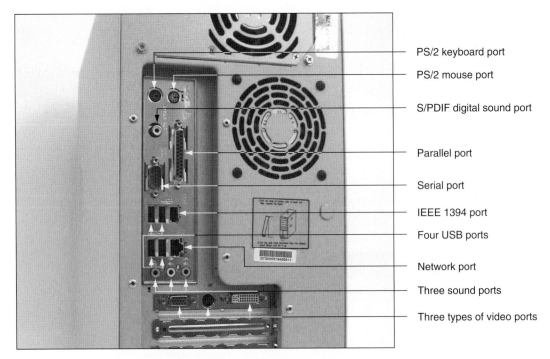

PS/2 keyboard port

PS/2 mouse port

S/PDIF digital sound port

Parallel port

Serial port

IEEE 1394 port

Four USB ports

Network port

Three sound ports

Three types of video ports

Figure 8-34 Rear of computer case showing ports; only the video ports are not coming directly off the motherboard

Port Type	Maximum Speed
1394b (FireWire)*	1.2 Gbps (gigabits per second) or 800 Mbps (megabits per second)**
Hi-Speed USB 2.0	480 Mbps
1394a (FireWire)	400 Mbps
Original USB	12 Mbps
Parallel	1.5 Mbps
Serial	115.2 Kbps (kilobits per second)

*IEEE 1394b has been designed to run at 3.2 Gbps, but products using this speed are not yet manufactured.

**FireWire 800 is the industry name for 1394b running at 800 Mbps.

Table 8-6 Data transmission speeds for various port types

USING SERIAL PORTS

Serial ports were originally intended for input and output devices such as a mouse or an external modem. Recall from Chapter 1 that a serial port transmits data in single bits, one bit following the next. You can identify these ports on the back of a PC case by (1) counting the pins and (2) determining whether the port is male or female. Serial ports have been mostly outdated by USB ports, and many new computers don't have a serial port.

Figure 8-35 shows two serial ports, one parallel port, and one game port for comparison. Serial ports are sometimes called DB9 and DB25 connectors. DB stands for data bus and refers to the number of pins on the connector. Serial ports are almost always male ports, and parallel ports are almost always female ports.

A+ ESS
1.1
4.1

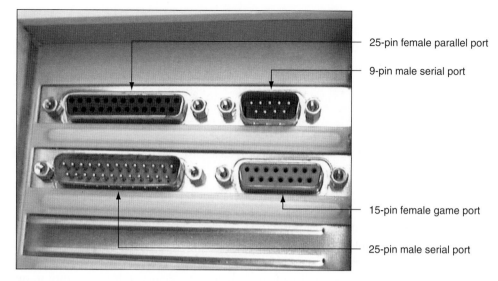

25-pin female parallel port

9-pin male serial port

15-pin female game port

25-pin male serial port

Figure 8-35 Serial, parallel, and game ports

A serial port conforms to the interface standard called RS-232c (Reference Standard 232 revision c), which is why a serial port is sometimes called the RS-232 port. The maximum cable length for a serial cable according to RS-232 standards is 50 feet. This interface standard originally called for 25 pins, but because microcomputers use only nine of those pins, manufacturers often installed a modified 9-pin port. You almost never see a 25-pin serial port on today's PCs. However, if you ever see one on a very old PC, know that the 25-pin port uses only nine pins; the other pins are unused. You can buy an adapter to convert a 25-pin port to a 9-pin port, and vice versa, to accommodate a cable you already have.

Recall that an internal device or a port that an external device is using needs an IRQ to hail the attention of the CPU and the CPU needs a range of I/O addresses to communicate with the device or port. To simplify how computer and I/O device manufacturers assign these system resources to ports, the industry has designated two configurations for system resources that apply to serial ports and designated them as COM1 (Communications Port 1) and COM2. Later, two more configurations were designated as COM3 and COM4. These COM assignments each represent a designated IRQ and an I/O address range, as shown in Table 8-7.

> **Notes**
>
> A **null modem cable** is an older type of cable that uses serial ports to connect two computers so they can communicate. A null modem cable looks and works like a serial cable except the read and write lines in the cable are reversed so that one computer writes data to a pin in the cable that is read by the other computer. Null modem cables were used before most computers had network ports. Today, use a crossover cable and network ports to connect two computers. You'll learn how to use crossover cables in Chapter 10.

Port	IRQ	I/O Address (in Hex)	Type
COM1	IRQ 4	03F8–03FF	Serial
COM2	IRQ 3	02F8–02FF	Serial
COM3	IRQ 4	03E8–03EF	Serial
COM4	IRQ 3	02E8–02EF	Serial
LPT1	IRQ 7	0378–037F	Parallel
LPT2	IRQ 5	0278–027F	Parallel

Table 8-7 Default port assignments on many computers

Most serial and parallel ports today connect directly to the motherboard, and the COM and LPT assignments are made in CMOS setup. The ports can also be enabled and disabled in setup. Sometimes the setup screen shows the COM assignments, and sometimes you see the actual I/O address and IRQ assignments (see Figure 8-36). In addition, one or more serial, parallel, USB, or game ports can be provided by an I/O **controller card**. Older I/O controller cards used jumpers and DIP switches to configure the serial and parallel ports on the card.

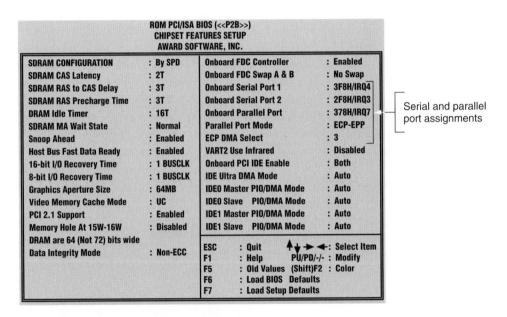

Figure 8-36 CMOS Setup screen for chipset features

To verify that the port is working with no errors for any Windows OS, you can use Device Manager. To do so, click the + sign beside Ports to show the list of ports, click a communications port, such as COM1, and click Properties. You will then see the Properties dialog box shown in Figure 8-37, if you are using Windows XP (other Windows OSs look similar).

When a serial port is used by an external modem, you need to know that in documentation, the serial port is called the DTE (Data Terminal Equipment) and the modem is called the DCE (Data Communications Equipment). When supporting an external modem using a serial port, it's important to know that communication is controlled by both the modem and the serial port, and settings must be correct for both the device and the port. The settings that control serial-port communication are called **port settings**.

A+ ESS
1.1
4.1

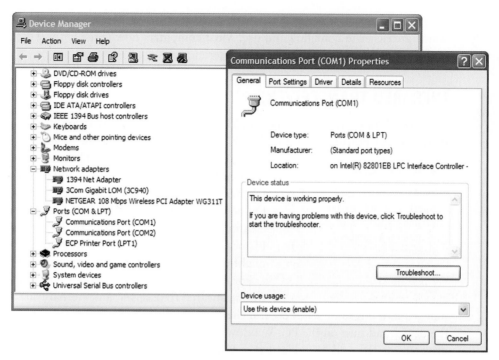

Figure 8-37 Properties of the COM1 serial port in Windows XP

To view the port setting for an external modem using a serial port, in Device Manager, right-click the serial port, labeled **Communications Port (COM1)**, and select **Properties**. The serial port's Properties dialog box opens. Select the **Port Settings** tab as shown in Figure 8-38. Note that the first drop-down list shows the bits per second of the port, which is currently set at 128,000 bps. Unless you have reason to do otherwise, verify that Bits per second is set to the highest value, Data bits is set to 8 (data is sent in 8-bit segments), Parity is set to None (no error checking by the port), Stop bits is set to 1 (bit used to control flow), and Flow control is set to Hardware (let the modem control data flow). Click **OK** when you're done.

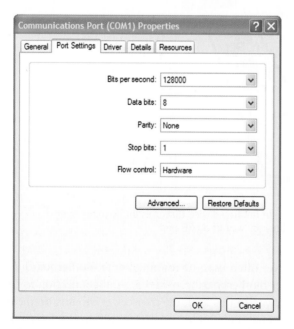

Figure 8-38 Port settings for a Windows XP serial port used by an external modem

Serial ports are fast becoming outdated because they are being replaced by USB ports, which are easier to configure and use. Most computers now come with two or more USB ports, and might or might not have one serial port.

INFRARED TRANSCEIVERS

An infrared transceiver, also called an IrDA (Infrared Data Association) transceiver or an IR transceiver provides an infrared port for wireless communication. Television remote controls communicate with the TV or set top box using infrared transmission. On desktop and notebook computers, infrared is used by wireless keyboards, mice, and printers. On notebooks, an infrared receiver is often used for communication between the notebook and a PDA (such as a Pocket PC or Blackberry) to transfer information. Also, an older PC might use an infrared device to connect to a network.

> **A+ Exam Tip**
>
> The A+ Essentials exam expects you to know how an infrared transceiver might be used on a notebook computer.

For a motherboard that does not have built-in support for an infrared transceiver, an external transceiver can be plugged into a USB or serial port. If the transceiver is Plug and Play, you need only connect the device and turn on the PC. Windows automatically detects and installs the infrared driver, using the Add New Hardware Wizard. Figure 8-39 shows a remote control that can be used with multimedia applications installed on a notebook computer. The remote communicates with the notebook by way of an IR transceiver connected to a USB port.

Figure 8-39 This remote control is an infrared device that uses an IR transceiver connected to a notebook by way of a USB port

An onboard infrared transceiver often uses the resources on a motherboard designated for a serial port. Sometimes an older motherboard provides a 5-pin connection for a proprietary IrDA-compliant infrared transceiver. In this case, the transceiver mounts on the outside of the case, and a wire goes through a small hole in the case to connect to the 5-pin connection. The motherboard manual will then instruct you to use CMOS setup to enable "UART2 Use

A+ ESS
1.1
2.1
4.1
5.1

A+
220-602
2.1

Infrared." UART (universal asynchronous receiver-transmitter) refers to the logic on the motherboard that controls the serial ports on the board, and is sometimes referred to as the UART 16550. When you enable "UART2 Use Infrared," the infrared transceiver uses system resources assigned to COM2. Because the infrared transceiver is now using these resources, the COM2 serial port does not have access to the resources and is disabled.

For legacy transceivers, install the transceiver using the Add New Hardware applet in the Control Panel, or run the device driver setup program. For serial port transceivers, the transceiver uses the resources of the serial port for communication and creates a virtual infrared serial port and a virtual infrared parallel port for infrared devices. During the installation, you are told what these virtual ports are and given the opportunity to change them. For example, if you physically connect the transceiver to COM2, the virtual ports will be COM4 for infrared serial devices and LPT3 for an infrared printer. The IRQ and I/O addresses for the infrared system are those that have been previously assigned to COM2. To activate the transceiver, you double-click the Infrared icon in Control Panel. If the icon is not visible, press F5 to refresh Control Panel.

Infrared wireless is becoming obsolete because of the line-of-sight issue: There must be an unobstructed "view" between the infrared device and the receiver. Short-range radio technology such as Bluetooth is becoming the most popular way to connect a wireless I/O device to a nearby computer, because with radio waves there is no line-of-sight issue.

> **Notes**
>
> Infrared standards are defined by the Infrared Data Association (IrDA). Their Web site is *www.irda.org*.

A+ ESS
1.1
4.1

USING PARALLEL PORTS

Parallel ports, commonly used by older printers, transmit data in parallel, eight bits at a time. Most parallel cables are only six feet (1.8 meters) long, though no established standard sets maximum cable length. However, to ensure data integrity, you should avoid using a parallel cable longer than 15 feet (4.5 meters). (In fact, Hewlett-Packard recommends that cables be no longer than 10 feet, or 3 meters.) If the data is transmitted in parallel over a very long cable, the data integrity is sometimes lost.

Parallel ports were originally intended to be used only for printers to receive data. However, some parallel ports are used for input/output devices, such as older tape drives and older external CD-ROM drives. Parallel ports that can handle communication in both directions are called bidirectional parallel ports. Also, today's printers and OSs expect the printer to be able to communicate with the OS such as when it needs to hail the OS that it is out of paper. These printers require bidirectional parallel ports.

TYPES OF PARALLEL PORTS

Parallel ports fall into three categories: standard parallel port (SPP), EPP (Enhanced Parallel Port), and ECP (Extended Capabilities Port). The standard parallel port is sometimes called a normal parallel port or a Centronics port, named after the 36-pin Centronics connection used by printers (see Figure 8-40). A standard port allows data to flow in only one direction and is the slowest of the three types of parallel ports. In contrast to a standard port, EPP and ECP are both bidirectional. ECP was designed to increase speed over EPP by using a DMA channel; therefore, when using ECP mode you are using a DMA channel.

A+ ESS
1.1
4.1

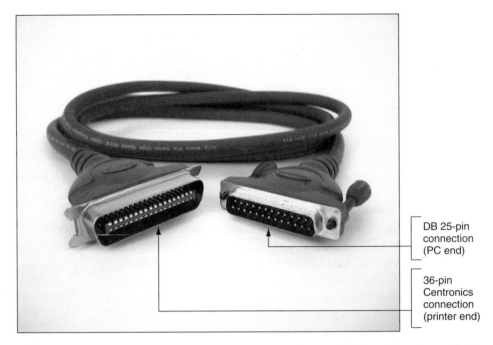

DB 25-pin
connection
(PC end)

36-pin
Centronics
connection
(printer end)

Figure 8-40 A parallel cable has a DB25 connection at the PC end of the cable and a 36-pin Centronics connection at the printer end of the cable

Over the years, both hardware and software manufacturers have implemented several parallel port designs, all attempting to increase speed and performance. To help establish industry standards, a committee supported by the Institute of Electrical and Electronics Engineers (IEEE) was formed in the early 1990s and created the IEEE 1284 standards for parallel ports. These standards require backward compatibility with previous parallel port technology. Both EPP and ECP are covered under the IEEE 1284 specifications.

There is little interest in developing better parallel ports. The interest isn't there because USB ports are faster and easier to configure. In fact, the evolution of parallel ports has pretty much come to a halt. Note, however, that although USB ports are replacing parallel ports, most computers still come with one parallel port.

> ✏ **Notes**
>
> When using EPP or ECP printers and parallel ports, be sure to use a printer cable that is IEEE 1284–compliant. Older, noncompliant cables will not work properly with these printers. To find out if a cable is compliant, look for the label somewhere on the cable. Also, note that a printer using a parallel port can use a 36-pin Centronics connector, or some newer printers use the smaller 36-pin Micro-Centronics or mini-Centronics connector.

CONFIGURING PARALLEL PORTS

Before you configure a parallel port, you need to determine whether the port is using an I/O card or whether it is connecting off the motherboard. If the port is on an I/O card, look to the card documentation to learn how to assign system resources to the port. If the parallel port is coming directly off the motherboard, use CMOS setup to configure the port (look back at Figure 8-36). In CMOS setup, you can set the port's resources to use LPT1 (Line Printer Terminal 1) or LPT2. On the other hand, for some BIOSs such as the one in Figure 8-36, you can assign an IRQ and I/O address range (see the fifth row in the second column).

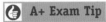 **A+ Exam Tip**

The A+Essentials exam expects you to be familiar with serial and parallel ports found on motherboards.

A+ ESS
1.1
4.1

Setup can have up to four different settings for parallel port modes. For the BIOS in Figure 8-36, choices for parallel port mode are Normal, EPP, ECP, and EPP + ECP (see the sixth row in the second column). If you select ECP or EPP + ECP, you must also make an ECP DMA selection. Choices for the DMA selection are DMA Channel 1 or 3.

> **Notes**
>
> If you have trouble using a motherboard port, such as a serial, parallel, USB, or 1394 port, check CMOS setup to make sure the port is enabled. If you have problems with resource conflicts, try disabling ECP mode for the parallel port. EPP mode gives good results and does not tie up a DMA channel.

A+ ESS
1.1
2.2
4.1
5.1

A+
220-602
2.2
3.3

USING USB PORTS

USB (Universal Serial Bus) ports are fast becoming the most popular ports for slower I/O devices such as printers and modems. USB is much faster than regular serial or parallel ports and uses higher-quality cabling. USB is also much easier to manage because it eliminates the need to resolve resource conflicts manually.

> **Notes**
>
> USB was originally created by a seven-member consortium, including Compaq, Digital Equipment, IBM, Intel, Microsoft, NEC, and Northern Telecom, and was designed to make the installation of slow peripheral devices as effortless as possible.

USB allows for hot-swapping and hot-pluggable devices. These two terms mean that a device can be plugged into a USB port while the computer is running, and the host controller will sense the device and configure it without your having to reboot the computer. Some I/O devices that use a USB connection are mice, joysticks, keyboards, printers, scanners, monitors, modems, digital cameras, fax machines, barcode readers, and digital telephones.

One to four USB ports are found on most new motherboards (see Figure 8-41). Older motherboards that have no USB ports or not enough USB ports can be upgraded by adding a PCI-to-USB controller card in a PCI slot to provide one or more USB ports. Sometimes a motherboard will have a USB port on the front of the case for easy access (see Figure 8-42).

> **Caution**
>
> Even though USB devices are hot-swappable, it's not always a good idea to plug or unplug a device while it is turned on. If you do so, especially when using a low-quality USB cable, you can fry the port or the device if wires in the USB connectors touch (creating a short) as you plug or unplug the connectors.

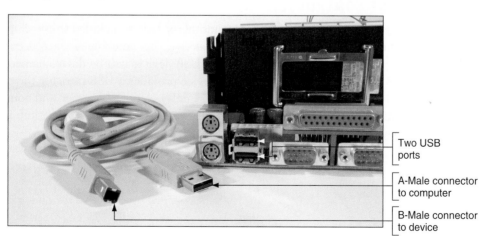

Two USB ports

A-Male connector to computer

B-Male connector to device

Figure 8-41 A motherboard with two USB ports and a USB cable; note the rectangular shape of the connection as compared to the nearby serial and parallel D-shaped ports

A+ ESS
1.1
2.2
4.1
5.1

A+
220-602
2.2
3.3

Figure 8-42 One or more USB ports on the front of a computer case make for easy access

USB VERSIONS

USB Version 1.1 (sometimes called Basic Speed USB or Original USB) allows for two speeds, 1.5 Mbps and 12 Mbps, and works well for slow I/O devices. USB Version 2.0 (sometimes called Hi-Speed USB or USB2) allows for up to 480 Mbps, which is 40 times faster than Original USB. Hi-Speed USB is backward-compatible with slower USB devices. The USB Implementers Forum, Inc. (*www.usb.org*), the organization responsible for developing USB, has adopted the symbols shown in Figure 8-43 to indicate if the product is certified by the organization as compliant with Original USB or Hi-Speed USB.

Figure 8-43 Hi-Speed and Original USB logos appear on products certified by the USB forum

USB HOST CONTROLLER

A USB host controller, which for most motherboards is included in the chipset, manages the USB bus. Sometimes a motherboard has two USB controllers; each is enabled and disabled in CMOS setup. As many as 127 USB devices can be daisy chained together using USB cables. In a daisy chain, one device provides a USB port for the next device. Figure 8-44 shows a keyboard and a mouse daisy chained together and connecting to a single USB port on an iMac computer. There can also be a standalone hub into which several devices can be plugged.

Figure 8-44   A keyboard and a mouse using a USB port daisy chained together

A USB cable has four wires, two for power and two for communication. The two power wires (one carries voltage and the other is a ground) allow the host controller to provide power to a device. The connector on the host computer or hub end is called the A-Male connector, and the connector on the device end of the cable is called the B-Male connector. The A-Male connector is flat and wide, and the B-Male connector is square. (Look back at Figure 8-41 to see both these connectors.) In addition, because some devices such as a digital camera are so small, USB standards allow for mini-A connectors and mini-B connectors. You can see one of these mini-B connectors in Figure 8-45 used with a digital camera. The A-Male connector of this USB cable is regular size to connect to a computer's USB port.

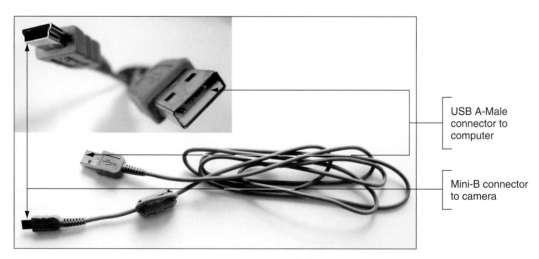

USB A-Male connector to computer

Mini-B connector to camera

Figure 8-45   The digital camera USB cable uses a mini-B connector and a regular size A-Male connector

USB cables for Original USB can be up to 3 meters (9 feet, 10 inches) and Hi-Speed USB cables can be up to 5 meters (16 feet, 5 inches). If you need to put a USB device farther from the PC than the cable is long, you can use a USB hub in the middle to effectively double the distance.

In USB technology, the host controller polls each device, asking if data is ready to be sent or requesting to send data to the device. The host controller manages communication to the CPU for all devices, using only a single IRQ (see Figure 8-46), I/O address range, and DMA channel to do so.

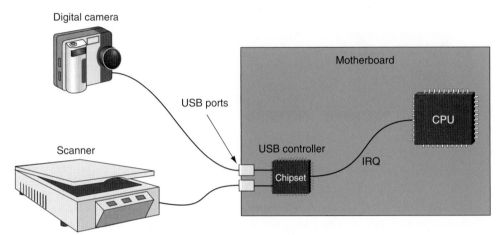

Figure 8-46 The USB controller has a single IRQ line that it uses when any USB device needs attention

Windows 95 OSR 2.1 was the first Microsoft OS to support USB, although Windows 98 offers much improved USB support. Besides Windows 95 with the USB update and Windows 98, Windows 2000 and Windows XP support Original USB, but Windows NT does not. Windows XP, with service packs applied, supports Hi-Speed USB.

PREPARING TO INSTALL A USB DEVICE

To install a USB device, you need:

- A motherboard or expansion card that provides a USB port
- An OS that supports USB
- A USB device
- A USB device driver

Recall that device drivers come from Windows or from the device manufacturer. Whenever possible, use drivers from the manufacturer. However, make sure you are using drivers written for the Windows OS you are using.

INSTALLING A USB DEVICE

Some USB devices such as printers require that you plug in the device before installing the drivers, and some USB devices such as scanners require you to install the drivers before plugging in the device. For some devices, it doesn't matter which is installed first. Carefully read and follow the device documentation. For example, the documentation for one digital camera says that if you install the camera before installing the driver, the drivers will not install properly.

A+ ESS
1.1
1.4
2.2
4.1
5.1

A+
220-602
2.2
3.3

Follow these general steps to install a USB device such as a scanner, where the scanner is plugged in before installing the drivers:

1. Using Device Manager, verify that the USB host controller driver is installed under Windows. For example, Figure 8-47 shows Windows XP Device Manager displaying the Properties dialog box for a USB controller. Note in the figure the symbol for USB. Also notice the first entry in the Universal Serial Bus controllers list. An entry of "Standard Enhanced" means that this controller supports Hi-Speed USB. If the controller is not installed, install it from the Control Panel by double-clicking the **Add New Hardware** icon.

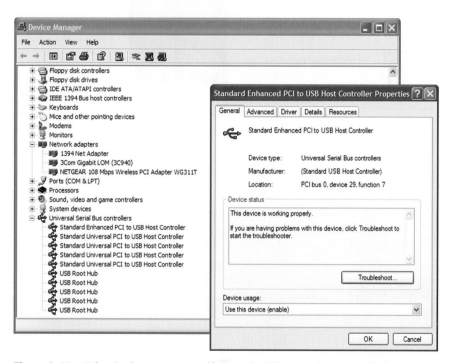

Figure 8-47 Using Device Manager, verify that the USB controller is installed and working properly

If you have a problem installing the controller, verify that support for USB is enabled in setup. You also might check the motherboard documentation or the drivers CD that came with your motherboard for help when troubleshooting problems with the USB controller. For example, if none of the USB ports work, you can update the USB controller drivers. To do that, on the USB controller properties window, click the **Driver** tab and then click **Update Driver**. The Hardware Update Wizard launches, as shown in Figure 8-48. When given the opportunity, point to the drivers on CD that came with your motherboard or download new drivers from the motherboard manufacturer Web site.

2. Plug in the USB device. Within a few seconds, Windows should launch the Found New Hardware Wizard to install the device drivers. If the wizard does not launch automatically, go to Control Panel and double-click the **Add New Hardware** icon. If you still have problems, try turning off the PC, plugging in the device, and rebooting. If that fails to install the drivers, look for and run the setup program on the CD or floppy disk that came with the device. After the drivers are installed, for most devices, you should see the device

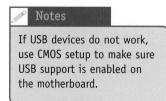

Notes

If USB devices do not work, use CMOS setup to make sure USB support is enabled on the motherboard.

A+ ESS
1.1
1.4
2.2
4.1
5.1

A+
220-602
2.2
3.3

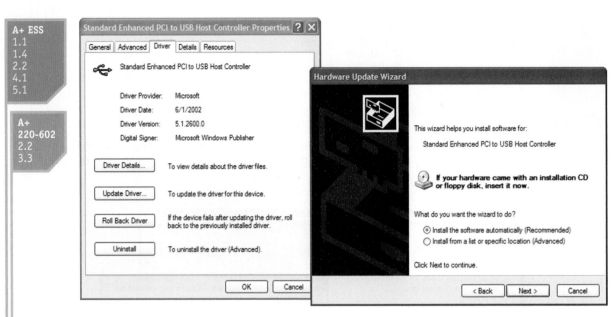

Figure 8-48   Updating drivers

listed in Device Manager. Verify that Windows sees the device with no conflicts and no errors.

3. Install the application software to use the device. For example, most scanners come with some software to scan and edit images. After you install the software, use it to scan an image.

> **Notes**
>
> Some motherboards provide extra ports that can be installed in faceplate openings off the back of the case. For example, Figure 8-49 shows a module that has a game port and two USB ports. To install the module, remove a faceplate and install the module in its place. Then connect the cable from the module to the connector on the motherboard.

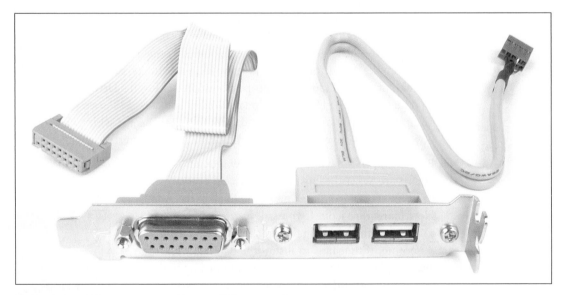

Figure 8-49   This connector provides two USB ports and one game port

A+ ESS
1.1
4.1
5.1

A+
220-602
2.2

USING IEEE 1394 PORTS

FireWire and i.Link are common names for another peripheral bus officially named IEEE 1394 (or sometimes simply called 1394). The name is derived from the name of the group that designed the bus. IEEE was primarily led by Apple Computer and Texas Instruments in the initial design.

FireWire is similar in design to USB, using serial transmission of data, but it is faster. In fact, FireWire supports data speeds as high as 3.2 Gbps (gigabits per second), which is much faster than USB. FireWire is likely to replace SCSI as a solution for high-volume, multimedia external devices such as digital camcorders, DVDs, and hard drives. SCSI is a very fast, but difficult-to-configure, peripheral bus.

FireWire devices are hot-pluggable and can be daisy chained together and managed by a host controller using a single set of system resources (an IRQ, an I/O address range, and a DMA channel). One host controller can support up to 63 FireWire devices.

The two standards for IEEE 1394 are IEEE 1394a and 1394b, although IEEE 1394c is on the drawing board. 1394a supports speeds up to 400 Mbps and is sometimes called FireWire 400. 1394a allows for cable lengths up to 4.5 meters (15 feet) and for up to 16 cables daisy chained together. 1394a supports two types of connectors and cables: a 4-pin connector that does not provide voltage to a device and a 6-pin connector that does (see Figure 8-50). The cable for a 6-pin port is wider than the 4-pin cable.

Notes

For interesting information about 1394, surf the 1394 Trade Association's Web site at *www.1394ta.org*.

Tip

Windows XP, Windows 2000, and Windows 98 all support FireWire. (Windows 95 and Windows NT do not.)

Tip

IEEE 1394a ports are common on newer, high-end motherboards and are expected to become standard ports on all new motherboards and to become as commonplace as USB ports are now.

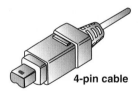
(Device requires AC adapter)

4-pin cable

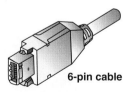
(Two pins are used for voltage and ground)

6-pin cable

Figure 8-50 Two types of IEEE 1394a cable connectors; the 6-pin cable provides voltage to the device from the PC

The newer standard, 1394b, supports speeds up to 3.2 Gbps, but current devices on the market are running at only 800 Mbps, which is why 1394b is also called FireWire 800. 1394b can use cables up to 100 meters (328 feet), and uses a 9-pin connector. You can use a 1394 cable that has a 9-pin connector at one end and 4-pin or 6-pin connector at the other end to connect a 1394a device to a 1394b computer port, causing the port to run at the slower speed. Figure 8-51 shows a FireWire 800 adapter that provides three 1394 ports: two 1394b 9-pin ports and one 1394a 6-pin port.

A+ ESS
1.1
4.1
5.1

A+
220-602
2.2

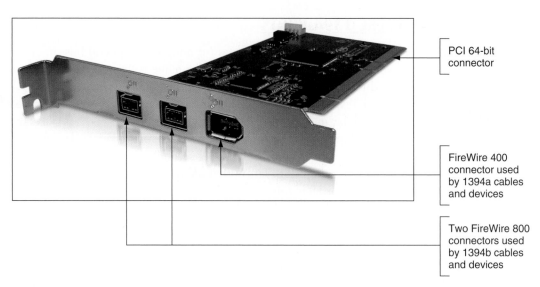

PCI 64-bit
connector

FireWire 400
connector used
by 1394a cables
and devices

Two FireWire 800
connectors used
by 1394b cables
and devices

Figure 8-51 This 1394 adapter card supports both 1394a and 1394b and uses a 64-bit PCI bus connector

> ✎ **Notes**
>
> A variation of 1394 is **IEEE 1394.3**, which is designed for peer-to-peer data transmission. Using this standard, imaging devices such as scanners and digital cameras can send images and photos directly to printers without involving a computer.

IEEE 1394 uses isochronous data transfer, meaning that data is transferred continuously without breaks. This works well when transferring real-time data such as that received by television transmission. Because of the real-time data transfer and the fact that data can be transferred from one device to another without involving the CPU, IEEE 1394 is an ideal medium for data transfers between consumer electronics products, such as camcorders, VCRs, TVs, and digital cameras.

Figure 8-52 shows an example of how this data transfer might work. A person can record a home movie using a digital camcorder and download the data through a digital VCR to a 1394-compliant external hard drive. The 1394-compliant digital VCR can connect to and send data to the hard drive without involving the PC. The PC can later read the data off the hard drive and use it as input to video-editing application software. A user can edit the data

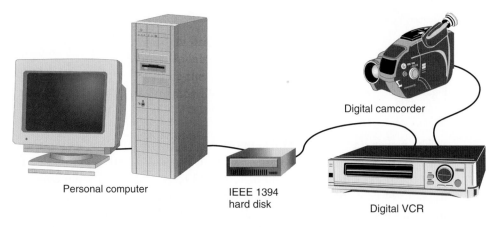

Personal computer

Digital camcorder

IEEE 1394
hard disk

Digital VCR

Figure 8-52 IEEE 1394 can be used as the interface technology to connect consumer audio/visual equipment to a PC

A+ ESS
1.1
4.1
5.1

A+
220-602
2.2

and design a professional video presentation complete with captioning and special effects. Furthermore, if the digital camcorder is also 1394-compliant, it can download the data directly to the PC by way of a 1394 port on the PC. The PC can then save the data to a regular internal hard drive.

Windows 98, Windows 2000, and Windows XP support IEEE 1394 storage devices, printers, scanners, and other devices. Windows 98 Second Edition supports IEEE 1394 storage devices but not IEEE 1394 printers and scanners. For Windows 98 Second Edition, you can also download an update from the Microsoft Web site (*windowsupdate. microsoft.com*) to solve problems that occurred when devices were removed while the PC was still running.

To use a 1394 port with Windows, follow these steps:

1. You first need to verify that Windows recognizes that an IEEE 1394 controller is present on the motherboard. To do this, open **Device Manager** and look for the 1394 Bus Controller listed as an installed device. Click the **+** sign beside the controller in Device Manager to see the specific brand of 1394 controller that the board contains. If the controller is not installed or is not working, reinstall the driver. Then, in Control Panel, double-click the **Add New Hardware** icon. If you have problems installing the driver, verify that 1394 support is enabled in setup.

2. Read the device documentation to decide if you install the drivers first or plug in the device first.

3. If you plug in the device first, plug it into the 1394 port. Then, install the device drivers for the 1394-compliant device. Without rebooting, you should be able to use the Add New Hardware icon in the Control Panel. For example, after you have installed the drivers for a camcorder, you should see the device listed in Device Manager under Sound, video, and game controllers. If you don't see the device listed, turn the device off and then on again.

4. If you need to install the drivers first, use the Add New Hardware icon in Control Panel or follow the documentation instructions to run a setup program on CD. After the drivers are installed, plug the device into the 1394 port. The device should immediately be recognized by Windows.

5. Install the application software to use the device. A 1394-compliant camcorder is likely to come bundled with video-editing software, for example. Run the software to use the device.

APPLYING CONCEPTS

For motherboards that provide FireWire ports, the board might come with an internal connector for an internal FireWire hard drive. This connector can also be used for a module that provides additional FireWire ports off the back of the PC case. Figure 8-53 shows a motherboard with the pinouts of the FireWire

A+ ESS
1.1
4.1
5.1

A+
220-602
2.2

connector labeled. The module is also shown in the figure. To install this module, remove a face-plate and install the module in its place. Then connect the cable to the motherboard connector.

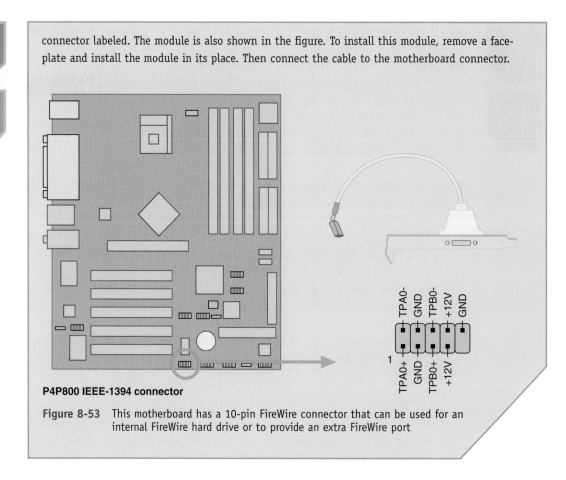

P4P800 IEEE-1394 connector

Figure 8-53 This motherboard has a 10-pin FireWire connector that can be used for an internal FireWire hard drive or to provide an extra FireWire port

INSTALLING AND SUPPORTING EXPANSION CARDS

Most motherboards today have three or more regular PCI slots and one slot designed for a video card. The slot intended for the video card is an AGP slot or a PCI Express x16 (pronounced "by sixteen") slot. For example, the motherboard in Figure 8-54 has three regular PCI slots, one PCI Express x16 slot with a video card installed, and two PCI Express x1 slots. (See Figure 4-1 in Chapter 4 for a close-up of this same motherboard.)

You'll see all kinds of expansion cards on the market, such as video cards, modem cards, network cards, IEEE 1394 controllers, USB controllers, floppy drive controllers, hard drive controllers, wireless NICs, sound cards, and many more. Today, all these cards are Plug and Play (PnP), meaning you don't have to set jumpers or DIP switches on the card to use system resources and installations should be easy to do using the Windows Found New Hardware Wizard. To know how to support the older expansion cards that are not Plug and Play and use the legacy ISA expansion slots, see Appendix C, "Supporting Legacy Devices."

In this section, you'll learn how to select an expansion card, install the card (a modem card in our example) in a PCI expansion slot, and support PCI cards. Recall that earlier in the chapter you learned about the specifics of installing a video card in an AGP slot.

SELECTING PCI CARDS

When selecting a PCI card for your motherboard, recall from Chapter 5 that there are several PCI and PCI Express standards. For PCI cards, you must match the notches on the card to the keys in the PCI slot so that the voltage requirements of the card will match the voltage provided by the slot. Also, know that you can install a 32-bit PCI card into a longer 64-bit PCI slot. In this case, the extended end of the long PCI slot is unused.

A+ ESS
1.2
3.2

A+
220-602
1.1

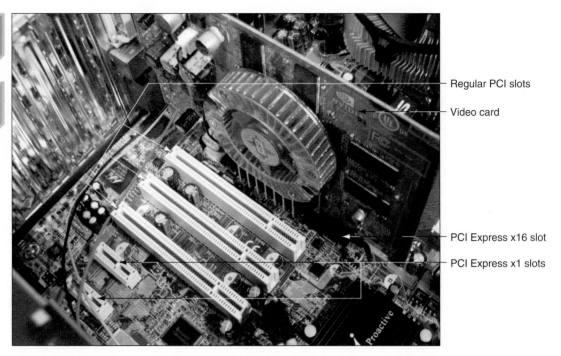

— Regular PCI slots

— Video card

— PCI Express x16 slot

— PCI Express x1 slots

Proactive

Figure 8-54 Asus P5AD2 motherboard with the MSI GeForce FX5750 video card installed in a PCI Express x16 slot

For motherboards that support the PCI-X standards, these PCI slots might support several different speeds. But know that when more than one PCI card is installed in PCI slots using the same PCI bus, the PCI bus runs at the speed of the slowest PCI card.

INSTALLING AND CONFIGURING A PCI MODEM CARD

A+ ESS
1.1
1.2
1.4
3.2
5.1

A+
220-602
1.1
5.1

A **modem** is a device used by a PC to communicate over a phone line. A modem can be an external device (see Figure 8-55) connected to a USB or serial port, a modem card (see Figure 8-56) using either a PCI or PCI Express slot, or a smaller and less expensive modem riser card. Also, some motherboards have a modem port as an on-board component. On notebook computers, a modem is an embedded component on the motherboard or is a PC Card installed in a PC Card slot.

A modem provides one or two RJ-11 (registered jack 11) ports used by phone lines. Modems are rated by speed; the most common modem speed is 56.6 Kbps, although a few modems are

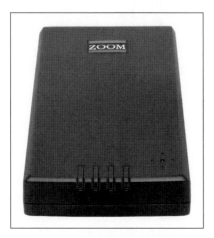

ZOOM

Figure 8-55 Zoom V.92 Mini Fax External Modem uses a USB connection

A+ ESS
1.1
1.2
1.4
3.2
5.1

A+
220-602
1.1
5.1

Figure 8-56 This 56K V.92 PCI modem card comes bundled with a phone cord and setup CD

still rated at 28.8 Kbps or 33.6 Kbps. Other than speed, other features supported by modems are the ability to compress data, provide error checking, and support video conferencing. The latest modem standard is **V.92**, which allows for quick connect (reduces handshake time), modem on hold (allows call waiting without breaking the connection to the ISP), and improved upload speeds for large files.

 Notes

Because of the sampling rate (8,000 samples every second) used by phone companies when converting an analog signal to digital, and taking into account the overhead of data transmission (bits and bytes sent with the data that are used to control and define transmissions), the maximum transmission rate that a modem can attain over a regular phone line is about 56,000 bps or 56 Kbps. Although theoretically possible, most modem connections don't actually attain this speed. When connecting to an ISP using a dial-up connection, to achieve 56 Kbps, the ISP must use a digital connection to the phone company.

A+ ESS
1.2
1.4
3.2
5.1

A+
220-602
1.1
5.1

APPLYING CONCEPTS Bill was hurriedly setting up a computer for a friend. When he got to the modem, he installed it as he had installed many modems in the past. He put the modem card in the PCI slot and turned on the PC for Plug and Play to do its job. When the Found New Hardware Wizard launched, he installed the drivers, but the modem wouldn't work. He tried again and again to reinstall the modem, but still it didn't work. After four hours of trying to get the modem to work, he concluded the modem was bad. Then it hit him to read the instructions that came with the modem. He opened the booklet and in very large letters on the very first page it said, "The modem WILL NOT WORK if you install the card first and the software second." Bill took the card out and followed the instructions and within five minutes he was surfing the Net. Bill says that from that day forward he *always* reads *all* instructions first and leaves his ego at the door!

Follow these general steps to install a modem card:

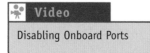
Disabling Onboard Ports

◢ Read the modem documentation. The manufacturer's instructions to install the modem might be different from those listed here.
◢ If you are installing the modem card to replace an onboard modem port, enter CMOS setup and disable the onboard modem port.

A+ ESS
1.2
1.4
3.2
5.1

A+
220-602
1.1
5.1

⊿ Protect the PC from ESD by using an antistatic bracelet and ground mat.

⊿ Power down the PC and unplug it. Open the computer case, locate the slot you plan to use, and remove the faceplate from the slot. Sometimes a faceplate punches or snaps out, and sometimes you have to remove a faceplate screw to remove the faceplate.

⊿ Insert the card in the expansion slot. Be careful to push the card directly into the slot, without rocking it from side to side. Rocking it from side to side can widen the expansion slot, making it more difficult to keep a good contact. If you have a problem getting the card into the slot, you can insert the end away from the side of the case in the slot first and gently rock the card from front to rear into the slot. The card should feel snug in the slot. You can almost feel it snap into place. If you find out later that the card does not work, most likely it is not seated securely in the slot. Check that first and then, if possible, try a different slot.

⊿ Insert the screw that connects the card to the case (refer back to Figure 8-32). Be sure to use this screw; if it's not present, the card can creep out of the slot over time.

⊿ Replace the case cover, power cord, and other peripherals. (If you want, you can leave the case cover off until you've tested the device, in case it doesn't work and you need to reseat it.)

⊿ Plug the telephone line from the house into the line jack on the modem (see Figure 8-57). The second RJ-11 jack on the modem is for an optional telephone. It connects a phone so that you can more easily use this same phone jack for voice communication.

Figure 8-57 An RJ-11 connection on a modem is the same as that used for a regular phone connection

Turn on your computer and follow these steps to configure the modem using Windows XP:

⊿ Be aware that when Windows 2000/XP installs a new hardware device, if any interaction with the user is required during the installation, the user must be logged into the system with a user account that has administrative privileges.

⊿ When you turn on the PC, Windows Plug and Play detects a new hardware device. In most cases, Windows XP will install its own drivers without giving you the opportunity to use manufacturer's drivers on CD. You might have to boot twice: once to allow Plug and Play to detect firmware on the modem card that runs the modem (called the UART which stands for universal asynchronous receiver-transmitter) and again to detect the modem. Also, if your modem has add-on features such as a Fax service, you might have to reboot again as this feature is installed. Follow onscreen directions until you reach the Windows desktop.

⬛ In most cases, Windows XP installs a modem card without giving you the opportunity to use the modem manufacturer drivers on the modem setup CD. After Windows XP completes the installation, to install the drivers on CD, open **Device Manager**. Right-click the modem and select **Properties** from the shortcut menu. The modem Properties window opens. Click the **Driver** tab and then click **Update Driver**. When the Hardware Update Wizard launches and asks permission to connect to Windows Update Web site to search for updated drivers, select **No, not this time** and click **Next** (see Figure 8-58).

Figure 8-58   Use the Hardware Update Wizard to install the modem manufacturer drivers

⬛ Insert the CD that came bundled with the modem. On the next wizard screen, select **Install from a list or specific location (Advanced)** and click **Next**.

⬛ On the next screen shown in Figure 8-59, select **Search for the best driver in these locations**. Also select **Include this location in the search**, but don't select any other option on this screen. Click the **Browse** button and point to the location of the Windows XP drivers on the CD. Click **OK** and then click **Next**. Click **Finish** to complete the wizard and update the modem drivers. Reboot the system so the updated drivers will be loaded.

> **Notes**
>
> Keep in mind that during a hardware installation, if the drivers are not digitally signed by Microsoft, Windows will ask if you want to continue the installation using unsigned drivers. In this situation, choose to continue. Later, if the device doesn't work or gives problems, you can try to find Microsoft-certified drivers for the device.

⬛ After the modem drivers are installed, verify the OS configured the modem correctly. Once again open **Device Manager** and the modem **Properties** window. Verify that Windows says the modem is working.

⬛ If you want to use Windows to make calls without using other software, create a dial-up Networking Connection. Right-click **My Network Places** and select **Properties** on the shortcut menu. The Network Connections window opens (see Figure 8-60).

⬛ Click **Create a new connection**. The New Connection Wizard launches. Click **Next**. The Network Connection Type dialog box opens (also shown in Figure 8-60). Select the type of connection and click **Next**. For example, if you want to connect to the

A+ ESS
1.2
1.4
3.2
5.1

A+
220-602
1.1
5.1

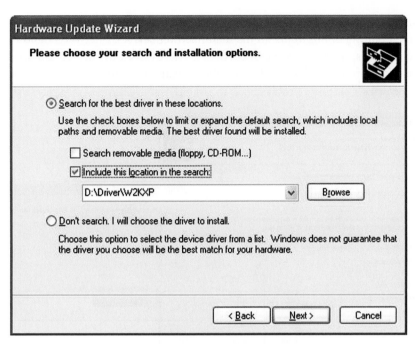

Figure 8-59 In the Hardware Update Wizard, point to the location of driver files on the modem setup CD

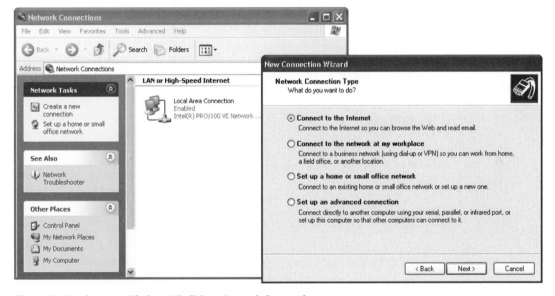

Figure 8-60 Create a Windows XP dial-up Network Connection

Internet through your ISP, click **Connect to the Internet**. Complete the wizard. You need to know the phone number of your ISP, your user name, and password.

▲ For easy access, you can copy the Network Connection you just created from the Network Connections window to your desktop as a shortcut.

▲ Test the modem by making a dial-up connection to your ISP.

For Windows 2000 and Windows 9x/Me, installing and configuring the modem is the

 Notes

Sometimes an installation disk has several directories, one for each operating system it supports. For example, for Windows 2000, look for a directory named \WIN2K or \W2KXP. The OS is looking for a directory that has a file with an .inf extension.

same as Windows XP except it will be easier to use manufacturer's drivers on the installation CD. For Windows 2000, to install the manufacturer drivers, after the Found New Hardware Wizard launches, when given the opportunity, select **CD-ROM drives** and **Specify a location** to point to the location of driver files on the modem installation CD (see Figure 8-61).

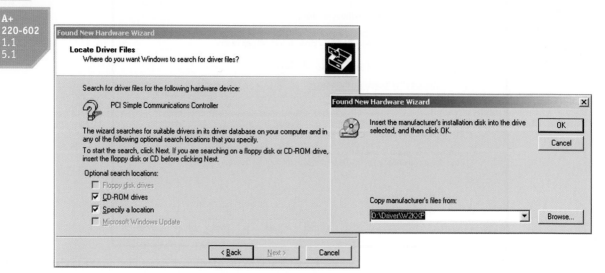

Figure 8-61 Install a modem under Windows 2000 using the modem drivers on the manufacturer installation CD

After a modem is installed, if you have problems using the modem, try these things:

1. Verify the phone line is connected to a modem port. The phone line might be plugged into the network port by mistake.

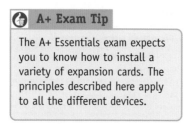

A+ Exam Tip

The A+ Essentials exam expects you to know how to install a variety of expansion cards. The principles described here apply to all the different devices.

2. Check the phone line. Can you make a call using a telephone? Do you need to dial a 9 or 8 to get an outside line?

3. Perform a diagnostic test on the modem. For Windows 2000/XP, open **Device Manager**, right-click the modem, and select **Properties** on the shortcut menu. The modem's Properties dialog box opens. Click the **Diagnostics** tab and then click the **Query Modem** button. See Figure 8-62. If the OS cannot communicate with the modem, nothing appears in the Command and Response box. However, if the OS receives responses from the modem, the dialog box appears. These commands, called AT commands, are used by software to communicate with a modem.

4. Try updating the modem drivers. To do that, right-click the modem in Device Manager and choose **Update Driver** from the shortcut menu. Follow directions onscreen. First try using the drivers that came with the modem on CD. If that doesn't work, try downloading new device drivers from the modem manufacturer's Web site.

5. Try uninstalling and reinstalling the modem. To uninstall the modem, right-click it in Device Manager and select **Uninstall** from the shortcut menu. To reinstall the modem, reboot to launch the Found New Hardware Wizard.

6. Read the modem's documentation for more things to do and try. Try moving the modem to a different PCI slot.

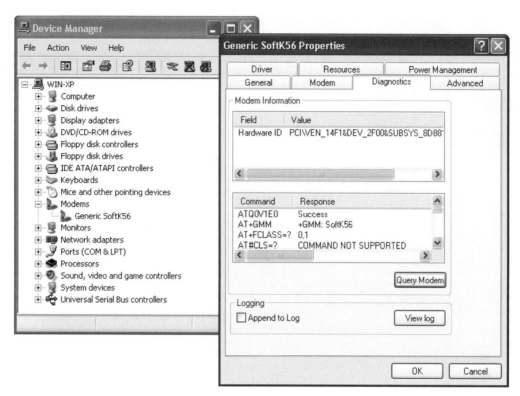

Figure 8-62 Windows XP uses AT commands to perform a diagnostic test of a modem

---

✎ Notes

Sometimes an external specialized device, such as a CAD/CAM device or security reader, comes bundled with an expansion card that provides a port for the device. When installing such devices, always read the documentation carefully before you begin. Also, motherboards sometimes offer special slots or connectors to be used for such things as IDE controllers, RAID controllers, USB controllers, temperature sensors, and internal audio input. Follow the motherboard documentation and the device documentation to install these devices.

SUPPORTING MULTIPLE PCI CARDS

Know that the PCI controller, which is part of the motherboard chipset, manages the PCI bus, the expansion slots, and all the PCI cards. The startup BIOS assigns IRQs to the PCI bus controller during the boot process. A PCI card does not need exclusive use of an IRQ because the PCI controller uses interrupt levels to manage the interrupt needs of a card. The controller assigns each PCI expansion slot an interrupt level, named level A, B, C, D, and so forth. When a PCI card in one of these slots requests an interrupt, the interrupt level is passed to the PCI controller, which uses an IRQ to hail the CPU for attention.

However, if you use Device Manager to see the resources assigned to a PCI card, Device Manager reports an IRQ assigned to it. For example, in Figure 8-63, Device Manager is displaying the resources assigned to a PCI network card for Windows XP. Notice that the IRQ assigned to the card is IRQ 9. You need to realize that this IRQ can also be used by other devices on the PCI bus.

If two heavy-demand PCI devices end up sharing an IRQ, they might not work properly. If you suspect a shared IRQ is the source of a problem, try moving one of the devices to a different PCI slot, so that a device with a heavy demand (such as a 1394 adapter) is matched with a low-demand device (such as a modem).

A+ ESS
1.2
1.4
3.2
5.1

A+
220-602
1.1
5.1

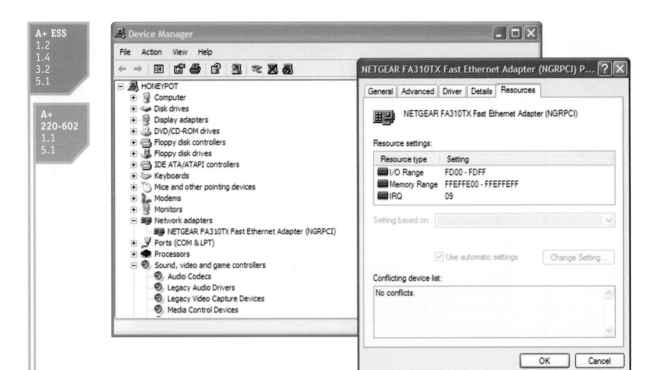

Figure 8-63 Use Device Manager to determine which IRQ has been assigned to a PCI device

TROUBLESHOOTING I/O DEVICES

A+ ESS
1.3
1.4
2.3

A+
220-602
1.2
1.3
2.3

Generally, when troubleshooting an I/O device, follow these steps:

1. For a new installation, suspect the drivers are not installed correctly, the device is not plugged in or set in the expansion slot correctly, or the application software does not work. Start at the beginning of the installation and redo and recheck each step.

2. For problems after an installation, ask the user what has just changed in the system. For example, if there has been a recent thunderstorm, the device might have been damaged by electricity. Maybe the user has just installed some software or changed Windows settings.

3. Analyze the situation and try to isolate the problem. For example, decide if the problem is most likely caused by hardware or software.

4. Check simple things first. Is the device getting power? Is it turned on? Is the data connection secure? Try rebooting the system to get a fresh start

5. Try using Device Manager to uninstall the device. Then reboot and install the drivers again.

6. Exchange the device for a known good one or install the suspected device in a working system.

7. After the problem is fixed, document the symptoms, the source of the problem, and the solution so you have that to take into the next troubleshooting situation.

Let's now look at specific instructions for troubleshooting a keyboard, a mouse, and other I/O devices.

8

A+ ESS
1.3
1.4
2.3

A+
220-602
1.2
1.3
2.3

TROUBLESHOOTING KEYBOARDS

Keyboards can give problems if they are not kept clean. If dirt, food, or drink are allowed to build up, one or more keys might stick or not work properly. Chips inside the keyboard can fail, and the keyboard cable or port connector can go bad. Because of its low cost, when a keyboard doesn't work, the solution is most often to replace it. However, you can try a few simple things to repair one, as described next.

A FEW KEYS DON'T WORK

For keypads on regular keyboards or notebook computers, is the Num Lock key set correctly? For regular keyboards, if a few keys don't work, try turning the keyboard upside down and lightly bumping multiple keys with your flat palm to help loosen and remove debris. Next, you can remove the caps on the bad keys with a chip extractor. Spray contact cleaner into the key well. Repeatedly depress the contact to clean it. Don't use rubbing alcohol to clean the key well, because it can leave a residue on the contact. If this method of cleaning solves the problem, clean the adjacent keys as well.

THE KEYBOARD DOES NOT WORK AT ALL

If the keyboard does not work at all, first check to see if the cable is plugged in. Maybe it's plugged into the mouse port by mistake. PC keyboard cables can become loose or disconnected. If the cable connection is good and the keyboard still does not work, swap it with another keyboard of the same type that you know is in good condition, to verify that the problem is in the keyboard, not the computer.

If the problem is in the keyboard, check the cable. If possible, swap the cable with a known good one, perhaps from an old discarded keyboard. Sometimes a wire in a PC keyboard cable becomes pinched or broken. Most cables can be easily detached from the keyboard by removing the few screws that hold the keyboard case together, then simply unplugging the cable. Be careful as you work; don't allow the keycaps to fall

> **⚡ Caution**
>
> Always power down a PC before plugging in a keyboard. The keyboard must be detected during the boot.

out! In Appendix B, "Electricity and Multimeters," you can learn how to use a multimeter to test a cable for continuity. You can use this method to verify that the cable is good.

On the motherboard, the chipset and the ROM BIOS chip both affect keyboard functions. You might choose to flash BIOS to verify that system BIOS is not the source of the problem. Otherwise, the entire motherboard might have to be replaced, or you can try substituting a USB keyboard for the PS/2 keyboard.

KEY CONTINUES TO REPEAT AFTER BEING RELEASED

This problem can be caused by a dirty contact. Some debris can have conductive properties, short the gap between the contacts, and cause the key to repeat. Try cleaning the key switch with contact cleaner.

Very high humidity and excess moisture sometimes short key switch contacts and cause keys to repeat because water is an electrical conductor. The problem usually resolves itself after the humidity level returns to normal. You can hasten the drying process by using a fan (not a hot hair dryer) to blow air at the keyboard.

KEYS PRODUCE THE WRONG CHARACTERS

This problem is usually caused by a bad chip. PC keyboards actually have a processor mounted on the logic board inside the keyboard. Try swapping the keyboard for one you know is good. If the problem goes away, replace the original keyboard.

MAJOR SPILLS ON THE KEYBOARD

When coffee or sugary drinks spill on the keyboard, they create a sticky mess. The best solution to stay up and running is to simply replace the keyboard. You can try to save the keyboard by thoroughly rinsing it in running water, perhaps from a bathroom shower. Make sure the keyboard dries thoroughly before you use it. Let it dry for two days on its own, or fewer if you set it out in the sun or in front of a fan. In some situations, such as a factory setting where dust and dirt are everywhere, consider using a clear, plastic keyboard cover.

TROUBLESHOOTING A TOUCH SCREEN

If a touch screen does not work, here are some things you can try:

- Check that the touch screen cable is connected to the PC and Device Manager recognizes the device with no errors.
- Examine the screen for excessive scratches. Too many scratches might mean the screen needs replacing. Instruct the user to only use fingers or a stylus approved by the touch screen manufacturer on the screen. Also, check with the touch screen manufacturer to see if a screen protector is available.
- Examine the edges of the touch screen for crumbs or other particles that might have lodged between the touch screen grid and the monitor screen. You can use a clean and dry toothbrush to gently clean around the edges of the touch screen to dislodge these particles.
- If the touch screen is not accurate, recalibrate the screen. See the touch screen documentation for instructions. If the monitor screen resolution needs changing, follow instructions in the touch screen documentation to know how to do this.
- Try uninstalling and reinstalling the touch screen under Windows.

TROUBLESHOOTING A MOUSE OR TOUCHPAD

If the mouse or touchpad on a notebook computer does not work or the pointer moves like crazy over the screen, do the following to troubleshoot the device:

- Check the mouse port connection. Is it secure? The mouse might be accidentally plugged into the keyboard port.
- Check for dust or dirt inside the mouse. Reboot the PC.
- In Control Panel, open the **Mouse** applet and verify settings. (Note these settings apply to a mouse on any type computer as well as a touchpad on a notebook computer.) To update the mouse drivers, click the **Hardware** tab and then click **Properties**. On the mouse properties window, click the **Driver** tab and then click **Update Drivers**.
- Try a new mouse.
- Using Device Manager and the Add New Hardware icon in the Control Panel, first uninstall and then reinstall the mouse driver. Reboot the PC.
- Reboot the PC and select the logged option from the startup menu to create the Ntbtlog.txt file. Continue to boot and check the log for errors.
- For a notebook touchpad, was an external mouse connected to the notebook when it was first booted? Check CMOS setup to see if the touchpad was set to be disabled if a mouse is present at startup.

A+ ESS
1.3
2.3

A+
220-602
1.2
1.3
2.3

TROUBLESHOOTING MONITORS AND VIDEO CARDS

For monitors as well as other devices, if you have problems, try doing the easy things first. For instance, try to make simple hardware and software adjustments. Many monitor problems are caused by poor cable connections or bad contrast/brightness adjustments.

 Tip

A user very much appreciates a PC support technician who takes a little extra time to clean a system being serviced. When servicing a monitor, take the time to clean the screen with a soft dry cloth.

Typical monitor problems and how to troubleshoot them are described next.

POWER LIGHT (LED) DOES NOT GO ON; NO PICTURE

For this problem, try the following:

- ◢ Is the monitor plugged in? Verify that the wall outlet works by plugging in a lamp, radio, or similar device. Is the monitor turned on? Look for a cutoff switch on the front and on the back.
- ◢ If the monitor power cord is plugged into a power strip or surge protector, verify that the power strip is turned on and working and that the monitor is also turned on. Look for an on/off switch on the front and back of the monitor. Some monitors have both.
- ◢ If the monitor power cord is plugged into the back of the computer, verify that the connection is tight and the computer is turned on.
- ◢ A blown fuse could be the problem. Some monitors have a fuse that is visible from the back of the monitor. It looks like a black knob that you can remove (no need to go inside the monitor cover). Remove the fuse and look for the broken wire indicating a bad fuse.
- ◢ The monitor might have a switch on the back for choosing between 110 volts and 220 volts. Check that the switch is in the right position.

 Caution

A monitor retains a charge even after the power cord is unplugged. If you are trained to open a monitor case to replace a fuse, unplug the monitor and wait at least 60 minutes before opening the case so that capacitors have completely discharged.

 Notes

When you turn on your PC, the first thing you see on the screen is the firmware on the video card identifying itself. You can use this information to search the Web, especially the manufacturer's Web site, for troubleshooting information about the card.

If none of these solutions solves the problem, the next step is to take the monitor to a service center.

POWER LED IS ON, NO PICTURE ON POWER-UP

For this problem, try the following:

- ◢ Check the contrast adjustment. If there's no change, leave it at a middle setting.
- ◢ Check the brightness or backlight adjustment. If there's no change, leave it at a middle setting.

A+ ESS
1.3
2.3

A+
220-602
1.2
1.3
2.3

◢ Make sure the cable is connected securely to the computer.

◢ If the monitor-to-computer cable detaches from the monitor, exchange it for a cable you know is good, or check the cable for continuity.

◢ If this solves the problem, reattach the old cable to verify that the problem was not simply a bad connection.

◢ Confirm that the proper system configuration has been set up. Some older motherboards have a jumper or DIP switch you can use to select the monitor type.

◢ Test a monitor you know is good on the computer you suspect to be bad. Do this and the previous step to identify the problem. If you think the monitor is bad, make sure that it also fails to work on a good computer.

◢ Check the CMOS settings or software configuration on the computer. When using Windows 2000/XP or Windows 9x/Me, boot into Safe Mode. For Windows 2000/XP, press F8 and then choose Safe Mode from the menu, and for Windows 9x/Me press F5 during the boot. This allows the OS to select a generic display driver and low resolution. If this works, change the driver and resolution.

◢ Reseat the video card. For a PCI card, move the card to a different expansion slot. Clean the card's edge connectors, using a contact cleaner purchased from a computer supply store.

◢ If there are socketed chips on the video card, remove the card from the expansion slot and then use a screwdriver to press down firmly on each corner of each socketed chip on the card. Chips sometimes loosen because of thermal changes; this condition is called chip creep.

◢ Trade a good video card for the video card you suspect is bad. Test the video card you think is bad on a computer that works. Test a video card you know is good on the computer that you suspect is bad. Whenever possible, do both.

◢ If the video card has socketed chips that appear dirty or corroded, consider removing them and trying to clean the pins with contact cleaner. Normally, however, if the problem is a bad video card, the most cost-effective measure is to replace the card.

◢ Go into CMOS setup and disable the shadowing of video ROM.

◢ Test the RAM on the motherboard with diagnostic software.

◢ For a motherboard that is using an AGP or a PCI-Express video card, try using a PCI video card in a PCI slot.

◢ Trade the motherboard for one you know is good. Sometimes, though rarely, a peripheral chip on the motherboard of the computer can cause the problem.

◢ For notebook computers, is the LCD switch turned on? Function keys are sometimes used for this purpose.

◢ For notebook computers, try connecting a second monitor to the notebook and use the function key to toggle between the LCD panel and the second monitor. If the second monitor works, but the LCD panel does not work, the problem might be with the LCD panel hardware. How to solve problems with notebook computers is covered in Chapter 11.

POWER IS ON, BUT MONITOR DISPLAYS THE WRONG CHARACTERS

For this problem, try the following:

◢ Wrong characters are usually not the result of a bad monitor but of a problem with the video card. Trade the video card for one you know is good.

◢ Exchange the motherboard. Sometimes a bad ROM or RAM chip on the motherboard displays the wrong characters on the monitor.

MONITOR FLICKERS, HAS WAVY LINES, OR BOTH

A+ ESS
1.3
2.3

A+
220-602
1.2
1.3
2.3

For this problem, try the following:

▲ Monitor flicker can be caused by poor cable connections. Check that the cable connections are snug.

▲ Does the monitor have a degauss button to eliminate accumulated or stray magnetic fields? If so, press it.

▲ Check if something in the office is causing a high amount of electrical noise. For example, you might be able to stop a flicker by moving the office fan to a different outlet. Bad fluorescent lights or large speakers can also produce interference. Two monitors placed very close together can also cause problems.

▲ If the vertical scan frequency (the refresh rate at which the screen is drawn) is below 60 Hz, a screen flicker might appear. To change the refresh rate, right-click the desktop and select **Properties** from the shortcut menu. The Display Properties window opens. Click the **Settings** tab, and then click the **Advanced** button. The video hardware properties window opens. Click the **Monitor** tab (see Figure 8-64). For best results, make sure the option, **Hide modes that this monitor cannot display** is checked. Then select the highest screen refresh rate listed in the drop-down list.

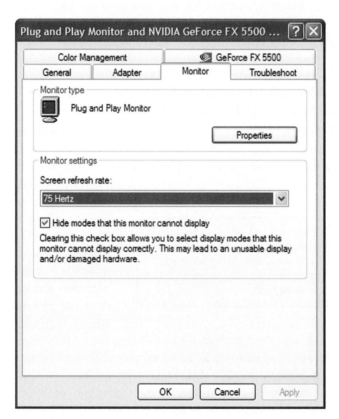

Figure 8-64 To reduce monitor flicker, increase the screen refresh rate

▲ For older monitors that do not support a high enough refresh rate, your only cure might be to purchase a new monitor. Before making a purchase, verify that the new monitor will solve the problem.

▲ For older monitors, use the controls on the monitor to check vertical hold (V-hold) which can cause the display to scroll.

A+ ESS
1.3
2.3

A+
220-602
1.2
1.3
2.3

- Using other controls on the monitor, you can change brightness, contrast, and horizontal and vertical display positions on the screen.
- Open Control Panel, click **Display**, and then click **Settings** to see if a high resolution (greater than 800 x 600) is selected. Consider these issues:

1. The video card might not support this resolution or color setting.

2. There might not be enough video RAM; see the video card documentation for the recommended amount.

3. The added (socketed) video RAM might be a different speed than the soldered memory.

NO GRAPHICS DISPLAY OR THE SCREEN GOES BLANK WHEN LOADING CERTAIN PROGRAMS

For this problem, try the following:

- A special graphics or video accelerator card is not present or is defective.
- Software is not configured to do graphics, or the software does not recognize the installed graphics card.
- The video card does not support the resolution and/or color setting.
- There might not be enough video RAM; see the video card for the recommended amount.
- The added (socketed) video RAM might be a different speed than the soldered memory.
- The wrong adapter/display type is selected. Start Windows from Safe Mode to reset the display.

SCREEN GOES BLANK 30 SECONDS OR ONE MINUTE AFTER THE KEYBOARD IS LEFT UNTOUCHED

A Green motherboard (one that follows energy-saving standards) used with an Energy Saver monitor can be configured to go into standby or doze mode after a period of inactivity. This might be the case if the monitor resumes after you press a key or move the mouse. Video might be set to doze after a period set as short as 20 seconds to as long as one hour. The power LED normally changes from green to orange to indicate doze mode. Monitors and video cards using these energy-saving features are addressed in Chapter 3.

> **Notes**
>
> Problems might occur if the motherboard power-saving features are turning off the monitor, and Windows screen saver is also turning off the monitor. If the system hangs when you try to get the monitor going again, try disabling one or the other. If this doesn't work, disable both.

You might be able to change the doze features by entering the CMOS menu and looking for an option such as Power Management. In addition, note that some monitors have a Power Save switch on the back. Make sure this is set as you want.

The screen saver feature of Windows can also set the monitor to turn off after so many minutes of inactivity. The number of minutes is set in the Display Properties window. Open Control Panel, select Display, and then select Screen Saver.

POOR COLOR DISPLAY

For this problem, try the following:

- Read the monitor documentation to learn how to use the color-adjusting buttons to fine-tune the color.
- Exchange video cards.

▲ Add more video RAM; see the video card for the recommended amount.

▲ Check if a fan, a large speaker (speakers have large magnets), or a nearby monitor could be causing interference.

▲ If the monitor displays blue and green, but no red, then the red electron gun might be bad. Replace the monitor. Same for missing blue or green colors.

▲ Odd-colored blotches on the screen might indicate a device such as a speaker or fan is sitting too close to the monitor and emitting EMI. Move any suspected device away from the monitor.

PICTURE OUT OF FOCUS OR OUT OF ADJUSTMENT

For this problem, try the following:

▲ Check the adjustment knobs on the control panel on the outside of the monitor.

▲ Change the refresh rate. Sometimes this can make the picture appear more focused.

▲ You can also make adjustments inside the monitor that might solve the problem. If you have not been trained to work inside the monitor, take it to a service center.

> **Notes**
>
> For LCD monitors, you can improve how fonts are displayed on the screen. On the Display Properties window, click the **Appearance** tab and then click **Effects**. The Effects dialog box appears (see Figure 8-65). Check **Use the following method to smooth edges of screen fonts**. Then, from the drop-down list, select **ClearType**. Click **OK** twice to close both windows.

CRACKLING SOUND

Dirt or dust inside the unit might be the cause. Someone at a computer monitor service center trained to work on the inside of the monitor can vacuum inside it. Recall from Chapter 3 that a monitor holds a dangerous charge of electricity and you should not open one unless trained to do so.

> **Tip**
>
> For LCD monitors, you can adjust the brightness of the display using function keys. See your notebook user manual to find out how.

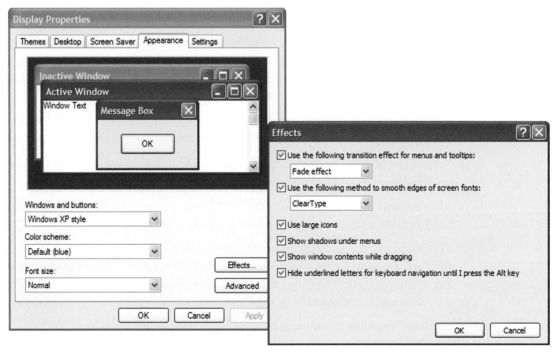

Figure 8-65   Use the Effects dialog box to improve displayed fonts using an LCD monitor

A+ ESS
1.3
2.3

A+
220-602
1.2
1.3
2.3

DISPLAY SETTINGS MAKE THE SCREEN UNREADABLE

When the display settings don't work, you can easily return to standard VGA settings, which include a resolution of 640 x 480. Do the following:

- For Windows 2000/XP or Windows 9x/Me, reboot the system and press the **F8** key after the first beep.
- When the Windows 2000/XP Advanced Options menu or the Windows 9x/Me startup menu appears, select **Safe Mode** to boot up with minimal configurations and standard VGA display mode. For Windows 2000/XP, you can also try Enable VGA Mode from the Advanced Options menu.
- Double-click the **Display** icon in Control Panel, and reset to the correct video configuration.

> **Caution**
>
> A CRT monitor screen is made of leaded glass, and a monitor contains capacitors that can hold a charge even after the monitor is unplugged. Therefore, it's important to dispose of a monitor correctly. For capacitors to fully discharge, it is not safe to remove the cover of a monitor until it has remained unplugged for at least one hour. To know how to dispose of a monitor, check with local county or environment officials for laws and regulations that apply to your area.

>> CHAPTER SUMMARY

- Adding new devices to a computer requires installing hardware and software. Even if you know how to generally install an I/O device, always follow the specific instructions of the product manufacturer.
- Use Device Manager under Windows to determine what resources currently installed devices use.
- A keyboard can use a DIN, PS/2, USB, or wireless connection.
- Biometric input devices, such as a fingerprint reader or iris scanner, collect biological data and compare it to that recorded about the person to authenticate the person's access to a system.
- Features to consider when purchasing a monitor are the screen size, refresh rate, interlacing, response time, dot pitch or pixel pitch, resolution, multiscan ability, color quality, contrast ratio, viewing angle, display type (active or passive matrix), backlighting, and type of connector (analog or digital) used by the monitor.
- A video card is rated by the bus that it uses and the amount of video RAM on the card. Both features affect the overall speed and performance of the card.
- Some types of video memory are VRAM, SGRAM, WRAM, 3-D RAM, MDRAM, G-DDR, G-DDR2, G-DDR3, and DRDRAM.
- Most computers provide one or more USB ports, one parallel port, and perhaps an IEEE 1394 port or serial port to be used for a variety of devices.
- The PCI bus is presently the most popular local bus. The VESA local bus is an outdated standard designed by the Video Electronics Standards Association for video cards. For video cards, the VESA bus was replaced by PCI, which was then replaced by the AGP bus, and more recently by the PCI Express bus.
- Generally, expansion cards use PCI Express or PCI slots.
- UART logic on a motherboard chipset controls serial ports.

◢ Because data might become corrupted, parallel cables should not exceed 15 feet (4.5 meters) in length. HP recommends that the cables not exceed 10 feet (3 meters).

◢ Three types of parallel ports are standard, EPP, and ECP. The ECP type uses a DMA channel.

◢ Serial ports are sometimes configured as COM1, COM2, COM3, or COM4, and parallel ports can be configured as LPT1, LPT2, or LPT3.

◢ The USB bus only uses one set of system resources for all USB devices connected to it, and USB devices are hot-pluggable.

◢ The IEEE 1394 bus provides 4-pin, 6-pin, or 9-pin connectors, uses only one set of system resources, and is hot-pluggable.

◢ The PCI bus runs in sync with the CPU, and the PCI controller manages system resources for all PCI cards. Resources are assigned to PCI slots during startup.

>> KEY TERMS

For explanations of key terms, see the Glossary near the end of the book.

3-D RAM	hot-pluggable	passive matrix display
active matrix display	hot-swapping	pixel
bus mouse	hub	PS/2-compatible mouse
chip creep	i.Link	refresh rate
DCE (Data Communications Equipment)	I/O controller card	resolution
	IEEE 1284	serial mouse
Direct RDRAM (DRDRAM)	IEEE 1394	SGRAM (synchronous graphics RAM)
dot pitch	IEEE 1394.3	
DSTN (dual-scan twisted nematic)	infrared transceiver	TFT (thin film transistor)
	interlaced	touch screen
DTE (Data Terminal Equipment)	IR transceiver	triad
ECP (Extended Capabilities Port)	IrDA (Infrared Data Association) transceiver	UART (universal asynchronous receiver-transmitter)
EPP (Enhanced Parallel Port)	isochronous data transfer	USB host controller
FireWire	LCD monitor	VRAM (video RAM)
flat panel monitor	motherboard mouse	WRAM (window RAM)
graphics accelerator	MultiBank DRAM (MDRAM)	
Graphics DDR (G-DDR)	noninterlaced	
Graphics DDR2 (G-DDR2)	null modem cable	
Graphics DDR3 (G-DDR3)		

>> REVIEWING THE BASICS

1. Identify three things that may cause monitor flicker.

2. Describe what to do if you've just spilled soda pop on your keyboard.

3. Explain how to check that chips on a video card are properly seated in their sockets.

4. When troubleshooting problems with a monitor in Windows XP, why would you enter Safe Mode?

5. Describe how to boot Windows XP into Safe Mode.

6. Why would an external modem cost more than an internal modem?

7. Name three possible ways a scanner might interface with a motherboard.

8. By definition, what system resources does COM1 use? COM2? COM3? COM4?

9. What is the display resolution for standard VGA settings?

10. What is the maximum length of a serial cable?

11. To what does RS-232 refer?

12. How many pins are on a typical serial port?

13. What is the name of a barcode reader that is a gun-type reader that can be handheld and is often used at a checkout counter?

14. What is the purpose of a keyboard wedge?

15. What is the name of the technology within the chipset that controls the speed of serial ports?

16. Why might you choose to use ECP mode for your parallel port rather than EPP mode?

17. When might you need to disable ECP mode for a parallel port?

18. How would you disable a serial port on a motherboard?

19. What Windows OSs support USB? Include the OS version numbers where that information is important.

20. What is the maximum speed of Original USB? Of Hi-Speed USB?

21. What is the maximum length of a USB Hi-Speed cable?

22. What are two other names for FireWire? What is the highest data throughput approved for FireWire?

23. When selecting a motherboard, why would you prefer to use PCI Express for the video card rather than AGP?

24. What is the most important disadvantage of using biometric devices to authenticate a person to have access to a system?

25. What criteria affect how much video RAM is needed for a video card to hold one frame buffer?

26. Give three examples of monitor screen sizes. How are monitor screen sizes measured?

27. What are two advantages of setting an LCD monitor to run in its native resolution?

28. What type of CRT monitor can offer a variety of refresh rates?

29. How many pins are used in the IEEE 1394 connector that supports the IEEE 1394b standard?

30. How many keyed notches does an AGP universal slot have?

31. What makes a device an ergonomic device?

32. How many pins are there on a DIN connector and a PS/2 connector for a keyboard?

33. What three colors are used to build all colors on a color monitor screen?

34. Which gives better image quality, a .25-mm dot pitch monitor or a .28-mm dot pitch monitor? Why?

35. If a mouse begins to be difficult to operate, what simple thing can you do to help?

>> *THINKING CRITICALLY*

1. You plug a new scanner into a USB port on your Windows XP system. When you first turn on the scanner, what should you expect to see?

   a. A message displayed by the scanner software telling you to reboot your system.

   b. You see the Found New Hardware Wizard launch.

   c. Your system automatically reboots.

   d. An error message from the USB controller.

2. You install the software bundled with your digital camera to download pictures from your camera to your system using a serial port. Next, you plug up the camera to the port using a serial cable and turn on your camera. You attempt to use the software to download pictures, but the software does not recognize the camera is present. What do you do next?

   a. Return the camera and purchase one that uses a USB port for downloading.

   b. Reinstall the bundled software.

   c. Access CMOS setup and verify that the serial port is enabled.

   d. Use Device Manager to verify that the OS recognizes the serial port.

   e. Replace the serial cable.

3. You turn on your Windows XP computer and see the system display POST messages. Then the screen turns blue with no text. Which of the following items could be the source of the problem?

   a. The video card

   b. The monitor

   c. Windows

   d. WordPerfect software installed on the system

>> *HANDS-ON PROJECTS*

Unless you follow proper procedures, working inside your computer can damage it seriously. Before you attempt to try these projects, be sure to use precautions outlined in Chapter 2, which include wearing an antistatic bracelet when working inside a PC.

PROJECT 8-1:   Installing a Device

Install a device on a computer. If you are working in a classroom environment, you can simulate an installation by moving a device from one computer to another.

PROJECT 8-2:   Researching a Computer Ad

Pick a current magazine ad for a complete, working computer system, including computer, monitor, keyboard, and software, together with extra devices such as a mouse or printer. Research the details of the ad and write a four- to eight-page report describing and explaining these details. This project provides a good opportunity to learn about the latest offerings on the market as well as current pricing.

PROJECT 8-3: Comparing Two Computer Ads

Find two ads for computer systems containing the same processor. Compare the two ads. Include in your comparison the different features offered and the weaknesses and strengths of each system.

PROJECT 8-4: Searching the Internet for a Video Driver

You are about to upgrade your PC from Windows 98 to Windows XP. Before performing the upgrade, search the Internet for a new video driver for your Matrox G200 MMS graphics card. What is the name of the file you need to download from the Matrox Web site for the upgrade?

PROJECT 8-5: Exploring Parallel Port Modes

Examine CMOS setup on your PC, and answer the following questions about your parallel port:

1. Is a parallel port coming directly off the motherboard?
2. What modes are available for the parallel port?
3. What is the currently selected mode?
4. If the parallel port supports ECP, what DMA channels can you select for this mode?
5. Disable the parallel port using CMOS setup. Reboot the PC and attempt to use the port by executing a print command. What error message do you get?

PROJECT 8-6: Preparing for Windows Vista

Microsoft says that to get the best video experience from Windows Vista, your graphics card must qualify for the OS. Do the following to find out if your system qualifies:

1. Find out what graphics card is installed your computer. What card is installed and how did you find out?
2. Search the Microsoft Web site (*www.windowsmarketplace.com*) for your card. If your card qualifies, print the Web page that shows your card qualifies for Vista.
3. If your card does not qualify, print the Web page of another video card that will work in your computer and that does qualify for Vista. How much does the upgrade card cost?

PROJECT 8-7: Working with a Monitor

1. Using a Windows OS, list the steps to change the monitor resolution.
2. Using the Display icon in the Windows Control Panel, practice changing the background, screen saver, and appearance. If you are not using your own computer, be sure to restore each setting after making changes.
3. Pretend you have made a mistake and selected a combination of foreground and background colors that makes reading the screen impossible. Solve the problem by booting Windows into Safe Mode. Correct the problem and then reboot.

4. From the Display Properties dialog box, change the resolution using the sliding bar under Display area. Make a change and then make the change permanent. You can go back and adjust it later if you want.

5. Work with a partner who is using a different computer. Unplug the monitor in the computer lab or classroom, loosen or disconnect the computer monitor cable, or turn the contrast and brightness all the way down, while your partner does something similar to the other PC. Trade PCs and troubleshoot the problems.

6. Turn off the PC, remove the case, and loosen the video card. Turn on the PC and write down the problem as a user would describe it. Turn off the PC, reseat the card, and verify that everything works.

7. Turn off your system. Insert into the system a defective video card provided by your instructor. Turn on the system. Describe the resulting problem in writing, as a user would.

>> REAL PROBLEMS, REAL SOLUTIONS

REAL PROBLEM 8-1:   Helping with Upgrade Decisions

Upgrading an existing system can sometimes be a wise thing to do, but sometimes the upgrade costs more than the system is worth. Also, if existing components are old, they might not be compatible with components you want to use for the upgrade. A friend, Renata, asks your advice about several upgrades she is considering. Answer these questions:

1. Renata has a Windows 2000 PC that does not have a FireWire port. She wants to use a camcorder that has a FireWire 400 interface with her PC. How would she perform the upgrade and what is the cost? Print Web pages to support your answers.

2. Renata has a Windows XP computer that has one USB port, but she wants to use her USB printer at the same time she uses her USB scanner. How can she do this and how much will it cost? Print Web pages to support your answers.

3. Renata also uses her Windows XP computer for gaming. The computer has an AGP 2.0 1.5-V video slot. What is the fastest and best graphics card she can buy to install in this slot? How much does it cost? Print Web pages to support your answer.

Multimedia Devices and Mass Storage

The ability to create output in a vast array of media—audio, video, and animation, as well as text and graphics—has turned PCs into multimedia machines. The multimedia computer has much to offer, from videoconferencing for executives to tools for teaching the alphabet to four-year-olds. This chapter examines multimedia devices, what they can do, how they work, and how to support them. You will also learn about storage devices such as CDs, DVDs, removable drives, and tape drives, including installation and troubleshooting. These mass storage devices are used to hold multimedia data and, in some cases, to store backups.

MULTIMEDIA ON A PC

The goal of multimedia technology is to use sights, sounds, and animation to make computer output look as much like real life as possible. Remember that computers store data digitally and ultimately as a stream of only two numbers: 0 and 1. In contrast, sights and sounds have an infinite number of variations and are analog in nature. The challenge for multimedia technology is to bridge these two worlds.

In this section, you'll first learn about the CPU technologies designed specifically for processing multimedia data and then we'll turn our attention to learning about some cool multimedia devices, including sound cards, digital cameras, MP3 players, TV tuners, and video capture cards.

CPU TECHNOLOGIES FOR MULTIMEDIA

Intel and AMD clearly dominate the CPU market, and both companies have made strides toward better CPU technologies used for multimedia.

Three early CPU improvements Intel made to its processors with multimedia applications in mind are MMX (Multimedia Extensions), used by the Pentium MMX and Pentium II; SSE (Streaming SIMD Extension), used by the Pentium III; and SSE2, SSE3, and Hyper-Threading for the Pentium 4. **SIMD**, which stands for "single instruction, multiple data," is a process that allows the CPU to receive a single instruction and then execute it on multiple pieces of data rather than receiving the same instruction each time each piece of data is received.

An instruction set is the group of operations that a CPU knows how to perform. These operations are preprogrammed into the processor logic when the CPU is manufactured. SSE2 has a larger instruction set than SSE, and SSE3 improves on SSE2. The Pentium 4 can use MMX, SSE, SSE2, SSE3, and Hyper-Threading. MMX and SSE help with repetitive looping, which happens a lot when the CPU is managing audio and graphics data. SSE also improves on 3D graphics.

 A+ Tip

The A+ Essentials exam expects you to be familiar with the characteristics of the different processors. Know the purposes of MMX, Hyper-Threading, and dual-core processing.

AMD is a favorite CPU manufacturer for gamers and hobbyists. For its processors, AMD uses 3DNow!, a processor instruction set designed to improve performance with 3D graphics and other multimedia data. In addition, AMD uses HyperTransport! to increase bandwidth and PowerNow! to improve a processor's performance and lower power requirements. AMD was first to market with 64-bit processors for the desktop, and AMD also uses dual-core processing.

SOUND CARDS AND ONBOARD SOUND

A sound card (an expansion card with sound ports) or onboard sound (sound ports embedded on a motherboard) can record sound, save it in a file on your hard drive, and play it back. Some sound cards and onboard sound give you the ability to mix and edit sound, and even to edit the sound using standard music score notation. Sound cards or motherboards with onboard sound have output ports for external speakers and input ports for a microphone, CD or DVD player, or other digital sound equipment.

The number and type of sound ports on a motherboard or sound card depend on the sound standards the card or board supports. For good sound, you definitely need two or more external speakers and an amplifier. Most cards sold today support the audio compression method also used by HDTV (high-definition TV) called Dolby AC-3 sound compression. Other names

A+ ESS
1.1

A+
220-602
1.1

given to this standard are Dolby Digital Surround, Dolby Surround Sound, or, the most common name, Surround Sound. The Surround Sound standard supports up to eight separate sound channels of sound information for up to eight different speakers, each producing a different sound. The number of speakers depends on the version of Surround Sound the motherboard or card supports. These speakers are known as Front Left and Right, Front Center, Rear Left and Right, and Subwoofer. Surround Sound Version 7.1 added two rear speakers in addition to the ones just mentioned. Because each channel is digital, there is no background noise on the channel, and a sound engineer can place sound on any one of these speakers. The sound effects can be awesome! The latest version of Surround Sound is Version 10.1.

The motherboard shown in Figure 9-1 contains onboard sound. Device drivers and a user manual for sound come bundled with the motherboard on CD. The purposes of the eight sound ports are listed in Table 9-1 for 2-, 4-, 6-, and 8-channel sound. The two S/PDIF (Sony/Philips Digital Interconnect Format) ports are used to connect to external sound equipment such as a CD or DVD player.

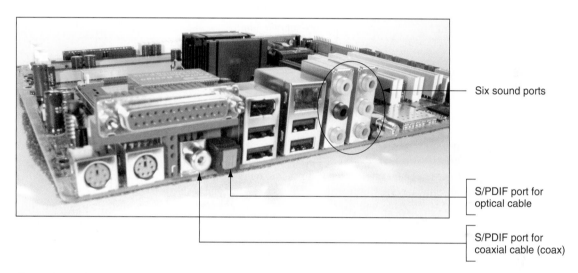

Six sound ports

S/PDIF port for
optical cable

S/PDIF port for
coaxial cable (coax)

Figure 9-1   This motherboard with onboard sound has eight sound ports

Port	2-Channel (Headset)	4-Channel	6-Channel	8-Channel
Light blue	Line in	Line in	Line in	Line in
Lime	Line out	Front speaker out	Front speaker out	Front speaker out
Pink	Mic in	Mic in	Mic in	Mic in
Gray	N/A	Rear speaker out	Rear speaker out	Rear speaker out
Black	N/A	N/A	N/A	Side speaker out
Yellow-orange	N/A	N/A	Center or subwoofer	Center or subwoofer
Gray half-oval	Optical S/PDIF out port connects an external audio output device using a fiber-optic S/PDIF cable			
Yellow	Coaxial S/PDIF out port connects an external audio output device using a coaxial S/PDIF cable			

Table 9-1   Sound ports on a motherboard

Also, sound cards might be Sound Blaster-compatible, meaning that they understand the commands sent to them that have been written for a Sound Blaster card, which is generally considered the standard for PC sound cards. In addition, some cards have internal input connectors to connect to a CD or DVD drive or TV Tuner card so that analog or digital sound goes directly from the device to the sound card, bypassing the CPU. Table 9-2 lists some sound card manufacturers.

Manufacturer	Web Site
Aopen	*www.aopen.com*
Chaintech	*www.chaintechusa.com*
Creative	*www.creative.com* and *www.soundblaster.com*
Diamond Multimedia	*www.diamondmm.com*
Guillemot Corporation	*www.hercules.com*
PPA	*www.ppa-usa.com*
Sabrent	*www.sabrent.com*
SIIG	*www.siig.com*
Turtle Beach	*www.tbeach.com*

Table 9-2 Sound card manufacturers

> **Notes**
>
> A good source for information about hardware devices (and software) is a site that offers product reviews and technical specifications and compares product prices and features. Check out these sites: CNET Networks (*www.cnet.com*), Price Watch (*www.pricewatch.com*), Tom's Hardware Guide (*www.tomshardware.com*), and Epinions, Inc. (*www.epinions.com*).

SAMPLING AND DIGITIZING THE SOUND

Sound passes through three stages when it is computerized: first, the sound is digitized— that is, converted from analog to digital; next, the digital data is stored in a compressed data file; later, the sound is reproduced or synthesized (digital to analog or digital out).

Sound is converted from analog to digital storage by first sampling the sound and then digitizing it. When you record sound, the analog sound is converted to analog voltage by a microphone and passed to the sound card, where it is digitized. The sound is sampled at set intervals. Each sample taken is stored as a number. The number of bits used to store the sample is called the sample size and greatly affects the quality of the digitized sound. Common sample sizes are 8, 16, and 24 bits.

The sampling rate of a sound card, which is the number of samples taken of the analog signal over a period of time, is usually expressed as samples (cycles) per second, or hertz (Hz). One thousand hertz (one kilohertz) is written as kHz. A low sampling rate provides a less-accurate representation of the sound than a high sampling rate. Our ears detect up to about 22,000 samples per second, or hertz. Studies show that in order to preserve the original sound, a digital sampling rate must be twice the frequency of the analog signal. Therefore, the sampling rate of music CDs is 44,100 Hz, or 44.1 kHz, although the sampling rates of high-end sound cards can be higher. When you record sound on a PC, the sampling rate is controlled by the recording software.

The larger the sample size is, the more accurate the sampling. If 8 bits are used to hold one number, the sample range can be from -128 to +127. This is because 1111 1111 in

A+ ESS
1.1

A+
220-602
1.1

binary (FF in hex) equals 255 in decimal, which, combined with zero, equals 256 values. Sound samples are considered both positive and negative numbers, so the range is -128 to +127 rather than 0 to 255. However, if 16 bits are used to hold the range of numbers, then the sample range increases dramatically, because 1111 1111 1111 1111 in binary (FFFF in hex) is 65,535 in decimal, meaning that the sample size can be -32,768 to +32,767, or a total of 65,536 values. High-fidelity music CDs use this 16-bit sample size. Samples can also be recorded on a single channel (mono) or on two channels (stereo). After the sound is recorded and digitized, many sound cards convert the digitized sound to MP3 format, which takes up less space on a hard drive or other media than does raw digitized sound.

INSTALLING A SOUND CARD

A+ ESS
1.2

Most sound cards come with device drivers as well as all the software needed for normal use, such as application software to play music CDs or record music. Later in this part of the chapter, you'll see how to install a sound card. The card that will be used is shown in Figure 9-2. It's a 24-bit Creative Labs Sound Blaster card that has a universal PCI connector and works under Windows NT/2000/XP, Windows 9x/Me, and DOS. The card comes with a user manual, drivers, and application software all on a CD.

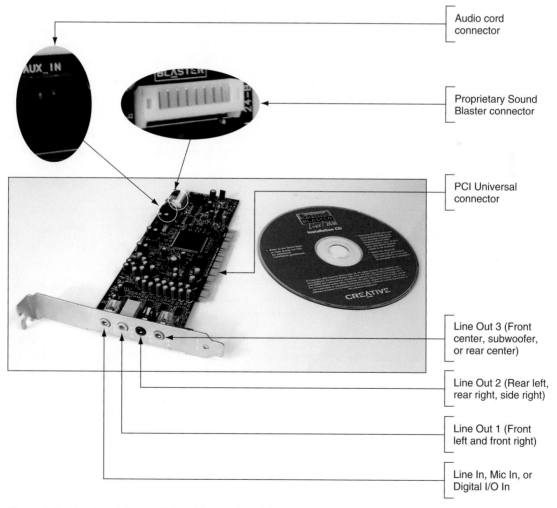

Audio cord connector

Proprietary Sound Blaster connector

PCI Universal connector

Line Out 3 (Front center, subwoofer, or rear center)

Line Out 2 (Rear left, rear right, side right)

Line Out 1 (Front left and front right)

Line In, Mic In, or Digital I/O In

Figure 9-2 The Sound Blaster PCI 24-bit sound card has two internal connections and four ports

The Sound Blaster card shown in Figure 9-2 has several ports that are labeled in the figure. The sound-out ports can support analog speakers or amplifiers that are externally powered. Typical color codes for these ports are:

 A+ Tip

The A+ Essentials exam expects you to know the characteristics of adapter cards used in multimedia applications and how to install these cards. You need to know about a sound card, video card, TV tuner card, SCSI, FireWire (1394), and USB adapter cards. The detailed installation learned in this section applies to other adapters as well as a sound card.

▲ *Blue.* Line in for music synthesizers, a microphone, DVD player, CD player, or other external device producing sound. It can also be used with a Digital I/O Module available from Creative. (If a card has a separate port for a microphone other than the Line-in port, most likely the microphone port will be red.)

▲ *Green.* Line out (Front speakers out, usually center port on the card). Use this port for a single speaker.

▲ *Black.* Rear out and Side Right out (for a sound system that uses a 7.1 speaker system).

▲ *Orange (sometimes yellow on other sound cards).* Front Center out, Subwoofer speaker, or Side Left (for a sound system that uses a 7.1 speaker system).

 Notes

The trend for today's motherboards is to embed sound capability on the board. If this onboard sound is giving problems, try using Device Manager to uninstall the sound drivers and then use the setup CD that came bundled with the motherboard to reinstall the drivers. If you want to upgrade to better sound by using a sound card, you can use CMOS setup to disable the onboard sound and then install a sound card.

The sound card has two internal connections (connections to something inside the case). The AUX In connector is used to connect devices that provide audio into the card, including a CD drive, DVD drive, TV Tuner card, and MPEG decoder card. The second internal connector is a proprietary connector used for other Creative devices.

APPLYING CONCEPTS Generally, the main steps to install a sound card are to install the card in an empty PCI slot on the motherboard and install the drivers on the CD that comes with the sound card. Also, on the CD you might find applications to install. Follow these steps to install a sound card:

1. Wear a ground bracelet to protect against ESD, as described in Chapter 2.

2. Turn off the PC, remove the cover, and locate an empty expansion slot for the card. Because this installation uses the connecting wire from the sound card to the CD drive (the wire comes with the sound card), place the sound card near enough to the CD drive so that the wire can reach between them.

3. Attach the wire to the sound card (see Figure 9-3) and to the CD drive or DVD drive.

CD drive

Audio cord and connector to optical drive

Figure 9-3 Connect the wire to the sound card that will make the direct audio connection from the CD drive

4. Remove the cover from the slot opening at the rear of the PC case, and place the card into the PCI slot, making sure that the card is seated firmly. Use the screw taken from the slot cover to secure the card to the back of the PC case.

5. Check again that both ends of the wire are still securely connected and that the wire is not hampering the CPU fan, and then replace the case cover.

$\frac{1}{2}$

Notes

Some high-end sound cards have a power connector to provide extra power to the card. For this type of card, connect a power cable with a miniature 4-pin connector to the card. Be careful! Know for certain the purpose of the connector is for power. Don't make the mistake of attaching a miniature power cord designed for a $3\frac{1}{2}$-inch disk drive coming from the power supply to the audio input connector on the sound card. The connections appear to fit, but you'll probably destroy the card by making this connection.

6. Plug in the speakers to the ports at the back of the sound card, and turn on the PC. The speakers might or might not require their own power source. Check the product documentation or manufacturer's Web site for more information.

Notes

In this installation, we connected the audio cord from the sound card to a CD drive. However, sometimes you might connect the audio cord to a DVD drive or TV Tuner card.

Notes

Some sound cards have a built-in amplifier. If this is the case and you are using a speaker system that includes an amplifier, disable the amplifier on the card either by setting a jumper on the card or by using the utility software that comes with the card. See the card's documentation for instructions.

A+ ESS
1.2

A+
220-602
1.1

Installing the Sound Card Driver

After the card is installed, the device drivers must be installed. This installation uses Windows XP, but a Windows 2000 or Windows 9x/Me installation works about the same way (important differences are noted in the steps). That being said, follow these steps using Windows XP to install the sound card drivers:

1. After physically installing the card, turn on the system. When Windows XP starts, it detects that new audio hardware is present. A bubble message appears on the system tray (see Figure 9-4) and the Found New Hardware Wizard opens (see Figure 9-5).

Figure 9-4   Windows XP detects new hardware is present

Figure 9-5   The Windows XP Found New Hardware Wizard steps you through a hardware installation

2. To use the drivers on the CD that came with the sound card, select **Install from a list or specific location (Advanced)** and click **Next.** (For Windows 9x/Me, in the New Hardware Wizard window, select **Search for the Best Driver for Your Device (Recommended)** and click **Next.**)

> 📝 **Notes**
>
> When Windows 2000/XP is searching for drivers, it is looking for a driver information file that has an .inf extension.

3. The next window in the wizard opens (see Figure 9-6). Select **Search for the best driver in these locations**, and check **Search removable media**. Also check **Include this location in the**

search and verify the CD drive letter is showing. In Figure 9-6, that drive is D:\. Click **Next**. (For Windows 9x/Me, check **Specify a Location**. Click the **Browse** button and point to the driver path, such as **D:\Audio\English\Win98drv** for Windows 98 or **D:\Audio\English\Win2k** for Windows 2000. Click **Next**.)

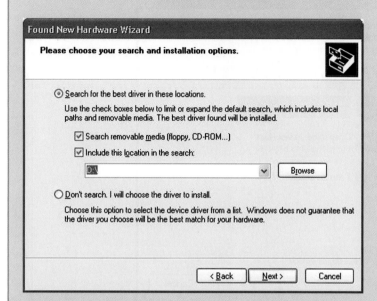

Figure 9-6   The Found New Hardware Wizard asks for directions for locating driver files

4. Windows XP locates the driver files and loads them. On the final screen of the wizard shown in Figure 9-7, click **Finish**. You're now ready to test the sound card.

Figure 9-7   The Found New Hardware Wizard has successfully finished the installation

5. To test the sound card, insert a music CD in the optical drive. Depending on how Windows XP is configured, the CD might automatically play, nothing will happen, or, if this is the

first time a music CD has been used with the system, the Audio CD window opens, as shown in Figure 9-8.

Figure 9-8 Windows XP asks what to do with the detected music CD

6. Select **Play Audio CD using Windows Media Player** and click **OK**. Windows Media Player launches to play the CD (see Figure 9-9).

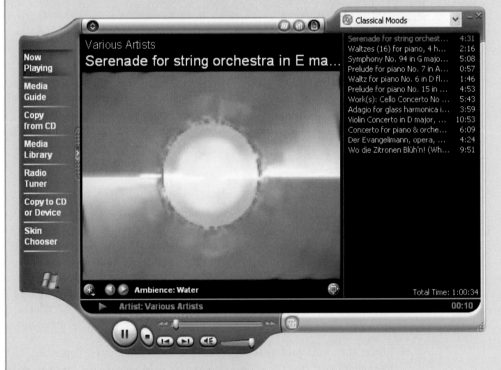

Figure 9-9 Windows Media Player playing a CD

A+ ESS
1.2

A+
220-602
1.1

7. The volume might need adjusting. You can adjust the volume by several methods and you might have to use more than one of them to get it right. Here are the ways:

▲ Windows Media Player has a volume control sliding bar, as shown at the bottom of Figure 9-9.

▲ To use the Windows XP volume control, click **Start, All Programs, Accessories, Entertainment, Volume Control**. The Volume Control window opens, as shown in Figure 9-10. Uncheck the **Mute** boxes and adjust the balance and volume.

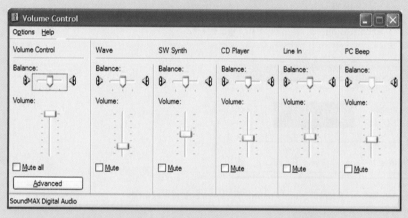

Figure 9-10 Windows XP Volume Control window controls volume

▲ You can also use a volume control icon on the taskbar. To create the icon, open the **Sounds and Audio Devices** applet in Control Panel. The Sounds and Audio Devices Properties window opens, as shown in Figure 9-11. Check **Place volume icon in the taskbar** and click **OK.** Adjust or mute the volume using this icon.

Figure 9-11 Use the Sounds and Audio Devices Properties window to place a volume control icon on the taskbar

▲ Many speakers and amplifiers have on/off switches and volume control buttons used to adjust the noise volume. Also, for notebook computers, look for buttons on the keyboard to adjust volume.

Recording Sound

As a final test of your sound card, if you have a microphone available, do the following to record a sample sound:

1. Click **Start, All Programs, Accessories, Entertainment**, and **Sound Recorder**. The Sound Recorder opens, as shown in Figure 9-12.

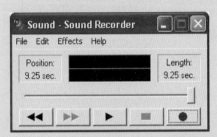

Figure 9-12   Record sounds using Windows Sound Recorder

2. Click the **Record** button (the red dot in the lower-right corner) to record, and click the Stop button (the black rectangle next to the red dot) when you're done. As a fun test of recording sound, create a welcome message in your own voice. Then, to save the message in a sound file, click **File, Save As**. When you save the sound to a file, Windows uses a Wave file format with the .wav file extension.

3. If you want, you can substitute this .wav file for one of the Windows sounds that plays when you open or close applications, shut down Windows, or perform many other Windows activities that can be accompanied by sound. To change the sounds for various Windows events, go to the Control Panel, open the **Sounds and Audio Devices applet**, and select the **Sounds** tab.

> **Notes**
>
> With most sound cards, the CD containing the sound card driver has application software for the special features offered by the card. Launch the sound card CD to install this software and also look for user manuals stored on the CD and diagnostic software to use if you have a problem with the sound card.

Notes on Windows 2000/XP Installations

Here are a few additional tips you need to know about installing hardware using Windows 2000/XP:

▲ When installing a hardware device, the Windows XP Found New Hardware Wizard might proceed with the installation using Microsoft drivers without giving you the opportunity to select manufacturer drivers. To prevent this from happening, run the setup program on the manufacturer's CD that is bundled with the card before installing the card. Later, after the card is installed, Windows will use the manufacturer's installed drivers for the card.

A+ ESS
1.2

A+
220-602
1.1

◢ When Windows XP installs a device, it verifies that Microsoft has digitally signed the drivers. Depending on how the OS is configured, you might or might not be allowed to keep going if the drivers are not digitally signed. If the drivers have been written for Windows XP, even though they are not certified by Microsoft, they should still work in a Windows XP system.

◢ You must be signed onto Windows XP using an account that has administrative privileges in order to use the Found New Hardware Wizard and install a hardware device.

◢ After the installation, you can use Device Manager to verify there are no errors. Open Device Manager, select the device, right-click it, and select Properties on the shortcut menu. Troubleshooting problems with sound cards is covered later in the chapter.

A+ ESS
1.1

DIGITAL CAMERAS AND FLASH MEMORY DEVICES

Digital cameras are becoming more popular as quality improves and prices go down. Digital camera technology works much like scanner technology, except it is much faster. It essentially scans the field of image set by the picture taker and translates the light signals into digital values, which can be stored as a file and viewed, manipulated, and printed with software that interprets the stored values appropriately.

TWAIN is a standard format used by digital cameras and scanners for transferring images. You can transfer images from the camera to your computer's hard drive using a cable supplied with the camera. The cable might attach directly to the camera or connect to a cradle the camera sits in to recharge or upload images. The cable can use a USB, FireWire (IEEE 1394), serial, or parallel connection. Also, some cameras use an infrared or other wireless connection. Or, if your computer has a flash card reader and your camera uses a compatible flash card, you can remove the flash card from the camera, insert it in the reader, and upload the images.

Digital cameras can hold their images both in embedded memory that cannot be removed or exchanged and in removable flash memory devices. Both these types of memory retain data without a battery.

🎥 **Video**

Types of Memory Cards

A storage device that uses memory chips to store data instead of spinning disks (such as those used by hard drives and CD drives) is called a solid state device (SSD), also called a solid state disk. Examples of solid state devices are jump drives (also called key drives or thumb drives), flash memory cards, and solid state disks used as hard drives in notebook computers designed for the most rugged uses.

Several types of flash memory cards on the market today are shown and described in Table 9-3. These cards might be used in digital cameras, cell phones, MP3 players, handheld computers, digital camcorders, and other portable devices.

Flash Memory Device	Example
Secure Digital (SD) cards are the most popular flash memory cards, and currently hold up to 4 GB of data.	![SanDisk 2.0GB SD card]
Multimedia Cards (MMC) look like SD cards, but the technology is different and they are not interchangeable. Generally, SD cards are faster than MMC cards.	![SanDisk 64MB MultiMediaCard]

Table 9-3 Flash memory devices

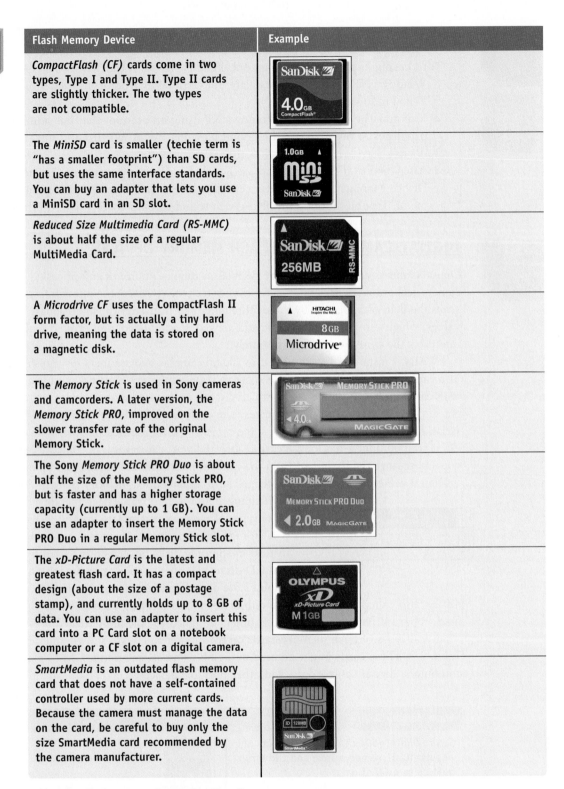

A+ ESS 1.1	Flash Memory Device	Example
	CompactFlash (CF) cards come in two types, Type I and Type II. Type II cards are slightly thicker. The two types are not compatible.	
	The *MiniSD* card is smaller (techie term is "has a smaller footprint") than SD cards, but uses the same interface standards. You can buy an adapter that lets you use a MiniSD card in an SD slot.	
	Reduced Size Multimedia Card (RS-MMC) is about half the size of a regular MultiMedia Card.	
	A *Microdrive CF* uses the CompactFlash II form factor, but is actually a tiny hard drive, meaning the data is stored on a magnetic disk.	
	The *Memory Stick* is used in Sony cameras and camcorders. A later version, the *Memory Stick PRO*, improved on the slower transfer rate of the original Memory Stick.	
	The Sony *Memory Stick PRO Duo* is about half the size of the Memory Stick PRO, but is faster and has a higher storage capacity (currently up to 1 GB). You can use an adapter to insert the Memory Stick PRO Duo in a regular Memory Stick slot.	
	The *xD-Picture Card* is the latest and greatest flash card. It has a compact design (about the size of a postage stamp), and currently holds up to 8 GB of data. You can use an adapter to insert this card into a PC Card slot on a notebook computer or a CF slot on a digital camera.	
	SmartMedia is an outdated flash memory card that does not have a self-contained controller used by more current cards. Because the camera must manage the data on the card, be careful to buy only the size SmartMedia card recommended by the camera manufacturer.	

Table 9-3 Flash memory devices (continued)

Figure 9-13 shows a digital camera that uses an xD Picture Card and a USB cable for uploading images, and in Figure 9-14, you can see a Sony digital camera that has a Memory Stick PRO slot. An adapter allows a Memory Stick PRO Duo to use the slot. Another option for storage in a digital camera is a Mini CD-R/RW, which is installed in the digital camera and can also be moved to a computer and read by a regular CD drive.

Figure 9-13 This digital camera uses an xD Picture Card and uploads images by way of a USB cable

Figure 9-14 This Sony digital camera has a Memory Stick PRO slot that can accommodate a Memory Stick PRO Duo with adapter; images upload by way of a USB cable

You can use a Web site such as *www.cdnet.com* or *www.compusa.com* to find and compare other digital cameras, storage media, and flash card readers. Select the camera first and then purchase the card storage device the camera supports. Some cameras might come bundled with the storage device.

To transfer images to your PC, to use the software that is bundled with your camera, first install the software. If the camera is designed to work with Windows XP, Windows XP can upload images from the camera without any additional software.

After the images are on the PC, use the camera's image-editing software, or another program such as Adobe PhotoShop, to view, touch up, and print the picture. The picture file, which is usually in JPEG (Joint Photographic Experts Group) format, can then be imported into documents. JPEG is a common compression standard for storing photos. Most JPEG files have a .jpg file extension. In addition, a high-end camera might support the uncompressed TIFF format. TIFF (Tagged Image File Format) files are larger, but retain more image information and give better results when printing photographs.

> **A+ Tip**
>
> The A+ Essentials exam expects you to know how to install the software bundled with your digital camera before attaching the camera to your PC.

Most digital cameras have a video-out port that allows you to attach the camera to any TV, using a cable provided with the camera. You can then display pictures on TV or copy them to videotape. Table 9-4 lists manufacturers of digital cameras.

Manufacturer	Web Site
Canon	*www.usa.canon.com*
Casio	*www.casio.com*
Epson	*www.epson.com*
Fujifilm	*www.fujifilm.com*
Hewlett-Packard	*www.photosmart.com*
Kodak	*www.kodak.com*
Minolta	*www.minolta.com*
Nikon	*www.nikonusa.com*
Olympus	*www.olympusamerica.com*
Sony	*www.sonystyle.com*
Toshiba	*www.toshiba.com*

Table 9-4 Digital camera manufacturers

WEB CAMERAS AND MICROPHONES

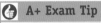

> **A+ Exam Tip**
>
> The A+ Essentials exam expects you to know the purposes and characteristics of digital cameras, Web cameras, and microphones.

A Web camera is a video camera that is used to capture digital video that can be used to feed live video on the Internet. The camera usually connects to a computer by way of a USB, FireWire, composite video, or S-video port. A Web cam refers to both a digital video camera and a Web site that provides a live or prerecorded video broadcast. One interesting Web site, Web Cam Central (*www.camcentral.com*), tracks other Web sites that have Web cams and provides some Web cams of its own. For example, one of the Web cams listed by Web Cam Central is the live Web cam at a marina in Cape Cod, Massachusetts (see Figure 9-15).

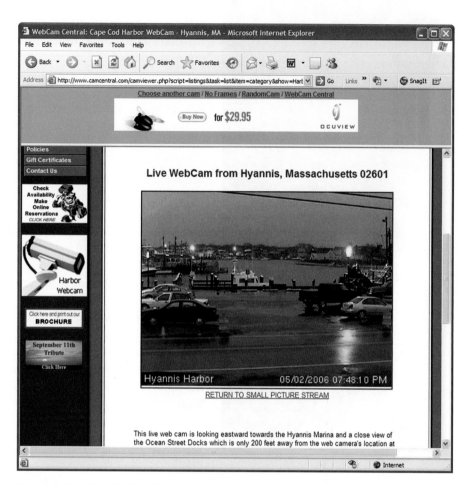

Figure 9-15 Use this live Web cam to watch the Nantucket and Martha's Vineyard ferry boats come and go

Besides the larger Web cameras used to produce live video for Web cam sites, you can buy an inexpensive Web camera to use for personal chat sessions and video conferencing such as the one shown in Figure 9-16.

Figure 9-16 This personal Web camera clips to the top of your notebook and comes packaged with an ear clip headset that includes a microphone and speaker

First, use the setup CD to install the software and then plug in the Web camera to a USB port. You can use the camera with or without the headset. If you want to include sound in your chat sessions, plug the two sound connectors into the speaker out and microphone in ports on your computer. These ports are embedded in notebook computers, as shown in Figure 9-16. For desktop computers, the ports are part of the sound card or they are onboard ports.

Next, use chat software such as MSN Messenger to create a live video session. For example, when you open MSN Messenger, if you or your chat friend has a Web camera installed, a small camera icon appears in the lower-left corner of your photo (see Figure 9-17). Click it to invite your friend to view your Web camera streaming video.

If you both have a speaker and microphone connected, you can also create a video conferencing session with video and voice. To begin a video conversation with sound, on the menu at the top of the MSN Messenger window, click **Voice**.

MP3 PLAYERS

A popular audio compression method is MP3, a method that can reduce the size of a sound file as much as 1:24 without much loss of quality. An MP3 player is a device or software that plays MP3 files. MP3 players are small but can store a lot of information. Figure 9-18 shows a typical MP3 player.

COMPRESSION METHODS USED WITH MP3 PLAYERS

One of the better-known multimedia data compression standards is MPEG, an international standard for data compression for motion pictures, video, and audio. Developed by the Moving Pictures Experts Group (MPEG), it tracks movement from one frame to the next and stores only what changes, rather than compressing individual frames. MPEG compression can yield a compression ratio of 100:1 for full-motion video (30 frames per second, or 30 fps).

A+ ESS
1.1

Use this icon to start a video session

Figure 9-17 Instant Messenger session using a Web camera

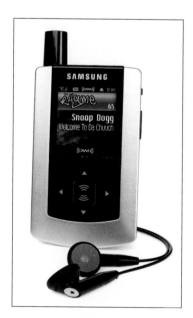

Figure 9-18 The portable Samsung Helix XM2go is an XM Satellite Radio and MP3 player

Currently, several MPEG standards are available: MPEG-1, MPEG-2, and MPEG-4. MPEG-1 is used to compress audio on CD and is the basis for MP3. MPEG-2 is used to compress video films on DVD. MPEG-3 was never fully developed or used. MPEG-4 is used for video transmissions over the Internet.

MPEG compression is possible because it cuts out or drastically reduces sound that is not normally heard by the human ear. In the regular audio CD format (uncompressed), one minute of music takes up about 10 MB of storage. The same minute of music in MP3 format takes only about 1 MB of memory. This makes it possible to download music in minutes rather than hours. Sound files downloaded from the Internet are most often MP3 files. MP3 files have an .mp3 file extension. For more information about MPEG and MP3, see *www.mpeg.org*.

HOW MP3 PLAYERS WORK

Most portable MP3 players today store MP3 files in onboard memory or hard drives, which can be expanded using an add-on flash memory card, such as SecureDigital, CompactFlash, or Memory Stick. MP3 files are downloaded from the PC to the MP3 player, in contrast to a digital camera, which transfers or uploads data to the PC.

You can purchase and download MP3 music files from Web sites such as EMusic (*www.emusic.com*) and MP3.com (*www.mp3.com*). After the files are downloaded to your PC, you can play them on your PC using MP3 player software such as Windows Media Player or MusicMatch Jukebox (see *www.musicmatch.com*), transfer them to a portable MP3 player, or convert them into an audio CD if your computer has a writable CD drive. There are also CD/MP3 players that can play CDs in either standard audio format or MP3-format. A CD can store 10 hours or more of music in MP3 format. You can also play the MP3 files directly from the Internet without first downloading them, which is called streaming audio. MP3 files are generally transferred to portable devices using a USB or FireWire cable.

Also, you can convert files from your regular music CDs into MP3 files (a process called ripping because the copyright owner of the music is considered to be ripped off), and play them on your computer or download them to an MP3 player. "Ripper" software copies the music file from the CD, and encoder software compresses the file into MP3 format. CD rippers, MP3 encoders, and MP3 player software can be downloaded from the Internet. For example, see the MusicMatch site at *www.musicmatch.com*.

Table 9-5 lists some manufacturers of MP3 players.

Manufacturer	Web Site
Apple Computers	*www.apple.com*
Creative Labs	*www.creative.com*
Dell	*www.dell.com*
Intel	*www.intel.com*
MachSpeed	*www.machspeed.com*
Panasonic	*www.panasonic.com*
Pine Technology	*www.xfxforce.com*
Rio (was SONICblue)	*www.rioaudio.com*
Samsung	*www.samsungusa.com*
SanDisk	*www.sandisk.com*
Sony	*www.sonystyle.com*

Table 9-5 MP3 player manufacturers

A+ ESS
1.1

MIDI DEVICES

MIDI (stands for "musical instrument digital interface" and pronounced "middy") is a set of standards that are used to represent music in digital form. Whereas MP3 is a method of storing a sound file in compressed format, MIDI is a method of digitally describing and storing every individual note played by each individual instrument used in making music. With MIDI files and MIDI software, you can choose to listen to only a single instrument being played or change one note played by that instrument. MIDI can be used to creatively produce synthesized music, mute one instrument or voice, and edit a song with your own voice or instrument. MIDI standards are used to connect electronic music equipment, such as keyboards and mixers, or to connect this equipment to a PC for input and output. Most sound cards can play MIDI files, and most electronic instruments have MIDI ports. To mix and edit music using MIDI on your PC, you'll need MIDI editing software such as JAMMER Professional by SoundTrek (*www.soundtrek.com*).

> **A+ Exam Tip**
>
> The A+ Essentials exam expects you to know about MIDI input devices, ports, and cables.

A MIDI port is a 5-pin DIN port that looks like a keyboard port, only larger. Figure 9-19 shows MIDI ports on electronic drums. A MIDI port is either an input port or an output port, but not both. Normally, you would connect the MIDI output port to a mixer, but you can also use it to connect to a PC. If your PC does not have MIDI ports, you can use a MIDI-to-USB cable like the one in Figure 9-20. The two MIDI connectors on the cable are for input and output.

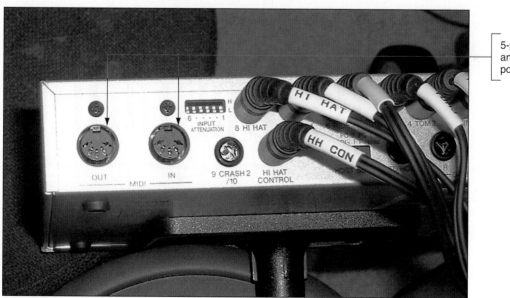

5-pin MIDI-out and MIDI-in ports

Figure 9-19 MIDI ports on an electronic drum set

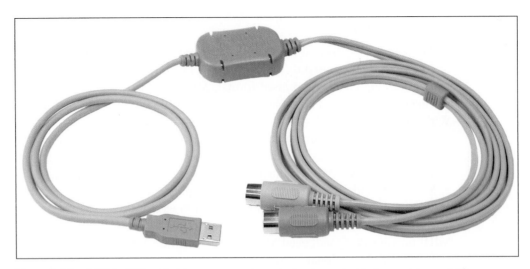

Figure 9-20 MIDI-to-USB cable lets you connect an electronic musical instrument to your PC

Some keyboards have a USB port to interface with a PC using MIDI data transmissions. For example, the keyboard shown in Figure 9-21 has a USB port and can output sound to a PC or receive standard MIDI files (SMF) to play.

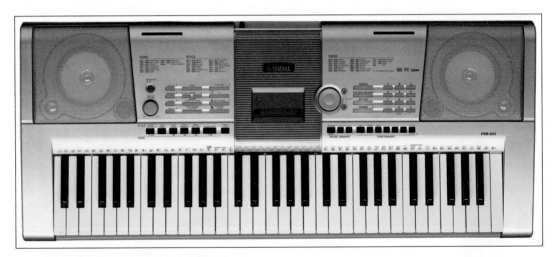

Figure 9-21 This keyboard by Yamaha has a USB port to be used as a MIDI interface

TV TUNER AND VIDEO CAPTURE CARDS

A TV tuner card can turn your computer into a television. A port on the card receives input from a TV cable and lets you view television on your computer monitor. A video capture card lets you capture this video input and save it to a file on your hard drive. Some cards are a combination TV tuner card and video capture card, making it possible for you to receive television input and save that input to your hard drive. A high-end TV tuner/video capture card might also serve as your video card. And, too, some motherboards and notebook computers have onboard TV tuners and TV captures, such as the notebook shown in Figure 9-22.

A+ ESS
1.1

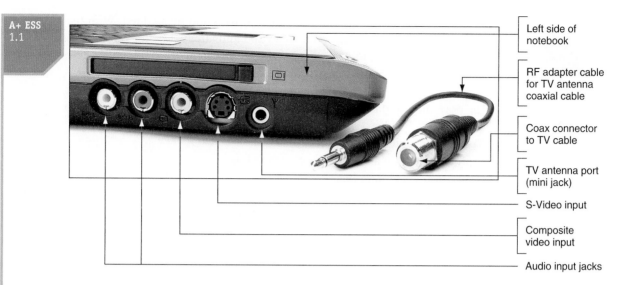

Left side of
notebook

RF adapter cable
for TV antenna
coaxial cable

Coax connector
to TV cable

TV antenna port
(mini jack)

S-Video input

Composite
video input

Audio input jacks

Figure 9-22   This notebook computer has embedded TV tuner and video capture abilities

To use this notebook to watch TV and capture live TV, plug in a TV coaxial cable (also called "coax" for short) to the RF adapter that is included, which plugs into the antenna mini-jack. Other ports labeled in Figure 9-22 can be used to capture input from a camcorder or VCR or input data from other audio and video equipment that use these audio input, composite video, and S-video ports. Using a cable with a standard RCA cable harness (red, white, and yellow ports), such as the one in Figure 9-23, you can use this notebook to display and/or record data from a DVD player or game box. The cable in Figure 9-23 connects to an Xbox.

Figure 9-23   Standard RCA cable harness connects to digital game box

A+ ESS
1.1

Captured video can be saved as motion clips or stills and then edited. With the right card and software, you can create your own video and animated CDs and DVDs. To help you select a video capture card, look for these features on the card, which follow the standards created by the NTSC (National Television Standards Committee) for the USA:

- ◢ The port and interface the camera uses with your PC, which might be a FireWire (IEEE 1394), S-video, or composite video port
- ◢ Data transfer rates, which affect price
- ◢ Capture resolution and color-depth capabilities
- ◢ Ability to transfer data back to a digital camcorder or VCR
- ◢ Stereo audio jacks
- ◢ Video-editing software bundled with the card

For a TV tuner card, look for these features:

- ◢ Ability to do instant replay and program scheduling
- ◢ Input ports for coaxial cable TV, TV antenna, video equipment, and game boxes
- ◢ TV or VCR port for output
- ◢ Remote control so you can flip TV channels from across the room

For a desktop system, expect a TV tuner or video capture card to fit into a PCI, PCI Express x16, or AGP slot. Some take the place of your regular video card and some install beside it. One example of a TV tuner and video capture card is the AVerTV PVR 150 Plus PCI card shown in Figure 9-24.

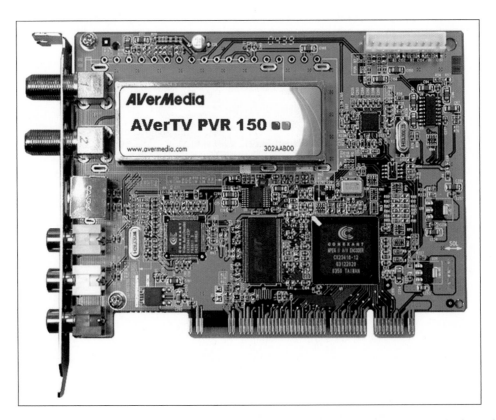

Figure 9-24   The AVerTV PVR 150 video capture and TV tuner card by AVerMedia uses a PCI slot and works alongside a regular video card

A+ ESS
1.1

Also, an external device can be used as a TV tuner and to capture video and stills. For notebook computers, the device can use the PC Card slot, or it can use a USB port. One example is the WinTV-USB device by Hauppauge Computer Works shown in Figure 9-25. It connects to a USB port and comes with a cord to connect to the Line-in port of a sound card.

Figure 9-25 Use this USB device to watch TV on your desktop or notebook computer and capture video and stills

Table 9-6 lists some manufacturers of TV tuner and video capture cards.

Manufacturer	Web Site
ASUS	www.asus.com
ATI	www.ati.com
AVerMedia	www.aver.com
Creative Labs	www.creative.com
Hauppauge Computer Works	www.hauppauge.com
Matrox	www.matrox.com
Pinnacle Systems	www.pinnaclesys.com
Sabrent	www.sabrent.com

Table 9-6 Video capture card manufacturers

OPTICAL STORAGE TECHNOLOGY

A+ ESS
1.1

A+
220-602
1.1

CDs and DVDs are popular storage media for multimedia data, and CDs are the most popular way of distributing software. Both DVD and CD technologies use patterns of tiny pits on the surface of a disc to represent bits, which a laser beam can then read. This is why they are called optical storage technologies. CD (compact disc) drives use the CDFS (Compact Disc File System) or the UDF (Universal Disk Format) file system, and DVD drives use the newer UDF file system.

Windows supports both file systems, which include several standards used for audio, photographs, video, and other data. Most CD drives support several CDFS formats, and most DVD drives support several UDF formats and the CDFS format for backward compatibility. In this section, you will learn about the major optical storage technologies, including their similarities and differences, their storage capacities, and variations within each type.

USING CDs

Of the multimedia components discussed in this chapter, the most popular is the CD drive. CDs are used to distribute software, sound files, and other multimedia files. CD drives are read-only devices or read/writable.

During the manufacturing process, data can be written to a CD only once because the data is actually embedded in the surface of the disc. Figure 9-26 shows a CD surface laid out as one continuous spiral of sectors of equal length that hold equal amounts of data. If laid out in a straight line, this spiral would be 3.5 miles long. The surface of a CD stores data as pits and lands. Lands are raised areas or bumps, and pits are recessed areas on the surface; each represents either a 1 or a 0, respectively. The bits are read by the drive with a laser beam that distinguishes between a pit and a land by the amount of deflection or scattering that occurs when the light beam hits the surface.

Figure 9-26 The spiral layout of sectors on a CD surface

During manufacturing, the plastic CD is imprinted with lands and pits (the process is called burning the CD) and then covered with a thin coat of aluminum (see Figure 9-27). An acrylic surface is added to protect the data, and finally a label is imprinted on the top of the CD.

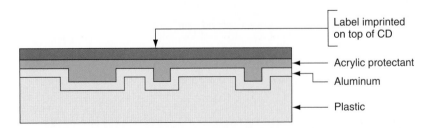

Figure 9-27 A CD is constructed of plastic, aluminum, and acrylic

When a CD drive reads a CD, a small motor with an actuator arm moves the laser beam to the sector on the track it needs to read. If the disc were spinning at a constant speed, the speed near the center of the disc would be greater than the speed at the outer edge. However, the laser beam needs to read each sector at the same constant speed. To create this effect of constant speed as the disc turns, called constant linear velocity (CLV), the CD drive uses a mechanism that slows down the disc when the laser beam is near the center of the disc, and speeds up the disc when the laser beam is near the outer edge. Thus, the beam is over a sector for the same amount of time, no matter where the sector is.

The transfer rate of the first CD drives was about 150 kilobytes per second of data (150 KBps), with the rpm (revolutions per minute) set to 200 when the laser was near the center of the disc and 500 at the outer edge. This transfer rate was about right for audio CDs. To show video and motion without a choppy effect, however, the speed of the drives was increased to double speed (150KBps x 2), quad speed (150KBps x 4), and so on. CD drives with speeds at 52x and 56x (52 and 56 times the audio speed) are not uncommon now. Audio CDs must still drop to the original speeds of 200 to 500 rpm and a transfer rate of 150 KBps.

 Notes

When you choose a CD drive, look for the multisession feature, which means that the drive can read a disc that has been created in multiple sessions. To say a disc was created in **multisessions** means that data was written to the disc at different times rather than in a single long session.

Tip

Some CD drives have power-saving features controlled by the device driver. For example, when the drive waits for a command for more than five minutes, it enters Power Save Mode, causing the spindle motor to stop. The restart is automatic when the drive receives a command.

Some later CD drives use CLV technology in combination with constant angular velocity (CAV). With CAV, the disc rotates at a constant speed, just as is done with hard drives.

CD-ROM, CD-R, AND CD-RW

If a CD drive can only read a CD and not write to it, the drive is called a CD-ROM drive. Two types of CD drives that can record or write to a CD are CD-R (CD-recordable) drives and CD-RW (CD-rewritable) drives, the latter of which allow you to overwrite old data with new data. CD-RW drives have made CD-R drives outdated.

You can buy three different kinds of discs: a regular CD disc (purchased with data already burned on it), a CD-R disc (to write to once), or a CD-RW disc (to write and overwrite). CD-RW discs cost more than CD-R discs. You can tell the difference between a CD and a CD-R or CD-RW disc by the color of the bottom of the disc. CD-R and CD-RW discs are blue, black, or some other color, and CDs are silver. A CD-RW drive can burn either a CD-R or CD-RW disc, but for the drive to overwrite old data, you must use a more expensive CD-RW disc. One drawback of using CD-RW discs is that these discs cannot be read by some older CD-ROM drives or audio CD players.

 Notes

CD-RW discs are useful in developing CDs for distribution. A developer can create a disc, test for errors, and rewrite to the disc without wasting many discs during development. After the disc is fully tested, CD-R discs can be burned for distribution. These discs cost less than CD-RW discs and are more likely to work with older CD drives.

A+ ESS
1.1

A+
220-602
1.1

APPLYING CONCEPTS

Windows XP can burn a CD without any extra software installed. It's very simple; first select all files you want to burn on the CD. To do that, right-click a file and select Send To from the shortcut menu, or you can drag and drop the file onto the CD-RW drive. Then select CD-RW drive (see Figure 9-28). After all files are selected, the next step is to burn the CD. Using My Computer, double-click the CD-RW drive. The files you have selected will appear in the right pane (see Figure 9-29). To burn the CD, click **Write these files to CD**.

If you plan to burn a lot of CDs or want to create music or video CDs, you might want to use software designed for that purpose to make your job easier. Some CD-RW drives come bundled with burn software. One example is Nero by Nero Inc. (*www.nero.com*).

When purchasing a CD-R/RW drive, know that some drives are multisession drives, and some are not. Also many CD-RW drives can also read a DVD. These drives are called combo drives, and are becoming popular as the prices of optical drives continue to drop.

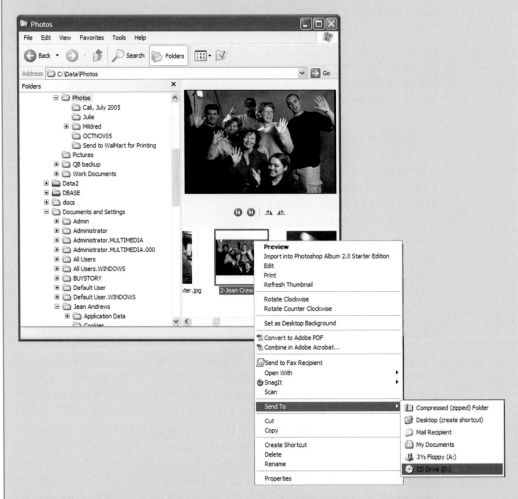

Figure 9-28 Using Windows XP, the first step to burn a CD is to select files for the CD

A+ ESS
1.1

A+
220-602
1.1

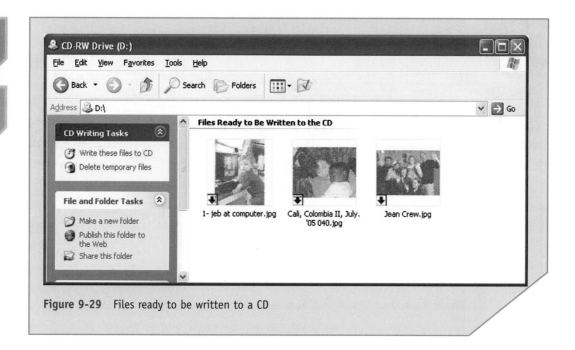

Figure 9-29 Files ready to be written to a CD

HOW AN OPTICAL DRIVE CAN INTERFACE WITH THE MOTHERBOARD

When you purchase a CD or DVD drive, consider how the drive will interface with the system. Optical drives can interface with the motherboard in several ways:

- Using a parallel ATA interface (also called an EIDE interface); the drive can share an EIDE connection and cable with another drive. However, know that if the other drive is a hard drive, hard drive performance might suffer. Parallel ATA is the most popular interface method for CD and DVD drives, and is also used by tape drives and Zip drives.
- Using a serial ATA interface (also called a SATA interface); the drive is the only drive on the serial ATA cable. Serial ATA optical drives are not yet commonplace, but are expected to eventually be more popular than parallel ATA drives.
- Using a SCSI interface with a SCSI host adapter.
- Using a portable drive and plugging into an external port on your PC, such as a USB port, FireWire port, or SCSI port.

INSTALLING A CD DRIVE

A+ ESS
1.1
1.2

Once installed, the CD or CD-RW drive becomes another drive on your system, such as drive D or E. After it is installed, you access it just like any other drive by typing D: or E: at the command prompt, or by accessing the drive through Windows Explorer or My Computer.

Currently, the most popular interface for an optical drive is parallel ATA, also called EIDE. Figure 9-30 shows the rear of an EIDE CD drive. Note the jumper bank that can be set to cable select, slave, or master. Recall from Chapter 7 that, for EIDE, there are four choices for drive installations: primary master, primary slave, secondary master, and secondary slave. If the drive will be the second drive installed on the cable, then set the drive to slave. If the drive is the only drive on

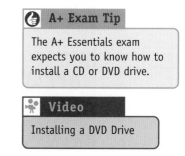

A+ Exam Tip

The A+ Essentials exam expects you to know how to install a CD or DVD drive.

Video

Installing a DVD Drive

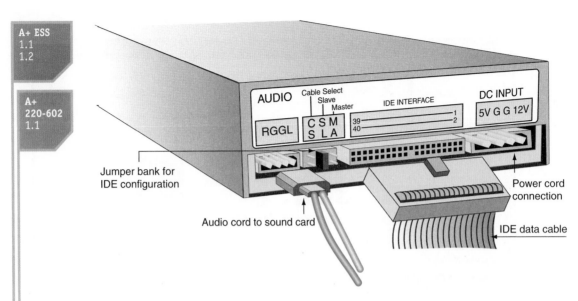

Figure 9-30   Rear view of an EIDE CD drive

the cable, choose master, because single is not a choice. The cable select setting is used if a special EIDE cable-select cable determines which drive is master or slave. If the CD drive shares an IDE channel with a hard drive, make the hard drive the master and the CD drive the slave.

> **Notes**
>
> Computer standards can have confusing and often contradicting names. To be correct, the standard for the drive interface in Figure 9-30 is parallel ATA, but the industry loosely uses the term EIDE to describe the standard. And sometimes a manufacturer uses an incorrect term to describe its products. Look at Figure 9-30 where the manufacturer labeled its CD drive's interface as an IDE connection when it really meant an EIDE connection. You should also know that most motherboard manufacturers label their EIDE connections as IDE connections.

> **Notes**
>
> For ATA/100 hard drives and above, you use an 80-conductor IDE cable for the hard drive on one channel and a regular 40-conductor cable for the CD drive on the other channel.

When given the choice of putting the CD drive on the same cable with a hard drive or on its own cable, choose to use its own cable. A CD drive that shares a cable with a hard drive can slow down the hard drive's performance. Most systems today have two EIDE connections on the motherboard, probably labeled IDE1 and IDE2, so most likely you will be able to use IDE2 for the CD drive.

APPLYING CONCEPTS   Follow these general steps to install a CD or DVD drive, using safety precautions to protect the system against ESD:

1. A computer case has some wide bays for DVD and CD drives and some narrow ones for hard drives, Zip drives, and floppy drives. Open the case and decide which large bay to use for the drive. If you use the top bay, the drive will be up and out of the way of other components inside the case.

A+ ESS
1.1
1.2

A+
220-602
1.1

2. Older cases use screws to secure the drive to the sides of the bay, and some bays have a clipping mechanism to secure the drive. The bay in Figure 9-31 has a clipping mechanism. For this bay, using two fingers, squeeze the two clips on each side of the bay together to release them and pull them forward. Remove the faceplate from the front of the bay.

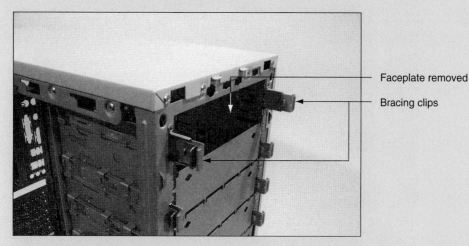

Faceplate removed

Bracing clips

Figure 9-31   To prepare a large bay for an optical drive, punch out the faceplate and pull the bracing clips forward

3. Slide the drive into the bay (see Figure 9-32). To see how far to push the drive into the bay, align it with the front of the case, as shown in Figure 9-33.

Figure 9-32   Slide the optical drive into the bay

Figure 9-33 To judge how far to insert the optical drive in the bay, align it with the front of the case

4. To secure the drive, push the clips back into position. For bays that use screws, put two screws on each side of the drive, tightening the screws so the drive can't shift, but avoiding overtightening them. Use the screws that come with the drive; screws that are too long can damage the drive. If necessary, buy a mounting kit to extend the sides of the drive so that it fits into the bay and attaches securely.

5. Connect a power cord to the drive.

6. For EIDE drives, connect the 40-pin cable to the IDE motherboard connector and the drive, being careful to follow the pin 1 rule: Match the edge color on the cable to pin 1 on both the adapter card and the drive. Generally, the colored edge is closest to the power connector.

7. Attach one end of the audio cord to the drive and the other end to the sound card or, for onboard sound, to the motherboard. Figure 9-34 shows an audio cord connected to the motherboard.

Figure 9-34 The audio cable connected to the audio connector on the motherboard; the other end of the cable is connected to the optical drive

A+ ESS
1.1
1.2

A+
220-602
1.1

9

8. Some drives have a ground connection, with one end of the ground cable attaching to the computer case. Follow the directions included with the drive.

9. Check all connections and turn on the power. Press the eject button on the front of the drive. If it works, then you know power is getting to the drive. Put the case cover back on.

10. Turn on the PC. Windows launches the Found New Hardware Wizard. Windows supports EIDE CD drives using its own internal drivers without add-on drivers, so the installation of drivers requires little intervention on your part. If the Found New Hardware Wizard does not launch, go to Control Panel and double-click the **Add Hardware** icon to launch the Add New Hardware Wizard. Click **Next** when you are prompted to begin installing the software for the new device. Complete the installation by following the directions of the Add New Hardware Wizard.

11. The drive is now ready to use. Press the eject button to open the drive shelf, and place a CD or DVD in the drive. Now access the disc using Windows Explorer.

> **✏ Notes**
>
> If you have a problem reading a CD, verify that you placed the CD in the tray label-side-up and that the format is compatible with your drive. If one CD doesn't work, try another—the first CD might be defective or scratched. When installing an optical drive that burns CDs or DVDs, after you have verified the drive can read a disc, if you are using Windows XP, you can burn a CD to verify that function. If burning software came bundled with the drive, now is the time to install it.

> **✏ Notes**
>
> A CD drive can be set so that when you insert a CD, software on the CD automatically executes, a feature called Autorun or Autoplay. To turn the feature on using Windows 9x/Me, open **Device Manager**, right-click the CD drive, and select **Properties**. In the Properties dialog box, select the **Settings** tab and then select **Auto insert notification**. For Windows XP, many options for managing content on CDs are available. To customize how Windows XP handles a CD, open **My Computer**, right-click the drive, and select **Properties** from the shortcut menu. The CD drive Properties dialog box opens; click the **Autoplay** tab (see Figure 9-35).
>
> To prevent a CD from automatically playing when Autoplay is enabled, hold down the Shift key when inserting the CD.

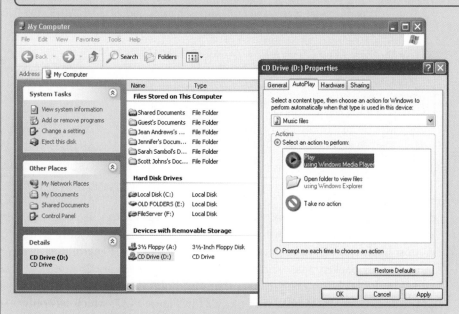

Figure 9-35 For Windows XP, use My Computer to tell the OS how to handle the Autoplay feature for your CD drive

USING DVDs

For years, the multimedia industry struggled to come up with an inexpensive storage media that would conveniently hold a full-length movie. That goal was met by more than one technology, but the technology that has clearly taken the lead is DVD (digital video disc or digital versatile disc); see Figure 9-36. It takes up to seven CDs to store a full-length movie, but it only requires one DVD. A DVD can hold 8.5 GB of data, and if both the top and bottom surfaces are used, it can hold 17 GB of data, which is enough for more than eight hours of video storage. Recall that DVD uses the Universal Disk Format (UDF) file system.

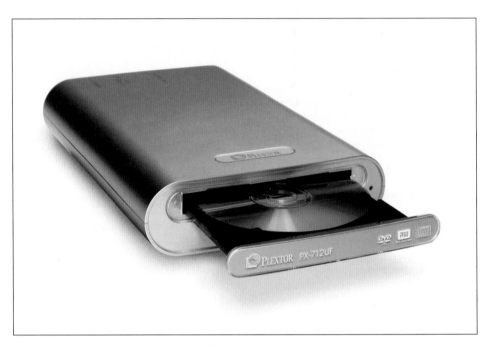

Figure 9-36   This external DVD drive by Plextor can use an IEEE 1394 or Hi-Speed USB connection and supports several speeds and read/write standards, including 8X DVD+R, 16X DVD+R/RW, 12X DVD-ROM, 16X CD-R write, 48X CD-RW rewrite, and 40X CD read

---

📝 **Notes**

The discrepancy in the computer industry between one billion bytes (1,000,000,000 bytes) and 1 GB (1,073,741,824 bytes) exists because 1 KB equals 1,024 bytes. Even though documentation might say that a DVD holds 17 GB, in fact it holds 17 billion bytes, which is only 15.90 GB.

DISTINGUISHING BETWEEN A DVD AND A CD

When you look at the surface of a CD and a DVD, it is difficult to distinguish between the two. They both have the same 5-inch diameter and 1.2-mm thickness, and the same shiny surface. However, a DVD can use both the top and bottom surface for data. If the top of the disc has no label, data is probably written on it, and it is most likely a DVD. Because a DVD uses a shorter wavelength laser, it can read smaller, more densely packed pits, which increases the disc's capacity. In addition, a second layer is added to the DVD, an opaque layer that also holds data and almost doubles the capacity of the disc. Compare the drawing of a CD in Figure 9-27, which has only a single layer of data on the bottom of the disc to the drawing of a DVD in Figure 9-37, in which the DVD has double layers on both the top and bottom.

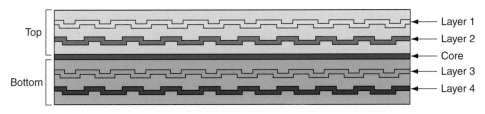

Figure 9-37 A DVD can hold data in double layers on both the top and bottom of the disc yielding a maximum capacity of 17 GB

STORAGE ON A DVD

The different amounts of data that can be stored on a DVD depend on these factors:

Single-sided, single-layer DVD can hold 4.7 GB of data

Single-sided, double-layer DVD can hold 8.5 GB of data

Double-sided, single-layer DVD can hold 9.4 GB of data

Double-sided, double-layer DVD can hold 17 GB of data

A DVD-ROM drive should be able to read a DVD that uses any one of the four methods of storing data.

Audio data is stored on a DVD in Dolby AC-3 compression or Surround Sound format discussed earlier in the chapter. For video data, DVD uses MPEG-2 video compression and requires MPEG-2 decoder software to decompress and decode the DVD compressed data. Current DVD drives use MPEG decoder software that comes bundled with the drive, and Windows XP has its own internal decoder software. For earlier DVD drives, this MPEG software was stored as firmware on an MPEG decoder card that came bundled with the DVD drive. The MPEG decoder card and the drive were installed at the same time. For detailed instructions for installing a DVD drive and decoder card, see the online content, "Installing a DVD Drive and MPEG Decoder Card."

DVD STANDARDS

Besides DVD-ROM drives that read DVDs, some DVD drives can write to DVD discs. Table 9-7 describes the DVD standards used for reading and writing. All have similar but

DVD Standard	Description
DVD-ROM	Read-only. A DVD-ROM drive can also read CDs.
DVD-R	DVD recordable. Uses a similar technology to CD-R drives. Holds about 4.7 GB of data.
DVD-R Dual Layer (DL)	DVD recordable in two layers. Doubles storage to 8.5 GB of data on one surface.
DVD-RW	Rewritable DVD. Also known as erasable, recordable device. Media can be read by most DVD-ROM drives.
DVD+R	DVD recordable is similar to and competes with DVD-R. Holds about 4.7 GB of data.
DVD+R Double Layer (DL)	DVD recordable in two layers. Doubles storage to 8.5 GB of data on one surface.
DVD+RW	Rewritable DVD. Uses DVD+R technology.
DVD-RAM	Recordable and erasable. DVD-RAM discs are sometimes stored in cartridges. The standard is supported by Toshiba, Hitachi, and Panasonic, who say future DVD-RAM discs will hold up to 50 GB of data.

Table 9-7 DVD standards

A+ ESS
1.1

not identical features, so compatibility of standards is an issue. Most DVD drives support several competing standards. When buying a DVD drive, look for the standards it supports and also look for its ability to burn CDs.

To be sure your DVD burner is compatible with most discs, choose one that supports both DVD-R and DVD+R formats. For rewriteable formats, the best DVD burners sup-

A+
220-602
1.1

port DVD-RW and DVD+RW. (DVD-RAM is not yet that common.) When selecting a DVD drive, also consider the write-once speeds and the rewriteable speeds. Current maximum speeds for write-once are 16X for DVD-R SL and DVD+R SL, 6X for DVD-R DL, and 8X for DVD+R DL. Current maximum speeds for rewritable burners are 6X for DVD-RW, 8X for DVD+RW, and 12X for DVD-RAM.

> **⏱ A+ Exam Tip**
>
> The A+ Essentials exam expects you to know about the drive speeds and media types of CD and DVD drives.

> **✎ Notes**
>
> A DVD combo drive supports many formats and speeds. For example, the Plextor PX-716SA Dual Layer DVD Writer supports DVD+R, DVD-R, DVD+RW, DVD-RW, CD-R, and CD-RW. It has double layer capability, burns at 6X to 48X speeds, and uses a serial ATA interface to the motherboard.

Two new and competing DVD formats are HD-DVD (high-density DVD) and Blu-ray Disc, both using blue laser formats. HD-DVD can hold up to 30 GB of data, and Blu-ray can hold up to 50 GB of data. Each standard is backed by a strong consortium of industry leaders, and both groups claim to be the solution for the confusing and complex DVD standards that plague the current market. For more information about HD-DVD, see *www.dvdsite.org*, and for information about Blu-ray, see *www.blu-raydisc.com*.

INSTALLING A DVD DRIVE

A+ ESS
1.1
1.2

A DVD drive looks like a CD drive and is installed the same way. Instructions for installing an optical drive are given earlier in the chapter, and there's no need to repeat them here.

Figure 9-38 shows the front and rear of a DVD drive. Just as with a CD drive, you will need to connect the power cord, EIDE data cable, and audio cord to the drive. This DVD drive has two connectors for the audio cord. The 4-pin connector is used for analog sound and the 2-pin connector is used for digital sound. Most often you'll use the 4-pin analog connection to connect to a sound card or to the motherboard. The 2-pin connector is seldom used because Windows XP transfers digital sound from the drive to the sound card without the use of a direct cable connection.

A+ ESS
1.1
1.2

A+
220-602
1.1

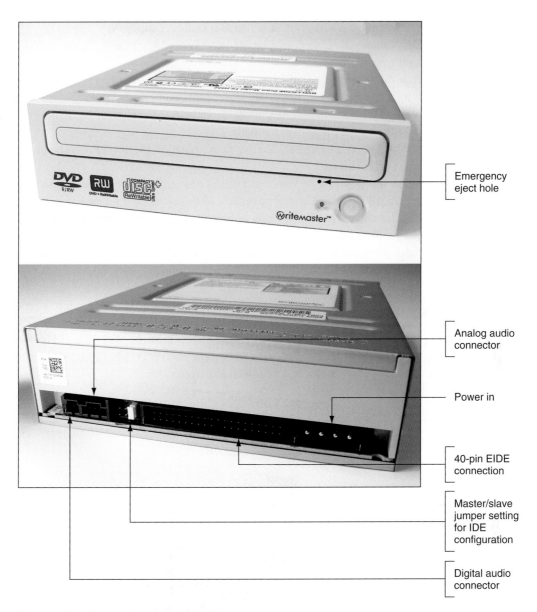

Emergency
eject hole

Analog audio
connector

Power in

40-pin EIDE
connection

Master/slave
jumper setting
for IDE
configuration

Digital audio
connector

Figure 9-38   Front and rear of a DVD drive

A+ ESS
1.1
1.2
1.4

A+
220-602
1.1
1.2
1.3

CARING FOR OPTICAL DRIVES AND DISCS

Most problems with CD and DVD discs are caused by dust, fingerprints, scratches, surface defects, or random electrical noise. Also, a CD or DVD drive will not properly read a CD or DVD when the drive is standing vertically, such as when someone turns a desktop PC case on its side to save desk space.

Use these precautions when handling CDs or DVDs:

- ◢ Hold the disc by the edge; do not touch the bright side of the disc where data is stored.
- ◢ To remove dust or fingerprints, use a clean, soft, dry cloth. Don't wipe the disc in a circular motion. Always wipe from the center of the disc out toward the edge.
- ◢ Don't paste paper on the surface of a CD. Don't paste any labels on the top of the CD, because this can imbalance the CD and cause the drive to vibrate. You can label a CD using a felt-tip pin. Don't label a DVD if both sides hold data.

A+ ESS
1.1
1.2
1.4

A+
220-602
1.1
1.2
1.3

◢ Don't subject a disc to heat or leave it in direct sunlight.

◢ Don't make the center hole larger.

◢ Don't bend a disc.

◢ Don't drop a disc or subject it to shock.

◢ If a disc gets stuck in the drive, use the emergency eject hole to remove it. Turn off the power to the PC first. Then insert an instrument such as a straightened paper clip into the hole to eject the tray manually.

◢ When closing a CD or DVD tray, don't push on the tray. Press the close button on the front of the drive.

◢ Don't use cleaners, alcohol, and the like on a disc unless you use a cleaning solution specifically designed for optical discs like the cleaning kit in Figure 9-39. Using this kit, you can spray the cleaning solution on a disc and then wipe it off with the soft purple cloth. To fix a scratch on a disc, use the repair solution made of aluminum oxide. Apply a small amount to the scratch and gently rub it with the yellow cloth. Then clean the disc using the cleaning solution.

> **Notes**
>
> A CD, CD-R, CD-RW, or DVD is expected to hold its data for many years; however, you can prolong the life of a disc by protecting it from exposure to light.

Optical drive technologies are interesting to study. For the tech-hungry reader, I suggest you check out the animated explanation at the Web site of HowStuffWorks, Inc. (*www.howstuffworks.com*). Table 9-8 lists manufacturers of optical drives.

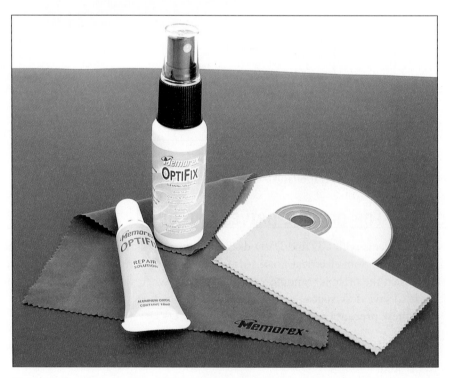

Figure 9-39 Use a cleaning solution and repair solution to clean and repair scratches on optical discs

Manufacturer	Web Site
Addonics	www.addonics.com
ASUS	www.asus.com
BenQ	www.benq.com
Creative Labs	www.creative.com
Hewlett-Packard	www.hp.com
IBM	www.ibm.com
Intel	www.intel.com
Panasonic	www.panasonic.com
Pioneer	www.pioneerelectronics.com
Plextor	www.plextor.com
Samsung	www.samsung.com
Sony Electronics	www.sonystyle.com
Toshiba	www.toshiba.com

Table 9-8 Optical drive manufacturers

HARDWARE USED FOR BACKUPS AND FAULT TOLERANCE

**A+ ESS
1.1**

**A+
220-602
1.1**

How valuable is your data? How valuable is your software? In many cases, the most valuable component on the desktop is not the hardware or the software, but the data. Think about each computer you support. What would happen if the hard drive failed? You should create backups to prepare for that situation. Whether your hard drive contains a large database or just a few word-processing files, make backups. Never keep an important file on only one medium. Make a copy to a disc, file server, or tape backup. In addition, consider keeping some of your backups in an off-site location.

Your backup policy depends on what you are backing up and your organization's policies. If you use your PC to interface with a server, for example, and all data is stored on the server and not on the PC, then you will only back up software. (The person responsible for the server usually backs up the data. You might want to check with the responsible party in your organization to make sure this is being done.) If you keep original application CDs in a safe place, and if you have multiple copies of them, you might decide not to back up the applications. In this case, if a hard drive fails, your chore is to reload several software packages.

In a business environment, if you keep important data on your PC, the easiest way to maintain a backup is to back up the data to another computer on the network. In this situation, there's always the chance that data on both the PC and the other computer can become corrupted. However, if the other computer is a file server, most likely it has its own automated backup utility to back up to either tape or a larger mainframe computer. Before you back up to the server, check with the server administrator to make sure that space is available and company policy allows you to do this.

If you keep important data on your PC in your home or small office, you need to seriously consider a sophisticated backup method. Plan for the worst case! You might decide to install a second hard drive and back up the data to this drive, or you could use an external hard drive. Another solution is a good tape backup system or other removable media such as CDs or DVDs. If your computer is networked to other computers, you can back up to another computer on the network. Of all the backup methods, backing up to another computer on a LAN is probably the simplest.

If you travel a lot, keeping good backups of data on your notebook computer might be a problem. Several Internet companies have solved this backup-on-the-go problem by providing remote backup services over the Internet. In a hotel room or other remote location, connect to the Internet and back up your data to a Web site's file server. If data is lost, you can easily recover it by connecting to the Internet and logging on to your backup service Web site. Two online backup services are @ Backup (*www.backup.com*) and Remote Backup Systems (*www.remote-backup.com*). Also, some high-end notebooks have two hard drives installed; you can use one to back up the other.

> **Notes**
>
> For backing up large amounts of data to a file server or other media, invest in backup software such as Ghost by Symantec (*www.symantec.com*) or PC BackUp by StompSoft (*www.stompsoft.com*).

Regardless of the backup method you use, back up the data after about four to ten hours of data entry. For a small office, this might mean you should make backups every night.

This section first discusses using tape drives and then using removable drives for backups.

TAPE DRIVES

Tape drives (see Figure 9-40) are an inexpensive way of backing up an entire hard drive or portions of it. Tape drives are more convenient and less expensive for backups than CDs, DVDs, or flash drives. Tapes currently have capacities of 20 to 800 GB compressed and come in several types and formats. Although tape drives don't require that you use special backup software to manage them, you might want to invest in specialized backup software to make backups as efficient and effortless as possible. Many tape drives come with bundled software, and Windows offers a Backup utility that can use tape drives. Several of the more common standards and types of tape drives and tapes are described in this section.

Figure 9-40 This Quantum Travan 40 tape drive holds up to 40 GB of data; it comes with backup software, data cartridge, USB 2.0 cable, power supply, power cord, and documentation

The biggest disadvantage of using tape drives is that data is stored on tape by sequential access; to read data from anywhere on the tape, you must start at the beginning of the tape and read until you come to the sought-after data. Sequential access makes recovering files slow and inconvenient, which is why tapes are not used for general-purpose data storage.

A+ ESS
1.1

A+
220-602
1.1

Table 9-9 lists some manufacturers of tape drives.

Manufacturer	Web Site
DLT	www.dlttape.com
Exabyte	www.exabyte.com
Hewlett Packard	www.hp.com
Imation	www.imation.com
Iomega	www.iomega.com
Quantum Corporation	www.quantum.com
Seagate	www.seagate.com
Sony	www.sony.com

Table 9-9   Tape drive manufacturers

HOW A TAPE DRIVE INTERFACES WITH A COMPUTER

A tape drive can be external or internal. An external tape drive costs more but can be used by more than one computer. A tape drive can interface with a computer in these ways:

▲ An external or internal drive can use a SCSI bus. This method works well if the tape drive and the hard drive are on the same SCSI bus, which contains a data pass-through just to the SCSI system.

▲ An external or internal drive can use a USB connection, its own proprietary controller card, or a parallel port.

▲ An internal drive can use the parallel ATA or serial ATA interface.

Currently, the most popular tape drive interfaces for internal drives are parallel ATA, SCSI, and serial ATA; for external drives, USB and SCSI are the most popular, and external serial ATA tape drives are expected to be available soon. Figure 9-41 shows the rear of a parallel ATA tape drive. You can see the connections for a power supply and a 40-pin IDE cable as well as jumpers to set the drive to master, slave, or cable select. This setup is similar for any EIDE device.

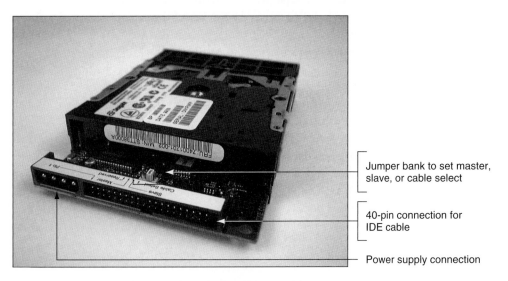

Jumper bank to set master, slave, or cable select

40-pin connection for IDE cable

Power supply connection

Figure 9-41   The rear of a parallel ATA (IDE ATAPI) tape drive

📝 **Notes**

When installing a parallel ATA tape drive, don't put the drive on the same IDE data cable as the hard drive, or it might hinder the hard drive's performance. A typical configuration is to install the hard drive as the sole device on the primary IDE channel and let a CD or DVD drive and tape drive share the second channel. Then, you can set the optical drive to master and the tape drive to slave on that channel.

THE TAPES USED BY A TAPE DRIVE

Tape drives accommodate one of two kinds of tapes: full-sized data cartridges are $4 \times 6 \times \frac{5}{8}$ inches, and the smaller minicartridges, like the one in Figure 9-42, are $3\frac{1}{4} \times 2\frac{1}{2} \times \frac{3}{5}$ inches. Minicartridges are more popular because their drives can fit into a standard $3\frac{1}{2}$-inch drive bay of a PC case.

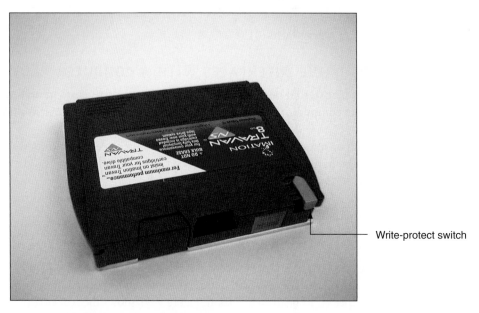

Write-protect switch

Figure 9-42 Minicartridge for a tape drive has a write-protect switch

The technology used by tape drives to write to tapes is similar to that used by floppy drives (see Chapter 7). A FAT at the beginning of the tape tracks the location of data and bad sectors on the tape. The tape must be formatted before data can be written to it. You can purchase factory-formatted tapes to save time.

When purchasing tapes, carefully match tapes to tape drives because several standards and sizes exist. One standard developed by 3M is Travan, which is backed by many leaders in the tape drive industry. There are different levels of Travan standards, called TR-1 through TR-8. Other tape standards include DDS, DAT, VXA-1, VXA-2, AIT-2, AIT-3, AIT-4, Super AIT, DLT (Digital Linear Tape), LTO, SDLT (Super DLT), SLR, and MLR QIC cartridges. Quarter-Inch Cartridge Drive Standards, Inc. (QIC at *www.qic.org*) is a trade association responsible for shaping many of these standards. One of the more current tape standards is the LTO Ultrium 3. For example, the Maxell LTO Ultrium 3 data tape cartridge can hold 400 GB of data or 800 GB of compressed data (see Figure 9-43). It can be used by the Quantum LTO-3 tape drive shown in Figure 9-44. DDS tapes and drives, a version of DAT, are also popular.

9

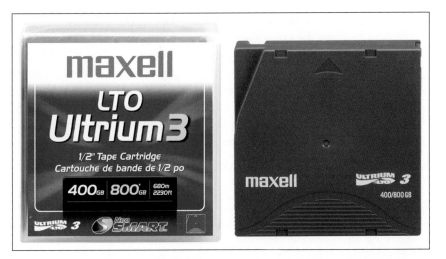

Figure 9-43 This Maxell LTO Ultrium 3 data tape cartridge can hold up to 800 GB of compressed data

Figure 9-44 Quantum Ultrium LTO-3 tape drive

Note that tape drives are likely to be able to read other formats than the formats they use for writing. For example, the Seagate Certance 40-GB tape drive writes to and reads 40-GB TR-6 tapes, and can read from 20-GB TR-5 tapes. Your best bet is to read the tape drive documentation to know what tapes the drive supports.

Here are some tips about how to care for and clean tapes and tape drives:

Tip

For an interesting photo gallery of tape media, see *www.BackupWorks.com*.

- ◢ Keep tapes away from magnetic fields.
- ◢ Don't expose tapes to heat, the sun, extreme cold, or sudden changes in temperature.

A+ ESS
1.1
1.4

A+
220-602
1.1
1.2
1.3

◢ Newer tape drives don't need cleaning as often as the older ones did. To know when and how to clean the tape drive heads, read the documentation that comes with the drive or check the Web site of the drive manufacturer. You might be told to use a cleaning tape in the drive (see Figure 9-45). Keep track of how often you use the cleaning tape, because they are only designed to work a certain number of times and then thrown away. (Look on the cleaning tape package to know how many times it can clean). Some drive heads can also be cleaned with a wet-type head-cleaning spray designed for magnetic tape such as the cleaner in Figure 9-46.

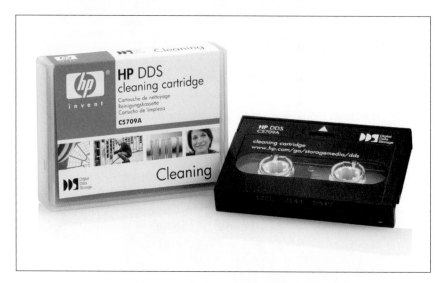

Figure 9-45 HP says this cleaning cartridge is good for 50 cleanings

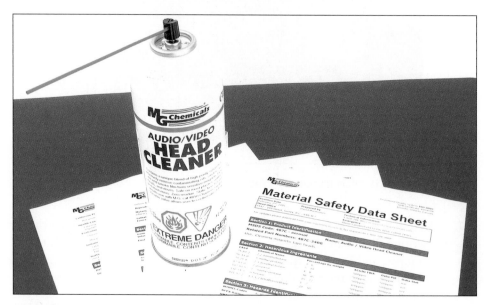

Figure 9-46 Head cleaner for magnetic tape by MG Chemicals

◢ Although you can manually clean individual tapes with head-cleaning spray, it's pretty time-consuming and probably not worth the effort. If a tape starts to give errors, buy a new one. If you are responsible for managing a lot of tapes, consider buying a magnetic tape cleaning machine that retensions, vacuums, inspects, and wipes tapes automatically. Do a google search on "magnetic tape cleaners" to turn up several cleaning devices with a wide variety of prices and features.

9

A+ ESS
1.1

A+
220-602
1.1

REMOVABLE DRIVES

A removable drive can be either an external or internal drive. Using a removable drive provides several advantages:

◢ Increases the overall storage capacity of a system
◢ Makes it easy to move large files from one computer to another
◢ Serves as a convenient medium for making backups of hard drive data
◢ Makes it easy to secure important files (To keep important files secure, keep the removable drive locked in a safe when it is not being used.)

When purchasing a removable drive, consider how susceptible the drive is when dropped. The drop height is the height from which the manufacturer says you can drop the drive without making it unusable. Also consider how long the data will last on the drive. The half-life (sometimes called life expectancy or shelf life) of the disk is the time it takes for the magnetic strength of the medium to weaken by half. Magnetic media, including traditional hard drives and floppy disks, have a half-life of five to seven years, but writable optical media such as CD-Rs have a half-life of 30 years.

TYPES OF REMOVABLE DRIVES

This section covers several of the newer and older removable drives on the market. One newer drive is the Microdrive CF introduced earlier in this chapter. The drive comes in several sizes up to 4 GB. It uses the CompactFlash II form factor, and you can purchase a PC Card adapter to make it convenient to use in a laptop computer (see Figure 9-47).

Figure 9-47 The Microdrive CF inserts into a PC Card adapter, which fits into a notebook PC Card slot

A less expensive and more convenient type of drive, ranging in size from 1 GB to 60 GB, is a flash drive that goes by many names, including a flash pen drive, jump drive, thumb drive, and key drive. These flash drives are a solid state device made of flash memory rather than a rotating disk. One popular example of a flash pen drive is the JumpDrive by Lexar Media (*www.card-media.co.uk*). The drive (see Figure 9-48) offers 64 MB to 4 GB of storage, conveniently fits on a keychain, and snaps into a USB port.

Figure 9-48   This JumpDrive holds 128 MB of data and snaps into a USB port

Another removable drive is the Iomega HDD drive by Iomega (*www.iomega.com*). The drive (see Figure 9-49) is small enough to fit into your shirt pocket and uses a USB or 1394 connection. It comes bundled with Iomega Automatic Backup and Symantec Norton Ghost software, holds from 20 GB to 250 GB of data, and is a great backup solution for a PC hard drive. Iomega says it's rugged enough that you don't have to worry about dropping it.

Figure 9-49   This 60-GB HDD portable hard drive by Iomega has a USB 2.0 and FireWire
connection and is small enough to fit in your pocket

One type of older removable drive is the Iomega $3\frac{1}{2}$-inch Zip drive, which stores 100 MB, 250 MB, or 750 MB of data on each of its disks, and has a drop height of 8 feet (see Figure 9-50). An internal Zip drive uses an EIDE interface. The external Zip drive plugs into a USB, FireWire, parallel, or SCSI port. The drive and disk look like a traditional

Figure 9-50   An internal Zip drive kit includes the IDE Zip drive, documentation,
drivers on floppy disk, and one Zip disk

A+ ESS
1.1

A+
220-602
1.1

$3\frac{1}{2}$-inch floppy disk drive and disk, but the disk is slightly larger. Zip drives can't read standard $3\frac{1}{2}$-inch floppy disks.

Another removable drive is SuperDisk, originally developed by Imation, which stores 120 MB or 240 MB of data. The drives are currently made by other manufacturers, but Imation still makes the removable disks. SuperDisk 120-MB drives are backward-compatible with double-density (720K) and high-density (1.44 MB) floppy disks, and SuperDisk 240-MB drives are backward-compatible with SuperDisk 120-MB drives and both sizes of floppy disks.

The SuperDisk is really two disk drives in one. It can use the old technology to read from and write to regular floppy disks, and it can use laser technology to read and write 120-MB or 240-MB disks. SuperDisk is up to 27 times faster than regular floppy drives. SuperDisk drives can be purchased as external (USB or parallel port) or internal drives. As internal drives, they are installed using the 40-pin EIDE connection, and not using the 34-pin floppy drive connection.

SuperDisk and Zip drives are considered fading, out-of-date technologies. For removable data storage, it's best to purchase the newer flash drive devices.

INSTALLING A REMOVABLE DRIVE

Installing an internal removable drive such as a Zip drive is similar to installing a hard drive. For an EIDE drive, set the drive to master or slave on an IDE channel. If the external or internal drive is a SCSI drive, the SCSI host adapter must already be installed and configured.

Do the following to install a removable drive:

1. Read the documentation about how to install the drive. Some USB or 1394 devices require you to install the software before plugging up the device. Other installations plug up the device and then install the software. The documentation will tell you the correct order to use. When using Windows XP, most likely no software is needed; just plug in the drive and Windows recognizes it immediately.

2. If software is needed and you install the software before you install the device, install the software now.

3. Identify the connectors. Many removable drives use either a USB port, a FireWire port, or a SCSI port for connection.

4. For a USB or FireWire device, connect the USB or FireWire cable to the USB or FireWire port. Go to Step 9.

5. For a SCSI device, with the SCSI host adapter installed, connect the SCSI cable to the drive and to the SCSI port on the host adapter.

6. For a SCSI drive, set the drive's SCSI ID. If the device is the last one on a SCSI chain, install a terminator on the device.

7. You might also need to set the host adapter to recognize an external device. See the documentation for the host adapter. (SCSI is covered in Chapter 7.)

8. Check all your connections and plug the AC power cord for the drive into a wall socket.

9. Turn on your PC. If you have not yet installed the software, do that now.

10. If you have problems, turn everything off and check all connections. Power up and try again. You can use Device Manager to uninstall the device drivers and get a fresh start.

A+ ESS
1.2

A+
220-602
1.1

FAULT TOLERANCE, DYNAMIC VOLUMES, AND RAID

Fault tolerance is a computer's ability to respond to a fault or catastrophe, such as a hardware failure or power outage, so that data is not lost. If data is important enough to justify the cost, you can protect the data by continuously writing two copies of it, each to a different hard drive. This method is most often used on high-end, expensive file servers, but it is occasionally appropriate for a single-user workstation. In addition, sometimes you can improve performance by writing data to two or more hard drives so that a single drive is not excessively used.

Collectively, the methods used to improve performance and automatically recover from a failure are called RAID (redundant array of inexpensive disks or redundant array of independent disks). There are several levels of RAID, but here we discuss only the most commonly used levels. We first look at how an operating system supports fault tolerance and improves hard drive performance, and then at how these methods are implemented with RAID hardware.

DYNAMIC VOLUMES UNDER WINDOWS

Windows 2000/XP implements fault tolerance by using a type of hard drive configuration called dynamic volumes or dynamic disks. Using this method of organizing hard drives, you can also write data across multiple hard drives to improve performance. In this part of the chapter, we first explain what basic disks and dynamic disks are and then look at different ways to implement fault tolerance under each OS.

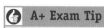
A+ Exam Tip

The A+ Essentials exam expects you to know about adding, removing, and configuring hard drives that use imaging technologies.

Basic Disks and Dynamic Disks

Windows 2000/XP offers two ways to configure a hard drive: as a basic disk or a dynamic disk. A basic disk is the same as the configuration used with DOS, Windows 9x/Me, and Windows NT. By default, Windows 2000/XP uses basic disk configuration. With basic disk configuration, you generally create partitions of a set size and then do not change them. If you want to change the size of a partition, you either have to reinstall Windows (if Windows is installed on that partition) or use special third-party software that allows you to change the size of a partition without losing your data. Within partitions, you create logical drives (sometimes called basic volumes) of set size.

Dynamic disks don't use partitions or logical drives; instead, they use dynamic volumes, which are called dynamic because you can change their size. Data to configure the disk is stored in a disk management database that resides in the last 1 MB of storage space at the end of a hard drive. DOS, Windows 9x/Me, and Windows NT cannot read dynamic disks. Dynamic disks are compatible only with Windows 2000 and Windows XP.

Notes

Because a dynamic disk requires 1 MB of storage for the disk management database, if you are partitioning a basic disk and expect that one day you might want to convert it to a dynamic disk, leave 1 MB of space on the drive unpartitioned, to be used later for the disk management database.

Ways to Use Windows Dynamic Disks

Dynamic disks can be used to improve performance or for fault tolerance. A dynamic volume is contained within a dynamic disk and is a logical volume similar to a logical drive in a basic disk. There are five types of dynamic volumes; the third type is used to improve performance and the last two types are used for fault tolerance:

▲ A simple volume corresponds to a primary partition on a basic disk and consists of disk space on a single physical disk.

A+ ESS
1.2

A+
220-602
1.1

▲ A spanned volume appears as a simple volume but can use space from two or more physical disks. It fills the space allotted on one physical disk before moving on to the next. This increases the amount of disk space available for a volume. However, if one physical disk on which data that is part of a spanned volume fails, all data in the volume is lost. Spanned volumes are sometimes called JBOD (just a bunch of drives).

▲ A striped volume (also called RAID 0) also can use space from two or more physical disks and increases the disk space available for a single volume. The difference between a spanned volume and a striped volume is that a striped volume writes to the physical disks evenly rather than filling allotted space on one and then moving on to the next. This increases disk performance as compared to access time with a spanned volume.

▲ A mirrored volume (also called RAID 1 or drive imaging) duplicates data on another drive and is used for fault tolerance. Each drive has its own volume, and the two volumes are called mirrors. If one drive fails, the other continues to operate and data is not lost. A variation of mirroring is disk duplexing, which uses two controllers, one for each drive, thus providing more fault tolerance than mirroring. Mirrored volumes are supported only by server OSs (such as Windows Server 2003 and Windows 2000 Server).

▲ A RAID-5 volume is striped across three or more drives and uses parity checking, so that if one drive fails, the other drives can re-create the data stored on the failed drive. Data is not duplicated, and, therefore, RAID-5 makes better use of volume capacity. RAID-5 volumes increase performance and provide fault tolerance. RAID-5 volumes are only supported by server OSs (such as Windows Server 2003 and Windows 2000 Server).

Figure 9-51 shows the difference between basic disk and dynamic disk organization. A basic disk or a dynamic disk can use any file system supported by Windows 2000/XP (FAT16, FAT32, and NTFS). Note that Windows 2000 Professional and Windows XP do not support the types of dynamic disks that provide fault tolerance (mirrored volume and RAID-5), so the only reasons to use dynamic disks under these OSs are to improve disk performance and to increase the size of a single volume. Dynamic drives offer little advantage for a system with only a single hard drive, and they are not supported at all on laptop computers.

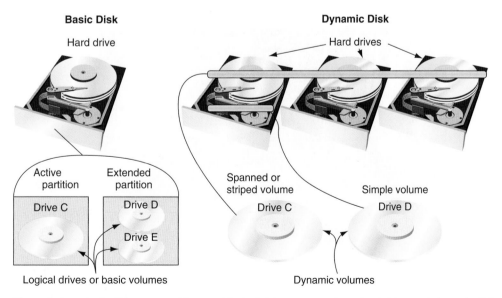

Figure 9-51 Basic disks use partitions and logical drives to organize a hard drive, and dynamic disks use dynamic volumes to organize multiple hard drives

✏ **Notes**

After Windows 2000/XP is installed, you can use the Windows 2000/XP Disk Management utility to switch from basic to dynamic or dynamic to basic, and change the file system on either type of disk. For a striped volume using Windows 2000/XP, each hard drive in the array must have the same amount of free space available to the volume and must use the same file system (FAT16, FAT32, or NTFS).

Table 9-10 summarizes which methods are used by the various OSs. The table uses the same terms used in the documentation for each OS to describe the methods supported.

Windows Version	Volume and RAID Types Supported
Windows 9x/Me	—
Windows NT Workstation	RAID 0 (striped)
Windows 2000 Professional	Simple, spanned, and striped (RAID 0)
Windows XP Professional	Simple, spanned, and striped (RAID 0)
Windows NT Server, Windows 2000 Server, and Windows Server 2003	Simple, spanned, striped (RAID 0), mirrored (RAID 1), and RAID 5

Table 9-10 Types of volumes and RAID used in different versions of Windows

HARDWARE RAID

Another way to implement RAID is to use hardware. In order to use hardware RAID, your hard drive controller or motherboard must support RAID. (The OS is not aware of a hardware RAID implementation.) A group of hard drives implementing RAID is called an array. Here are the different ways your motherboard or adapter can support a RAID array:

▲ *The motherboard IDE controller supports RAID*. Figure 9-52 shows a motherboard that has two regular IDE connectors, two serial ATA connectors that can be configured for RAID, and two parallel RAID connectors. This board supports spanning,

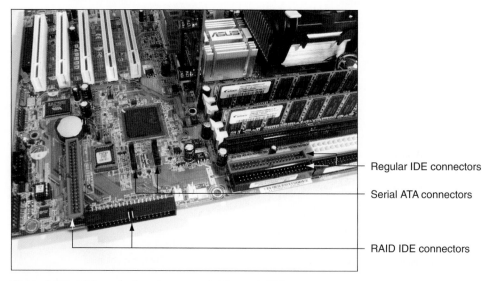

Regular IDE connectors

Serial ATA connectors

RAID IDE connectors

Figure 9-52 This motherboard supports RAID 0 and RAID 1

RAID 0, RAID 1, and a combination of RAID 0 and RAID 1. First, you install the drives and then use CMOS setup to configure the RAID array.

▲ *Install a RAID-compliant IDE controller card and disable the IDE controller on your motherboard.* Use this option if your motherboard does not support RAID. Install the controller card and drives and then use the software bundled with the controller card to configure the RAID array.

▲ *The motherboard SCSI controller supports RAID or you install a SCSI host adapter that supports RAID.* SCSI was introduced in Chapter 7.

When installing a hardware RAID system, for best performance, all hard drives in an array must be identical in brand, size, speed, and other features. As with installing any hardware, first read the documentation that comes with the motherboard or RAID controller and follow those specific directions rather than the general guidelines given here. Generally, to set up a RAID array, first install the hard drives, connecting the data cables to the RAID connectors on the motherboard or controller. Next, if your motherboard is controlling the RAID array, enter CMOS setup and verify that the RAID drives were autodetected correctly and the correct RAID type is selected. When using serial ATA for your RAID drives, you'll need to configure the serial ATA ports to hold a RAID array, as shown in Figure 9-53.

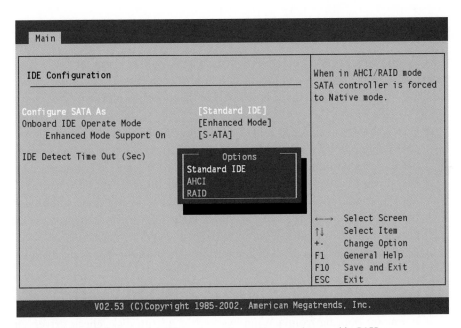

Figure 9-53 Configure serial ATA ports on the motherboard to enable RAID

When using a RAID controller card, use the software that came bundled with the card to configure your RAID array. For some RAID controllers, whether on a card or on a motherboard, a RAID driver is installed from within Windows after Windows has been installed on one of the RAID drives. After everything is set up, the OS and applications see the RAID array as a single volume such as drive D. Later, if errors occur on one of the drives in the RAID array, the RAID drivers notify the OS and thereafter direct all data to the good drives.

For file servers using RAID 5 that must work continuously and hold important data, it might be practical to use hardware that allows for hard drive hot-swapping, which means you can remove one hard drive and insert another without powering down the computer. However, hard drives that can be hot-swapped cost significantly more than regular hard drives. RAID hard drive arrays are sometimes used as part of a storage area network (SAN). A SAN is a network that has the primary purpose of providing large amounts of data storage.

A+ ESS
1.2

A+
220-602
1.1

> ✎ **Notes**
>
> For best performance and reliability, use a hardware RAID implementation instead of software RAID. Using hardware RAID, the RAID controller duplicates the data so the OS is not involved. Also, for an OS implementation of RAID, the OS active partition cannot be part of the RAID array, so you must have a non-RAID drive in your system as well as the RAID array. If this drive fails, then the system goes down regardless of the health of the RAID array. Therefore, for the best fault tolerance, use hardware RAID.

TROUBLESHOOTING MULTIMEDIA DEVICES

A+
220-602
1.2

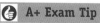 **A+ Exam Tip**

The A+ Essentials and A+ 220-602 exams expect you to be a good PC troubleshooter and present different troubleshooting scenarios for you to solve. This section is good preparation for that skill.

This section covers some troubleshooting guidelines for CD, CD-RW, DVD, DVD-RW, tape drives, and sound cards. As with other components you have learned about, remember not to touch chips on circuit boards or disk surfaces where data is stored, stack components on top of one another, or subject them to magnetic fields or ESD.

PROBLEMS WITH CD, CD-RW, DVD, OR DVD-RW INSTALLATION

Use the following general guidelines when a CD, CD-RW, DVD, or DVD-RW drive installation causes problems. These guidelines are useful even if your computer does not recognize the drive (for example, no drive D is listed in Windows Explorer):

◢ Check the data cable and power cord connections to the drive. Is the stripe on the data cable correctly aligned to pin 1? (Look for an arrow or small 1 printed on the drive. For a best guess, pin 1 is usually next to the power connector.)

◢ For an EIDE drive, is the correct master/slave jumper set? For example, if both the hard drive and the CD or DVD drive are hooked to the same ribbon cable, one must be set to master and the other to slave. If the CD or DVD drive is the only drive connected to the cable, then it should be set to single or master.

◢ For an EIDE drive, is the IDE connection on the motherboard disabled in CMOS setup? If so, enable it.

◢ If you are using a SCSI drive, are the proper IDs set? Is the device terminated if it is the last item in the SCSI chain? Are the correct SCSI drivers installed?

◢ If you are booting from a Windows 9x/Me startup disk, check drivers, including entries in Config.sys and Autoexec.bat, and verify that Mscdex.exe is in the correct directory.

◢ Is another device using the same port settings? Check system resources listed in Device Manager. Is there an IRQ conflict with the IDE primary or secondary channel or the SCSI host the drive is using?

◢ Suspect a boot virus. This is a common problem. Run a virus scan program.

PROBLEMS WHEN BURNING A CD

When trying to burn a CD, sometimes Windows refuses to perform the burn or the burned CD is not readable. Here are some things that might go wrong and what to do about them:

◢ A CD can hold about 700 MB of data. Be sure your total file sizes don't exceed this amount.

A+
220-602
1.2

◢ The hard drive needs some temporary holding space for the write process. Make sure you have at least 1 GB of free space.

◢ If something interrupts the write process before the burning is done, you might end up with a bad CD. Disable any screen saver and close other programs before you begin.

◢ If several CDs give you problems, try a different brand of CDs.

◢ The burn process requires a constant flow of data to the CD. If you have a sluggish Windows system, a CD might not burn correctly. Try using a slower burn rate to adjust for a slow data transfer rate. To slow the burn rate, right-click the CD-RW drive and select **Properties** from the shortcut menu. Click the **Recording** tab (see Figure 9-54). Choose a slower write speed from the drop-down menu. Notice in the Recording tab window you can also point to a drive different from drive C to hold temporary files for burning. Use this option if drive C is full, and another drive has more available space.

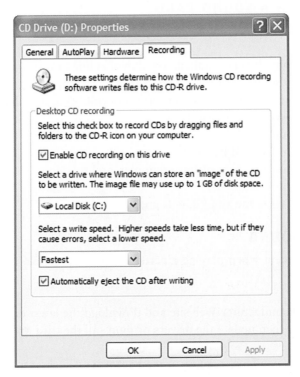

Figure 9-54 Slow down the CD-RW write speed to account for a slow Windows system

TROUBLESHOOTING SOUND PROBLEMS

Problems with sound can be caused by a problem with the sound card itself, but you might also have problems with system settings, bad connections, or a number of other factors. Here are some questions you can try to answer to diagnose the problem:

◢ Are the speakers plugged into the correct line "Out" or the "Spkr" port of the sound card (the middle port or green port)? Most problems with sound are caused by not properly connecting the speaker cables to the correct speaker ports.

◢ Is the audio cord attached between the optical drive and the analog audio connector on the sound card?

◢ Are the speakers turned on?

◢ Is the speaker volume turned up?

◢ Is the transformer for the speaker plugged into an electrical outlet on one end and into the speakers on the other end?

◢ Is the volume control for Windows turned up? Are the Mute check boxes unchecked? (To check for Windows XP, click Start, All Programs, Accessories, Entertainment, and Volume Control. To check for Windows 98, click Start, Programs, Accessories, Multimedia, and Volume Control.)

◢ Check Device Manager to verify the sound card is installed and shows no problems or conflicts.

◢ Does the sound card have a "diagnose" file on the install disk?

◢ Does the sound card have manufacturer configuration utility software installed? If so, open the utility and verify the sound card ports you are using are enabled and other settings are correct.

◢ Verify your speakers work. Try connecting them to a CD player.

PROBLEMS INSTALLING A SOUND CARD

If you have just installed a sound card, and it doesn't produce sound, try these things:

◢ You might have the wrong drivers installed. Try downloading new or updated drivers. (Once I tried to install a sound card using drivers on the accompanying CD, but the CD bundled with the card was for the wrong card. Downloading new drivers from the sound card Web site solved the problem.)

◢ Using Device Manager, uninstall the sound card and then reinstall it using the Add New Hardware applet in Control Panel.

◢ To check for a bad connection, turn off the computer, and then remove and reinstall the sound card.

◢ Replace the sound card with one you know is good.

GAMES DON'T HAVE SOUND

If your sound card works except when playing a certain really cool game, try these things:

◢ Go to the sound card manufacturer Web site and download the latest drivers for the card. Using Device Manager, update the drivers or uninstall the card and then install it using the latest drivers.

◢ Try disabling all utilities you have running in the background such as a screen saver program or antivirus software. If this solves the problem, then enable first one and then the next until you find the utility causing the problem.

◢ Try reducing sound acceleration. To do that, in Control Panel, open the **Sounds and Audio Devices** applet. On the Volume tab, Speaker settings, click **Advanced** (see Figure 9-55). The Advanced Audio Properties window opens. Click the **Performance** tab. Move the Hardware acceleration slide to the left one click. Try the game again. If it still doesn't make noise, move the slide one more click. You might have to move it all the way to the left.

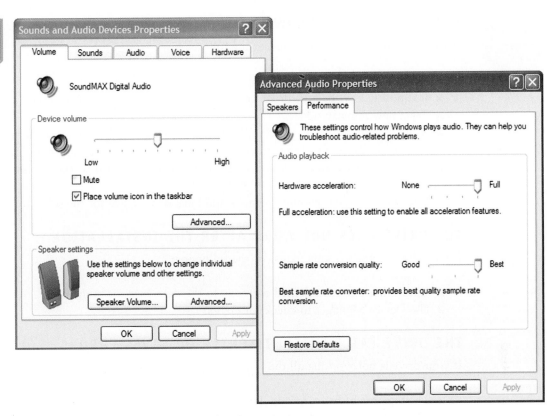

Figure 9-55 Adjust sound hardware acceleration

TROUBLESHOOTING TAPE DRIVES

The following list describes tape drive problems you might encounter and suggestions for dealing with them.

A MINICARTRIDGE DOES NOT WORK

If your minicartridge is not working, consider the following:

- ▲ If you are trying to write data, verify that the minicartridge is write-enabled.
- ▲ Are you inserting the minicartridge correctly? Check the user guide.
- ▲ Check that you are using the correct type of minicartridge. See the user guide.
- ▲ Is the minicartridge formatted? The software performs the format, which can take an hour or more.
- ▲ Use the backup software to retension the tape. Some tape drives require this, and others do not. Retensioning fast-forwards and rewinds the tape to eliminate loose spots.
- ▲ Take the minicartridge out and reboot. Try the minicartridge again.
- ▲ Try using a new minicartridge. The old one might have worn out.
- ▲ The tape might be unspooled, a problem usually caused by dust inside the drive. Blow all dust out of the drive and use a new tape.
- ▲ As with floppy disks, if the tape was removed from the drive while the drive light was on, the data being written at that time might not be readable.

DATA TRANSFER IS SLOW

If your data transfer is slow, consider the following:

- ◢ Change tape software settings for speed and data compression.
- ◢ If supported by the tape drive, try an accelerator card to improve speed.
- ◢ Try a new minicartridge.
- ◢ If the tape drive can do so, completely erase the tape and reformat it. Be sure that the tape drive can perform this procedure before you tell the software to do it.
- ◢ If you have installed an accelerator card, verify that the card is connected to the tape drive.
- ◢ Check that there is enough memory and hard drive space for the software to run.

THE DRIVE DOES NOT WORK AFTER THE INSTALLATION

If your drive is not working, consider the following:

- ◢ Check that pin 1 is oriented correctly to the data cable at both ends.
- ◢ Use Device Manager to check for errors.

THE DRIVE FAILS INTERMITTENTLY OR GIVES ERRORS

If your drive is not working all the time, consider the following:

- ◢ The tape might be worn out. Try a new tape.
- ◢ Clean the read/write head of the tape drive. See the tape drive user guide for directions.
- ◢ For an external tape drive, move the drive as far as you can from the monitor and computer case.
- ◢ Reformat the tape.
- ◢ Retension the tape.
- ◢ Verify that you are using the correct tape type and tape format.

>> CHAPTER SUMMARY

- ◢ Multimedia PCs and devices are designed to create and reproduce lifelike presentations of sight and sound.

- ◢ MMX, SSE, SSE2, SSE3, and Hyper-Threading by Intel and 3DNow!, HyperTransport!, and PowerNow! by AMD improve the speed of processing graphics, video, and sound, using improved methods of handling high-volume repetition during I/O operations. Dual-core processing is also used by Intel and AMD.

- ◢ To take full advantage of MMX, SSE, or 3DNow! technology, software must be written to use its specific capabilities.

- ◢ All computer communication is digital. To be converted to digital from analog, sound and images are sampled, which means their data is measured at a series of representative points. More accurate sampling requires more space for data storage.

- ◢ Installing a sound card includes physically installing the card, and then installing the sound card driver and sound application software.

- ◢ If only one speaker connection is used, connect it to the green sound port on the sound card, which is usually a middle port.

▲ Digital cameras use light sensors to detect light and convert it to a digital signal stored in an image file (usually JPEG format).

▲ MP3 is a version of MPEG compression used for audio files. Portable MP3 players store and play MP3 files downloaded from a PC, using internal memory and flash storage devices.

▲ A TV tuner card turns your PC or notebook into a television. A video capture card allows you to capture input from a camcorder or directly from TV. Combo cards have both abilities.

▲ CDs and DVDs are optical devices with data physically embedded into the surface of the disc. Laser beams are used to read data off the disc by measuring light reflection.

▲ The speed of CD and DVD drives slows down as the laser beam moves from the inside to the outside of the disc.

▲ Internal CD and DVD drives can have an EIDE, serial ATA, or SCSI interface, and external optical drives can use a USB port, 1394 port, or SCSI port.

▲ The most common interfaces for internal optical drives are parallel ATA and serial ATA.

▲ Data is only written to the shiny underside of a CD, which should be protected from damage. Data can be written to both sides of a DVD.

▲ A DVD can store a full-length movie and uses software or an accompanying decoder card to decode the MPEG-compressed video data and Surround Sound compressed audio.

▲ Tape drives are an inexpensive way to back up an entire hard drive or portions of it. Tape drives are more convenient for backups than removable disks.

▲ The most convenient backup media is another hard drive on the same or another computer. For traveling with a notebook, some Web sites provide online remote backup.

▲ Some examples of removable drives are Microdrive, JumpDrive, Iomega HDD, Zip drive, and SuperDisk.

▲ Five types of dynamic volumes used by Windows 2003/2000 Server are simple volume, spanned volume, striped volume (RAID 0), mirrored volume (RAID 1), and RAID 5.

▲ Windows XP supports spanned and striped (RAID 0) volumes.

▲ Hardware RAID is considered a better solution for fault tolerance than software RAID.

>> KEY TERMS

For explanations of key terms, see the Glossary near the end of the book.

array
basic disk
CDFS (Compact Disc File System)
CD-R (CD-recordable)
CD-RW (CD-rewritable)
constant angular velocity (CAV)
constant linear velocity (CLV)
data cartridge
drop height
DVD (digital video disc or digital versatile disc)
dynamic disk

dynamic volume
fault tolerance
half-life
hertz (Hz)
JPEG (Joint Photographic Experts Group)
lands
minicartridge
mirrored volume
MMX (Multimedia Extensions)
Moving Pictures Experts Group (MPEG)
MP3

multisession
pits
RAID (redundant array of inexpensive disks or redundant array of independent disks)
RAID 0
RAID 1
RAID-5 volume
sampling rate
sequential access
SIMD (single instruction, multiple data)
simple volume

>> KEY TERMS CONTINUED

solid state device (SSD)	streaming audio	TV tuner card
solid state disk (SSD)	striped volume	UDF (Universal Disk Format) file
spanned volume	Surround Sound	system
SSE (Streaming SIMD Extension)	TIFF (Tagged Image File Format)	video capture card

>> REVIEWING THE BASICS

1. What must be true before MMX, SSE, SSE2, and 3DNow! technology can improve multimedia performance on a PC?

2. What is the significance of the multisession feature on a CD drive?

3. Name three ways a CD drive can interface with a motherboard.

4. Which side of a CD contains data?

5. If a CD drive and a hard drive are sharing the same data cable in a computer system, what type of connection is the CD drive using? Which of the two drives should be set to master? Which to slave?

6. What unit of measure is used to express the sampling rate of a sound card?

7. Why must sound and video input into a PC be converted from analog to digital?

8. What is the sampling rate (in Hz) of music CDs?

9. How many samples can be stored in 8 bits?

10. What would be a quick, short test to see if a sound card was successfully installed?

11. In a system that uses a CD drive, the audio wire connects the _____ to the _____.

12. Why would you want to retension a backup tape?

13. Which holds more data, a Microdrive or a Zip drive?

14. How is the direction of data flow different for data transfers for MP3 players and digital cameras?

15. What is the significance of Sound Blaster compatibility for a sound card?

16. When using a single speaker, which port on a sound card is used to send sound out?

17. What is the difference between MPEG, JPEG, and MP3? Explain what each one is used for.

18. Name at least four features you should look for when buying a video capture card.

19. When connecting cords to the rear of a sound card and the card has a blue, red, yellow, and black port, which port is most likely to be used for the microphone?

20. In the preceding question, which port is likely to be used for sound input from a DVD player sitting beside the computer?

21. What are the three ways that data on a DVD can be decoded?

22. What is the most popular way an internal DVD drive interfaces with a motherboard?

23. What is the difference between CD, CD-R, and CD-RW drives?

24. Rank these storage methods in order of their storage capacity: DVD, floppy disk, CD, tape.

25. How many unique speakers can Surround Sound 7.1 support?

26. Which type of flash memory device is typically used on a Sony digital camera?

27. What is currently the most popular memory device used in a digital camera?

28. Of the flash memory device used in digital cameras, which uses the latest technology and holds the most data?

29. Current DVD recordable drives for personal computers can write only 8.5 GB of data on a DVD. How many layers and how many sides or surfaces of the disc are used for the data?

30. Which version of RAID is supported by Windows XP? Does this RAID version provide fault tolerance?

>> THINKING CRITICALLY

1. You have just installed a new sound card and its drivers and connected the speakers and amplifier. You insert a music CD into the drive to test the drive. Windows Media Player launches and says it is playing the CD, but you don't hear music. What do you do first?

   a. Check the volume controls on the speaker amplifier.

   b. Check the connections of the amplifier and speakers to the card.

   c. Check Device Manager for errors with the sound card.

   d. Verify that the amplifier has power.

2. You have just upgraded your computer from Windows 98 to Windows XP. Now your system has no sound. What are the first two things you do?

   a. Check Device Manager to see if the sound card is recognized and has no errors.

   b. Reinstall Windows 98.

   c. Use Device Manager to uninstall the sound card.

   d. Identify your sound card by opening the case and looking on the card for manufacturer and model.

   e. Identify your sound card by finding the documentation and driver CD that came with the card.

   f. Download Windows XP drivers for the sound card from the sound card manufacturer's Web site.

3. You have just installed a new DVD drive and its drivers, but the drive does not work. You check the power and data cables and feel comfortable that the hardware installation is correct. You then decide to reload the device drivers. What is the first thing you do?

   a. Open Control Panel and launch the Add New Hardware Wizard.

   b. Open Device Manager and choose Update Driver.

   c. Remove the data cable from the DVD drive so Windows will no longer recognize the drive and allow you to reinstall the drivers.

   d. Open Device Manager and uninstall the drive.

4. Which method of fault tolerance is the least expensive per MB of storage, disk duplexing or disk striping with parity? Explain your answer.

5. Does RAID 0 provide fault tolerance? Explain your answer.

>> HANDS-ON PROJECTS

PROJECT 9-1:   Practicing Troubleshooting Skills

1. A friend calls to say that he just purchased a new sound card and speakers to install in his PC. He wants some help from you over the phone. The PC already has a CD drive installed. Your friend installed the sound card in an expansion slot and connected the audio wire to the sound card and the CD drive. List the steps you would guide him through to complete the installation.

2. Suppose that the audio wire connection in Step 1 does not fit the connection on the CD drive. You think that if the problem is a wrong fit, perhaps you can improvise to connect audio from the CD drive directly to the sound card. Your friend tells you that the CD drive has a port for a headphone connection and the sound card has a port for audio in. How might you improvise to provide this direct connection? Check your theory using the appropriate audio wire.

3. Work with a partner. Each of you should set up a problem with sound on a PC and have the other troubleshoot it. Suggestions for a problem to set up include:

   ◢ Speaker cables disconnected

   ◢ Speaker turned off

   ◢ Speaker cable plugged into the wrong jack

   ◢ Volume turned down all the way

   As you troubleshoot the problem, write down its initial symptoms as a user would describe them, and the steps you take toward the solution.

PROJECT 9-2:   Installing a Sound Card

Install a sound card in your lab computer. Verify that the card works by playing a music CD or playing music from the Internet.

PROJECT 9-3:   Using the Internet for Research

Make a presentation or write a paper about digital cameras. Cover what features to look for when buying one and how to compare quality from one camera to another. Use the following Web sites, as well as three other Web sites in your research.

◢ *www.imaging-resource.com*

◢ *www.pcphotoreview.com*

◢ *www.steves-digicams.com*

PROJECT 9-4:   Exploring Multimedia on the Web

Do the following to investigate how to experience multimedia on the Web:

1. Go to the Adobe Web site (*www.adobe.com*) and download the latest version of Macromedia Flash Player, software used to add animation, video, and sound to Web sites.

2. Using a search engine, find at least two Flash-enabled Web sites, and then use Flash to explore these sites.

3. Go to the Microsoft Web site (*www.microsoft.com*) and download the latest version of Windows Media Player, software used to play music and video stored locally or online.

4. Use Media Player to play a music CD, a radio station on the Web, and a video clip on the Web.

5. Answer these questions:

   a. What are the two sites you found that use Macromedia Flash?

   b. What music CD did you play?

   c. What radio station did you play? What was the station's Web site URL?

   d. What video clip did you play? At which Web site did you locate the clip?

>> REAL PROBLEMS, REAL SOLUTIONS

<u>REAL PROBLEM 9-1:</u>   Using Hardware RAID

You work as a PC technician for a boss who believes you are really bright and can solve just about any problem he throws at you. Folks in the company have complained one time too many that the file server downtime is just killing them, so he asks you to solve this problem. He wants you to figure out what hardware is needed to implement hardware RAID for fault tolerance. Here are the first steps you take:

1. You check the file server's configuration and discover it has a single hard drive using a serial ATA connection with Windows Server 2003 installed. There are four empty bays in the computer case and four extra power cords.

2. You discover the server's motherboard has an empty 64-bit PCI slot. You think it might accommodate a RAID controller.

3. After doing a little searching on the Web, you find the Intel RAID Controller SRCS14L (*www.intel.com/design/servers/raid/srcs14l/*). You think it might work.

4. The next steps are to read the documentation about this controller, decide on which RAID configuration you should use and how many and what kind of hard drives you should buy.

Complete the investigation and do the following:

1. Decide what hardware you must purchase and print Web pages showing the products and their cost.

2. What levels of RAID does this controller support? Which RAID level is best to use? Print any important information in the RAID controller documentation that supports your decisions. If you prefer, you can recommend a different RAID controller.

3. What is the total hardware cost of implementing RAID? Estimate how much time you think it will take for you to install the devices and test the setup.

PCs on a Network

In this chapter, we discuss how to connect PCs in networks and how to access resources on a network. You'll learn about the technologies used to build networks and how Windows supports and manages a network connection, including how computers are identified and addressed on a network. You'll also learn to connect a computer to a network.

Local networks are often large and complex, and few local networks exist today that are isolated from other networks. In this chapter, you'll learn how switches and routers work to manage large local networks and connect to other networks. You'll also learn how to set up and secure a wireless network. And you'll learn to troubleshoot a network connection.

PHYSICAL NETWORK ARCHITECTURES

A+ ESS
5.1

A+
220-602
5.1

In this first part of the chapter, you'll learn about the various types of networking technologies and designs. We'll first look at the different sizes of networks, the different technologies used by networks, and some networking terms. Then, we'll turn our attention to the details of the types of networks you are most likely to encounter as a PC repair technician, which include Ethernet, wireless networks, telephone networks, and the mostly outdated token ring and FDDI networks.

SIZES OF NETWORKS

A computer network is created when two or more computers can communicate with each other. Networks can be categorized by several methods, including the technology used and the size of the network. When networks are categorized by size or physical area they cover, these are the categories used:

- *PAN.* A **PAN (personal area network)** consisting of personal devices at close range such as a cell phone, PDA, and notebook computer in communication. PANs can use wired connections (such as USB or FireWire) or wireless connections (such as Bluetooth or infrared).
- *LAN.* A **LAN (local area network)** covers a small local area such as a home, office, or other building or small group of buildings. LANs can use wired (most likely Ethernet) or wireless (most likely 802.11) technologies. A LAN is used for workstations, servers, printers, and other devices to communicate and share resources.
- *MAN.* A **MAN (metropolitan area network)** covers a large campus or city. (A small MAN is sometimes called a CAN or campus area network.) Newer technologies used are wireless and Ethernet with fiber-optic cabling. Older technologies used are ATM and FDDI.
- *WAN.* A **WAN (wide area network)** covers a large geographical area and is made up of many smaller networks. The best known WAN is the Internet.

NETWORKING TECHNOLOGIES

Networking technologies have evolved over time based on the type of data the network is intended to support, the data capacity on the network, and how a network is to fit among other networks. When you study the different network technologies, much attention is given to how much data can travel over a given communication system in a given amount of time. This measure of data capacity is called **bandwidth** (or **data throughput** or **line speed**). The greater the bandwidth is, the faster the communication. In analog systems, bandwidth is the difference between the highest and lowest frequency that a device can transmit. Frequencies are measured in cycles per second, or hertz (Hz). In digital systems such as computers and computer networks, bandwidth is a measure of data transmission in bits per second (bps), thousands of bits per second (Kbps), or millions of bits per second (Mbps).

Interconnecting networks (for example, the Internet) are built using technologies that provide varying degrees of bandwidth, each serving a different purpose and following a different set of standards. Generally, the larger the network, the more bandwidth it requires, which dictates which technology is used. Table 10-1 lists bandwidth technologies, their speeds, and their uses. The table is more or less ordered from slowest to fastest bandwidth, although there is some overlap and several factors can affect the actual bandwidth of a particular network.

10

A+ ESS
5.1

A+
220-602
5.1

Technology	Maximum Throughput Speeds	Common Uses
GSM mobile telephone service	9.6 to 14.4 Kbps	Wireless technology used for mobile phones
Regular telephone (POTS, for plain old telephone service)	Up to 56 Kbps	Home and small business access to an ISP using a modem
Frame Relay	56 Kbps to 45 Mbps	Businesses that need to communicate internationally or across the country
Fractional T-1	n times 64 Kbps (where n = number of channels or portions of a T-1 leased)	Companies expecting to grow into a T-1 line, but not yet ready for a T-1
X.25	56 Kbps	Outdated technology that provided communication between mainframes and terminals
ISDN	64 Kbps to 128 Kbps	Mostly outdated small to medium-sized business access to an ISP
IDSL (ISDN Digital Subscriber Line)	128 Kbps	Home and small business access to an ISP
ADSL (Asymmetric Digital Subscriber Line)	640 Kbps upstream and up to 24 Mbps downstream	Most bandwidth is from ISP to user. Slower versions of ADSL are called ADSL Lite or DSL Lite. ISP customers pay according to a bandwidth scale. ADSL is a type of broadband technology. (Broadband refers to a networking technology that carries more than one type of signal such as DSL and telephone.)
T-1	1.544 Mbps	To connect large companies to branch offices or an ISP. E-1, which is used in Europe, is a similar technology.
SDSL (Symmetric DSL)	Up to 2.3 Mbps	Equal bandwidths in both directions
Cable modem	512 Kbps to 5 Mbps	Connects a home or small business to an ISP; is usually purchased with cable television subscription. Cable modem is a type of broadband technology that is used in conjunction with television on the same cable.
Token Ring	4 or 16 Mbps	Outdated technology once used on a LAN
T-3	45 Mbps	Large companies that require a lot of bandwidth and transmit extensive amounts of data

Table 10-1 Bandwidth technologies

A+ ESS
5.1

A+
220-602
5.1

Technology	Maximum Throughput Speeds	Common Uses
OC-1	52 Mbps	Base rate of transmission used by SONET and ATM. Multiples are called Optical Carrier levels (OCx).
802.11b wireless	Up to 11 Mbps	First 802.11 standard that was widely used, but is being replaced by 802.11g
802.11a wireless	Up to 54 Mbps	Shorter range than 802.11b, but faster
802.11g wireless	Up to 54 Mbps	Compatible with and replacing 802.11b
VDSL (Very-high-rate DSL)	Up to 200 Mbps	This latest version of DSL can be asymmetric or symmetric DSL.
Ethernet	10, 100, or 1,000 Mbps	Most popular technology for a local network. 1,000-Mbps Ethernet is called Gigabit Ethernet.
FDDI	100 Mbps	Older network backbones. FDDI is being replaced by Gigabit Ethernet.
ATM	25, 45, 155, or 622 Mbps	ATM (Asynchronous Transfer Mode) networks are used for large business networks and LAN backbones. ATM is being replaced by Gigabit Ethernet.
OC-3, OC-24, OC-256	155 Mbps, 1.23 Gbps, 13 Gbps	Internet backbones; they use optical fiber
Gigabit Ethernet	1 Gbps	Latest Ethernet standard
10-gigabit Ethernet	10 Gbps	Newest Ethernet standard expected to largely replace SONET, OC, and ATM because of its speed, simplicity, and lower cost
OC-768	40 Gbps	Currently, this is the fastest OC level.
SONET (Synchronous Optical Network)	52 Mbps to 20 Gbps	Major backbones make use of different OC levels.

Table 10-1   Bandwidth technologies (continued)

Notes

The **Institute of Electrical and Electronics Engineers (IEEE)** creates standards for computer and electronics industries. Of those standards, IEEE 802 applies to networking. For example, IEEE 802.2 describes the standard for Logical Link Control, which defines how networks that use different protocols communicate with each other. For more information on the IEEE 802 standards, see the IEEE Web site, *www.ieee.org*.

10

A+ ESS
5.1

A+
220-602
5.1

ADDITIONAL TERMS USED IN NETWORKING

Before we get into the details of network architecture, you need to know a few terms and what they mean:

▲ A node, or host, is one device on the network. It can be a workstation, server, printer, or other device.

▲ A PC makes a direct connection to a network by way of a network adapter, which might be a network port embedded on the motherboard or a network interface card (NIC), using a PCI slot, such as the one shown in Figure 10-1. In addition, the adapter might also be an external device connecting to the PC using a USB port, SCSI external port, or serial port. The adapter might provide a port for a network cable or an antenna for a wireless connection. The adapter must match the type and speed of the physical network being used, and the network port must match the type of connectors used on the network. Laptops can make connections to a network through a PC Card NIC, a built-in network port, a wireless connection, or an external device that connects to the laptop by way of a USB port. (You will learn about PC Cards in Chapter 11.)

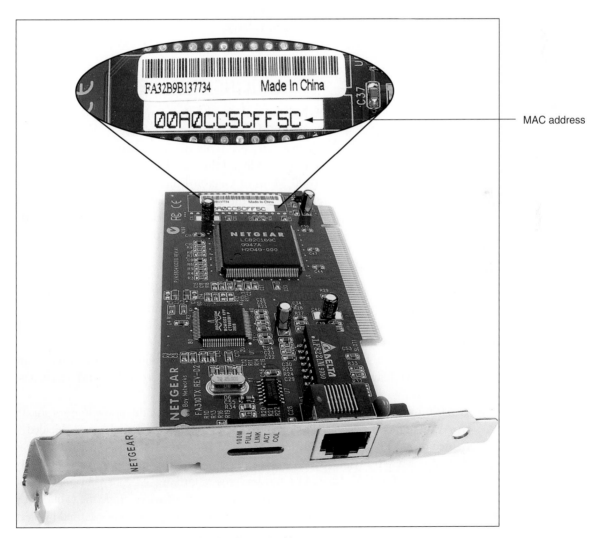

MAC address

Figure 10-1 Ethernet network card showing its MAC address

A+ ESS
5.1

A+
220-602
5.1

▲ Every network adapter (including a network card, onboard wireless, or wireless NIC) has a 48-bit (6-byte) number hard-coded on the card by its manufacturer that is unique for that adapter, and this number is used to identify the adapter on the network. The number is often written in hex and is called the MAC (Media Access Control) address, hardware address, physical address, adapter address, or Ethernet address. An example of a MAC address is 00-0C-6E-4E-AB-A5. Part of the MAC address refers to the manufacturer; therefore, no two adapters should have the same MAC address. Most likely the MAC address is written on the card, as shown in Figure 10-1.

▲ Communication on a network follows rules of communication called network protocols. Communication over a network happens in layers. The OS on one PC communicates with the OS on another PC using one set of protocols, and the network card communicates with other hardware devices on the network using another set of networking protocols. Examples of OS protocols are TCP/IP and NetBEUI, and examples of hardware protocols are Ethernet and Token Ring. You'll learn more about these protocols later in the chapter.

▲ Data is transmitted on a network in pieces called packets, datagrams, or frames. Information about the packet that identifies the type of data, where it came from, and where it's going is placed at the beginning and end of the data. Information at the beginning of the data is called a header, and information at the end of the data is called a trailer. If the data to be sent is large, it is first divided into several packets small enough to travel on the network.

A+ ESS
2.1
5.1

A+
220-602
2.1
5.1
5.3

 A+ Tip

The A+ Essentials exam expects you to be familiar with many networking terms. This chapter is full of key terms you need to know for the exam.

INTRODUCING ETHERNET

Ethernet (sometimes abbreviated ENET) is the most popular network architecture used today. The three variations of Ethernet are primarily distinguished from one another by speed: 10-Mbps Ethernet, 100-Mbps or Fast Ethernet, and 1000-Mbps or Gigabit Ethernet. In the following sections, we'll look at the several variations of Ethernet, the ways nodes on an Ethernet network can be connected, and how repeaters perform on a network.

VARIATIONS OF ETHERNET

Several variations of Ethernet have evolved over the years, which are primarily identified by their speeds and the types of cables and connectors used to wire these networks. Each variation of Ethernet can use more than one cabling method. Table 10-2 compares cable types and Ethernet versions.

As you can see from Table 10-2, the three main types of cabling used by Ethernet are twisted-pair, coaxial, and fiber-optic. Within each category, there are several variations:

▲ *Twisted-pair cable.* Twisted-pair cable is the most popular cabling method for local networks. It comes in two varieties: unshielded twisted pair (UTP) cable and shielded twisted pair (STP) cable. UTP cable is the most common and least expensive. UTP is rated by category: CAT-3 (Category 3) is less expensive than the more popular CAT-5 cable or enhanced CAT-5 (CAT-5e). CAT-6 has less crosstalk than CAT-5 or CAT-5e. STP uses a covering around the pairs of wires inside the cable that protects it from electromagnetic interference caused by electrical motors, transmitters, or high-tension lines. It costs more than unshielded cable, so it's used only when the situation demands it. Twisted-pair cable has four pairs of twisted wires for a total of eight wires and uses a connector called an

 A+ Tip

The A+ Essentials exam expects you to know the details shown in Table 10-2.

A+ ESS
2.1
5.1

A+
220-602
2.1
5.1
5.3

RJ-45 connector (RJ stands for registered jack) that looks like a large phone jack. Figure 10-2 shows unshielded twisted pair cables and the RJ-45 connector.

Cable System	Speed	Cables and Connectors	Example of Connectors	Maximum Cable Length
10Base2 (ThinNet)	10 Mbps	Coaxial uses a BNC connector		185 meters or 607 feet
10Base5 (ThickNet)	10 Mbps	Coaxial uses an AUI 15-pin D-shaped connector		500 meters or 1,640 feet
10BaseT, 100BaseT (Twisted-pair), and Gigabit Ethernet	10, 100, or 1,000 Mbps	UTP or STP uses an RJ-45 connector		100 meters or 328 feet
10BaseF, 10BaseFL, 100BaseFL, 100BaseFX, 1000BaseFX, or 1000BaseX (fiber-optic)	10, 100, or 1,000 Mbps	Fiber-optic cable uses ST or SC connectors (shown to the right) or LC and MT-RJ connectors (not shown)		500 meters up to 2 kilometers (6,562 feet)

Table 10-2 Variations of Ethernet and Ethernet cabling

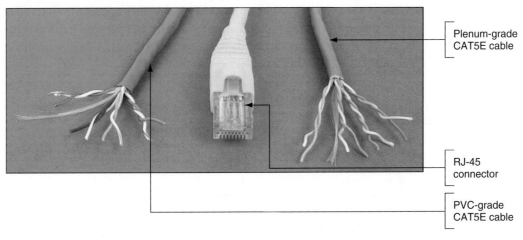

Figure 10-2 The most common networking cable for a local network is UTP cable using an RJ-45 connector

Notes

Normally, the plastic covering of a cable is made of PVC (polyvinyl chloride), which is not safe when used inside plenums (areas between the floors of buildings). In these situations, plenum cable covered with Teflon is used because it does not give off toxic fumes when burned. Plenum cable is two or three times more expensive than PVC cable. Figure 10-2 shows plenum cable and PVC cable, both of which are unshielded twisted pair CAT5e cables.

A+ ESS
2.1
5.1

A+
220-602
2.1
5.1
5.3

▲ *Coaxial cable.* **Coaxial cable** has a single copper wire down the middle and a braided shield around it (see Figure 10-3). Because it's stiff and difficult to manage, it's not as popular as twisted pair for local networking, although maximum cable lengths for coaxial cable are longer than twisted pair maximum lengths. There are two thicknesses of coaxial cables used for networking: thick and thin. Thick cabling (called RG8 cabling) is used by ThickNet Ethernet, and thin cabling (called RG58 cabling) is used by ThinNet Ethernet. Each type cable uses a different type connector, as shown in Table 10-2. The more popular of the two is thin coaxial cable using a **BNC connector**.

Other important coaxial cables you should know about are RG59, which is used for cable TV and VCR transmission and RG6, which is used for satellite dish signals and video applications requiring greater shielding than RG59.

Figure 10-3   Coaxial cable and a BNC connector are used with ThinNet Ethernet

▲ *Fiber optic.* **Fiber-optic** cables transmit signals as pulses of light over glass strands inside protected tubing, as illustrated in Figure 10-4. Fiber-optic cable comes in two types: single-mode (thin, difficult to connect, expensive, and best performing) and multimode (most popular). A single-mode cable uses a single strand of glass fiber and multimode cable uses multiple strands of glass. Both single-mode and multimode fiber-optic cables can be constructed as loose-tube cables for outdoor use or tight-buffered cable for indoor or outdoor use. Loose-tube cables are filled with gel to prevent water from soaking into the cable, and tight-buffered cables are filled with yarn to protect the fiber-optic strands, as shown in Figure 10-4.

Fiber-optic cables can use one of four connectors, all shown in Figure 10-5. The two older types are ST (straight tip) and SC (subscriber connector or standard connector). Two newer types are LC (local connector) and MT-RJ (mechanical transfer registered jack) connectors. Any one of the four connectors can be used with either single-mode or multimode fiber-optic cable.

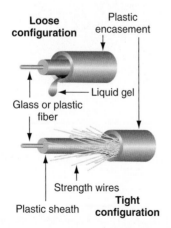

Loose configuration
Plastic encasement
Liquid gel
Glass or plastic fiber
Strength wires
Plastic sheath
Tight configuration

⚙ A+ Tip

The A+ Essentials exam expects you to know about these cable types: Plenum, PVC, UTP, CAT3, CAT5, CAT5e, CAT6, STP, single-mode fiber, multimode fiber, ST, SC, and LC.

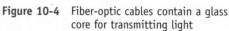

Figure 10-4   Fiber-optic cables contain a glass core for transmitting light

A+ ESS
2.1
5.1

A+
220-602
2.1
5.1
5.3

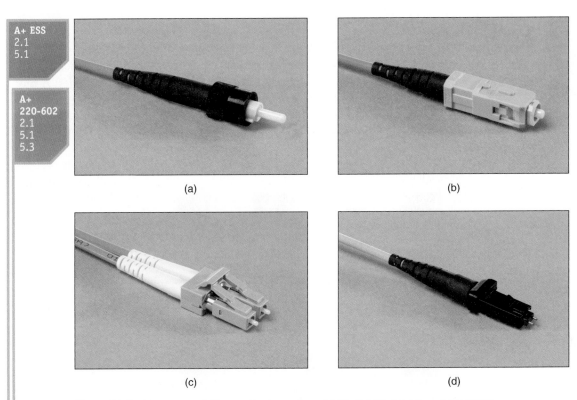

(a)

(b)

(c)

(d)

Figure 10-5 Four types of fiber-optic connectors: (a) ST, (b) SC, (c) LC, and (d) MT-RJ

Each version of Ethernet can use more than one cabling method. Here is a brief description of the types of Ethernet identified by the cabling methods they use:

▲ *10-Mbps Ethernet.* The first Ethernet specification was invented by Xerox Corporation in the 1970s, and in 1980 it was enhanced and became known as Ethernet IEEE 802.3. This type of Ethernet operates at 10 Mbps (megabits per second). This speed of Ethernet can use three different cabling methods: 10BaseT Ethernet uses twisted-pair cabling rated CAT-3 or higher and an RJ-45 connector. 10Base5 Ethernet (sometimes called ThickNet) uses thick RG8 coaxial cable with an AUI connector. 10Base2 Ethernet (sometimes called ThinNet) uses a thin RG58 coaxial cable with a BNC connector.

▲ *100-Mbps Ethernet or Fast Ethernet.* This improved version of Ethernet (sometimes called 100BaseT or Fast Ethernet) operates at 100 Mbps and uses STP or UTP cabling rated CAT-5 or higher. 100BaseT networks can support slower speeds of 10 Mbps so that devices that run at either 10 Mbps or 100 Mbps can coexist on the same LAN. Two variations of 100BaseT are 100BaseTX and 100BaseFX. The most popular variation is 100BaseTX. 100BaseFX uses fiber-optic cable.

▲ *1000-Mbps Ethernet or Gigabit Ethernet.* This up-and-coming version of Ethernet operates at 1000 Mbps and uses twisted-pair cable and fiber-optic cable. Gigabit Ethernet is currently replacing 100BaseT Ethernet as the choice for LAN technology. Because it can use the same cabling and connectors as 100BaseT, a company can upgrade from 100BaseT to Gigabit without great expense.

▲ *10-Gigabit Ethernet.* This version of Ethernet operates at 10 billion bits per second (10 Gbps) and uses fiber cable. It can be used on LANs, WANs, and MANs, and is also a good choice for backbone networks. (A backbone network is a channel whereby local networks can connect to wide area networks.)

A+ ESS
2.1
5.1

A+
220-602
2.1
5.1
5.3

ETHERNET TOPOLOGY

The topology of a network refers to the arrangement or shape used to physically connect devices on a network to one another. Ethernet networks can be configured as either a bus topology or a star topology. Figure 10-6 shows examples of bus and star topologies. A **bus topology** connects each node in a line and has no central connection point. Cables just go from one computer to the next, and then the next. A **star topology** connects all nodes to a centralized hub or switch. PCs on the LAN are like points of a star around the hub or switch in the middle, which connects the nodes on the LAN.

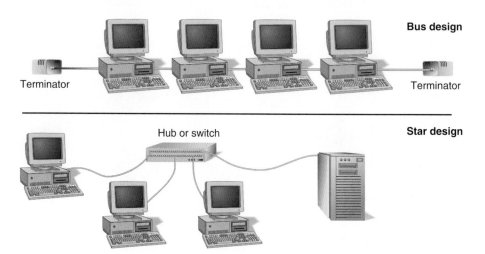

Figure 10-6 Nodes on an Ethernet network can be connected to one another in a star or bus formation

The star arrangement is more popular because it is easier to maintain than the bus arrangement. In a star topology that uses a hub, the hub passes all data that flows to it to every device connected to it. An Ethernet hub **broadcasts** the data packet to every device, as shown in Figure 10-7.

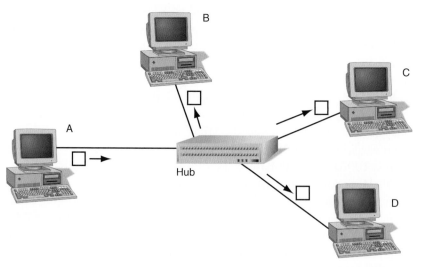

Figure 10-7 Any data received by a hub is replicated and passed on to every device connected to it

In Figure 10-7, when computer A sends data to the hub, the hub replicates the data and sends it to every device connected to it. Computers B, C, and D each get a copy of the data. It's up to these computers to decide if the data is intended for them. For this reason, a hub can generate a lot of unnecessary traffic on a LAN, which can result in slow performance when several nodes are connected to the hub.

You can think of a hub as just a pass-through and distribution point for every device connected to it, without regard for what kind of data is passing through and where the data might be going. See Figure 10-8.

Figure 10-8 A hub is a pass-through device to connect nodes on a network

A switch (see Figure 10-9) is smarter and more efficient than a hub and keeps a table of all the devices connected to it. It uses this table to determine which path to use when sending packets. The switch only passes data to the device to which the data is addressed. In the past, because switches were so much more expensive than hubs, most networks used mostly hubs and only used a switch when needed to improve a bottleneck in network performance. Now, because the prices of switches have dramatically decreased and networks built with switches are much faster than those built with hubs, most networks use all switches and no hubs.

Figure 10-9 An eight-port switch by Netgear

A+ ESS
2.1
5.1

A+
220-602
2.1
5.1
5.3

As network needs grow, you can add a switch or hub so that you can connect more devices to the network. Figure 10-10 shows an example of a network that uses three switches in sequence. The switches themselves form a bus network, but the computers connected to each switch form a star. This network configuration, which uses a logical bus for data delivery but is wired as a physical star, is an example of a **star bus topology**.

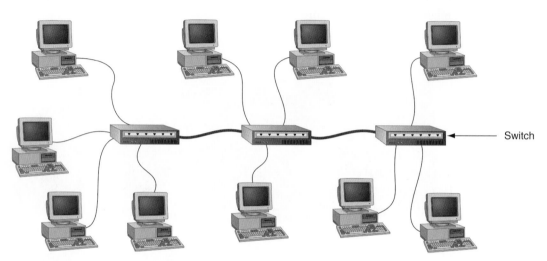

Switch

Figure 10-10   A star bus network uses more than one switch

APPLYING | CONCEPTS   PATCH CABLES, CROSSOVER CABLES, AND CABLE TESTERS

Two types of network cables can be used when building a network: a patch cable and a crossover cable. A **patch cable** (also called a straight-through cable) is used to connect a computer to a hub or switch. A **crossover cable** is used to connect two PCs (when a hub or switch is not used) to make the simplest network of all.

The difference in a patch cable and a crossover cable is the way the read and write lines are wired in the connectors at each end of the cables. A crossover cable has the read and write lines reversed so that one computer reads off the line to which the other computer writes. For older hubs, it was necessary to use a crossover cable to connect a hub to another hub. However, today you can connect a hub or switch to another hub or switch using the more common patch cables because these devices have a special port (called the uplink port) to use for the connection. Also, most switches use auto-uplinking, which means you can connect a switch to a switch using a patch cable on any port.

A patch cable and a crossover cable look identical and have identical connectors. One way to tell them apart is to look for the labeling imprinted on the cables, as shown in Figure 10-11.

If a cable is not labeled, you can use a cable tester to determine the type of cable. A cable tester can have two components. Connect each component to the ends of the cable and turn on the tester. Lights on the tester will show you if the cable is good and what type of cable you have. You'll need to read the user manual that comes with the cable tester to know how to interpret the lights.

10

A+ ESS
2.1
5.1

A+
220-602
2.1
5.1
5.3

You can also use cable testers like the one in Figure 10-12 to trace a network cable through a building. Suppose you see several network jacks on walls in a building but you don't know which jacks connect. Install a short cable in each of two jacks and then use the cable tester to test the

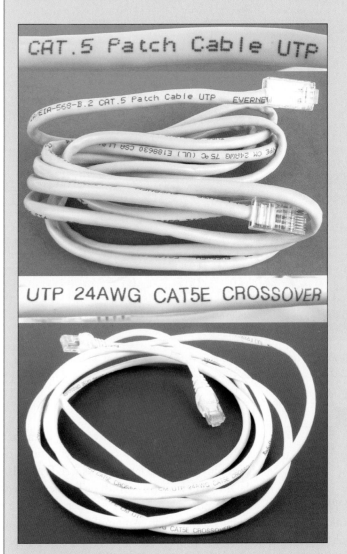

Figure 10-11 Patch cables and crossover cables look the same but are labeled differently

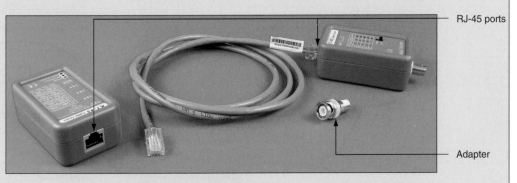

Figure 10-12 Use a cable tester pair to determine the type of cable and if the cable is good

continuity, as shown in Figure 10-13. You might damage a cable tester if you connect it to a live circuit, so before you start connecting the cable tester to wall jacks, be sure that you turn off all devices on the network.

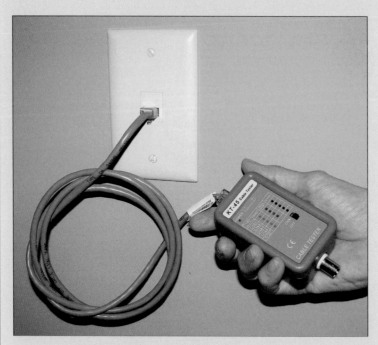

Figure 10-13   Use cable testers to trace network cables through a building

Video

Ethernet Cables

REPEATERS

Because signals transmitted over long distances on a network can weaken (in a process called attenuation), devices are added to amplify signals in large LANs (see Figure 10-14). For example, if two devices on a 100BaseT Ethernet network are more than 100 meters (328 feet) apart, amplification is required. A repeater is a device that amplifies signals on a network. There are two kinds of repeaters. An amplifier repeater simply amplifies the incoming signal, noise and all. A signal-regenerating repeater reads the signal and then creates an exact duplicate of the original signal before sending it on. Ethernet uses a signal-regenerating repeater. For the typical Ethernet network, a switch or hub acts as a signal-regenerating repeater.

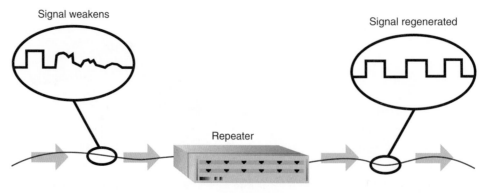

Figure 10-14   A repeater on a network restores the clarity of the signal, which degrades over a distance because of attenuation

A+ ESS
2.1
5.1
6.1

A+
220-602
2.1
5.1
6.2
6.3

WIRELESS NETWORKS

 A+ Tip

The A+ Essentials exam expects you to be familiar with these wireless technologies: 802.11, infrared, Bluetooth, and cellular.

Wireless networks, as the name implies, use radio waves or infrared light instead of cables or wires to connect computers or other devices. A **Wireless LAN (WLAN)** covers a limited geographical area and is popular in places where networking cables are difficult to install, such as outdoors, in public places, and in homes that are not wired for networks. They are also useful in hotel rooms.

Three current wireless technologies are 802.11 (also called WiFi), WiMAX, and Bluetooth. Recall from Chapter 8 that an earlier and outdated wireless technology is infrared. Although wireless networks have some obvious advantages in places where running cables would be difficult or overly expensive, wireless networks tend to be slower than wired networks, especially when they are busy. Another problem with wireless networks is security. In this section, you'll learn about the three most popular wireless technologies used primarily to transmit data. In this next section, you'll learn about some wireless telephone networks primarily dedicated to voice communication.

802.11 WIRELESS

By far, the most popular technology for desktop and notebook computer wireless connections is IEEE 802.11, first published in 1990. Most new wireless LAN devices operate under the IEEE 802.11g standard, which is backward compatible with the earlier and slower IEEE 802.11b standard. These standards are also called **Wi-Fi (Wireless Fidelity)**.

802.11g and 802.11b use a frequency range of 2.4 GHz in the radio band and have a distance range of about 100 meters. 802.11b/g has the disadvantage that many cordless phones use the 2.4-GHz frequency range and cause network interference. 802.11g runs at 54 Mbps and 802.11b runs at 11Mbps. Apple Computer calls 802.11b **AirPort**, and it calls 802.11g AirPort Extreme.

Another IEEE standard is 802.11a, which works in the 5.0-GHz frequency range and is, therefore, not compatible with 802.11b/g. It has a shorter range from a wireless device to an access point (50 meters compared with 100 meters for 802.11b/g), supports 54 Mbps, and does not encounter interference from cordless phones, microwave ovens, and Bluetooth devices, as does 802.11b/g. Most wireless devices today support all three IEEE standards; look for **802.11a/b/g** on the packages. Another standard is 802.11d, which is designed to run in countries outside the United States where other 802.11 versions do not meet the legal requirements for radio band technologies.

As wireless networks become more and more popular and our wireless devices become more mobile, new IEEE standards are being developed to deal with the new demands on the technology. 802.11k and 802.11r are two standards designed to help manage connections between wireless devices and access points. Normally, if a wireless device senses more than one access point, by default, it connects to the access point with the strongest signal, which can cause an overload on some access points while other access points are idle. The 802.11k standard defines how wireless network traffic can better be distributed over multiple access points covering a wide area so that the access point with the strongest signal is not overloaded. The 802.11r standard defines how a mobile wireless device can easily and quickly transition as it moves out of range of one access point and into the range of another.

Wireless connections using 802.11b/g/a can be made with a variety of devices, four of which are shown in Figure 10-15. Notice in the figure the different types of antennae.

Video

Wireless Network Cards

A+ ESS
2.1
5.1
6.1

A+
220-602
2.1
5.1
6.2
6.3

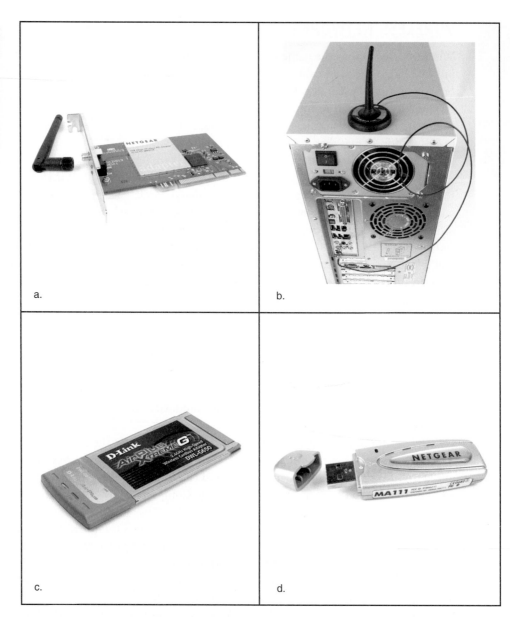

a.

b.

c.

d.

Figure 10-15 Four different types of wireless network adapters: (a) wireless NIC that fits in a PCI slot; (b) onboard wireless with an antenna that can be moved; (c) PC Card wireless NIC with embedded antenna; and (d) wireless NIC that uses a USB port on a desktop or notebook computer

Wireless devices can communicate directly (such as a PC to a PC, which is called Ad Hoc mode), or they can connect to a LAN by way of a wireless **access point (AP)**, as shown in Figure 10-16. Multiple access points can be positioned so that nodes can access at least one access point from anywhere in the covered area. When devices use an access point, they communicate through the access point instead of communicating directly. Often a wireless access point is doing double duty as a router, a device that connects one network to another (see Figure 10-17). This access point uses two antennae to strengthen the wireless signal. Later in the chapter, you will learn how to install a wireless device in a computer and connect it to a wireless network.

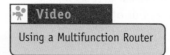

Video

Using a Multifunction Router

10

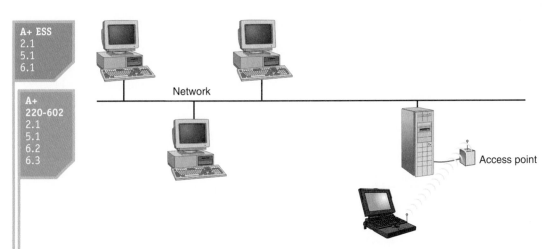

Network

Access point

Figure 10-16 Nodes on a wireless LAN connect to a cabled network by way of an access point

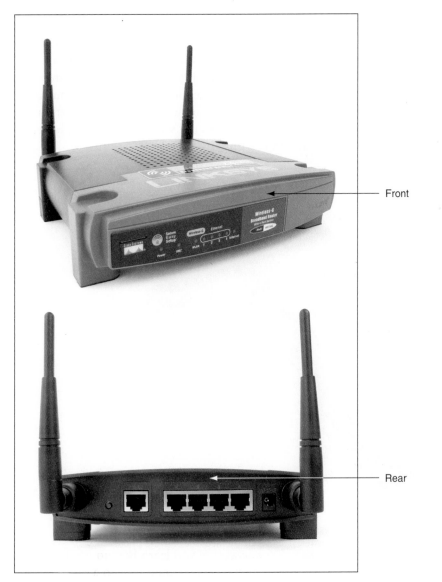

Front

Rear

Figure 10-17 This multifunction device is a router and also serves as a wireless access point to connect computers wirelessly to the local network

A+ ESS
2.1
5.1
6.1

A+
220-602
2.1
5.1
6.2
6.3

> ✏ **Notes**
>
> A LAN is often depicted in a logic diagram as a straight line with devices connecting to it. This method merely shows that devices are connected and is a nondescriptive way of drawing a LAN that might use a bus, ring, or star topology.

WIMAX OR 802.16 WIRELESS

A newer IEEE wireless standard is WiMAX, which is defined under IEEE 802.16d and 802.16e. WiMAX supports up to 75 Mbps with a range up to 6 miles and uses 2- to 11-GHz frequency. It is used in public hot spots and as a wireless broadband solution for business and residential use. It is often used as a last-mile solution for DSL and cable modem technologies, which means that the DSL or cable connection goes into a central point in an area, and WiMAX is used for the final leg to the consumer.

BLUETOOTH

Bluetooth is a standard for short-range wireless communication and data synchronization between devices. This standard was developed by a group of electronics manufacturers, including Ericsson, IBM, Intel, Nokia, and Toshiba, and it is overseen by the Bluetooth Special Interest Group (*www.bluetooth.com* and *www.bluetooth.org*). Bluetooth, which has a range of only 10 meters, also works in the 2.4-GHz frequency range, transfers data at up to 3 Mbps, is easy to configure, and is considered a viable option for short-range connections. For security, Bluetooth transmissions are encrypted. Examples of Bluetooth connections include connecting a printer to a PC or connecting a notebook computer or PDA to a cell phone so that the PDA or notebook computer can connect to a remote network by way of the cell phone's cellular network. Figure 10-18 shows a cordless Bluetooth headset that you can purchase to use with your mobile phone. The wireless headset clips over your ear and is battery powered.

Figure 10-18   This wireless headset accessory for a mobile phone uses Bluetooth wireless between the headset and the phone

10

A+ ESS
2.1
5.1

A+
220-602
2.1
5.1

TELEPHONE NETWORKS

As wireless networking technologies and the Internet technologies continue to improve, they are becoming more integrated with telephone and voice communications. In this section, we'll look at different telephone technologies, both wired and wireless, and see how they are integrated with our computer networks.

> **Notes**
>
> For more information on Wi-Fi, see *www.wi-fi.org*, and for more information on AirPort, see *www.apple.com*. For information on Bluetooth, see *www.bluetooth.com*. For information on WiMAX, see *www.wimaxforum.org*.

PLAIN OLD TELEPHONE SERVICE (POTS)

Almost all wireless and Internet phone systems connect to the regular, wired public phone system, which is called the PSTN (Public Switched Telephone Network) or POTS (plain old telephone service). This system uses a series of switches to create a closed circuit between two telephones; the circuit remains closed and in use as long as the callers are connected. For this reason, charges for calls are made according to the connect time.

VoIP

VoIP (Voice over Internet Protocol), also called Internet telephone, was once a novelty on the Internet, but not very useful because of all the problems with poor voice quality and dropped connections. However, VoIP has recently come of age and has become a viable residential and business alternative to regular phone service. Using VoIP, voice is converted to digital data for transmission over the Internet and to connect to POTS so that people can make and receive calls to VoIP subscribers as well as those using regular telephone service.

Just as with Ethernet, VoIP uses packets of data to communicate, and these voice packets can travel over the Internet using various paths rather than using a single closed circuit as does the PSTN network. Therefore, charges for VoIP are usually based on data sent rather than connect time.

To use VoIP, you need a broadband Internet connection such as a cable modem or DSL and a subscription to a VoIP provider. Regular analog or digital telephones can be used, which connect to the Internet by way of a network cable just as your computer connects, as shown in Figure 10-19. The digital phone is this figure connects to a network port on a router or to a network wall jack using an RJ-45 connector labeled in the figure. The AC power adapter plugs into a power outlet and provides power to the phone by way of the one cord to the phone. This one cord is doing double duty as a power cord and a network cable. Also, WiFi telephones are beginning to appear on the market that can use a WiFi hot spot to send and receive VoIP wireless data. Because a WiFi phone is a node on a wireless network, it can have an always-up connection to the Internet. Some expect WiFi phones to ultimately replace cell phones, which are discussed next.

A+ ESS
2.1
5.1

A+
220-602
2.1
5.1

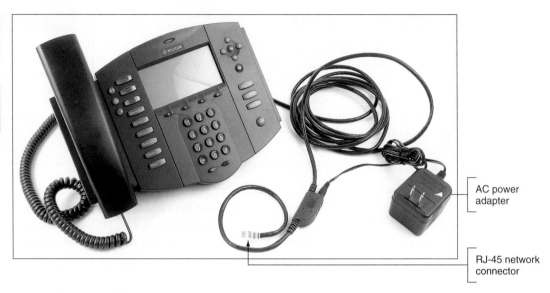

AC power adapter

RJ-45 network connector

Figure 10-19 This VoIP digital telephone connects to a local network and on to the Internet by way of a network cable

CELLULAR WAN

A cellular network or cellular WAN is a wireless network that is designed to cover a wide area and is made up of numerous cells, which are sometimes called radio cells (see Figure 10-20). A cell is a geographical area that offers connectivity and is created by a fixed transceiver and antenna, also called a base station. Each cell can transmit using many different frequencies, making it possible for many users to be connected at the same time. Also, because each cell is limited to a small geographical area, one cell does not interfere with the transmissions of another cell in the same cellular WAN. Access points for WiMAX or 802.11 wireless networks are sometimes strategically positioned over a wide area to form a cellular WAN.

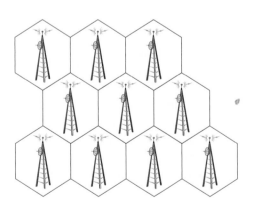

Figure 10-20 A cellular WAN is made up of many cells that provide coverage over a wide area

The most common cellular WAN is one used to provide mobile phone service for cell phones, and one technological system to provide this service is GSM (Global System for Mobile Communications). GSM is an open standard that uses digital communication of data, and is accepted and used worldwide. Because of this widespread use, it is possible for subscribers to use their GSM mobile phones in over 200 countries around the world. And, because GSM is digital, it can be used to transmit text messages, video files, and other digital data. Besides GSM, two other systems used for mobile phone cellular WAN transmissions are CDMA (Code Division Multiple Access) and TDMA (Time Division Multiple Access). Most cell phone service providers in the United States use either CDMA or TDMA for domestic calls. If your cell phone supports the technology, you might be able to purchase a GSM plan for international calling at a higher rate.

Normally, charges for cell phone service are made according to connect time, similar to PSTN calling, because cellular calls create a type of closed circuit or channel that is used for

A+ ESS
2.1
5.1

A+
220-602
2.1
5.1

the duration of the call. However, a new communication protocol used with GSM and TDMA is called General Packet Radio Service (GPRS), which sends voice, text, or video data in packets similar to VoIP. Using GPRS, charges for a call are based on packets of data sent rather than connect time. Using GPRS, a cell phone could conceivably have an always-on connection to the Internet similar to a WiFi phone.

All wireless phone systems, including cellular, use full-duplex transmission, which means both persons in a conversation can talk or transmit at the same time. This is possible because the cell phones are using one frequency to transmit data and another to receive data. In contrast, walkie-talkies use half-duplex transmission, which means transmission works in only one direction at a time because the walkie-talkies are using the same frequency to both send and receive data. Full-duplex and half-duplex transmissions are illustrated in Figure 10-21.

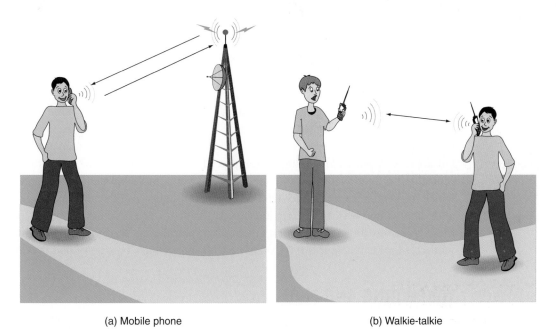

(a) Mobile phone
(b) Walkie-talkie

Figure 10-21 Full-duplex and half-duplex transmission

Cellular phones sometimes use Bluetooth wireless technology to make the short wireless hop between the phone and a wireless headset. In this case, the phone serves as the base station for the headset. Also, a cellular phone might use Bluetooth to communicate with a notebook computer, as shown in Figure 10-22. The notebook communicates with the nearby cellular phone, which communicates with the cellular WAN to provide Internet access for the notebook.

Bluetooth

Cellular WAN

Figure 10-22 Bluetooth can be used for short transmissions between personal devices such as a cell phone and notebook computer

A+ ESS
2.1
5.1

A+
220-602
2.1
5.1

SATELLITE PHONE

An alternative to a cellular mobile phone is a satellite phone. A satellite phone communicates directly with satellites orbiting the earth at a low level, which is why a satellite phone is also called an LEO (low earth orbit) phone. The advantages of a satellite phone over a cellular phone are that there are fewer gaps in coverage and these phones can more likely be used around the world. One disadvantage of a satellite phone is that, because it must communicate with a satellite, its antenna must be longer than that used by cellular phones. Also, from personal experience, I can tell you that for best reception, you must be outdoors.

CORDLESS PHONE

A cordless phone is a wireless telephone that sets in a cradle of a phone base station that connects to a regular house phone line. Cordless phones can be used only within a short range of the base station. They typically use one of these frequency ranges: 900 MHz, 2.4 GHz, or 5.8 GHz. One problem with cordless phones is that a cordless phone operating at 2.4 GHz might interfere with 802.11b/g wireless LANs.

RADIO PHONE

Another type of wireless phone is a radio phone. Service for a radio phone is provided by the Mobile Telephone Service (MTS) that uses VHF (very high frequency) radio waves. This radio frequency (RF) range is also used by FM radio. Radio phones were once used as car phones, but are mostly outdated, having been replaced by cellular phones. MTS uses high-powered centralized radio towers, and to connect to a tower, a radio phone needs a large transmitter, which means that radio phones tend to be big and bulky. Another disadvantage is that there are a limited number of radio frequencies available for MTS, so not too many people can use these phones at the same time in a given geographical area. Radio phones might still be used in wilderness areas where it is too expensive to install cellular base stations for cellular phones.

TOKEN RING AND FDDI

Token Ring is an older, almost totally outdated LAN technology developed by IBM that transmits data at 4 Mbps or 16 Mbps. Physically, a Token Ring network is arranged in a star topology because each node connects to a centralized device and not to other nodes in the network. However, a token actually travels in a ring on the network. The token is either free or busy, and a node must have the token to communicate. Because it is physically a star and logically a ring, it is sometimes called a star ring topology. The centralized device to which the network nodes connect is called a Controlled Access Unit (CAU), a Multistation Access Unit (MSAU or sometimes just MAU), or a Smart Multistation Access Unit (SMAU).

Each workstation contains a Token Ring LAN card (see Figure 10-23) that connects each workstation to an MSAU. Token Ring cables can be either UTP or STP cables that have two twisted pairs, for a total of four wires in the cable. Token Ring connectors can be RJ-45 connectors, but the connector pins are not the same as RJ-45 connectors used on Ethernet. Token Ring can also use another type of connector that has no "male" or "female" version, known as a Universal Data Connector (UDC) or an IBM Data Connector (IDC). Because there is no "male" or "female" connector, any connector can connect to any other connector.

Fiber Distributed Data Interface (FDDI, pronounced *fiddy*) uses a token that travels in a ring like Token Ring. But with FDDI, data frames travel on the ring without the token, and multiple nodes can have data on the ring at the same time. Nodes on a FDDI network can be connected in a ring using a **ring topology**, meaning that each node is connected to two

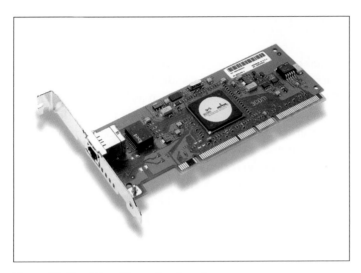

Figure 10-23   Token Ring network card

other nodes, although most FDDI networks use hubs in a physical star topology. FDDI provides data transfer at 100 Mbps, which is much faster than Token Ring and a little faster than Fast Ethernet, which also runs at about 100 Mbps. It was once used as a network technology for a large LAN in a large company, but more commonly is used as a backbone network to connect several LANs in a large building. Figure 10-24 shows a FDDI network card.

Figure 10-24   FDDI network card

So far in the chapter, we've looked at all the different hardware devices and hardware technologies to build networks. Each hardware device on a network such as a NIC, switch, router, or Internet telephone uses a hardware protocol to communicate on the network. For most wired LANs, that protocol is Ethernet. However, in addition to the hardware protocol, there is a layer of network communication at the operating system level. The OS can use one of several communication protocols such as TCP/IP or AppleTalk. For example, a Windows network might use TCP/IP to communicate at the OS level, and the devices on the LAN (NICs and switches) might use Ethernet. The next section looks at the different OS networking protocols, how they work, and how to configure a computer to use them.

WINDOWS ON A NETWORK

As a system of interlinked computers, a network needs both software and hardware to work. Software includes an operating system installed on each computer on the network, and perhaps an NOS (network operating system) such as Windows Server 2003 or Unix to control the entire network and its resources. If the network is small (fewer than 10 computers), it can be a peer-to-peer network, in which each computer on the network has the same authority as the other computers. A Windows peer-to-peer network is called a workgroup.

Larger networks use the client/server model, in which access to a network is controlled by an NOS using a centralized database. A client computer provides a user ID and password to a server that validates the data against the security database. In a Windows network, this server is called the domain controller, and the network model is called a domain. Popular network operating systems are Windows 2003 Server, Novell NetWare, Open Enterprise Server, Unix, and Linux. Windows has client software built in for Windows and Novell NetWare servers. Alternately, for Novell NetWare, you can install Novell client software.

> **⊘ A+ Tip**
>
> The A+ Essentials exam expects you to understand the differences between a peer-to-peer network and a client/server network.

A network can have more than one workgroup or domain in operation, and some computers might not belong to any workgroup or domain. A computer joins a workgroup or domain in order to share resources with other computers and devices in the group or domain. Company policy controls how many workgroups or domains can exist within the company network. This number is based on user needs, security concerns, and administrative overhead required to manage the groups.

FOUR SUITES OF PROTOCOLS

At the physical network level, Windows supports Ethernet, ATM, Token Ring, and other networking protocols. At the operating system level, Windows supports the four suites of protocols shown in Figure 10-25 and described in the following list. The figure also shows the different ways a computer or other device on the network can be addressed.

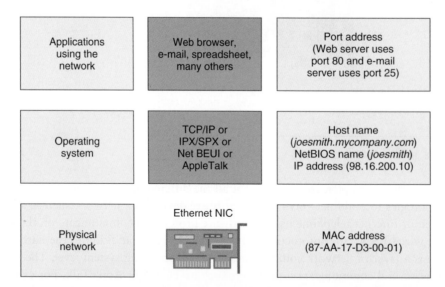

Figure 10-25 An operating system can use more than one method to address a computer on the network, but at the network level, a MAC address is always used to address a device on the network

Use Figure 10-25 as a reference point throughout this section to understand the way the protocols and addresses relate on the network.

- ◢ TCP/IP (Transmission Control Protocol/Internet Protocol) is the protocol suite used on the Internet and so should be your choice if you want to connect your network to the Internet, with each workstation having Internet access. Novell NetWare, Linux, Unix, and Mac OS also support TCP/IP.
- ◢ IPX/SPX (Internetwork Packet Exchange/Sequenced Packet Exchange) is an NWLink protocol suite designed for use with the Novell NetWare operating system. IPX/SPX is similar to TCP/IP but is not supported on the Internet. NWLink is Microsoft's version of the IPX/SPX protocol suite used by Novell NetWare. When a Windows PC is a client on a Novell NetWare network, the Windows PC must be configured to use NWLink, which includes the IPX/SPX protocol.
- ◢ NetBEUI (NetBIOS Extended User Interface, pronounced *net-bouie*) is a proprietary Windows protocol suite used only by Windows computers. NetBEUI supports NetBIOS (Network Basic Input/Output System), a protocol that applications use to communicate with each other. NetBEUI is faster than TCP/IP and easier to configure but does not support routing to other networks, and, therefore, is not supported on the Internet. It should be used only on an isolated network. Windows XP does not automatically install NetBEUI, because Microsoft considers NetBEUI and NetBIOS to both be legacy protocols.
- ◢ AppleTalk is a proprietary networking protocol suite for Macintosh computers by Apple Corporation.

To use one of these protocols on a network, the first step is to physically connect the computer to the network by installing the NIC in the computer and connecting the network cable to the switch, router, or other network device. (For wireless LANs, after installing the NIC, you put the computer within range of an access point.) After the drivers for the NIC are installed, the NIC is automatically associated with an OS networking protocol in a process called binding. Binding occurs when an operating system–level protocol such as TCP/IP associates itself with a lower-level hardware protocol such as Ethernet. When the two protocols are bound, communication continues between them until they are unbound, or released.

 A+ Tip

The A+ Essentials exam expects you to be familiar with these networking protocols: TCP/IP, IPX/SPX, NWLink, and NetBIOS.

You can determine which protocols are installed in Windows by looking at the properties of a network connection. For example, in Windows XP you can right-click **My Network Places** and select **Properties** from the shortcut menu to open the Network Connections window, as shown on the left side of Figure 10-26. Then right-click the **Local Area Connection** icon and select **Properties** from the shortcut menu. The Local Area Connection Properties dialog box opens, as shown on the right side of the figure.

You can see that two of the three available protocols are bound to the NIC because they are checked. In this situation, the PC is using a TCP/IP network, but one network printer uses IPX/SPX and does not support TCP/IP. Because the PC uses that printer, it must have IPX/SPX installed. (A network printer is a printer that any user on the network can access using one of those methods: (1) through its own network card and connection to the network, (2) through a connection to a standalone print server, or (3) through a connection to a computer as a local printer, which is shared on the network.)

There is no problem with more than one operating system protocol operating on the network at the same time. Also, if you want to use a protocol and it is not listed, click **Install** in the Local Area Connection Properties window to select the protocol and install it.

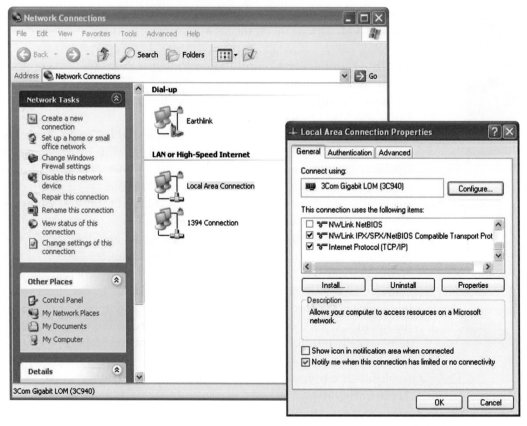

Figure 10-26 Three Windows XP network protocols are installed and two protocols are bound to this network card

ADDRESSING ON A NETWORK

Every device on a network has a unique address. Part of learning about a network is learning how a device (such as a computer or a printer) or a program (such as a Web server) is identified on the network. On a network, four methods are used to identify devices and programs:

- *Using a MAC address.* As you learned earlier, a MAC address is a unique, 48-bit address permanently embedded in a NIC and identifying a device on a LAN. The MAC address is used only by devices inside the local network, and is not used outside the LAN.
- *Using an IP address.* An IP address is a 32-bit address consisting of a series of four 8-bit numbers separated by periods. An IP address identifies a computer, printer, or other device on a TCP/IP network such as the Internet or an intranet. (An intranet is a private or corporate network that uses TCP/IP.) Because the largest possible 8-bit number is 255, each of the four numbers can be no larger than 255. An example of an IP address is 109.168.0.104. Consider a MAC address a local address and an IP address a long-distance address, as shown in Figure 10-27.
- *Using character-based names.* Character-based names include domain names, host names, and NetBIOS names used to identify a PC on a network with easy-to-remember letters rather than numbers. (Host names and NetBIOS names are often just called computer names.)
- *Using a port address.* A port address is a number that one application uses to address another application installed on a remote computer on the network.

> **🔵 A+ Tip**
>
> The A+ Essentials exam expects you to know each of the methods of identifying devices and programs on a network.

10

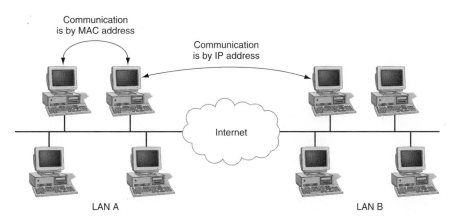

A+ ESS
5.1

A+
220-602
5.1

Communication
is by MAC address

Communication
is by IP address

Internet

LAN A

LAN B

Figure 10-27 Computers on the same LAN use MAC addresses to communicate, but computers on different LANs use IP addresses to communicate over the Internet

APPLYING CONCEPTS

EXAMINING YOUR NETWORK CONFIGURATION

If your PC is connected to the Internet or any other TCP/IP network, you can use some Windows utilities to report how the network connection is configured. For Windows 2000/XP, to display the IP address and the MAC addresses of all installed NICs, in a command prompt window, use the command **ipconfig /all**. The screen shown in Figure 10-28 appears.

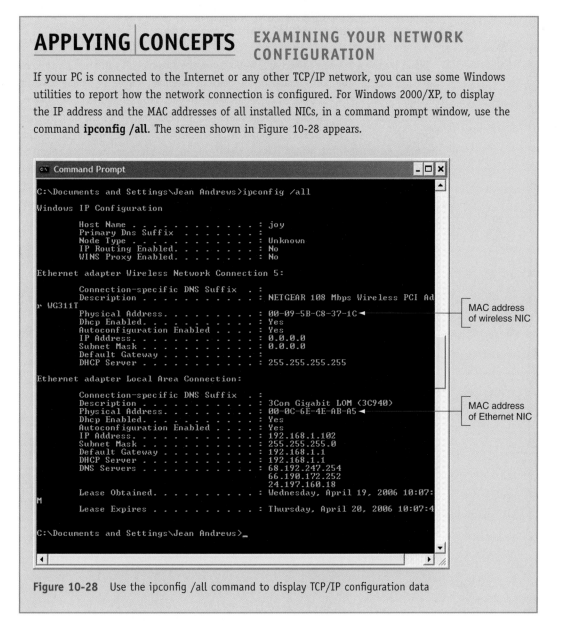

Figure 10-28 Use the ipconfig /all command to display TCP/IP configuration data

A+ ESS
5.1

A+
220-602
5.1

For Windows 9x/Me, use the Winipcfg utility instead of Ipconfig. Enter **winipcfg** in the Run dialog box and press **Enter**. The IP Configuration window opens (see Figure 10-29). Select the NIC in the drop-down list of network devices.

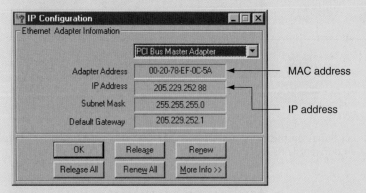

Figure 10-29   Use the Windows 9x/Me Winipcfg utility to display a PC's
IP address and MAC address

When we use a browser to access a Web site on the Internet, it's interesting to know that we can use an IP address and port number in the place of a domain name. For example, you can access the Microsoft Web site by entering this domain name in your browser address box: *www.microsoft.com*. However, you can also use the IP address and port number instead of the domain name (see Figure 10-30). The IP address (207.46.20.30 in the browser address box) identifies the computer and the port number (80, which follows the IP address and is separated by a colon) identifies the application. The application, service, or program that is responding to requests made to port 80 on this computer is a Web server program that is serving up Web pages. An example of a Web server program is Internet Information Services (IIS) by Microsoft. Also note that if you enter an IP address without a port number in a browser address box, port 80 is assumed.

Figure 10-30   A Web site can be accessed by its IP address and port number

A+ ESS
5.1

A+
220-602
5.1

Now let's turn our attention to the details of understanding how IP addresses and computer names are used on a network.

IP ADDRESSES

All protocols of the TCP/IP suite identify a device on the Internet or an intranet by its IP address. An IP address is 32 bits long, made up of 4 bytes separated by periods, as in this address: 190.180.40.120. The largest possible 8-bit number is 11111111, which is equal to 255 in decimal, so the largest possible IP address in decimal is 255.255.255.255, which in binary is 11111111.11111111.11111111.11111111. Each of the four numbers separated by periods is called an octet (for 8 bits) and can be any number from 0 to 255, making a total of 4.3 billion potential IP addresses (256 x 256 x 256 x 256). Because of the allocation scheme used to assign these addresses, not all of them are available for use.

The first part of an IP address identifies the network, and the last part identifies the host. It's important to understand how the bits of an IP address are used in order to understand how routing happens over interconnected networks such as the Internet, and how TCP/IP can locate an IP address anywhere on the globe. When data is routed over interconnected networks, the network portion of the IP address is used to locate the right network. After the data arrives at the local network, the host portion of the IP address is used to identify the one computer on the network that is to receive the data. Finally, the IP address of the host must be used to identify its MAC address so the data can travel on the host's LAN to that host. Now that you are familiar with both the hardware and OS components of networking, we turn our attention to the details of connecting a PC to a network.

INSTALLING A NIC AND CONNECTING TO A NETWORK

A+ ESS
5.2

A+
220-602
5.2
5.3

To connect a PC to a network, you'll need a patch cable and a device for the PC to connect to, such as a switch or router. For most corporate environments, the switch is located in an electrical closet centrally located in the building, and patch cables connect the device to network wall jacks. In this situation, the patch cable connects from the PC to the wall jack.

Installed on the PC, you'll need a network card (NIC), an onboard network port, or a wireless network card or device. When selecting a NIC or wireless device, consider these things:

▲ Match the NIC to the type of bus on the motherboard you plan to use (PCI Express x4, PCI Express x1, or PCI). In most cases, you'll use a PCI slot.
▲ Match the NIC to the speed and type of network to which you are attaching. In most cases, you'll be using a 100BaseT or Gigabit Ethernet network with UTP CAT5e cables using RJ-45 connectors. If the switch uses Gigabit Ethernet, it will also support a 100BaseT NIC, although the network connection will run at the slower rate.

> 📹 **Video**
>
> Setting up a Network with Crossover Cables

▲ For wireless connections, match the wireless NIC or other device to the type of network technology used by the access point you plan to use. In most cases, that will be 802.11g/b.

Installing a network card and connecting the PC to a network involves three general steps: (1) Put the NIC in the PC, and install the NIC's drivers; (2) configure the NIC using Windows, so that it has the appropriate addresses on the network and the correct network

A+ ESS
5.2

A+
220-602
5.2
5.3

protocols; and (3) test the NIC to verify that the PC can access resources on the network. This section discusses these steps to install a wired NIC using Windows 2000/XP and Windows 9x/Me. It also discusses how to install a wireless NIC in a notebook.

INSTALLING A NIC USING WINDOWS 2000/XP

To install a NIC using Windows 2000/XP, do the following:

> **🖒 A+ Tip**
>
> The A+ Essentials exam expects you to know how to configure a Windows 2000/XP network connection.

1. Read the instructions that come bundled with the NIC. Should you install the NIC first or the drivers first? In these steps, we are installing the NIC first, but always follow specific instructions of the manufacturer.

2. Physically install the network card in the PC.

3. Turn on the PC. The Found New Hardware Wizard launches to begin the process of loading the necessary drivers to use the new device. It is better to use the manufacturer's drivers, not the Windows drivers. If given the opportunity to choose between Windows drivers and the manufacturer drivers on CD, choose the manufacturer drivers. If Windows completes the installation using its own drivers without giving you the opportunity to install the manufacturer's drivers, after the NIC is installed, you can use Device Manager to update the drivers using the manufacturer's drivers.

4. After the Windows desktop loads, verify that the drivers installed successfully. Open **Device Manager**, right-click the card from the list of devices, and click **Properties**. The card's Properties dialog box opens (see Figure 10-31). Look for any conflicts or other errors reported by Device Manager on the General tab and the Resources tab of this dialog box.

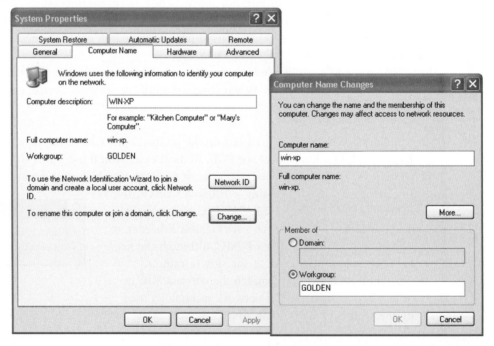

Figure 10-31   A network adapter's resources show in the Properties dialog box of the Device Manager window

A+ ESS
5.2

A+
220-602
5.2
5.3

5. If errors are reported or you want to replace Windows drivers with the manufacturer's drivers, click the **Driver** tab and then click **Update Driver**. Follow the instructions onscreen to use the network card manufacturer's drivers. You'll find other troubleshooting tips for installing NICs later in this chapter.

Video

Setting up a Network with Hub and Patch Cables

6. Connect a network patch cable to the NIC port and to the network switch or a wall jack connected to a switch. You are now ready to configure the NIC to access the network.

APPLYING | CONCEPTS

Incidentally, there are three ways to access the network adapter Properties dialog box:

◢ As described earlier, open **Device Manager**, right-click the network adapter, and select **Properties** from the shortcut menu.

◢ From Control Panel, launch the Windows XP **Network Connections** applet or the Windows 2000 **Network and Dial-up Connections** applet. Right-click the **Local Area Connection** icon and select **Properties** from the shortcut menu. Click **Configure**.

◢ Right-click **My Network Places** and select **Properties** from the shortcut menu. The Windows XP Network Connections applet or Windows 2000 Network and Dial-up Connections applet launches. Right-click the **Local Area Connection** icon and select **Properties** from the shortcut menu. Click **Configure**.

CONFIGURING WINDOWS 2000/XP TO USE A NETWORK

The first step to configure Windows 2000/XP to use a network is to give the computer a name. If you plan to use NetBEUI as a networking protocol instead of TCP/IP, limit the computer name to 15 characters. For Windows 2000/XP, the protocol is TCP/IP by default. Follow these directions to name a computer:

1. Right-click **My Computer** and select **Properties** from the shortcut menu. The System Properties dialog box opens.

2. For Windows XP, click the **Computer Name** tab, then click the **Change** button. The Computer Name Changes dialog box opens (see Figure 10-32). For Windows 2000, click the **Network Identification** tab, and then click the **Properties** button. The Identification Changes window opens.

3. Enter the Computer name (**win-xp** in the example shown in Figure 10-32). Each computer name must be unique within a workgroup or domain.

4. If the computer is connecting to a workgroup, select **Workgroup** and enter the name of the workgroup (**GOLDEN** in this example). Recall that a workgroup is a group of computers on a network that shares files, folders, and printers. All users in the workgroup must have the same workgroup name entered in this window. If the PC is to join a domain (a network where logging on is controlled by a server), select **Domain** and enter the name of the domain here, such as *mycompany.com*. When configuring a PC on a network, always follow the specific directions of the network administrator responsible for the network.

A+ ESS
5.2

A+
220-602
5.2
5.3

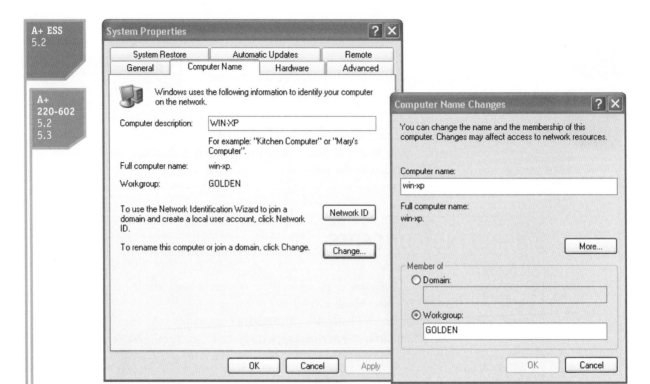

Figure 10-32 Windows XP uses the Computer Name Changes dialog box to assign a host name to a computer on a network

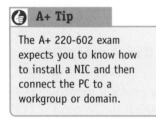

A+ Tip

The A+ 220-602 exam expects you to know how to install a NIC and then connect the PC to a workgroup or domain.

5. Click **OK** to exit the Windows XP Computer Name Changes dialog box or the Windows 2000 Identification Changes window, and click **OK** to exit the System Properties dialog box. You will be asked to reboot the computer for changes to take effect.

6. After rebooting a Windows XP system, click **Start, My Network Places**, and then click **View workgroup computers** to view this computer and others on the network. On the Windows 2000 desktop, open **My Network Places**, and double-click **Computers Near Me.** Figure 10-33 shows an example of My Network Places.

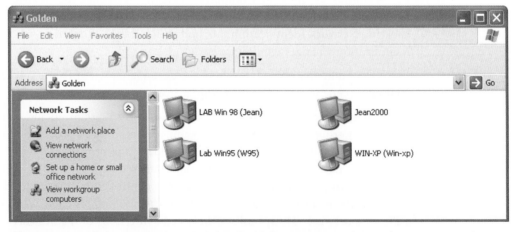

Figure 10-33 Windows XP My Network Places shows all computers on the LAN in a common workgroup

A+ ESS
5.2

A+
220-602
5.2
5.3

CONFIGURING TCP/IP USING WINDOWS 2000/XP

When a network card is installed in Windows 2000/XP, TCP/IP is installed by default. However, if TCP/IP has been uninstalled or gives you problems, you can install it again.

> **Notes**
>
> My Network Places for Windows 2000/XP and Network Neighborhood for Windows 9x/Me can be viewed on the desktop and in Windows Explorer. By default, Windows XP puts My Network Places only in Windows Explorer, Windows 2000 puts My Network Places in both places, and Windows 98 puts Network Neighborhood in both places.

Also, Windows makes some assumptions about how TCP/IP is configured, and these settings might not be appropriate for your network. This section addresses all these concerns.

Before you configure TCP/IP, you might need to ask the network administrator the following questions:

1. Will the PC use dynamic or static IP addressing?

2. If static IP addressing is used, what are the IP address, subnet mask, and default gateway for this computer?

3. Do you use DNS? If so, what are the IP addresses of your DNS servers?

4. Is a proxy server used to connect to other networks (including the Internet)? If so, what is the IP address of the proxy server?

A few definitions are needed: a DNS (Domain Name System, also called Domain Name Service) server tracks relationships between character-based names and IP addresses. A subnet mask is a group of four dotted decimal numbers that tells TCP/IP if a computer's IP address is on the same network as another computer or on a different network. A static IP address is an IP address permanently assigned to a computer. A dynamic IP address is an IP address that is assigned to a computer each time the computer connects to the network; the assignment is made by a DHCP (Dynamic Host Configuration Protocol) server running on the network. The server also gives the PC its subnet

> **A+ Tip**
>
> The A+ 220-602 exam expects you to be familiar with a gateway, subnet mask, and static and dynamic (or automatic) address assignments.

mask and default gateway, so that the computer knows how to communicate with other hosts that are not on its own network. A gateway is a computer or other device that allows a computer on one network to communicate with a computer on another network. A default gateway is the gateway a computer uses to access another network if it does not have a better option.

Most likely, you will be using dynamic IP addressing, and you will obtain the DNS server address automatically. The DHCP server might also act as the proxy server so that computers inside the network can make connections to computers outside the network using the proxy server's public IP address. A proxy server accesses the Internet on behalf of other computers on the local network using a service called NAT (Network Address Translation). The proxy server presents its own public IP address to the Internet in place of local private IP addresses used on the network.

To set the TCP/IP properties for a connection, follow these steps:

1. For Windows XP, open the **Network Connections** applet, and for Windows 2000, open the **Network and Dial-up Connections** applet. Right-click the **Local Area Connection** icon, and then select **Properties** from the shortcut menu. See Figure 10-34.

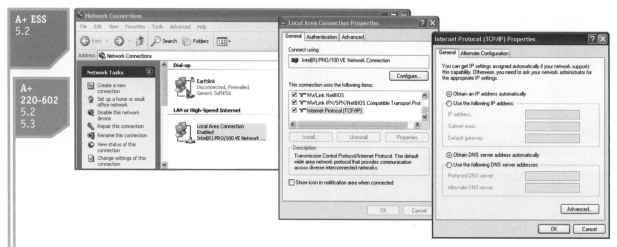

Figure 10-34 To configure TCP/IP under Windows XP, use the Internet Protocol (TCP/IP) Properties dialog box

2. Select **Internet Protocol (TCP/IP)** from the list of installed components, and then click the **Properties** button. The Internet Protocol (TCP/IP) Properties dialog box opens, which is also shown in Figure 10-34.

3. For dynamic IP addressing, select **Obtain an IP address automatically**. (This is the most likely choice.) For static IP addressing, select **Use the following IP address**, and enter the IP address, subnet mask, and default gateway.

4. To disable DNS until the DHCP server gives the computer the DNS server address, select **Obtain DNS server address automatically**. (This is the most likely choice.) If you have the IP addresses of the DNS servers, click **Use the following DNS server addresses**, and enter the IP addresses. Click **OK** twice to close both windows.

5. Open **My Network Places** and verify that your computer and other computers on the network are visible. If you don't see other computers on the network, reboot the PC.

CONFIGURING THE NWLINK AND NETBEUI PROTOCOLS

 A+ Tip

The A+ 220-602 exam expects you to know how to configure a computer to be a client on a Novell network using NWLink.

Instead of or in addition to TCP/IP, a computer might use the NWLink or NetBEUI protocol. These protocols can be used to communicate on a network, but not over the Internet, and a computer can use a combination of TCP/IP, NWLink, and NetBEUI.

A Novell network can use TCP/IP or IPX/SPX. If the network is using IPX/SPX, each Windows computer on the network must be configured to use the NWLink protocol. Do the following to install and use NWLink:

1. NWLink is not normally installed. To install it, right-click the **Local Area Connection** icon in the Network Connections window and select **Properties**. The properties dialog box opens, which lists the installed protocols (refer back to Figure 10-34). If NWLink is not listed, click **Install**. The Select Network Component Type dialog box opens, as shown in Figure 10-35. Select **Protocol** and click **Add**.

2. In the dialog box that opens, also shown in Figure 10-35, select **NWLink IPX/SPX/NetBIOS Compatible Transport Protocol** and click **OK**.

10

A+ ESS
5.2

A+
220-602
5.2
5.3

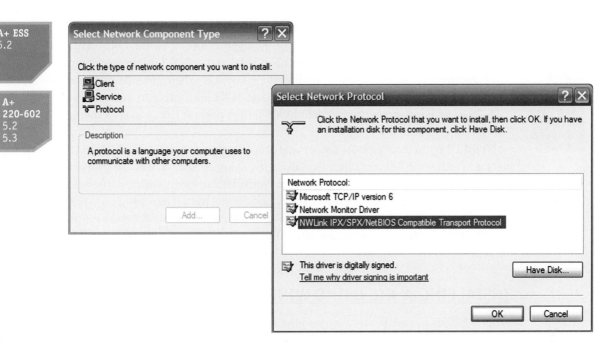

Figure 10-35 Installing network components

3. You should now see NWLink listed as an installed protocol in the Local Area Connection Properties dialog box (see the left side of Figure 10-36). Make sure that when the NIC used for your network connection is displayed near the top of the properties dialog box, the NWLink IPX/SPX/NetBIOS Compatible Transport Protocol is checked and, therefore, bound to the selected NIC.

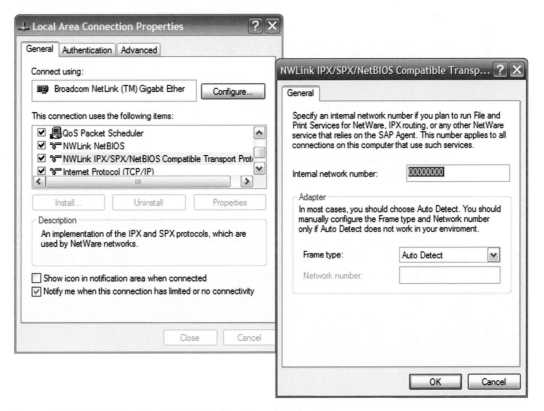

Figure 10-36 NWLink protocol is installed and bound to the NIC

A+ ESS
5.2

A+
220-602
5.2
5.3

4. Check for network connectivity by opening My Network Places and browsing the network. If you have problems with the connection, open the **Local Area Connection Properties** dialog box (see Figure 10-36), select the **NWLink** protocol, and click **Properties**. On the resulting dialog box, shown on the right side of Figure 10-36, verify that **Auto Detect** is selected so that NWLink is able to automatically detect the type of hardware network technology that is present (most likely Ethernet).

NetBEUI is used to support legacy applications that require a NetBIOS interface. To connect a Windows 2000 computer to a network using NetBEUI, use the Properties dialog box of the local area connection to install the NetBEUI Protocol, which automatically binds itself to the NIC providing this local network connection. Then assign a name to the computer. Remember to limit the name to 15 characters. Windows XP does not normally support NetBEUI. However, you can manually install it using the Windows XP Setup CD. For directions, see the Microsoft Knowledge Base Article 301041 at *support.microsoft.com*.

INSTALLING A NIC USING WINDOWS 9X/ME

After a NIC is physically installed and the PC is turned on, Windows 9x/Me automatically detects the card and guides you through the process of installing drivers. After the installation, verify that the card is installed with no errors by using Device Manager. In Device Manager, the network card should be listed under Network adapters. Right-click the card and select **Properties** to view the card's properties. Last, connect a network patch cable to the NIC port and to the network hub or a wall jack connected to a hub. You are now ready to configure the NIC to access the network.

> **Notes**
>
> The 2006 A+ exams do not cover Windows 9x/Me. However, this book covers Windows 9x/Me because technicians are sometimes called on to support this legacy OS and, at the time this book went to print, the 2003 A+ exams were still live.

ASSIGNING A COMPUTER NAME

To assign a name to a Windows 9x/Me computer, follow these directions:

1. Access **Control Panel** and double-click the **Network** icon.

2. Click the **Identification** tab (see Figure 10-37).

3. Enter the computer name (**Patricia** in this example). Enter the name of the workgroup (**Golden** in this example). Each computer name must be unique within the workgroup.

4. Click **OK** to exit the window. You will be asked to reboot the system.

5. After you have rebooted, open **Network Neighborhood** on the Windows desktop. You should be able to see this computer and others on the network. Figure 10-38 shows an example of Network Neighborhood. If you cannot see other computers, you might have to install and configure TCP/IP, as described next.

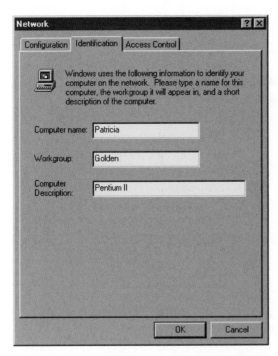

Figure 10-37 Each computer in a workgroup in Windows 98 must be assigned a name that other users on the network will see in their Network Neighborhood window

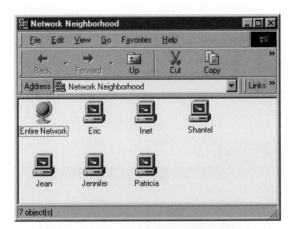

Figure 10-38 Windows 98 Network Neighborhood shows all computers on the LAN in a common workgroup

INSTALLING AND CONFIGURING TCP/IP USING WINDOWS 98

If TCP/IP is not already installed, you must install it. For Windows 98, do the following:

1. Access **Control Panel** and double-click the **Network** icon. The Network window opens.

2. Click Add to display the Select Network Component Type window, as shown in Figure 10-39.

3. Select **Protocol** and click **Add**. The Select Network Protocol window opens. Select **Microsoft** on the left and **TCP/IP** on the right (see Figure 10-39). Click **OK**. The system asks for the Microsoft Windows 98 CD and requests that you reboot the system.

4. When you return to the Network window, notice that TCP/IP is automatically bound to any network cards or modems that it finds installed.

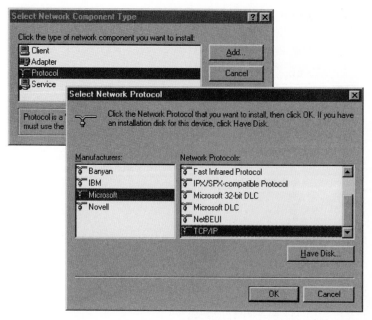

Figure 10-39 To install TCP/IP in Windows 98, use the Select Network Component Type window

The next step is to configure TCP/IP. Most likely, you will be using dynamic IP addressing, and the DNS service is initially disabled (later the DHCP server will tell the PC to enable it). In Windows 98, do the following to configure TCP/IP that has been bound to a NIC to communicate over a local network:

1. In the Network window, select the item where TCP/IP is bound to the NIC. (On the left side of Figure 10-40, that item is TCP/IP->NETGEAR FA311 Fast Ethernet PCI Adapter.) Then, click **Properties**. The TCP/IP Properties dialog box opens, as shown on the right side of the figure.

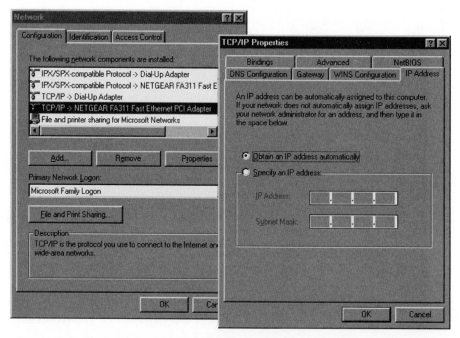

Figure 10-40 To configure TCP/IP in Windows 98, select the binding and click Properties to view the TCP/IP Properties dialog box

10

2. If static IP addressing is used, click **Specify an IP address**, and then enter the IP address and subnet mask supplied by your administrator. If dynamic IP addressing is used (as is usually the case), click **Obtain an IP address automatically**.

3. Click the **DNS Configuration** tab and choose to enable or disable DNS (see Figure 10-41). If you enable DNS, enter the IP addresses of your DNS servers. If your network administrator gave you other specific values for the TCP/IP configuration, you will find the tabs for these settings on this window. But in most cases, the above steps will work for you to configure TCP/IP.

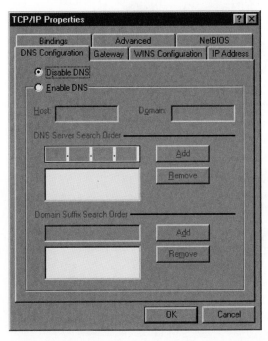

Figure 10-41 Configure DNS service under TCP/IP for Windows 98

4. When finished, click **OK** to exit the Properties dialog box, and then click **OK** to exit the Network window.

5. On the desktop, verify that you can see your computer and others on the network in Network Neighborhood. If you don't see others on the network, reboot the PC.

INSTALLING A WIRELESS ADAPTER IN A NOTEBOOK

For a notebook computer, a wireless adapter will use a USB port or a PC Card slot. Most new adapters use the USB port, such as the wireless adapter shown in Figure 10-42. The adapter will come with a setup CD and some documentation and maybe an accessory or two.

Do the following to install the adapter:

1. Read the installation directions that come with the wireless adapter to find out if you install the software first or the adapter first. For the Linksys wireless adapter used in this example, the instructions clearly say to first install the software (see Figure 10-43).

> **Notes**
>
> To use NetBEUI on a Windows 9x/Me network, first verify that NetBEUI is installed or install it as you do TCP/IP. It should automatically bind itself to any network adapters installed. NetBEUI needs no other configuration.

A+ ESS
2.1
3.2
5.2
6.1

A+
220-602
2.3
5.2
6.2
6.3

Figure 10-42 This 802.11g wireless adapter by Linksys uses a USB port to connect to a notebook or desktop computer

Figure 10-43 This label makes it clear you need to install the software before installing the wireless adapter

2. Insert the CD in the CD drive. The opening screen for this adapter is shown in Figure 10-44. Click **Click Here to Start** and follow the directions onscreen to install the device drivers and the utility to configure the wireless connection.

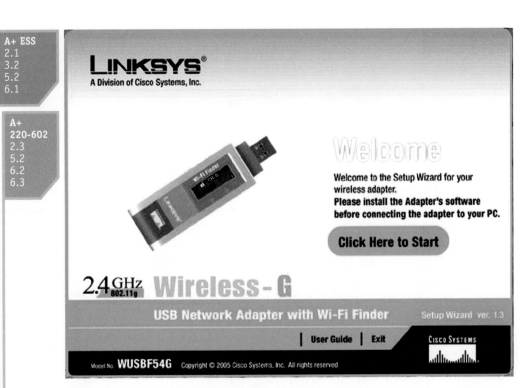

Figure 10-44 Install the wireless adapter software

3. Next, plug the wireless adapter into a USB port. See Figure 10-45. The Found New Hardware bubble appears. See Figure 10-46. Click the bubble to launch the Found New Hardware Wizard. Follow the wizard to install the device.

Figure 10-45 Plug the wireless USB adapter into the USB port

A+ ESS
2.1
3.2
5.2
6.1

A+
220-602
2.3
5.2
6.2
6.3

Figure 10-46   Windows XP recognizes the presence of a new USB device

When a new device is being installed, Windows might recognize that the drivers were not digitally signed by Microsoft. If this is the case, it displays a dialog box similar to that in Figure 10-47 (for a Netgear wireless adapter). Now you have a decision to make. You can stop the installation and go to the manufacturer's Web site to try to find approved drivers, or you can continue with the installation. For most devices, it is safe to continue the installation using unsigned drivers. To do that, click **Continue Anyway**.

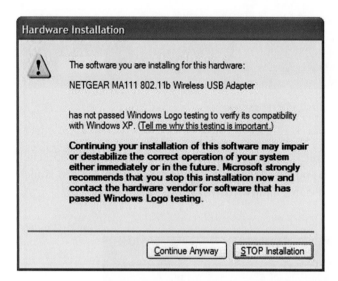

Figure 10-47   Windows asks you for a decision about using unsigned drivers

At another point in the installation, the wizard might ask if you want to disable the Windows XP Configuration Manager, which means you are choosing to use the manufacturer's utility to configure the wireless adapter (see Figure 10-48). Unless you have a good reason to do otherwise, click **Yes** to choose to use the manufacturer's utility. This utility will most likely be easier to use and allow you to better manage the wireless NIC than would the Windows XP Network Connections window. (Later, if you change your mind about which utility to use, you might have to uninstall and reinstall the device.)

A+ ESS
2.1
3.2
5.2
6.1

A+
220-602
2.3
5.2
6.2
6.3

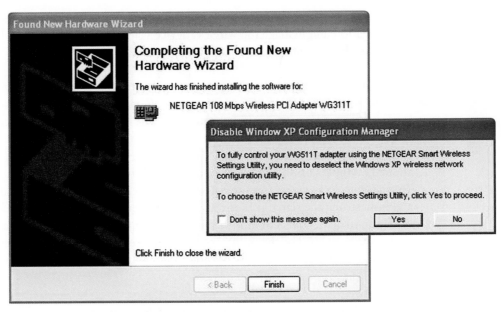

Figure 10-48 During the wireless NIC installation, you are asked which utility you want to use to configure the NIC

After the wireless adapter is installed, the next step is to configure it. Read the adapter's documentation to find out how to use the software. Most likely during installation an icon was added to your system tray. Double-click the icon to open the configuration window. Figure 10-49 shows the configuration window for the Linksys wireless adapter. Click **Manual Setup** to configure the adapter.

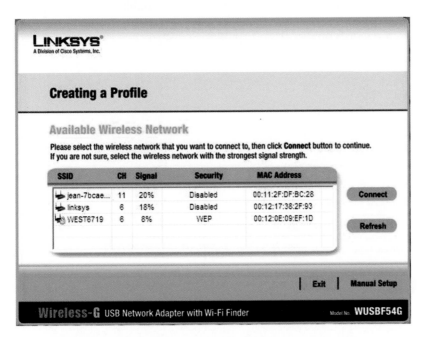

Figure 10-49 Opening screen to configure a Linksys wireless adapter

A+ ESS
2.1
3.2
5.2
6.1

A+
220-602
2.3
5.2
6.2
6.3

Each manufacturer has a different configuration utility, but all utilities should allow you to view information and manage the wireless device using these parameters. Information displayed about the current connection should include:

▲ *The MAC address of the access point device that the adapter is currently using.*
▲ *The current channel the connection is using.* 802.11b/g uses 14 different channels. The United States can use channels 1 through 11. The access point device is configured to use one of these 11 channels.
▲ *Current transmission rate.* For 802.11b networks, the transmission rate (Tx rate) is about 11 Mbps. For 802.11g, expect about 54 Mbps.
▲ *Throughput, link quality,* and *signal strength.* These values indicate throughput rate and how strong the signal is. For most wireless devices, there is nothing for you to configure to get a connection. If the signal strength is poor, look for a way to scan for a new access point. For the utility shown in Figure 10-49, click the **Refresh** button. If the wireless signal strength is still not good enough, try moving your notebook around a bit.

Configuration changes you can make for a wireless device include:

▲ *Mode or network type.* The mode indicates whether the computer is to communicate through an access point (Infrastructure mode) or directly with another wireless device (Ad Hoc mode).
▲ *SSID.* The SSID (service set identifier) is set to ANY by default, which means the NIC is free to connect to any access point it finds. You can enter the name of an access point to specify that this NIC should connect only to a specific access point. If you don't know the name assigned to a particular access point, ask the network administrator responsible for managing the wireless network. For public hot spots, if you don't know the SSID, try "Hotspot". For some public hot spots, the access point is hidden so you must pay to know its name. Figure 10-50 shows the configuration screen for the Linksys adapter where you can choose the mode and enter an SSID.

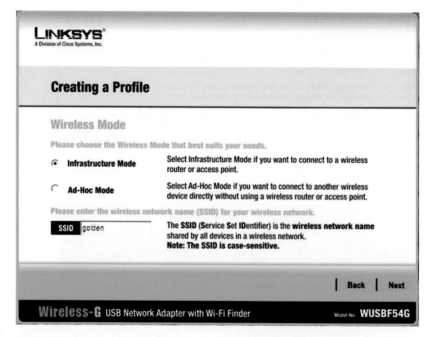

Figure 10-50 Configure the wireless mode and the SSID of the access point

A+ ESS
2.1
3.2
5.2
6.1

A+
220-602
2.3
5.2
6.2
6.3

▲ *Encryption settings.* Most wireless devices today support one or more standards for encrypted wireless transmission. When you try to connect to a secured network, if the connection is set for encryption, you'll be required to enter a secret passphrase or key to be used for the encryption. This passphrase is a word, such as "ourpassphrase," which generates a digital key used for encryption. Every computer user on the same wireless network must enter the same passphrase or key, which an administrator can change at any time.

▲ *Tx rate.* For some adapters, you can specify the transmission rate or leave it at fully automatic so that the adapter is free to use the best transmission rate possible.

▲ *TCP/IP configuration.* Some wireless configuration utilities provide a screen to configure the TCP/IP settings to static or dynamic IP addressing. If your utility does not do that, after you configure the adapter, you'll need to use the Network Connections window to verify the TCP/IP settings. Initially, they'll be set for dynamic IP configuration.

After you have made all configuration changes, you should immediately be able to use your browser. If you can't, then try rebooting the computer. Also, try moving the computer to a better hot spot and click the button to reconnect.

Here are the steps to connect to a public hot spot for a notebook computer that has embedded wireless ability and uses Windows XP network configuration:

1. Turn on your wireless device. For one notebook, that's done by a switch on the keyboard (see Figure 10-51).

Figure 10-51 Turn on the wireless switch on your notebook

2. Right-click **My Network Places** and select **Properties**. The Network Connections window opens. Right-click the **Wireless Network Connection** icon and select **View Available Wireless Networks** from the shortcut menu. The Wireless Network Connection window opens (see Figure 10-52).

3. Select an unsecured network from those listed and click **Connect**. (Incidentally, if you select a secured network that is protected with an encryption key, to continue, you must enter the key in a dialog box shown in Figure 10-53.)

A+ ESS
2.1
3.2
5.2
6.1

A+
220-602
2.3
5.2
6.2
6.3

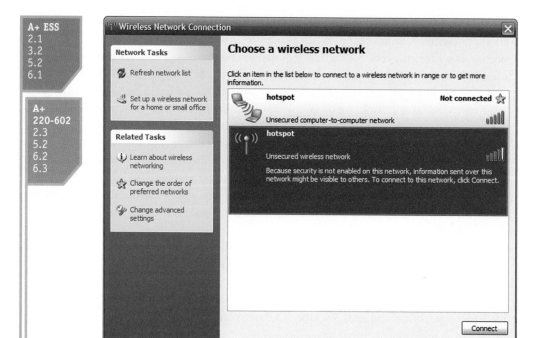

Figure 10-52 Available wireless hot spots

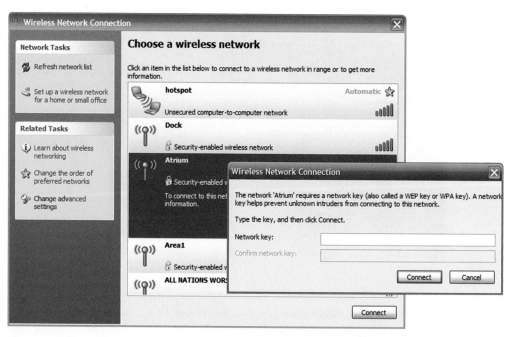

Figure 10-53 To use a secured wireless network, you must know the encryption key

4. Open your browser to test the connection. For some hot spots, a home page appears and you must enter a code or ticket number to proceed (see Figure 10-54).

5. You can see the status of the wireless connection by double-clicking the Wireless Network Connection icon in the Network Connections window or by double-clicking the wireless icon in the system tray. Either way, the status window shown in Figure 10-55 appears.

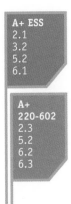

A+ ESS
2.1
3.2
5.2
6.1

A+
220-602
2.3
5.2
6.2
6.3

Figure 10-54 This hot spot requires a ticket number or code to use the wireless network

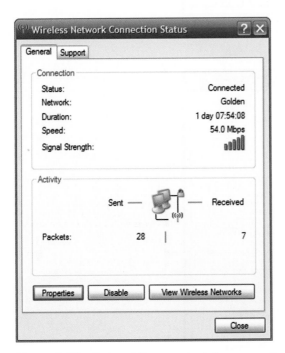

Figure 10-55 Status of the current wireless connection

If you have problems connecting, do the following:

1. If you know the SSID of the hot spot, on the Wireless Network Connection window, click **Change advanced settings**. The Wireless Network Connection Properties dialog box opens. Click the **Wireless Networks** tab (see Figure 10-56).

2. Click **Add**. The Wireless network properties window opens (see Figure 10-57). Enter the SSID of the network and make sure that Network Authentication is set to **Open** and Data encryption is set to **Disabled**. Click **OK**. When a dialog box opens to warn you of the dangers of disabling encryption, click **Continue Anyway**. Click **OK** to close the Wireless Network Connection Properties dialog box.

A+ ESS
2.1
3.2
5.2
6.1

A+
220-602
2.3
5.2
6.2
6.3

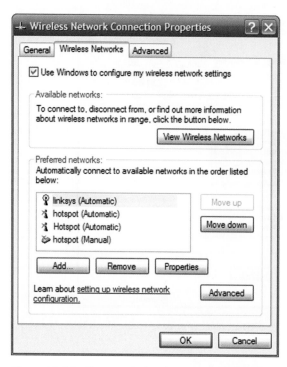

Figure 10-56 Manage wireless hot spots using the Wireless Network Connection Properties dialog box

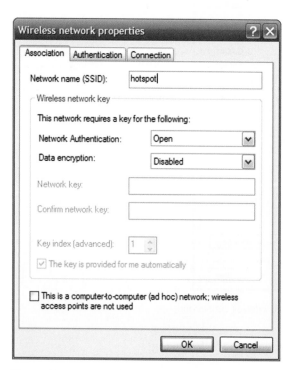

Figure 10-57 Enter the SSID of a hot spot to which you want to connect

3. In the Network Connections window, right-click the **Wireless Network Connection** icon and select **View Available Wireless Networks**. You should now be able to connect to the hot spot.

4. If you still can't connect, it is possible that a private and secured wireless access point has been configured for MAC address filtering in order to control which wireless

A+ ESS
2.1
3.2
5.2
6.1

A+
220-602
2.3
5.2
6.2
6.3

adapters can use the access point. Check with the network administrator to determine if this is the case; if necessary, give the administrator the adapter's MAC address to be entered into a table of acceptable MAC addresses.

5. To know the MAC address of your wireless adapter, you can look on the back of the adapter itself (see Figure 10-58) or in the adapter documentation. Also, if the adapter is installed on your computer, you can use the command **ipconfig /all** in a command prompt window. By the way, if you're running Windows XP Professional, you can also display your MAC address using the Getmac command.

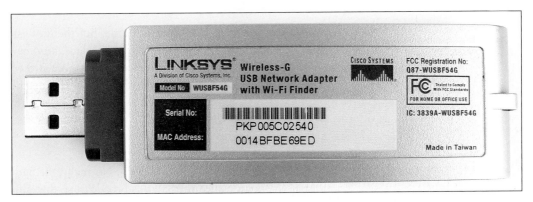

Figure 10-58   The MAC address is printed on the back of this USB wireless adapter

> **Notes**
>
> For a desktop computer, know that a wireless NIC uses an internal or external antenna. To install a NIC that uses an external antenna, remove the antenna from the NIC. Turn off the computer, unplug the power cord, open the case, and install the NIC. For an external antenna, screw the antenna on the NIC and raise it to an upright position (see Figure 10-59). Turn on the computer. The computer immediately detects the device and launches the Found New Hardware Wizard. The installation then proceeds the same way as for a wireless NIC installed in a notebook computer.

Video

Installing a Wireless NIC

Figure 10-59   Raise the antenna on a NIC to an upright position

HOW TO SET UP YOUR OWN WIRELESS NETWORK

**A+ ESS
6.1**

**A+
220-602
6.2
6.3**

Setting up your own wireless network involves buying a wireless access point and configuring it and your wireless computers for communication. The key to successful wireless networking is good security. This section first looks at what you need to know about securing a wireless network, then shows how to choose the equipment you'll need and how to set up a wireless network.

SECURITY ON A WIRELESS LAN

Wireless LANs are so convenient for us at work and at home, but the downside of having a wireless network is that if we don't have the proper security in place, anyone with a wireless computer within range of your access point can use the network—and, if they know how, can intercept and read all the data sent across the network. They might even be able to hack into our computers by using our own wireless network against us. For all these reasons, it's terribly important to secure your wireless network.

Securing a wireless network is generally done in these ways:

Video

Securing a Wireless LAN

▲ *Disable SSID broadcasting.* Normally, the name of the access point (called the SSID) is broadcast so that anyone with a wireless computer can see the name and use the network. If you hide the SSID, a computer can see the wireless network, but can't use it unless the SSID is entered in the wireless adapter configuration.

▲ *Filter MAC addresses.* A wireless access point can filter the MAC addresses of wireless NICs that are allowed to use the access point. This type of security prevents uninvited guests from using the wireless LAN, but does not prevent others from receiving data in the air.

▲ *Data encryption.* Data sent over a wireless connection can be encrypted. The three main methods of encryption for 802.11 wireless networks are WEP (Wired Equivalent Privacy), WPA (WiFi Protected Access), and WPA2. With either method, data is encrypted using a firmware program on the wireless device and is only encrypted while the data is wireless; the data is decrypted before placing it on the wired network. With WEP encryption, data is encrypted using either 64-bit or 128-bit encryption keys. (Because the user can configure only 40 bits of the 64 bits, 64-bit WEP encryption is sometimes called 40-bit WEP encryption.) Because the key used for encryption is static (doesn't change), a hacker who spends enough time examining data packets can eventually find enough patterns in the coding to decrypt the code and read WEP-encrypted data. WPA encryption, also called TKIP (Temporal Key Integrity Protocol) encryption, is stronger than WEP and was designed to replace it. With WPA encryption, encryption keys are changed at set intervals. The latest and best wireless encryption standard is WPA2, also called the 802.11i standard or the AES (Advanced Encryption Standard) protocol. As of March 2006, for a wireless device to be WiFi certified, it must support the WPA2 standard, which is included in Windows XP Service Pack 2. When buying wireless devices, be sure the encryption methods used are compatible!

▲ *Change firmware default settings.* Default settings are easy to guess. For example, a default password is often set to "password" and the default SSID is often set to the brand name of the device, such as Linksys or Netgear. For added security, be sure to change all default settings so they are not so easy to guess. Change the SSID to keep someone from guessing the SSID when it is not broadcasted. Also, change the default password and username for the configuration utility. You can also disable DHCP and use static IP addressing so others cannot obtain an IP address.

A+ ESS
6.1

A+
220-602
6.2
6.3

▲ *Update firmware.* For added security, keep the firmware on your wireless access point updated with downloads from the device manufacturer.

▲ *Use a firewall.* If the access point has firewall capability, be sure to turn it on. In addition, be sure to use a software firewall on every computer using the wireless network.

▲ *Virtual private network (VPN).* A VPN requires a password for entrance and encrypts data over both wired and wireless networks. The basic difference between WEP or WPA encryption and VPN encryption is that VPN encryption applies from the user's PC all the way to the host computer regardless of the type of network used. A VPN uses a technique called tunneling, in which a packet of data is encrypted, as shown in Figure 10-60. The encryption methods used by VPN are stronger than WEP or WPA and are the preferred method when transmitting sensitive data over a wireless connection. How to set up a VPN is beyond the scope of this chapter.

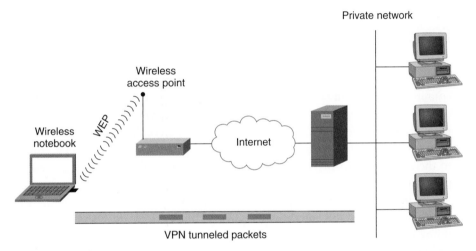

Figure 10-60 With tunneling, packets can travel over a wireless LAN and the Internet in a virtual private network (VPN), but WEP or WPA applies only to the wireless connection

CHOOSING A WIRELESS ACCESS POINT

When selecting a wireless access point, look for the ability to use all the security measures listed in the previous section. Also, be sure the access point supports 802.11 b/g. And, as always, before you buy, search the Internet to read hardware reviews about the device. Only buy a device that consistently gets good reviews. If you're also in need of a wireless adapter to use for the computers that will use your wireless networks, for best results, try to find adapters and an access point made by the same manufacturer.

A wireless access point can be a standalone device such as the one in Figure 10-61 by D-Link, which supports 802.11b/g. This particular access point advertises that it can support transfer rates up to 108 Mbps, but be aware that to get this high rate, you must use a compatible D-Link wireless adapter on your notebook or desktop computer. An access point can also serve more than one purpose, such as the Linksys router shown earlier in Figure 10-17.

Figure 10-61   This wireless access point by D-Link supports 802.11b/g

CONFIGURE AND TEST YOUR WIRELESS NETWORK

To install a standalone access point, position it centrally located to where you want your hot spot to be and plug it in. It will have a network or USB cable that you can connect to a computer so you can configure the access point. A wireless access point includes firmware. (You might be able to update or flash the firmware with updates downloaded from the manufacturer's Web site.) The firmware includes a configuration utility. You access this utility by entering the IP address of the access point in a browser on a computer connected to the access point. Any changes you make to the configuration are stored on the access point device.

Run the setup CD that comes with the access point. If you don't have the setup CD, you can open your browser and enter the IP address of the device, which should launch a firmware utility you can use to configure it. All changes you make to the access point configuration will be saved on the device firmware memory.

Go through the following steps to configure the wireless access point:

1. It's very important to change the default password to the administrative utility to configure the access point. Unless you have disabled or secured the wireless access point, anyone outside your building can use your wireless network. If they guess the default password to the access point, they can change the password to hijack your wireless network. Also, your wireless network can be used for criminal activity. When you first install an access point, before you do anything else, change your password.

2. Look for a way to select the channel the access point will use, the ability to change the SSID of the access point, and the ability to disable SSID broadcasting. Figure 10-62 shows these three settings for one Linksys access point. Figure 10-63 shows how a wireless computer sees a wireless access point that is not broadcasting its SSID. This computer would not be able to use this access point until you entered the SSID in the configuration window shown in Figure 10-64.

A+ ESS
6.1

A+
220-602
6.2
6.3

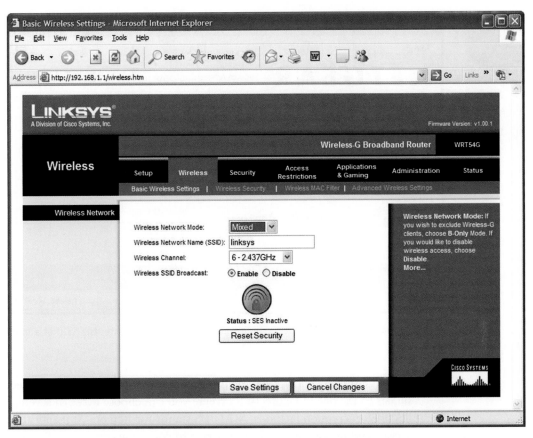

Figure 10-62 Look for the ability of the access point to disable SSID broadcasting

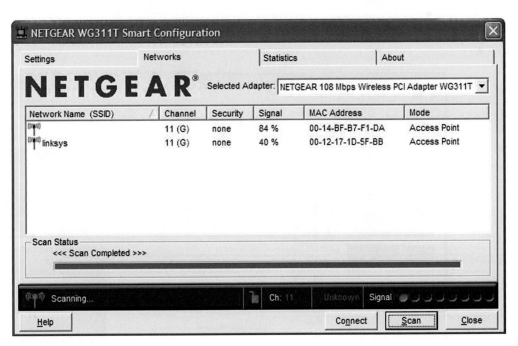

Figure 10-63 A wireless NIC shows it has located two access points, but one is not broadcasting its SSID

Figure 10-64　This wireless adapter configuration screen lets you enter the SSID of a hidden access point and also configure the wireless connection for WEP encryption

3. To configure data encryption on your access point, look for a wireless security screen similar to the one in Figure 10-65 where you can choose between several WPA, WEP, or RADIUS encryption methods. (RADIUS stands for Remote Authentication Dial-In User Service and uses an authentication server to control access.) WPA Personal is the one to choose unless one of your wireless adapters doesn't support it. For example, the wireless adapter configuration screen in Figure 10-64 shows it supports only WEP encryption, so your access point is forced to use that method. Enter the same passphrase for WEP encryption on the access point screen and all your wireless adapter configuration screens.

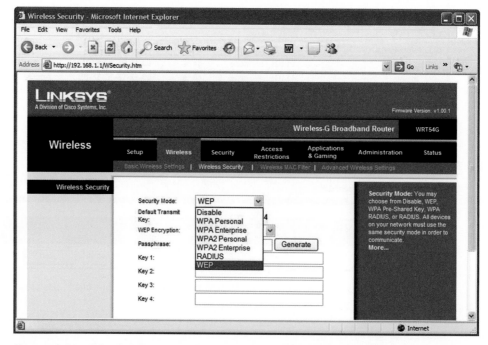

Figure 10-65　This wireless access point supports several encryption methods

10

A+ ESS
6.1

4. Look for MAC filtering on your access point, similar to the screen in Figure 10-66. On this access point, you can enter a table of MAC addresses and decide if this list of MAC addresses is to be used to prevent or permit use of the access point.

A+
220-602
6.2
6.3

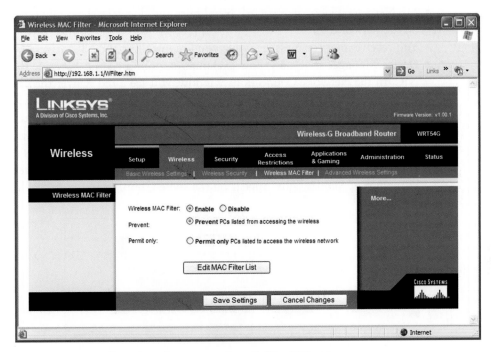

Figure 10-66   Configure how the access point will filter MAC addresses

5. Save all your settings for the access point and test the connection. To test it, on one of your wireless computers, open the configuration window for the wireless adapter and scan for access points. If the scan does not detect your access point, verify the wireless adapter is set to scan all channels or the selected channel of your access point. Try moving your access point or the computer. If you still can't get a connection, remove all security measures and try again. Then restore the security features one at a time until you discover the one causing the problem, or use encryption.

We've just configured your wireless access point to use several security features. Is it really necessary to use them all? Well, not really, but it can't hurt. Encryption is essential to keep others from hacking into your wireless data, and to keep others out of your network, you need to disable SSID broadcasting, filter MAC addresses, or use encryption.

TROUBLESHOOTING A NETWORK CONNECTION

A+ ESS
1.3
5.1
5.3

APPLYING CONCEPTS   T.J. has just used a crossover cable to connect his two computers together. My Network Places on both computers refuses to display the other computer. What should T.J. check?

A+
220-602
1.2
3.1
5.3

A+ ESS
1.3
5.1
5.3

A+
220-602
1.2
3.1
5.3

If you have problems connecting to the network, follow the guidelines in this section. First, here are some symptoms that might indicate the NIC is faulty:

◢ You cannot make a connection to the network.

◢ My Network Places or Network Neighborhood does not show any other computers on the network.

◢ You receive an error message while you are installing the NIC drivers.

◢ Device Manager shows a yellow exclamation point or a red X beside the name of the NIC. In the Network Connections window, you see a red X over the network icon.

◢ There are at least two lights on a NIC: One stays on steadily to let you know there is a physical connection (labeled LINK in Figure 10-67), and another blinks to let you know there is activity (labeled ACT in Figure 10-67). If you see no lights, you know there is no physical connection between the NIC and the network. This means there is a problem with the network cable, the card, or the switch, hub, or router to which the PC connects. Similar lights appear on the switch, hub, or router for each network port.

Figure 10-67 Lights on the back of a NIC can be used for troubleshooting

◢ The problem might not be caused by the NIC. You can check to see if a network cable is good using a cable tester such as the one shown earlier in Figure 10-12. Electrical interference might be a problem. If you suspect interference, you can install a ferrite clamp close to the device end of the cable. The clamp helps to eliminate electromagnetic interference and is shown in Figure 10-68.

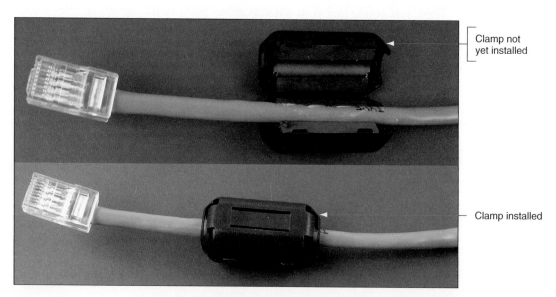

Clamp not yet installed

Clamp installed

Figure 10-68 Install a ferrite clamp on a network cable to protect against electrical interference

A+ ESS
1.3
5.1
5.3

A+
220-602
1.2
3.1
5.3

Sometimes you might have trouble with a network connection due to a TCP/IP problem. Windows TCP/IP includes several diagnostic tools that are useful in troubleshooting problems with TCP/IP. The most useful is Ping (Packet Internet Groper), which tests connectivity and is discussed here. Ping sends a signal to a remote computer. If the remote computer is online and hears the signal, it responds. Ipconfig under Windows 2000/XP and Winipcfg under Windows 9x/Me test the TCP/IP configuration.

Try these things to test TCP/IP configuration and connectivity:

1. For Windows 2000/XP, enter **Ipconfig /all** at the command prompt. For Windows 9x/Me, click **Start,** click **Run,** enter **Winipcfg** in the Run dialog box, and then click **OK.** If the TCP/IP configuration is correct and an IP address is assigned, the IP address, subnet mask, and default gateway appear along with the adapter address. For dynamic IP addressing, if the PC cannot reach the DHCP server, then it assigns itself an IP address. This is called IP autoconfiguration and the IP address is called an Automatic Private IP Address (APIPA). In this situation, the Winipcfg window and the results of the Ipconfig command both show the IP address as the IP Autoconfiguration Address, and the address begins with 169.254. In this case, suspect that the PC is not able to reach the network or the DHCP server is down.

2. Try to release the current IP address and lease a new address. To do this for Windows 9x/Me Winipcfg, select the network card, click the **Release** button, and then click the **Renew** button. For Windows 2000/XP, first use the **Ipconfig /release** command, and then use the **Ipconfig /renew** command. Or you can open the Network Connections window, right-click the network connection, and click **Repair** on the shortcut menu (see Figure 10-69).

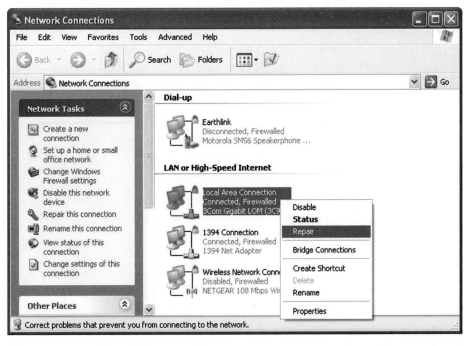

Figure 10-69 Use the Repair command to release and renew the IP address of a network connection

3. Next, try the loopback address test. At a command prompt, enter the command **Ping 127.0.0.1** (with no period after the final 1). This IP address always refers to your local computer. It should respond with a reply message from your computer. If this works, TCP/IP is likely to be configured correctly. If you get any errors up to this point, then assume that the problem is on your PC. Check the installation and configuration of each component, such as the network card and the TCP/IP protocol suite. Remove and reinstall each component, and watch for error messages, writing them down so that you can recognize or research them later as necessary. Compare the configuration to that of a working PC on the same network.

4. Next, ping the IP address of your default gateway. If it does not respond, the problem might be with the gateway or with the network to the gateway.

5. Now try to ping the host computer you are trying to reach. If it does not respond, the problem might be with the host computer or with the network to the computer.

6. If you have Internet access and substitute a domain name for the IP address in the Ping command, and Ping works, you can conclude that DNS works. If an IP address works, but the domain name does not work, the problem lies with DNS. Try this command: **ping www.course.com**.

7. Determine whether other computers on the network are having trouble with their connections. If the entire network is down, the problem is not isolated to the PC and the NIC you are working on. Check the hub or switch controlling the network.

8. Make sure the NIC and its drivers are installed by checking for the NIC in Device Manager. Try uninstalling and reinstalling the NIC drivers.

9. If the drivers still install with errors, try downloading new drivers from the Web site of the network card manufacturer. Also, look on the installation CD that came bundled with the NIC for a setup program. If you find one, uninstall the NIC and run this setup program.

10. Some network cards have diagnostic programs on the installation CD. Try running the program from the CD. Look in the documentation that came with the card for instructions on how to install and run the program.

11. Check the network cable to make sure it is not damaged and that it does not exceed the recommended length for the type of network you are using. If the cable is frayed, twisted, or damaged, replace it. Be sure all network cables are securely attached to the wall or are up and out of harm's way so they will not be tripped over, stepped on, twisted, or otherwise damaged.

12. Connect the network cable to a different port on the hub. If that doesn't help, you might have a problem with the cable or the NIC itself. Uninstall the NIC drivers, replace the NIC, and then install new drivers.

13. Check to see whether you have the most current version of your motherboard BIOS. The motherboard manufacturer should have information on its Web site about whether an upgrade is available.

A+ ESS
1.3
5.1
5.3

A+
220-602
1.2
3.1
5.3

APPLYING CONCEPTS   Back to T.J.'s problem connecting his two computers. The problem might be the hardware or software. Begin with the hardware. Are the lights displayed correctly on the NICs? If so, T.J. can assume the hardware is functioning. Next, check the driver installation. Does Device Manager on both computers show no errors or conflicts with each network adapter? Next, check the configuration. In this situation, T.J. should have used static IP addressing. What is the IP address of each PC? Open a command window and try to ping the local computer, and then try to ping the remote computer. Does each computer have a computer name? Try rebooting each computer.

>> CHAPTER SUMMARY

- Networks are categorized in size as a PAN, LAN, MAN, or WAN.

- Bandwidth measures how much data can travel over a given communications system in a given amount of time. Common bandwidth technologies for personal or small business networks include Ethernet, WiFi, regular telephone lines, cable modem, ISDN, DSL, and satellite access.

- The most popular physical network architecture for LANs is Ethernet.

- Ethernet uses a logical bus and can be configured as a star topology, in which all nodes connect to a centralized switch or hub, or a bus topology, which connects nodes in a line and has no central connection point.

- An Ethernet hub broadcasts all data that flows through it to every node connected to it. It does not make decisions about where to send packets. Switches keep switching tables of nodes on the network and send packets only to the designated node.

- The most popular Ethernet networks are 100BaseT and Gigabit Ethernet, which both use STP or UTP cabling with RJ-45 connectors.

- Wireless LANs make connections using radio or infrared technology. A wireless LAN can be used in combination with a wired LAN. The most popular wireless technology for a LAN is 802.11b/g, also called Wi-Fi.

- Telephone networks include POTS, VoIP, cellular WAN, satellite phone, and radio phone. Another type of wireless telephone is a cordless phone that communicates with a base station at close range.

- A PC connects to a network using a NIC (network interface card) or network adapter, which communicates with NICs on other PCs using a set of hardware protocols (such as Ethernet). The OSs on the two computers use a different set of protocols (such as TCP/IP or NetBEUI) to communicate.

- NICs and the device drivers that control them are designed to work with a particular network architecture and are the only PC components that are aware of the type of physical network being used.

- The three protocols that Windows supports for network communications are TCP/IP (the protocol suite for the Internet), IPX/SPX (designed for use with Novell NetWare), and NetBEUI (a proprietary Windows protocol for use on networks isolated from the Internet). Only TCP/IP is supported on the Internet.

▲ The four types of addresses on a Windows network are MAC addresses, IP addresses, character-based names (such as NetBIOS names, host names, domain names), and port addresses.

▲ MAC addresses are used only for communication within a local network.

▲ IP addresses identify devices on the Internet and other TCP/IP networks. They consist of four numbers separated by periods. The first part of an IP address identifies the network, and the last identifies the host.

▲ When installing a NIC, physically install the card, install the device drivers, install the OS networking protocol you intend to use (it might already be installed by default), configure the OS protocol, and give the computer a name.

▲ When configuring TCP/IP, you must know if IP addresses are statically or dynamically assigned.

▲ When setting up a wireless network, configure the wireless access point to secure the network from unauthorized access. Use encryption to keep data from being stolen in transmission.

▲ When troubleshooting a NIC on a PC, check connections in the rest of the network, cabling and ports for the PC, the NIC itself (substituting one known to be working, if necessary), the BIOS, and the device drivers.

▲ Ping is a useful TCP/IP utility to check network connectivity.

▲ Two other useful troubleshooting tools are Ipconfig (Windows 2000 and Windows XP) and Winipcfg (Windows 9x/Me), which test TCP/IP configuration.

>> KEY TERMS

For explanations of key terms, see the Glossary near the end of the book.

100BaseT	data throughput	hardware address
10Base2	datagram	host
10Base5	default gateway	host name
10BaseT	DHCP (Dynamic Host	hub
802.11a/b/g	Configuration Protocol)	IBM Data Connector (IDC)
access point (AP)	DNS (Domain Name System, or	Institute of Electrical and
adapter address	Domain Name Service)	Electronics Engineers (IEEE)
AirPort	DNS server	intranet
amplifier repeater	domain name	IP address
attenuation	dynamic IP address	IPX/SPX (Internetwork Packet
bandwidth	Ethernet	Exchange/Sequenced Packet
base station	Fast Ethernet	Exchange)
binding	ferrite clamp	LAN (local area network)
Bluetooth	Fiber Distributed Data Interface	line speed
BNC connector	(FDDI)	MAC (Media Access Control)
broadband	fiber optic	address
broadcast	frame	MAN (metropolitan area
bus topology	full duplex	network)
CDMA (Code Division Multiple	fully qualified domain name	multicasting
Access)	(FQDN)	NAT (Network Address
cellular network	gateway	Translation)
cellular WAN	General Packet Radio Service	NetBEUI (NetBIOS Extended
client	(GPRS)	User Interface)
client/server	Gigabit Ethernet	NetBIOS (Network Basic
coaxial cable	GSM (Global System for Mobile	Input/Output System)
computer name	Communications)	network adapter
crossover cable	half duplex	network interface card (NIC)

network operating system (NOS)
network printer
node
NWLink
octet
packet
PAN (personal area network)
patch cable
peer-to-peer network
physical address
Ping (Packet Internet Groper)
proxy server
repeater
ring topology

RJ-45 connector
server
shielded twisted-pair (STP) cable
signal-regenerating repeater
star bus topology
star ring topology
star topology
static IP address
subnet mask
switch
TCP/IP (Transmission Control
   Protocol/Internet Protocol)
TDMA (Time Division Multiple
   Access)

ThickNet
ThinNet
Token Ring
Universal Data Connector (UDC)
unshielded twisted pair (UTP)
   cable
WAN (wide area network)
WEP (Wired Equivalent
   Privacy)
Wi-Fi (Wireless Fidelity)
wireless LAN (WLAN)
WPA (WiFi Protected Access)
WPA2 (WiFi Protected
   Access 2)

>> REVIEWING THE BASICS

1. Name three types of Ethernet. What transmission speed does each support?

2. What is the maximum length of a cable on a 100BaseT network?

3. What does the 100 in the name 100BaseT indicate?

4. What is broadcasting? Name a network connection device that relies on it and one that does not rely on it.

5. What IEEE standards describe Ethernet? What IEEE standards describe wireless LANs?

6. What are three ways a wireless network can be secured?

7. What connecting device do you use for a small LAN? For two or more connected networks?

8. Describe the structure of an IP address. How is it different from a MAC address?

9. Which provides stronger security for a wireless network, WEP or WPA?

10. What advantage does a VPN have over WPA encryption when a notebook computer is using a wireless connection to connect to the Internet and on to a private corporate network?

11. When you secure a wireless network using MAC address filtering, is data sent over the network secure? Why or why not?

12. Why might a wireless access point have more than one antenna?

13. Which Windows operating system does not automatically include the NetBEUI protocol?

14. What are the two ways an IP address can be assigned to a PC? What is one advantage of each?

15. What are the Ping, Ipconfig, and Winipcfg utilities used for?

16. Of IPX/SPX, TCP/IP, and NetBEUI, which is routable and which is not?

17. Place the following bandwidth technologies in the order of their highest speed, from slowest to fastest: SDSL, ISDN, regular telephone lines, cable modem, Gigabit Ethernet, ATM.

18. When using DSL to connect to the Internet, the data transmission shares the cabling with what other technology?

19. Give two examples of broadband technology.

20. Which is more expensive, UTP CAT5e cabling or STP CAT5e cabling?

21. What is the most common type connector used with coaxial cable on a ThinNet Ethernet network?

22. If you wanted to upgrade your 100BaseT Ethernet network so that it will run about 10 times the current speed, what technology would you use?

23. What networking protocol was first used by Novell NetWare and is not supported on the Internet?

24. If you were going to connect two PCs together in a simple network using the network ports on each PC, what type of cable would you use?

25. When using a cable modem to connect to the Internet, the data transmission shares the cabling with what other technology?

>> THINKING CRITICALLY

1. You have just installed a network adapter and have booted up the system, installing the drivers. You open My Network Places on a remote computer and don't see the computer on which you just installed the NIC. What is the first thing you check?

   a. Is File and Printer Sharing installed?

   b. Is the NetBEUI protocol installed?

   c. Are the lights on the adapter functioning correctly?

   d. Has the computer been assigned a computer name?

2. You work in the Accounting Department and have been using a network drive to post Excel spreadsheets to your workgroup as you complete them. When you attempt to save a spreadsheet to the drive, you see the error message, "You do not have access to the folder 'J:\'. See your administrator for access to this folder." What should you do first? Second?

   a. Ask your network administrator to give you permission to access the folder.

   b. Check My Network Places to verify that you can connect to the network.

   c. Save the spreadsheet to your hard drive.

   d. Using Windows Explorer, remap the network drive.

   e. Reboot your PC.

3. Linda has been assigned the job of connecting five computers to a network. The room holding the five computers has three network ports that connect to a switch in an electrical closet down the hallway. Linda decides to install a second switch in the room. The new switch has four network ports. She uses a crossover cable to connect one of the four ports on the switch to a wall jack. Now she has five ports available (two wall jacks and three switch ports). While installing and configuring the NICs in the five computers, she discovers that the PCs connected to the two wall jacks work fine, but the three connected to the switch refuse to communicate with the network. What could be wrong and what should she try next?

>> HANDS-ON PROJECTS

PROJECT 10-1:   Investigating Your PC

If you are connected to the Internet or a network, answer these questions:

1. What is the hardware device used to make this connection (modem or network card)? List the device's name as Windows sees it.

10

2. If you are connected to a LAN, what is the MAC address of the NIC? Print the screen that shows the address.

3. What is the IP address of your PC?

4. What Windows utilities did you use to answer the first three questions?

5. Print the screen that shows which network protocols are installed on your PC.

PROJECT 10-2:   Researching Switches

A PC support technician is often called on to research equipment to maintain or improve a PC or network and make recommendations for purchase. Find four Web pages advertising switches that meet these criteria:

1. Find two switches by different manufacturers that support Gigabit Ethernet and have at least five ports.

2. Find two switches by different manufacturers that support Fast Ethernet and have at least five ports.

3. Compare the features and prices of each switch. Which brand and type switch would you recommend for a small business network? What information might you want to know before you make your recommendation?

PROJECT 10-3:   Installing a NIC

Some motherboards come with an onboard network port. If this port goes bad, you can use CMOS setup to disable the port and then install a NIC on the motherboard. Using a computer that has onboard networking, disable the network port and install a NIC. Then verify the computer has network connectivity and is able to use the network. Next, remove the NIC, enable the onboard networking, and again verify the computer can access the network.

PROJECT 10-4:   Researching a Wireless LAN

Suppose you want to connect two computers to your company LAN using a wireless connection. Use the Internet to research the equipment needed to create the wireless LAN, and answer the following:

1. Print a Web page showing an access point device that can connect to an Ethernet LAN.

2. How much does the device cost? How many wireless devices can the access point support at one time? How is the device powered?

3. Print three Web pages showing three different network adapters a computer can use to connect to the access point. Include one external device that uses a USB port and one internal device. How much does each device cost?

4. What is the total cost of implementing a wireless LAN with two computers using the wireless connection?

>> REAL PROBLEMS, REAL SOLUTIONS

REAL PROBLEM 10-1: Setting Up a Small Network

You've been using a Windows 98 desktop computer for several years, but finally the day has come! You purchase a wonderful and new Windows XP notebook computer complete with all the bells and whistles. Now you are faced with the task of transferring all your e-mail addresses, favorite Web site links, and files to your notebook.

Your old desktop doesn't have a CD burner, so burning a CD is out of the question. You considered the possibility of e-mailing everything from one computer to another or using floppy disks, but both solutions are not good options. Then the thought dawns on you to purchase a crossover cable and connect the two computers in the simplest possible network. Practice this solution by using a crossover cable to connect a Windows XP computer to a Windows 98 computer and share files between them.

REAL PROBLEM 10-2: Connecting to the Internet

Jack is a PC support technician in training who makes house calls. He appeared for an appointment at a business where he expected to set up a small network of three computers. However, he found out he was expected to connect one computer to the Internet using cable modem. Being new at supporting computers, Jack had never tackled this job. Here's a great opportunity for Jack to apply what he does know to find out what he doesn't know.

When configuring a PC to connect to the Internet using a LAN, DSL, cable modem, ISDN, satellite, or wireless connection, the most common method is to use a NIC in the PC that connects to the LAN, DSL converter box, cable modem, ISDN converter box (called a TA or terminal adapter), or satellite converter box. On the other hand, the connection might be by way of a USB port. To make the connection, follow specific directions that came bundled with the converter box or modem. When a network connection is used, generally you connect the PC to the modem and connect the modem to the phone jack (for DSL) or the TV jack (for cable modem). Plug up the power and turn on the modem. Then configure the TCP/IP settings for the connection to the ISP. When the PC is rebooted, it will receive a dynamic IP address from the ISP or will use a static IP address provided by the ISP. Test the connection by using a browser to surf the Web. If a USB connection is used between your computer and the modem, you need to first install the modem drivers before you connect the modem to your PC.

Here is what Jack did:

1. Jack connected the cable modem to the TV jack and plugged it in.

2. He connected the cable modem to the PC by way of a network cable.

3. He booted up the PC and then configured the network connection for static IP addressing, assigning an IP address of 192.168.1.1 to the PC.

4. Next, he tried to surf the Web, but could not connect.

Answer the following questions to solve Jack's connectivity problem:

1. What, if anything, is wrong with Jack's TCP/IP configuration?

2. What, if anything, is wrong with Jack's physical connections?

3. What are the first three things you would do if you were solving the problem?

CHAPTER 11

Notebooks, Tablet PCs, and PDAs

So far in this book, you've learned how computers work, explored some of the devices used to work with them, examined operating systems, and discovered how to connect a PC to a network. Most devices and software you've learned about relate to desktop computers, which are stationary and cannot be moved easily. However, recent statistics show that more than half of personal computers purchased today are notebook computers, and almost 30 percent of personal computers in use today are notebooks. As notebooks become more and more popular, PC service technicians will need to know how to support them. In this chapter, you'll learn about supporting, upgrading, and troubleshooting notebooks. You'll also learn about other portable devices, including tablet PCs and personal digital assistants (PDAs).

SUPPORTING NOTEBOOKS

A notebook or laptop computer is a computer designed to be portable (see Figure 11-1). Notebooks use the same technology as PCs but with modifications to use less power, consume less space, and operate on the move.

Figure 11-1 A notebook is a computer designed for portability

In many situations, the task of troubleshooting, upgrading, and maintaining a notebook computer requires the same skills, knowledge, and procedures as when servicing a desktop computer. However, you should take some special considerations into account when purchasing, caring for, supporting, upgrading, and troubleshooting notebooks. When you think of all the new notebooks sold this past year or so, learning about notebooks and how to support them can position you for some great career opportunities supporting notebooks!

Now let's turn our attention to some useful tips when selecting and purchasing a notebook and the special considerations when servicing them. Then you'll learn how to care for notebooks and how to connect peripheral equipment to them.

TIPS FOR BUYING A NOTEBOOK

A PC repair technician is often called on to help customers select and buy computer and networking products. Listed below are some special considerations you need to keep in mind when selecting a notebook computer:

◢ The main advantage a notebook has over a desktop is portability. A notebook computer generally costs about twice as much as a comparable desktop system, when comparing speed, computing power, and features. Notebooks are generally slower than desktops because of slower processors, motherboards, hard drives, and video systems. Notebooks generally cannot be upgraded as easily as a desktop and the upgrades cost more. In addition, notebooks tend to drop in value over three or four years faster than do desktops. For all these reasons, if the computer is to remain at one location, buy a desktop rather than a notebook.

11

◢ Most people buy a desktop expecting to be able to upgrade it over the course of its lifetime. Not so with notebooks. It is unlikely that you will be able to upgrade the processor, motherboard, or video, although you can upgrade memory or add a new Mini PCI card. In general, buy a notebook without expecting to upgrade internal components.

◢ Because added features cost more on a notebook than a desktop and add to the weight of the notebook, don't buy these extra features unless you really need them.

◢ Servicing your own notebook when internal components break might not be possible because you might not be able to purchase the parts or obtain the instructions for disassembling the notebook. Therefore, it's probably a good idea to pay for the extended warranty on a notebook that will last the three or four years that the notebook still has value. After about four years, any notebook is most likely not going to be worth more than $400. At that time, you can buy a new one.

◢ Selecting the brand of notebook is your most important decision when selecting a notebook. As with any buying decision, do your research. Read online reviews of notebooks and their manufacturer. Pay special attention to how satisfied customers are with the service when the notebook breaks.

◢ Keep these key points about notebook components in mind:

- Buy the fastest processor that you can afford. Mobile processors are built to conserve power and take up less space. Chapter 4 discusses mobile processors in detail.
- For the LCD panel, active matrix is better than dual scan. Also consider the resolution, backlighting, and size. For more information on selecting an LCD panel, see Chapter 8.
- Buy as much memory as you plan to use later. Sometimes, to upgrade memory on a notebook, you must replace a module that has low RAM with one that has more RAM, which can make upgrading memory more expensive.
- The best type of battery to buy is a lithium battery.
- Also consider the weight and size of the notebook, keyboard, pointing device, optical drives, and other features.

SPECIAL CONSIDERATIONS WHEN SERVICING NOTEBOOKS

A+ ESS
1.4
2.4

Notebooks and their replacement parts cost more than desktop PCs with similar features because their components are designed to be more compact and stand up to travel. They use thin LCD panels instead of CRT monitors for display, compact hard drives, and small memory modules and CPUs that require less power than regular components. Whereas a desktop computer is often assembled from parts made by a variety of manufacturers, notebook computers are almost always sold by a vendor that either manufactured the notebook or had it manufactured as a consolidated system. Factors to consider that generally apply more to notebook computers than desktop computers are the original equipment manufacturer's warranty, the service manuals and diagnostic software provided by the OEM, and the customized installation of the OS that is unique to notebooks.

WARRANTY CONCERNS

Most manufacturers or retailers of notebooks offer at least a one-year warranty and the option to purchase an extended warranty. Therefore, when problems arise while the notebook is under warranty, you are dealing with a single manufacturer or retailer to get support or parts. After

A+ ESS
1.4
2.4

the notebook is out of warranty, this manufacturer or retailer can still be your one-stop shop for support and parts.

The warranty often applies to all components in the system, but it can be voided if someone other than an authorized service center services the notebook. Therefore, you as a service technician must be very careful not to void a warranty that the customer has purchased. Warranties can be voided by opening the case, removing part labels, installing other-vendor parts, upgrading the OS, or disassembling the system unless directly instructed to do so by the service center help desk personnel.

Before you begin servicing a notebook, to avoid problems with a warranty, always ask the customer, "Is the notebook under warranty?" If the notebook is under warranty, look at the documentation to find out how to get technical support. Options are phone numbers, chat rooms on the Web, and e-mail. Use the most appropriate option. Before you contact technical support, have the notebook model and serial number ready (see Figure 11-2). You'll also need the name, phone number, and address of the person or company that made the purchase.

Figure 11-2 The model and serial number stamped on the bottom of a notebook are used to identify the notebook to service desk personnel

Based on the type of warranty purchased by the notebook's owner, the manufacturer might send an on-site service technician, ask you to ship or take the notebook to an authorized service center, or help you solve the problem over the phone. Table 11-1 lists manufacturers of notebooks and tablet PCs. Tablet PCs are discussed later in the chapter.

A+ ESS
1.4
2.4

Manufacturer	Web Site
Acer America	*global.acer.com*
Apple Computer	*www.apple.com*
Compaq and HP	*www.hp.com*
Dell Computer	*www.dell.com*
eMachines by Gateway	*www.emachines.com*
Fujitsu/Fuji	*www.fujitsu.com*
Gateway	*www.gateway.com*
Lenovo (formally IBM Thinkpads)	*www.lenovo.com*
MPC Computers	*www.mpccorp.com*
NEC	*www.nec.com*
PC Notebook	*www.pcnotebook.com*
Sony (VAIO)	*www.sonystyle.com*
Toshiba America	*www.csd.toshiba.com*
WinBook	*www.winbook.com*

Table 11-1 Notebook and tablet PC manufacturers

SERVICE MANUALS AND OTHER SOURCES OF INFORMATION

Desktop computer cases tend to be similar to one another, and components in desktop systems tend to be interchangeable among manufacturers. Not so with notebooks. Notebook manufacturers tend to take great liberty in creating their own unique computer cases, buses, cables, connectors, drives, circuit boards, fans, and even screws, all of which are likely to be proprietary in design.

Every notebook model has a unique case. Components are installed in unique ways and opening the case for each notebook model is done differently. Because of these differences, servicing notebooks can be very complicated and time consuming. For example, a hard drive on one notebook is accessed by popping open a side panel and sliding the drive out of its bay. However, to access the hard drive on another model notebook, you must remove the keyboard, video card, memory modules, internal antennae, and even the LCD panel. If you are not familiar with a particular notebook model, you can do damage to the case as you pry and push trying to open it. Trial and error is likely to damage a case. Even though you might successfully replace a broken component, the damaged case can result in an unhappy customer.

Fortunately, a notebook service manual can save you much time and effort—if you can locate one (see Figure 11-3). Two notebook manufacturers, Lenovo (formally IBM) and Dell, provide their service manuals online free of charge. In addition, Compaq offers detailed information on its Web site to help you service its notebooks (see Figure 11-4). For all notebook manufacturers, check the FAQ pages of their Web sites for help in tasks such as opening a case without damaging it and locating and replacing a component.

Sometimes, you can find service manuals on the Web. One useful and very interesting Web site that contains service manuals for several different brands of notebooks as well as service manuals for lots of other electronic devices is *www.eserviceinfo.com*. It is published out of Bulgaria. Some of these service manuals are presented as files with an .rar file extension. An RAR file is a compressed file similar to a Zip file, except a very large file can be broken into two or more RAR files. You can download a trial version of the software to manage RAR files from RARLAB at *www.rarlab.com*.

A+ ESS
1.4
2.4

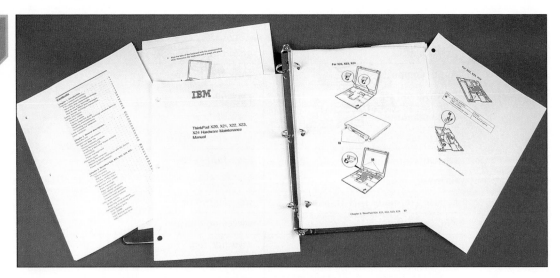

Figure 11-3   A notebook service manual tells you how to use diagnostic tools, troubleshoot a notebook, and replace components

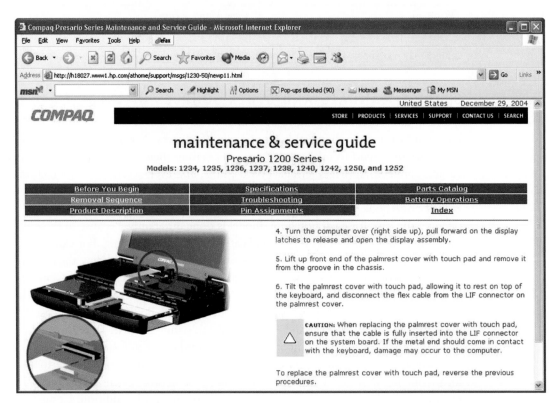

Figure 11-4   The Compaq Web site (*www.hp.com*) provides detailed instructions for troubleshooting and replacing components

Of course, don't forget about the user manuals. They might contain directions for upgrading and replacing components that do not require disassembling the case, such as how to upgrade memory. User manuals also include troubleshooting tips and procedures and possibly descriptions of CMOS settings. In addition, you can use a Web search engine (for example,

> **Notes**
>
> Just as with desktop computers, you might be able to solve a problem with an unstable system or a motherboard component by flashing BIOS. Be sure to download BIOS updates only from the motherboard manufacturer Web site.

A+ ESS
1.4
2.4

Google at *www.google.com*) to search on the computer model and component that is giving you the problem.

DIAGNOSTIC TOOLS PROVIDED BY MANUFACTURERS

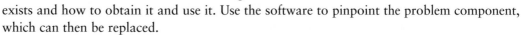

Notes

When you purchase a replacement part for a notebook from the notebook's manufacturer, most often the manufacturer also sends you detailed instructions for exchanging the part.

Most notebook manufacturers provide diagnostic software that can help you test components to determine which component needs replacing. As one of the first steps when servicing a notebook, check the user manual, service manual, or manufacturer Web site to determine if diagnostic software exists and how to obtain it and use it. Use the software to pinpoint the problem component, which can then be replaced.

For older notebooks, the software is usually contained on a floppy disk and run from the disk. This test disk might come with the notebook or can be purchased from the manufacturer as a separate item. Check the manufacturer Web site for test software that can be downloaded for a particular model notebook. For newer notebooks, the software is stored on CDs bundled with the notebook or on the hard drive and accessed by pressing certain keys during the boot process.

One example of diagnostic software is PC-Doctor, which is used by several Lenovo and IBM ThinkPad models. The test software is stored on a floppy disk, CD, or hard drive. If stored on a floppy disk or CD, you can boot from the device to run the tests. If the software is stored on the hard drive, you can run it from the Windows Start menu or by pressing a function key at startup before Windows loads. Either way, PC-Doctor can run tests on the keyboard, video, speakers, mouse, joystick, floppy disk drive, CD drive, DVD drive, wireless LAN, motherboard, processor, serial and parallel ports, hard drive, Zip drive, and memory. To learn how to use the software, see the notebook's service manual or user manual.

A+ ESS
1.4
2.4
3.2
3.3

A+
220-602
3.3

THE OEM OPERATING SYSTEM BUILD

Notebook computers are sold with an operating system preinstalled at the factory. The OS installation is tailored by the manufacturer to satisfy the specific needs of the notebook. In this situation, the manufacturer is called the OEM (original equipment manufacturer) and the customized installation of the OS is called the operating system build or OS build. Drivers installed are also specific to proprietary devices installed in the notebook. Diagnostic software is often written specifically for a notebook and its installed OS. For all these reasons, use caution when deciding to upgrade to a new OS and know that, if you have problems with a device, in most circumstances, you must turn to the OEM for solutions and updates for device drivers. Now let's look at some OS features designed with notebooks in mind, tools helpful when notebook OS problems arise, and special considerations to be aware of when upgrading notebook operating systems.

Windows Notebook Features

Windows 2000/XP and Windows 98 include several features that can be useful when supporting notebooks:

- *Channel aggregation.* This OS feature allows you to use two modem connections at the same time to speed up data throughput when connected over phone lines. To use the feature, you must have two phone lines and two modem cards that are physically designed to connect two phone lines at the same time.
- *Power management.* Some power-management features include automatically powering down a PC Card when it is not in use, support for multiple battery packs, and individual power profiles. Power profiles are described later in this chapter.
- *Support for PC Cards.* This support includes many Windows drivers for PC Card devices.

A+ ESS
1.4
2.4
3.2
3.3

A+
220-602
3.3

▲ *Windows 9x/Me Briefcase.* When returning from a trip with a notebook, you might want to update your desktop PC with all e-mail documents and other files created or updated during the trip. To do this, use Windows 9x/Me Briefcase, a system folder used to synchronize files between two computers. Briefcase automatically updates files on the original computer to the most recent version. You can use a null modem cable, disk, or network for the file transfer.

▲ *Windows 2000/XP Offline Files and Folders.* Offline Files and Folders replaces Windows 9x/Me Briefcase and stores shared network files and folders in a cache on the notebook hard drive so that you can use them offline. When you reconnect to the network, Offline Files and Folders synchronizes the files in the cache with those on the network.

▲ *Folder redirection under Windows 2000/XP.* Folder redirection lets you point to an alternate location on a network for a folder. This feature can make the location of a folder transparent to the user. For example, a user's My Documents folder is normally located on the local computer's logical drive C. Using folder redirection, an administrator can put this My Documents folder on a file server. Having this folder on a shared file server has two important benefits:

- Regardless of which computer a user logs on to, her My Documents folder is available.
- A company routinely backs up data on a shared file server so backing up the user's data happens without her having to do anything.

  When using folder redirection with Offline Files and Folders, a user can access her My Documents folder even when the notebook is not attached to the company network.

▲ *Hardware profiles under Windows 2000/XP.* Hardware profiles let you specify which devices are to be loaded on startup for a particular user or set of circumstances. For example, you might set two different hardware profiles for a notebook computer, one for when it is on the road and one for when it is at home connected to a home network.

The Recovery CDs and Recovery Partitions

Most notebook computers come with one or more support CDs provided by the manufacturer. This CD might or might not contain an installable version of the OS preinstalled on the notebook. If you need to install the OS again, such as when you are replacing a faulty hard drive, you might have to request that the notebook manufacturer provide you with a recovery CD for the OS installation (see Figure 11-5).

Figure 11-5 The Recovery CD is an important tool needed to recover from a failed notebook hard drive

Some notebooks come with the utilities and system files needed to install a new copy of the OS stored on the hard drive in a separate partition. This partition might or might not be hidden. Figure 11-6 shows the Disk Management information for a hard drive on one notebook that has a 3.95-GB recovery partition that is not hidden. The files stored on this partition are protected from access when using Windows Explorer, as shown in Figure 11-7.

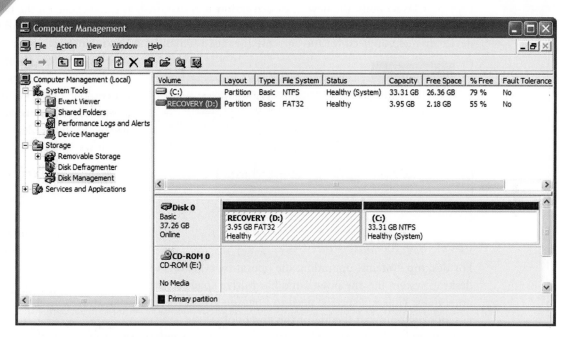

Figure 11-6 This notebook hard drive has a recovery partition that can be used to recover the system

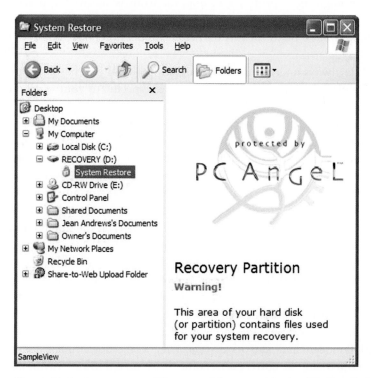

Figure 11-7 A recovery partition cannot be accessed using Windows Explorer

A+ ESS
1.4
2.4
3.2
3.3

A+
220-602
3.3

To know how to access the recovery tools stored on a recovery partition, see the user reference manual. Most likely, you'll see a message at the beginning of the boot, such as "Press ESC for diagnostics," or "Press F12 to recover the system." When you press the key, a menu appears giving you options to diagnose the problem, to repair the current OS installation, or to completely rebuild the entire hard drive to its state when the notebook was first purchased. Of course, this won't work if your hard drive is broken and/or the recovery partition is damaged. In this situation, you're dependent on the OS recovery CD and other support CDs to build the new hard drive after it is installed.

The support CDs that come bundled with a notebook should definitely contain all the device drivers you need for the currently installed OS and might contain device drivers for another OS. For example, if Windows 98 is installed on a system, one of the support CDs most likely contains device drivers for Windows 98 and Windows 2000. The CDs might also include setup programs for the applications that come preinstalled on the notebook.

> ✎ **Notes**
>
> When you first purchase a notebook, make sure you have a recovery CD containing the installed OS so you can recover from a failed hard drive. If one doesn't come bundled with the notebook, purchase it from the notebook manufacturer. (The price should be less than $20.) Do this before problems arise. If the notebook is more than three years old, the manufacturer might no longer provide the CD.

Operating System Upgrades

For desktop systems, upgrading the operating system is usually a good thing to do if the desktop system has the power and hard drive space to support the new OS. Not so with notebooks. Unless a specific need to upgrade arises, the operating system preinstalled on the notebook should last the life of the notebook.

As an example of a specific reason to upgrade, consider a situation in which a notebook holds private data and you need to provide the best possible security on the notebook. In this situation, it might be appropriate to upgrade from Windows 98 to Windows XP. However, Windows 2000 might be the appropriate second choice if the notebook manufacturer has a Windows 2000 build for this particular model notebook, but does not have a Windows XP build for it.

If at all possible, always upgrade the OS using an OS build purchased from the notebook manufacturer complete with supporting device drivers specific to your notebook. In addition, carefully follow their specific instructions for the installation.

If you decide to upgrade the OS using an off-the-shelf version of Windows 2000 or Windows XP, first determine that all components in the system are compatible with the upgrade. Be certain to have available all the device drivers you need for the new OS before you upgrade. Download the drivers from the notebook manufacturer's Web site and store them in a folder on the hard drive. After you upgrade the OS, install the drivers from this folder. The notebook manufacturer might also suggest you first flash the BIOS before you perform the upgrade. And, if applications came preinstalled on the notebook, find out if you have the applications' setup CDs and if they will install under the new OS.

An interesting situation occurred when I attempted to upgrade a notebook computer from Windows 98 to Windows 2000. This situation demonstrates the importance of having the notebook manufacturer's correct device drivers for the OS. The support CD that came with the notebook claimed to have on it device drivers for the internal modem and network cards for both OSs. I performed the OS upgrade and then attempted to use this support CD to install the Windows 2000 modem and network drivers. They would not install. I discovered the drivers on the CD were not the correct drivers for this system. However, without the modem or network ports working, I could not connect to the Internet to download good drivers.

A+ ESS
1.4
2.4
3.2
3.3

A+
220-602
3.3

A+ ESS
1.4
2.4
7.1

A+
220-602
1.2
1.3
7.1

The solution was to download the drivers onto another computer and burn a CD with the drivers. Then, I used that CD on the notebook to install the drivers.

CARING FOR NOTEBOOKS

Notebook computers tend to not last as long as desktop computers because they are portable and, therefore, subjected to more wear and tear. Also, notebooks are more susceptible to worms and viruses than desktop systems, because you are more likely to use them on a public network such as when you sit down at a coffee shop hot spot to work. A notebook's user manual gives specific instructions on how to care for the notebook. Generally, however, follow these guidelines:

▲ LCD panels on notebooks are fragile and can be damaged fairly easily. Take precautions against damaging a notebook's LCD panel. Don't touch it with sharp objects like a ballpoint pen.

▲ Don't connect the notebook to a phone line during an electrical storm.

▲ Run antivirus software and always keep the software current.

▲ Never, ever connect to the Internet using a public wireless connection or ISP without first turning on a software firewall.

▲ Only use battery packs recommended by the notebook manufacturer. Keep the battery pack away from moisture or heat, and don't attempt to take the pack apart. When it no longer works, dispose of it correctly. Chapter 2 covers how to dispose of batteries. Best practices to prolong the life of your battery are discussed in the next section of this chapter.

▲ Use an administrator password to protect the system from unauthorized entry, especially if you are connected to a public network.

▲ Don't tightly pack the notebook in a suitcase because the LCD panel might get damaged. Use a good-quality carrying case and make it a habit of always transporting the notebook in the carrying case. Don't place heavy objects on top of the notebook case.

▲ Don't pick up or hold the notebook by the display panel. Pick it up and hold it by the bottom. Keep the lid closed when the notebook is not in use.

▲ Don't move the notebook while the hard drive is being accessed (the drive indicator light is on). Wait until the light goes off.

▲ Don't put the notebook close to an appliance such as a TV, large audio speakers, or refrigerator that generates a strong magnetic field, and don't place your cell phone on a notebook while the phone is in use.

▲ As with any computer, keep the OS current with the latest Windows updates.

▲ Keep your notebook at a controlled temperature. For example, never leave it in a car overnight when it is cold, and don't leave it in a car during the day when it's hot. Don't expose your notebook to direct sunlight for an extended time.

▲ Don't leave the notebook in a dusty or smoke-filled area. Don't use it in a wet area such as near a swimming pool or in the bathtub. Don't use it at the beach where sand can get in it.

▲ Don't power it up and down unnecessarily.

▲ Protect the notebook from overheating by not running it when it's still inside the case, resting on a pillow, or partially covered with a blanket or anything else that would prevent proper air circulation around it.

▲ Don't connect a modem in a notebook to a private branch exchange (PBX) or other digital telephone service such as that used in some hotels because these private telephone systems often carry too much voltage on the phone line, which can damage the modem.

A+ ESS
1.4
2.4
7.1

A+
220-602
1.2
1.3
7.1

▲ If a notebook has just come indoors from the cold, don't turn it on until it reaches room temperature. In some cases, condensation on the hard drive platters can cause problems. Some manufacturers recommend that when you receive a new notebook shipped to you during the winter, you should leave it in its shipping carton for several hours before you open the carton to prevent subjecting the notebook to a temperature shock.

▲ Protect a notebook against ESD. If you have just come in from the cold on a low-humidity day when there is the possibility that you are carrying ESD, don't touch the notebook until you have grounded yourself.

▲ Before placing a notebook in a carrying case for travel, remove any CDs, DVDs, or PC Cards and put them in protective covers. Verify that the system is powered down and not in suspend or standby mode.

A well-used notebook, especially one that is used in dusty or dirty areas, needs cleaning occasionally. Here are some cleaning tips:

▲ It is not necessary to disassemble a notebook for routine cleaning. In fact, you can clean the LCD panel, battery connections, keyboard, touch pad, or even memory contacts as needed without opening the notebook case.

▲ Clean the LCD panel with a soft dry cloth. If the panel is very dirty, you can dampen the cloth with water. Even though some books advise using a mixture of isopropyl alcohol and water to clean an LCD panel, notebook manufacturers say not to.

▲ Use a can of compressed air meant to be used around computer equipment to blow dust and small particles out of the keyboard, track ball, and touch pad. Turn the notebook at an angle and direct the air into the sides of the keyboard. Then use a soft, damp cloth to clean key caps and touch pad.

▲ Use compressed air to blow out all air vents on the notebook to make sure they are clean and unobstructed.

▲ If keys are sticking, remove the keyboard so you can better spray under the key with compressed air. If you can remove the key cap, remove it and clean the key contact area with contact cleaner. One example of a contact cleaner you can use for this purpose is Stabilant 22 (*www.stabilant.com*). Reinstall the keyboard and test it. If the key still sticks, replace the keyboard.

▲ Remove the battery and clean the battery connections with a contact cleaner.

SECURING A NOTEBOOK AND ITS DATA

A+ ESS
6.1
6.3

A+
220-602
6.3

Because a notebook computer is smaller and lighter than a desktop system and is carried out into public places, it is more susceptible to being stolen. In addition, many times the most valuable thing in the notebook is the data. For these reasons, it is important for a PC support technician to know about ways to protect the notebook and its data.

Security Devices

According to the Safeware Insurance Group, the owner of a notebook computer has a 1 in 14 chance of it being stolen. Some commonsense rules can help protect your notebook. When traveling, always know where your notebook is. If you're standing at an airport counter, tuck your notebook case securely between your ankles. When flying, never check in your notebook as baggage, and don't store it in airplane overhead bins; keep it at your feet. Never leave a notebook in an unlocked car or hotel room and, when you're using it, always log off the

11

A+ ESS
6.1
6.3

A+
220-602
6.3

network before you walk away from it. When leaving work, lock your notebook in a secure place or use a notebook cable lock to secure it to your desk. Figure 11-8 shows a cable lock system. Most notebooks have a security slot on the case to connect the cable lock.

Figure 11-8 Use a cable lock system to secure a notebook computer to a desk to help prevent it from being stolen

Another security device you can use is a theft-prevention plate that includes a label identifying the notebook, which is permanently engraved into your notebook case. The identifying numbers or bar code identify you, the owner, and can also clearly establish to police that the notebook has been stolen. Two sources of theft-prevention plates and cable locks are Computer Security Products, Inc. (*www.computersecurity.com*) and Flexguard Security System (*www.flexguard.com*).

Power-On and Hard Drive Passwords

On CMOS setup screens, you can set a supervisor password and a user password (also called a power-on password). These passwords can be configured so they are required to boot the system, view CMOS setup, or make changes to setup. In addition, some notebooks give you the option of setting a hard drive password, which is written on the hard drive. Data on the hard drive cannot be changed without entering this password. The advantage of using a hard drive password over a power-on password or Windows password is that if the hard drive is removed and installed in another notebook, it still protects the hard drive's data. Just as with the power-on password, the hard drive password is requested by the system when it is powering up.

To know if your notebook supports these three types of power-on passwords, look on the CMOS setup screens. Figure 11-9 shows one notebook CMOS screen that shows the options to set four passwords (supervisor password, user password, and a hard drive password for each of two hard drives in the system). To set a hard drive password or the user password, you must first set a supervisor password. After that is set, to set a hard drive password, on the Security menu, select Hard Disk Security. The submenu in Figure 11-10 shows where you can choose to set a password for either or both hard drives.

Video
Configuring a Motherboard

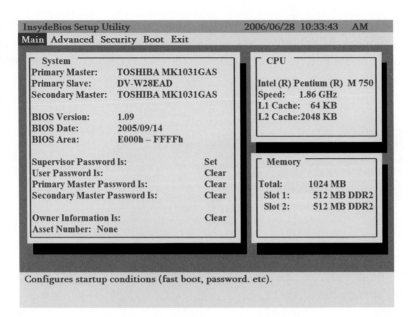

Figure 11-9 CMOS setup main menu shows support for four power-on passwords

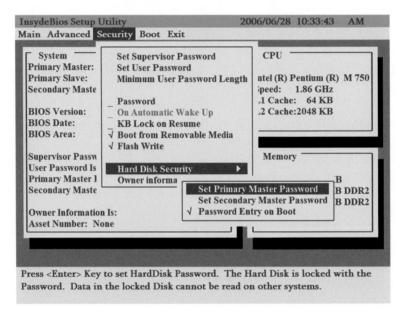

Figure 11-10 Submenu shows how to set a hard drive password that will be written on the drive

Data Backups

As discussed earlier in the book, if you can't get along without the data, back it up. Don't trust your hard drive with data you can't do without; back it up to another media.

One problem with backups on notebook computers is that standard backup techniques often rely on company file servers, CD burners, or other media that are not always available when traveling with your notebook. If you need to back up data or have access to this backed-up data while traveling, one solution is an online backup service such as @Backup (*www.backup.com*) or Computer Security Products, Inc. (*www.computersecurity.com*). Also, some high-end notebooks have two hard drives. For these systems, you can back up data from one hard drive to the other, although, if your notebook is stolen, so is your backup.

A+ ESS
2.1
2.2

A+
220-602
1.3
2.2

POWER MANAGEMENT

A notebook can be powered in several ways, including an AC adapter (which uses regular house current to power the notebook), a DC adapter (which uses DC power such as that provided by automobile cigarette lighters), and a battery pack. Some AC adapters are capable of auto-switching from 110 V to 220 V AC power, in contrast to fixed-input AC adapters that can handle only one type of AC voltage.

Types of batteries include the older and mostly outdated Ni-Cad (nickel-cadmium) battery, the longer-life NiMH (nickel-metal-hydride) battery, and the current Lithium Ion battery, which is more efficient than earlier batteries. A future battery solution is a fuel cell battery, technically called a Direct Methanol Fuel Cell (DMFC) battery. A DMFC initially provides up to five hours of battery life, and future versions will provide up to 10 hours of battery life. A notebook user might need one or more batteries and a DC adapter for travel and an AC adapter at home and for recharging the batteries.

Here are some general dos and don'ts for switching power sources and protecting the battery and notebook, which apply to most notebooks. See a notebook's user manual for specific instructions.

> **Notes**
>
> If you're using the AC adapter to power your notebook when the power goes out, the installed battery serves as a built-in UPS. The battery immediately takes over as your uninterruptible power supply.

◢ If you need to use the notebook for extended periods away from an electrical outlet, you can use extra battery packs. When the notebook signals that power is low, remove the old battery and replace it with a charged one. To remove a battery, generally, you release a latch and then remove the battery, as shown in Figure 11-11.

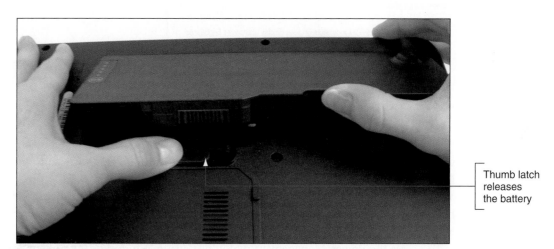

Thumb latch releases the battery

Figure 11-11 Release a latch to remove the battery from a notebook

◢ For some notebook batteries, don't recharge the battery pack until all the power is used. Recharging too soon can shorten the battery life. For other batteries, it doesn't matter how often you recharge them. Check your user manual to learn how and when to recharge your battery.

◢ For some older batteries, when you're recharging the battery, don't use it until it's fully recharged. Also, some manufacturers of older batteries recommend that you don't leave the battery in the notebook while the notebook is turned on and connected to an electrical outlet.

A+ ESS
2.1
2.2

A+
220-602
1.3
2.1

⬧ If you're not using the notebook for a long time (more than a month), remove the battery from the notebook and store the notebook and battery in a cool, dry place. Leaving a battery in a notebook for extended periods when it is not used can damage the battery.

⬧ Use power-management features of your OS, which are covered later in this chapter. Also, to make a battery charge last longer while working with your notebook, you can dim the LCD panel and remove any PC Cards you're not using.

⬧ CD and DVD drives use a lot of power. Therefore, whenever possible, connect the notebook to an electrical outlet to play a movie on DVD or burn a CD.

⬧ Use standby or hibernate mode whenever you are not using the notebook.

⬧ While working with your notebook and using the battery, if you get a message that the battery is low, you can immediately plug in the AC or DC adapter without first powering down your notebook.

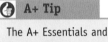

A+ Tip

The A+ Essentials and A+ 220-602 exams expect you to know how notebooks get their power and about conserving power to prolong battery life.

⬧ To conserve power when the battery is running, a notebook sometimes reduces LCD panel brightness. For example, when you unplug the AC adapter on one notebook, a message appears (see Figure 11-12) telling you brightness has been reduced. To save even more power, lower the brightness even more.

⬧ A notebook has an internal surge protector. However, for extra protection, you might want to use a power strip for added surge protection.

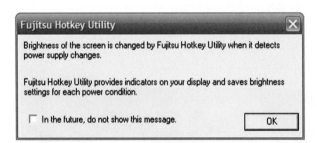

Figure 11-12 Reduce LCD panel brightness to conserve power when running the battery

A notebook ACPI-compliant BIOS supports features to help manage power consumption, which were all discussed in Chapter 3. The goal is to minimize power consumption to increase the time before a battery pack needs recharging. Using CMOS setup, you can disable and enable some power-management features, and configuring power management is best done in Windows. Instructions are given next for Windows 2000/XP, but Windows 9x/Me works about the same way.

To access the Power Management dialog box using Windows 2000/XP, open **Control Panel**, and double-click the **Power Options** applet (in Windows 9x/Me, the applet is named Power Management). Figure 11-13 shows the Power Options Properties dialog box for one Windows XP notebook. (A different brand of notebook might have different tabs in its Properties dialog box.) Notice there is one set of power-management options for when an AC or DC adapter is plugged in and when the battery is running. Use this dialog box to create, delete, and modify multiple power-management schemes to customize how Windows 2000/XP manages power consumption.

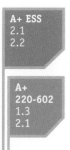

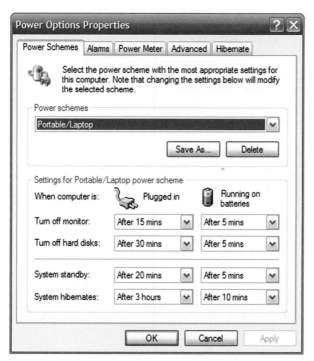

Figure 11-13 The Power Options Properties dialog box of Windows 2000/XP allows you to create and manage multiple power schemes

For example, one power-saving feature of Windows 2000/XP and Windows 9x/Me puts a notebook into hibernation, as discussed in Chapter 3. Before you direct a notebook to hibernate, make sure you know the keystrokes or buttons required to restore the system to an active state without turning off the computer. For many computers, pressing the power button or a function key wakes up a system from hibernation.

If the notebook supports hibernating, you can configure Windows 2000/XP to cause the notebook to hibernate after a set period of time, when you press the power button, or when you close the lid of the notebook. Do the following:

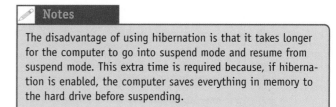

Notes

The disadvantage of using hibernation is that it takes longer for the computer to go into suspend mode and resume from suspend mode. This extra time is required because, if hibernation is enabled, the computer saves everything in memory to the hard drive before suspending.

1. In the Power Options Properties dialog box, click the **Hibernate** tab (see Figure 11-14), and verify that hibernate support is enabled. If there is no Hibernate tab, your notebook does not support hibernating.

2. Click the **Advanced** tab, as shown in Figure 11-15. With the options on this tab, you can control what happens when you press the power button or close the lid of the notebook.

3. Click the **When I close the lid of my portable computer** list arrow and select **Hibernate**. (Other choices are Standby, Power Off, and None.)

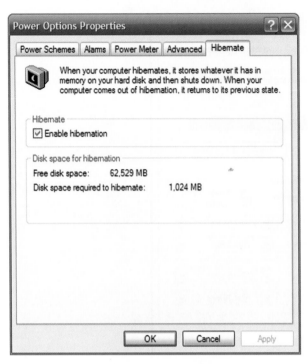

Figure 11-14 Verify that hibernate support is enabled

Figure 11-15 The Advanced tab of the Power Options Properties dialog box allows you to control the behavior of the power button and what happens when you close the lid of your notebook

4. You can also control what happens when you press the power button. You can see your choices in Figure 11-16. When you're done, click **Apply** and then click **OK** to close the Power Options dialog box and save your changes.

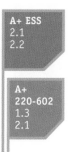

A+ ESS
2.1
2.2

A+
220-602
1.3
2.1

Figure 11-16 Choices of action when you press the power button of your notebook

Using Windows 2000/XP, you can monitor and manage batteries on notebooks that are ACPI- and APM-enabled. You can access the battery meter directly by adding the battery status icon to the taskbar. Follow these steps:

1. From the **Start** menu, open **Control Panel**.
2. Double-click **Power Options** to open the Power Options Properties dialog box.
3. Click the **Advanced** tab.
4. Click the **Always show icon on the taskbar** check box (refer to Figure 11-16), and then click **OK**.

Note that the Power Options Properties dialog box also offers the Alarms tab on which you can set alarms to alert you when battery power is low or critical.

PORT REPLICATORS AND DOCKING STATIONS

Some notebooks have a connector on the bottom of the notebook to connect to a port replicator, such as the one shown in Figure 11-17, or a docking station, shown in Figure 11-18. A port replicator provides a means to connect a notebook to a power outlet and provides additional ports to allow a notebook to easily connect to a full-sized monitor, keyboard, and other peripheral devices. A docking station provides the same functions as a port replicator, but also adds secondary storage, such as an extra hard drive, a floppy drive, or a DVD drive.

A+ Tip

The A+ Essentials exam expects you to know the difference between a port replicator and a docking station.

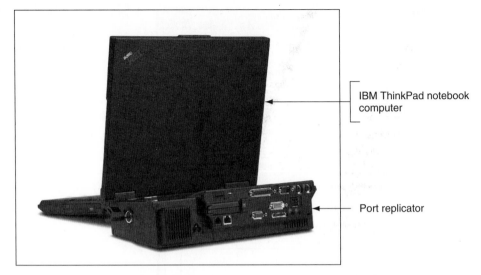

IBM ThinkPad notebook computer

Port replicator

Figure 11-17 A port replicator makes it convenient to connect a notebook computer to resources and peripherals at your office

Figure 11-18 An IBM ThinkPad dock, an example of a docking station

If a notebook has a docking station, you can set up one hardware profile to use the docking station and another when you are on the road and don't have access to it. To create a hardware profile in Windows 2000/XP for a mobile user:

1. Open the **System Properties** window and click the **Hardware** tab.

2. Click the **Hardware Profiles** button at the bottom of the Hardware tab. The Hardware Profiles dialog box opens (Figure 11-19).

3. Select a profile from the list of available hardware profiles and then click the **Copy** button.

4. Type a new name for the profile, and then click **OK**.

5. Under *When Windows starts*, select either the option for Windows 2000/XP to wait for you to select a hardware profile or the option for Windows 2000/XP to start with the first profile listed if you don't select one in the specified number of seconds. Close all open windows.

6. Restart the computer and, when prompted, select the new hardware profile.

7. Open the **System Properties** dialog box. Click the **Hardware** tab, click **Device Manager,** and then double-click the icon for a device that you want enabled or disabled in the new profile. For example, you might set one profile to access a second hard drive that is installed on the docking station, which is not available when traveling.

A+ ESS
2.1
2.2

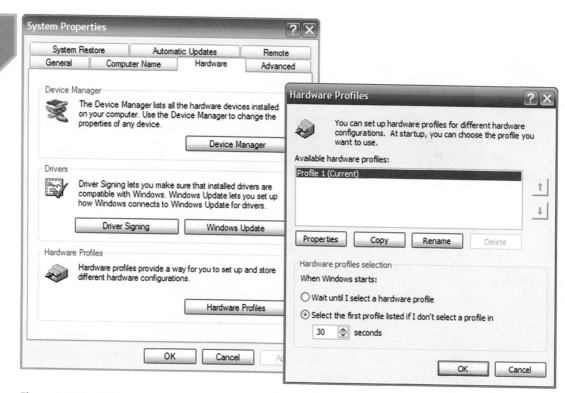

Figure 11-19 Windows XP allows you to set a hardware profile for different hardware configurations

8. Click the **General** tab in the Properties dialog box for the device. In the area for Device usage, select the option to enable or disable the device for the current profile or for all hardware profiles. Close all open dialog boxes.

A+
220-602
2.2

CONNECTING PERIPHERAL DEVICES TO NOTEBOOKS

A notebook provides ports on its back or sides (see Figure 11-20), which are used for connecting peripherals.

In addition to the ports labeled in Figure 11-20, a notebook might have these slots, switches, and ports, several of which are discussed in the following subsections:

▲ PC Card or CardBus slot with lock switch and eject button
▲ ExpressCard slot with slot protective cover
▲ USB and FireWire ports
▲ Network port (RJ-45) and modem port (RJ-11)
▲ Headphone jack and microphone jack
▲ Volume control
▲ Secure Digital (SD) or CompactFlash Card slot
▲ Wireless antenna on/off switch (for onboard wireless, the antenna is inside the notebook case)
▲ 15-pin VGA video port
▲ Audio input and video input jacks if the notebook has an embedded TV tuner
▲ Airflow vents
▲ Power jack for DC or AC power adapter
▲ Security lock for installing a chain and lock
▲ Older notebooks might have a parallel port, serial port, PS/2 port, or infrared port

A+ ESS
2.1
2.2

A+
220-602
2.2

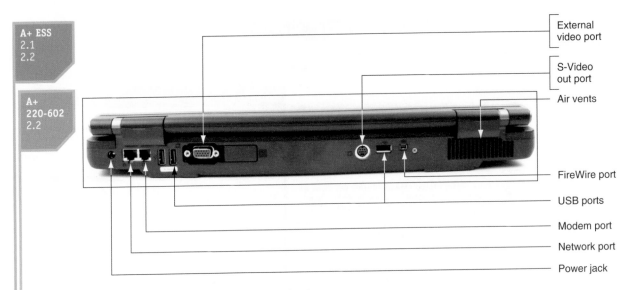

Figure 11-20 Ports on the back of a notebook

Before we get into the discussion of ports used primarily on notebooks, keep in mind that USB ports have become a popular way of adding devices to all types of computers, including notebooks. For example, if the notebook does not have an RJ-45 port for an Ethernet connection, you can buy a device that plugs into the USB port and provides the Ethernet port. Another example shown in Figure 11-21 involves a wireless mouse and keypad that use a receiver connected to a USB port. Installing this mouse and keypad on a Windows 2000/XP notebook is very simple. You plug the receiver into the port. Windows displays a message that it has located the device, and the mouse and keypad are ready to use. This ease of installation is quickly making USB the preferred method of connecting peripheral devices.

Figure 11-21 This wireless mouse and keypad use a receiver that connects to a USB port

PC CARD, CARDBUS, AND EXPRESSCARD SLOTS

Notebook computers typically have one or more I/O card slots, which can accommodate one or more standards of I/O cards. These card standards have evolved over the years and

A+ ESS
2.1
2.2

A+
220-602
2.2

have been designed and supported by the PCMCIA (Personal Computer Memory Card International Association). PCMCIA standards include one or more variations of PC Card, CardBus, and ExpressCard.

PC Card and CardBus

A PC Card is about the size of a credit card, but thicker, and inserts into a PC Card slot. Originally, PC Cards were called **PCMCIA (Personal Computer Memory Card International Association) Cards** and the first of these cards were used to add memory to a notebook. For example, Figure 11-22 shows a modem PC Card being inserted into a PC Card slot. The card provides a phone line port for the telephone line to the modem, as shown in Figure 11-23.

Figure 11-22 Many peripheral devices are added to a notebook using a PC Card slot; here, a modem PC Card is inserted in a PC Card slot

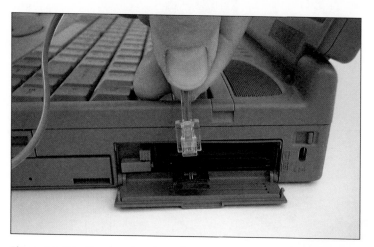

Figure 11-23 Connect the phone line to the modem PC Card

Some docking station PCs also have a PC Card slot, so that the device you use with your notebook can also be attached to the docking station. PC Card slots are considered standard equipment on notebooks, although the trend is moving from using PC Card slots toward using USB ports to connect peripheral equipment to a notebook. PC Card slots are used by many devices, including modems, network cards for wired or wireless networks, sound

> **A+ Exam Tip**
>
> The A+ Essentials exam expects you to know about PCMCIA Type I, II, and III, CardBus, and ExpressCard slots and cards.

cards, SCSI host adapters, IEEE 1394 controllers, USB controllers, flash memory adapters, TV tuners, and hard disks.

The PCMCIA organization has developed four standards for these slots. The latest PCMCIA specification that can use the PC Card slot is CardBus, which improves I/O speed, increases the bus width to 32 bits, and supports lower-voltage PC Cards while maintaining backward compatibility with earlier standards. Three standards for PCMCIA slots pertain to size and are named Type I, Type II, and Type III. Generally, the thicker the PC Card, the higher the standard. A thick hard drive card might need a Type III slot, but a thin modem card might only need a Type II slot. Type I cards can be up to 3.3-mm thick and are primarily used for adding RAM to a notebook PC. Type II cards can be up to 5.5-mm thick and are often used as modem cards. Type III cards can be up to 10.5-mm thick, large enough to accommodate a portable disk drive. When buying a notebook PC, look for Type I, Type II, and Type III PC Card slots. Often, two slots are included, and a slot might support more than one type. Also, the motherboard bus used by the PC Card slot to communicate with the processor can be a 16-bit or 32-bit PCMCIA I/O bus. For improved performance, look for 32-bit CardBus slots.

Some PC Cards have dongles or pigtails such as the network PC Card shown in Figure 11-24. The RJ-45 connection is at the end of a dongle so that the thick RJ-45 connection does not have to fit flat against the PC Card. Other PC Cards are thick at the end so that the ports can be embedded directly on the card, such as the TV tuner PC Card shown in Figure 11-25.

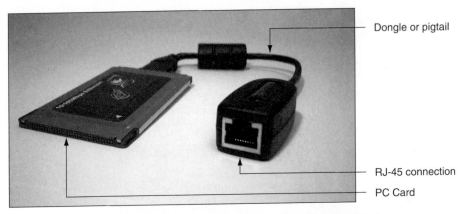

Dongle or pigtail

RJ-45 connection

PC Card

Figure 11-24 This PC Card serves as a NIC for an Ethernet 100BaseT network

Figure 11-25 This TV tuner card connects to a notebook by way of a PCMCIA CardBus slot

PC Cards are often used to provide proprietary ports or adapters that are not available on the notebook, such as those used for flash memory devices, including Secure Digital (SD) card, CompactFlash card, or Microdrive CF, all discussed in Chapter 9. One example is the PC Card shown in Figure 11-26 that contains a slot for a CompactFlash memory card.

Figure 11-26 The PC card contains an adapter for a CompactFlash memory card

The underlying technology for a PC Card slot is 16-bit ISA or 32-bit PCI. Before CardBus, all PC Card slots used the 16-bit ISA interface between the card slot and the processor. The CardBus technology uses 32-bit PCI for the interface standard. PCMCIA has announced that it no longer will present any new developments for the PC Card, because it is now promoting the ExpressCard slot as the replacement slot for the PC Card slot.

ExpressCard

The latest PCMCIA standard is ExpressCard, which was designed to use the same type of interface used by the PCI Express or USB 2.0 standard. Currently, two sizes of ExpressCards exist: ExpressCard/34 is 34-mm wide and ExpressCard/54 is 54-mm wide. Both of these types of cards are 75-mm long and 5-mm high. Figure 11-27 compares a CardBus PC Card to each of the two ExpressCard cards. An ExpressCard/34 card can fit into an ExpressCard/54 slot, but not vice versa.

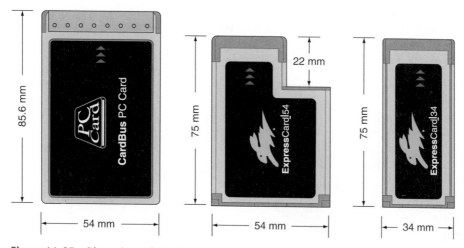

Figure 11-27 Dimensions of CardBus and ExpressCard cards

Just as PCI Express slots are not backward compatible with PCI slots on a desktop computer, ExpressCard slots are not backward compatible with PC Card slots on a notebook. Some notebooks will have both types of slots, such as the notebook in Figure 11-28. An ExpressCard slot is fully hot-pluggable, hot-swappable, and supports autoconfiguration, just as does a USB port. PCMCIA is also promoting the ExpressCard slot as an option for desktop computers, rather than using PCI or PCI Express slots for expansion cards.

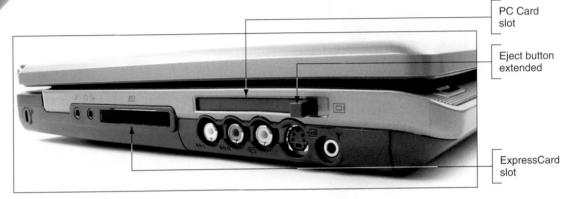

PC Card slot

Eject button extended

ExpressCard slot

Figure 11-28 This notebook has one PC Card and one ExpressCard slot

One example of an ExpressCard/34 card is the Gigabit Ethernet card shown in Figure 11-29. Figure 11-30 shows an ExpressCard/54 card that provides two eSATA ports for external SATA drives.

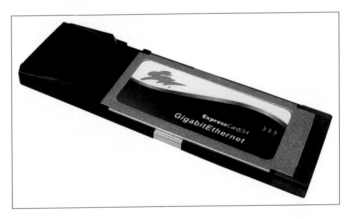

Figure 11-29 This ExpressCard/34 card supports Gigabit Ethernet

Figure 11-30 This ExpressCard/54 card supports two eSATA drives

A+ ESS
2.1
2.2

A+
220-602
2.2

USING PC CARD AND EXPRESSCARD SLOTS

The operating system must provide two services for a PC Card, ExpressCard, or another type of proprietary card: a socket service and a card service. The socket service establishes communication between the card and the notebook when the card is first inserted, and then disconnects communication when the card is removed. The card service provides the device driver to interface with the card after the socket is created.

To remove a device that is not hot-swappable, you must first power down the notebook. Hot-swapping allows you to remove one card and insert another without powering down. PC Cards and ExpressCards can be hot-swapped, but you must stop and then unplug one card before inserting another. For example, if you currently use a wireless network card in the PC Card slot of a Windows XP notebook and want to switch to a TV tuner card, first turn off the wireless network card, remove the network card, and then insert the TV tuner card and connect the TV cable to the card. Follow these directions to remove a card from a PC Card or ExpressCard slot:

1. For Windows XP, the easiest way to stop a card is to use the Unplug or Eject Hardware icon in the system tray, shown in Figure 11-31. Click the icon and the Safely Remove Hardware dialog box on the left side of Figure 11-32 opens.

Icon used to
stop a device

Figure 11-31   Use this icon in the Windows XP system tray to stop a hot-pluggable device before removing it

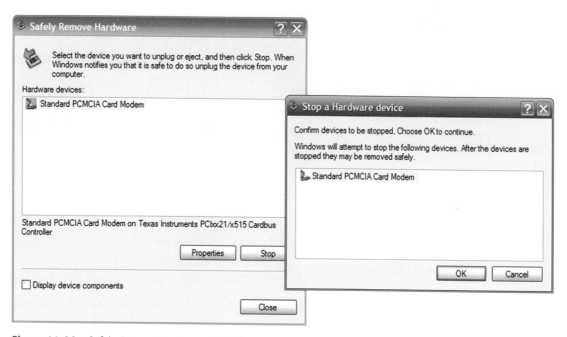

Figure 11-32   Safely Remove Hardware dialog box

2. Click **Stop**. The Stop a Hardware device dialog box opens, as shown on the right side of Figure 11-32. Click **OK** to continue. The bubble shown in Figure 11-33 appears telling you that you can now remove the device. If Windows tells you it cannot stop the device, you must shut down your computer before removing the card.

A+ ESS
2.1
2.2

A+
220-602
2.2

Figure 11-33 The stopped device can now be removed

> ### 👍 A+ Exam Tip
>
> The A+ Essentials exam expects you to know how to remove a hot-swappable and non-hot-swappable device from a notebook.

> ### ✎ Notes
>
> A bug in Windows XP causes the system to hang if you remove a PC Card while the system is in sleep mode or is hibernating. To solve the problem, download the latest service pack for Windows XP.

After you have stopped the card, press the eject button beside the PC Card slot, which causes the button to pop out. You can then press the button again to eject the card. For an ExpressCard, push on the card, which causes it to pop out of the slot. Then, you can remove the card.

For Windows 2000, to stop a PC Card, use the Add/Remove Hardware icon in Control Panel. The Add/Remove Hardware Wizard starts; click **Next,** and click **Uninstall/Unplug a device** in the next dialog box. Click **Next,** and then click **Unplug/Eject a device** in the next dialog box. A list of devices appears. Sometimes, only one item will be in the list, as shown in Figure 11-34. Select the device and click **Next.** The final window tells you that you can safely unplug the device and gives you the option to display an Unplug/Eject icon in the taskbar when the device is used again. For Windows 9x/Me, use the PC Card icon in Control Panel to stop a card.

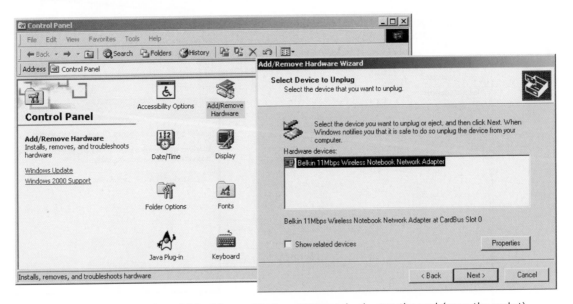

Figure 11-34 Before removing a PC Card from a Windows 2000 notebook, stop the card (open the socket)

The first time you insert a PC Card or ExpressCard in a notebook, the Found New Hardware Wizard starts (see Figure 11-35) and guides you through the installation steps in which you can use the drivers provided by the hardware manufacturer or use Windows drivers. The next time you insert the card in the notebook, the card is detected and starts without help.

11

A+ ESS
2.1
2.2

A+
220-602
2.2

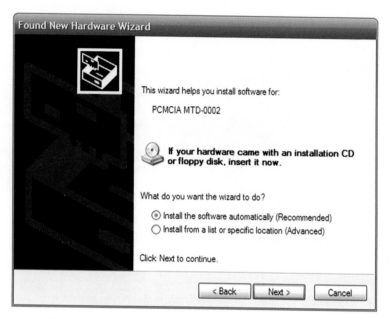

Figure 11-35 The Found New Hardware Wizard launches the first time you insert a PC Card or ExpressCard in the I/O slot

If you are having problems getting a notebook to recognize a PC Card or ExpressCard, try the following:

▲ Don't insert a card in a slot if the card is damaged or is wet. Doing so can damage the slot.
▲ Make sure the system is on and not in hibernation or standby mode when you insert the card.
▲ When you first insert a card and the notebook does not recognize it, the slot might be disabled in CMOS setup. Reboot the notebook and enter the CMOS setup program. Look for the feature to enable or disable a PC Card or ExpressCard slot on the Power Management screen or an Advanced Settings screen.
▲ In Device Manager, verify the PCMCIA or PC Card controller is functioning correctly with no errors. You can update the controller drivers; be sure to use drivers provided by the notebook manufacturer. Check the driver CD that came bundled with the notebook.
▲ A program, such as antivirus software, might be interfering with the Card Services program. Try disabling any software not certified for your OS by Microsoft.
▲ Try installing the card's drivers before you insert the card. Look for a setup program on the manufacturer's CD bundled with the card.

> **Caution**
>
> Inserting a card in a PC Card or ExpressCard slot while the notebook is shutting down or booting up can cause damage to the card and/or to the notebook.

Here are some additional tips when using an ExpressCard slot:

▲ When using an ExpressCard/54 slot, insert an ExpressCard/34 card in the left side of the slot. Push a card firmly into the slot until you feel it snap into the connector.
▲ When you're not using an ExpressCard slot, to protect the slot, insert the protective cover into the slot (see Figure 11-36).

A+ ESS
2.1
2.2

A+
220-602
2.2

Figure 11-36   An ExpressCard slot uses a protective cover in the slot to protect it

USING WIRELESS DEVICES WITH NOTEBOOKS

A+ ESS
2.1
2.2
5.1

A+
220-602
2.1
5.2

A notebook might have the ability to support a cellular WAN connection such as WiFi or a personal area network (PAN) connection such as Bluetooth or infrared. In Chapter 10, you learned how to set up and secure a WiFi connection, and infrared connections are covered in Chapter 8.

Because supporting WiFi connections on a notebook is such an important subject, let's briefly review some information you learned in Chapter 10. Recall that a wireless notebook can be configured to connect in ad hoc mode (to another computer) or in infrastructure mode (to a wireless access point). And, if a notebook has an internal wireless NIC, most likely the NIC is configured using Windows tools. To change wireless settings, use the Network Connections window. For example, to decide between using ad hoc mode or infrastructure mode, right-click the **Wireless Network Connection** icon in the Network Connections window and click **Properties** from the shortcut menu. In the properties dialog box, click the **Wireless Networks** tab, as shown on the left side of Figure 11-37. Click **Advanced** and then make your mode selection, as shown on the right side of Figure 11-37. Most likely, the first selection is the correct one because it allows you to connect using either mode. Click **Close** and **OK** to close both boxes.

To make the wireless connection, turn on the wireless switch on your notebook. Most likely, this is all that is necessary for the connection to be made unless you need to enter a passphrase to a secured network. If you have a problem connecting, double-click the wireless icon in the Network Connections window. A list of wireless networks appears. You can refresh the list by clicking **Refresh network list** (see Figure 11-38). Select a network and click **Connect**. If the network is secured, you'll be asked to enter a passphrase to use the network. To change networks, select the network you are connected to and click **Disconnect**, as shown in Figure 11-38. You can then connect to a different network.

> ✎ **Notes**
>
> By default, a wired or wireless network connection is set for dynamic IP addressing, which is the right choice for most public and corporate networks. However, you can configure a notebook for dynamic IP addressing when a DHCP server is available, but use static IP addressing when a DHCP server is not available. After you have configured the notebook for dynamic IP addressing, on the **Internet Protocol (TCP/IP) Properties** dialog box, click the **Alternate Configuration** tab and assign a static IP address, subnet mask, and DNS servers.

A+ ESS
2.1
2.2
5.1

A+
220-602
2.1
5.2

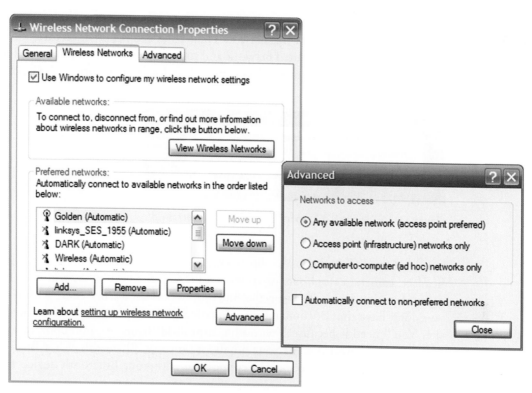

Figure 11-37 Use the Wireless Network Connection Properties dialog box to configure a wireless NIC installed in a notebook

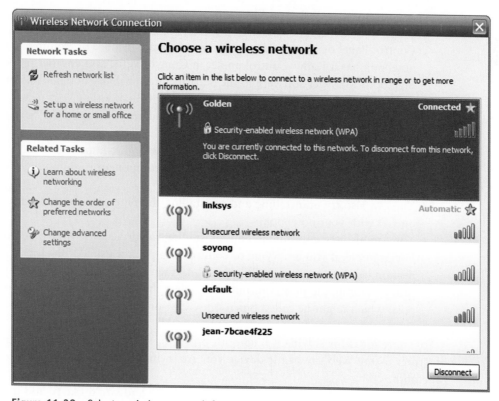

Figure 11-38 Select a wireless network from those in range

A+ ESS
2.1
2.2
5.1

A+
220-602
2.1
5.2

After the connection is made, a bubble appears identifying the network (see Figure 11-39). Notice in Figure 11-39 that this network connection is unsecured. Be careful to not transmit private data over an unsecured network and to keep your Windows Firewall fully enabled. For more information about wireless networks and wireless security, see Chapter 10.

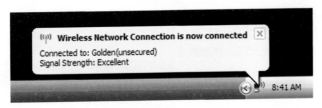

Figure 11-39 Windows XP reports the wireless connection

If your notebook supports a Bluetooth connection used to connect to a printer, mouse, headset, camera, cell phone, or connect a PDA to the notebook, you need to read the documentation for configuring the Bluetooth connection that came with the notebook. If you don't have that documentation, download it from the notebook manufacturer Web site. You'll need it because Bluetooth setups differ from one notebook to another. Following the directions for your notebook, turn on Bluetooth. After Bluetooth is turned on, you should be able to make a connection with your Bluetooth device when it is set close to the notebook.

If you are having problems getting the Bluetooth connection to work, try the following:

- Make sure the wireless switch is turned on (for some notebooks, this switch turns on and off both the WiFi and Bluetooth signal).
- Verify that Windows sees Bluetooth enabled. You might do this by using an applet in Control Panel or by using a program on the Start menu. For example, one Toshiba notebook has a Radio Control applet in Control Panel and another notebook uses Bluetooth Manager software in the Start menu. For many notebooks, you should see an icon in the system tray showing the status of Bluetooth.
- Be sure you have downloaded all Windows updates. (Windows XP Service Pack 2 is required for Bluetooth.)
- Look in Device Manager to make sure the Bluetooth component is recognized with no errors. For some notebooks, even though the component is an internal device, it is seen in Device Manager as a USB device.
- You can also try uninstalling and reinstalling the Bluetooth drivers that come bundled on CD with your notebook.
- You can also try uninstalling and reinstalling the drivers for your Bluetooth device. For example, if you are trying to connect to a printer using a Bluetooth wireless connection, try first turning on Bluetooth and then uninstalling and reinstalling the printer. During the printer installation, select the Bluetooth connection for the printer port, which might be called Bluetooth COM or something similar.

For more ideas for solving a Bluetooth problem, try the Web site of the notebook manufacturer or the Web site of the device you are trying to connect to your notebook using Bluetooth.

If your notebook doesn't have Bluetooth capability and you'd like to add it, you can buy a USB Bluetooth adapter like the one shown in Figure 11-40. After you have installed the drivers and the adapter, you can use it to wirelessly connect to any Bluetooth-enabled device.

A+ ESS
2.1
2.2
5.1

A+
220-602
2.1
5.2

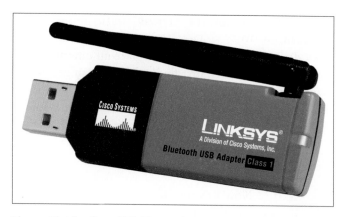

Figure 11-40 Use a USB Bluetooth adapter to add Bluetooth capability to a notebook

REPLACING AND UPGRADING INTERNAL PARTS

A+ ESS
2.3

A+
220-602
1.2

Sometimes it is necessary to open a notebook case so that you can upgrade memory, exchange a hard drive, or replace a broken component such as the LCD panel. Most notebooks sold today are designed so that you can easily get memory modules or drives to upgrade or exchange them. However, replacing a broken LCD panel can be a complex process, taking most of your day. In this section, we'll first look at the alternatives you need to consider before you decide to take on complex repair projects, and then we'll look at how to upgrade memory, exchange a drive, and perform other complex repair projects, including exchanging an LCD panel.

THREE APPROACHES TO DEALING WITH A BROKEN INTERNAL DEVICE

When a component on a notebook needs replacing or upgrading, first you need to consider the warranty and how much time the repair will take. Before you decide to upgrade or repair an internal component, take into consideration these two alternatives:

▲ *Return the notebook to the manufacturer or another service center for repair.* If the notebook is under warranty, you need to return it to the manufacturer to do any serious repair work such as fixing a broken LCD panel. However, for simple repair and upgrade tasks, such as upgrading memory or exchanging a hard drive, most likely you can do these simple jobs by yourself without concern for voiding a warranty. If you're not sure about the possibility of voiding the warranty, check with the manufacturer before you begin working on the notebook. If the notebook is not under warranty and you don't have the experience or time to fix a broken component, find out how much the manufacturer will charge to do the job. Also, consider using a generic notebook repair service. Know that some notebook manufacturers refuse to sell internal components for their notebooks except to authorized service centers. In this case, you have no option but to use the service center for repairs.

▲ *Substitute an external component for an internal component.* As you'll see later in the chapter, replacing components on notebooks can be time consuming and require a lot of patience and know-how. If the notebook is not under warranty, sometimes, it's wiser to simply avoid opening the case and working inside it. Instead, you could simply use CMOS setup to disable an internal component and then use an external device in its place. For example, if a keyboard fails, you can use a wireless keyboard with an access point connected to the USB port. Also, if an internal modem fails, the

A+ ESS
2.3

A+
220-602
1.2

simplest solution might be to disable the internal modem and replace it with a PC Card modem card.

▲ *Replace the internal device.* Before deciding to replace an internal device that is not easy to get to, such as an LCD panel, first find out if you can get the documentation necessary to know how to open the notebook case and exchange the component. How to find this documentation was discussed earlier in the chapter. Without the instructions or a lot of experience servicing notebooks, the project could be very frustrating and result in a notebook useful only as a paperweight.

> **Notes**
>
> Before making the decision to replace an internal part, ask the question, "Can an external device or PC Card substitute?" Many customers appreciate these solutions, because most often they are much less labor-intensive and less costly.

Now let's turn our attention to how to substitute an external device for an internal one and then how to prepare to work inside a notebook computer case.

SUBSTITUTE AN INTERNAL DEVICE WITH AN EXTERNAL DEVICE

To substitute an internal device with an external device, first go into CMOS setup and disable the internal device. For most notebooks, you enter CMOS setup when the notebook is booting. Table 11-2 lists how to access CMOS setup for different notebook computers.

Notebook Model	To Run CMOS Setup
Dell, Gateway, Fujitsu, Sony, Acer, and most other notebooks	During booting, press F2 when the logo appears.
Lenovo or IBM ThinkPad models series 240, 390, 570, iSeries 1200, 1300, 1400, 1500, 172x, A20, A21, A22, A30, A31, R30, R31, R32, S30, S31, T20, T21, T22, T23, T30, X20, X21, X23, X24, X30, X31	Press F1 when the ThinkPad logo appears during the boot.
Lenovo or IBM ThinkPad R40, R40e, T40	During startup, press the Access IBM button. Then select Start setup utility.
IBM ThinkPad 510, 300350500	Put the system in MS-DOS mode (not a DOS box under Windows) and then press Ctrl+Alt+F3 at a DOS prompt.
IBM ThinkPad 310, 315310E	Press F2 when the ThinkPad logo appears during booting.
IBM ThinkPad 365C, CS365CD, CSD365, ED	Put the system in MS-DOS mode (not a DOS box under Windows) and then press Ctrl+Alt+F11 at a DOS prompt.
IBM ThinkPad 365X, 365XD	During booting, press and hold down the F1 key until the Setup screen appears.
IBM ThinkPad 360, 355, 380, 385, 560, 600, 701x, 76x, 770	During booting, press and hold down the F1 key until the Setup screen appears. Also, for the 701 notebook, you can access CMOS setup at any time by pressing the Fn and F1 keys.
IBM ThinkPad 700x, 720x	During booting, press Ctrl+Alt+Ins right after the memory count.

Table 11-2 How to access CMOS setup for different notebooks

11

A+ ESS
2.3

A+
220-602
1.2

Notebook Model	To Run CMOS Setup
IBM ThinkPad 710T, 730T	During booting, press and hold down the suspend/resume switch.
Toshiba Satellite models 16xx, 17xx, 30xx, 100x, 19xx, 1000, 1200, 1100x	Turn the system off. Press the power button and then press and hold down F2 until the CMOS Setup screen appears.
Toshiba Satellite models 500x, 510x, 520x	A CMOS setup program is not included in the motherboard ROM. To access setup, after Windows is loaded, open Control Panel and double-click the HWSetup program.
Toshiba all Libretto, all Portege, and other Satellite models not listed earlier	Three ways to access setup: ▲ In Windows, double-click HWSetup in Control Panel. ▲ Power off and on the system. During the boot, when you see the message to press F1, press it. ▲ In MS-DOS mode (not a DOS box inside Windows), run the TSETUP program, which can be downloaded from the Toshiba Web site.
Compaq Presario models	During booting, press F2 when the logo screen appears.
Compaq Evo models	During booting, when the message "F10 = ROM Based Setup" appears, press F10.
Compaq Prosignia models	During booting, while the cursor is blinking, press F10.

Table 11-2 How to access CMOS setup for different notebooks (continued)

After you have disabled the internal device, install the external peripheral device as described earlier in the chapter.

PREPARATION FOR SERVICING A NOTEBOOK

Before attempting to replace or upgrade a component installed in a notebook, always do the following:

▲ If the computer is working, have the user back up any important data stored on the notebook.

▲ Ground yourself by using an antistatic ground strap. If no ground strap is available, periodically touch the port to discharge any static electricity on your body.

▲ Turn off any attached devices such as a printer and then shut down the notebook.

▲ Disconnect the AC adapter from the computer and from the electrical outlet.

▲ If the notebook is attached to a port replicator or docking station, release it to undock the computer.

▲ Remove the battery pack.

▲ Remove any PC Cards, CDs, or DVDs.

Caution

It is very important to unplug the AC adapter and remove the battery pack before working inside a notebook case. If the battery is still in the notebook, power provided by the battery could damage components as you work on them.

A+ ESS
2.3

A+
220-602
1.2

A+ ESS
1.1
2.1

A+
220-602
2.2

You are now ready to follow specific instructions for your particular notebook model to replace or upgrade an internal component. Some components can easily be accessed by either removing a panel to expose the component or by removing a screw or two and then sliding the component out the side of the case. When a component can be accessed this easily, most users can do the job if given detailed instructions. However, some components, such as the LCD panel or motherboard, are not so easily accessed. To get to these components requires opening the case and disassembling the notebook.

UPGRADING MEMORY

When deciding how much memory a notebook should have, several factors need to be taken into consideration:

- For most situations, the more memory the better. If memory is low, upgrading memory can make a dramatic improvement in performance.
- If a notebook has special features such as video-editing software or a TV tuner, you'll need additional memory to support these features. See the notebook user manual for recommendations about the amount of memory needed.
- A notebook might have dedicated video memory or the video system might use regular RAM for video data. Using regular RAM for video is called video sharing or shared memory. Video sharing can take from 1 MB to 8 MB of RAM for video depending on the screen resolution you are using. Shared memory reduces the amount of memory available for other tasks, which might mean you need to install more RAM. Using shared memory means that the system can cost less, produce less heat, weigh less, use less power, and help extend battery life.

> 👍 **A+ Tip**
>
> The A+ 220-602 exam expects you to know how sharing memory with video affects decisions made when upgrading memory.

In this section, you'll learn about the different types of memory modules used with notebook computers and how to upgrade memory.

TYPES OF MEMORY USED IN NOTEBOOKS

Notebooks use several types of memory, including SO-DIMMs (small outline DIMMs), SO-RIMMs (small outline RIMMs), credit card memory, and proprietary memory modules. Table 11-3 lists SO-DIMMs and SO-RIMMs. All of these memory modules are smaller than regular SIMMs, DIMMs, or RIMMs.

Memory Module Description	Sample Memory Module
2.66" 200-pin SO-DIMM contains DDR2 SDRAM. One notch is near the side of the module.	
2.66" 200-pin SO-DIMM contains DDR SDRAM. One notch near the side of the module is slightly offset from the notch on a DDR2 SDRAM module.	

Table 11-3   Memory modules used in notebook computers

A+ ESS
1.1
2.1

A+
220-602
2.2

Memory Module Description	Sample Memory Module
2.66" 144-pin SO-DIMM contains SDRAM. One notch is slightly offset from the center of the module.	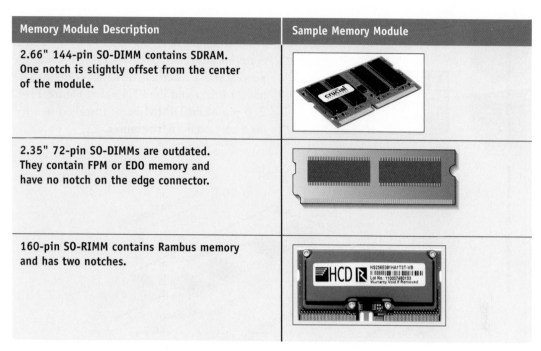
2.35" 72-pin SO-DIMMs are outdated. They contain FPM or EDO memory and have no notch on the edge connector.	
160-pin SO-RIMM contains Rambus memory and has two notches.	

Table 11-3 Memory modules used in notebook computers (continued)

In addition, some older notebooks use credit card memory or proprietary memory modules, both installed in slots inside the notebook case. Figure 11-41 shows credit card memory, proprietary memory, and SO-DIMMs for comparison.

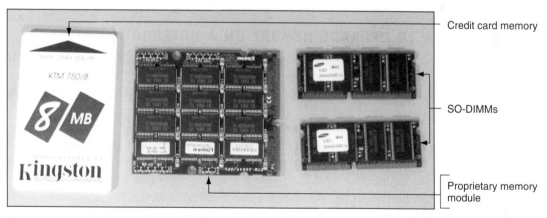

Figure 11-41 Older notebooks used credit card memory and proprietary memory modules, both larger than the current SO-DIMM modules

SO-DIMMs (small outline DIMMs, pronounced "sew-dims") come in several types. 72-pin SO-DIMMs, which support 32-bit data transfers, use FPM or EDO (which you learned about in Chapter 6), and could be used as single modules in 386 or 486 machines but must be used in pairs in Pentium machines. 144-pin SO-DIMMs, which support 64-bit data transfers, use EDO and SDRAM and can be used as single modules in Pentium machines. 200-pin SO-DIMMs are 2.625 inches wide and contain DDR SDRAM or DDR2 SDRAM. They have a single notch near the edge of one side of the module. A DDR SO-DIMM uses 2.5 volts of power, and a DDR2 SO-DIMM uses 1.8 volts. The notch of a DDR2 SO-DIMM is slightly offset from the DDR SO-DIMM's notch. Another type of memory for notebooks is the 160-pin SO-RIMM (small outline RIMM), which uses a 64-bit data path and the Rambus technology discussed in Chapter 6.

A+ ESS
1.1
2.1

Subnotebooks sometimes use MicroDIMMs that are smaller than SO-DIMMs and have a 64-bit data path. A MicroDIMM that contains SDRAM has 144 pins. A MicroDIMM that contains DDR SDRAM has 172 pins and uses 2.5 volts of power, and a MicroDIMM that contains DDR2 SDRAM has 214 pins and uses 1.8 volts. Figure 11-42 shows a 214-pin MicroDIMM being installed in a memory socket on a subnotebook computer.

A+
220-602
2.2

Video

Upgrading Memory on a Notebook

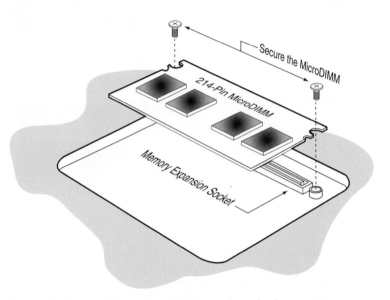

Figure 11-42 Installing a MicroDIMM in a subnotebook computer

A+ ESS
2.1

HOW TO UPGRADE MEMORY ON A NOTEBOOK

Before upgrading memory, make sure you are not voiding your warranty. Search for the best buy, but make sure you use memory modules made by or authorized by your notebook's manufacturer and designed for the exact model of your notebook. Installing generic memory might save money but might also void the notebook's warranty.

Upgrading memory on a notebook works about the same way as with upgrading memory on a desktop: Decide how much memory you can upgrade, purchase the memory, and install it. As with a desktop computer, be sure to match the type of memory to the type the notebook supports.

Most notebooks are designed for easier access to memory. For example, for the notebook shown in Figure 11-43, to replace a memory module, turn the notebook upside down. Remove the screws and the panel cover to expose the modules. Always check the notebook user guide for specific directions.

A+ ESS
2.1

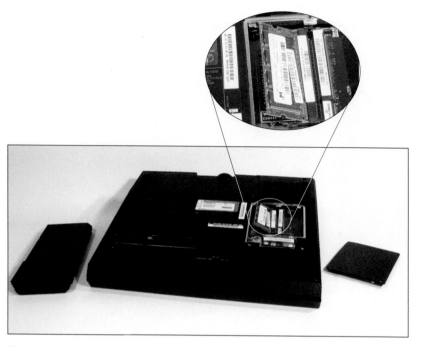

Figure 11-43   To access memory modules, remove a panel cover on the bottom of the notebook

APPLYING CONCEPTS   Older notebooks often make it much more difficult to upgrade memory. In this example, reaching the memory slots requires first removing the keyboard. Do the following:

1. Turn off the notebook and remove the battery pack and all cables.

2. Lift the keyboard brace, as shown in Figure 11-44. (Your notebook might have a different way to enter the system, such as from the bottom of the case.)

Figure 11-44   Lift the keyboard brace

3. Turn the keyboard over and toward the front of the notebook (see Figure 11-45). The keyboard is still connected to the notebook by the ribbon cable.

Ribbon cable connecting
keyboard to notebook

Figure 11-45 Turn the keyboard over toward the front of the notebook to expose the memory module socket

4. Lift the plastic sheet covering the memory module socket.

5. Insert the SO-DIMM module into the socket. See Figure 11-46. The socket braces should snap into place on each side of the module when the module is in position.

Figure 11-46 Install the SO-DIMM into the memory socket

6. Replace the keyboard and keyboard brace. (If you entered from the bottom, you might be replacing a cover on the bottom of the case in this step.)

7. Power up the notebook so that it can detect the new memory.

REPLACING A HARD DRIVE

When purchasing and installing an internal hard drive, floppy drive, CD/CD-RW drive, DVD/DVD-RW drive, or removable drive, see the notebook manufacturer's documentation about specific sizes and connectors that will fit the notebook. Also be aware of voiding a warranty if you don't follow the notebook manufacturer's directions. When purchasing a hard drive, know that hard drives for notebooks often use proprietary form factors and

A+ ESS
1.2
2.1

connectors, which means you must purchase a drive from the notebook manufacturer or at least buy one that uses the same connector and form factor. Here is what you need to know when shopping for a notebook hard drive:

◢ A desktop hard drive is 3.5 inches wide and a notebook drive is 2.5 inches wide. Figure 11-47 shows a comparison of the two sizes. Because the form factor of a notebook drive is more compact, it costs more than a desktop drive holding the same amount of data. (Notebook drives generally run at 4200 RPM or 5400 RPM, compared to 5400 RPM or 7200 RPM for desktop drives.)

Hard drive for a desktop computer

Hard drive for a notebook

Figure 11-47 Hard drives for notebooks are smaller than hard drives for desktop computers

◢ Most notebook hard drives sold today use a universal 40-pin connector for an IDE notebook. A few notebook manufacturers are making serial ATA hard drives for their notebooks. Check your notebook manual to know which to buy.

◢ For IDE drives, some notebooks use an adapter to interface between a proprietary connector on their hard drives and the 40-pin connector on the notebook motherboards. You'll need to remove the old drive and see how it's connected to know if an adapter is used. If you find an adapter, most likely, you can then connect the adapter to the new drive.

Before deciding to replace a hard drive, consider these issues:

◢ If the old drive has crashed, you'll need the recovery CD and notebook drivers CDs to reinstall Windows and the drivers. Make sure you have all these CDs before you start.

◢ If you are upgrading from a low-capacity drive to a higher-capacity drive, you need to consider how you will transfer data from the old drive to the new one. One way to do that is to use a USB to IDE converter that you first learned about in Chapter 7 (refer back to Figure 7-56). Using this converter, both drives can be up and working on the notebook at the same time so you can copy files. For less then $10, you can also purchase an even more convenient notebook hard drive enclosure case. Using one of these cases, you can slide the drive into the case and plug the case into the notebook's USB port.

To replace a hard drive, older notebook computers required that you disassemble the notebook. With newer notebooks, you can easily replace a drive. For example, to remove the IBM ThinkPad X20 hard drive, first power down the system and remove the battery pack. Then remove a coin screw that holds the drive in place (see Figure 11-48). Pull the drive out of its bay, and replace it with a new drive. Next, replace the screw and power up the system.

When the system boots up, if CMOS setup is set to autodetect hard drives, BIOS recognizes the new drive and searches for an operating system. If the drive is new, boot from the Windows recovery CD that came from the notebook manufacturer and install the OS.

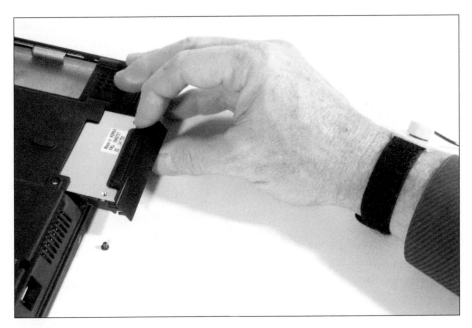

Figure 11-48 Replacing the hard drive in an IBM ThinkPad X20

Let's look at one more example. To replace the hard drive for the notebook shown in Figure 11-49, first remove the floppy disk drive to reveal the hard drive under it. Remove the screws holding the hard drive in place, remove the drive, and replace it with a drive designed to fit this particular cavity.

> **Notes**
>
> In other chapters, it is possible to give general directions on PC repair that apply to all kinds of brands, models, and systems. Not so with notebooks. Learning to repair notebooks involves learning unique ways to assemble, disassemble, and repair notebook components for specific brands and models of notebooks.

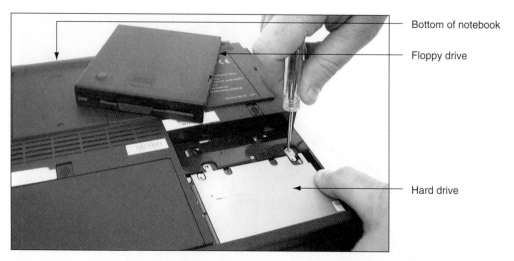

Bottom of notebook

Floppy drive

Hard drive

Figure 11-49 First remove the floppy drive to reveal the hard drive cavity

REPLACING THE LCD PANEL

Because the LCD panel is so fragile, it is one component that is likely to be broken when a notebook is not handled properly. If the LCD panel is dim or black when the notebook is running, first try to use the video port on the notebook to connect it to an external monitor. After you connect the monitor, use a function key to toggle between the LCD panel, the external monitor, and both the panel and monitor. If the external monitor works, but the LCD panel does not work, then most likely the problem is with the LCD panel assembly.

If the LCD display is entirely black, most likely you'll have to replace the entire LCD assembly. However, if the screen is dim, but you can make out that some display is present, the problem might be the video inverter card, which is the interface between the LCD panel and the motherboard (see Figure 11-50). Check with the notebook manufacturer to confirm that it makes sense to first try replacing just the relatively inexpensive inverter card before you replace the more expensive entire LCD panel assembly. If the entire assembly needs replacing, the cost of the assembly might exceed the value of the notebook.

XGA   FRU:26P8021
MADE IN THAILAND
EC: 013503

Figure 11-50 An IBM ThinkPad video inverter card

Let's first look at the special tools and procedures for disassembling a notebook and then we'll look at how to replace components in the LCD panel assembly.

DISASSEMBLING A NOTEBOOK

Working on notebooks requires special tools and extra patience. Just as when you are working with desktop systems, before opening the case of a notebook or touching sensitive components, you should always use a ground strap to protect the system against ESD. You can attach the alligator clip end of the ground strap to an unpainted metallic surface on the notebook. This surface could be, for instance, a port on the back of the notebook (see Figure 11-51). If a ground strap is not available, first dissipate any ESD between you and the notebook by touching a metallic unpainted part of the notebook, such as a port on the back before you touch a component inside the case.

A+ ESS
1.2
2.1

A+
220-602
2.1

A+ ESS
1.2
7.1
7.2

A+
220-602
1.2

A+ ESS
1.2
7.1
7.2

A+
220-602
1.2

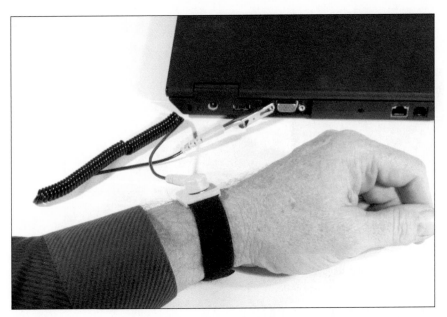

Figure 11-51   To protect the system against ESD, attach the alligator clip of a ground strap to an I/O port on the back of the notebook

Screws and nuts on a notebook are smaller than a desktop system and require smaller tools. You will need the following tools to disassemble a notebook, although you can get by without several of them. See Figure 11-52 for a display of some of these tools:

▲ Antistatic ground strap
▲ Small flat-head screwdriver
▲ Number 1 Phillips-head screwdriver
▲ Dental pick (useful for prying without damaging plastic cases, connectors, and screw covers such as the one in Figure 11-53)
▲ Torx screwdriver set, particularly size T5
▲ Something such as a pill box to keep screws and small parts organized
▲ Notebook for note taking or digital camera (optional)
▲ Flashlight (optional)
▲ Three-prong extractor to pick up tiny screws (optional)

Figure 11-52   Tools for disassembling a notebook computer

A+ ESS
1.2

Figure 11-53 Use a small screwdriver or dental pick to pry up the plastic cover hiding a screw

Notebooks contain many small screws of various sizes and lengths. When reassembling, put screws back where they came from so that when you reassemble the system, you won't use screws that are too long and that can protrude into a sensitive component and damage it. As you remove a screw, store or label it so you know where it goes when reassembling. One way to do that is to place screws in a pill box with each cell labeled. Another way is to place screws on a soft padded work surface and use white labeling tape to label each set of screws. A third way to organize screws is to put them on notebook paper and write beside them where the screw belongs (see Figure 11-54). Whatever method you use, work methodically to keep screws and components organized so you know what goes where when reassembling.

Figure 11-54 Using a notepad can help you organize screws so you know which screw goes where when reassembling

As you disassemble the computer, if you are not following directions from a service manual, keep notes as you work to help you reassemble later. Draw diagrams and label things carefully. Include in your drawings cable orientations and screw locations. You might consider using a digital camera. Take photos as you work and use the photos to guide you through the reassembly process.

When disassembling a notebook, consider the following tips:

▲ Take your time. Patience is needed to keep from scratching or marring plastic screw covers, hinges, and the case.

▲ As you work, don't force anything. If you find yourself forcing something, you're likely to break it.

▲ Always wear a ground strap or use other protection against ESD.

▲ When removing cables, know that sometimes cable connectors are ZIF connectors. To disconnect a cable from a ZIF connector, first pull up on the connector and then remove the cable, as shown in Figure 11-55. Figure 11-56 shows a notebook using three ZIF connectors that hold the three keyboard cables in place.

▲ Again, use a dental pick or very small screwdriver to pry up the plastic cover hiding a screw.

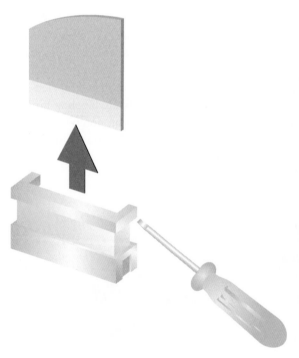

Figure 11-55 To disconnect a ZIF connector, first push up on the connector, release the latch, and then remove the cable

A+ ESS
1.2

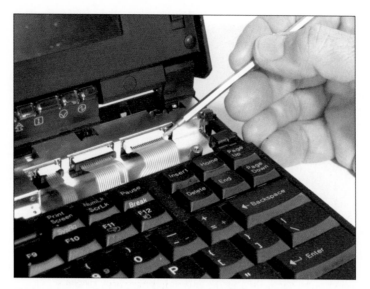

Figure 11-56 Three ZIF connectors hold the three keyboard cables in place

HOW TO REPLACE AN LCD PANEL ASSEMBLY

Sometimes, a notebook LCD panel including the entire cover and hinges are considered a single field replaceable unit, and sometimes components within the LCD assembly are considered an FRU. For example, the field replaceable units for the display panel in Figure 11-57 are the LCD front bezel, the hinges, the LCD panel, the inverter card, the LCD interface cables, the LCD USB cover, and the rear cover. Some high-end notebooks contain a video card that has embedded video memory. This video card might also need replacing. In most cases, you would replace only the LCD panel and perhaps the inverter card.

The following are some general directions to replace an LCD panel:

1. Remove the battery pack.

2. For many notebooks, to remove the LCD top cover, you must first remove the keyboard. A keyboard is sometimes removed by first removing screws on the bottom or top of the case and then prying up the keyboard using the edge of a blank key, as shown in Figure 11-58.

3. Sometimes, you must also remove screws in the back of the notebook to release the hinge assembly.

4. Remove the hinge covers; be careful not to break these plastic covers.

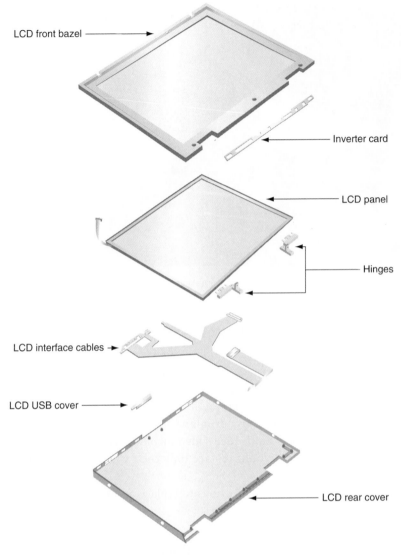

LCD front bazel

Inverter card

LCD panel

Hinges

LCD interface cables

LCD USB cover

LCD rear cover

Figure 11-57   Components in an LCD assembly

Figure 11-58   Pry up the keyboard using the edge of a screwdriver on the right of the keyboard

A+ ESS
1.2

5. After you remove the hinge screws, you should then be able to lift the cover off the notebook case (see Figure 11-59).

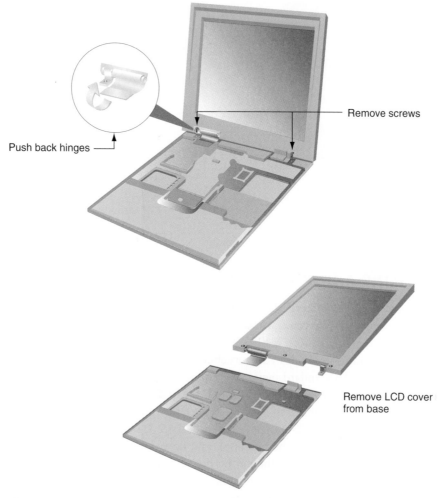

Push back hinges

Remove screws

Remove LCD cover from base

Figure 11-59 Remove the top LCD cover by first removing hinge screws and disconnecting the hinges; then lift off the cover

6. The LCD panel might connect to the notebook case by way of wires running through the hinge assembly, cables, or a pin connector. Cables might be connected to the motherboard using ZIF connectors. As you remove the LCD top cover, be careful to watch for how the panel is connected. Don't pull on wires or cables as you remove the cover, but first carefully disconnect them.

7. Next, remove screws that hold the top cover and LCD panel together. Sometimes, these screws are covered with black plastic circles. First use a dental pick or small screwdriver to pick off these covers. You should then be able to remove the front bezel and separate the rear cover from the LCD panel.

8. For notebooks that provide a USB connection on the top cover, the cable system might be complex. Carefully remove all connections (see Figure 11-60).

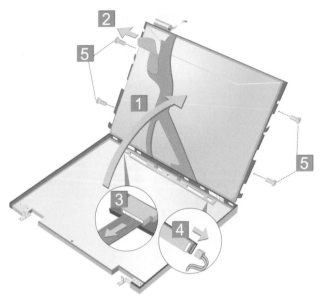

Figure 11-60 Removing the cable system from the rear of an LCD panel

REPLACING A MINI PCI CARD

A notebook does not contain the normal PCI Express, PCI, and ISA expansion slots found in desktop systems. Until recently, most internal cards, such as wired and wireless network adapters, SCSI host adapters, IEEE 1394 controllers, and USB controllers, used proprietary slots designed and supported by the notebook manufacturer. Recently, however, the industry has turned toward a standard method of connecting an internal card to a notebook using the Mini PCI specifications, which are based on the PCI industry standard for desktop computer expansion cards, but applied to a much smaller form factor for notebook expansion cards.

The standards include three types of cards—Type I, II, and III—that define how the internal card provides a port on the notebook and how the card connects to the motherboard. Type I and II cards connect to the motherboard using a 100-pin stacking connector, and Type III cards use a 124-pin stacking connector, are smaller than the Type I and II cards, and are expected to be the most popular. Figure 11-61 shows an example of a Mini-PCI card that you install inside a notebook to provide wireless WiFi connectivity.

Figure 11-61 This Cisco 802.11b wireless internal adapter is a Type III Mini-PCI card made by IBM

A+ ESS
1.2
2.1
2.3

Figure 11-62 shows how to remove a Mini PCI wireless network card in a Dell notebook. First, you must remove the hinged cover and the keyboard. Then disconnect the cable to the wireless antenna from the card. Next, pull outward on the securing tabs that hold the card in place. The card will pop up slightly. Lift it out of the cavity.

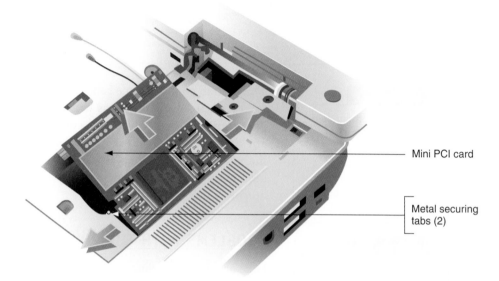

Mini PCI card

Metal securing tabs (2)

Figure 11-62 Remove a Mini PCI card

To replace the card, align the card in the cavity and press it down until it pops in place. Then reconnect the wireless antenna cable, as shown in Figure 11-63. Replace the keyboard and hinged cover.

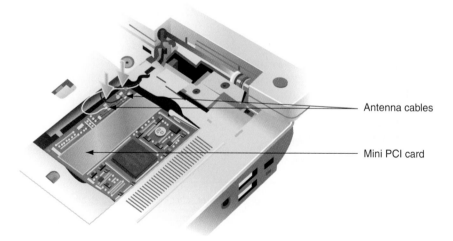

Antenna cables

Mini PCI card

Figure 11-63 Install a Mini PCI card

OTHER FIELD REPLACEABLE UNITS FOR NOTEBOOKS

Besides memory, hard drives, LCD panels, and Mini PCI cards, other field replaceable units (FRUs) for notebooks might be the motherboard, the CPU, the keyboard, the PC Card socket assembly, the optical drive (CD or DVD drive), the floppy drive, a sound card, a

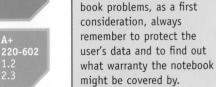

pointing device, the AC adapter, the battery pack, and the DC controller. Parts either made or approved by the notebook manufacturer must be used to replace all these parts. The DC controller is a card inside the notebook that converts voltage to CPU core voltage. The DC controller can support battery mode, AC adapter mode, and various sleep modes, and must be specifically rated for the notebook's processor. For more information about disassembling a notebook, see Appendix D.

TROUBLESHOOTING NOTEBOOKS

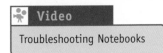

> **Notes**
>
> When troubleshooting notebook problems, as a first consideration, always remember to protect the user's data and to find out what warranty the notebook might be covered by.

> **Video**
>
> Troubleshooting Notebooks

This section contains some general troubleshooting steps to follow when solving problems with notebooks. Problems with software and hardware are covered. As when solving any computer problem, begin by interviewing the user and, if appropriate, backing up any important data. Be sure to keep notes as you go and document what you did and the outcome.

PROBLEMS WITH THE POWER SYSTEM

Here are some guidelines when troubleshooting problems with the power system:

◢ Check the power light. For many notebooks, a blinking light indicates the notebook has power and is in standby mode. If the power light is steady, the system has power. If the light is off, press the power button.

◢ The battery charge might be depleted. Connect the AC adapter.

◢ The AC adapter might not be solidly connected at both ends. Also check the connectors at the adapter unit, as shown in Figure 11-64.

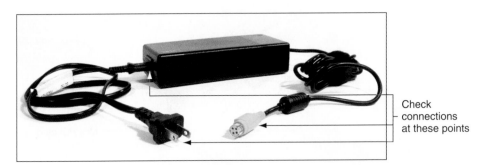

Check connections at these points

Figure 11-64 When troubleshooting an AC adapter, check connections at all points

◢ Eliminate power strips or other devices that might cause problems. Connect the AC adapter directly to an electrical outlet.

◢ Note that the memory modules might be defective or loose. Try reseating them.

◢ Too many peripherals might be drawing the system down. Try unplugging all unnecessary devices.

A+ ESS
1.3
2.3

A+
220-602
1.2
2.3

▲ If the system fails only when the AC adapter is connected, it might be defective. Try a new AC adapter, or, if you have a multimeter, use it to verify the voltage output of the adapter. Do the following for an adapter with a single center pin connector:

- Unplug the AC adapter from the computer, but leave it plugged into the electrical outlet.
- Using a multimeter set to measure voltage in the 1 to 20 V DC range, place the red probe of the multimeter in the center of the DC connector that would normally plug into the DC outlet on the notebook. Place the black probe on the outside cylinder of the DC connector (see Figure 11-65).

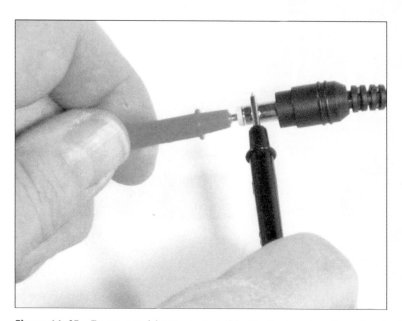

Figure 11-65 To use a multimeter to test this AC adapter, place the red probe (which, in the image, is in the person's left hand) in the center connector and the black probe on the outside

▲ The voltage range should be plus or minus five percent of the accepted voltage. For example, if a notebook is designed to use 16V, the voltage should measure somewhere between 15.2 and 16.8V DC.

▲ If you boot the notebook and discover CMOS setup has lost configuration information or the date and time are wrong, most likely the small battery inside the case that powers CMOS RAM needs replacing. Notebook manufacturers sometimes call this battery the backup battery or reserve battery. Notebook service manuals will provide instructions to exchange the battery. If you don't have a service manual, and you order the battery from the notebook manufacturer, most likely they will send you the battery along with detailed instructions on how to install it. Before you decide to replace the battery, if you have a multimeter, look on the battery for the voltage output and use the multimeter to determine if the voltage is correct. If not, replace the battery. If backup batteries need replacing often, replace the motherboard.

> 📹 **Video**
>
> Troubleshooting a Boot Problem 1

▲ Sometimes the backup battery is easy to get to, and sometimes it isn't. Figure 11-66 shows an example of one IBM ThinkPad in which the backup battery is easily accessed by removing a plate on the bottom of the notebook.

A+ ESS
1.3
2.3

A+
220-602
1.2
2.3

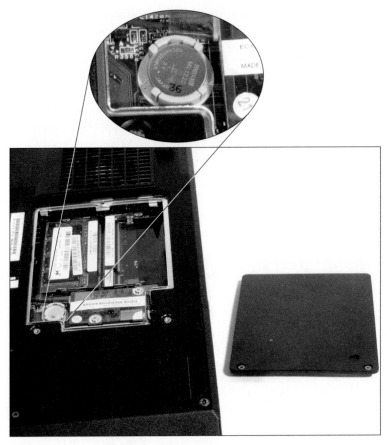

Figure 11-66   For this notebook, access the backup battery by removing a plate on the bottom
of the notebook

Notes

A backup battery is often a
lithium battery, which can
explode if not treated
correctly. Dispose of a used
battery by taking it to a
recycle center or following
other county regulations for
disposing of hazardous waste.

A+ Tip

The A+ Essentials and
A+ 220-602 exams expect
you to know how to diag-
nose and troubleshoot
problems with notebook
computers.

◢ If suspend mode or standby mode does not work, the
problem might be a faulty battery, DC controller, or
motherboard. Eliminate the battery as the problem by
trying suspend mode or standby mode while connected
to an electrical outlet. If the problem still persists,
first replace the DC controller and then replace the
motherboard.

◢ Some notebooks can hold suspend mode for a short time
while you exchange a battery pack or install an AC
adapter after the battery pack is discharged. These
systems use a standby battery. If the standby battery
does not work, first try replacing the standby battery,
then the DC controller. If this doesn't work and the
situation merits having the standby battery function,
replace the motherboard.

PROBLEMS WITH VIDEO

Problems with the video system can be caused by display
settings, the power system, or a faulty LCD panel or
inverter board. Use Table 11-4 as a starting point to troubleshoot video.

A+ ESS
1.3
2.3

A+
220-602
1.2
2.3

Problem	What to Do
Display is blank	◢ The problem might be caused by lack of power. Check the power light. Check the battery. Try another electrical outlet. Check the AC adapter. Check the power properties for incorrect settings.
	◢ Does the LCD panel have a cutoff switch that is turned off?
	◢ Perhaps display settings are turned down so low you cannot see the screen. Try using buttons on the keyboard to adjust brightness and contrast. See the user manual to learn how.
	◢ There might be a loose connection. Try reseating the LCD connector inside the notebook.
	◢ The LCD panel or inverter board might be broken. Try connecting a regular monitor to the system using the video port on the back of the notebook. Use a function key to toggle between the monitor and the LCD panel. If the monitor works, consider replacing the LCD assembly. Is the system under warranty?
	◢ The LCD panel might be set too dim, so it's hard to read. Try adjusting the brightness and contrast level.
Display is hard to read	◢ Consider electrical devices that might give interference, such as a powerful speaker system, stereo systems, fans, or halogen or fluorescent lights.
	◢ Is the notebook in direct sunlight? Try eliminating glare.
	◢ Try restoring the refresh rate, resolution, and other Windows display settings to default values.
Bright dots, dark dots, bright or dark vertical or horizontal lines, discoloration, dents, or bubbles appear on the LCD panel	◢ All these symptoms indicate a damaged LCD panel. A few defective dots on an LCD panel (for example, fewer than 11 dots) is considered a cosmetic problem, and notebook manufacturers generally will not replace the LCD panel under warranty. If the problems are disruptive, replace the LCD panel.
Screen flickers	◢ Most likely, display settings need adjusting and the LCD panel is not the problem.
LCD contrast and brightness cannot be adjusted	◢ Try reseating the LCD connector inside the notebook. ◢ Replace the LCD assembly.
LCD panel is unreadable, characters are missing, or incorrect characters appear	◢ Try reseating the LCD connector inside the notebook. ◢ Replace the LCD assembly.

Table 11-4 Problems with video and what to do about them

If you must replace the LCD panel or inverter board, be certain you purchase the same LCD assembly installed in the notebook. Variations in LCD panels are: some are monochrome; some are color; some have contrast and brightness adjustments; and some don't. In most cases, putting a different LCD assembly in a notebook other than the one it is designed to support will not work.

A+ ESS
1.3
2.3

A+
220-602
1.2
2.3

A NOTEBOOK GETS WET

To prevent a shock, if a notebook gets wet and is connected to an electrical outlet, turn off the electricity at the circuit breaker before touching the notebook or any cables connected to it. Then do the following:

- Turn off the computer and disconnect the AC adapter from the computer and from the electrical outlet.
- Turn off any attached devices such as a printer and disconnect them from the power source.
- Ground yourself by touching a metal unpainted part of the notebook such as a serial or parallel port on the back of the notebook.
- Remove any PC Cards or removable drives.
- Remove the battery pack.
- Remove the hard drive and memory modules.
- Open the notebook up and set it across two bricks or books so that air can circulate around it.
- Allow the notebook and all components to dry for at least 24 hours at room temperature. Don't use a hair dryer or fan to speed up the drying. Don't reassemble the components until you are sure all are dry. Then reinstall the hard drive and memory

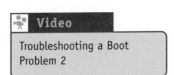

Video

Troubleshooting a Boot
Problem 2

modules. Connect the notebook to the AC adapter and turn it on. Verify that the notebook is working and then install the battery pack, removable drives, and PC Cards. If the notebook does not work correctly, begin troubleshooting the system that is not working.

THE NOTEBOOK IS DROPPED

If the notebook is dropped, do the following:

- If the system is still running, save your work and close any open files or applications. Shut down the computer.
- Disconnect the AC adapter from the notebook and from the electrical outlet.
- Turn off and disconnect any external devices such as a printer and remove the battery pack.
- Reinstall the battery pack or the AC adapter and turn on the notebook.
- If the notebook does not work, begin troubleshooting the system that is not working.

PROTECTING AND RETRIEVING DATA

Video

Recovering Data on a Laptop

Sometimes, the most important component in a notebook computer is the user data. If data is not backed up but the hard drive is not physically damaged, before you begin servicing the system, you can download the data to a hard drive in a desktop system. After the data is safe on another computer, the user can relax and you can focus on getting the notebook working. Follow these steps:

1. Obtain a notebook IDE adapter kit such as the one purchased from PC Cables (*www.pccables.com*, see Figure 11-67), used to install a notebook hard drive in a desktop system.

11

A+ ESS
1.3
2.3

A+
220-602
1.2
2.3

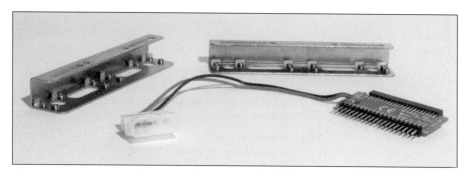

Figure 11-67 Use an IDE adapter kit to install a notebook hard drive into a desktop system

2. Remove the notebook hard drive from the notebook and connect the adapter to the drive. You can either set the drive on top of the PC case to make the connection or you can use the braces that come with the adapter kit to install the drive in a drive bay in the desktop. Just to copy data from the drive, it's really only necessary to set the drive on top of the desktop case.

3. Copy the data onto a hard drive in the desktop system.

4. If appropriate, you can then put the notebook hard drive back in the notebook to help you troubleshoot the system.

If you must replace the notebook hard drive, you can use the converter kit to install the drive in the desktop system and copy the data from the desktop system onto the new drive, before or after you have installed the OS on the drive.

MORE ERRORS AND WHAT TO DO ABOUT THEM

Table 11-5 contains a list of common and not-so-common error messages and what to do about them. In addition to this list, error messages given throughout the book that apply to desktop systems also might apply to notebooks. If you receive an error message that is not in the list or you are not familiar with, first check the Web site of the notebook manufacturer or the notebook service manual. Search on the error message to find out what to do. If this doesn't give results, do a general Web search using a search engine.

 Notes

Newsgroups can be an interesting source of information when repairing notebooks. Check out the Yahoo newsgroup "laptoprepair" at *groups.yahoo.com/group/Laptop_Repair/*.

A+ ESS
1.3
2.3

A+
220-602
1.2
2.3

Error Message	What to Do
Operating system not found	◢ Remove any bootable devices, such as a floppy disk or CD, and try a reboot.
	◢ Suspect damaged system files on the hard drive. For Windows 2000/XP, try booting to the Advanced Options menu by pressing F8 during the boot.
	◢ Try booting from a support CD or rescue disk for the OS and examine the hard drive for errors.
	◢ Go to CMOS setup and verify that the hard drive is correctly identified.
	◢ Reseat the hard drive.
	◢ Troubleshoot the operating system installed on the hard drive.
	◢ Flash BIOS and then reinstall the operating system.
	◢ Replace the motherboard.
Error reading PC Card	◢ Try reseating the card and rebooting.
	◢ Reinstall the drivers for the PC Card.
Keyboard controller error	◢ Try reseating the internal keyboard cable.
	◢ Try an external keyboard, disabling the internal keyboard.
	◢ Replace the keyboard.
Certain keys on the keyboard don't work	◢ Is the NumLock key set correctly?
	◢ An application might not be configured correctly. Try a different application.
One beep and the LCD panel is blank	◢ Reseat the LCD connectors.
	◢ Replace the LCD panel.
	◢ Replace the motherboard.
Wireless connectivity is not working or is weak	◢ Move the notebook to a better hot spot.
	◢ Is the wireless switch turned on?
	◢ The internal antenna might be loose. Check with the notebook manufacturer for a solution.
Touchpad or touch screen does not work	◢ Are you using the correct type of digital pen? Try rebooting the notebook.
	◢ Check Device Manager for errors.
	◢ Try updating device drivers and flashing BIOS.
Intermittent problems	◢ Intermittent problems might or might not have to do with hardware. Run diagnostic software. If a hardware component fails the diagnostic test, replace it. Then rerun the test.
	◢ Keep detailed records of what happened just before intermittent problems occur. Watch for patterns that might uncover the source of the problem.
The system does not detect a PC Card or ExpressCard	◢ Try a different card.
	◢ Reinstall the PCMCIA drivers.
	◢ Consider using a USB port for external devices rather than depending on the PC Card or ExpressCard slot.
	◢ Replace the PCMCIA assembly.
	◢ Replace the motherboard.

Table 11-5 Error messages and what to do about them

11

A+ ESS
1.3
2.3

A+
220-602
1.2
2.3

ONLINE RESOURCES FOR TROUBLESHOOTING NOTEBOOKS

Except for the differences discussed in this section, notebooks work identically to desktop PCs, and the troubleshooting guidelines in previous chapters also apply to notebooks. When troubleshooting notebooks, be especially conscious of warranty issues; know what you can do within the guidelines of the warranty. The documentation that comes with a notebook is much more comprehensive than what comes with a PC and most often contains troubleshooting guidelines for the notebook. Remember that the loaded OS and the hardware configuration are specific to the notebook, so you can rely on the notebook's manufacturer for support more than you can for a desktop PC. Support CDs that come bundled with a notebook include device drivers for all embedded devices. You can also download additional or updated drivers from the notebook manufacturer's Web site.

SURVEYING TABLET PCs

A tablet PC is a type of notebook computer that is designed for users who require a more graphical, user-friendly interface and need more portability than a full-size notebook allows. A tablet PC is a cross between a notebook computer and a pad and pencil. It costs about the same or more than a notebook, but is smaller, more portable, and provides many of the same features of a notebook, plus it lets you use a digital pen or stylus to write handwritten text on the LCD panel, which also serves as a touch screen. See Figure 11-68.

Figure 11-68   Tablet PC

Tablet PCs come in these forms:

▲ A convertible tablet PC looks like a regular clamshell notebook with LCD monitor and keyboard. To convert to a slate-top tablet PC, rotate the LCD panel 180 degrees and lay the back of the LCD panel flat against the bottom of the notebook. See Figure 11-69.

Figure 11-69   Acer TMC 110 tablet PC

▲ A slate model tablet PC such as the one shown in Figure 11-68 is slimmer and lighter than a notebook. It can easily dock to a desktop so you can use a regular monitor, mouse, and keyboard.

▲ A tablet PC with a docking station offers some interesting variations such as a grab-and-go docking station that lets you dock or undock your tablet PC without having to power down. (Microsoft calls this feature surprise hot docking.) Another type of docking station has dual-monitor support, which uses a regular monitor for some open applications, while others are shown on the tablet PC's LCD panel.

Using a digital pen, a user can write on the LCD panel/touch screen pad, comfortably resting her hand on it because the pad only picks up data written by the digital pen. Handwriting-recognition software interprets handwriting and can import it into Word documents, Excel spreadsheets, PowerPoint presentations, and other application files. Tablet PCs use Microsoft Windows XP Tablet PC Edition, which is Windows XP Professional with additional features included, such as voice-recognition and handwriting-recognition software. Features of a tablet PC include the following:

▲ A functioning Windows XP computer with the power of a full-sized notebook

▲ Onscreen writing ability for handwritten notes and drawings

▲ Voice-recognition and handwriting-recognition software that can import interpreted text into Word documents, Excel spreadsheets, and other application files

▲ Ability to record handwritten notes on top of other files, such as a handwritten note written on a PowerPoint presentation or photograph (see Figure 11-70)

▲ Built-in support for wireless, wired, and dial-up networking

▲ AC power adapter and rechargeable battery

▲ Windows XP Tablet PC Edition

▲ PC Card, USB ports, and VGA port for peripheral devices

▲ Hardware keyboard or onscreen software keyboard

▲ Accessories might include extra batteries, portfolio-style case, additional flash memory, screen protector, extra digital pens, or wireless keyboard

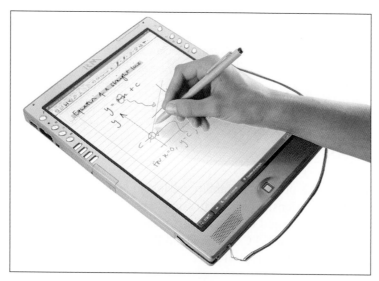

Figure 11-70   Handwritten note on a tablet PC document

Because a tablet PC uses Windows XP Tablet PC Edition operating system, which is an extension of Windows XP Professional, an application written for Windows XP Professional should have no problem working on a tablet PC. Also, many industries have software written specifically for the tablet PC, including real estate, legal, architecture, and medicine. An example of an application written specifically for a tablet PC is OmniForm Filler Solution for the Tablet PC by ScanSoft (*www.scansoft.com*) that uses the handwriting-recognition abilities built into Windows XP Tablet PC Edition to provide the ability to check boxes and radio buttons, select from drop-down lists, and add digital photographs or drawings to forms.

APPLYING CONCEPTS   As a PC support technician, many times you are called on to help people make good purchasing decisions. Choosing among a notebook, tablet PC, and PDA is most often a function of a user's lifestyle and job description. Here is a good example of a user finding just the right product to fit her needs:

Lacey is a successful real estate agent in a resort town on the Atlantic coast. She has many clients who live in distant cities and often works with these clients in long-distance relationships. Lacey tried to use a notebook computer, but found it awkward to carry a notebook when viewing real estate and working out of her car. She got frustrated with her notebook and sold it at an online auction Web site. Next, she tried using a PDA to track her clients and real estate listings, but the small screen also frustrated her. Then she came across an ad for a tablet PC and bought one. During the first week she owned the tablet PC, she was looking for a beach house for a client who lived in Oklahoma. She found just the right property, but it needed a lot of renovation. She took pictures with her digital camera and uploaded them to her tablet PC. Then she wrote several handwritten notes across each photograph pointing out problems that needed correcting and her ideas for renovation. She e-mailed the entire proposal to her client and made the sale!

Now Lacey has imported into her tablet PC all the forms necessary for a client to list or make an offer on a property. Clients can fill out these forms by hand on her tablet PC while on-site, and Lacey

can later convert them to typed text before printing the forms for the client's signature. Lacey also says she can informally take notes at a client meeting on her tablet PC without the raised LCD panel of her old notebook computer standing stiffly between her and her client.
She likes being able to appear professional, yet casual and friendly at the same time.

SURVEYING PDAs

Notebooks and tablet PCs provide portability or flexibility, but even the smallest can be cumbersome in some situations, especially for simple tasks such as checking addresses, viewing stock prices, or recording and receiving short messages. PDAs (personal digital assistants), sometimes called personal PCs or handheld PCs, provide greater ease of use for such situations. Figure 11-71 shows a typical PDA.

Figure 11-71   Garmin iQue M5 Color Pocket PC PDA and GPS

> **Notes**
>
> The GPS (Global Positioning System) is a group of 24 orbiting satellites. A GPS receiver can use signals received from three or more satellites to calculate its position and then use preinstalled software to give directions to a destination.

A PDA, such as a Palm Pilot, Pocket PC, BlackBerry, or Symbian, is a small, handheld computer with its own operating system and applications. A PDA connects to your desktop computer by way of Bluetooth wireless or a USB or serial port and is powered using an AC adapter or battery. Some PDAs come with more than one wireless technology such as Bluetooth (to sync with a notebook), a GPS receiver (to find your position and give directions to a destination), cellular WAN (to serve double duty as a cell phone), and WiFi. A PDA in combination with a cell phone is called a smart phone.

A PDA uses either a grayscale or color LCD panel, and can sometimes benefit from additional memory. Other PDA hardware includes a stylus used to operate the PDA by touching the screen. You tap the screen with the stylus to open applications or make menu selections. You can also hold down the stylus to scroll through menu options. For quick access to commonly used applications such as a calendar or an address book, most PDAs provide application buttons below the screen that you can press to open the application. A PDA might use an AC/DC adapter that can plug into the PDA itself or into the universal cradle. Some PDAs have optional accessories such as the fold-out keyboard shown in Figure 11-72.

PDA snaps in here

Figure 11-72   This fold-out keyboard attaches to a PDA

When purchasing a PDA, first decide how you will use it, and then match the features of the PDA to its intended purpose. Following are the main questions to consider when purchasing a PDA. The next sections cover several of these items.

- What applications come with the PDA, and what applications can be added later?
- How easy is the PDA to use, and how thorough is its documentation?
- How easy is it to keep the PDA synchronized with your desktop computer or notebook, and will your organization approve the type of PDA synchronization?
- What support is available on the manufacturer's Web site? What software for the PDA can be downloaded from this site? What is the cost of that software?
- What type of batteries does the PDA use, and what is the battery life?
- Can the PDA use e-mail and the Web, and what extra hardware and software is required to do that? How much will this service cost?
- What additional devices can be purchased to make the PDA more versatile and easier to use?
- What operating system does the PDA use? How easy is the OS to use?
- What is the warranty? Does the warranty cover such things as dropping the PDA or damaging the LCD panel by pressing too hard on it?
- What is the price of the PDA, and what is the price of additional years of warranty?

BATTERY LIFE ON A PDA

Battery life on a PDA varies by model, and short battery life is one of the largest complaints made about PDAs. Some PDAs use rechargeable batteries, and others do not. If your PDA's battery runs down all the way and discharges, you lose all the data and applications on the PDA! Many manufacturers suggest that you get in the habit of setting your PDA in its cradle whenever you are not carrying it, and that you never trust it with data or downloaded software for more than a few hours. It is a good idea to have a cradle and adapter wherever you use your PDA; you might want to keep one at your home, another at your office, and another in your briefcase.

APPLICATIONS ON A PDA

You can use a PDA to store addresses and phone numbers, manage a calendar, run word-processing software, send and receive e-mail, access Web sites, play music, find directions using a GPS receiver, and exchange information with a desktop computer. Some PDAs also serve double duty as a cell phone. A PDA can come with all application software prein-stalled or require the user to download applications at additional cost. Some PDAs support only the preinstalled applications and cannot download others. Some PDAs allow you to download e-mail or Web site content from a desktop computer or a notebook, and others can access the Internet directly by way of a modem or wireless connection. Not all Web sites are designed to be accessed by a PDA, and the Web content a PDA can read is more limited than the content a desktop or notebook computer can read.

CONNECTING A PDA TO A PC

Typically, a PDA comes with a universal cradle that has an attached cable to connect to a desk-top computer or notebook by way of a USB or serial port, or a PDA might use an infrared or Bluetooth wireless connection. For example, the ASUS MyPal shown in Figure 11-71 supports the Bluetooth standard introduced in Chapter 10.

The process by which the PDA and the PC "talk" to each other through the universal cradle, cable, or wireless connection is called synchro-nization. This process enables you to back up information on your PDA to the PC, work with PDA files on the PC, and download applications to the PDA that you downloaded from the Web using the PC.

> **Notes**
>
> Special software, such as ActiveSync by Microsoft, might be needed to synchronize a PDA and the other computer attached via the cable. You need to install this software before connecting the PDA to the PC. Follow the instructions in the PDA documentation and on the CD included with it to install the software.

To set up communication between a PDA and a PC, do the following:

◢ Read the PDA documentation about how to synchronize it with the PC and install on the PC the synchronization software that came bundled with the PDA. If the synchro-nization software must first be launched, launch it.

◢ For cable connections, connect the PDA to the PC by way of a USB cable or serial cable that most likely also came bundled with the PDA.

◢ For wireless connections, if the PDA and PC both use the same wireless standard (for example, Bluetooth, infrared, or WiFi), verify they are both set to the same standards, channel, and encryption methods. Also, both PDA and PC wireless abilities must be enabled and switches turned on.

◢ The PDA and PC should immediately synchronize. Data entered on one device should be reflected on the other.

If the PDA and PC have problems communicating, check out and try the following:

◢ Is the USB or serial cable plugged in at both ends?

◢ For a USB connection, verify the USB controller is working in Device Manager with no conflicts.

▲ Is the USB or serial port enabled in CMOS setup?

▲ Is the wireless switch turned on? Is wireless software enabled, and does Device Manager correctly recognize the wireless component?

▲ Is the PDA turned on?

▲ Check the PDA documentation for other things to do and try.

▲ Uninstall and reinstall the PDA software on the PC.

▲ Check the Web site of the PDA manufacturer for problems and solutions.

PDA MANUFACTURERS AND OPERATING SYSTEMS

Listed below are several operating systems for PDAs, together with the percentage of the market share they had in 2005, as reported by Gartner, Inc. When selecting a PDA, generally, you first decide what applications you intend to use on the PDA and then select the operating system that supports these applications. After you have decided on the applications and the OS, you're ready to select the PDA. Only one OS is installed on a PDA and generally it is not upgraded for the life of the PDA. Here is a list of operating systems used on PDAs:

▲ *Windows Mobile.* Windows Mobile by Microsoft (*www.microsoft.com*) with 49 percent of the market and increasing. Earlier handheld OSs by Microsoft are Pocket PC and Windows CE. A PDA that uses Windows Mobile is likely to be called a Pocket PC.

▲ *BlackBerry.* BlackBerry by Research in Motion (*www.rim.com*) with 25 percent of the market and increasing.

▲ *Palm OS.* Palm OS by Access Co (*www.access-us-inc.com*) with 15 percent of the market and decreasing.

▲ *Symbian OS.* Symbian OS by Symbian (*www.symbian.com*) with 6 percent of the market and increasing.

These operating systems support both smart phones and PDAs. The principle differences between the OSs are the hardware and applications they support. Windows Mobile is considered the more versatile OS that can better be used to download and run applications similar to those supported by Windows, such as Microsoft Word or Excel. The other OSs are generally tied to the hardware manufacturers of PDAs and smart phones. Table 11-6 lists some manufacturers of PDAs.

> **Notes**
> Hewlett-Packard sponsors a forum to promote open source software (programming code is made public and no royalties are paid) to use the Linux operating system on handheld computers. For more information, see *www.handhelds.org*.

Manufacturer	Web Site
ASUS	*www.asus.com*
Casio	*www.casio.com*
Compaq	*www.hp.com*
Hewlett-Packard	*www.hp.com*
Palm (was PalmOne)	*www.palm.com*
Sony	*www.sonystyle.com*
Samsung	*www.samsung.com*

Table 11-6 Manufacturers of PDAs

>> *CHAPTER SUMMARY*

▲ Notebook computers are designed for travel. They use the same technology as desktop computers, with modifications for space, portability, and power conservation. A notebook generally costs more than a desktop with the same specifications.

▲ When supporting notebooks, pay careful attention to what the warranty allows you to change on the computer.

▲ The notebook manufacturer service manual, diagnostic software, and Windows Recovery CD are useful when disassembling, troubleshooting, and repairing a notebook.

▲ A notebook uses a customized installation of the Windows OS, customized by the notebook manufacturer. For most situations, the OS does not need upgrading for the life of the notebook unless you need to use features of a new OS. To perform an upgrade, obtain a customized version of the new OS from the notebook manufacturer.

▲ Windows features useful on notebooks include Multilink Channel Aggregation, power management, PC Card support, Windows 9x/Me Briefcase, and Windows 2000/XP Offline Files, folder redirection, and hardware profiles.

▲ A notebook can be powered by its battery pack or by an AC or DC adapter connected to a power source.

▲ PC Cards are a popular way to add peripheral devices to notebooks. Types of PC Cards that vary in thickness are Types I, II, and III. CardBus cards can be used in PC Card slots. The latest I/O cards are ExpressCard/34 and ExpressCard/54, which are not backward compatible with the PC Card slots.

▲ When an internal component needs replacing, consider the possibility of disabling the component and using an external peripheral device in its place.

▲ Current notebooks use SO-DIMMs and SO-RIMMs for memory. SO-DIMMs can have 72 pins, 144 pins, or 200 pins and SO-RIMMs have 160 pins.

▲ When upgrading components on a notebook, including memory, use components that are the same brand as the notebook, or use only components recommended by the notebook's manufacturer.

▲ Notebook settings and procedures vary more widely from model to model than those of desktop computers. Check the manufacturer's documentation and Web site for information specific to your notebook model.

▲ A tablet PC is a notebook computer with a touch screen that can input handwritten notes, interpreting them as text.

▲ A tablet PC can be a convertible model or a slate model and can come with a docking station that supports surprise hot docking.

▲ Input on a tablet PC can be by handwriting, voice, keyboard, or an onscreen keyboard.

▲ A PDA provides even more portability than a notebook computer or tablet PC for applications such as address books and calendars. PDAs are designed to provide handheld computing power and can interface with a desktop or notebook computer to transfer files and applications.

▲ PDAs synchronize with PCs through a USB, serial, or wireless port. For wireless, check that the PC and PDA support the same wireless standard.

>> KEY TERMS

For explanations of key terms, see the Glossary near the end of the book.

CardBus
credit card memory
DC controller
docking station
ExpressCard
folder redirection
hardware profiles
laptop computer
MicroDIMM

Mini PCI
notebook
PC Card
PC Card slot
PCMCIA (Personal Computer
    Memory Card International
    Association) Card
PCMCIA slot
PDA (personal digital assistant)

port replicator
shared memory
SO-DIMM (small outline
    DIMM)
SO-RIMM (small outline
    RIMM)
synchronization
video sharing

>> REVIEWING THE BASICS

1. Why are notebooks usually more expensive than PCs with comparable power and features?

2. What are four types of SO-DIMMs used in a notebook?

3. List three types of batteries that might be used on notebooks.

4. What are three ways a notebook can receive its power?

5. What component that is part of the LCD panel assembly might be responsible for the LCD panel showing dim screens?

6. What is the thickness of a Type I PC Card? Of a Type III PC Card?

7. What term refers to a PC Card you can remove and replace without powering off?

8. What two services must an OS provide for a PC Card to work?

9. What is the small cord sometimes found on the end of a PC Card called?

10. What applet in the Windows 2000 Control Panel do you use to stop a PC Card before removing it? In Windows 98?

11. How do you solve the problem when a Windows XP notebook hangs after a PC Card has been removed while the notebook was in sleep mode?

12. What type of memory module used in notebooks has 160 pins?

13. List 10 devices that a notebook manufacturer might consider to be field replaceable units.

14. Why is understanding the warranty on notebooks so important?

15. What is the purpose of a DC controller on a notebook?

16. What happens if the battery on your PDA discharges?

17. What are the two most popular operating systems currently used by PDAs?

18. What is the difference between a port replicator and a docking station?

19. Which notebook component is most likely to be the easiest to replace: the hard drive or the LCD panel?

20. What are the three types of Mini PCI cards? How many pins does each type card have?

21. What is the purpose of the Multilink Channel Aggregation feature of Windows?

22. If you need to replace a hard drive in a notebook, why is it best not to use a standard Windows XP setup CD to install the OS on the new drive?

23. What is the best way to identify a notebook so that you can find the right documentation for the notebook on the manufacturer's Web site?

24. If you need to install an external peripheral to take the place of a failed internal component in a notebook, what do you first do to disable the internal component?

25. List the ways that a PDA can connect to a PC to synchronize with it.

>> THINKING CRITICALLY

1. Your friend has a Windows 98 notebook computer and has purchased Windows XP and installed it as an upgrade on his notebook. He calls to tell you about the upgrade and says that he cannot connect to the Internet. His notebook has an embedded modem that he uses for communication. What do you tell him to do?

    a. Reinstall Windows 98.

    b. Using another computer, download and install the Windows XP modem drivers from the notebook manufacturer's Web site.

    c. Search the CDs that come with the notebook for Windows XP modem drivers and install them.

    d. Perform a clean install of Windows XP.

2. A friend asks you for help in determining the best product to buy: a notebook, tablet PC, or PDA. She is a paralegal and spends a lot of time at the courthouse researching real estate titles. She wants a device to take notes with as she works. List three questions you would ask her to help her make her decision.

>> HANDS-ON PROJECTS

PROJECT 11-1: Observing Notebook Features

Examine a notebook, its documentation, and the manufacturer's Web site, and then answer these questions:

1. How do you exchange the battery pack on the notebook?

2. What type of SO-DIMM or SO-RIMM does the notebook use?

3. How much memory is currently installed?

4. What is the capacity of the hard drive?

5. What OS is installed?

6. What processor is installed?

7. What ports are on the notebook?

8. How many PC Card or ExpressCard slots does the notebook have?

9. How much does the notebook weigh?

10. What is the cost of a new battery pack?

11. Can you buy memory from the Web site? How much does it cost to upgrade the notebook's memory to full capacity?

PROJECT 11-2: Researching Wireless Notebook Systems

Use the Web for the following research:

1. Find a notebook that has integrated wireless technology. Print the Web page advertising the notebook.

2. Drill down to the detailed specifications for the notebook, and answer these questions:

   a. What type of wireless technology does the notebook support?

   b. Does the notebook have a built-in wireless access point, or is the wireless adapter an optional add-on? If the access point is built in, where is the antenna LED located on the notebook? If the adapter is optional, where is it installed?

   c. If the notebook requires you to buy additional devices to connect to a wireless network, what devices must you buy?

3. Suppose you have a PC with a USB port. Find a device that uses this USB port and provides a wireless access point for your notebook to connect to the PC. Make sure that the device is compatible with the notebook's wireless technology. Print a Web page about this device.

PROJECT 11-3: Researching PC Card Modems

Some employees in your company spend a lot of time on the road and, while traveling, need easy Internet access. Research how they can use a cellular phone to connect a notebook computer to the Internet. Using the Motorola Web site (*www.motorola.com*) or a similar site, do the following:

1. Print the Web page of a modem card or a USB device for a notebook computer that can accommodate a cellular phone connection.

2. Print the Web page of a cellular phone that can accommodate a modem card connection to a notebook.

3. Is the connection between the cellular phone and the notebook wireless or does it use a cable? If a cable is used, print the page that shows or describes the cable that connects the notebook to the cellular phone.

PROJECT 11-4: Researching PDAs

Select two different PDAs, one PDA that uses Windows Mobile and one BlackBerry, that cost about the same. Using information from the Web site of the manufacturer of each PDA, write the following:

1. Short description of the features of the PDA, including its model number

2. Price

3. Manufacturer

4. Type of battery and battery life

5. Ability for Web and e-mail access

6. Additional devices that can be purchased

7. Operating system

8. Built-in or bundled applications

9. Warranty

>> *REAL PROBLEMS, REAL SOLUTIONS*

REAL PROBLEM 11-1:   Upgrading Notebook Memory

You've had your HP Pavilion ze4145 for a couple of years and are looking for ways to improve its performance. You've cleaned up the hard drive and defragged it, and now you're considering the possibility of upgrading memory. Windows XP reports the system has 256 MB of RAM. You open the cover on the bottom of the case and discover that one SO-DIMM slot is filled and the other is empty. Imprinted on the one SO-DIMM is PC21005-2533-0-A1 SG, 256MB, DDR 266MHz, CL2.5. How much will the upgrade cost to bring total RAM in the system to 512 MB? Print the Web page to support your answer.

REAL PROBLEM 11-2:   Notebook Power Problems

Julie's Windows XP Dell Inspirion 6000 notebook has a failed modem. The modem port does not work, but Julie travels a lot and needs it to access her ISP when other options are not available. Download the service manual for her notebook from *www.dell.com* and print the page that shows the location of the modem card in the notebook. Do you think it best to replace the internal modem card or use a PC Card or USB modem instead? What is the cost of purchasing the internal modem card and about how much time do you think it will take to exchange the card? On the other hand, how much will an external modem cost? Print Web pages documenting your answers.

REAL PROBLEM 11-3:   Taking Apart a Notebook

If you enjoy putting together a thousand-piece jigsaw puzzle, you'll probably enjoy working on notebook computers. With desktop systems, replacing a component is not a time-consuming task, but with notebooks, the job could take several hours. If you take the time to carefully examine the notebook's case before attempting to open it, you will probably find markings provided by the manufacturer to assist you in locating components that are commonly upgraded. If you have a service manual, your work will be much easier than without one.

The best way to learn to disassemble a notebook is to practice on an old one that you can afford to break. Find an old Dell or IBM ThinkPad for which you can download the service manual from the Dell or IBM Web site. Then carefully and patiently follow the disassembly instructions and then reassemble it. When done, you can congratulate yourself and move on to newer notebooks.

Supporting Printers and Scanners

In this chapter, you will learn:

- How printers and scanners work

- How to install printers and scanners and how to share a printer over a local area network

- About routine maintenance tasks necessary to support printers and scanners

- How to trouble-shoot printer and scanner problems

This chapter discusses the most popular types of printers, how they work, and how to support them. You'll also learn about supporting scanners. As you work through the chapter, you'll learn how to install a printer and scanner and how to share a printer with others on a network. Then, you'll learn about maintaining printers and scanners and troubleshooting printer and scanner problems.

HOW PRINTERS AND SCANNERS WORK

A+ ESS
4.1

A+
220-602
4.1

Local printers and scanners connect directly to a computer by way of a USB port, parallel port, serial port, wireless connection (Bluetooth, infrared, or WiFi), IEEE 1394 (FireWire) port, SCSI port, PC Card, or ExpressCard connection, or a computer can access a network printer by way of the network. Some printers support more than one method. Printers can also be combined with fax machines, copiers, and scanners in the same machine. Most often, printers and scanners are powered by AC power or by using an AC adapter that converts power to DC. In addition, some printers are battery powered.

Printers can have a variety of options, including extra paper trays to hold different sizes of paper, special paper feeders or transparency feeders, staplers, collators, and sorters. Printers can print in color or black and white, and printers can print on one side of the page or automatically print on both sides (called duplex printing). Besides these features, printers are rated by the time it takes for the first page to print (warm-up time), the resolution (for example, 1200 x 1200 dpi), the maximum pages printed per month so as not to void the warranty (called the maximum duty cycle), the printing speed (for example, 35 PPM or 35 pages per minute), and the technology the printer uses to format a page before it is printed (choices are PCL, PostScript, and GDI).

> **A+ Tip**
>
> The A+ Essentials exam expects you to know that printers and scanners can connect using these interfaces: parallel, network, USB, SCSI, serial, IEEE 1394 (FireWire), and wireless (Bluetooth, 802.11, and infrared).

> **Notes**
>
> If you can afford it, the best practice is to purchase one machine for one purpose instead of bundling many functions into a single machine. For example, if you need a scanner and a printer, purchase a good printer and a good scanner rather than a combo machine. Routine maintenance and troubleshooting are easier and less expensive on single-purpose machines, although the initial cost is higher.

There are two major categories of printers: impact printers and nonimpact printers. An impact printer creates a printed page by using some mechanism that touches or hits the paper. An example of an impact printer is a dot matrix printer. A nonimpact printer does not use a mechanism to touch the page. Examples of nonimpact printers are laser, inkjet (ink dispersion), solid ink, dye sublimation, and thermal printers. In the following sections, we'll look at the different types of printers for desktop computing. Then we'll look at how a scanner works.

LASER PRINTERS

A laser printer is a type of electrophotographic printer that can range from a small, personal desktop model to a large, network printer capable of handling and printing large volumes continuously. Figure 12-1 shows an example of a typical laser printer for a desktop computer system.

> **A+ Exam Tip**
>
> The A+ Essentials exam expects you to be familiar with these types of printers: laser, inkjet, solid ink, thermal, and impact.

Laser printers require the interaction of mechanical, electrical, and optical technologies to work. Understanding how they work will help you support and service them. You'll also learn how to protect yourself and the printer while you work on it.

A+ ESS
4.1

A+
220-602
4.1

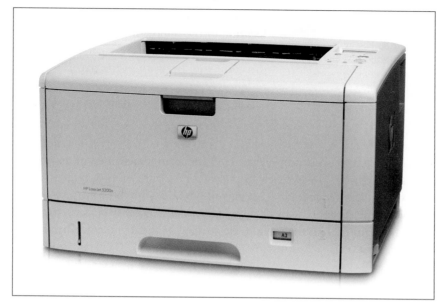

Figure 12-1 A desktop laser printer

Laser printers work by placing toner on an electrically charged rotating drum and then depositing the toner on paper as the paper moves through the system at the same speed the drum is turning. Figure 12-2 shows the six steps of laser printing. The first four use the printer components that undergo the most wear. These components are contained within the removable cartridge to increase the printer's life. The last two steps are performed outside the cartridge.

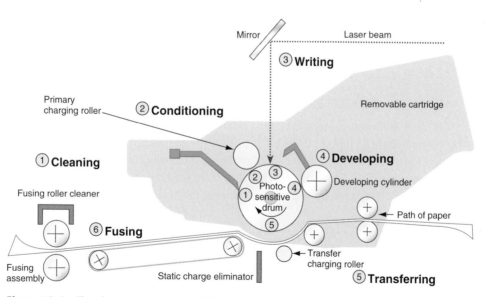

Figure 12-2 The six progressive steps of laser printing

Note that Figure 12-2 shows only a cross-section of the drum, mechanisms, and paper. Remember that the drum is as wide as a sheet of paper. The mirror, blades, and rollers in the drawing are also as wide as paper. Also know that toner responds to a charge and moves from one surface to another if the second surface has a more positive charge than the first.

A+ ESS
4.1

A+
220-602
4.1

A+ Tip

The A+ Essentials exam expects you to know the six steps in the printing process for a laser printer.

As you read about and visualize the process, first note the location of the removable cartridge in the drawing, the photosensitive drum inside the cartridge turning in a clockwise direction, and the path of the paper, which moves from right to left.

The six steps of laser printing are described next.

STEP 1: CLEANING

In the cleaning step, shown in Figure 12-3, the drum is cleaned of any residual toner and electrical charge. First, a sweeper strip cleans the drum of any residual toner, which is swept away by a sweeping blade. A cleaning blade completes the physical cleaning of the drum. Next, the drum is cleaned of any electrical charge by erase lamps in the hinged top cover of the printer. The lamps light the surface of the drum to neutralize any electrical charge left on it.

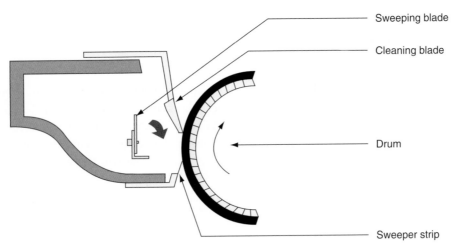

Sweeping blade

Cleaning blade

Drum

Sweeper strip

Figure 12-3 The cleaning step cleans the drum of toner and electrical charge

STEP 2: CONDITIONING

In the conditioning step, the drum is conditioned to contain a high electrical charge. A uniform electrical charge of -600 V is put on the surface of the drum. The charge is put there by a primary charging roller or primary corona, which is charged by a high-voltage power supply assembly. The primary charging roller in Figure 12-2 is inside the toner cartridge and regulates the charge on the drum, ensuring that it is a uniform -600 V.

STEP 3: WRITING

In the writing step, a laser beam discharges a lower charge only to places where toner should go. The uniform charge applied in Step 2 is discharged only where you want the printer to print. This is done by controlling mirrors to reflect laser beams onto the drum in a pattern that re-creates the image desired. This is the first step in which data from the computer must be transmitted to the printer. Figure 12-4 shows the process. Data from the PC is received by the formatter (1) and passed on to the DC controller (2), which controls the laser unit (3). The laser beam is initiated and directed toward the octagonal mirror called the scanning mirror. The scanning mirror (4) is turned by the scanning motor in a clockwise direction. There are eight mirrors on the eight sides of the scanning mirror. As the mirror turns, the laser beam is directed in a sweeping motion that can cover the entire length of the

A+ ESS
4.1

A+
220-602
4.1

drum. The laser beam is reflected off the scanning mirror, focused by the focusing lens (5), and sent on to the mirror (6), which is also shown in Figure 12-2. The mirror deflects the laser beam to a slit in the removable cartridge and onto the drum (7).

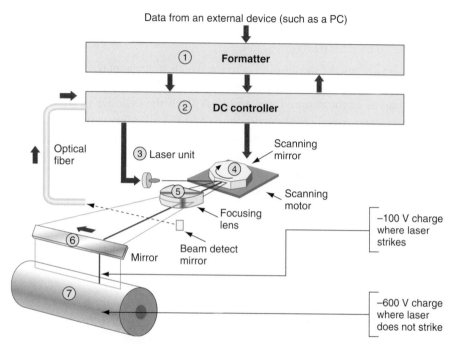

Figure 12-4 The writing step, done by an invisible laser beam, mirrors, and motors, causes a discharge on the drum where the images will be

The speed of the motor turning the drum and the speed of the scanning motor turning the scanning mirror are synchronized so that the laser beam completes one pass, or scanline, across the drum and returns to the beginning of the drum (right side of the drum in Figure 12-4) to begin a new pass, until it completes the correct number of passes for each inch of the drum circumference. For example, for a 1200 dots per inch (dpi) printer, the beam makes 1200 passes for every one inch of the drum circumference. The laser beam is turned on and off continually as it makes a single pass down the length of the drum, so that dots are written along the drum on every pass. For a 1200-dpi printer, 1200 dots are written along the drum for every inch of linear pass. The 1200 dots per inch down this single pass, combined with 1200 passes per inch of drum circumference, accomplish the resolution of 1200 x 1200 dots per square inch of many desktop laser printers.

> **Notes**
>
> A laser printer can produce better-quality printouts than a dot matrix printer, even when printing at the same dpi, because it can vary the size of the dots it prints, creating a sharp, clear image. Hewlett-Packard (HP) calls this technology of varying the size of dots **REt (Resolution Enhancement technology)**.

In a laser printer, where the laser beam strikes the surface of the drum, the drum discharges from its conditioned charge of -600 V down to -100 V where toner will be placed on the drum. Toner does not stick to the highly charged areas of the drum.

Just as the scanning laser beam is synchronized to the rotating drum, the data output is synchronized to the scanning beam. Before the beam begins moving across the scanline of the drum, the beam detect mirror detects the laser beam by reflecting it to an optical fiber. The light travels along the optical fiber to the DC controller, where it is converted to an electrical signal that synchronizes the data output. The signal is also used to diagnose problems with the laser or scanning motor.

The laser beam has written an image to the drum surface as a -100 V charge. The -100 V charge on this image area will be used in the developing stage to transmit toner to the drum surface.

STEP 4: DEVELOPING

Figure 12-5 shows the developing step, in which toner is placed on the drum where the charge has been reduced. Toner is applied by the developing cylinder to the discharged (-100 V) areas of the drum. Toner transfers from the cylinder to the drum as the two rotate very close together. The cylinder is coated with a layer of toner, made of black resin bonded to iron, which is similar to the toner used in photocopy machines. The toner is held on the cylinder surface by its attraction to a magnet inside the cylinder. (A toner cavity keeps the cylinder supplied with toner.) A **control blade** prevents too much toner from sticking to the cylinder surface. The toner on the cylinder surface takes on a negative charge (between -200 V and -500 V) because the surface is connected to a DC power supply, called the DC bias.

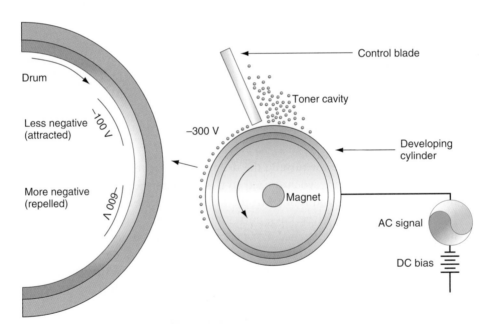

Figure 12-5 In the developing step, charged toner is deposited onto the drum surface

The negatively charged toner is more negative than the -100 V on the drum surface but less negative than the -600 V surface. This means that the toner is attracted to the -100 V area of the drum surface (the -100 V area is positive relative to the toner). The toner is repelled from the -600 V part of the drum surface, which is negative relative to the toner. The result is that toner sticks to the drum where the laser beam has hit and is repelled from the area where the laser beam has not hit.

You can adjust printer density manually at the printer or through software controlling the printer. When you adjust print density with laser printers, you are adjusting the DC bias charge on the developing cylinder, which controls the amount of toner attracted to the cylinder; this, in turn, results in a change in print density.

A+ ESS
4.1

A+
220-602
4.1

STEP 5: TRANSFERRING

In the transferring step (shown in Figure 12-2), a strong electrical charge draws the toner off the drum onto the paper. This is the first step that takes place outside the cartridge. The transfer charging roller, or transfer corona, produces a positive charge on the paper that pulls the toner from the drum onto the paper when it passes between the transfer charging roller and the drum. The static charge eliminator (refer again to Figure 12-2) weakens the positive charge on the paper and the negative charge on the drum so that the paper does not adhere to the drum, which it would otherwise do because of the difference in charge between the two. The stiffness of the paper and the small radius of the drum also help the paper move away from the drum and toward the fusing assembly. Very thin paper can wrap around the drum, which is why printer manuals usually instruct you to use only paper designated for laser printers.

STEP 6: FUSING

The fusing step uses heat and pressure to fuse the toner to the paper. Up to this point, the toner is merely sitting on the paper. The fusing rollers apply heat to the paper, which causes the toner to melt, and the rollers apply pressure to bond the melted toner into the paper. The temperature of the rollers is monitored by the printer. If the temperature exceeds an allowed maximum value (410 degrees F for some printers), the printer shuts down.

The previous steps describe how a black-and-white printer works. Color laser printers work in a similar way, but the writing process repeats four times, one for each toner color of cyan, magenta, yellow, and black. Then, the paper passes to the fusing stage, when the fuser bonds all toner to the paper and aids in blending the four tones to form specific colors.

INKJET PRINTERS

Inkjet printers use a type of ink-dispersion printing and don't normally provide the high-quality resolution of laser printers, but are popular because they are small and can print color inexpensively. Most inkjet printers today give photo-quality results, especially when used with photo-quality paper.

Earlier inkjet printers used 300 x 300 dpi, but inkjet printers today can use up to 4800 x 1200 dpi. Increasing the dpi has drawbacks. It increases the amount of data sent to the printer for a single page, and all those dots of ink can produce a wet page. An improved technology that gives photo-quality results mixes different colors of ink to produce a new color that then makes a single dot. Hewlett-Packard calls this PhotoREt II color technology. HP mixes as many as 16 drops of ink to produce a single dot of color on the page.

Inkjet printers tend to smudge on inexpensive paper, and they are slower than laser printers. If a printed page later gets damp, the ink can run and get quite messy. The quality of the paper used with inkjet printers significantly affects the quality of printed output. You should use only paper that is designed for an inkjet printer, and you should use a high-grade paper to get the best results. Figure 12-6 shows one example of an inkjet printer.

An inkjet printer uses a print head that moves across the paper, creating one line of text with each pass. The printer puts ink on the paper using a matrix of small dots. Different types of inkjet printers form their droplets of ink in different ways. Printer manufacturers use several technologies, but the most popular is the bubble-jet. Bubble-jet printers use tubes of ink that have tiny resistors near the end of each tube. These resistors heat up and cause the ink to boil. Then, a tiny air bubble of ionized ink (ink with an electrical charge) is ejected onto the paper. A typical bubble-jet print head has 64 or 128 tiny nozzles, all of which can fire a droplet simultaneously. (High-end printers can have as many as 3,000 nozzles.) Plates carrying a magnetic charge direct the path of ink onto the paper to form shapes.

Figure 12-6 An example of an inkjet printer

Inkjet printers include one or more ink cartridges. When purchasing an inkjet printer, look for the kind that uses two or four separate cartridges. One cartridge is used for black ink. In addition, some color printers use one cartridge for three-color printing (colors are yellow, blue, and red, better known as yellow, cyan, and magenta, sometimes written as CcMmY). Other less-expensive printers use three separate color cartridges. Some low-end inkjet printers use a single three-color cartridge and don't have a black ink cartridge. These printers must combine all colors of ink to produce a dull black. Having a separate cartridge for black ink means that it prints true black and, more important, does not use the more expensive colored ink. To save money, you should be able to replace an empty cartridge without having to replace all cartridges.

Figure 12-7 shows two ink cartridges. The black cartridge is on the left and the three-color cartridge is on the right. The print head assemblage moves across the page as it prints. When not in use, the assemblage sits in the far-right position shown in the figure, which is called the home position. This position helps protect the ink in the cartridges from drying out.

Figure 12-7 The ink cartridges of an inkjet printer

A+ ESS
4.1

A+
220-602
4.1

DOT MATRIX PRINTERS

Dot matrix printers are almost nonexistent now because they have been replaced with inkjet or laser printers. The two reasons you still see some around are: (1) they are impact printers and can print multicopy documents, which some businesses still find useful: and (2) they last forever. A dot matrix printer has a print head that moves across the width of the paper, using pins to print a matrix of dots on the page. The pins shoot against a cloth ribbon, which hits the paper, depositing the ink. The ribbon provides both the ink for printing and the lubrication for the pinheads.

Occasionally, you should replace the ribbon of a dot matrix printer. If the print head fails, check on the cost of replacing the head versus the cost of buying a new printer. Sometimes, the cost of the head is so high, it's best to just buy a new printer. Overheating can damage a print head (see Figure 12-8), so keep it as cool as possible to make it last longer. Keep the printer in a cool, well-ventilated area, and don't use it to print more than 50 to 75 pages without allowing the head to cool down.

Print head

Figure 12-8   Keep the print head of a dot matrix printer as cool as possible so that it will last longer

THERMAL PRINTERS AND SOLID INK PRINTERS

Two similar and relatively new technologies are thermal printers and solid ink printers. Both are nonimpact printers that use heat to produce printed output. Thermal printers use wax-based ink that is heated by heat pins that melt the ink onto paper. The print head containing these heat pins is as wide as the paper. The internal logic of the printer determines which pins get heated to produce the printed image. Thermal printers are popular in retail applications for printing bar codes and price tags. A thermal printer can burn dots onto special paper, as done by older fax machines (called direct thermal printing), or the printer can use a ribbon that contains the wax-based ink (called thermal wax transfer printing).

One variation of thermal printing uses thermal dye sublimation technology to print identification cards and access cards. A **dye-sublimation printer** uses solid dyes embedded on different transparent films. As the print head passes over each color film, it heats up, causing the dye to vaporize onto the glossy surface of the paper. Because the dye is vaporized onto the paper rather than jetted at it, the results are more photo-lab quality than with inkjet printing.

Solid ink printers such as the Xerox Phaser 8550 shown in Figure 12-9 use ink stored in solid blocks, which Xerox calls color sticks. The sticks or blocks are easy to handle and several can be inserted in the printer to be used as needed, avoiding the problem of running out of ink in the middle of a large print job. The solid ink is melted into the print head, which spans the width of the paper. The head jets the liquid ink onto the paper as it passes by on a drum. The design is simple, print quality is excellent, and solid ink printers are easy to set up and maintain. The greatest disadvantage to solid ink printing is the time it takes for the print head to heat up to begin a print job, which is about 15 minutes. For this reason, some solid ink printers anticipate that a print job might be coming based on previous use of the printer, and automatically heat up.

Figure 12-9 Phaser 8550 solid ink printer by Xerox

Table 12-1 lists some printer manufacturers.

Printer Manufacturer	Web Site
Brother	www.brother.com
Canon	usa.canon.com
Hewlett-Packard	www.hp.com
IBM	www.ibm.com
Lexmark	www.lexmark.com
Okidata	www.okidata.com
SATO	www.satoamerica.com
Seiko Epson	www.epson.com
Tally Genicom	www.tallygenicom.com
Xerox	www.xerox.com

Table 12-1 Printer manufacturers

A+ ESS
4.1

A+
220-602
4.1

INTRODUCING SCANNERS

A scanner is a device that allows a computer to convert a picture, drawing, bar code, or other image into digital data that can be input into the computer as a file. Some scanners have embedded optical character recognition (OCR) software that can interpret written text so that the text scanned in can be input into a word-processing program such as Microsoft Word.

Basically, there are three types of scanners:

▲ A flat-bed scanner has a glass bed on which you place a sheet of paper. Then, the scanning head moves across the glass, scanning the page. Figure 12-10 shows an example of a flat-bed scanner. One advantage of using a flat-bed scanner over a sheet-fed scanner is that you can scan pages in books and additional types of media other than single sheets of paper.

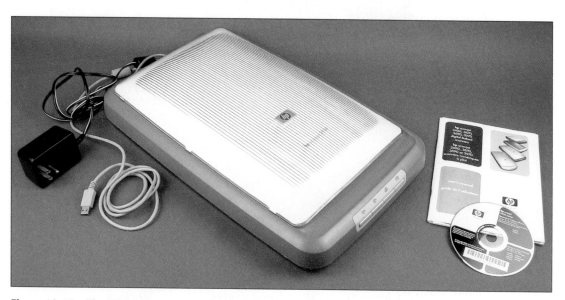

Figure 12-10 The HP Scanjet 3970 is a type of flat-bed scanner

▲ A sheet-fed scanner pulls a sheet of paper through the scanner mechanism similar to the way a fax machine works. In fact, a fax machine is actually a sheet-fed scanner in combination with a modem. Some high-end scanners are a combination sheet-fed and flat-bed scanner such as the one shown in Figure 12-11.

▲ A portable or handheld scanner can be a bar-code scanner or a sheet-fed scanner. You learned about bar-code scanners in Chapter 8. Figure 12-12 shows one example of a portable sheet-fed scanner that is designed to scan receipts and business cards and is useful for a traveling (and well-organized) businessperson.

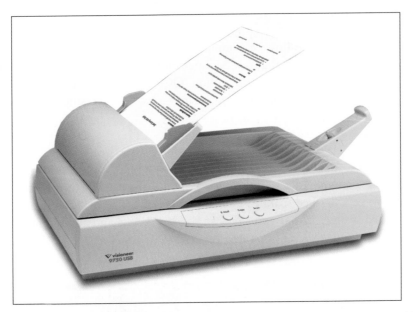

Figure 12-11 A combination flat-bed and sheet-fed scanner by Visioneer (*www.visioneer.com*)

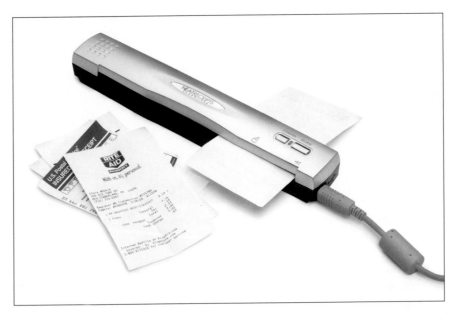

Figure 12-12 This portable scanner is a type of sheet-fed scanner useful for travelers to input receipts and business cards into a database

Besides the type of scanner, other features to look for when shopping for a scanner include:

- ◢ *Scanning speed.* How fast the scanner can scan is especially important if the scanner is to be used for high-volume input. Also, for high volume input, some sheet-fed scanners are stack loading, which means that you can put in a stack of paper and let it scan the entire stack as does a copier or fax machine.
- ◢ *Scanner resolution.* An example of scanner resolution is 400 dpi (dots per inch).
- ◢ *Scanning mode.* The scanning mode might be color, black and white, or grayscale. The best scanners work in all three modes.

▲ *Preview mode.* Most flat-bed scanners have a preview mode so that you can scan in a preview of the page and then select that portion of the page you want to include in the final scan.

▲ *Bundled software.* Examples of bundled software are OCR software and image-editing software.

▲ *Maximum document size.* The maximum document size might be $8\frac{1}{2}$ x 11 or larger.

▲ *File formats.* The file formats that the image can be saved into might be JPEG, TIFF, PDF, GIF, HTML, and others.

▲ *Connection to PC.* The type of connection to the PC a scanner uses might be a USB, FireWire, or SCSI connection. Some older scanners use a serial or parallel port connection.

A flat-bed scanner works by using a motor that moves the scanning head across the paper laid on the glass bed of the scanner, as shown in Figure 12-13. A type of fluorescent lamp is used to provide light under the glass that shines on the page. Reflected light is diverted by a series of mirrors into a lens. The lens focuses the light onto a series of diodes that converts the light into electrical current. At the heart of a scanner is this array of diodes called a CCD (charge-coupled device) array that senses light and converts it to electricity. The varying amounts of current are then digitized and sent to the PC where it is translated into a graphics file. If OCR software is involved, this software on the PC converts the graphics file into a text file.

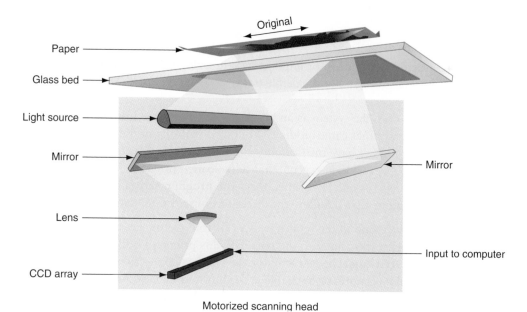

Figure 12-13 How a flat-bed scanner works

Also, for some less-expensive scanners, the light source and CCD array are replaced by a series of light-emitting diodes (LEDs) that produce the light, and a contact image sensor (CIS) converts the reflected light to electricity. Therefore, the two major technologies used by scanners are CCD (higher quality) and CIS (lower quality).

INSTALLING AND SHARING A PRINTER

A+ ESS
3.1
3.2
4.2

A+
220-602
4.2

When a printer is connected to a port on a computer, the computer can share the printer with others on the network. There are also network printers with Ethernet ports that can connect the printer directly to the network.

Each computer on a network that uses the printer must have printer drivers installed so the OS on each computer can communicate with the printer and provide the interface between applications it supports and the printer. This section covers how to install a local printer and how to share that printer with others on the network.

> ✎ **Notes**
>
> As you go through this part of the chapter, remember that a printer connected to a computer by way of a port on the computer is called a **local printer**, and a printer accessed by way of a network is called a **network printer**. A computer can have several printers installed. Of these, Windows designates one printer to be the **default printer**, which is the one Windows prints to unless another is selected.

> ⓔ **A+ Exam Tip**
>
> The A+ Essentials and A+ 220-602 exams expect you to know how to install a local and network printer.

INSTALLING A LOCAL PRINTER

Installing a local printer begins differently depending on the type of port you are using. For hot-pluggable ports such as a FireWire, USB, PC Card, ExpressCard, or wireless connection, you need to first install the software before connecting the printer. Remember that when using a hot-pluggable port, you don't need to power down a computer before plugging in or unplugging a hot-pluggable device. Follow these steps to install a local printer using a hot-pluggable port:

1. Log onto the system as an administrator. Begin the installation by running the setup program that came on the CD bundled with the printer before you install the printer. If you don't have the CD, download the printer drivers from the printer manufacturer Web site and then execute that downloaded program. The setup program installs the drivers. For one HP printer, the setup program shows its progress in a window shown in Figure 12-14. Follow the directions onscreen to complete the printer installation.

2. At one point in the setup, you will be told to connect the printer (see Figure 12-15). Connect the printer to the port. For this printer, a USB port is used. For wireless printers, verify that the software for the wireless connection on your PC is installed and the wireless connection is enabled. For infrared wireless printers, place the printer in line of sight of the infrared port on the PC. (Most wireless printers have a status light that stays lit when a wireless connection is active.) Turn on the printer.

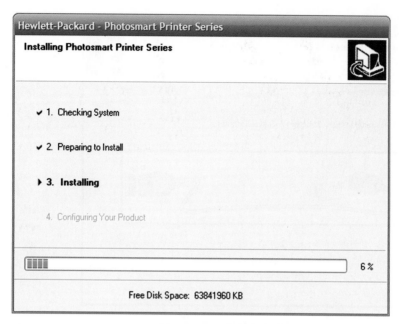

Figure 12-14 The printer setup program installs the drivers

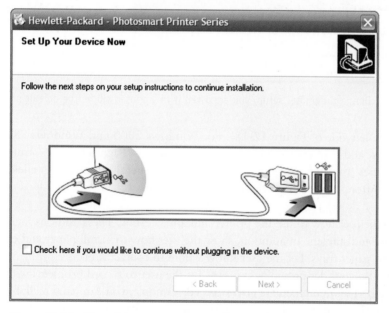

Figure 12-15 The printer setup program tells you when to connect the printer

3. The setup program detects the printer and tells you so, as shown in Figure 12-16. If Windows launches the Found New Hardware Wizard, it should close quickly. If not, cancel the wizard.

4. The setup program asks if you want this printer to be the default printer (see Figure 12-17). Click Yes or No to make your selection. The setup program finishes the installation.

5. You can now test the printer. For Windows XP, open the Printers and Faxes window by clicking **Start, Control Panel,** and **Printers and Faxes** (in Classic view) or **Printers and Other Hardware** (in Category view). The Printers and Faxes window opens

A+ ESS
3.1
3.2
4.2

A+
220-602
4.2

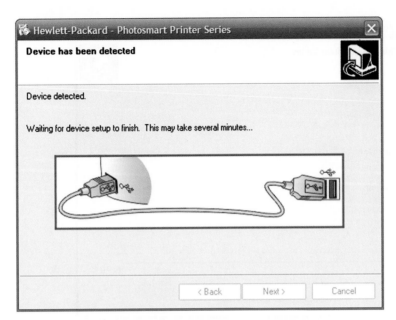

Figure 12-16 The printer setup program detects the printer

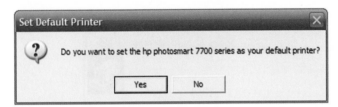

Figure 12-17 During the printer setup, you are asked if this printer will be the default printer

(see the left side of Figure 12-18). For Windows 2000 and Windows 98, click **Start, Settings,** and **Printers** to open the Printers window. Right-click the printer and select **Properties** from the shortcut menu. Click the **General** tab and then click the **Print Test Page** button, as shown on the right side of Figure 12-18.

6. Show the user how to use the printer and any add-ons. These add-ons include feeders, sorters, and staplers. In addition, show the user how to install paper and envelopes in the various paper trays. Let the user know whom to contact if printer problems arise. You might also consider providing a means for the user to record problems with the printer that don't require immediate attention. For example, you can hang a clipboard and paper close to the printer for the user to write questions that you can address at a later time.

Here are the directions to install a local printer using an older port, such as a SCSI, serial, or parallel port, that is not hot-pluggable:

1. Plug in the printer to the port and turn on the printer. Now, you must decide how you want to install the drivers. You can use the setup program from the printer manufacturer or use the Windows installation process. First try using the setup program that came on the printer's setup CD or downloaded from the manufacturer's Web site. If you have problems with the installation, you can then try the Windows approach.

2. To use the manufacturer's installation program, launch the printer setup program from the printer setup CD or downloaded from the manufacturer's Web site and follow the directions onscreen to install the printer.

Figure 12-18 To verify a printer installation, always print a test page as the last step in the installation

3. Alternately, you can use the Windows installation process to install the printer drivers. For Windows XP, open the Printers and Faxes window, or for Windows 2000 and Windows 98, open the Printers window. Click **Add a Printer**. The Add Printer Wizard launches, shown in Figure 12-19. Follow the directions onscreen to install the printer drivers.

4. To test the printer after it is installed, in the Printers and Faxes window or the Printers window, right-click the printer and select **Properties** from the shortcut menu. Click **Print Test Page**.

Notes

For Windows XP, by default, the Printers and Faxes window shows on the Start menu. If it is missing and you want to add it, right-click **Start** and select **Properties**. The Taskbar and Start Menu Properties dialog box opens. On the Start Menu tab, click **Customize** (see Figure 12-20). In the Customize Start Menu dialog box, click the **Advanced** tab. Check **Printers and Faxes**. Click **OK** to close the Customize Start Menu dialog box. Then click **Apply** and **OK** to apply your changes and close the Taskbar and Start Menu Properties dialog box.

A+ ESS
3.1
3.2
4.2

A+
220-602
4.2

Figure 12-19 Use the Add Printer Wizard to install a printer

Figure 12-20 Add the Printers and Faxes item to the Start menu

A+ ESS
3.1
4.2

SHARING A PRINTER WITH OTHERS IN A WORKGROUP

To share a local printer using Windows, File and Printer Sharing must be installed, and to use a shared printer on a remote PC, Client for Microsoft Networks must be installed. Using Windows 2000/XP, these components are installed by default.

A+ ESS
3.1
4.2

A+
220-602
4.2

To share a local printer connected to a Windows 2000/XP workstation, do the following:

1. Open the Printers and Faxes window or Printers window. Right-click the printer you want to share, and select **Sharing** from the shortcut menu. The printer's Properties dialog box opens, as shown in Figure 12-21 for Windows XP; the dialog box in Windows 2000 is similar. Select **Share this printer** and enter a name for the printer.

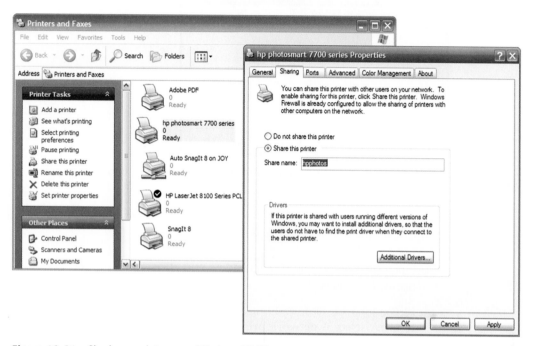

Figure 12-21   Sharing a printer on a Windows XP PC

2. If you want to make drivers for the printer available to remote users who are using an operating system other than the OS being used, click **Additional Drivers**.

3. The Additional Drivers window opens, as shown in Figure 12-22. Select the OS. In the figure, Windows 2000, XP, 95, 98, and Me are selected so that users of these OSs will have the printer drivers they need. Click **OK** twice to close both windows. You might be asked for the Windows installation CD or other access to the installation files. A shared printer shows a hand icon under it in the Printers and Faxes window, and the printer is listed in My Network Places or Network Neighborhood of other PCs on the network.

You can share a printer on a Windows 9x/Me computer in the same way as for Windows 2000/XP, except the Additional Drivers option is not available.

USING A SHARED PRINTER

Recall that for a remote PC to use a shared network printer, the drivers for that printer must be installed on the remote PC. There are two approaches to installing shared network printer drivers on a remote PC. You can perform the installation using the drivers on CD (either the Windows CD or printer manufacturer's CD), or you can perform the installation using the printer drivers on the host PC. The installations work about the same way for Windows 2000/XP and Windows 98. The Windows XP installation is shown here, but differences for Windows 2000 and Windows 98 are noted.

Figure 12-22 Make drivers for other operating systems available for the shared printer

To use a shared printer on the network by installing the manufacturer's printer drivers from CD, do the following using Windows XP:

1. Open the Printers and Faxes window and click **Add a printer**. The Add Printer Wizard opens. Click **Next**.

2. In response to the question, "Select the option that describes the printer you want to use:" select **A network printer, or a printer attached to another computer**. Click **Next**. The Specify a Printer page of the Add Printer Wizard opens, as shown in Figure 12-23.

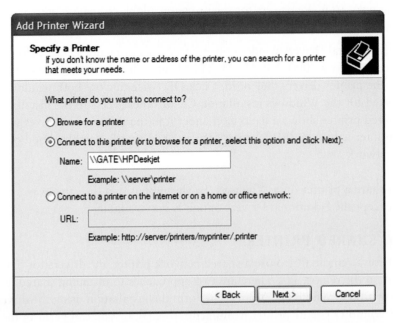

Figure 12-23 To use a network printer under Windows XP, enter the host computer name followed by the printer name, or have Windows XP browse the network for shared printers

A+ ESS
3.1
4.2

A+
220-602
4.2

3. Enter the host computer name and printer name. Begin with two backslashes and separate the computer name from the printer name with a backslash. Or, you can click **Browse**, search the list of shared printers on the network, and select the printer to install. (If your network is using static IP addressing and you know the IP address of the host PC, you can enter the IP address instead of the host name in this step.) Click **Next**.

4. Windows XP searches for Windows XP drivers on the host computer for this printer. If it finds them (meaning that the host computer is a Windows XP machine), the wizard skips to Step 6. If it doesn't find the drivers (the host computer is not a Windows XP machine), a message asks if you want to search for the proper driver. Click **OK**.

5. Click **Have Disk** to use the manufacturer's drivers, or to use Windows drivers, select the printer manufacturer and then the printer model from the list of supported printers. Click **OK** when you finish.

6. In response to the question, "Do you want to use this printer as the default printer?" answer **Yes** if you want Windows to send documents to this printer until you select a different one. Click **Next**. Click **Finish** to complete the wizard.

7. The printer icon appears in the Printers and Faxes window. To test the printer installation, right-click the icon and select **Properties** from the shortcut menu. Click the **General** tab and then click **Print Test Page**.

Here are some additional things to know about installing a network printer using the Windows 98 Add Printer Wizard:

◢ When the wizard asks, "Do you print from MS-DOS-based programs?" answer Yes if you have any intention of ever doing so.

◢ The wizard gives you the opportunity to name the printer. You might include the location of the printer, such as 3rd Floor Laser or John's Laser.

◢ Sometimes, a DOS-based program has problems printing to a network printer. You can choose to associate the network printer with a printer port such as LPT1 to satisfy the DOS application. Click **Capture Printer Port**, and then select the port from the drop-down menu in the Capture Printer Port dialog box (see Figure 12-24).

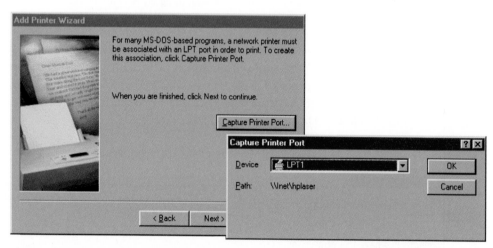

Figure 12-24 Associate a network printer with a printer port to help DOS applications in Windows 98

A+ ESS
3.1
4.2

A+
220-602
4.2

◢ The Windows 98 Add Printer Wizard gives you the opportunity to print a test page on the last window of the wizard. It's always a good idea to print this test page to verify that the printer is accessible.

◢ Know that the Windows 98 Add Printer Wizard does not attempt to use the printer drivers on the host PC, but always installs local Windows 9x/Me drivers or uses the manufacturer's CD.

Another way to install a shared printer is to first use My Network Places or Network Neighborhood to locate the printer on the network. This method is faster because the remote PCs can use the printer drivers on the host PC. Do the following:

1. On a remote PC that uses Windows 2000/XP, open **My Network Places** and find the printer. Right-click the printer and select **Connect** from the shortcut menu. See Figure 12-25. (For Windows 9x/Me, open **Network Neighborhood** and find the printer. Right-click the printer and select **Install** from the shortcut menu.)

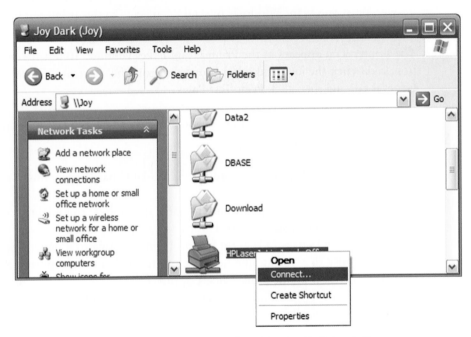

Figure 12-25 Install a shared printer in Windows XP using My Network Places

2. If the host computer is using the same OS as you are, or if you have a Windows 2000/XP host computer and the additional drivers for your OS have been installed, you can use those drivers for the installation. If Windows cannot find the right drivers, it sends you an error message and gives you the opportunity to install the drivers from your Windows CD or the printer manufacturer's CD.

 Notes

When installing a shared printer on a Windows 9x/Me PC where the host computer is also a Windows 9x/Me PC, you must first share the \Windows folder on the host PC so the remote PC can access the printer drivers. This is a security risk, so remove the share status on this important folder as soon as all remote PCs have the printer installed.

A+ ESS
3.1
4.2

A+
220-602
4.2

OTHER METHODS OF SHARING PRINTERS OVER A NETWORK

The three ways to make a printer available on a network are listed here:

◢ A regular printer can be attached to a PC using a port on the PC, and then that PC can share the printer with the network. (This method was described in the last section.)

◢ A network printer with embedded logic to manage network communication can be connected directly to a network with its own NIC.

◢ A dedicated device or computer called a print server can control several printers connected to a network. For example, HP has software called HP JetDirect, designed to support HP printers in this manner. For more information, see the HP Web site, *www.hp.com*.

If printers are available on the network using one of the last two methods, follow the printer manufacturer's directions to install the printer on each PC. If you don't have these directions, do the following:

1. Download the printer drivers from the printer manufacturer's Web site and decompress the downloaded file, if necessary.

2. Open the Printers and Faxes or Printers window and start the wizard to add a new printer. Select the option to install a local printer but do not ask Windows to automatically detect the printer.

3. On the next window shown in Figure 12-26, choose **Create a new port**. From the list of port types, select **Standard TCP/IP Port**. Click **Next** twice.

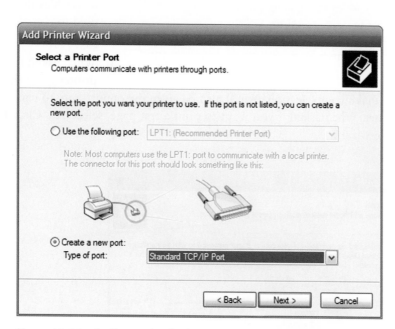

Figure 12-26 Configure a local printer to use a standard TCP/IP port

4. On the next window shown in Figure 12-27, you need to identify the printer on the network. If you know the IP address of the printer, enter it in the first box on this window and click **Next**. Some network printers have assigned printer names or the printer might have an assigned port name. To know how your network printer is configured, see the network printer's configuration window. How to access this window is discussed later in the chapter.

A+ ESS
3.1
4.2

A+
220-602
4.2

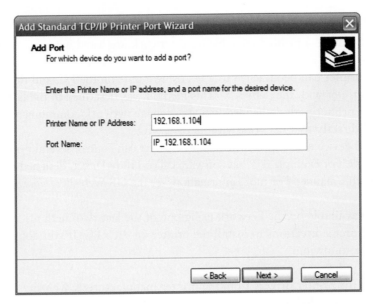

Figure 12-27 Enter the printer name or IP address to identify the printer on the network

Notes

To know the IP address of a network printer, look in the printer documentation. Or you can press a key on the front panel of the printer to instruct it to print setup information about the printer, which should include its IP address. To know which keys to press to print the setup report, see the printer documentation.

5. On the next window (see Figure 12-28), click **Have Disk** so you can point to and use the downloaded driver files that will then be used to complete the printer installation.

6. When asked if you want this printer to be the default

printer, make your selection. You'll also be given the opportunity to choose to share the printer. When asked if you want to print a test page, select **Yes**. Click **Finish** to close the wizard.

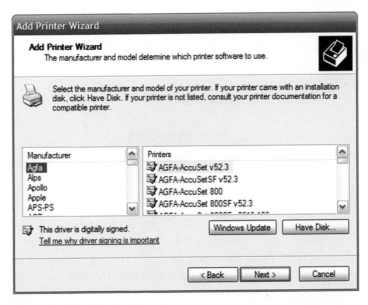

Figure 12-28 Select printer drivers

12

Notes

Because a network printer has no OS installed, the printer's NIC contains all the firmware needed to communicate over the network. For a PC, some of this software is part of Windows, including the network protocols TCP/IP and IPX/SPX. A network printer's NIC firmware usually supports TCP/IP and IPX/SPX. The network printer documentation will tell you which protocols are supported. One of these protocols must be installed on a PC using the printer.

One shortcut you might take to speed up the process of installing a printer connected directly to the network is to install the printer on one PC and then share it on the network. Then, you can install the printer on the other PCs by using My Network Places for Windows 2000/XP or Network Neighborhood for Windows 98, following the directions given earlier. Find the printer, right-click it, and then select **Connect** (for Windows 2000/XP) or **Install** (for Windows 9x/Me) from the shortcut menu. The disadvantage of using this method is that the computer sharing the printer must be turned on when other computers on the network want to use the printer.

MAINTAINING PRINTERS AND SCANNERS

A+ ESS
3.3
4.2

A+
220-602
3.3
4.2

Printers and scanners generally last for years if they are properly used and maintained. To get the most out of a printer or scanner, it's important to follow the manufacturer's directions when using the device and to perform the necessary routine maintenance. For example, the life of a printer can be shortened if you allow the printer to overheat, don't use approved paper, or don't install consumable maintenance kits when they are required.

When supporting printers using Windows, it is helpful to know about the protocols used by printers for communication between Windows and the printer, so we will begin our discussion of maintaining printers here. Then, we'll turn our attention to managing printers, including the routine maintenance that printers need. Finally, you'll learn how to install and support a scanner.

PRINTER LANGUAGES

Years ago, all printers were dot matrix printers that could only print simple text using only a single font. Communication between the OS and the printer was simple. Today's printers can produce beautiful colored graphics and text using a variety of fonts and symbols, and communication between the OS and a printer can get pretty complicated.

The languages or methods the OS and printer use for communication and building a page before it prints are listed in the following. The method used depends on what the printer is designed to support and the printer drivers installed. If the printer has sophisticated firmware, it might be able to support more than one method. In this case, the installed printer drivers determine which methods can be used:

▲ *The printer uses PostScript commands to build the page.* For Windows 2000/XP or Windows 9x/Me using a PostScript printer, the commands and data needed to build a page to print are sent to the printer using the PostScript language. The printer firmware then interprets these commands and draws and formats the page in the printer memory before it is printed. PostScript is a language used to communicate how a page is to print and was developed by Adobe Systems. PostScript is popular with desktop publishing, the typesetting industry, and the Macintosh OS.

A+ ESS
3.3
4.2

A+
220-602
3.3
4.2

◢ *The printer uses PCL commands to build the page.* For Windows 2000/XP, a printer language that competes with PostScript is PCL (Printer Control Language). PCL was developed by Hewlett-Packard but is considered a de facto standard in the printing industry. Many printer manufacturers use PCL.

◢ *The Windows GDI builds the page and then sends it to the printer.* For Windows 2000/XP or Windows 9x/Me, a less-sophisticated method of communicating to a printer is to use the GDI (Graphics Device Interface) component of Windows. GDI draws and formats the page and then sends the almost-ready-to-print page to the printer in bitmap form. Because Windows, rather than the printer, does most of the work of building the page, a GDI printer needs less firmware and memory, and, therefore, generally costs less than a PCL or PostScript printer. The downside of using the GDI method is that Windows performance can suffer when printing a lot of complicated pages. Most low-end inkjet and laser printers are GDI printers. If the printer specifications don't say PCL or PostScript, you can assume it's a GDI printer. Many high-end printers support more than one protocol and can handle GDI, PCL, or PostScript printing.

◢ *Raw data is printed with little-to-no formatting.* Text data that contains no embedded control characters is sent to the printer as is, and the printer can print it without any processing. The data is called raw data. Dot matrix printers that can only print simple text receive and print raw data.

Normally, when Windows receives a print job from an application, it places the job in a queue and prints from the queue, so that the application is released from the printing process as soon as possible. Several print jobs can accumulate in the queue, which you can view in the Printers and Faxes or Printers window. This process is called spooling. (The word spool is an acronym for *s*imultaneous *p*eripheral *o*perations *on*line.) Most printing from Windows uses spooling.

If the printer port, printer cable, and printer all support bidirectional communication, the printer can communicate with Windows. For example, Windows XP can ask the printer how much printer memory is available and what fonts are installed. The printer can send messages to the OS, such as an out-of-paper or paper-jam message.

USING WINDOWS TO MANAGE PRINTERS

From the Printers and Faxes window (for Windows XP) or the Printers window (for Windows 2000 and Windows 9x/Me), you can delete printers, change the Windows default printer, purge print jobs to troubleshoot failed printing, and perform other printer maintenance tasks. For example, to manage the print jobs for a printer, double-click the printer in the Printers and Faxes window. The printer window opens, and is similar to the one in Figure 12-29. From this window, you can see the status and order of the print jobs. If the printer reports a problem with printing, it will be displayed as the status for the first job in the print queue. To cancel a single print job, right-click the job and select **Cancel** from the shortcut menu, as shown in Figure 12-29. To cancel all print jobs, click **Printer** on the menu and select **Cancel All Documents**. (For Windows 9x/Me, click **Purge Print Documents**.)

> ✎ **Notes**
>
> When you use the Windows 2000/XP default settings, user accounts in the Everyone group are assigned the Print permission level, which means users can send documents to a printer. They cannot manage the print queue or change printer settings. Users in the Administrator and Power User groups are assigned the Manage Printers permission level, which means they have complete control over a printer, including printer settings and the print queue. A third permission level, Manage Documents, can be assigned to a user so that the user can manage the print queue while not being allowed to change printer settings.

A+ ESS
3.3
4.2

A+
220-602
3.3
4.2

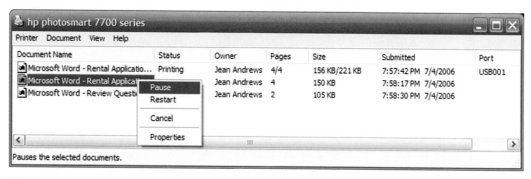

Figure 12-29 Manage print jobs using the printer window

The Printers and Faxes or Printers window can also be used to manage printer settings and options. For example, a printer that supports automatically printing on both sides of the paper (called duplex printing) needs to be configured in Windows to use this feature. On the printer's Properties window, click the **Configure** tab, shown in Figure 12-30. On this window, to enable duplexing, check **Duplexing Unit**. (Also notice the Mopier Enabled option on this window, which is the ability to print and collate multiple copies of a single print job.) To apply your changes, click **Apply** and then click **OK** to close the window. Now, when a user attempts to print from an application, the Print window gives the option to print on both sides of the paper. For example, when a user attempts to print a Word document, the Print window shown in Figure 12-31 appears. To print on both sides of the paper, the user can click **Properties** and then check **Print on Both Sides** in the window on the right side of Figure 12-31.

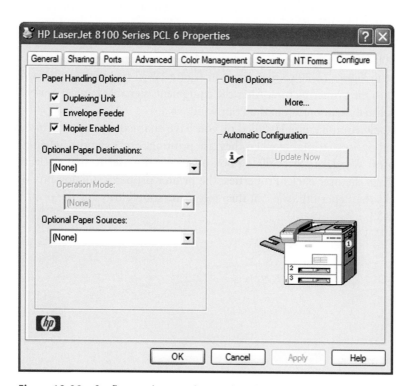

Figure 12-30 Configure printer options and settings using the printer's Properties window

A+ ESS
3.3
4.2

A+
220-602
3.3
4.2

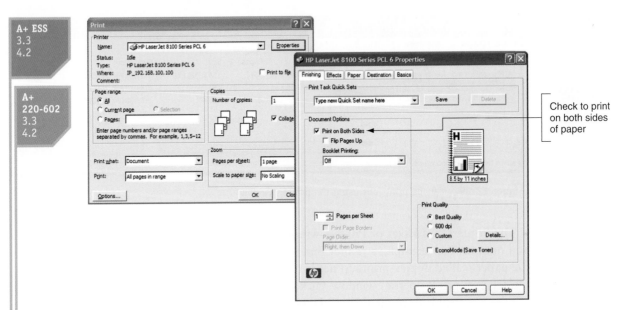

Figure 12-31 Printing on both sides of the paper

A printer might be able to accommodate different types of input trays and feeders for various envelopes, oversized paper, colored paper, transparencies, and other media. In addition, you can install on the printer staplers, sorters, stackers, binders, and output trays so that the printer can sort output by user (called mailboxes). After you have physically installed one of these devices, use the printer properties window to enable it. For example, suppose you have installed a 3,000-sheet stapler and stacker unit on the printer whose properties window is shown in Figure 12-30. To enable this equipment, in the drop-down list of Optional Paper Destinations, select **HP 3000-Sheet Stapler/Stacker** and click **Apply** (see Figure 12-32). Compare the picture of the printer in Figure 12-30 to the picture in Figure 12-32 where the equipment is enabled and drawn into the printer picture. After the equipment is enabled, when a user prints, the equipment is listed as an option in the Print window.

After this new equipment is installed or you have enabled a printer feature, users might see additional options available when they are printing. For example, when a user prints using Microsoft Word, the Print dialog box opens for the user to make selections for the print job. When the user clicks **Properties**, the printer properties dialog box opens. When the user clicks the **Paper** tab, she can then select the source tray for the print job, as shown in Figure 12-33.

Figure 12-32 Optional printer equipment has been installed by Windows

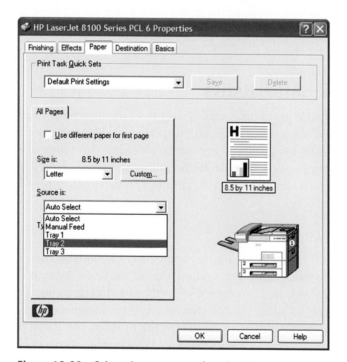

Figure 12-33 Select the source tray for print jobs

Some printers give you the option to install additional memory to hold fonts and print job buffers or a hard drive can be installed in some printers to give additional printer storage space. See the printer reference manual to find out how to install more memory or an internal hard drive. Most likely, you will use a screwdriver to remove a cover plate on the printer to expose a cavity where memory or a drive can be installed. After this equipment is installed, you must enable and configure it using the printer properties window. For example, for the HP 8100 printer properties window shown in Figure 12-30, when you click **More** under Other Options, the More Configuration Options dialog box opens, as shown in Figure 12-34. Using this dialog box, you can enable and configure the amount of additional printer memory or the size of a hard drive that you have just installed.

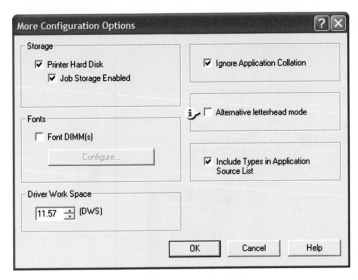

Figure 12-34   Enable and configure newly installed printer memory and hard drive

If a printer is giving you problems or you want to upgrade the printer drivers to add new functionality, search the printer manufacturer's Web site for the latest drivers for your printer and operating system. Download the drivers to a folder on the hard drive, such as C:\Downloads\Printer, and then double-click the driver file to extract files and launch the installation program to update the printer drivers.

ROUTINE PRINTER MAINTENANCE

Routine printer maintenance procedures vary widely from manufacturer to manufacturer and printer to printer. For each printer you support, research the printer documentation or the manufacturer's Web site for specific maintenance procedures and how often you should perform them for each printer you support. In the following sections, you'll learn about printer consumables, printer maintenance kits, cleaning printers, online help for printers, and updating printer firmware.

PRINTER CONSUMABLES

Make sure consumables for the printer are on hand. These consumables can include paper, ink ribbons, color sticks, toner cartridges, and ink cartridges. Know how to exchange these consumables and also know how to recognize when they need exchanging. Each printer's requirements are different, so you'll need to study the printer documentation to find out what your printer requires. Buy the products in advance of when you think you'll need them. Nothing is more frustrating to a user than to have a printer not working because the support technician responsible for the printer forgot to order extra toner cartridges.

Figure 12-35 shows an ink cartridge being installed in one inkjet printer. To replace a cartridge, turn on the printer and open the front cover. The printer releases the cartridges. You can then open the latch on top of the cartridge and remove it. Install the new cartridge as shown in the figure.

When a cartridge is not in use, put it in the cradle on the left side of the printer to protect it from drying out, as shown in Figure 12-36.

A+ ESS
1.4

A+
220-602
1.2
4.3
4.4

Figure 12-35 Installing an ink cartridge in an inkjet printer

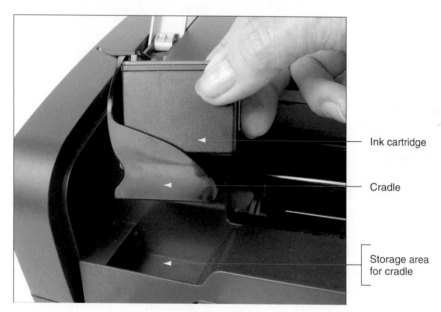

Ink cartridge

Cradle

Storage area
for cradle

Figure 12-36 Use the protective cradle to keep an ink cartridge from drying out
when it is not installed in the printer

PRINTER MAINTENANCE KITS

Manufacturers of high-end printers provide printer maintenance kits, which include specific
printer components, step-by-step instructions for performing maintenance, and any special tools
or equipment you need to do maintenance. For example, the maintenance plan for the HP
Color LaserJet 4600 printer says to replace the transfer roller
assembly after printing 120,000 pages and replace the fusing
assembly after 150,000 pages. The plan also says the black
ink cartridge should last for about 9,000 pages and the color
ink cartridge for about 8,000 pages. HP sells the image transfer kit, the image fuser kit, and the ink cartridges designed for
this printer.

> **A+ Tip**
>
> The A+ 220-602 exam expects
> you to know about the impor-
> tance of resetting the page
> count after installing a
> printer maintenance kit.

A+ ESS
1.4

A+
220-602
1.2
4.3
4.4

> **A+ Tip**
>
> The A+ Essentials exam expects you to know that printers use certain consumables and require routine preventive maintenance.

To find out how many pages a printer has printed so that you know if you need to do the maintenance, you need to have the printer give you the page count since the last maintenance. You can tell the printer to display the information or print a status report by using buttons on the front of the printer (see Figure 12-37) or you can use utility software from a computer connected to the printer. See the printer documentation to know how to get this report.

After you have performed the maintenance, be sure to reset the page count so it will be accurate to tell you when you need to do the next routine maintenance. Keep a written record of the maintenance and other service done. If a printer gives problems, one of the first things you can do is check this service documentation to find out if maintenance is due. You can also check for a history of prior problems and how they were resolved.

Figure 12-37 Use buttons on the front of the printer to display the page count

CLEANING A PRINTER

A printer gets dirty inside and outside as stray toner, ink, dust, and bits of paper accumulate. As part of routine printer maintenance, you need to regularly clean the printer. How often depends on how much the printer is used and the work environment. Some manufacturers suggest a heavily used printer be cleaned weekly, and others suggest you clean it whenever you exchange the toner or ink cartridges.

Clean the outside of the printer with a damp cloth. Don't use ammonia-based cleaners. Clean the inside of the printer with a dry cloth and remove dust, bits of paper, and stray toner. Picking up stray toner can be a problem. Don't try to blow it out with compressed air because you don't want the toner in the air. Also, don't use an antistatic vacuum cleaner. You can, however, use a vacuum cleaner designed to pick up toner, called a toner-certified vacuum cleaner. This type of vacuum does not allow the toner that it picks up to touch any conductive surface. Some printer manufacturers also suggest you use an **extension magnet brush**. The long-handled brush is made of nylon fibers that are charged with static electricity and easily attract the toner like a magnet. For a laser printer, wipe the rollers from side to side with a dry cloth to remove loose dirt and toner. Don't touch the soft

> **Notes**
>
> If you get toner on your clothes, dust it off and clean your clothes with cold water. Hot water will set the toner.

A+ ESS
1.4

A+
220-602
1.2
4.3
4.4

black roller (the transfer roller), or you might affect the print quality. You can find specific instructions for cleaning a printer on the printer Web site.

For some inkjet printers, you can use software to clean the inkjet nozzles or align the cartridges, which can help improve print quality when colors appear streaked or out of alignment. How to access these tools differs from one printer to another. For some printers, a Services tab is added to the printer properties window. Other printer installations might put utility programs in the Start menu. Here is one example of how to clean and calibrate an inkjet printer that adds a tab to the Printing Preferences window:

1. Open the Printers and Faxes or the Printers window. Right-click the **inkjet printer** icon, and select **Properties** from the shortcut menu.

2. On the General tab, click **Printing Preferences**. The Printing Preferences window opens. Click the **Services** tab and then click **Service this device**, as shown on the left side of Figure 12-38. The Toolbox window for the printer is displayed, as shown on the right side of the figure.

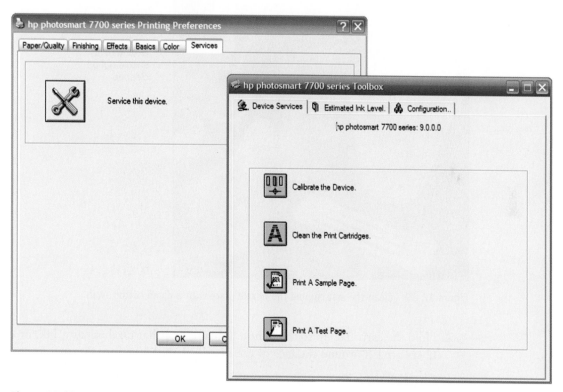

Figure 12-38 Use the Services tab in the Printing Preferences window to service this inkjet printer

3. To calibrate the printer, click **Calibrate the Device**. In the next window, click **Calibrate**. As the printer calibrates itself, a page prints. The page contains a test pattern. If the test pattern does not look straight and smooth, first try to calibrate the printer a second time. If it still does not produce a smooth test pattern, you might have to replace the ink cartridges.

4. To have the printer automatically clean the ink nozzles, click **Clean the Print Cartridges** in the Toolbox window shown in Figure 12-38.

5. A test page prints. If the page prints sharply with no missing dots or lines, you are finished. If the page does not print correctly, perform the auto-clean again.

6. You might need to perform the auto-clean procedure six or seven times to clean the nozzles completely.

If the printer still does not print with the quality printing you expect, you can try to manually clean the cartridge nozzles. Check the printer manufacturer Web site for directions. For most inkjet printers, you are directed to use clean, distilled water and cotton swabs to clean the face of the ink cartridge, being careful not to touch the nozzle plate. To prevent the inkjet nozzles from drying out, don't leave the ink cartridges out of their cradle for longer than 30 minutes. Here are some general directions:

1. Following manufacturer directions, remove the inkjet cartridges from the printer and lay them on their sides on a paper towel.

2. Dip a cotton swab in distilled water (not tap water) and squeeze out any excess water.

3. Hold an ink cartridge so that the nozzle plate faces up and use the swab to wipe clean the area around the nozzle plate, as shown in Figure 12-39. Do not clean the plate itself.

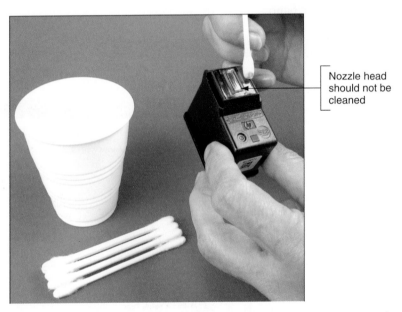

Nozzle head should not be cleaned

Figure 12-39 Clean the area around the nozzle plate with a damp cotton swab

4. Hold the cartridge up to the light and make sure that no dust, dirt, ink, or cotton fibers are left around the face of the nozzle plate. Make sure the area is clean.

5. Clean all the ink cartridges the same way and replace the cartridges in the printer.

6. Print a test page. If print quality is still poor, try repeating the automatic nozzle cleaning process using the printer Properties window described earlier.

7. If you still have problems, you need to replace the ink cartridges.

ONLINE SUPPORT FOR PRINTERS

The printer manufacturer's Web site is an important resource when supporting printers. Here are some things to look for:

▲ *Online documentation.* Expect the printer manufacturer's Web site to include documentation on installing, configuring, troubleshooting, using, upgrading, and maintaining the printer. Also look for information on printer parts and warranty, compatibility information, specifications and features of your printer, a way to register your printer,

A+ ESS
1.4

A+
220-602
1.2
4.3
4.4

and how to recycle or dispose of a printer. You might also be able to download your printer manual in PDF format.

▲ *A knowledge base of common problems and what to do about them.* Some Web sites also offer a newsgroup service or discussion group where you can communicate with others responsible for supporting a particular printer. Also look for a way to e-mail for technical support.

▲ *Updated device drivers.* Sometimes, you can solve printer problems by downloading and installing the latest drivers. Also, a manufacturer makes new features and options available through these drivers. Be sure you download files for the correct printer and OS.

▲ *Catalog of options and upgrades for purchase.* Look for memory upgrades, optional trays, feeders, sorters, staplers, printer stands, and other equipment to upgrade your printer. Expect to find the parts as well as how to install and maintain them.

▲ *Replacement parts.* When a printer part breaks, buy only parts made by or approved by the printer manufacturer. Manufacturers also sell consumable supplies such as toner and ink cartridges.

▲ *Printer maintenance kits.* The best practice is to buy everything you need for routine maintenance either from the printer manufacturer or an approved vendor. If you buy from a nonapproved vendor, you risk damaging the printer or shortening its lifespan.

▲ *Additional software.* Look for software to use with your printer, such as software to produce greeting cards or edit photographs.

▲ *Firmware updates.* Some high-end printers have firmware that can be flashed to solve problems and add features. Be careful to verify that you download the correct update for your printer.

UPDATING PRINTER FIRMWARE

Now let's look at one example of how to upgrade the firmware on one network printer. The printer we are using is an HP 8100 DN printer. Follow these directions:

1. To know how to access the firmware utility on the printer, see the printer documentation. For this network printer, you enter its IP address in a browser address box from any computer on the network. Recall that this is the same method used to access the firmware utility for a router, which is the method typically used for any network device. The opening window of the utility opens, as shown in Figure 12-40. On this window, you can see the MAC address of the printer, the firmware version installed, the IP address, and other basic information.

2. Click **Administration** and then click the **Configuration** tab, as shown in Figure 12-41. Notice in this window you can configure the printer for static or dynamic IP addressing, which is labeled in the figure as TCP Configuration Type. If you are addressing the printer by its IP address, choose **Manual** so that the IP address doesn't change.

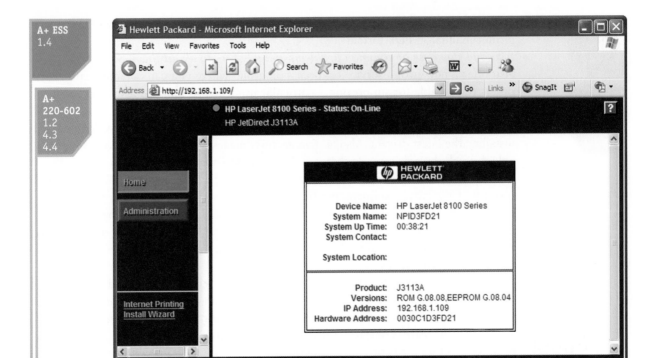

Figure 12-40   The network printer firmware is accessed on the network using a browser

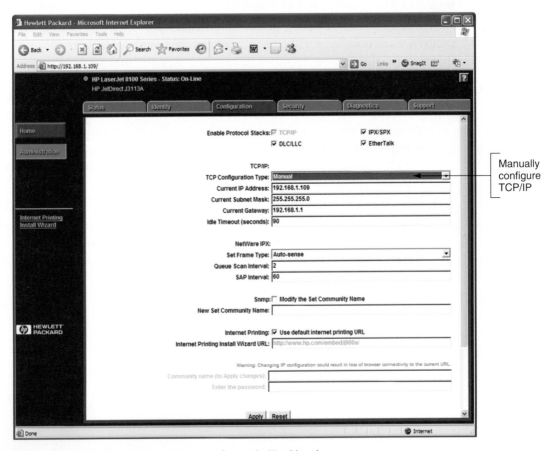

Figure 12-41   Configure a network printer for static IP addressing

3. To check for firmware upgrades, click the **Support** tab, which provides a connection to the HP Web site. Search the site for the printer downloads. Figure 12-42 shows the correct page for this printer. At the bottom of this page, click **Cross operating system (BIOS, Firmware, Diagnostics, etc.)**.

4. Follow the onscreen directions to download and install any available updates you select.

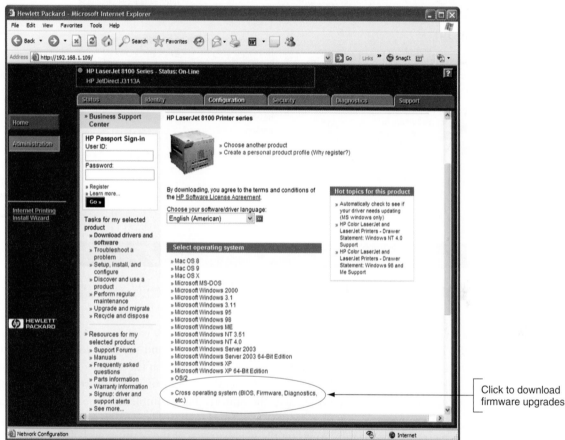

Figure 12-42 Locate any firmware updates for the printer on the HP Web site

SUPPORTING SCANNERS

In this part of the chapter, you'll learn how to install a scanner and about the routine maintenance a scanner might need.

HOW TO INSTALL A SCANNER

The most common type of connector for a scanner intended to be used with a desktop system is a USB port, which means the scanner is hot-pluggable. Here are general directions for installing a scanner:

1. Read the manufacturer setup instructions and follow them in detail rather than using the general directions here. For USB scanners or other scanners that are hot-pluggable, most likely you'll be told to first run the setup CD before connecting the scanner.

2. Log on to the Windows 2000/XP system as an administrator.

3. Launch the setup program on the scanner setup CD and follow the onscreen instructions to install device drivers and other software. Figure 12-43 shows the main menu of one installation program for an HP scanner.

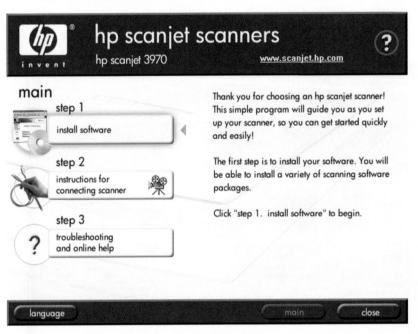

Figure 12-43 Main menu of a scanner setup program

4. Connect the scanner, plug it up, and turn it on.

5. Test the scanner by scanning a document or picture and saving it to a file. To scan an item, you can use the software that came bundled with the scanner or you can press a button on the front of the scanner. Generally, you have more control over scanning when you use the software rather than the buttons. For example, for one scanner, you launch the scanner software that displays a menu shown in Figure 12-44. To scan a picture, place the picture face down on the glass surface of the scanner and click **Scan Picture**.

Figure 12-44 Scanner software main menu

6. The next window shows a preview of the scanned image (see Figure 12-45). Adjust the area of the page you want to scan and select your output type. Then click **Accept**. The scanner rescans and saves the image to a file. You can select the file format on the next window.

Figure 12-45 Make adjustments before the final scan is made

For older scanners that use a serial or parallel port, first power down your PC and connect the scanner. Then restart your PC. The Found New Hardware Wizard should launch and you can then install the software. For some products, the scanner installation instructions might tell you to first install the scanner drivers from the setup CD before connecting the scanner.

For SCSI scanners, be sure to set the SCSI ID for the scanner as one SCSI device on the chain. Figure 12-46 shows the dial where you set the SCSI ID on one scanner.

Notes

Remember that you should not unplug a USB device from or plug a USB device into a USB port without first powering down or unplugging the device, turning off the device, or disconnecting it from its power source.

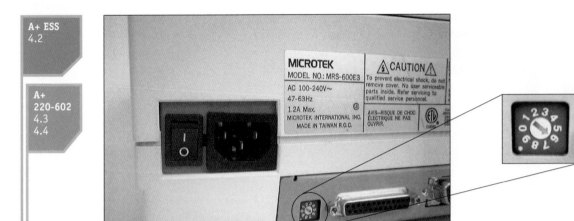

Figure 12-46 This rotary dial on the rear of a SCSI scanner is used to set the SCSI ID, which is now set to 6

SCANNER ROUTINE MAINTENANCE

Most scanners come bundled with utility software that you can use to adjust scanner settings. Look for ways to change the scanner resolution, output type (colors, black and white, or grayscale), destination folder for files, file format, automatic cropping, percentage scaling for slides and negatives, and image quality in a saved file. Figure 12-47 shows one settings window for an HP scanner. If you're not sure which setting gives the best results, first try restoring all default settings. Perhaps a user has made a setting that is causing odd scanning results. Restoring default settings might solve the problem.

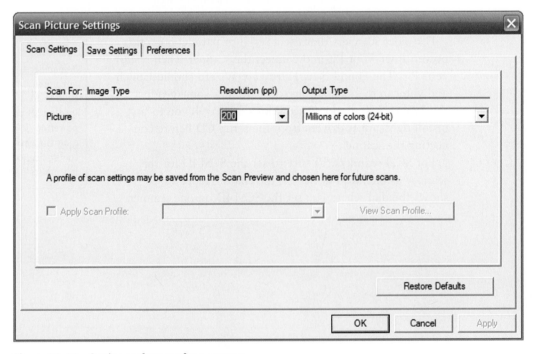

Figure 12-47 Setting preferences for a scanner

A+ ESS
1.4

A+
220-602
4.3
4.4

Besides changing settings, to find out about other routine maintenance chores for a scanner, read the scanner documentation. For flat-bed scanners, you can clean the glass window with a soft dry cloth or you can use mild glass cleaner. First unplug the scanner. Don't use acetone or isopropyl alcohol on the glass because these chemicals can leave streaks. Before you're done, make sure the glass is dry. If the underside of the glass needs cleaning, see the Web site of the scanner manufacturer for specific instructions to remove the glass to clean it.

Some scanners have a built-in device to scan negatives and slides such as the one shown in Figure 12-48. This device is underneath the scanner lid. Just as with the glass-scanning window, you can also clean this surface with a soft dry cloth or use mild glass cleaner.

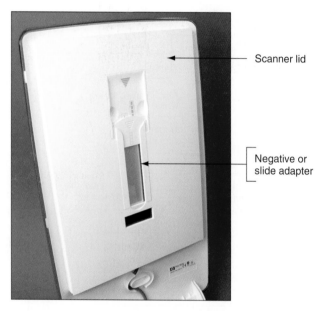

Scanner lid

Negative or slide adapter

Figure 12-48 An adapter in this scanner is used to scan negatives and slides

TROUBLESHOOTING PRINTERS AND SCANNERS

A+ ESS
1.3
3.3
4.3

A+
220-602
1.2
3.3
4.3
4.4

This section first discusses general printer troubleshooting and then explains how to troubleshoot problems specific to each of the three major types of printers. Then you'll see how to troubleshoot problems with scanners.

In these sections, you'll learn some general and specific troubleshooting tips. If you exhaust this list and still have a problem, turn to the manufacturer's Web site for additional information and support.

APPLYING CONCEPTS Jill is the PC support technician responsible for supporting 10 users, their peer-to-peer network, printers, and computers. Everything was working fine when Jill left work one evening, but the next morning three users meet her at the door, complaining that they cannot print to the network printer and that important work must be printed by noon. What do you think are the first three things Jill should check?

As with all computer problems, begin troubleshooting by interviewing the user, finding out what works and doesn't work, and making an initial determination of the problem. When you think the problem is solved, ask the user to check things out to make sure he is satisfied with your work. And, after the problem is solved, be sure to document the symptoms of the problem and what you did to solve it.

PRINTER DOES NOT PRINT

When a printer does not print, the problem can be caused by the printer, the PC hardware or OS, the application using the printer, the printer cable, or the network. Follow the steps in Figure 12-49 to isolate the problem.

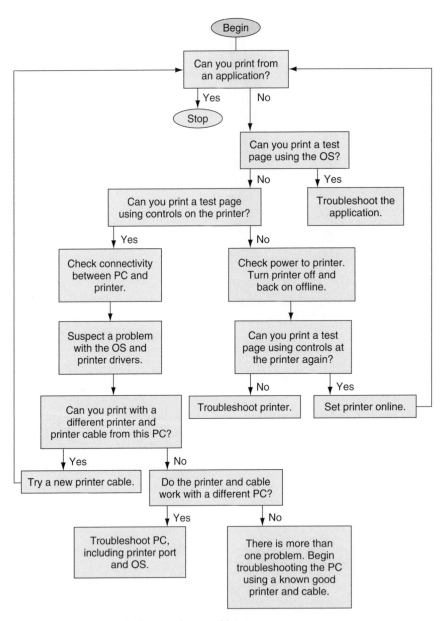

Figure 12-49   How to isolate a printer problem

As you can see in the figure, the problem can be isolated to one of the following areas:

▲ The printer itself
▲ Connectivity between the PC and its local printer

A+ ESS
1.3
3.3
4.3

A+
220-602
1.2
3.3
4.3
4.4

⊿ Connectivity between the PC and a network printer
⊿ The OS and printer drivers
⊿ The application attempting to use the printer

The following sections address printer problems caused by all of these categories, starting with hardware.

PROBLEMS WITH THE PRINTER ITSELF

To eliminate the printer as the problem, first check that the printer is on, and then print a self-test page. For directions to print a self-test page, see the printer's user guide. For example, you might need to hold down a button or buttons on the printer's front panel. If this test page prints correctly, then the printer works correctly.

A printer test page generally prints some text, some graphics, and some information about the printer, such as the printer resolution and how much memory is installed. Verify that the information on the test page is correct. For example, if you know that the printer should have 2 MB of on-board printer memory, but the test only reports 1 MB, then there is a problem with memory. If the information reported is not correct and the printer allows you to upgrade firmware on the printer, try doing that next.

If the self-test page does not print or prints incorrectly (for example, it has missing dots or smudged streaks through the page), then troubleshoot the printer until it prints correctly. Does the printer have paper? Is the paper installed correctly? Is there a paper jam? Is the paper damp or wrinkled, causing it to refuse to feed? Are the printer cover and rear access doors properly closed and locked? Try resetting the printer. For a laser printer, check that a toner cartridge is installed. For an inkjet printer, check that ink cartridges are installed. Has the protective tape been removed from the print cartridge? Check that power is getting to the printer. Try another power source. Check the user guide for the printer and the printer Web site for troubleshooting suggestions. For a laser printer, replace the toner cartridge. For inkjet printers, replace the ink cartridge. Check the service documentation and printer page count to find out if routine maintenance is due or if the printer has a history of similar problems. Other things to try to troubleshoot problems with laser, inkjet, and dot matrix printers are covered later in the chapter.

If none of these steps works, you might need to take the printer to a certified repair shop. Before you do, though, try contacting the manufacturer. The printer documentation can be very helpful and most often contains a phone number for technical support.

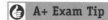 **A+ Exam Tip**

The A+ Essentials exam expects you to know the importance of printing a test page when solving printer problems. You also need to know about using diagnostic tools available on the Web.

PROBLEMS WITH A LOCAL PRINTER CABLE OR PORT

If the printer self-test worked, but the OS printer test did not work, check for connectivity problems between the printer and the PC. For a local printer connected directly to a PC, the problem might be with the printer cable or the port the printer is using. Do the following:

⊿ Check that the cable is firmly connected at both ends. For some parallel ports, you can use a screwdriver to securely anchor the cable to the parallel port with two screws on each side of the port. If you suspect the cable is bad, you can use a multimeter to check the cable.

⊿ A business might use an older switch box (sometimes called a T-switch) to share one printer between two computers. A printer cable connects to the printer port of each computer. The two cables connect to the switch box. A third cable connects from the switch box to the printer. A switch on the front of the box controls which computer has access to the printer. Switch boxes were built with older dot matrix printers in mind. Some

A+ ESS
1.3
3.3
4.3

A+
220-602
1.2
3.3
4.3
4.4

switch boxes are not recommended for inkjet or laser printers that use a bidirectional parallel cable, and can even damage a printer. For these printers, remove the switch box.

▲ Try a different cable. Use a shorter cable. (Parallel cables longer than 10 feet can sometimes cause problems.) Verify that a parallel cable is IEEE 1284-compliant.

▲ Try printing using the same printer and printer cable but a different PC.

▲ Enter Device Manager and verify the port the printer is using is enabled and working properly. Try another device on the same port to verify the problem is not with the port.

▲ Enter CMOS setup of the PC and check how the port is configured. Is it enabled? For a parallel port, is the port set to ECP or bidirectional? Recall that an ECP parallel port requires the use of a DMA channel. Try setting the port to bidirectional.

▲ If you have access to a port tester device, test the port.

PROBLEMS WITH CONNECTIVITY FOR A NETWORK PRINTER

If the self-test page prints but the OS test page does not print and the printer is a network printer, the problem might be with connectivity between the PC on the network and the network printer. Try the following:

▲ Is the printer online?

▲ Turn the printer off and back on. Try rebooting the PC.

▲ If the printer is installed directly to one computer and shared with other computers on the network, check that you can print a test page from the computer that has the printer attached to it locally. Right-click the printer you want to test, and choose **Properties** from the shortcut menu. Click the **Print Test Page** button to send a test page to the printer.

▲ If you cannot print from the local printer, solve the problem there before attempting to print over the network.

▲ Verify that the correct default printer is selected.

▲ Return to the remote computer, and verify that you can access the computer to which the printer is attached. Go to Network Neighborhood or My Network Places, and attempt to open shared folders on the printer's computer. Perhaps you have not entered a correct user ID and password to access this computer; if so, you will be unable to use the computer's resources.

▲ Using the Printers and Faxes window, delete the printer, and then use Windows 2000/XP My Network Places or Windows 9x/Me Network Neighborhood to reconnect the printer.

▲ Is the correct network printer selected on the remote PC?

▲ Can you print to another network printer? If so, there might be a problem with the printer. Look at the printer's configuration.

▲ Is enough hard drive space available on the remote PC?

▲ For printers connected directly to the network, try pinging the printer. Try using another network port, and try using another network cable for the printer.

▲ Run diagnostic software provided by the printer manufacturer.

▲ If a PC cannot communicate with a network printer connected directly to the network, try installing a second network protocol that the network printer supports, such as IPX/SPX. If this works, then suspect that the firmware on the NIC is having a problem with TCP/IP. Try flashing the network printer's firmware.

PROBLEMS PRINTING FROM WINDOWS

If a self-test page works and you have already stepped through checking the printer connectivity, but you still cannot print a test page from Windows, try the following:

▲ The print spool might be stalled. Try deleting all print jobs in the printer's queue. Double-click the printer icon in the Printers and Faxes or Printers window. Select **Printer** on the

A+ ESS
1.3
3.3
4.3

A+
220-602
1.2
3.3
4.3
4.4

menu bar, and then select **Cancel All Documents** (for Windows 2000/XP) or **Purge Print Documents** (for Windows 9x/Me). (It might take a moment for the print jobs to disappear.)

◢ Verify that the correct default printer is selected.

◢ Verify that the printer is online. See the printer documentation for information on how to determine the status from the control panel of the printer.

◢ If you still cannot print, reboot the PC. Verify that the printer cable or cable connections are solid.

◢ Try removing and reinstalling the printer driver. To uninstall the printer driver, right-click the printer icon in the Printers and Faxes or Printers window, and select **Delete**. Then reinstall the printer.

◢ Check the Web site of the printer manufacturer for an updated printer driver. Download and install the correct driver.

◢ Check Event Viewer for recorded events surrounding the printer or the port it is using. To access the log, in Control Panel, open the **Administrative Tools** applet and select **Event Viewer**. Then click **System**. For example, Figure 12-50 shows a recorded event about a print job.

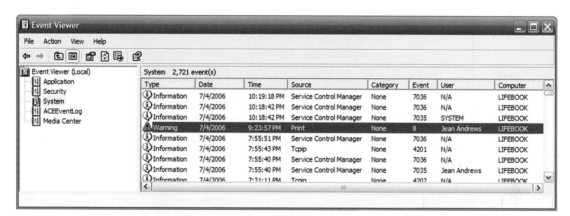

Figure 12-50 Check Event Viewer for recorded errors about the printer or its port

◢ In the printer's Properties dialog box, select the **Ports** tab (see Figure 12-51) and uncheck **Enable bidirectional support** for this printer. The PC and printer might have a problem with bidirectional communication.

◢ Verify printer properties. Try lowering the resolution.

◢ Try disabling printer spooling. On the printer's Properties dialog box, select the **Advanced** tab and then select **Print directly to the printer** (see Figure 12-52). Click **Apply**. Spooling holds print jobs in a queue for printing, so if spooling is disabled, printing from an application can be slower.

◢ If you have trouble printing from an application, you can also bypass spooling in the application by selecting the option to print to a file. Then drag that file to the icon representing your printer in the Printers and Faxes window.

◢ Verify that enough hard drive space is available for the OS to create temporary print files.

◢ Use Chkdsk, Error-checking (Windows 2000/XP), or ScanDisk (Windows 9x/Me) to verify that the hard drive does not have errors. Use Defragmenter to optimize the hard drive.

◢ Boot Windows into Safe Mode and attempt to print. If this step works, there might be a conflict between the printer driver and another driver or application.

◢ Check the printer documentation for troubleshooting steps to solve printer problems. Look for diagnostic software that you can download from the printer manufacturer Web site or diagnostic routines you can run from the printer menu.

A+ ESS
1.3
3.3
4.3

A+
220-602
1.2
3.3
4.3
4.4

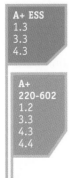

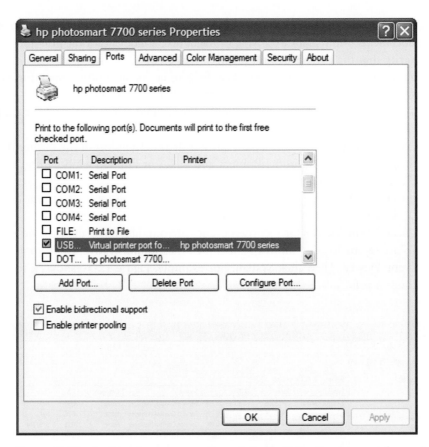

Figure 12-51 On this tab, you can enable and disable bidirectional support for a printer

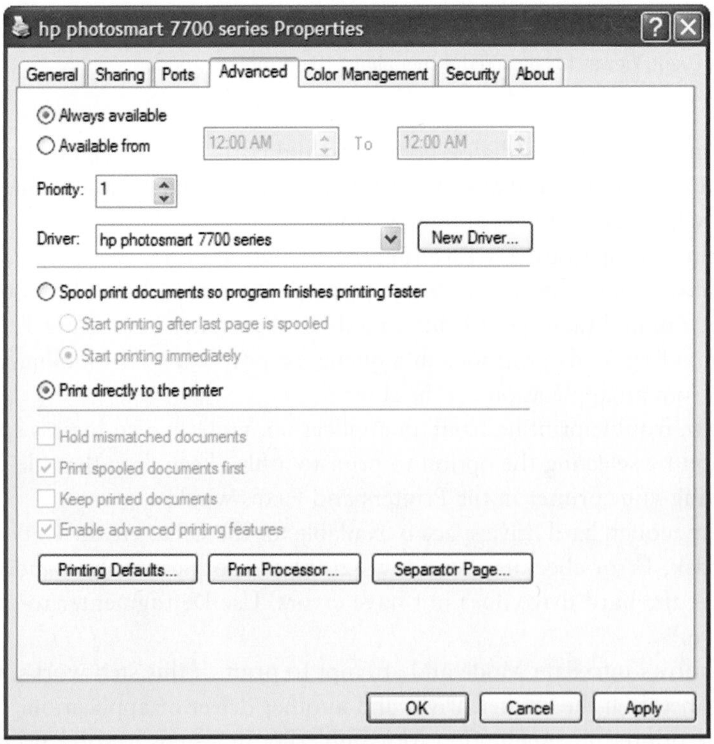

Figure 12-52 Disable printer spooling

A+ ESS
1.3
3.3
4.3

A+
220-602
1.2
3.3
4.3
4.4

PROBLEMS PRINTING FROM APPLICATIONS

If you can print a Windows test page, but you cannot print from an application, try the following:

- ◢ Verify that the correct printer is selected in the Print Setup dialog box.
- ◢ Try printing a different application file.
- ◢ Delete any files in the print spool. From the Printers and Faxes or Printers window, double-click the printer icon. Click **Printer** on the menu bar of the window that opens, and then click **Cancel All Documents** or **Purge Print Documents**.
- ◢ Reboot the PC. Immediately enter Notepad or WordPad, type some text, and print.
- ◢ Reopen the application giving the print error and attempt to print again.
- ◢ Try creating data in a new file and printing it. Keep the data simple.
- ◢ Try printing from another application.
- ◢ If you can print from other applications, consider reinstalling the problem application.
- ◢ Close any applications that are not being used.
- ◢ Add more memory to the printer.
- ◢ Remove and reinstall the printer drivers.
- ◢ For DOS applications, you might need to exit the application before printing will work. Verify that the printer is configured to handle DOS printing.

A+ ESS
4.3

PROBLEMS WITH LASER PRINTERS

This section covers some problems that can occur with laser printers. For more specific guidelines for your printer model, refer to the printer documentation or the manufacturer's Web site.

A+
220-602
1.2
4.3
4.4

POOR PRINT QUALITY OR A TONER LOW MESSAGE IS DISPLAYED

Poor print quality, including faded, smeared, wavy, speckled, or streaked printouts, often indicates that the toner is low. All major mechanical printer components that normally create problems are conveniently contained within the replaceable toner cartridge. In most cases, the solution to poor-quality printing is to replace this cartridge. Follow these general guidelines:

- ◢ If you suspect the printer is overheated, unplug it and allow it to cool.
- ◢ The toner cartridge might be low on toner or might not be installed correctly. Remove the toner cartridge and gently rock it from side to side to redistribute the toner. Replace the cartridge. To avoid flying toner, don't shake the cartridge too hard.
- ◢ If this doesn't solve the problem, try replacing the toner cartridge immediately.
- ◢ EconoMode (a mode that uses less toner) might be on; turn it off.
- ◢ The printer might need cleaning. Some printers have a cleaning utility program that you can run from the printer menu or from software downloaded to the PC. On some laser printers, you can clean the mirror. Check the user guide for directions.
- ◢ A single sheet of paper might be defective. Try new paper.
- ◢ The paper quality might not be high enough. Try a different brand of paper. Only use paper recommended for use with a laser printer. Also, some types of paper can receive print only on one side.
- ◢ Clean the inside of the printer with a dry, lint-free cloth. Don't touch the transfer roller, which is the soft, spongy black roller.
- ◢ If the transfer roller is dirty, the problem will probably correct itself after several sheets print. If not, take the printer to an authorized service center.

 Notes

Extreme humidity can cause the toner to clump in the cartridge and give a Toner Low message. If this is a consistent problem in your location, you might want to invest in a dehumidifier for the room where your printer is located.

A+ ESS
4.3

A+
220-602
1.2
4.3
4.4

▲ Does the printer require routine maintenance? Check the Web site of the printer manufacturer for how often to perform the maintenance and to purchase the required printer maintenance kit.

PRINTER STAYS IN WARM-UP MODE

The "warming up" message on the front panel of the printer (refer back to Figure 12-37) should turn off as soon as the printer establishes communication with the PC. If this doesn't happen, try the following:

1. Turn off the printer and disconnect the cable to the computer.

2. Turn on the printer. If it now displays a Ready message, the problem is communication between the printer and computer.

3. Verify that the cable is connected to the correct port.

4. Verify that data to the installed printer is being sent to the correct port. For example, open the Properties dialog box of the installed printer and click the Ports tab, as shown earlier in Figure 12-51.

5. Try rebooting the PC.

6. Consider the network connecting the printer and PC is down. Try printing from another PC.

A PAPER JAM OCCURS OR PAPER OUT MESSAGE APPEARS

If paper is jammed inside the printer, follow the directions in the printer documentation to remove the paper. Don't jerk the paper from the printer mechanism, but pull evenly on the paper, with care. Here are some guidelines:

▲ Check for jammed paper from both the input tray and the output bin. Check both sides.
▲ If there is no jammed paper, then remove the tray and check the metal plate at the bottom of the tray. Can it move up and down freely? If not, replace the tray.
▲ When you insert the tray in the printer, does the printer lift the plate as the tray is inserted? If not, the lift mechanism might need repair.
▲ Damp paper can cause paper jams. Be sure to only use dry paper in a printer.

ONE OR MORE WHITE STREAKS APPEAR IN THE PRINT

Do the following:

▲ Remove the toner cartridge, shake it from side to side to redistribute the toner supply, and replace the cartridge.
▲ Streaking is usually caused by a dirty developer unit or corona wire. The developer unit is contained in the toner cartridge. Replace the cartridge or check the printer documentation for directions on how to remove and clean the developer unit. Allow the corona wire to cool and clean it with a lint-free swab.

A+ ESS
4.3

A+
220-602
1.2
4.3
4.4

PRINT APPEARS SPECKLED

For this problem, do the following:

◢ Try replacing the cartridge. If the problem persists, the power supply assembly might be damaged.
◢ Replace the laser drum.

> **Notes**
>
> If loose toner comes out with your printout, the fuser is not reaching the proper temperature. Professional service is required.

PRINTED IMAGES ARE DISTORTED

If printed images are distorted and there is no paper jam, foreign material inside the printer might be interfering with the mechanical components. Check for debris that might be interfering with the printer operation. If the page has a gray background or gray print, the photoreceptor drum is worn out and needs to be replaced.

PRINTING IS SLOW

Laser printers are rated by two speed properties: the time it takes to print the first page (measured in seconds) and the print speed (measured in pages per minute). Try the following if the printer is slow:

◢ Space is needed on the hard drive to manage print jobs. Clean up the drive. Install a larger drive if necessary.
◢ Add more memory to the printer. See the printer manual for directions.
◢ Lower the printer resolution and the print quality (which lowers the REt settings).
◢ Verify that the hard drive has enough space.
◢ Upgrade the computer's memory or the CPU.

A PORTION OF THE PAGE DOES NOT PRINT

For some laser printers, an error occurs if the printer does not have enough memory to hold the entire page. For other printers, only a part of the page prints. Some might signal this problem by flashing a light or displaying an error message on their display panels. (Some HP LaserJet printers have a control panel and send an error message for low memory, "20 Mem Overflow.") The solution is to install more memory or to print only simple pages with few graphics. Print a self-test page to verify how much memory is installed. Check the user guide to determine how much memory the printer can support and what kind of memory to buy.

PROBLEMS WITH INKJET PRINTERS

This section covers some problems that can occur with inkjet printers. For more specific guidelines for your printer, refer to the printer documentation or the manufacturer's Web site.

PRINT QUALITY IS POOR

Is the correct paper for inkjet printers being used? The quality of paper determines the final print quality, especially with inkjet printers. In general, the better the quality of the paper used with an inkjet printer, the better the print quality. Do not use less than 20-LB paper in any type of printer, unless the printer documentation specifically says that a lower weight is satisfactory. Here are some more things to check:

◢ Is the ink supply low, or is there a partially clogged nozzle?
◢ Remove and reinstall the cartridge.

◢ Follow the printer's documentation to clean each nozzle.
◢ In the Printer Setup dialog box, click the Media/Quality tab, then change the Print Quality selection. Try different settings with sample prints.
◢ Is the print head too close to or too far from the paper?
◢ There is a little sponge in some printers near the carriage rest that can become clogged with ink. It should be removed and cleaned.
◢ If you are printing transparencies, try changing the fill pattern in your application.

PRINTING IS INTERMITTENT OR ABSENT

For these problems, do the following:

◢ Make sure the correct printer driver is installed.
◢ Is the ink supply low?
◢ Are nozzles clogged?
◢ Replace the ink cartridges or replenish the ink supply.
◢ Sometimes, leaving the printer on for a while will heat up the ink nozzles and unclog them.

LINES OR DOTS ARE MISSING FROM THE PRINTED PAGE

The ink nozzles on an inkjet cartridge occasionally dry out, especially when the printer sits unused for a long time. Symptoms are missing lines or dots on the printed page. Follow directions given earlier in the chapter for cleaning inkjet nozzles.

INK STREAKS APPEAR ON THE PRINTED PAGE

Sometimes, dust or dirt gets down into the print head assemblage, causing streaks or lines on the printed page. Follow the manufacturer's directions to clean the inkjet nozzles.

PAPER IS JAMMED

Inkjet printers have a door in the back of the printer that you can open to gently remove jammed paper, as shown in Figure 12-53. Don't try to pull the paper out from the front of the printer because doing so can tear the paper, leaving pieces inside the printer.

Figure 12-53 Open the door on the back of an inkjet printer to remove jammed paper

A+ ESS
4.3

A+
220-602
1.2
4.3
4.4

PROBLEMS WITH DOT MATRIX PRINTERS

This section covers some problems that can occur with dot matrix printers. Again, for more specific guidelines for your printer, see the printer documentation or the manufacturer's Web site.

PRINT QUALITY IS POOR

For poor print quality, do the following:

- Begin with the ribbon. Does it advance normally while the carriage moves back and forth? If not, replace the ribbon.
- If the new ribbon still does not advance properly, check the printer's advance mechanism.
- Adjust the print head spacing. Look for a lever adjustment you can use to change the distance between the print head and plate.
- Check the print head for dirt. Make sure it's not hot before you touch it. If debris has built up, wipe each wire with a cotton swab dipped in alcohol or contact cleaner.

PRINT HEAD MOVES BACK AND FORTH BUT NOTHING PRINTS

Do the following:

- Check the ribbon. Is it installed correctly between the plate and print head?
- Does the ribbon advance properly? Is it jammed? If the ribbon is dried out, it needs to be replaced.

APPLYING | CONCEPTS

Now back to Jill and her company's network printer problem. Generally, Jill should focus on finding out what works and what doesn't work, always remembering to check the simple things first. Jill should first go to the printer and check that the printer is online and has no error messages, such as a Paper Out message. Then, Jill should ask, "Can anyone print to this printer?" To find out, she should go to the closest PC and try to print a Windows test page. If the test page prints, she should next go to one of the three PCs that do not print and begin troubleshooting that PC's connection to the network. If the test page did not print at the closest PC, the problem is still not necessarily the printer. To eliminate the printer as the problem, the next step is to print a self-test page at the printer. If that self-test page prints, then Jill should check other PCs on the network. Is the entire network down? Can one PC see another PC on the network? Perhaps part of the network is down (maybe because of a switch or hub serving one part of the network).

TROUBLESHOOTING SCANNERS

Here are some troubleshooting tips if Windows cannot find an installed scanner or the scanner refuses to scan:

- Try turning off the scanner or unplugging it from its power source and then turning it back on.
- Try disconnecting the USB cable and then reconnecting it. If you are using a USB hub, remove the hub and connect the scanner directly to the PC.
- Try rebooting your computer.
- Is there enough free hard drive space? If necessary, clean up the hard drive.

A+ ESS
4.3

A+
220-602
1.2
4.3
4.4

▲ Many scanners have a repair utility and troubleshooting software that installs when the setup program runs. For example, looking back at Figure 12-43, to get help, click **troubleshooting and online help**. The resulting instructions give you suggestions of things to check. It also tells you that a repair utility is available from the Add or Remove Programs applet in Control Panel. In Control Panel, open the applet and select the scanner. Click **Change**. The installation wizard launches and gives you the opportunity to repair or remove the software (see Figure 12-54).

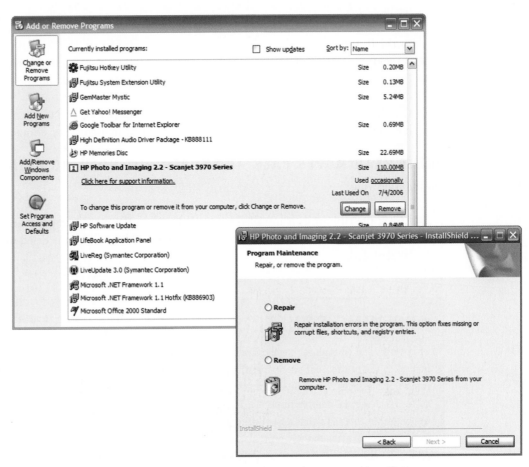

Figure 12-54 When a scanner gives problems, you can repair or remove the software

▲ Check the Web site of the scanner manufacturer for troubleshooting guidelines and other help. You might be able to post a question to a newsgroup on the site or start a chat session with technical support. Figure 12-55 shows help given at the HP site for one flat-bed scanner. Notice the two links to chat with an online technician and to e-mail technical support. Also notice the link to download drivers. Try downloading and installing new drivers for the scanner.

▲ Try uninstalling and reinstalling the scanner software. To uninstall the software, use the Add or Remove Programs applet in Control Panel.

▲ Install the scanner on another computer to determine if the problem is with the computer or the scanner.

A+ ESS
4.3

A+
220-602
1.2
4.3
4.4

Figure 12-55 Online help for a scanner

>> CHAPTER SUMMARY

▲ The two most popular types of printers are laser and inkjet. Other types of printers are solid ink, dye sublimation, thermal printers, and dot matrix. Laser printers produce the highest quality, followed by inkjet printers. Dot matrix printers have the advantage of being able to print multicopy documents.

▲ The six steps that a laser printer performs to print are cleaning, conditioning, writing, developing, transferring, and fusing. The first four steps take place inside the removable toner cartridge.

▲ Inkjet printers print by shooting ionized ink at a sheet of paper.

▲ The nozzles of an inkjet printer tend to clog or dry out, especially when the printer remains unused. The nozzles can be cleaned automatically by means of printer software or buttons on the front panel of the printer.

▲ Dot matrix printers print by projecting pins from the print head against an inked ribbon that deposits ink on the paper.

▲ Three types of scanners are flat-bed, sheet-fed, and portable scanners.

▲ A printer is installed as a local printer connected directly to a computer, a network printer that works as a device on the network, or a network printer connected to a print server. A local printer can be shared so that others can use it as a resource on the network.

▲ Printers can process print jobs using PostScript, PCL (Printer Control Language), or GDI input. In addition, printers can receive raw data that can be printed with no processing.

◢ Windows manages and configures a printer using the Windows XP Printers and Faxes window or the Windows 2000 or Windows 9x/Me Printers window.

◢ Routine maintenance and cleaning help a printer or scanner to last longer and work better.

◢ When troubleshooting printers, first isolate the problem. Narrow the source to the printer, cable, PC hardware, operating system including the device driver, application software, or network. Test pages printed directly at the printer or within Windows can help narrow down the source of the problem.

>> KEY TERMS

For explanations of key terms, see the Glossary near the end of the book.

beam detect mirror	inkjet printer	REt (Resolution Enhancement
control blade	laser printer	technology)
default printer	local printer	scanner
dye-sublimation printer	network printer	scanning mirror
extension magnet brush	PCL (Printer Control Language)	solid ink printer
GDI (Graphics Device	PostScript	spooling
Interface)	printer maintenance kit	thermal printer

>> REVIEWING THE BASICS

1. List the six steps used by a laser printer to print a page.

2. Which document exhibits better quality, one printed with 600 dpi or one printed with 1200 dpi? Why?

3. What type of port will a desktop scanner most likely use?

4. What two types of scanning technologies does a scanner use?

5. What are two possible settings in CMOS for parallel port mode?

6. During the laser printing process, what determines when the toner sticks to the drum and when it does not stick to the drum?

7. Why is it less expensive to maintain an inkjet printer that has a black ink cartridge than one that does not?

8. What technology makes an inkjet printer a photo-quality printer?

9. What should you do if an inkjet printer prints with missing dots or lines on the page?

10. What can you do to help a dot matrix printer last longer?

11. List two possible ways to improve printing speed.

12. When a laser printer is short on memory, what is a possible symptom of this problem?

13. What two Windows components are used to share resources on a network and access those shared resources?

14. How do you share a local printer with others in the workgroup?

15. What are two ways to install a printer that is being shared by another computer on the network?

16. What company developed PostScript? PCL?

17. When you are isolating a printer problem, what are the four major possible sources of the problem?

18. How can you eliminate the printer as the source of a printing problem?

19. How can you be sure that a printer cable is not the source of a printer problem?

20. Why is it important not to remove ink cartridges from an inkjet printer and leave the cartridges outside the printer for an extended period of time?

>> THINKING CRITICALLY

1. A Windows XP computer has a locally installed printer that you must make available to eight other Windows XP computers on the network. What is the best way to do this?

   a. Use the Add Printer icon in the Printers window for each of the eight PCs.

   b. Use My Network Places to install the printer on each of the eight PCs.

   c. Use the printer manufacturer's setup program from the printer's CD on each of the eight PCs.

   d. Install the printer on each of the eight PCs while sitting at the host PC. Use My Network Places on the host PC.

2. You are not able to print a Word document on a Windows XP computer to a network printer. The network printer is connected directly to the network, but when you look at the Printers and Faxes window, you see the name of the printer as \\SMITHWIN2K\HP LaserJet 8100. In the following list, select the possible sources of the problem.

   a. The SMITHWIN2K computer is not turned on.

   b. The HP LaserJet 8100 printer is not online.

   c. The SMITHWIN2K printer is not online.

   d. The Windows XP computer has a stalled printer spool.

   e. The HP LaserJet 8100 computer is not logged on to the workgroup.

3. You are not able to print a test page from your Windows 2000 PC to your local HP DeskJet printer. Which of the following are possible causes of the problem?

   a. The network is down.

   b. The printer cable is not connected properly.

   c. The Windows print spool is stalled.

   d. You have the wrong printer drivers installed.

   e. File and Printer Sharing is not enabled.

>> HANDS-ON PROJECTS

PROJECT 12-1:   Practicing Printer Maintenance

For an inkjet printer, follow the procedures in the printer's user guide to clean the printer nozzles and ink cartridges. For a laser printer, follow the procedures in its user guide to clean the inside of the printer where the toner cartridge is installed.

PROJECT 12-2:   Sharing a Local Printer

Practice networking skills using Windows 2000/XP or Windows 9x/Me:

1. Share a local printer with others on the network.

2. Install a shared printer on a remote PC. Verify that you can print to the printer.

PROJECT 12-3:   Researching Printer Web Sites

Your company plans to purchase a new printer, and you want to evaluate the printer manufacturers' Web sites to determine which site offers the best support. Research three Web sites listed in Table 12-1 and answer these questions, supporting your answers with printed pages from the Web site:

1. Which Web site made it easiest for you to select a new printer based on your criteria for its use?

2. Which Web site made it easiest for you to find help for troubleshooting printer problems?

3. Which Web site gave you the best information about routine maintenance for its printers?

4. Which Web site gave you the best information about how to clean its printers?

PROJECT 12-4:   Researching a Printer Maintenance Plan

You have been asked to recommend a maintenance plan for a laser printer. Search the manufacturer's Web site for information, and then write a maintenance plan. Include in the plan the tasks that need to be done, how often they need doing, and what tools and components are needed to perform the tasks. Use the Hewlett-Packard LaserJet 8100 DN printer unless your instructor tells you to use a different printer, perhaps one that is available in your lab.

>> REAL PROBLEMS, REAL SOLUTIONS

REAL PROBLEM 12-1:   Selecting a Color Printer for a Small Business

Jack owns a small real estate firm and has come to you asking for help with his printing needs. Currently, he has a color inkjet printer that he is using to print flyers, business cards, brochures, and other marketing materials. However, he is not satisfied with the print quality and wants to invest in a printer that produces more professional-looking hard copy. He expects to print no more than 8,000 sheets per month and needs the ability to print envelopes, letter-size and legal-size pages, and business cards. He wants to be able to automatically print on both sides of a legal-size page to produce a three-column brochure. Research printer solutions and do the following:

1. Print Web pages showing three printers to present to Jack that satisfy his needs. Include at least one laser printer and at least one other printer technology other than laser in your selections.

2. Print Web pages showing the routine maintenance requirements of these printers.

3. Print Web pages showing all the consumable products (other than paper) that Jack should expect to have to purchase in the first year of use.

4. Calculate the initial cost of the equipment and the total cost of consumables for one year (other than paper) for each printer solution.

5. Prepare a list of advantages and disadvantages for each solution.

6. Based on your research, which of the three solutions do you recommend? Why?

APPENDIX A

How an OS Uses System Resources

A system resource is a tool used by either hardware or software to communicate with the other. When BIOS or a driver wants to send data to a device (such as when you save a file to the hard drive), or when a device needs attention (such as when you press a key on the keyboard), the device or software uses system resources to communicate. When you install a hardware device under DOS or Windows 9x/Me, it is sometimes necessary to configure which system resources a device will use. Therefore, for these operating systems, a technician needs a general understanding about system resources discussed in this appendix.

There are four types of system resources: interrupt request numbers (IRQs), memory addresses, I/O addresses, and direct memory access (DMA) channels. Table A-1 lists these system resources used by software and hardware, and defines each.

As you can see in Table A-1, all four resources are used for communication between hardware and software. Hardware devices signal the CPU for attention using an IRQ. Software addresses a device by one of its I/O addresses. Software looks at memory as a hardware device and addresses it with memory addresses, and DMA channels pass data back and forth between a hardware device and memory.

All four system resources depend on certain lines on a bus on the motherboard (see Figure A-1). A bus such as the system bus has three components: the data bus carries data, the address bus communicates addresses (both memory addresses and I/O addresses), and the control bus controls communication. (IRQs and DMA channels are controlled by this portion of the bus.)

System Resource	Definition
IRQ	A line of a motherboard bus that a hardware device can use to signal the CPU that the device needs attention. Some lines have a higher priority for attention than others. Each IRQ line is assigned a number (0 to 15) to identify it.
Memory addresses	Numbers assigned to physical memory located either in RAM or ROM chips. Software can access this memory by using these addresses. Memory addresses are communicated on the address bus.
I/O addresses	Numbers assigned to hardware devices that software uses to send a command to a device. Each device "listens" for these numbers and responds to the ones assigned to it. I/O addresses are communicated on the address bus.
DMA channel	A number designating a channel on which the device can pass data to memory without involving the CPU. Think of a DMA channel as a shortcut for data moving to and from the device and memory.

Table A-1   System resources used by software and hardware

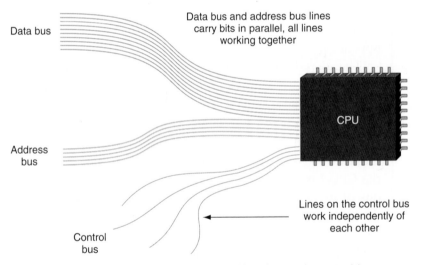

Figure A-1   A bus consists of a data bus, an address bus, and a control bus

Let's turn our attention to a more detailed description of the four resources and how they work.

INTERRUPT REQUEST NUMBER (IRQ)

When a hardware device needs the CPU to do something—for instance, when the keyboard needs the CPU to process a keystroke after a key has been pressed—the device needs a way to get the CPU's attention, and the CPU must know what to do once it turns its attention to the device. Getting the CPU's attention is known as a hardware interrupt, and the device creates a hardware interrupt by placing voltage on the designated interrupt request (IRQ) line assigned to the device. This voltage on the line serves as a signal to the CPU that the device has a request that needs processing. Often, a hardware device that needs attention from the CPU is referred to as "needing servicing." Interrupts initiate many processes that the CPU carries out, and these processes are said to be "interrupt-driven."

A

Table A-2 lists common uses for the sixteen available IRQs. The respective I/O addresses, which are listed in the second column of the table, are discussed in the third section of this appendix.

IRQ	I/O Address	Device
0	0040–005F	System timer
1	0060–006F	Keyboard controller
2	00A0–00AF	Access to IRQs above 7
3	02F8–02FF	COM2 (covered in Chapter 8)
3	02E8–02EF	COM4 (covered in Chapter 8)
4	03F8–03FF	COM1 (covered in Chapter 8)
4	03E8–03EF	COM3 (covered in Chapter 8)
5	0278–027F	Sound card or parallel port LPT2 (covered in Chapter 8)
6	03F0–03F7	Floppy drive controller
7	0378–037F	Printer parallel port LPT1 (covered in Chapter 8)
8	0070–007F	Real-time clock
9–10	N/A	Available
11	N/A	SCSI or available
12	0238–023F	Motherboard mouse
13	00F8–00FF	Math coprocessor
14	01F0–01F7	IDE hard drive (covered in Chapter 7)
15	0170–017F	Secondary IDE hard drive or available (covered in Chapter 7)

Table A-2   IRQs and I/O addresses for devices

In Table A-2, notice the COM and LPT assignments. Recall from Chapter 8 that a COM or LPT assignment is an agreed-on grouping of I/O addresses and an IRQ value. In the industry, it is agreed that when a device is configured to use COM1, it is using I/O addresses 03F8 through 03FF and IRQ 4. When all device and motherboard manufacturers agree to this and other COM and LPT assignments, it is less likely that devices will attempt to use conflicting resources, and it makes it easier to configure a device.

COM1 and COM2 are predetermined assignments that can be made to serial devices such as modems, and LPT1 and LPT2 are predetermined assignments that can be made to parallel devices such as printers. For example, a modem is built so that you can choose between using COM1 or COM2 for its resource assignments, rather than having to specify a particular IRQ or range of I/O addresses.

On motherboards, part of the chipset called the interrupt controller manages the IRQs for the CPU. The CPU actually doesn't know which IRQ is "up" because the interrupt controller manages that. If more than one IRQ is up at the same time, the interrupt controller selects the IRQ that has the lowest value to process first. For example, if a user presses a key on the keyboard at the same time that she moves the mouse configured to use COM1, the keystroke is processed before the mouse action, because the keyboard is using IRQ 1 and the mouse on COM1 is using IRQ 4. In other words, the interrupt controller is sort of the doorman to the CPU's apartment building. All devices wait outside the door while the interrupt controller decides who should be "let in" first, according to the IRQ value each holds in his hand.

The interrupt controller on early motherboards was designed to handle only eight different IRQs. To accommodate the need for more devices, a second group of IRQs was later added (IRQs 8 through 15), and a second interrupt controller was added to manage these new IRQs. This second controller did not have access to the CPU, so it had to communicate with the CPU through the first controller (see Figure A-2). To signal the first controller, the second controller used one of the first controller's IRQ values (IRQ 2). These last eight IRQs plug into the system using IRQ 2. Because of this, the IRQ priority level became: 0, 1, (8, 9, 10, 11, 12, 13, 14, 15), 3, 4, 5, 6, 7.

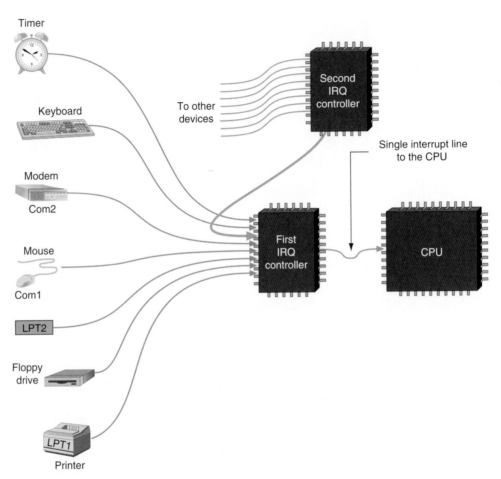

Figure A-2   The second IRQ controller uses IRQ 2 to signal the first IRQ controller

APPLYING | CONCEPTS   To see how the IRQs are assigned on your computer, you can use Device Manager for Windows 2000/XP and Windows 9x/Me. (For DOS, use a utility called MSD.) For Windows XP, click **Start**, right-click **My Computer**, and select **Properties** on the shortcut menu. For Windows 2000, right-click **My Computer** on the desktop and select **Properties** on the shortcut menu. The System Properties dialog box opens, as shown in Figure A-3. Click the **Hardware** tab and then click the **Device Manager** button. On the menu, click **View**, and then click **Resources by Type**, if necessary. Click the plus sign next to Interrupt request (IRQ) to open the list of assigned IRQs. Notice in the figure that IRQs 9 and 11 are each being shared by two devices.

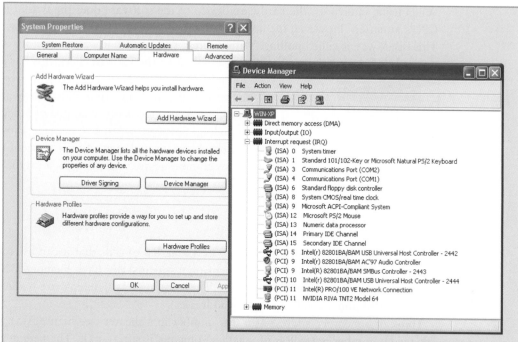

Figure A-3   Use Device Manager to see how your system is using IRQs and other system resources

To see current assignments in Windows 9x/Me, click **Start**, point to **Settings**, click **Control Panel**, and double-click **System**. Click the **Device Manager** tab, select **Computer,** and then click **Properties**. Figure A-4 shows the Computer Properties dialog box. Notice that IRQ 2 is assigned to the programmable interrupt controller because it is being used to manage IRQs 8 through 15.

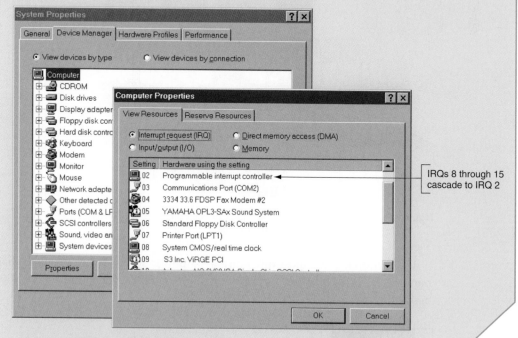

Figure A-4   Windows 9x/Me Device Manager shows current assignments for system resources

When using interrupts, the hardware device or the software does the work of getting the CPU's attention. However, the flow of "attention getting" can go the other way as well. This other way is called polling. With polling, software that was written for a specific hardware device constantly runs and occasionally asks the CPU to check this hardware device to see if it needs service. Not very many devices use polling as the method of communication; most hardware devices use interrupts. A joystick is one example of a device that does use polling. Software written to manage a joystick has the CPU check the joystick periodically to see if the device has data to communicate, which is why a joystick does not need an IRQ to work.

> **Notes**
>
> Sharing IRQs is not possible with ISA devices on the ISA bus. However, newer buses are designed to allow more than one device to share an IRQ.

MEMORY ADDRESSES

An operating system relates to memory as a long list of cells that it can use to hold data and instructions, somewhat like a one-dimensional spreadsheet. Each memory location or cell is assigned a number beginning with zero. These number assignments are made when the OS is first loaded and are called memory addresses.

Think of a memory address as a seat number in a theater (see Figure A-5). Each seat is assigned a number regardless of whether someone is sitting in it. The person sitting in a seat can be data or instructions, and the OS does not refer to the person by name, but only by the seat number. For example, the OS might say, "I want to print the data in memory addresses 500 through 650."

Figure A-5   Memory addresses are assigned to each location in memory, and these locations can store data or instructions

These addresses are most often displayed on the screen as hexadecimal (base 16 or hex) numbers in segment: offset form (for example, C800:5, which in hex is C8005 and in decimal is 819,205).

> **Notes**
>
> Windows offers a calculator that can quickly convert numbers in binary, digital, and hexadecimal. Enter a number in one number system, and then click another number system to make the conversion. To access the calculator in Windows 2000/XP or Windows 9x/Me, click **Start, Programs** (**All Programs** in Windows XP), **Accessories**, and then **Calculator**. To view the version of the calculator that can convert number systems, click **View, Scientific**.

I/O ADDRESSES

Another system resource made available to hardware devices is the input/output address, which is also known as an I/O address, a port address, or a port. I/O addresses are numbers the CPU can use to access hardware devices, in much the same way it uses memory addresses to access physical memory. Each device needs a range of I/O addresses so that the CPU can communicate more than one type of command to it.

Notes

For more information on the hexadecimal number system and how it applies to memory addresses, see "The Hexadecimal Number System and Memory Addressing" in the online content.

The address bus on the motherboard sometimes carries memory addresses and sometimes carries I/O addresses. If the address bus has been set to carry I/O addresses, then each device "listens" to this bus (see Figure A-6). If a device (such as a hard drive, floppy drive, or keyboard) hears an address that belongs to it, then it responds; otherwise, it ignores the request for information. In short, the CPU "knows" a hardware device as a group of I/O addresses. If it wants to know the status of a printer or a CD drive, for example, it places a particular I/O address on the address bus on the motherboard.

Because IBM made many address assignments when it manufactured the first PC in the late 1970s, common devices such as a hard drive, a floppy drive, or a keyboard use a range of predetermined I/O addresses that never change. Their BIOS is simply programmed to use these standard addresses and standard IRQs. Legacy devices (devices that use older technologies) were designed to use more than one group of addresses and IRQs, depending on how jumpers or DIP switches were set on the device. Newer devices, called Plug and Play devices, can use any I/O addresses or IRQ assigned to them during startup.

Notes

Refer back to Table A-2 for a listing of a few common assignments for I/O addresses. Because these addresses are usually written as hex numbers, you sometimes see them written with 0x first, such as 0x0040, or with the h last, like this: 0040h.

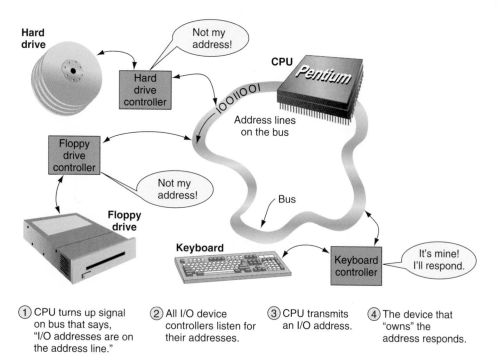

① CPU turns up signal on bus that says, "I/O addresses are on the address line."

② All I/O device controllers listen for their addresses.

③ CPU transmits an I/O address.

④ The device that "owns" the address responds.

Figure A-6 I/O address lines on a bus work much like people sitting in a waiting room waiting for their number to be called; all devices "hear" the addresses, but only one responds

DMA CHANNELS

Another system resource used by hardware and software is a direct memory access (DMA) channel, a shortcut method that lets an I/O device send data directly to memory. This bypasses the CPU and improves performance.

A chip on the motherboard contains the DMA logic and manages the process. Earlier computers had four DMA channels numbered 0, 1, 2, and 3. Later, channels 5, 6, and 7 were added. DMA channel 4 is used as IRQ 2 was used, as the entry point for the higher DMA channels to connect to the lower channels. This allows the higher channels a way to connect to the DMA controller on the motherboard and on to the CPU. In Figure A-7, you can see that DMA channel 4 is used to point to or cascade into the lower DMA channels.

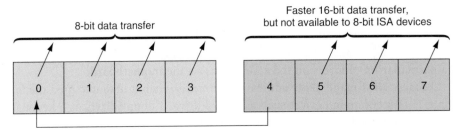

Figure A-7   DMA channel 4 is not available for I/O use because it is used to cascade into the lower-four DMA channels

Some devices, such as a printer, are designed to use DMA channels, and others, such as the mouse, are not. Those that use the channels might be able to use only a certain channel, say channel 3, and no other. Alternately, the BIOS might have the option of changing a DMA channel number to avoid conflicts with other devices. Conflicts occur when more than one device uses the same channel. DMA channels are not as popular as they once were, because their design makes them slower than newer methods such as a faster I/O bus. However, slower devices such as floppy drives, sound cards, and tape drives might still use DMA channels.

Electricity and Multimeters

This appendix gives you a general introduction to what electricity is and how it is measured. In addition, you will learn how to use a multimeter to measure the voltage output of a power supply. Knowing the basics of electricity and how it works with your equipment will make you a stronger PC support technician. In addition, a multimeter can be a handy little tool to help you identify an unknown cable, test continuity in a fuse or other device, or test the voltage output of a notebook AC adapter or PC power supply.

ELECTRICITY: A BASIC INTRODUCTION

Notes

To most people, volts, ohms, watts, and amps are vague words that have to do with electricity. If these terms are mysterious to you, they will become clearer in this section, which discusses electricity in nontechnical language and uses simple analogies to illustrate the underlying concepts.

Electricity is energy and water is matter, but the two have enough in common to make some comparisons, as shown in Figure B-1. The water system shown in the top part of the figure is closed; that is, the amount of water in the system remains the same because no water enters and no water leaves the system. The electrical system in the lower part of the figure is closed as well.

Just as water flows down because of the force of gravity, electricity flows from negative to positive because of the force of like charges repelling one another. The water pump produces water pressure in the system by lifting the water, and a battery produces electrical pressure in the system by creating a buildup of negative charges (in the form of electrons) in one location, which are driven to move. This difference in charge, which is similar to water pressure in a water system, is called potential difference. Water seeks a place of rest, moving from a high to a low elevation, and electrons seek a place of rest by moving from a negatively charged location (sometimes called "hot") to a positively charged location (sometimes called "ground"). In the figure, as water flows through the closed system, the water wheel harnesses some of its force and converts it to a form of energy, motion. Also in the figure, as the electrons flow in the closed electrical system called a circuit, the light bulb harnesses some of the force of the moving electrons and converts it to another form of energy, light. When the water returns to the pool, water pressure

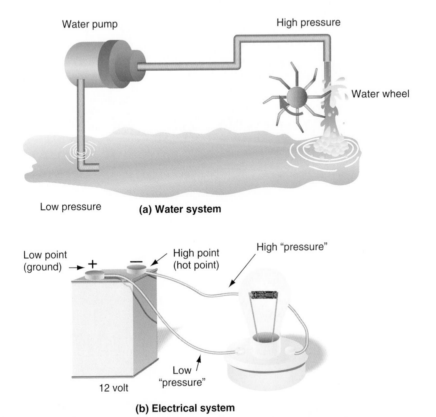

Figure B-1   Two closed systems: (a) water system with pump, wheel, and pool; (b) electrical system with battery and light bulb

decreases and the water is at rest. When the electrons arrive at the positive side of the battery, electrical potential difference decreases, and the system is at rest.

Electrical energy has properties that you can measure in various ways. Table B-1 defines four properties of electricity, how they can be measured, and some examples of each. These properties are explained in detail later in this appendix.

 Notes

Electron flow goes from the hot point, or negative terminal, to the ground, or positive terminal. Because early theories of electricity assumed that electricity flowed from positive to negative, most electronics books show the current flowing from positive to negative. This theory is called conventional current flow; if it were used in Figure B-1, the figure would show reversed positive and negative symbols.

Unit	Definition and Measurement	Computer Example
Volt (measures potential difference)	Abbreviated as V (for example, 110 V). Volts are measured by finding the potential difference between the electrical charges on either side of an electrical device in an electrical system.	An AT power supply provides four separate voltages: +12 V, -12 V, +5 V, and -5 V. An ATX or BTX power supply provides these voltages and +3.3 V as well.
Amp or ampere (measures electrical current)	Abbreviated as A (for example, 1.5 A). Amps are measured by placing an ammeter in the flow of current and measuring that current.	A 17-inch monitor requires less than 2 A to operate. A small laser printer uses about 2 A. A CD-ROM drive uses about 1 A.
Ohm (measures resistance)	Abbreviated with the symbol Ω (for example, 20 Ω). Devices are rated according to how much resistance to electrical current they offer. The ohm rating of a resistor or other electrical device is often written somewhere on the device. The resistance of a device is measured when the device is not connected to an electrical system.	Current can flow in typical computer cables and wires with a resistance of near zero Ω.
Watt (measures power)	Abbreviated W (for example, 20 W). Watts are calculated by multiplying volts by amps.	A computer power supply is rated at 200 to 600 W.

Table B-1 Measures of electricity

VOLTAGE

Consider how to measure the water pressure in Figure B-1. If you measure the pressure of the water directly above the water wheel and then measure the pressure just as the water lands in the pool, you find that the water pressure above the wheel is greater than the water pressure below it.

Now consider the electrical system. If you measure the electrical charge on one side of the light bulb and compare it with the electrical charge on the other side of the bulb, you see a difference in charge. The potential difference in charge creates an electrical force called voltage, which drives the electrons through the system between two points. Voltage is measured in units called volts (V).

In Figure B-2, the leads of a voltmeter, a device for measuring electrical voltage, are placed on either side of a light bulb that consumes some electrical power. The potential difference between the two points on either side of the device is the voltage in the closed system. Voltage is measured when the power is on.

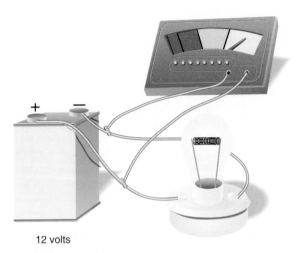

12 volts

Figure B-2   A voltmeter measuring the voltage across a bulb and a battery

AMPS

The volume of electrons (or electricity) flowing through an electrical system is called current. Look back at Figure B-1. The volume or amount of water flowing through the water system does not change, although the water pressure changes at different points in the system. To measure that volume, you pick one point in the system and measure the volume of water passing through that point over a period of time. The electrical system is similar. If you measure the number of electrons, or electrical current, at any point in this system, you find the same value as at any other point, because the current is constant throughout the system. (This assumes that the entire closed water or electrical system has only a single pipe or a single wire.)

Electrical current is measured in amperes (A), abbreviated amps. Figure B-3 shows an ammeter, a device that measures electrical current in amps. You place the ammeter in the path of the electrical flow so that the electrons must flow through the ammeter. The measurement, which you take with the power on, might not be completely accurate because the ammeter can influence the circuit. Nonetheless, the measurement still provides useful information.

Because the current flows through an ammeter, check the rating of the ammeter before measuring amps to make sure it can handle the flow of electricity. More flow than the ammeter is designed to handle can blow the meter's fuse.

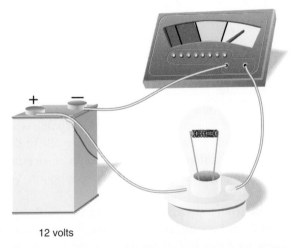

12 volts

Figure B-3   Battery and bulb circuit with ammeter in line

Notes

Refer again to the water system in Figure B-1. To increase the volume of water flowing through the system, you increase the difference in water pressure between the low and high points (which is called the pressure differential). As the pressure differential increases, the water flow (or current) increases, and as the water pressure differential decreases, the water flow (or current) decreases. In other words, there is a direct relationship between pressure differential and current. An electrical system works the same way. As the electrical potential difference (or voltage) increases, the electrical current increases; as the voltage decreases, the current decreases. There is a direct relationship between voltage and current.

OHMS

Suppose you are working your water pump to full capacity. If you still want to increase the overall power of your water system—so the wheel turns faster to produce more mechanical energy—you could decrease the resistance to water flow, allowing more water to flow to push the wheel faster. You might use a larger pipe or a lighter water wheel, or, if the system has a partially open water valve, you could open the valve more; these alternatives all would lower resistance to water flow. As resistance decreases, current increases. As resistance increases (smaller pipes, heavier wheel, partially closed valve), current decreases.

Similarly, resistance in an electrical system is a property that opposes the flow of electricity. As electrical resistance increases, the flow of electrons decreases. As resistance decreases, the electricity increases. (A condition of low resistance that allows current to flow in a completed circuit is called continuity.) When too much electricity flows through a wire, it creates heat energy (similar to friction) in the wire. This heat energy can cause the wire to melt or burn, which can result in an electrical fire, just as too much water current can cause a pipe to burst. Reducing the size of a wire reduces the amount of electricity that can safely flow through it. Electrical resistance is measured in ohms (Ω).

Resistors are devices used in electrical circuits to resist the flow of electricity. These devices control the flow of electricity in a circuit, much as partially closed valves control the flow of water.

 Notes

Voltage and current have a direct relationship. This means that when voltage increases, current increases. Resistance has an inverse relationship with current and a direct relationship with voltage. This means that as resistance increases, current decreases if voltage remains constant, such as when you use a dimmer switch to dim a light. As a general rule, the more voltage you expect in an electrical system, in order for current to remain constant, the more resistance you must add in the form of a larger-capacity resistor. This last statement is known as Ohm's Law. A similar statement defines the relationship among the units of measure: volts, amps, and ohms. One volt drives a current of one amp through a resistance of one ohm.

WATTAGE

Wattage is the total amount of power needed to operate an electrical device. When thinking of the water system, you recognize that the amount of water power used to turn the water wheel is not just a measure of the water pressure that forces current through the system. The amount of power also depends on the amount of water available to flow. For a given water pressure, you have more power with more water flow and less power with less water flow. A lot of power results when you have a lot of pressure and a lot of current.

As with the water system, electrical power increases as both voltage and current increase. Wattage, measured in watts (W), is calculated by multiplying volts by amps in a system (W = V x A). For example, 120 volts times 5 amps is 600 watts. Note that while volts and amps are measured to determine their value, watts are calculated from those values.

MEASURING THE VOLTAGE OF A POWER SUPPLY

If you suspect a problem with a power supply, the simplest and preferred solution is to replace it with a new one. However, in some situations, you might want to measure the voltage output first. You will learn how to do so in this part of the appendix.

> ✎ **Notes**
>
> When a power supply works properly, voltages all fall within an acceptable range (plus or minus 10 percent). However, be aware that even if measured voltage falls within the appropriate range, a power supply can still cause problems. This is because problems with power supplies can be intermittent—in other words, they come and go. Therefore, if the voltages are correct, you should still suspect the power supply is the problem when certain symptoms are present. To learn for certain whether the power supply is the problem, replace it with a unit you know is good.

USING A MULTIMETER

A voltmeter measures the difference in electrical potential between two points, in volts, and an ammeter measures electrical current in amps. A multimeter, as shown in Figure B-4, can make a variety of measurements, depending on the dial or function switch setting.

Multimeters are sometimes small, portable, battery-powered units. Larger ones are designed to sit on a countertop and are powered by a wall outlet. A multimeter can provide either a digital or an analog display. A digital display shows the readings as digits on an LCD (liquid crystal display) panel. A digital multimeter is sometimes called a DMM (digital

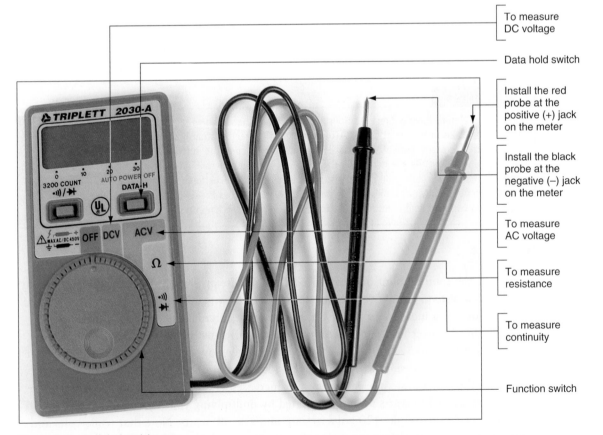

Figure B-4 A digital multimeter

multimeter) or a DVM (digital voltage meter). An analog
display shows the readings as a needle moving across a
scale of values.

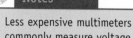

> **Notes**
>
> Less expensive multimeters commonly measure voltage, resistance, and continuity, but not amps.

Before you begin to use a multimeter, you must tell it
three things: (1) what you want it to measure (voltage,
current, or resistance); (2) whether the current is AC or DC;
and (3) what range of values it should expect. If you are
measuring the voltage output from a wall outlet (110–120 V), the range should be much
higher than when you are measuring the voltage output of a computer power supply
(3–12 V). Setting the range high assures you that the meter can handle a large input
without pegging the needle (exceeding the highest value the meter is designed to measure)
or damaging the meter. However, if you set the range too high, you might not see the
voltage register at all. Set the range low enough to ensure that the measure is as accurate
as you need but not lower than the expected voltage. When you set the range too low on
some digital multimeters, the meter reads "OL" on the display.

For example, to measure the voltage of house current, if you expect the voltage to be
115 volts, set the voltage range from 0 to somewhere between 120 and 130 volts. You
want the high end of the range to be slightly higher than the expected voltage. To protect
themselves, most meters do not allow a very large voltage or current into the meter when
the range is set low. Some multimeters are autorange meters, which sense the quantity of
input and set the range accordingly.

HOW TO MEASURE VOLTAGE

To measure voltage, place the other end of the black probe at the ground point and the
other end of the red probe at the hot point, without disconnecting anything in the circuit
and with the power on. For example, to measure voltage
using the multimeter in Figure B-4, turn the function
switch dial to DCV for DC voltage measurement. This
meter is autoranging, so that's all that needs to be set. With
the power on, place the two probes in position and read
the voltage from the LCD panel. The DATA-H (data hold)
switch allows you to freeze the displayed reading.

> **Caution**
>
> When using a multimeter to measure voltage, current, or resistance, be careful not to touch a chip with the probes.

HOW TO MEASURE CURRENT

In most troubleshooting situations, you will measure voltage, not current. However, you
should still know how to measure current. To measure current in amps, the multimeter
itself must be part of the circuit. Disconnect the circuit at some point so that you can
connect the multimeter in line to find a measure in amps. Note that not all multimeters
can measure amps.

HOW TO MEASURE CONTINUITY

You can also use a multimeter to measure continuity. If there is little or no resistance (less
than 20 ohms gives continuity in a PC) in a wire or a closed connection between two
points, the path for electricity between the two points is unhindered or "continuous." This
measurement is taken with no electricity present in the circuit.

For example, if you want to know that pin 2 on one end of a serial cable is connected to
pin 3 on the other end of the cable, set the multimeter to measure continuity, and work
without connecting the cable to anything. Put one probe on pin 2 at one end of the cable
and the other probe on pin 3 at the other end. If the two pins connect, the multimeter
shows a reading on the LCD panel, or a buzzer sounds (see the multimeter documentation).

In this situation, you might find that the probe is too large to extend into the pinhole of the female connection of the cable. A straightened small paper clip works well here to extend the probe. However, be very careful not to use a paper clip that is too thick and might widen the size of the pinhole, because this can later prevent the pinhole from making a good connection.

One way to determine if a fuse is good is to measure continuity. Set a multimeter to measure continuity, and place its probes on each end of the fuse. If the fuse has continuity, then it is good. If the multimeter has no continuity setting, set it to measure resistance. If the reading in ohms is approximately zero, there is no resistance and the fuse is good. If the reading is infinity, resistance is infinite; the fuse is blown and should not be used.

HOW TO MEASURE THE VOLTAGE OF A POWER SUPPLY

To determine whether a power supply is working properly, measure the voltage of each circuit the power supply supports. To do so, first open the computer case and identify all power cords coming from the power supply. Look for the cords from the power supply to the motherboard and other power cords to the drives (see Figure B-5).

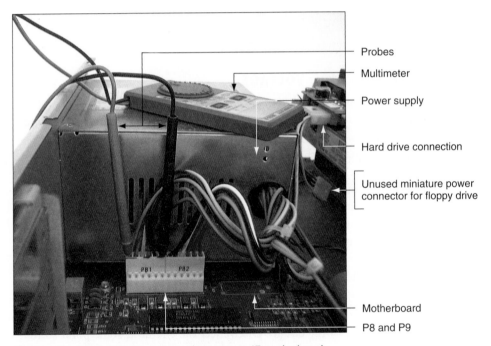

Probes

Multimeter

Power supply

Hard drive connection

Unused miniature power connector for floppy drive

Motherboard

P8 and P9

Figure B-5 Multimeter measuring voltage on an AT motherboard

The computer must be turned on to test the power supply output. Be very careful not to touch any chips or disturb any circuit boards as you work. The voltage output from the power supply is no more than 14 volts, not enough to seriously hurt you if you accidentally touch a hot probe. However, you can damage the computer if you are not careful.

You can hurt yourself if you accidentally create a short circuit from the power supply to ground through the probe. If you touch the probe to the hot circuit and to ground, you divert current from the computer circuit and through the probe to ground. This short might be enough to cause a spark or to melt the probe, which can happen if you allow the two probes to touch while one of them is attached to the hot circuit and the other is attached to ground. Make sure the probes only touch one metal object, preferably only a single power pin on a connector, or you could cause a short.

Because of the danger of touching a hot probe to a ground probe, you might prefer not to put the black probe into a ground lead too close to the hot probe. Instead, when the directions say to place the black probe on a lead very close to the hot probe, you can use a black wire lead on an unused power supply connection meant for a hard drive. The idea is that the black probe should always be placed on a ground or black lead.

All ground leads are considered at ground, no matter what number they are assigned. Therefore, you can consider all black leads to be equal. For an AT motherboard, the ground leads for P8 and P9 are the four black center leads 5, 6, 7, and 8. For an ATX motherboard, the ground leads are seven black leads in center positions on the ATX P1 power connector. The ground leads for a hard drive power connection are the two black center leads, 2 and 3.

The following sections first discuss how to measure the power output for AT, ATX, and BTX motherboards and then discuss the procedure for a secondary storage device.

MEASURING VOLTAGE OUTPUT TO AN AT MOTHERBOARD

1. Remove the cover of the computer. The voltage range for each connection is often written on the top of the power supply. The two power connections to the motherboard are often labeled P8 and P9. Figure B-6 shows a close-up of the two connections, P8 and P9, coming from the power supply to the motherboard. Each connection has six leads, for a total of 12 leads. Of these 12, four are ground connections and lead 1 is a "power good" pin, used to indicate that the motherboard is receiving power. Table B-2 lists the purposes of these 12 leads.

2. Set the multimeter to measure voltage in a range of 20 volts, and set the AC/DC switch to DC. Insert the black probe into the negative (-) jack and the red probe into the positive (+) jack of the meter.

> **⚡ Caution**
>
> Be certain the multimeter is set to measure voltage and not current (amps). If the multimeter is set to measure current, you might damage the power supply or motherboard or both.

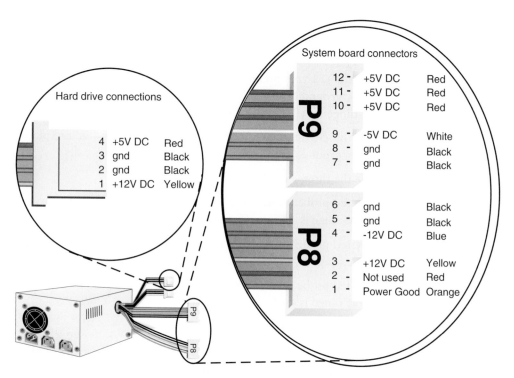

Figure B-6   AT power supply connections

Connection	Lead	Description	Acceptable Range
P8	1	"Power Good"	
	2	Not used or +5 volts	+4.4 to +5.2 volts
	3	+12 volts	+10.8 to +13.2 volts
	4	-12 volts	-10.8 to -13.2 volts
	5	Black ground	
	6	Black ground	
P9	7	Black ground	
	8	Black ground	
	9	-5 volts	-4.5 to -5.5 volts
	10	+5 volts	+4.5 to +5.5 volts
	11	+5 volts	+4.5 to +5.5 volts
	12	+5 volts	+4.5 to +5.5 volts

Table B-2   Twelve leads to the AT motherboard from the AT power supply

3. Turn on the multimeter and turn on the computer.

4. To measure the +12-volt circuit and all four ground leads:

   a. Place the red probe on lead 3. The probe is shaped like a needle. (Alligator clips don't work too well here.) Insert the needle down into the lead housing as far as you can. Place the black probe on lead 5. The acceptable range is +10.8 to +13.2 volts.

   b. Place the red probe on lead 3, and place the black probe on lead 6. The acceptable range is +10.8 to +13.2 volts.

   c. Place the red probe on lead 3, and place the black probe on lead 7. The acceptable range is +10.8 to +13.2 volts.

   d. Place the red probe on lead 3, and place the black probe on lead 8. The acceptable range is +10.8 to +13.2 volts.

5. To measure the -12-volt circuit, place the red probe on lead 4, and place the black probe on any ground lead or on the computer case, which is also grounded. The acceptable range is -10.8 to -13.2 volts.

6. To measure the -5-volt circuit, place the red probe on lead 9, and place the black probe on any ground. The acceptable range is -4.5 to -5.5 volts.

7. To measure the three +5-volt circuits:

   a. Place the red probe on lead 10, and place the black probe on any ground. The acceptable range is +4.5 to +5.5 volts.

   b. Place the red probe on lead 11, and place the black probe on any ground. The acceptable range is +4.5 to +5.5 volts.

   c. Place the red probe on lead 12, and place the black probe on any ground. The acceptable range is +4.5 to +5.5 volts.

8. Turn off the PC and replace the cover.

MEASURING VOLTAGE OUTPUT TO AN ATX MOTHERBOARD

To measure the output to the ATX motherboard, follow the procedure just described for the AT motherboard. Recall that the ATX board uses 3.3, 5, and 12 volts coming from the power supply. Figure B-7 shows the power output of each pin on the connector. Looking at Figure B-7, you can see the distinguishing shape of each side of the connector. Notice the different hole shapes (square or rounded) on each side of the connector, ensuring that the plug from the power supply is oriented correctly in the connector. Also notice the notch on the connector and on the pinout diagram on the right side of the figure. This notch helps orient you as you read the pinouts. You can also use the color of the wires coming from the power supply to each pin on the P1 connector to help orient the connector. Table B-3 lists the leads to the motherboard and their acceptable voltage ranges.

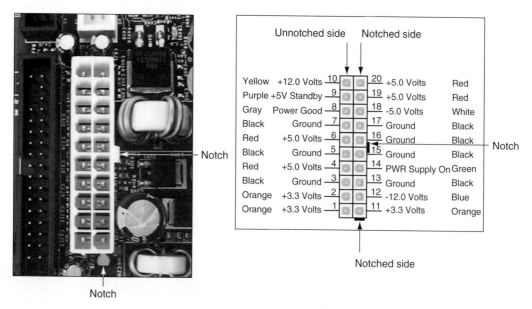

Figure B-7 Power connection on an ATX motherboard

Unnotched Side			Notched Side		
Lead	Description	Acceptable Range (Volts)	Lead	Description	Acceptable Range (Volts)
1	+3.3 volts	+3.1 to +3.5 V	11	+3.3 volts	+3.1 to +3.5 V
2	+3.3 volts	+3.1 to +3.5 V	12	-12 volts	-10.8 to -13.2 V
3	Black ground		13	Black ground	
4	+5 volts	+4.5 to +5.5 V	14	Power supply on	
5	Black ground		15	Black ground	
6	+5 volts	+4.5 to +5.5 V	16	Black ground	
7	Black ground		17	Black ground	
8	Power Good		18	-5 volts	-4.5 to -5.5 V
9	+5 volts standby	+4.5 to +5.5 V	19	+5 volts	+4.5 to +5.5 V
10	+12 volts	+10.8 to +13.2 V	20	+5 volts	+4.5 to +5.5 V

Table B-3 Twenty leads to the ATX motherboard from the ATX power supply

---

✎ Notes

Dell ATX power supplies and motherboards made after 1998 might not use the standard P1 pinouts for ATX, although the power connectors look the same. For this reason, never use a Dell power supply with a non-Dell motherboard, or a Dell motherboard with a non-Dell power supply, without first verifying that the power connector pinouts match; otherwise, you might destroy the power supply, the motherboard, or both. End PC Noise (*www.endpcnoise.com*) sells a pinout converter to convert the P1 connector of a Dell power supply or motherboard to standard ATX. Also, PC Power and Cooling (*www.pcpowerandcooling.com*) makes power supplies modified to work with a Dell motherboard.

MEASURING VOLTAGE OUTPUT TO AN ENHANCED ATX OR BTX MOTHERBOARD

An Enhanced ATX (ATX version 2.2) or BTX motherboard has a 24-pin P1 power connector, which is diagrammed in Figure B-8. The purposes for the pins for this power connector are listed in Table B-4. These motherboards and power supplies are designed so that the power supply monitors the range of voltages provided to the motherboard and halts the motherboard if voltages are inadequate. Therefore, measuring voltages for these systems is usually not necessary.

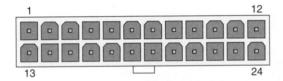

Figure B-8   Enhanced ATX or BTX 24-pin power connector on the motherboard

Unnotched Side			Notched Side		
Lead	**Description**	**Acceptable Range (Volts)**	**Lead**	**Description**	**Acceptable Range (Volts)**
1	+3.3 volts	3.2 to 3.5 V	13	+3.3 volts	3.2 to 3.5 V
2	+3.3 volts	3.2 to 3.5 V	14	-12 volts	-10.8 to -13.2 V
3	COM		15	COM	
4	+5 volts	4.75 to 5.25 V	16	PS ON	Power supply is on
5	COM		17	COM	
6	+5 volts	4.75 to 5.25 V	18	COM	
7	COM		19	COM	
8	Power OK	All voltages are in acceptable ranges	20	NC	
9	+5 volts	Standby voltage is always on	21	+5 volts	4.75 to 5.25 V
10	+12 volts	11.4 to 12.6 V	22	+5 volts	4.75 to 5.25 V
11	+12 volts	11.4 to 12.6 V	23	+5 volts	4.75 to 5.25 V
12	+3.3 volts	3.2 to 3.5 V	24	COM	

Table B-4   Twenty-four leads to the Enhanced ATX or BTX motherboard from the power supply

TESTING THE POWER OUTPUT TO A FLOPPY OR HARD DRIVE

The power cords to the hard drive, CD-ROM drive, floppy drive, and other drives all supply the same voltage: one +5-volt circuit and one +12-volt circuit. These connectors use four leads; the two outside connections are hot, and the two inside connections are ground (see Figure B-6). The power connection to a 3.5-inch floppy disk drive is usually a miniature connection, slightly smaller than other drive connections, but still with four pins. Follow these steps to measure the voltage to any drive:

1. With the drive plugged in, turn on the computer.

2. Set the multimeter to measure voltage, as described earlier.

3. Place the red probe on lead 1, shown in the drive connection callout in Figure B-6, and place the black probe on lead 2 or 3 (ground). The acceptable range is +10.8 to +13.2 volts.

4. Place the red probe on lead 4, and place the black probe on lead 2 or 3 (ground). The acceptable range is +4.5 to +5.5 volts.

You may choose to alter the method you use to ground the black probe. In Step 4, the red probe and black probe are very close to each other. You may choose to keep them farther apart by placing the black probe in a ground lead of an unused hard drive connection.

PRACTICING MEASURING THE OUTPUT OF YOUR POWER SUPPLY

To practice, measure the power output to your motherboard and to the hard drive. As you do so, fill in the following charts as appropriate. Note that the "red" and "black" designations in the column headers refer to the color of the physical probes.

AT MOTHERBOARD

Red Lead	Black Lead	Voltage Measure
3	5	
3	6	
3	7	
3	8	
4	Ground	
9	Ground	
10	Ground	
11	Ground	
12	Ground	

ATX MOTHERBOARD

Red Lead	Black Lead	Voltage Measure
10	7	
10	5	
10	3	
10	17	
10	16	
10	15	
10	13	
9	Ground	
6	Ground	
4	Ground	
2	Ground	
1	Ground	
20	Ground	
19	Ground	
18	Ground	
12	Ground	
11	Ground	

HARD DRIVE

Red Lead	Black Lead	Voltage Measure
1	3	
4	2	

Supporting SCSI and Legacy Devices

In Chapter 7, you were introduced to SCSI, an interface standard used by hard drives, CD and DVD drives, scanners, printers, and other devices. Because devices that use a SCSI interface are more expensive and more difficult to install than devices that use other interfaces, they are mostly used in corporate settings and are seldom seen in the small office or used on home PCs. SCSI is slowly being replaced by SATA, FireWire, and USB interfaces. However, because you may find yourself working with SCSI on older systems, the first half of this appendix discusses how SCSI technology works, as well as advantages and disadvantages of SCSI.

In Chapter 8, you learned how to install various external and internal devices using motherboard ports such as a USB port, serial port, or parallel port, and also using AGP, PCI, and PCI Express expansion slots. However, occasionally, as a PC repair technician, you'll be called on to install devices in the older ISA expansions slots. In addition, when supporting Windows 95 or Windows 98, you might have to use legacy 16-bit drivers for an ISA card or an external device that uses a serial or parallel port. The second half of this appendix covers supporting these older ISA cards and 16-bit drivers under Windows 95/98.

ALL ABOUT SCSI

The two general categories of all SCSI standards used on PCs have to do with the width in bits of the SCSI data bus, either 8 bits (narrow SCSI) or 16 bits (wide SCSI). In almost every case, if the SCSI standard is 16 bits, then the word *wide* is in the name for the standard. In most cases, the word *narrow* is not mentioned in names for 8-bit standards. Narrow SCSI uses a cable with a 50-pin connector (also called an A cable), and wide SCSI uses a cable with a 68-pin connector (also called a P cable).

> ✎ **Notes**
>
> The wide SCSI specification allows for a data path of 32 bits, although this is not broadly implemented in PCs. When you see a SCSI device referred to as wide, you can generally assume 16 bits.

SIGNALING METHODS USED ON SCSI CABLES

A SCSI cable can be built in two different ways, depending on the method by which the electrical signal is placed on the cable: single-ended and differential. Both types of cables send a signal on a pair of twisted wires. In single-ended (SE) cables, one of the wires carries voltage and the other is a ground; in differential cables, both wires carry voltage and the signal is calculated to be the difference between the two voltages (see Figure C-1).

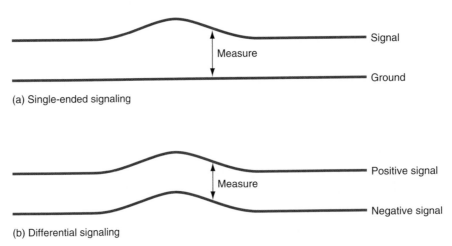

(a) Single-ended signaling

(b) Differential signaling

Figure C-1 A SCSI pair of wires can carry a signal using (a) ground and a signal, or (b) a positive and negative signal, but differential signaling is less likely to be affected by noise on the line

A single-ended cable is less expensive than a differential cable, but the maximum cable length cannot be as long because data integrity is not as great. With differential cabling, signal accuracy is better; noise on the line and electromagnetic interference are less likely to affect signaling because the reading is the difference between the two signals rather than the amplitude of one signal. Differential signaling also sends an extra verifying signal for each bit, providing greater reliability and reducing the chance of data errors.

When differential signaling was first introduced, the difference in voltage between the two wires was high (called High Voltage Differential, or HVD). This required a large amount of power and circuitry and made it impossible to mix differential and single-ended devices on a system without burning out the hardware. HVD became obsolete with the introduction of the SCSI-3 standard. The introduction of Low Voltage Differential (LVD) signaling and termination made it possible to develop less expensive, low-voltage interfaces on the device, host adapter, cables, and terminators. As its name implies, LVD signaling uses lower voltages on the two-wire pair. It provides for cable lengths up to 12 meters (about 39.4 feet) and is required with Ultra SCSI standards. There is a type of LVD signaling called LVD/SE multimode that can work with SE devices and cables. If an LVD/SE device is used on a bus with SE devices, it uses the SE signaling method, which is slower and cannot accommodate longer cable lengths. Table C-1 lists and describes the four types of cables.

SCSI Cable	Maximum Length (meters and feet)	Maximum Speed	Transfer Rate	Description
Single-ended (SE)	3 M (10 ft.) for wide or 6 M (20 ft.) for narrow SCSI	20 MHz	40 Mbps	One wire in the pair is ground.
High voltage differential (HVD)	25 M (82 ft.)	20 or 40 MHz	40 Mbps	Both wires in the pair have high voltage.
Low voltage differential (LVD)	12 M (40 ft.) for 15 devices or 25 M (80 ft.) for 7 devices	320 MHz	80 Mbps	Both wires in the pair have low voltage.
LVD/SE multimode				If one SE device is on the bus, the smaller length and speed apply.

Table C-1   SCSI cables

Cables for both narrow SCSI and wide SCSI can be either single-ended or differential. Single-ended, HVD, and LVD cables look the same, so you must make sure that you use the correct cable. It's important to know that you cannot look at a cable, the cable connector, or the connector on a device and know what type of signaling it uses. Connecting an HVD device to a SCSI bus using SE or LVD devices could burn the SE or LVD devices with the high voltage from the HVD device. Look at the device documentation to learn what type of signaling a device uses, or look for a symbol on the device that indicates the signaling method. Figure C-2 shows the different symbols used on devices and cables to show what kind of signaling they use.

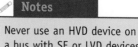

Notes

Never use an HVD device on a bus with SE or LVD devices, because the high voltage put on the cable by the HVD device can destroy the low-voltage devices.

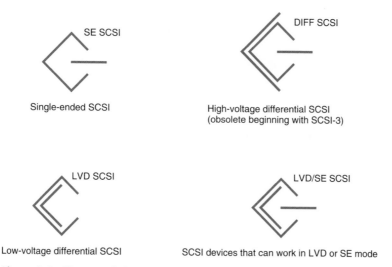

SE SCSI

Single-ended SCSI

DIFF SCSI

High-voltage differential SCSI
(obsolete beginning with SCSI-3)

LVD SCSI

Low-voltage differential SCSI

LVD/SE SCSI

SCSI devices that can work in LVD or SE mode

Figure C-2   These symbols tell what type of signaling a device or cable uses

Adapters are available for mixing single-ended and differential devices and cables, but using them is not recommended. Mixing single-ended and differential signaling types is not a good idea because of the different ways they transmit data. Even with adapters, incompatible connections between single-ended and differential signals can damage both the host adapter and the devices connected to it. An exception to this principle is LVD/SE devices designed to work with either LVD or SE and revert to SE mode whenever the two are connected. Even then, however, know that the device is running at a slower speed than it could run if connected to an all-LVD signaling system, and that all cables in the system must meet the shorter SE standard lengths.

CONNECTORS USED WITH SCSI CABLES

The connector type or the number of pins on a SCSI cable connector are not affected by the signaling method used. Within each signaling method, the number of pins can vary. Figure C-3 shows just a few of the many types of SCSI connectors. Although there are two main types of SCSI connectors, 50-pin (A cable) and 68-pin (P cable), there are other, less common types as well, such as the 80-pin SCA (Single Connector Attachment) connector used with some hot-swapping drives. Only 80-pin connectors supply power to the device in the connector; other devices require separate power connections. A SCSI bus can support more than one type of connector, and you can use connector adapters in order to plug a cable with one type of connector into a port using another type of connector.

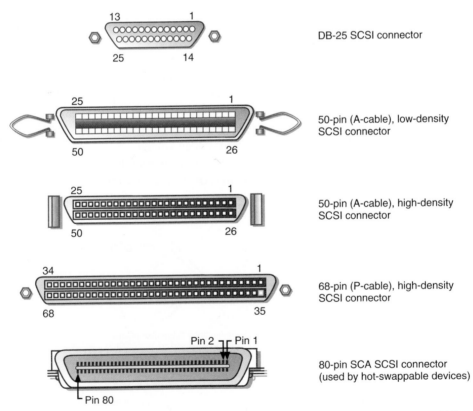

Figure C-3   The most popular SCSI connectors are 50-pin, A cable connectors for narrow SCSI and 68-pin, P cable connectors for wide SCSI

For each type of connector, there can be variations in shape and pin density. Different companies and device manufacturers can make different connector types. For example, in an attempt to trim the size of the connector, a 25-pin SCSI connector was designed for narrow SCSI. The problem was that this connector looked like a parallel port connector. Never plug a SCSI connector into a parallel port or vice versa; you can damage equipment, because the signals work completely differently.

The good news in all this variety is that adapters are generally available to connect one type of connector to another, meaning that you can mix wide and narrow SCSI devices that use different connector variations. If you have any wide devices on your system at all, the cable from the host adapter must have a 68-pin connector, and you will need to use converters to attach 50-pin narrow devices.

Most recent SCSI devices and buses use D-shaped 50-pin or 68-pin connectors that cannot be plugged in incorrectly. Older 50-pin connectors did not have this shape and could be oriented incorrectly. To line up a 50-pin connector to an internal SCSI device, look for a red or blue stripe on one side of the cable; this stripe lines up with pin 1 on the connector. Look also for a tab on one edge of the connector and a corresponding notch where you are to insert it.

The SCSI bus inside a computer is a ribbon or round cable, and the device connectors for internal devices are plugs at different positions on the cable. Having multiple connectors on the SCSI bus (see Figure C-4) enables you to connect multiple internal devices easily. One end of the bus attaches to the host adapter, and for best results, you should always plug a device into the last connector on the cable.

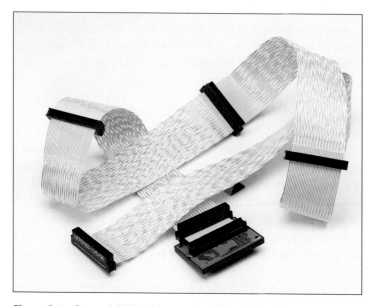

Figure C-4 Internal SCSI cables can be ribbon cables or round cables and can support several devices. This 68-pin ribbon cable by Adaptec supports single-ended and LVD connections.

For external SCSI chains, there are two connectors on each device; both can send or receive information. That means it doesn't matter which connector on one device is linked to which connector on the next. A cable goes from the host adapter to a connector on the first device, and then another cable goes from the second connector on the first device to a connector on the second device, and so on. The last connector on the last device must be filled with a terminator, unless that device provides software termination. External SCSI chains work like some Christmas lights: if one goes out, they all go out. Therefore, when connecting devices in an external SCSI chain, you should make sure to snap in the retaining clips or wires to complete the connection.

TERMINATION

Termination prevents an echo effect from electrical noise and reflected data at the end of the SCSI daisy chain, which can cause interference with data transmission. Each end of a SCSI chain must be terminated, and there are several ways to do that:

- ▲ The host adapter can have a switch setting that activates or deactivates a terminating resistor on the card, depending on whether or not the adapter is at one end of the chain.
- ▲ A device can have either a single SCSI connection requiring that the device be placed at the end of the chain, or the device can have two connections. When a device has two connections, the second connection can be used to connect another device or to terminate the chain by placing an external terminator on the connection. This external terminator serves as the terminating resistor.
- ▲ The device at the end of the chain can also be terminated by a resistor physically mounted on that device in a specially designated socket.
- ▲ Some devices have built-in terminators (internal terminators) that you can turn on or off with a jumper setting on the device.
- ▲ Termination can be controlled by software. Sometimes this software uses automatic termination that does not require your intervention.

Termination is needed at the end of both internal and external SCSI chains. If the host adapter is at the end of the SCSI chain, it must be terminated. Only when you have both internal and external devices attached to a host adapter do you remove termination from the host adapter.

There are several types of terminators:

- ▲ Passive terminators, the least reliable type, are used with SCSI-1 devices that operate at low speed and at short distances. They use simple resistors only and are rarely used today, because they are not sufficient for today's faster SCSI devices and longer cabling distances. Passive termination should only be used with narrow SCSI.
- ▲ Active terminators include voltage regulators in addition to the simple resistors used with passive termination. Most of today's single-ended SCSI cables use active termination, which was recommended with SCSI-2. Active termination is used with wide SCSI and is required with fast SCSI. It also works better over longer distances than passive termination.
- ▲ Forced perfect terminators (FPTs) are a more advanced version of active terminators and include a mechanism to force signal termination to the correct voltage, eliminating most signal echoes and interference. FPTs are more expensive and more reliable than passive and active terminators.

Passive terminators, active terminators, and FPTs are all used with single-ended SCSI cables. Differential cables use either HVD or LVD terminators.

SCSI-1, SCSI-2, AND SCSI-3

Recall that the three major versions of SCSI are SCSI-1, SCSI-2, and SCSI-3, commonly known as Regular SCSI, Fast SCSI, and Ultra SCSI. SCSI-1 was the original version of the SCSI standard. It covered the design of wiring on the SCSI bus but did not include a common command set. Therefore, there were still a lot of incompatibilities between SCSI-1 devices. With SCSI-1, only an 8-bit data bus was used, and there could be only seven devices besides the host adapter.

SCSI-2 improved the standard by developing a common command set so that devices could communicate with each other more easily. It also introduced wide SCSI, which expanded the width of the data bus to 16 bits and the number of possible devices to 15. SCSI-2 also made parity checking of the data bus mandatory.

SCSI-3, which has grown to be a set of standards rather than a single standard, supports both parallel and serial data transmission, supports FireWire connections, and increases the possible rate of data transfer to 320 MB/sec and higher. The SPI (SCSI Parallel Interface) standard is part of SCSI-3 and specifies how SCSI devices are connected. There have been three versions of SPI; the latest is Ultra 320 SCSI. SCSI-3 uses an 8-, 16-, or 32-bit data bus and supports up to 32 devices on a system.

Because SCSI standards vary, when you buy a new SCSI device, you must be sure that it is compatible with the SCSI bus you already have, taking into consideration that some SCSI standards are backward-compatible. If the new SCSI device is not compatible, you cannot use the same SCSI bus, and you must buy a new host adapter to build a second SCSI bus system, increasing the overall cost of adding the new device.

Table C-2 summarizes characteristics of the different SCSI standards. Other names used in the industry for these standards are also listed in the table. Note that both Fast SCSI (SCSI-2) and Ultra SCSI (SCSI-3) have narrow and wide versions.

Standard Name	Standard Number	Bus Width (Narrow = 8 bits, Wide = 16 bits)	Transfer Rate (MB/sec)	Maximum Number of Devices
Regular SCSI	SCSI-1	Narrow	5	8
Fast SCSI or Fast Narrow	SCSI-2	Narrow	10	8
Fast Wide SCSI or Wide SCSI	SCSI-2	Wide	20	16
Ultra SCSI, Ultra Narrow, or Fast-20 SCSI	SCSI-3	Narrow	20	8
Wide Ultra SCSI or Fast Wide 20	SCSI-3	Wide	40	16
Ultra2 SCSI or SPI-2	SCSI-3	Narrow	40	8
Wide Ultra2 SCSI	SCSI-3	Wide	80	16
Ultra3 SCSI or SPI-3	SCSI-3	Narrow	80	8
Wide Ultra3 SCSI or Ultra 160 SCSI	SCSI-3	Wide	160	16
Ultra 320 SCSI (Ultra4 SCSI or SPI-4)	SCSI-3	Wide	320*	16

*SPI-4 is expected to soon be rated at 640 MBps and then 1280 MBps.

Table C-2 Summary of SCSI standards

Notes

The latest SCSI standard, serial SCSI, also called serial attached SCSI (SAS), allows for more than 15 devices on a single SCSI chain, uses smaller, longer, round cables, and uses smaller hard drive form factors that can support larger capacities. Serial SCSI is compatible with serial ATA drives in the same system, and claims to be more reliable and better performing than serial ATA. For more information on serial SCSI, see the SCSI Trade Association's Web site at *www.serialattachedscsi.com*.

Table C-3 summarizes cable specifications for the SCSI standards listed in Table C-2. Note that 8-bit narrow SCSI uses a 50-pin cable and 16-bit wide SCSI uses a 68-pin cable.

SCSI Standard Name	Maximum Length of Single-Ended Cable (Meters)	Maximum Length of Differential Cable (Meters)	Cable Type
Regular SCSI	6	25	50-pin
Fast SCSI or Fast Narrow	3	25	50-pin
Fast Wide SCSI or Wide SCSI	3	25	68-pin
Ultra SCSI, Ultra Narrow, or Fast-20 SCSI	1.5	25	50-pin
Wide Ultra SCSI or Fast Wide 20	1.5	25	68-pin
Ultra2 SCSI or SPI-2		12 LVD	50-pin
Wide Ultra2 SCSI			68-pin
Ultra3 SCSI or SPI-3		12 LVD	50-pin
Wide Ultra3 SCSI or Ultra 160 SCSI		12 LVD	68-pin
Ultra 320 SCSI (Ultra4 SCSI or SPI-4)		12 LVD	68-pin

Table C-3   SCSI standard cable specifications

USING ISA EXPANSION SLOTS

Using legacy ISA expansion slots is a little more difficult than using PCI slots because the configuration is not as automated. The ISA bus itself does not manage system resources, as does the PCI bus controller. It is up to the ISA device to request system resources at startup. If the ISA device does not support Plug and Play (PnP), you select the I/O address, DMA channel, and IRQ by setting jumpers or DIP switches on the card. If the ISA device is PnP-compliant, then at startup, PnP allocates the required resources to the device. After the device and its drivers are installed, look at Device Manager to find out what resources it is using.

 A+ Tip

To discover if a device is PnP-compliant, look for "Ready for Windows" on the box or read the documentation.

When adding a legacy ISA expansion card to a system, the most difficult problems you are likely to encounter are resource conflicts between two legacy devices or problems using legacy device drivers. For example, suppose you install a legacy network card in a system, and the card does not work and the modem card has stopped working. Most likely you have a resource conflict. The tool to use for help in resolving hardware conflicts in Windows is Device Manager.

Follow this general approach when installing a legacy device:

Notes

Device Manager is not infallible because it depends on what the OS knows about resources being used, and sometimes a legacy device does not tell the OS what it is using.

1. Recall that Windows 95 and 98 allow legacy 16-bit drivers, but Windows Me and Windows 2000/XP do not. For Windows Me or Windows 2000/XP, search the manufacturer's Web site for 32-bit drivers. If you cannot find them, the device will not work in this system.

2. Know the system resources already in use. See the documentation for devices already installed, use Device Manager, or try both. It's important to keep a notebook dedicated to your PC, in which you keep records of each device and its present settings, as well as any changes you make to your system.

3. Know what resources the device will need (see the documentation). Install the device using resources that are not already used by your system. If the device is set to use a resource already in use, read the documentation to see if you can set a jumper or DIP switch to use an alternate resource. For example, Figure C-5 shows a diagram of a modem card pictured in Figure C-6. The card has a bank of DIP switches on the back of the card and a bank of jumpers on the card itself. By using combinations of these DIP switches and jumpers, you can configure this modem to use a specific set of IRQ and I/O addresses.

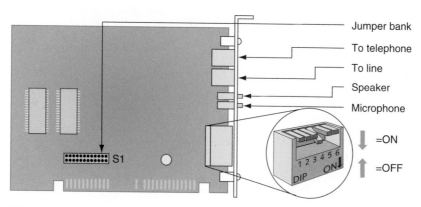

Figure C-5 Diagram of a modem card

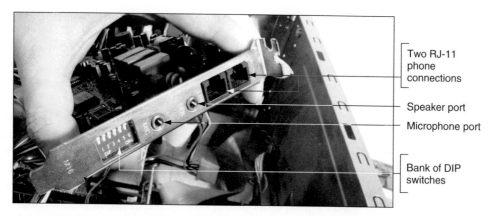

Figure C-6 Ports and DIP switches on the back of an internal legacy modem

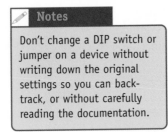

Notes

Don't change a DIP switch or jumper on a device without writing down the original settings so you can backtrack, or without carefully reading the documentation.

4. If a card does not work after you install it, try reseating the card in the slot or using a different slot.
5. If the device still does not work or another device stops working, suspect a resource conflict. If you do have a conflict, use Device Manager, CMOS setup, and documentation for the motherboard and devices to first identify and then resolve the conflict. To find out what resources your system is using for Windows 9x/Me, follow Step 6.

6. Click **Start**, point to Settings, click **Control Panel, System**, and then click **Device Manager**. Click **Computer** and then **Properties**. Select the **View Resources** tab. The window in Figure C-7 is displayed. From it, you can view current assignments for IRQs, I/O addresses, DMA channels, and upper memory addresses.

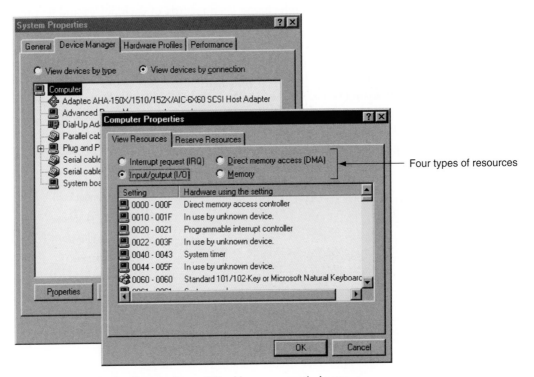

Figure C-7   Use Device Manager to see I/O addresses currently in use

After you have found the conflicting resource, try the following to resolve the conflict:

1. If the device is a legacy ISA device, physically set the device's jumpers or DIP switches to use a different resource.
2. If a legacy device can only use one IRQ, use CMOS setup to reserve that IRQ for the device.
3. If your BIOS supports PCI bus IRQ steering, enable the feature. That alone might solve the problem. In Device Manager, go to the device's Properties dialog box, click the **IRQ Steering** tab, and check **Use IRQ Steering**. Windows 9x/Me is then allowed to assign the IRQ based on what it knows about IRQs currently being used.
4. Using PCI bus IRQ steering, tell Windows 98 to use a different IRQ for a PCI device. To do that, use the Properties dialog box for the device in Device Manager.
5. Move the device to a different slot. Use the slot closest to the CPU, if you can.

6. Disable PCI bus IRQ steering.
7. Suspect that the documentation for the device is wrong, that the device is faulty, or that there is a problem with the motherboard or the OS. Try a new device in this system, or try this device in another working system.

Sometimes the problem might be that an ISA card can use only a certain IRQ, but that IRQ is not available. When ISA slots and PCI slots exist on the same motherboard, know that the PCI controller is managing the IRQ assignments. These IRQs are the ones left over after legacy ISA bus devices claim their IRQs. However, sometimes BIOS gives the PCI bus controller an IRQ that a legacy ISA device needs, which can prevent either device from working. You can counteract this conflict by going into CMOS setup, where you can specify which IRQ to assign to a PCI slot. You can also tell setup that a particular IRQ is reserved for a legacy device, and thereby prevent the PCI bus from using it, as shown in Figure C-8.

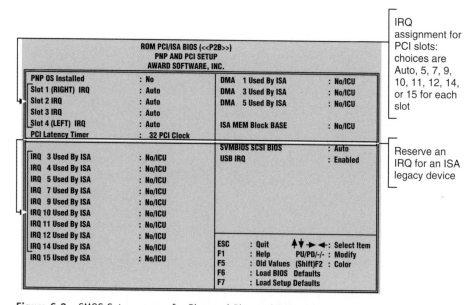

Figure C-8   CMOS Setup screen for Plug and Play and PCI options

USING LEGACY DRIVERS

Windows 9x/Me contains 32-bit drivers for hundreds of hardware devices, and even more are provided by the device manufacturers. However, some older legacy devices, including ISA cards and external devices that use serial or parallel ports, do not have 32-bit drivers. In this situation, for Windows 95/98, you are forced to use a 16-bit, real-mode device driver. These 16-bit drivers are loaded by entries in the Config.sys, Autoexec.bat, or System.ini file and probably use upper memory addresses.

If you decide to install 16-bit drivers, be sure to back up these files before you begin the installation. Then run a setup program on the floppy disk or CD provided with the device. Next, use the Run dialog box or double-click the program filename in Explorer. The setup program copies the driver files to the hard drive and adds the DEVICE= command to Config.sys. In addition, it might make entries in Autoexec.bat, or, for drivers written for Windows 3.x, it might make entries in System.ini. After you have verified that the device is working, note the changes made to Autoexec.bat, Config.sys, and System.ini. You might want to keep a record of the commands the setup program put in these files, in case you need it for future troubleshooting.

If you have problems with installing or running a legacy driver, do the following:

1. Make every effort to locate a 32-bit driver for the device. Check the Microsoft Web site at *support.microsoft.com*, and check the device manufacturer's Web site. Use a search engine to search the Web for shareware drivers.
2. If you cannot find 32-bit drivers, create an empty copy of Autoexec.bat and Config.sys on your hard drive. Boot up into MS-DOS mode and run the 16-bit setup program from the command prompt. Look at the entries it puts into Autoexec.bat and Config.sys and copy these command lines into your original versions of Autoexec.bat and Config.sys.

APPENDIX D

Disassembling a Notebook

If you enjoy putting together a thousand-piece jigsaw puzzle, you'll probably enjoy working on notebook computers. With desktop systems, replacing a component is not a time-consuming task, but with notebooks, the job could take several hours. This appendix gives you some tips and procedures to help make your work easier.

If you take the time to carefully examine the notebook's case before attempting to open it, you will probably find markings provided by the manufacturer to assist you in locating components that are commonly upgraded. If you have a service manual, your work will be much easier than without one. However, after a little practice, you'll see that notebook assemblies have some things in common and disassembling one gets easier with experience.

The best way to learn to disassemble a notebook is to practice on an old one that you can afford to break. Find an old Dell or IBM ThinkPad for which you can download the service manual from the Dell (*www.dell.com*) or IBM Web sites (*www.ibm.com* or *www.lenovo.com*). Then carefully and patiently follow the disassembly instructions and then reassemble it. When done, you can congratulate yourself and move on to newer notebooks. One advantage of starting out this way is that the older notebooks are often more difficult to disassemble than the newer ones. By starting with an older one, you learn skills that will make disassembling a new notebook much easier. One caution is worth repeating: Always make sure the notebook you are disassembling is not under warranty. You don't want to void that warranty.

When disassembling a notebook, consider the following tips, which are also covered in Chapter 11:

- ▲ Take your time. Patience is needed to keep from scratching or marring plastic screw covers, hinges, and the case.
- ▲ As you work, don't force anything. If you find yourself forcing something, you're likely to break it.
- ▲ Always wear a ground strap or use other protection against ESD.
- ▲ When removing cables, know that sometimes cable connectors are ZIF connectors. To disconnect a cable from a ZIF connector, first lift up the sides of the connector, which releases the cable from the connector, and then remove the cable.
- ▲ Use a dental pick or very small screwdriver to pry up the plastic cover hiding a screw. Screws around the LCD panel and keyboard are often hidden beneath plastic circles pasted on top of the screw. This plastic can easily be damaged or lost.

DISASSEMBLING AN OLDER THINKPAD

As a general rule, the older the notebook is, the more difficult it will be to disassemble, and the ThinkPad is no exception. Fortunately, though, the older IBM ThinkPad 755c notebook, which uses a 486 processor, uses some disassembly procedures that are typical to several older notebooks. Generally, follow these steps to disassemble the notebook:

1. The easy-to-get-to drives and battery pack are hidden under the keyboard. Release the spring latches on both sides of the keyboard and raise it. You can then use a ribbon or handle connected to the battery, hard drive, and floppy drive to remove each (see Figure D-1).

Figure D-1 Raise the keyboard as a lid, which exposes drives and the battery inside the case

2. To remove the keyboard, pry up the black plastic covers near the keyboard hinges, and remove the screws under these covers, which allows you to then remove the keyboard hinges. Next, remove the plastic cover at the top of the keyboard, which exposes the three cable connectors for the keyboard (see Figure D-2). Disconnect these three ZIF connectors by first using a small screwdriver or dental pick to raise the sides of the connector, which releases pressure on the cable. Then remove the cable.

3. This notebook uses a DRAM credit card memory module. The module is removed by sliding it out of its motherboard slot (see Figure D-3).

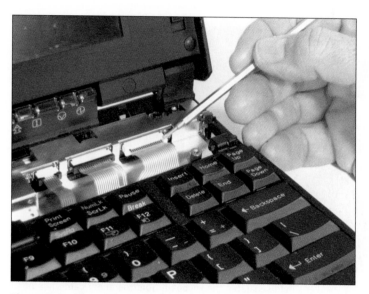

Figure D-2 Three ZIF connectors hold the three keyboard cables in place

Figure D-3 Remove the DRAM memory module

4. To remove the modem card, audio card, or DC controller card, you must first remove a speaker shield located just under the top half of the keyboard (see Figure D-4). The shield is secured with 10 screws. Remove the screws and then the shield. Take care to record where each screw goes because they are not all the same size.

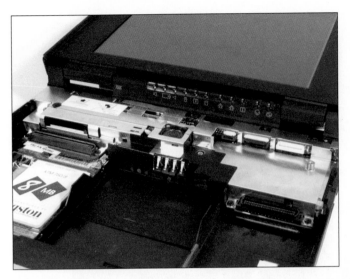

Figure D-4   A speaker shield separates the keyboard from the audio card underneath

5. The audio card is now exposed. Lift it up, gently disconnecting it from its slot on the motherboard (see Figure D-5). Then disconnect the audio cable.

Figure D-5   Remove the audio card and then disconnect the audio cable

6. If you need to remove the DC controller, first remove the LCD panel assembly, which is rather tedious because the LCD panel is connected to the motherboard by several small wires and cables. After they are removed, the DC controller is exposed and can be removed by first removing two screws and a bracket that hold it in place.

7. Next, the backup and standby batteries can be removed and then the motherboard. (These batteries are covered in the next section.) The motherboard comes out of the case with the rear panel assembly still connected (see Figure D-6). The PCMCIA slot assembly is then exposed and can be removed.

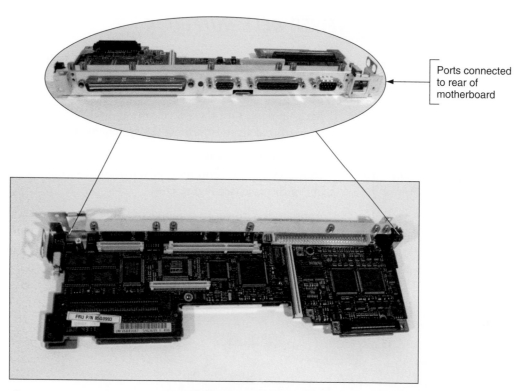

Ports connected
to rear of
motherboard

Figure D-6 The motherboard is removed from the case with the rear panel assembly connected, which can then be removed

This notebook is one of the more difficult to disassemble. Figure D-7 shows all parts ready to be reassembled in reverse order.

> 📝 **Notes**
>
> After assembling a notebook, before powering it up, turn the notebook upside down a couple of times and listen for any rattles that might indicate a loose screw, spring, or other small part. If you hear any rattles, disassemble the notebook and correct the problem.

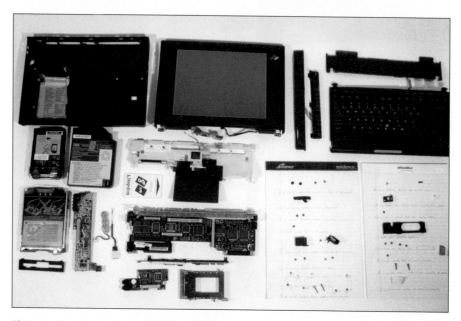

Figure D-7 Notebook parts disassembled

DISASSEMBLING A NEWER DELL NOTEBOOK

In this next example, we'll disassemble a Pentium II notebook, the Dell Latitude CPi. This notebook is more typical of newer notebooks because there are not so many small brackets and screws.

> **Notes**
>
> If you plan to disassemble a Dell Latitude computer, download the entire service manual from the Dell Web site so that you will have the complete details of the procedures. In this appendix, to conserve space, some details have been omitted.

1. Back up data, turn the system off, and remove the battery pack. Put on a ground strap to protect the system against ESD.

2. Remove the hard drive by turning the computer over and removing two screws on the bottom near the hard drive door. Then pull the drive out of the case (see Figure D-8).

3. Another easy-to-get-to component is the memory card. First remove the plate on the bottom of the computer. Then gently push the two clips outward on each side of the memory card. Rotate it up and out of the slot (see Figure D-9).

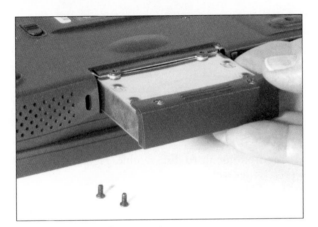

Figure D-8   Remove the hard drive by first removing two screws that hold the drive in place

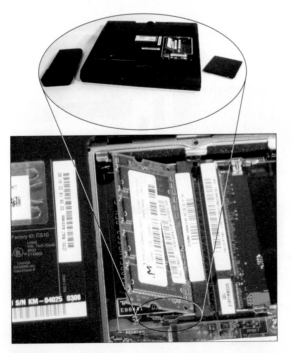

Figure D-9   Remove the memory module card by first releasing clips on both sides of the card

4. You can now open the case. Figure D-10 shows the order of components to be removed. First, on the bottom of the computer, remove six screws that hold the keyboard to the case.

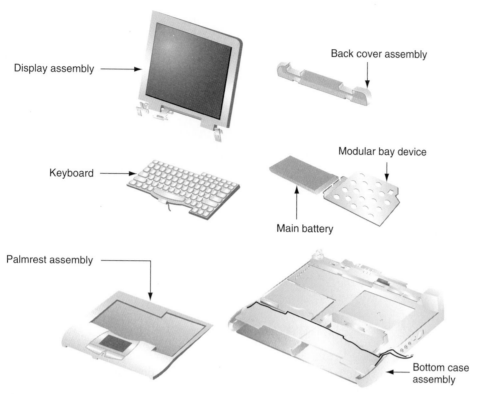

Display assembly

Back cover assembly

Keyboard

Modular bay device

Main battery

Palmrest assembly

Bottom case assembly

Figure D-10 Exploded view of Dell Latitude notebook

5. Next, push the latches on the palm rest assembly outward to release the assembly from the keyboard.

6. Insert a small screwdriver under the edge of the blank key on the right edge of the keyboard and push up on the keyboard (see Figure D-11). Lift the keyboard up and out.

Figure D-11 Pry up the keyboard using a screwdriver on the right of the keyboard

7. The rear assembly is removed next. To do that, remove the 12 screws on each side of a port and on the right and left sides of the back cover. The back cover can then be removed (see Figure D-12).

Figure D-12 Twelve screws hold the back cover in place

8. The palm rest assembly is removed next by first disconnecting the touch pad cable from the ZIF connector, removing six screws that hold the assembly in place, and then removing the assembly itself.

9. The display assembly is removed next. Its components are shown in Figure D-13. First remove the grounding screw from the LCD interface cable and disconnect the interface cable from the connector on the motherboard. Close the display.

10. Remove the four hinge screws, two on each side, and lift the display assembly from the case.

11. To disassemble the LCD panel assembly, first remove the four screws along the top of the assembly and the two screws on the bottom (refer to Figure D-13). Be certain to keep track of which screw goes where; they are not all the same size.

12. Separate the front bezel from the LCD panel by first prying them apart slightly. You can then see hidden snaps holding them together. Release the hidden snaps and remove the bezel.

 Caution

As you work, be careful to not put pressure on the LCD panel. If it breaks, and fluid gets on your skin or in your eyes, run water over your skin or eyes for at least 15 minutes.

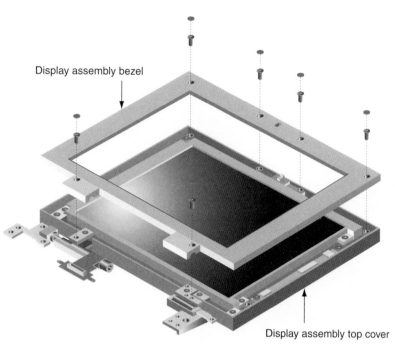

Figure D-13 Exploded LCD panel assembly

13. Next, remove the audio card (see Figure D-14). To do that, remove the screw holding the speaker shield in place and then remove the shield. Next, disconnect the audio wires and microphone wires from the audio board, and lift the audio board from the case.

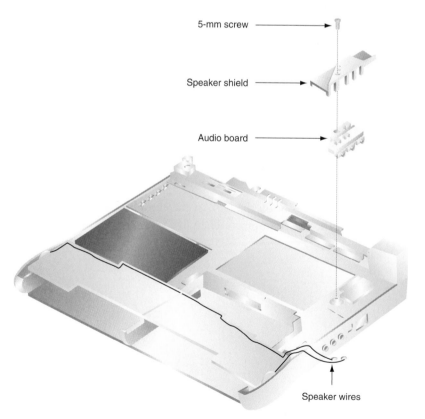

Figure D-14 To remove the audio board, first remove the speaker shield

14. The motherboard is removed next (see Figure D-15). First remove the two screws holding the thermal cooling assembly in place and then remove the assembly, which is on top of the processor. Then remove the air flow duct.

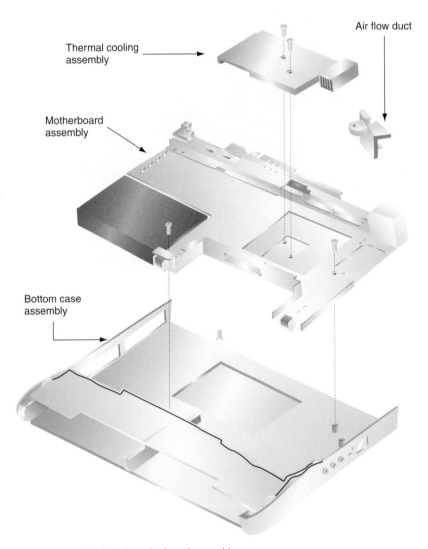

Air flow duct

Thermal cooling assembly

Motherboard assembly

Bottom case assembly

Figure D-15 Exploded motherboard assembly

15. Remove the left rear foot on the base of the computer and then remove the two screws holding the motherboard in place. Then lift it out of the case.

CompTIA A+ Acronyms

CompTIA provides a list of acronyms which you need to know before you sit for the A+ exams. You can download the list from the CompTIA Web site at *www.comptia.org*. The list is included here for your convenience. However, CompTIA occasionally updates the list, so be sure to check the CompTIA Web site for the latest version.

Acronym	Spelled Out
AC	alternating current
ACPI	advanced configuration and power interface
ACT	activity
ADSL	asymmetrical digital subscriber line
AGP	accelerated graphics port
AMD	advanced micro devices
AMR	audio modem riser
APIPA	automatic private Internet protocol addressing
ARP	address resolution protocol
ASR	automated system recovery
AT	advanced technology
ATA	advanced technology attachment
ATAPI	advanced technology attachment packet interface
ATM	asynchronous transfer mode
ATX	advanced technology extended
BIOS	basic input/output system
BNC	Bayonet-Neill-Concelman or British navel connector
BRI	basic rate interface
BTX	balanced technology extended
CD	compact disc
CD-ROM	compact disc-read-only memory
CD-RW	compact disc-rewritable
CDFS	compact disc file system
CGA	color/graphics adapter
CMOS	complementary metal-oxide semiconductor
COM1	communication port 1
CPU	central processing unit
CRIMM	continuity-Rambus inline memory module
CRT	cathode-ray tube
DB-25	serial communications D-shell connector, 25 pins
DC	direct current
DDR	double data-rate
DDR RAM	double data-rate random access memory
DDR SDRAM	double data-rate symmetric dynamic random access memory
DFS	distributed file system
DHCP	dynamic host configuration protocol
DIMM	dual inline memory module
DIN	Deutsche Industrie Norm
DIP	dual inline package

Acronym	Spelled Out
DMA	direct memory access
DNS	domain name service or domain name server
DOS	disk operating system
DB-9	9-pin D shell connector
DRAM	dynamic random access memory
DSL	digital subscriber line
DVD	digital video disc
DVD-RAM	digital versatile disc-random access memory
DVD-ROM	digital video disc-read only memory
DVD-R	digital video disc-recordable
DVD-RW	digital video disc-rewritable
DVI	digital visual interface
ECC	error correction code
ECP	extended capabilities port
EDO SDRAM	extended data out symmetric dynamic random access memory
EEPROM	electrically erasable programmable read-only memory
EFS	encrypting file system
EGA	enhanced graphics adapter
EIDE	enhanced integrated drive electronics
EISA	extended industry standard architecture
EMI	electromagnetic interference
ENET	Ethernet
EPP	enhanced parallel port
ERD	emergency repair disk
ESD	electrostatic discharge
ESDI	enhanced small device interface
EVGA	extended video graphics adapter/array
EVDO	evolution data optimized or evolution data only
FAT	file allocation table
FAT12	12-bit file allocation table
FAT16	16-bit file allocation table
FAT32	32-bit file allocation table
FCC	Federal Communications Commission
FDD	floppy disk drive
FERPA	Family Educational Rights and Privacy Act
FPM	fast page-mode
FPM SDRAM	fast page-mode symmetric dynamic random access memory
FRU	field replaceable unit
FTP	file transfer protocol

Acronym	Spelled Out
GB	gigabyte
GDI	graphics device interface
GHz	gigahertz
GUI	graphical user interface
GRPS	general radio packet system
GSM	global system manager or graphics size modification or graphics screen manager
HCL	hardware compatibility list
HDD	hard disk drive
HDMi	high definition media interface
HPFS	high performance file system
HTML	hypertext markup language
HTTP	hypertext transfer protocol
HTTPS	hypertext transfer protocol over secure sockets layer
I/O	input/output
ICMP	Internet control message protocol
ICS	Internet connection sharing
IDE	integrated drive electronics
IEEE	Institute of Electrical and Electronics Engineers
IIS	Internet information server
IMAP	Internet mail access protocol
IP	Internet protocol
IPSEC	Internet protocol security
IPX	internetwork packet exchange
IPX/SPX	internetwork packet exchange/sequenced packet exchange
IR	infrared
IrDA	Infrared Data Association
IRQ	interrupt request
ISA	industry standard architecture
ISDN	integrated services digital network
ISO	Industry Standards Organization
ISP	Internet service provider
KB	kilobyte
LAN	local area network
LAT	local area transport
LCD	liquid crystal display
LED	light emitting diode
LPT	line printer terminal
LPT1	line printer terminal 1
LPX	low profile extended

Acronym	Spelled Out
LVD	low voltage differential
MAC	media access control
MAN	metropolitan area network
Mb	megabit
MB	megabyte
MBR	master boot record
MCA	micro channel architecture
MHz	megahertz
MicroDIMM	micro dual inline memory module
MIDI	musical instrument digital interface
MLI	multiple link interface
MMC	Microsoft management console
MMX	multimedia extensions
MP3	Moving Picture Experts Group Layer 3 Audio
MPEG	Moving Picture Experts Group
MSDS	material safety data sheet
MUI	multilingual user interface
NAS	network-attached storage
NAT	network address translation
NetBIOS	networked basic input/output system
NetBEUI	networked basic input/output system extended user interface
NFS	network file system
NIC	network interface card
NLI	not logged in or natural language interface
NLX	new low-profile extended
NNTP	network news transfer protocol
NTFS	new technology file system
NTLDR	new technology loader
OEM	original equipment manufacturer
OS	operating system
OSR	original equipment manufacturer service release
PAN	personal area network
PATA	parallel advanced technology attachment
PCI	peripheral component interconnect
PCIX	peripheral component interconnect extended
PCL	printer control language
PCMCIA	Personal Computer Memory Card International Association
PDA	personal digital assistant
PGA	pin grid array

Acronym	Spelled Out
PGA2	pin grid array 2
PIN	personal identification number
PnP	plug and play
POP	post office protocol
POP3	post office protocol 3
POST	power-on self test
PPP	point-to-point protocol
PPTP	point-to-point tunneling protocol
PRI	primary rate interface
PROM	programmable read-only memory
PS/2	personal system/2 connector
PSTN	public switched telephone network
PVC	permanent virtual circuit
QoS	quality of service
RAID	redundant array of independent disks
RAM	random access memory
RAMBUS	trademarked term
RAS	remote access service
RDRAM	Rambus dynamic random access memory
RF	radio frequency
RGB	red green blue
RIMM	Rambus inline memory module
RIP	routing information protocol
RIS	remote installation service
RISC	reduced instruction set computer
RJ	registered jack
RJ-11	registered jack function 11
RJ-45	registered jack-45
ROM	read only memory
RS-232	recommended standard 232
RTC	real-time clock
SAN	storage area network
SATA	serial advanced technology attachment
SCSI	small computer system interface
SCSI ID	small computer system interface identifier
SD card	secure digital card
SDRAM	symmetric dynamic random access memory
SEC	single edge connector
SFC	system file checker

Acronym	Spelled Out
SGRAM	synchronous graphics random access memory
SIMM	single inline memory module
SLI	scalable link interface or system level integration or scanline interleave mode
SMB	server message block
SMTP	simple mail transport protocol
SNMP	simple network management protocol
SoDIMM	small outline dual inline memory module
SOHO	small office/home office
SP	service pack
SP1	service pack 1
SP2	service pack 2
SPDIF	Sony-Philips digital interface format
SPGA	staggered pin grid array
SPX	sequenced package exchange
SRAM	static random access memory
SSH	secure shell
SSID	service set identifier
SSL	secure sockets layer
ST	straight tip
STP	shielded twisted pair
SVGA	super video graphics array
SXGA	super extended graphics array
TB	terabyte
TCP/IP	transmission control protocol/Internet protocol
TFTP	trivial file transfer protocol
UART	universal asynchronous receiver transmitter
UDF	user-defined functions or universal disk format or universal data format
UDMA	ultra direct memory access
UDP	user datagram protocol
UFS	universal file system
UPS	uninterruptible power supply
URL	uniform resource locator
USB	universal serial bus
UTP	unshielded twisted pair
UXGA	ultra extended graphics array
VESA	Video Electronics Standards Association
VFAT	virtual file allocation table
VGA	video graphics array
VoIP	voice over Internet protocol

Acronym	Spelled Out
VPN	virtual private network
VRAM	video random access memory
WAN	wide area network
WAP	wireless application protocol
WEP	wired equivalent privacy
WIFI	wireless fidelity
WINS	Windows Internet name service
WLAN	wireless local area network
WPA	wireless protected access
WUXGA	wide ultra extended graphics array
XGA	extended graphics array
XPR	is an AIX command-line utility
ZIF	zero-insertion-force
ZIP	zigzag inline package

GLOSSARY

This glossary defines the key terms listed at the end of each chapter and other terms related to managing and maintaining a personal computer.

100BaseT An Ethernet standard that operates at 100 Mbps and uses STP cabling. Also called Fast Ethernet. Variations of 100BaseT are 100BaseTX and 100BaseFX.

10Base2 An Ethernet standard that operates at 10 Mbps and uses small coaxial cable up to 200 meters long. Also called ThinNet.

10Base5 An Ethernet standard that operates at 10 Mbps and uses thick coaxial cable up to 500 meters long. Also called ThickNet.

32-bit flat memory mode A protected processing mode used by Windows NT/2000/XP to process programs written in 32-bit code early in the boot process.

3-D RAM Special video RAM designed to improve 3-D graphics simulation.

80 conductor IDE cable An IDE cable that has 40 pins but uses 80 wires, 40 of which are ground wires designed to reduce crosstalk on the cable. The cable is used by ATA/100 and ATA/133 IDE drives.

802.11a/b/g See IEEE 802.11a/b/g.

A+ Certification A certification awarded by CompTIA (The Computer Technology Industry Association) that measures a PC technician's knowledge and skills.

access point (AP) A device connected to a LAN that provides wireless communication so that computers, printers, and other wireless devices can communicate with devices on the LAN.

ACPI (Advanced Configuration and Power Interface) Specification developed by Intel, Compaq, Phoenix, Microsoft, and Toshiba to control power on notebooks and other devices. Windows 98 and Windows 2000/XP support ACPI.

active backplane A type of backplane system in which there is some circuitry, including bus connectors, buffers, and driver circuits, on the backplane.

active matrix A type of video display that amplifies the signal at every intersection in the grid of electrodes, which enhances the pixel quality over that of a dual-scan passive matrix display.

active partition The primary partition on the hard drive that boots the OS. Windows NT/2000/XP calls the active partition the system partition.

active terminator A type of terminator for single-ended SCSI cables that includes voltage regulators in addition to the simple resistors used with passive termination.

adapter address See MAC address.

adapter card A small circuit board inserted in an expansion slot and used to communicate between the system bus and a peripheral device. Also called an interface card.

administrator account In Windows NT/ 2000/XP, an account that grants to the administrator(s) rights and permissions to all hardware and software resources, such as the right to add, delete, and change accounts and to change hardware configurations.

Advanced Options menu A Windows 2000/XP menu that appears when you press F8 when Windows starts. The menu can be used to troubleshoot problems when loading Windows 2000/XP.

Advanced SCSI Programming Interface (ASPI) A popular device driver that enables operating systems to communicate with a SCSI host adapter. (The "A" originally stood for Adaptec.)

Advanced Transfer Cache (ATC) A type of L2 cache contained within the Pentium processor housing that is embedded on the same core processor die as the CPU itself.

adware Software installed on a computer that produces pop-up ads using your browser; the ads are often based on your browsing habits.

AirPort The term Apple computers use to describe the IEEE 802.11b standard.

alternating current (AC) Current that cycles back and forth rather than traveling in only one direction. In the United States, the AC voltage from a standard wall outlet is normally between 110 and 115 V. In Europe, the standard AC voltage from a wall outlet is 220 V.

ammeter A meter that measures electrical current in amps.

ampere or amp (A) A unit of measurement for electrical current. One volt across a resistance of one ohm will produce a flow of one amp.

amplifier repeater A repeater that does not distinguish between noise and signal; it amplifies both.

ANSI (American National Standards Institute) A nonprofit organization dedicated to creating trade and communications standards.

answer file A text file that contains information that Windows NT/2000/XP requires in order to do an unattended installation.

antivirus (AV) software Utility programs that prevent infection or scan a system to detect and remove viruses. McAfee Associates' VirusScan and Norton AntiVirus are two popular AV packages.

application program interface (API) call A request from software to the OS to access hardware or other software using a previously defined procedure that both the software and the OS understand.

ARP (Address Resolution Protocol) A protocol that TCP/IP uses to translate IP addresses into physical network addresses (MAC addresses).

ASCII (American Standard Code for Information Interchange) A popular standard for writing letters and other characters in binary code. Originally, ASCII characters were seven bits, so there were 127 possible values. ASCII has been expanded to an 8-bit version, allowing 128 additional values.

asynchronous SRAM Static RAM that does not work in step with the CPU clock and is, therefore, slower than synchronous SRAM.

AT A form factor, generally no longer produced, in which the motherboard requires a full-size case. Because of their dimensions and configuration, AT systems are difficult to install, service, and upgrade. Also called full AT.

AT command set A set of commands that a PC uses to control a modem and that a user can enter to troubleshoot the modem.

ATAPI (Advanced Technology Attachment Packet Interface) An interface standard, part of the IDE/ATA standards, that allows tape drives, CD-ROM drives, and other drives to be treated like an IDE hard drive by the system.

attenuation Signal degeneration over distance. Attenuation is solved on a network by adding repeaters to the network.

ATX The most common form factor for PC systems presently in use, originally introduced by Intel in 1995. ATX motherboards and cases make better use of space and resources than did the AT form factor.

ATX12 V power supply A power supply that provides a 12 V power cord with a 4-pin connector to be used by the auxiliary 4-pin power connector on motherboards used to provide extra power for processors.

audio/modem riser (AMR) A specification for a small slot on a motherboard to accommodate an audio or modem riser card. A controller on the motherboard contains some of the logic for the audio or modem functionality.

authentication The process of proving an individual is who they say they are before they are allowed access to a computer, file, folder, or network. The process might use a password, PIN, smart card, or biometric data.

authorization Controlling what an individual can or cannot do with resources on a computer network. Using Windows, authorization is granted by the rights and permissions assigned to user accounts.

autodetection A feature of system BIOS and hard drives that automatically identifies and configures a new drive in CMOS setup.

Autoexec.bat A startup text file once used by DOS and used by Windows to provide backward-compatibility. It executes commands automatically during the boot process and is used to create a16-bit environment.

Automated System Recovery (ASR) The Windows XP process that allows you to restore an entire hard drive volume or logical drive to its state at the time the backup of the volume was made.

Automatic Private IP Address (APIPA) An IP address in the address range 169.254.x.x, used by a computer when it cannot successfully lease an IP address from a DHCP server.

autorange meter A multimeter that senses the quantity of input and sets the range accordingly.

Baby AT An improved and more flexible version of the AT form factor. Baby AT was the industry standard from approximately 1993 to 1997 and can fit into some ATX cases.

back side bus The bus between the CPU and the L2 cache inside the CPU housing.

backplane system A form factor in which there is no true motherboard. Instead, motherboard components are included on an adapter card plugged into a slot on a board called the backplane.

backup An extra copy of a file, used in the event that the original becomes damaged or destroyed.

backup domain controller (BDC) In Windows NT, a computer on a network that holds a read-only copy of the SAM (security accounts manager) database.

Backup Operator A Windows 2000/XP user account that can back up and restore any files on the system regardless of its having access to these files.

bandwidth In relation to analog communication, the range of frequencies that a communications channel or cable can carry. In general use, the term refers to the volume of data that can travel on a bus or over a cable stated in bits per second (bps), kilobits per second (Kbps), or megabits per second (Mbps). Also called data throughput or line speed.

bank An area on the motherboard that contains slots for memory modules (typically labeled bank 0, 1, 2, and 3).

baseline The level of performance expected from a system, which can be compared to current measurements to determine what needs upgrading or tuning.

basic disk A way to partition a hard drive, used by DOS and all versions of Windows, that stores information about the drive in a partition table at the beginning of the drive. Compare to dynamic disk.

batch file A text file containing a series of OS commands. Autoexec.bat is a batch file.

baud rate A measure of line speed between two devices such as a computer and a printer or a modem. This speed is measured in the number of times a signal changes in one second. *See also* bits per second (bps).

beam detect mirror Detects the initial presence of a laser printer's laser beam by reflecting the beam to an optical fiber.

best-effort protocol *See* connectionless protocol.

binary number system The number system used by computers; it has only two numbers, 0 and 1, called binary digits, or bits.

binding The process by which a protocol is associated with a network card or a modem card.

BIOS (basic input/output system) Firmware that can control much of a computer's input/output functions, such as communication with the floppy drive and the monitor. Also called ROM BIOS.

bit (binary digit) A 0 or 1 used by the binary number system.

bits per second (bps) A measure of data transmission speed. For example, a common modem speed is 56,000 bps, or 56 Kbps.

block mode A method of data transfer between hard drive and memory that allows multiple data transfers on a single software interrupt.

blue screen A Windows NT/2000/XP error that displays against a blue screen and causes the system to halt. Also called a stop error.

Bluetooth A standard for wireless communication and data synchronization between devices, developed by a group of electronics manufacturers and overseen by the Bluetooth Special Interest Group. Bluetooth uses the same frequency range as 802.11b, but does not have as wide a range.

BNC connector A connector used with thin coaxial cable. Some BNC connectors are T-shaped and called T-connectors. One end of the T connects to the NIC, and the two other ends can connect to cables or end a bus formation with a terminator.

boot loader menu A startup menu that gives the user the choice of which operating system to load such as Windows 98 or Windows XP which are both installed on the same system, creating a dual boot.

boot partition The hard drive partition where the Windows NT/2000/XP OS is stored. The system partition and the boot partition may be different partitions.

boot record The first sector of a floppy disk or logical drive in a partition; it contains information about the disk or logical drive. On a hard drive, if the boot record is in the active partition, then it is used to boot the OS. Also called boot sector.

boot sector *See* boot record.

boot sector virus An infectious program that can replace the boot program with a modified, infected version, often causing boot and data retrieval problems.

Boot.ini A Windows NT/2000/XP hidden text file that contains information needed to start the boot and build the boot loader menu.

bootable disk For DOS and Windows, a floppy disk that can upload the OS files necessary for computer startup. For DOS or Windows 9x/Me, it must contain the files Io.sys, Msdos.sys, and Command.com.

bootstrap loader A small program at the end of the boot record that can be used to boot an OS from the disk or logical drive.

bridge A device used to connect two or more network segments. It can make decisions about allowing a packet to pass based on the packet's destination MAC address.

bridging protocol *See* line protocol.

Briefcase A system folder in Windows 9x/Me that is used to synchronize files between two computers.

broadband A transmission technique that carries more than one type of transmission on the same medium, such as cable modem or DSL.

broadcast Process by which a message is sent from a single host to all hosts on the network, without regard to the kind of data being sent or the destination of the data.

brouter A device that functions as both a bridge and a router. A brouter acts as a router when handling packets using routable protocols such as TCP/IP and IPX/SPX. It acts as a bridge when handling packets using nonroutable protocols such as NetBEUI.

brownouts Temporary reductions in voltage, which can sometimes cause data loss. *Also called* sags.

browser hijacker A malicious program that infects your Web browser and can change your home page or browser settings. It can also redirect your browser to unwanted sites, produce pop-up ads, and set unwanted bookmarks. Also called a home page hijacker.

BTX (Balanced Technology Extended) The latest form factor expected to replace ATX. It has higher quality fans, is designed for better air flow, and has improved structural support for the motherboard.

buffer A temporary memory area where data is kept before being written to a hard drive or sent to a printer, thus reducing the number of writes to the devices.

built-in user account An administrator account and a guest account that are set up when Windows NT/2000/XP is first installed.

burst EDO (BEDO) A refined version of EDO memory that significantly improved access time over EDO. BEDO was not widely used because Intel chose not to support it. BEDO memory is stored on 168-pin DIMM modules.

burst SRAM Memory that is more expensive and slightly faster than pipelined burst SRAM. Data is sent in a two-step process; the data address is sent, and then the data itself is sent without interruption.

bus The paths, or lines, on the motherboard on which data, instructions, and electrical power move from component to component.

bus mouse A mouse that plugs into a bus adapter card and has a round, 9-pin mini-DIN connector.

bus riser *See* riser card.

bus speed The speed, or frequency, at which the data on the motherboard is written and read.

bus topology A LAN architecture in which all the devices are connected to a bus, or one communication line. Bus topology does not have a central connection point.

byte A collection of eight bits that can represent a single character.

cabinet file A file with a .cab extension that contains one or more compressed files and is often used to

distribute software on disk. The Extract command is used to extract files from the cabinet file.

cable modem A technology that uses cable TV lines for data transmission requiring a modem at each end. From the modem, a network cable connects to an NIC in the user's PC, or a USB cable connects to a USB port.

call tracking A system that tracks the dates, times, and transactions of help-desk or on-site PC support calls, including the problem presented, the issues addressed, who did what, and when and how each call was resolved.

CAM (Common Access Method) A standard adapter driver used by SCSI.

capacitor An electronic device that can maintain an electrical charge for a period of time and is used to smooth out the flow of electrical current. Capacitors are often found in computer power supplies.

CardBus A PCMCIA specification that improved on the earlier PC Card standards. It improves I/O speed, increases the bus width to 32 bits, and supports lower-voltage PC Cards, while maintaining backward compatibility with earlier standards.

cards Adapter boards or interface cards placed into expansion slots to expand the functions of a computer, allowing it to communicate with external devices such as monitors or speakers.

carrier A signal used to activate a phone line to confirm a continuous frequency; used to indicate that two computers are ready to receive or transmit data via modems.

CAS Latency (CL) A feature of memory that reflects the number of clock cycles that pass while data is written to memory.

CAU (Controlled-Access Unit) *See* Multistation Access Unit.

CCITT (Comité Consultatif International Télégraphique et Téléphonique) An international organization that was responsible for developing standards for international communications. This organization has been incorporated into the ITU. *See also* ITU.

CD (change directory) command A command given at the command prompt that changes the default directory, for example CD \Windows.

CDFS (Compact Disc File System) The 32-bit file system for CD discs and some CD-R and CD-RW discs that replaced the older 16-bit mscdex file system used by DOS. *See also* Universal Disk Format (UDF).

CDMA (code-division multiple access) A protocol standard used by cellular WANs and cell phones

CD-R (CD-recordable) A CD drive that can record or write data to a CD. The drive may or may not be multisession, but the data cannot be erased once it is written.

CD-RW (CD-rewritable) A CD drive that can record or write data to a CD. The data can be erased and overwritten. The drive may or may not be multisession.

central processing unit (CPU) Also called a microprocessor or processor. The heart and brain of the computer, which receives data input, processes information, and executes instructions.

chain A group of clusters used to hold a single file.

CHAP (Challenge Handshake Authentication Protocol) A protocol used to encrypt account names and passwords that are sent to a network controller for validation.

checksum A method of checking transmitted data for errors, whereby the digits are added and their sum compared to an expected sum.

child directory *See* subdirectory.

child, parent, grandparent backup method A plan for backing up and reusing tapes or removable disks by rotating them each day (child), week (parent), and month (grandparent).

chip creep A condition in which chips loosen because of thermal changes.

chipset A group of chips on the motherboard that controls the timing and flow of data and instructions to and from the CPU.

CHS (cylinder, head, sector) mode An outdated method by which BIOS reads from and writes to hard drives by addressing the correct cylinder, head, and sector. Also called normal mode.

circuit board A computer component, such as the main motherboard or an adapter board, that has electronic circuits and chips.

CISC (complex instruction set computing) Earlier CPU type of instruction set.

clamping voltage The maximum voltage allowed through a surge suppressor, such as 175 or 330 volts.

clean install Installing an OS on a new hard drive or on a hard drive that has a previous OS installed, but without carrying forward any settings kept by the old OS, including information about hardware, software, or user preferences. A fresh installation.

client/server A computer concept whereby one computer (the client) requests information from another computer (the server).

client/server application An application that has two components. The client software requests data from the server software on the same or another computer.

clock speed The speed, or frequency, expressed in MHz, that controls activity on the motherboard and is generated by a crystal or oscillator located somewhere on the motherboard.

clone A computer that is a no-name Intel- and Microsoft-compatible PC.

cluster One or more sectors that constitute the smallest unit of space on a disk for storing data (also referred to as a file allocation unit). Files are written to a disk as groups of whole clusters.

CMOS (complementary metal-oxide semiconductor) The technology used to manufacture microchips. CMOS chips require less electricity, hold data longer after the electricity is turned off, are slower, and produce less heat than earlier technologies. The configuration, or setup, chip is a CMOS chip.

CMOS configuration chip A chip on the motherboard that contains a very small amount of memory, or RAM   enough to hold configuration, or setup, information about the computer The chip is powered by a battery when the PC is turned off. Also called CMOS setup chip or CMOS RAM chip.

CMOS setup (1) The CMOS configuration chip. (2) The program in system BIOS that can change the values in CMOS RAM.

CMOS setup chip *See* CMOS configuration chip.

COAST (cache on a stick) Memory modules that hold memory used as a memory cache. *See* memory cache.

coaxial cable Networking cable used with 10-Mbps Ethernet ThinNet or ThickNet.

cold boot *See* hard boot.

combo card An outdated Ethernet card that contains more than one transceiver, each with a different port on the back of the card, in order to accommodate different cabling media.

Command.com Along with Msdos.sys and Io.sys, one of the three files that are the core components of the real-mode portion of Windows 9x/Me. Command.com provides a command prompt and interprets commands.

comment A line or part of a line in a program that is intended as a remark or comment and is ignored when the program runs. A semicolon or an REM is often used to mark a line as a comment.

communication and networking riser (CNR) A specification for a small expansion slot on a motherboard that accommodates a small audio, modem, or network riser card.

compact case   A type of case used in low-end desktop systems. Compact cases, also called low-profile or slimline cases, follow either the NLX, LPX, or Mini LPX form factor. They are likely to have fewer drive bays, but they generally still provide for some expansion.

Compact.exe   Windows 2000/XP command and program to compress or uncompress a volume, folder, or file.

compressed drive   A drive whose format has been reorganized in order to store more data. A Windows 9x compressed drive is really not a drive at all; it's actually a type of file, typically with a host drive called H.

compression   To store data in a file, folder, or logical drive using a coding format that reduces the size of files in order to save space on a drive or shorten transport time when sending a file over the Internet or network.

computer name   Character-based host name or NetBIOS name assigned to a computer.

Config.sys   A text file used by DOS and supported by Windows 9x/Me that lists device drivers to be loaded at startup. It can also set system variables to be used by DOS and Windows.

Configuration Manager   A component of Windows Plug and Play that controls the configuration process of all devices and communicates these configurations to the devices.

connectionless protocol   A protocol such as UDP that does not require a connection before sending a packet and does not guarantee delivery. An example of a UDP transmission is streaming video over the Web. Also called a best-effort protocol.

connection-oriented protocol   In networking, a protocol that confirms that a good connection has been made before transmitting data to the other end. An example of a connection-oriented protocol is TCP.

console   A window in which one or more Windows 2000/XP utility programs have been installed. The window is created using Microsoft Management Console, and installed utilities are called snap-ins.

constant angular velocity (CAV)   A technology used by hard drives and newer CD-ROM drives whereby the disk rotates at a constant speed.

constant linear velocity (CLV)   A CD-ROM format in which the spacing of data is consistent on the CD, but the speed of the disc varies depending on whether the data being read is near the center or the edge of the disc.

continuity   A continuous, unbroken path for the flow of electricity. A continuity test can determine whether or not internal wiring is still intact, or whether a fuse is good or bad.

control blade   A laser printer component that prevents too much toner from sticking to the cylinder surface.

conventional memory   DOS and Windows 9x/Me memory addresses between 0 and 640 K. Also called base memory.

cooler   A combination cooling fan and heat sink mounted on the top or side of a processor to keep it cool.

copyright   An individual's right to copy his/her own work. No one else, other than the copyright owner, is legally allowed to do so without permission.

CRC (cyclical redundancy check)   A process in which calculations are performed on bytes of data before and after they are transmitted to check for corruption during transmission.

credit card memory   A type of memory used on older notebooks that could upgrade existing memory by way of a specialized memory slot.

C-RIMM (Continuity RIMM)   A placeholder RIMM module that provides continuity so that every RIMM slot is filled.

cross-linked clusters   Errors caused when more than one file points to a cluster, and the files appear to share the same disk space, according to the file allocation table.

crossover cable   A cable used to connect two PCs into the simplest network possible. Also used to connect two hubs.

CVF (compressed volume file)   The Windows 9x/Me file on the host drive of a compressed drive that holds all compressed data.

data bus   The lines on the system bus that the CPU uses to send and receive data.

data cartridge   A type of tape medium typically used for backups. Full-sized data cartridges are $4 \times 6 \times 2\frac{5}{8}$ inches in size. A minicartridge is only $3\frac{1}{4} \times 2\frac{1}{2} \times 2\frac{3}{5}$ inches in size.

data line protector   A surge protector designed to work with the telephone line to a modem.

data migration   Moving data from one application to another application or from one storage media to another, and most often involves a change in the way the data is formatted.

data path   The number of bits transported into and out of the processor.

data path size   The number of lines on a bus that can hold data, for example, 8, 16, 32, and 64 lines, which can accommodate 8, 16, 32, and 64 bits at a time.

data throughput   *See* bandwidth.

datagram   *See* packet.

DC controller   A card inside a notebook that converts voltage to CPU voltage. Some notebook manufacturers consider the card to be an FRU.

DCE (Data Communications Equipment)   The hardware, usually a dial-up modem, that provides the connection between a data terminal and a communications line. *See also* DTE.

DDR SDRAM   *See* Double Data Rate SDRAM.

DDR2 SDRAM   A version of SDRAM that is faster than DDR and uses less power.

default gateway   The gateway a computer on a network will use to access another network unless it knows to specifically use another gateway for quicker access to that network.

default printer   The printer Windows prints to unless another printer is selected.

Defrag.exe   Windows program and command to defragment a logical drive.

defragment   To "optimize" or rewrite a file to a disk in one contiguous chain of clusters, thus speeding up data retrieval.

demodulation   The process by which digital data that has been converted to analog data is converted back to digital data. *See* modulation.

desktop   The initial screen that is displayed when an OS has a GUI interface loaded.

device driver   A program stored on the hard drive that tells the computer how to communicate with an input/output device such as a printer or modem.

DHCP (Dynamic Host Configuration Protocol) server   A service that assigns dynamic IP addresses to computers on a network when they first access the network.

diagnostic cards   Adapter cards designed to discover and report computer errors and conflicts at POST time (before the computer boots up), often by displaying a number on the card.

diagnostic software   Utility programs that help troubleshoot computer systems. Some Windows diagnostic utilities are CHKDSK and SCANDISK. PC-Technician is an example of a third-party diagnostic program.

dialer   Malicious software installed on your PC that disconnects your phone line from your ISP and dials up an expensive pay-per-minute phone number without your knowledge.

dial-up networking   A Windows 9x/Me and Windows NT/2000/XP utility that uses a modem and telephone line to connect to a network.

differential backup   Backup method that backs up only files that have changed or have been created since the last full backup. When recovering data, only two backups are needed: the full backup and the last differential backup.

differential cable   A SCSI cable in which a signal is carried on two wires, each carrying voltage, and the signal is the difference between the two. Differential signaling provides for error checking and greater data integrity. Compare to single-ended cable.

digital certificate   A code used to authenticate the source of a file or document or to identify and authenticate a person or organization sending data over the Internet. The code is assigned by a certificate authority such as VeriSign and includes a public key for encryption. Also called *digital ID* or *digital signature*.

digital ID   See digital certificate.

digital signature   *See* digital certificate.

DIMM (dual inline memory module)   A miniature circuit board installed on a motherboard to hold memory. DIMMs can hold up to 2 GB of RAM on a single module.

diode   An electronic device that allows electricity to flow in only one direction. Used in a rectifier circuit.

DIP (dual inline package) switch   A switch on a circuit board or other device that can be set on or off to hold configuration or setup information.

direct current (DC)   Current that travels in only one direction (the type of electricity provided by batteries). Computer power supplies transform AC to low DC.

Direct Rambus DRAM   A memory technology by Rambus and Intel that uses a narrow network-type system bus. Memory is stored on a RIMM module. Also called RDRAM or Direct RDRAM.

Direct RDRAM   *See* Direct Rambus DRAM.

directory table   An OS table that contains file information such as the name, size, time and date of last modification, and cluster number of the file's beginning location.

discrete L2 cache   A type of L2 cache contained within the Pentium processor housing, but on a different die, with a cache bus between the processor and the cache.

disk cache   A method whereby recently retrieved data and adjacent data are read into memory in advance, anticipating the next CPU request.

disk cloning   *See* drive imaging.

disk compression   Compressing data on a hard drive to allow more data to be written to the drive.

disk imaging *See* drive imaging.

Disk Management A Windows 2000/XP utility used to display, create, and format partitions on basic disks and volumes on dynamic disks.

disk quota A limit placed on the amount of disk space that is available to users. Requires a Windows 2000/XP NTFS volume.

disk thrashing A condition that results when the hard drive is excessively used for virtual memory because RAM is full. It dramatically slows down processing and can cause premature hard drive failure.

Display Power Management Signaling (DPMS) Energy Star standard specifications that allow for the video card and monitor to go into sleep mode simultaneously. *See also* Energy Star.

distribution server A file server holding Windows setup files used to install Windows on computers networked to the server.

DMA (direct memory access) channel A number identifying a channel whereby a device can pass data to memory without involving the CPU. Think of a DMA channel as a shortcut for data moving to/from the device and memory.

DMA transfer mode A transfer mode used by devices, including the hard drive, to transfer data to memory without involving the CPU.

DNS (domain name service or domain name system) A distributed pool of information (called the name space) that keeps track of assigned domain names and their corresponding IP addresses, and the system that allows a host to locate information in the pool. Compare to WINS.

DNS server A computer that can find an IP address for another computer when only the domain name is known.

docking station A device that receives a notebook computer and provides additional secondary storage and easy connection to peripheral devices.

domain In Windows NT/2000/XP, a logical group of networked computers, such as those on a college campus, that share a centralized directory database of user account information and security for the entire domain.

domain controller A Windows NT/2000 or Windows Server 2003 computer which holds and controls a database of (1) user accounts, (2) group accounts, and (3) computer accounts used to manage access to the network.

domain name A unique, text-based name that identifies a network.

DOS box A command window.

Dosstart.bat A type of Autoexec.bat file that is executed by Windows 9x/Me in two situations: when you select Restart the computer in MS-DOS mode from the shutdown menu or you run a program in MS-DOS mode.

dot pitch The distance between the dots that the electronic beam hits on a monitor screen.

Double Data Rate SDRAM (DDR SDRAM) A type of memory technology used on DIMMs that runs at twice the speed of the system clock.

doze time The time before an Energy Star or "Green" system will reduce 80 percent of its activity.

drive imaging Making an exact image of a hard-drive, including partition information, boot sectors, operating system installation, and application software to replicate the hard drive on another system or recover from a hard drive crash. Also called *disk cloning* and *disk imaging*.

DriveSpace A Windows 9x/Me utility that compresses files so that they take up less space on a disk drive, creating a single large file on the disk to hold all the compressed files.

drop height The height from which a manufacturer states that its device, such as a hard drive, can be dropped without making the device unusable.

DSL (Digital Subscriber Line) A telephone line that carries digital data from end to end, and can be leased from the telephone company for individual use. Some DSL lines are rated at 5 Mbps, about 50 times faster than regular telephone lines.

DTE (Data Terminal Equipment) Both the computer and a remote terminal or other computer to which it is attached. *See also* DCE.

dual boot The ability to boot using either of two different OSs, such as Windows 98 and Windows XP.

dual channel A motherboard feature that improves memory performance by providing two 64-bit channels between memory and the chipset. DDR and DDR2 memory can use dual channels.

dual-core processing Two processors contained in the same processor housing that share the interface with the chipset and memory.

dual-scan passive matrix A type of video display that is less expensive than an active-matrix display and does not provide as high-quality an image. With dual-scan display, two columns of electrodes are activated at the same time.

dual-voltage CPU A CPU that requires two different voltages, one for internal processing and the other for I/O processing.

dump file A file that contains information captured from memory at the time a stop error occurred.

DVD (digital video disc or digital versatile disk) A faster, larger CD format that can read older CDs, store over 8 GB of data, and hold full-length motion picture videos.

dye-sublimation printer A type of printer with photo-lab-quality results that uses transparent dyed film. The film is heated, which causes the dye to vaporize onto glossy paper.

dynamic disk A way to partition one or more hard drives, introduced with Windows 2000, in which information about the drive is stored in a database at the end of the drive. Compare to basic disk.

dynamic IP address An assigned IP address that is used for the current session only. When the session is terminated, the IP address is returned to the list of available addresses.

dynamic RAM (DRAM) The most common type of system memory, it requires refreshing every few milliseconds.

dynamic volume A volume type used with dynamic disks for which you can change the size of the volume after you have created it.

dynamic VxD A VxD that is loaded and unloaded from memory as needed.

ECC (error-correcting code) A chipset feature on a motherboard that checks the integrity of data stored on DIMMs or RIMMs and can correct single-bit errors in a byte. More advanced ECC schemas can detect, but not correct, double-bit errors in a byte.

ECHS (extended CHS) mode *See* large mode.

ECP (Extended Capabilities Port) A bidirectional parallel port mode that uses a DMA channel to speed up data flow.

EDO (extended data out) A type of outdated RAM that was faster than conventional RAM because it eliminated the delay before it issued the next memory address.

EEPROM (electrically erasable programmable ROM) A type of chip in which higher voltage may be applied to one of the pins to erase its previous memory before a new instruction set is electronically written.

EIDE (Enhanced IDE) A standard for managing the interface between secondary storage devices and a computer system. A system can support up to six serial ATA and parallel ATA IDE devices or up to four parallel ATA IDE devices such as hard drives, CD-ROM drives, and DVD drives.

electromagnetic interference (EMI) A magnetic field produced as a side effect from the flow of electric-

ity. EMI can cause corrupted data in data lines that are not properly shielded.

electrostatic discharge (ESD) Another name for static electricity, which can damage chips and destroy motherboards, even though it might not be felt or seen with the naked eye.

Emergency Repair Disk (ERD) A Windows NT record of critical information about your system that can be used to fix a problem with the OS. The ERD enables restoration of the Windows NT registry on your hard drive.

Emergency Repair Process A Windows 2000 process that restores the OS to its state at the completion of a successful installation.

emergency startup disk (ESD) *See* rescue disk.

Emm386.exe A DOS and Windows 9x/Me utility that provides access to upper memory for 16-bit device drivers and other software.

Encrypted File System (EFS) A way to use a key to encode a file or folder on an NTFS volume to protect sensitive data. Because it is an inte-grated system service, EFS is transparent to users and applications and is difficult to attack.

encrypting virus A type of virus that transforms itself into a nonreplicating program in order to avoid detection. It transforms itself back into a replicating program in order to spread.

encryption The process of putting readable data into an encoded form that can only be decoded (or decrypted) through use of a key.

Energy Star "Green" systems that satisfy the EPA requirements to decrease the overall consumption of electricity. *See also* Green Standards.

enhanced BIOS A system BIOS that has been written to accommodate large-capacity drives (over 504 MB, usually in the gigabyte range).

EPIC (explicitly parallel instruction computing) The CPU architecture used by the Intel Itanium chip that bundles programming instructions with instructions on how to use multiprocessing abili-ties to do two instructions in parallel.

EPP (Enhanced Parallel Port) A parallel port that allows data to flow in both directions (bidirectional port) and is faster than original parallel ports on PCs that allowed communication only in one direction.

EPROM (erasable programmable ROM) A type of chip with a special window that allows the current memory contents to be erased with special ultravi-olet light so that the chip can be reprogrammed.

error correction The ability of a modem to identify transmission errors and then automatically request another transmission.

escalate When a technician passes a customer's problem to higher organizational levels because he or she cannot solve the problem.

Ethernet The most popular LAN architecture that can run at 10 Mbps (ThinNet or ThickNet), 100 Mbps (Fast Ethernet), or 1 Gbps (Gigabit Ethernet).

Execution Trace Cache A type of Level 1 cache used by some CPUs to hold decoded operations waiting to be executed.

executive services In Windows NT/2000/XP, a group of components running in kernel mode that interfaces between the subsystems in user mode and the HAL.

expansion bus A bus that does not run in sync with the system clock.

expansion card A circuit board inserted into a slot on the motherboard to enhance the capability of the computer.

expansion slot A narrow slot on the motherboard where an expansion card can be inserted. Expansion slots connect to a bus on the motherboard.

expert systems Software that uses a database of known facts and rules to simulate a human expert's reasoning and decision-making processes.

ExpressCard The latest PCMCIA standard for notebook I/O cards that uses the PCI Express and USB 2.0 data transfer standards. Two types of Express-Cards are ExpressCard/34 (34 mm wide) and ExpressCard/54 (54 mm wide).

extended memory Memory above 1024 K used in a DOS or Windows 9x/Me system.

extended partition The only partition on a hard drive that can contain more than one logical drive.

extension magnet brush A long-handled brush made of nylon fibers that are charged with static electricity to pick up stray toner inside a printer.

external cache Static cache memory, stored on the motherboard or inside the CPU housing, that is not part of the CPU (also called L2 or L3 cache).

external command Commands that have their own program files.

faceplate A metal or plastic plate that comes with the computer case and fits over the empty drive bays or slots for expansion cards to create a well-fitted enclosure around them.

Fast Ethernet *See* 100BaseT.

FAT (file allocation table) A table on a hard drive or floppy disk that tracks the clusters used to contain a file.

FAT12 The 12-bit wide, one-column file allocation table for a floppy disk, containing information about how each cluster or file allocation unit on the disk is currently used.

fault tolerance The degree to which a system can tolerate failures. Adding redundant components, such as disk mirroring or disk duplexing, is a way to build in fault tolerance.

Fiber Distributed Data Interface (FDDI) A ring-based network that does not require a centralized hub and can transfer data at a rate of 100 Mbps.

field replaceable unit (FRU) A component in a computer or device that can be replaced with a new component without sending the computer or device back to the manufacturer. Examples: power supply, DIMM, motherboard, floppy disk drive.

file allocation unit *See* cluster.

file extension A three-character portion of the name of a file that is used to identify the file type. In command lines, the file extension follows the filename and is separated from it by a period. For example, Msd.exe, where exe is the file extension.

file system The overall structure that an OS uses to name, store, and organize files on a disk. Examples of file systems are FAT32 and NTFS.

file virus A virus that inserts virus code into an executable program file and can spread whenever that program is executed.

filename The first part of the name assigned to a file. In DOS, the filename can be no more than eight characters long and is followed by the file extension. In Windows, a filename can be up to 255 characters.

firewall Hardware or software that protects a computer or network from unauthorized access.

FireWire *See* IEEE 1394.

firmware Software that is permanently stored in a chip. The BIOS on a motherboard is an example of firmware.

flash ROM ROM that can be reprogrammed or changed without replacing chips.

flat panel monitor A desktop monitor that uses an LCD panel.

FlexATX A version of the ATX form factor that allows for maximum flexibility in the size and shape of cases and motherboards. FlexATX is ideal for custom systems.

floppy disk drive (FDD) A drive that can hold either a $5\frac{1}{4}$ inch or $3\frac{1}{2}$ floppy disk.

flow control When using modems, a method of controlling the flow of data to adjust for problems with data transmission. Xon/Xoff is an example of a flow control protocol.

folder *See* subdirectory.

folder redirection A Windows XP feature that allows a user to point to a folder that can be on the local PC or somewhere on the network, and its location can be transparent to the user.

forced perfect terminator (FPT) A type of SCSI active terminator that includes a mechanism to force signal termination to the correct voltage, eliminating most signal echoes and interference.

forgotten password floppy disk A Windows XP disk created to be used in the event the user forgets the user account password to the system.

form factor A set of specifications on the size, shape, and configuration of a computer hardware component such as a case, power supply, or motherboard.

formatting Preparing a hard drive volume or floppy disk for use by placing tracks and sectors on its surface to store information (for example, FORMAT A:).

FPM (fast page mode) An outdated memory mode used before the introduction of EDO memory. FPM improved on earlier memory types by sending the row address just once for many accesses to memory near that row.

fragmentation The distribution of data files on a hard drive or floppy disk such that they are stored in noncontiguous clusters.

fragmented file A file that has been written to different portions of the disk so that it is not in contiguous clusters.

frame The header and trailer information added to data to form a data packet to be sent over a network.

front-side bus (FSB) *See* system bus.

FTP (File Transfer Protocol) The protocol used to transfer files over a TCP/IP network such that the file does not need to be converted to ASCII format before transferring it.

full AT *See* AT.

full backup A complete backup, whereby all of the files on the hard drive are backed up each time the backup procedure is performed. It is the safest backup method, but it takes the most time.

full-duplex Communication that happens in two directions at the same time.

fully qualified domain name (FQDN) A host name and a domain name such as *jsmith.amazon.com*. Sometimes loosely referred to as a domain name.

gateway A computer or other device that connects networks.

GDI (Graphics Device Interface) A core Windows component responsible for building graphics data to display or print. A GDI printer relies on Windows to construct a page to print and then receives the constructed page as bitmap data.

General Packet Radio Service (GPRS) A protocol standard that can be used by GSM or TDMA on a cellular WAN to send voice, text, or video data in packets similar to VoIP.

General Protection Fault (GPF) A Windows error that occurs when a program attempts to access a memory address that is not available or is no longer assigned to it.

Gigabit Ethernet The next generation of Ethernet. Gigabit Ethernet supports rates of data transfer up to 1 gigabit per second but is not yet widely used.

gigahertz (GHz) One thousand MHz, or one billion cycles per second.

global user account Sometimes called a domain user account, the account is used at the domain level, created by an administrator, and stored in the SAM (security accounts manager) database on a Windows 2000 or Windows 2003 domain controller.

graphics accelerator A type of video card that has an on-board processor that can substantially increase speed and boost graphical and video performance.

graphics DDR (G-DDR), graphics DDR2, graphics DDR3 Types of DDR, DDR2, and DDR3 memory specifically designed to be used in graphics cards.

grayware A program that AV software recognizes to be potentially harmful or potentially unwanted.

Green Standards A computer or device that conforms to these standards can go into sleep or doze mode when not in use, thus saving energy and helping the environment. Devices that carry the Green Star or Energy Star comply with these standards.

ground bracelet A strap you wear around your wrist that is attached to the computer case, ground mat, or another ground so that ESD is discharged from your body before you touch sensitive components inside a computer. Also called static strap, ground strap, ESD bracelet.

group profile A group of user profiles. All profiles in the group can be changed by changing the group profile.

GSM (Global System for Mobile communication) An open standard for cellular WANs and cell phones that uses digital communication of data and is accepted and used worldwide.

guard tone   A tone that an answering modem sends when it first answers the phone, to tell the calling modem that a modem is on the other end of the line.

Guest user   A user who has limited permissions on a system and cannot make changes to it. Guest user accounts are intended for one-time or infrequent users of a workstation.

HAL (hardware abstraction layer)   The low-level part of Windows NT/2000/XP, written specifically for each CPU technology, so that only the HAL must change when platform components change.

half life   The time it takes for a medium storing data to weaken to half of its strength. Magnetic media, including traditional hard drives and floppy disks, have a half-life of five to seven years.

half-duplex   Communication between two devices whereby transmission takes place in only one direction at a time.

handshaking   When two modems begin to communicate, the initial agreement made as to how to send and receive data.

hard boot   Restart the computer by turning off the power or by pressing the Reset button. Also called a cold boot.

hard copy   Output from a printer to paper.

hard drive   The main secondary storage device of a PC, a small case that contains magnetic coated platters that rotate at high speed.

hard drive controller   The firmware that controls access to a hard drive contained on a circuit board mounted on or inside the hard drive housing. Older hard drives used firmware on a controller card that connected to the drive by way of two cables, one for data and one for control.

hard drive standby time   The amount of time before a hard drive will shut down to conserve energy.

hard-disk loading   The illegal practice of installing unauthorized software on computers for sale. Hard-disk loading can typically be identified by the absence of original software disks in the original system's shipment.

hardware   The physical components that constitute the computer system, such as the monitor, the keyboard, the motherboard, and the printer.

hardware address   *See* MAC address.

hardware cache   A disk cache that is contained in RAM chips built right on the disk controller. Also called a buffer.

hardware interrupt   An event caused by a hardware device signaling the CPU that it requires service.

hardware profile   A set of hardware configuration information that Windows keeps in the registry. Windows can maintain more than one hardware profile for the same PC.

HCL (hardware compatibility list)   The list of all computers and peripheral devices that have been tested and are officially supported by Windows NT/2000/XP (see *www.microsoft.com/whdc/hcl/default.mspx*).

head   The top or bottom surface of one platter on a hard drive. Each platter has two heads.

heat sink   A piece of metal, with cooling fins, that can be attached to or mounted on an integrated chip (such as the CPU) to dissipate heat.

hertz (Hz)   Unit of measurement for frequency, calculated in terms of vibrations, or cycles per second. For example, for 16-bit stereo sound, a frequency of 44,000 Hz is used. *See also* megahertz.

hexadecimal notation (hex)   A numbering system that uses 16 digits, the numerals 0–9, and the letters A–F. Hexadecimal notation is often used to display memory addresses.

hibernation   A notebook OS feature that conserves power by using a small trickle of electricity. Before the notebook begins to hibernate, everything currently stored in memory is saved to the hard drive. When the notebook is brought out of hibernation, open applications and their data are returned to the state before hibernation.

hidden file   A file that is not displayed in a directory list. Whether to hide or display a file is one of the file's attributes kept by the OS.

high memory area (HMA)   In DOS or Windows 9x/Me, the first 64K of extended memory.

High Voltage Differential (HVD)   A type of SCSI differential signaling requiring more expensive hardware to handle the higher voltage. HVD became obsolete with the introduction of SCSI-3.

high-level formatting   Formatting performed by means of the DOS or Windows Format program (for example, FORMAT C:/S creates the boot record, FAT, and root directory on drive C and makes the drive bootable). Also called OS formatting.

Himem.sys   The DOS and Windows 9x/Me memory manager extension that allowed access to memory addresses above 1 MB.

hive   Physical segment of the Windows NT/2000/XP registry that is stored in a file.

hop count   *See* time to live (TTL).

host   Any computer or other device on a network that has been assigned an IP address. Also called node.

host adapter The circuit board that controls a SCSI bus supporting as many as seven or fifteen separate devices. The host adapter controls communication between the SCSI bus and the PC.

host bus *See* system bus.

host drive Using Windows 9x, typically drive H on a compressed drive. *See* compressed drive.

host name A name that identifies a computer, printer, or other device on a network.

hot-pluggable *See* hot-swappable.

hot-swappable A device that can be plugged into a computer while it is turned on and the computer will sense the device and configure it without rebooting, or the device can be removed without an OS error. Also called hot-pluggable.

HTML (HyperText Markup Language) A markup language used for hypertext documents on the World Wide Web. This language uses tags to format the document, create hyperlinks, and mark locations for graphics.

HTTP (HyperText Transfer Protocol) The communications protocol used by the World Wide Web.

HTTPS (HTTP secure) A version of the HTTP protocol that includes data encryption for security.

hub A network device or box that provides a central location to connect cables.

hypertext Text that contains links to remote points in the document or to other files, documents, or graphics. Hypertext is created using HTML and is commonly distributed from Web sites.

i.Link *See* IEEE 1394.

I/O addresses Numbers that are used by devices and the CPU to manage communication between them. Also called ports or port addresses.

I/O controller card An older card that can contain serial, parallel, and game ports and floppy drive and IDE connectors.

IBM Data Connector *See* IDC.

IBM-compatible PC A computer that uses an Intel (or compatible) processor and can run DOS and Windows.

ICMP (Internet Control Message Protocol) Part of the IP layer that is used to transmit error messages and other control messages to hosts and routers.

IDC (IBM Data Connector) A connector used with STP cable on a Token Ring network. Also called a *UDC (Universal Data Connector)*.

IDE (Integrated Drive Electronics or Integrated Device Electronics) A hard drive whose disk controller is integrated into the drive, eliminating the need for a controller cable and thus increasing speed, as well as reducing price. *See also* EIDE.

IEEE 1284 A standard for parallel ports and cables developed by the Institute for Electrical and Electronics Engineers and supported by many hardware manufacturers.

IEEE 1394 Standards for an expansion bus that can also be configured to work as a local bus. It is expected to replace the SCSI bus, providing an easy method to install and configure fast I/O devices. Also called FireWire and i.Link.

IEEE 1394.3 A standard, developed by the 1394 Trade Association, that is designed for peer-to-peer data transmission and allows imaging devices to send images and photos directly to printers without involving a computer.

IEEE 802.11a/b/g IEEE specifications for wireless communication and data synchronization. Also known as Wi-Fi. Apple Computer's versions of 802.11b/g are called AirPort and AirPort Extreme.

IFS (Installable File System) The Windows 9x/Me component that configures all devices and communicates these configurations to the device drivers.

IMAP4 (Internet Message Access Protocol version 4) Version 4 of the IMAP protocol, which is an e-mail protocol that has more functionality than its predecessor, POP. IMAP can archive messages in folders on the e-mail server and can allow the user to choose not to download attachments to messages.

incremental backup A time-saving backup method that only backs up files changed or newly created since the last full or incremental backup. Multiple incremental backups might be required when recovering lost data.

infestation Any unwanted program that is transmitted to a computer without the user's knowledge and that is designed to do varying degrees of damage to data and software. There are a number of different types of infestations, including viruses, Trojan horses, worms, and logic bombs. *See* malicious software.

information (.inf) file Text file with an .inf file extension, such as Msbatch.inf, that contains information about a hardware or software installation.

infrared transceiver A wireless transceiver that uses infrared technology to support some wireless devices such as keyboards, mice, and printers. A motherboard might have an embedded infrared transceiver, or the transceiver might plug into a USB or serial port. The technology is defined by the Infrared Data Association (IrDA). Also called an *IrDA transceiver* or *infrared port*.

initialization files   Configuration information files for Windows. System.ini is one of the most important Windows 9x/Me initialization files.

inkjet printer   A type of ink dispersion printer that uses cartridges of ink. The ink is heated to a boiling point and then ejected onto the paper through tiny nozzles.

Institute of Electrical and Electronics Engineers (IEEE)   A nonprofit organization that develops standards for the computer and electronics industries.

instruction set   The set of instructions, on the CPU chip, that the computer can perform directly (such as ADD and MOVE).

intelligent UPS   A UPS connected to a computer by way of a USB or serial cable so that software on the computer can monitor and control the UPS. Also called *smart UPS*.

interlaced   A type of display in which the electronic beam of a monitor draws every other line with each pass, which lessens the overall effect of a lower refresh rate.

internal bus   The bus inside the CPU that is used for communication between the CPU's internal components.

internal cache   Memory cache that is faster than external cache, and is contained inside CPU chips (also referred to as primary, Level 1, or L1 cache).

internal command   Commands that are embedded in the Command.com file.

Internet Connection Firewall (ICF)   Windows XP software designed to protect a PC from unauthorized access from the Internet. Windows XP Service Pack 2 improved on ICF and renamed it Windows Firewall.

Internet Connection Sharing (ICS)   A Windows 98 and Windows XP utility that uses NAT and acts as a proxy server to manage two or more computers connected to the Internet.

Internet service provider (ISP)   A commercial group that provides Internet access for a monthly fee. AOL, Earthlink, and CompuServe are large ISPs.

intranet   A private network that uses the TCP/IP protocols.

Io.sys   Along with Msdos.sys and Command.com, one of the three files that are the core components of the real mode portion of Windows 9x/Me. It is the first program file of the OS.

IP (Internet Protocol)   The rules of communication in the TCP/IP stack that control segmenting data into packets, routing those packets across networks, and then reassembling the packets once they reach their destination.

IP address   A 32-bit address consisting of four numbers separated by periods, used to uniquely identify a device on a network that uses TCP/IP protocols. The first numbers identify the network; the last numbers identify a host. An example of an IP address is 206.96.103.114.

IPX/SPX (Internetwork Packet Exchange/Sequenced Packet Exchange)   A networking protocol suite first used by Novell NetWare, and which corresponds to the TCP/IP protocols.

IrDA transceiver   *See* infrared transceiver.

IRQ (interrupt request) line   A line on a bus that is assigned to a device and is used to signal the CPU for servicing. These lines are assigned a reference number (for example, the normal IRQ for a printer is IRQ 7).

ISA (Industry Standard Architecture) slot   An older slot on the motherboard used for slower I/O devices, which can support an 8-bit or a 16-bit data path. ISA slots are mostly replaced by PCI slots.

ISDN (Integrated Services Digital Network)   A digital telephone line that can carry data at about five times the speed of regular telephone lines. Two channels (telephone numbers) share a single pair of wires.

isochronous data transfer   A method used by IEEE 1394 to transfer data continuously without breaks.

ITU (International Telecommunications Union)   The international organization responsible for developing international standards of communication. Formerly CCITT.

joule   A measure of work or energy. One joule of energy produces one watt of power for one second.

JPEG (Joint Photographic Experts Group)   A graphical compression scheme that allows the user to control the amount of data that is averaged and sacrificed as file size is reduced. It is a common Internet file format. Most JPEG files have a .jpg extension.

jumper   Two wires that stick up side by side on the motherboard and are used to hold configuration information. The jumper is considered closed if a cover is over the wires, and open if the cover is missing.

Kerberos   A protocol used to encrypt account names and passwords that are sent to a network controller for validation. Kerberos is the default protocol used by Windows 2000/XP.

kernel   The portion of an OS that is responsible for interacting with the hardware.

kernel mode   A Windows NT/2000/XP "privileged" processing mode that has access to hardware components.

key (1) In encryption, a secret number or code used to encode and decode data. (2) In Windows, a section name of the Windows registry.

key fob A device, such as a type of smart card, that can fit conveniently on a key chain.

keyboard A common input device through which data and instructions may be typed into computer memory.

keylogger A type of spyware that tracks your keystrokes, including passwords, chat room sessions, e-mail messages, documents, online purchases, and anything else you type on your PC. Text is logged to a text file and transmitted over the Internet without your knowledge.

LAN (local area network) A computer network that covers only a small area, usually within one building.

land grid array (LGA) A feature of a CPU socket whereby pads, called lands, are used to make contact in uniform rows over the socket. Compare to *pin grid array (PGA)*.

lands Microscopic flat areas on the surface of a CD or DVD that separate pits. Lands and pits are used to represent data on the disk.

laptop computer *See* notebook.

large mode A mode of addressing information on hard drives that range from 504 MB to 8.4 GB, addressing information on a hard drive by translating cylinder, head, and sector information in order to break the 528-MB hard drive barrier. Also called ECHS mode.

large-capacity drive A hard drive larger than 504 MB.

laser printer A type of printer that uses a laser beam to control how toner is placed on the page and then uses heat to fuse the toner to the page.

Last Known Good configuration In Windows NT/2000/XP, registry settings and device drivers that were in effect when the computer last booted successfully. These settings can be restored during the startup process to recover from errors during the last boot.

LBA (logical block addressing) mode A mode of addressing information on hard drives in which the BIOS and operating system view the drive as one long linear list of LBAs or addressable sectors, permitting drives to be larger than 8.4 GB (LBA 0 is cylinder 0, head 0, and sector 1).

Level 1 (L1) cache *See* internal cache.

Level 2 (L2) cache *See* external cache.

Level 3 (L3) cache *See* external cache.

license Permission for an individual to use a product or service. A manufacturer's method of maintaining ownership, while granting permission for use to others.

Limited user Windows XP user accounts known as Users in Windows NT/2000, which have read-write access only on their own folders, read-only access to most system folders, and no access to other users' data.

line conditioner A device that regulates, or conditions, power, providing continuous voltage during brownouts and spikes.

line protocol A protocol used to send data packets destined for a network over telephone lines. PPP and SLIP are examples of line protocols.

line speed *See* bandwidth.

line-interactive UPS A variation of a standby UPS that shortens switching time by always keeping the inverter that converts AC to DC working, so that there is no charge-up time for the inverter.

LMHosts A text file located in the Windows folder that contains NetBIOS names and their associated IP addresses. This file is used for name resolution for a NetBEUI network.

local bus A bus that operates at a speed synchronized with the CPU frequency. The system bus is a local bus.

local I/O bus A local bus that provides I/O devices with fast access to the CPU. The PCI bus is a local I/O bus.

local printer A printer connected to a computer by way of a port on the computer. Compare to network printer.

local profile User profile that is stored on a local computer and cannot be accessed from another computer on the network.

local user account A user account that applies only to a local computer and cannot be used to access resources from other computers on the network.

logic bomb —A type of malicious software that is dormant code added to software and triggered at a predetermined time or by a predetermined event.

logical drive A portion or all of a hard drive partition that is treated by the operating system as though it were a physical drive. Each logical drive is assigned a drive letter, such as drive C, and contains a file system. Also called a volume.

logical geometry The number of heads, tracks, and sectors that the BIOS on the hard drive controller presents to the system BIOS and the OS. The logical geometry does not consist of the same values as the physical geometry, although calculations of drive capacity yield the same results. The use of communicating logical geometry is outdated.

Logical Unit Number (LUN) A number assigned to a logical device (such as a tray in a CD changer) that is part of a physical SCSI device, which is assigned a SCSI ID.

long mode A CPU processing mode that processes 64 bits at a time. The AMD Athlon 64 and the Intel Itaninum CPUs use this mode.

lost allocation units *See* lost clusters.

lost clusters File fragments that, according to the file allocation table, contain data that does not belong to any file. The command CHKDSK/F can free these fragments. Also called lost allocation units.

low insertion force (LIF) socket A socket that requires the installer to manually apply an even force over the microchip when inserting the chip into the socket.

Low Voltage Differential (LVD) A type of differential signaling that uses lower voltage than does HVD, is less expensive, and can be compatible with single-ended signaling on the same SCSI bus.

low-level formatting A process (usually performed at the factory) that electronically creates the hard drive tracks and sectors and tests for bad spots on the disk surface.

low-profile case *See* compact case.

LPX A form factor in which expansion cards are mounted on a riser card that plugs into a motherboard. The expansion cards in LPX systems are mounted parallel to the motherboard, rather than perpendicular to it as in AT and ATX systems.

MAC (Media Access Control) address A 48-bit hardware address unique to each NIC card and assigned by the manufacturer. The address is often printed on the adapter as hexadecimal numbers. An example is 00 00 0C 08 2F 35. Also called a physical address, an adapter address, or a hardware address.

macro A small sequence of commands, contained within a document, that can be automatically executed when the document is loaded, or executed later by using a predetermined keystroke.

macro virus A virus that can hide in the macros of a document file.

main board *See* motherboard.

malicious software Any unwanted program that is transmitted to a computer without the user's knowledge and that is designed to do varying degrees of damage to data and software. Types of infestations include viruses, Trojan horses, worms, adware, spyware, keyloggers, browser hijackers, dialers, and downloaders. Also called malware or an infestation.

malware *See* malicious software.

mandatory user profile A roaming user profile that applies to all users in a user group, and individual users cannot change that profile.

Master Boot Record (MBR) The first sector on a hard drive, which contains the partition table and a program the BIOS uses to boot an OS from the drive.

master file table (MFT) The database used by the NTFS file system to track the contents of a logical drive.

material safety data sheet (MSDS) A document that explains how to properly handle substances such as chemical solvents; it includes information such as physical data, toxicity, health effects, first aid, storage, disposal, and spill procedures.

megahertz (MHz) One million Hz, or one million cycles per second. *See* hertz (Hz).

memory Physical microchips that can hold data and programming, located on the motherboard or expansion cards.

memory address A number assigned to each byte in memory. The CPU can use memory addresses to track where information is stored in RAM. Memory addresses are usually displayed as hexadecimal numbers in segment/offset form.

memory bus *See* system bus.

memory cache A small amount of faster RAM that stores recently retrieved data, in anticipation of what the CPU will request next, thus speeding up access. *See also* system bus.

memory dump The contents of memory saved to a file at the time an event halted the system. Support technicians can analyze the dump file to help understand the source of the problem.

memory extender For DOS and Windows 9x/Me, a device driver named Himem.sys that manages RAM, giving access to memory addresses above 1 MB.

memory paging In Windows, swapping blocks of RAM memory to an area of the hard drive to serve as virtual memory when RAM is low.

memory-resident virus A virus that can stay lurking in memory even after its host program is terminated.

microATX A version of the ATX form factor. MicroATX addresses some new technologies that were developed after the original introduction of ATX.

microcode A programming instruction that can be executed by a CPU without breaking the instruction down into simpler instructions. Typically, a single command line in a Visual Basic or C++ program must be broken down into numerous microcode commands.

MicroDIMM A type of memory module used on sub-notebooks that has 144 pins and uses a 64-bit data path.

microprocessor *See* central processing unit (CPU).

Microsoft Management Console (MMC) A utility to build customized consoles. These consoles can be saved to a file with an .msc file extension.

Mini PCI The PCI industry standard for desktop computer expansion cards, applied to a much smaller form factor for notebook expansion cards.

Mini-ATX A smaller ATX board that can be used with regular ATX cases and power supplies.

minicartridge A tape drive cartridge that is only $3\frac{1}{4}$ x $2\frac{1}{2}$ x $\frac{3}{5}$ inches. It is small enough to allow two drives to fit into a standard $5\frac{1}{2}$-inch drive bay of a PC case.

minifile system In Windows NT/2000/XP, a simplified file system that is started so that Ntldr (NT Loader) can read files from any file system the OS supports.

Mini-LPX A smaller version of the LPX motherboard.

mixed mode A Windows 2000 mode for domain controllers used when there is at least one Windows NT domain controller on the network.

MMX (Multimedia Extensions) Multimedia instructions built into Intel processors to add functionality such as better processing of multimedia, SIMD support, and increased cache.

modem From MOdulate/DEModulate. A device that modulates digital data from a computer to an analog format that can be sent over telephone lines, then demodulates it back into digital form.

modem eliminator *See* null modem cable.

modem riser card A small modem card that uses an AMR or CNR slot. Part of the modem logic is contained in a controller on the motherboard.

modem speed The speed at which a modem can transmit data along a phone line, measured in bits per second (bps). Also called line speed.

modulation Converting binary or digital data into an analog signal that can be sent over standard telephone lines.

monitor The most commonly used output device for displaying text and graphics on a computer.

motherboard The main board in the computer, also called the system board. The CPU, ROM chips, SIMMs, DIMMs, RIMMs, and interface cards are plugged into the motherboard.

motherboard bus *See* system bus.

motherboard mouse *See* PS/2-compatible mouse.

mouse A pointing and input device that allows the user to move a cursor around a screen and select items with the click of a button.

MP3 A method to compress audio files that uses MPEG level 1. It can reduce sound files as low as a 1:24 ratio without losing much sound quality.

MPEG (Moving Pictures Experts Group) A processing-intensive standard for data compression for motion pictures that tracks movement from one frame to the next and only stores the data that has changed.

Msdos.sys In Windows 9x/Me, a text file that contains settings used by Io.sys during booting. In DOS, the Msdos.sys file was a program file that contained part of the DOS core.

MultiBank DRAM (MDRAM) A type of video memory that is faster than VRAM and WRAM, but can be more economical because it can be installed on a video card in smaller increments.

multicasting A process in which a message is sent by one host to multiple hosts, such as when a video conference is broadcast to several hosts on the Internet.

multimeter A device used to measure the various components of an electrical circuit. The most common measurements are voltage, current, and resistance.

multipartite virus A combination of a boot sector virus and a file virus. It can hide in either type of program.

multiplier The factor by which the bus speed or frequency is multiplied to get the CPU clock speed.

multi-processor platform A system that contains more than one processor. The motherboard has more than one processor socket and the processors must be rated to work in this multi-processor environment.

multiscan monitor A monitor that can work within a range of frequencies and thus can work with different standards and video cards. It offers a variety of refresh rates.

multisession A feature that allows data to be read from or written to a CD during more than one session. This is important if the disk was only partially filled during the first write.

Multistation Access Unit (MSAU or MAU) A centralized hub used in Token Ring networks to connect stations. Also called CAU.

multitasking Doing more than one thing at a time. A true multitasking system requires two or more CPUs, each processing a different thread at the same time. Compare to cooperative multitasking and preemptive multitasking.

multithreading   The ability to pass more than one function (thread) to the OS kernel at the same time, such as when one thread is performing a print job while another reads a file.

name resolution   The process of associating a NetBIOS name or host name to an IP address.

narrow SCSI   One of the two main SCSI specifications. Narrow SCSI has an 8-bit data bus. The word "narrow" is not usually included in the names of narrow SCSI devices.

NAT (Network Address Translation)   A process that converts private IP addresses on a LAN to the proxy server's IP address before a data packet is sent over the Internet.

native mode   A Windows 2000 mode used by domain controllers when there are no Windows NT domain controllers present on the network.

NetBEUI (NetBIOS Extended User Interface)   A fast, proprietary Microsoft networking protocol used only by Windows-based systems, and limited to LANs because it does not support routing.

NetBIOS (Network Basic Input/Output System)   An API protocol used by some applications to communicate over a NetBEUI network. NetBIOS has largely been replaced by Windows Sockets over a TCP/IP network.

network adapter   *See* network interface card.

network drive map   Mounting a drive to a computer, such as drive E, that is actually hard drive space on another host computer on the network.

network interface card (NIC)   An expansion card that plugs into a computer's motherboard and provides a port on the back of the card to connect a PC to a network. Also called a network adapter.

network operating system (NOS)   An operating system that resides on the controlling computer in the network. The NOS controls what software, data, and devices a user on the network can access. Examples of an NOS are Novell Netware and Windows Server 2003.

network printer   A printer that any user on the network can access, through its own network card and connection to the network, through a connection to a standalone print server, or through a connection to a computer as a local printer, which is shared on the network.

NLX   A low-end form factor that is similar to LPX but provides greater support for current and emerging processor technologies. NLX was designed for flexibility and efficiency of space.

NNTP (Network News Transfer Protocol)   The protocol used by newsgroup server and client software.

node   *See* host

noise   An extraneous, unwanted signal, often over an analog phone line, that can cause communication interference or transmission errors. Possible sources are fluorescent lighting, radios, TVs, lightning, or bad wiring.

noninterlaced   A type of display in which the electronic beam of a monitor draws every line on the screen with each pass.

non-memory-resident virus   A virus that is terminated when the host program is closed. Compare to memory-resident virus.

nonparity memory   Eight-bit memory without error checking. A SIMM part number with a 32 in it (4 x 8 bits) is nonparity.

nonvolatile   Refers to a kind of RAM that is stable and can hold data as long as electricity is powering the memory.

normal mode   *See* CHS mode.

North Bridge   That portion of the chipset hub that connects faster I/O buses (for example, AGP bus) to the system bus. Compare to South Bridge.

notebook   A portable computer that is designed for travel and mobility. Notebooks use the same technology as desktop PCs, with modifications for conserving voltage, taking up less space, and operating while on the move. Also called a laptop computer.

NTFS (NT file system)   The file system for the Windows NT/2000/XP operating systems. NTFS cannot be accessed by other operating systems such as DOS. It provides increased reliability and security in comparison to other methods of organizing and accessing files. There are several versions of NTFS that might or might not be compatible.

Ntldr (NT Loader)   In Windows NT/2000/XP, the OS loader used on Intel systems.

NTVDM (NT virtual DOS machine)   An emulated environment in which a 16-bit DOS application resides within Windows NT/2000/XP with its own memory space or WOW (Win16 on Win32).

null modem cable   A cable that allows two data terminal equipment (DTE) devices to communicate in which the transmit and receive wires are crossconnected and no modems are necessary.

NWLink   Microsoft's version of the IPX/SPX protocol suite used by Novell NetWare operating systems.

octet   Term for each of the four 8-bit numbers that make up an IP address. For example, the IP address 206.96.103.114 has four octets.

ohm (Ω)   The standard unit of measurement for electrical resistance. Resistors are rated in ohms.

on-board ports Ports that are directly on the motherboard, such as a built-in keyboard port or on-board serial port.

operating system (OS) Software that controls a computer. An OS controls how system resources are used and provides a user interface, a way of managing hardware and software, and ways to work with files.

operating system formatting *See* high-level formatting.

overclocking Running a processor at a higher frequency than is recommended by the manufacturer, which can result in an unstable system, but is a popular thing to do when a computer is used for gaming.

P1 connector Power connection on an ATX or BTX motherboard.

P8 connector One of two power connectors on an AT motherboard.

P9 connector One of two power connectors on an AT motherboard.

packet Segment of network data that also includes header, destination address, and trailer information that is sent as a unit. Also called data packet or datagram.

page fault An OS interrupt that occurs when the OS is forced to access the hard drive to satisfy the demands for virtual memory.

page file *See* swap file.

Pagefile.sys The Windows NT/2000/XP swap file.

page-in The process in which the memory manager goes to the hard drive to return the data from a swap file to RAM.

page-out The process in which, when RAM is full, the memory manager takes a page and moves it to the swap file.

pages 4K segments in which Windows NT/2000/XP allocates memory.

parallel ATA (PATA) An older IDE cabling method that uses a 40-pin flat data cable or an 80-conductor cable and a 40-pin IDE connector. *See also* serial ATA.

parallel port A female 25-pin port on a computer that can transmit data in parallel, 8 bits at a time, and is usually used with a printer. The names for parallel ports are LPT1 and LPT2.

parity An error-checking scheme in which a ninth, or "parity," bit is added. The value of the parity bit is set to either 0 or 1 to provide an even number of ones for even parity and an odd number of ones for odd parity.

parity error An error that occurs when the number of 1s in the byte is not in agreement with the expected number.

parity memory Nine-bit memory in which the ninth bit is used for error checking. A SIMM part number with a 36 in it (4 x 9 bits) is parity. Older PCs almost always use parity chips.

partition A division of a hard drive that can be used to hold logical drives.

partition table A table at the beginning of the hard drive that contains information about each partition on the drive. The partition table is contained in the Master Boot Record.

passive backplane A type of backplane system in which the backplane contains no circuitry at all. All circuitry in a passive backplane system is contained on a mothercard plugged into a backplane.

passive terminator A type of terminator for single-ended SCSI cables. Simple resistors are used to provide termination of a signal. Passive termination is not reliable over long distances and should only be used with narrow SCSI.

passphrase A type of password that can contain a phrase where spaces are allowed. A passphrase is stronger than a one-word password.

patch An update to software that corrects an error, adds a feature, or addresses security issues. Also called an update or service pack.

patch cable A network cable that is used to connect a PC to a hub, switch, or router.

path (1) A drive and list of directories pointing to a file such as C:\Windows\command. (2) The OS command to provide a list of paths to the system for finding program files to execute.

PC Card A credit-card-sized adapter card that can be slid into a slot in the side of many notebook computers and is used by modems, network cards, and other devices. Also called PCMCIA Card.

PC Card slot An expansion slot on a notebook computer, into which a PC Card is inserted. Also called a PCMCIA Card slot.

PCI (Peripheral Component Interconnect) bus A bus common on Pentium computers that runs at speeds of up to 33 MHz or 66 MHz, with a 32-bit-wide or 64-bit-wide data path. PCI-X, released in September 1999, enables PCI to run at 133 MHz. For some chipsets, it serves as the middle layer between the memory bus and expansion buses.

PCL (Printer Control Language) A printer language developed by Hewlett-Packard that communicates to a printer how to print a page.

PCMCIA (Personal Computer Memory Card International Association) Card   *See* PC Card.

PCMCIA Card slot   *See* PC Card slot.

PDA (Personal Digital Assistant)   A small, handheld computer that has its own operating system and applications.

peer-to-peer network   A network of computers that are all equals, or peers. Each computer has the same amount of authority, and each can act as a server to the other computers.

peripheral devices   Devices that communicate with the CPU but are not located directly on the motherboard, such as the monitor, floppy drive, printer, and mouse.

phishing   (1) A type of identity theft where a person is baited into giving personal data to a Web site that appears to be the Web site of a reputable company with which the person has an account. (2) Sending an e-mail message with the intent of getting the user to reveal private information that can be used for identify theft.

physical address   *See* MAC address.

physical geometry   The actual layout of heads, tracks, and sectors on a hard drive. Compare to logical geometry.

PIF (program information file)   A file used by Windows to describe the environment for a DOS program to use.

pin grid array (PGA)   A feature of a CPU socket whereby the pins are aligned in uniform rows around the socket.

Ping (Packet Internet Groper)   A Windows and Unix command used to troubleshoot network connections. It verifies that the host can communicate with another host on the network.

pinout   A description of how each pin on a bus, connection, plug, slot, or socket is used.

PIO (Programmed I/O) transfer mode   A transfer mode that uses the CPU to transfer data from the hard drive to memory. PIO mode is slower than DMA mode.

pipelined burst SRAM   A less expensive SRAM that uses more clock cycles per transfer than non-pipelined burst but does not significantly slow down the process.

pits   Recessed areas on the surface of a CD or DVD, separating lands, or flat areas. Lands and pits are used to represent data on a disc.

pixel   A small spot on a fine horizontal scan line. Pixels are illuminated to create an image on the monitor.

PKI (public key infrastructure)   The standards used to encrypt, transport, and validate digital certificates over the Internet.

Plug and Play (PnP)   A standard designed to make the installation of new hardware devices easier by automatically configuring devices to eliminate system resource conflicts (such as IRQ or I/O address conflicts). PnP is supported by Windows 9x/Me, Windows 2000, and Windows XP.

polling   A process by which the CPU checks the status of connected devices to determine if they are ready to send or receive data.

polymorphic virus   A type of virus that changes its distinguishing characteristics as it replicates itself. Mutating in this way makes it more difficult for AV software to recognize the presence of the virus.

POP (Post Office Protocol)   The protocol that an e-mail server and client use when the client requests the downloading of e-mail messages. The most recent version is POP3. POP is being replaced by IMAP.

port   (1) As applied to services running on a computer, a number assigned to a process on a computer so that the process can be found by TCP/IP. Also called a port address or port number. (2) Another name for an I/O address. *See also* I/O address. (3) A physical connector, usually at the back of a computer, that allows a cable from a peripheral device, such as a printer, mouse, or modem, to be attached.

port address   *See* I/O address.

port forwarding   A technique that allows a computer on the Internet to reach a computer on a private network using a certain port when the private network is protected by a router using NAT as a proxy server. Port forwarding is also called tunneling.

port number   *See* port.

port replicator   A device designed to connect to a notebook computer in order to make it easy to connect the notebook to peripheral devices.

port settings   The configuration parameters of communications devices such as COM1, COM2, or LPT1, including IRQ settings.

port speed   The communication speed between a DTE (computer) and a DCE (modem). As a general rule, the port speed should be at least four times as fast as the modem speed.

POST (power-on self test)   A self-diagnostic program used to perform a simple test of the CPU, RAM, and various I/O devices. The POST is performed by startup BIOS when the computer is first turned on, and is stored in ROM-BIOS.

PostScript   A printer language developed by Adobe Systems which tells a printer how to print a page.

power conditioner   A line conditioner that regulates, or conditions, power, providing continuous voltage during brownouts.

power scheme   A feature of Windows XP support for notebooks that allows the user to create groups of power settings for specific sets of conditions.

power supply   A box inside the computer case that supplies power to the motherboard and other installed devices. Power supplies provide 3.3, 5, and 12 volts DC.

power-on password   A password that a computer uses to control access during the boot process.

PPP (Point-to-Point Protocol)   A protocol that governs the methods for communicating via modems and dial-up telephone lines. The Windows Dial-up Networking utility uses PPP.

PPPoE (Point-to-Point Protocol over Ethernet)   The protocol that describes how a PC is to interact with a broadband converter box, such as cable modem, when the two are connected by an Ethernet cable, connected to a NIC in a PC.

preemptive multitasking   A type of pseudo-multitasking whereby the CPU allows an application a specified period of time and then preempts the processing to give time to another application.

primary cache   *See* internal cache.

primary domain controller (PDC)   In a Windows NT network, the computer that controls the directory database of user accounts, group accounts, and computer accounts on a domain. *See also* backup domain controller.

primary partition   A hard disk partition that can contain only one logical drive.

primary storage   Temporary storage on the motherboard used by the CPU to process data and instructions. Memory is considered primary storage.

printer   A peripheral output device that produces printed output to paper. Different types include dot matrix, ink-jet, and laser printers.

printer maintenance kit   A kit purchased from a printer manufacturer that contains the parts, tools, and instructions needed to perform routine printer maintenance.

private IP address   An IP address that is used on a private TCP/IP network that is isolated from the Internet.

process   An executing instance of a program together with the program resources. There can be more than one process running for a program at the same time. One process for a program happens each time the program is loaded into memory or executed.

processor   *See* central processing unit (CPU).

processor speed   The speed, or frequency, at which the CPU operates. Usually expressed in GHz.

product activation   The process that Microsoft uses to prevent software piracy. For example, once Windows XP is activated for a particular computer, it cannot be legally installed on another computer.

program   A set of step-by-step instructions to a computer. Some are burned directly into chips, while others are stored as program files. Programs are written in languages such as BASIC and C++.

program file   A file that contains instructions designed to be executed by the CPU.

protected mode   An operating mode that supports preemptive multitasking, the OS manages memory and other hardware devices, and programs can use a 32-bit data path. Also called 32-bit mode.

protocol   A set of rules and standards that two entities use for communication.

Protocol.ini   A Windows initialization file that contains network configuration information.

proxy server   A server that acts as an intermediary between another computer and the Internet. The proxy server substitutes its own IP address for the IP address of the computer on the network making a request, so that all traffic over the Internet appears to be coming from only the IP address of the proxy server.

PS/2-compatible mouse   A mouse that plugs into a round mouse PS/2 port on the motherboard. Sometimes called a motherboard mouse.

public IP address   An IP address available to the Internet.

QIC (Quarter-Inch Committee or quarter-inch cartridge)   A name of a standardized method used to write data to tape. These backup files have a .qic extension.

Quality of Service (QoS)   A measure of the success of communication over the Internet. Communication is degraded on the Internet when packets are dropped, delayed, delivered out of order, or corrupted. VoIP requires a high QoS.

RAID (redundant array of inexpensive disks or redundant array of independent disks)   Several methods of configuring multiple hard drives to store data to increase logical volume size and improve performance, or to ensure that if one hard drive fails, the data is still available from another hard drive.

RAM (random access memory) Memory modules on the motherboard containing microchips used to temporarily hold data and programs while the CPU processes both. Information in RAM is lost when the PC is turned off.

RAM drive An area of memory that is treated as though it were a hard drive, but works much faster than a hard drive. The Windows 9x/Me startup disk uses a RAM drive. Compare to virtual memory.

RARP (Reverse Address Resolution Protocol) A protocol used to translate the unique hardware NIC addresses (MAC addresses) into IP addresses (the reverse of ARP).

RDRAM *See* Direct Rambus DRAM.

read/write head A sealed, magnetic coil device that moves across the surface of a disk either reading data from or writing data to the disk.

real mode A single-tasking operating mode whereby a program can use 1024 K of memory addresses, has direct access to RAM, and uses a 16-bit data path. Using a memory extender (Himem.sys) a program in real mode can access memory above 1024 K. Also called 16-bit mode.

Recovery Console A Windows 2000/XP command interface utility and OS that can be used to solve problems when Windows cannot load from the hard drive.

rectifier An electrical device that converts AC to DC. A PC power supply contains a rectifier.

refresh The process of periodically rewriting data, such as on dynamic RAM.

refresh rate As applied to monitors, the number of times in one second an electronic beam can fill the screen with lines from top to bottom. Also called vertical scan rate.

registry A database that Windows uses to store hardware and software configuration information, user preferences, and setup information.

re-marked chips Chips that have been used and returned to the factory, marked again, and resold. The surface of the chips may be dull or scratched.

Remote Assistance A Windows XP feature that allows a support technician at a remote location to have full access to the Windows XP desktop.

repeater A device that amplifies signals on a network so they can be transmitted further down the line.

rescue disk A floppy disk that can be used to start up a computer when the hard drive fails to boot. Also called emergency startup disk (ESD) or startup disk.

resistance The degree to which a device opposes or resists the flow of electricity. As the electrical resistance increases, the current decreases. *See* ohm and resistor.

resistor An electronic device that resists or opposes the flow of electricity. A resistor can be used to reduce the amount of electricity being supplied to an electronic component.

resolution The number of pixels on a monitor screen that are addressable by software (example: 1024 x 768 pixels).

restore point A snapshot of the Windows Me/XP system state, usually made before installation of new hardware or applications.

REt (Resolution Enhancement technology) The term used by Hewlett-Packard to describe the way a laser printer varies the size of the dots used to create an image. This technology partly accounts for the sharp, clear image created by a laser printer.

RIMM A type of memory module developed by Rambus, Inc.

ring topology A network topology in which the nodes in a network form a ring. Each node is connected only to two other nodes, and a centralized hub is not required.

RISC (Reduced Instruction Set Computing) chips Chips that incorporate only the most frequently used instructions, so that the computer operates faster (for example, the PowerPC uses RISC chips).

riser card A card that plugs into a motherboard and allows for expansion cards to be mounted parallel to the motherboard. Expansion cards are plugged into slots on the riser card.

RJ-11 A phone line connection found on modems, telephones, and house phone outlets.

RJ-45 connector A connector used with twisted-pair cable that connects the cable to the NIC.

roaming user profile A user profile for a roaming user. Roaming user profiles are stored on a server so that the user can access the profile from anywhere on the network.

ROM (read-only memory) Chips that contain programming code and cannot be erased.

ROM BIOS *See* BIOS.

root directory The main directory created when a hard drive or disk is first formatted. In Linux, it's indicated by a forward slash. In DOS and Windows, it's indicated by a backward slash.

rootkit A type of malicious software that loads itself before the OS boot is complete and can hijack internal Windows components so that it masks information Windows provides to user-mode utilities such as Windows Explorer or Task Manager.

routable protocol   A protocol that can be routed to interconnected networks on the basis of a network address. TCP/IP is a routable protocol, but NetBEUI is not.

router   A device that connects networks and makes decisions as to the best routes to use when forwarding packets.

sags   *See* brownouts.

sampling rate   The rate of samples taken of an analog signal over a period of time, usually expressed as samples per second, or hertz.

SBAC (SCSI bus adapter chip)   The SCSI chip within a device housing that controls data transfer over the SCSI bus.

SCAM (SCSI Configuration AutoMatically)   A method of configuring SCSI device settings that follows the Plug and Play standard. SCAM makes installation of SCSI devices much easier, provided that the devices are SCAM-compliant.

scam e-mail   E-mail sent by a scam artist intended to lure you into a scheme.

scanner   A device that allows a computer to convert a picture, drawing, barcode, or other image into digital data that can be input into the computer.

scanning mirror   A component of a laser printer consisting of an octagonal mirror that can be directed in a sweeping motion to cover the entire length of a laser printer drum.

script virus   A type of virus that hides in a script which might execute when you click a link on a Web page or in an HTML e-mail message, or when you attempt to open an e-mail attachment.

SCSI (Small Computer System Interface)   A fast interface between a host adapter and the CPU that can daisy chain as many as 7 or 15 devices on a single bus.

SCSI ID   A number from 0 to 15 assigned to each SCSI device attached to the daisy chain.

SDRAM II   *See* Double Data Rate SDRAM (DDR SDRAM).

secondary storage   Storage that is remote to the CPU and permanently holds data, even when the PC is turned off, such as a hard drive.

sector   On a disk surface one segment of a track, which almost always contains 512 bytes of data.

security accounts manager (SAM)   A portion of the Windows NT/2000/XP registry that manages the account database that contains accounts, policies, and other pertinent information about local accounts.

sequential access   A method of data access used by tape drives, whereby data is written or read sequentially from the beginning to the end of the tape or until the desired data is found.

serial ATA (SATA)   An ATAPI cabling method that uses a narrower and more reliable cable than the 80-conductor cable. *See also* parallel ATA.

serial ATA cable   An IDE cable that is narrower and has fewer pins than the parallel IDE 80-conductor cable.

serial mouse   A mouse that uses a serial port and has a female 9-pin DB-9 connector.

serial port   A male 9-pin or 25-pin port on a computer system used by slower I/O devices such as a mouse or modem. Data travels serially, one bit at a time, through the port. Serial ports are sometimes configured as COM1, COM2, COM3, or COM4.

service   A program that runs in the background to support or serve Windows or an application.

service pack   *See* patch.

session   An established communication link between two software programs. On the Internet, a session is created by TCP.

SFC (System File Checker)   A Windows tool that checks to make sure Windows is using the correct versions of system files.

SGRAM (synchronous graphics RAM)   Memory designed especially for video card processing that can synchronize itself with the CPU bus clock.

shadow RAM or shadowing ROM   ROM programming code copied into RAM to speed up the system operation, because of the faster access speed of RAM.

shared memory   When the video system does not have dedicated video memory, but is using regular RAM instead. A system with shared memory generally costs less than having dedicated video memory. Also called *video sharing*.

shell   The portion of an OS that relates to the user and to applications.

shielded twisted-pair (STP) cable   A cable that is made of one or more twisted pairs of wires and is surrounded by a metal shield.

shortcut   An icon on the desktop that points to a program that can be executed or to a file or folder.

signal-regenerating repeater   A repeater that is able to distinguish between noise and signal. It reads the signal and retransmits it without the accompanying noise.

Sigverif.exe   A Windows 2000/XP utility that allows you to search for digital signatures.

SIMD (single instruction, multiple data)   A process that allows the CPU to execute a single instruction simultaneously on multiple pieces of data, rather than by repetitive looping.

SIMM (single inline memory module)   A miniature circuit board used in older computers to hold RAM. SIMMs hold 8, 16, 32, or 64 MB on a single module.

simple volume   A type of dynamic volume used on a single hard drive that corresponds to a primary partition on a basic disk.

single-ended (SE) cable   A type of SCSI cable in which two wires are used to carry a signal, one of which carries the signal itself; the other is a ground for the signal.

single-voltage CPU   A CPU that requires one voltage for both internal and I/O operations.

site license   A license that allows a company to install multiple copies of software, or to allow multiple employees to execute the software from a file server.

slack   Wasted space on a hard drive caused by not using all available space at the end of clusters.

sleep mode   A mode used in many "Green" systems that allows them to be configured through CMOS to suspend the monitor or even the drive, if the keyboard and/or CPU have been inactive for a set number of minutes. *See also* Green Standards.

slimline case   *See* compact case.

SLIP (Serial Line Internet Protocol)   A line protocol used by regular telephone lines that has largely been replaced by PPP.

smart card   Any small device that contains authentication information that can be keyed into a logon window or read by a reader to authenticate a user on a network.

smart card reader   A device that can read a smart card used to authenticate a person onto a network.

Smart Multistation Access Unit (SMAU)   *See* MAU.

smart UPS   *See* intelligent UPS.

SMARTDrive   A hard drive cache program that came with Windows 3.x and DOS and can be executed as a TSR from the Autoexec.bat file (for example, Device = Smartdrv.sys 2048).

SMTP (Simple Mail Transfer Protocol)   The protocol used by e-mail clients and servers to send e-mail messages over the Internet. *See* POP and IMAP4.

SMTP AUTH (SMTP Authentication)   A protocol that is used to authenticate or prove that a client who attempts to use an email server to send email is

authorized to use the server. The protocol is based on the Simple Authentication and Security Layer (SASL) protocol.

snap-ins   A Windows utility that can be installed in a console window by Microsoft Management Console.

SNMP (Simple Network Management Protocol)   A protocol used to monitor and manage network traffic on a workstation. SNMP works with TCP/IP and IPX/SPX networks.

social engineering   The practice of tricking people into giving out private information or allowing unsafe programs into the network or computer.

socket   *See* session.

SO-DIMM (small outline DIMM)   A type of memory module used in notebook computers that uses DIMM technology and can have either 72 pins or 144 pins.

soft boot   To restart a PC without turning off the power, for example, in Windows XP, by clicking Start, Turn Off Computer, and Restart. Also called warm boot.

soft power   *See* soft switch.

soft switch   A feature on an ATX or BTX system that allows an OS to power down the system and allows for activity such as a keystroke or network activity to power up the system. Also called soft power.

software   Computer programs, or instructions to perform a specific task. Software may be BIOS, OSs, or applications software such as a word-processing or spreadsheet program.

software cache   Cache controlled by software whereby the cache is stored in RAM.

solid ink printer   A type of printer that uses sticks or blocks of solid ink. The ink is melted and then jetted onto the paper as the paper passes by on a drum.

solid state device (SSD)   A storage device that uses memory chips to store data instead of spinning disks (such as those used by hard drives and CD drives). Examples of solid state devices are jump drives (also called key drives or thumb drives), flash memory cards, and solid state disks used as hard drives in notebook computers designed for the most rugged uses. Also called solid state disk (SSD).

solid state disk (SSD)   *See* solid state device.

SO-RIMM (small outline RIMM)   A 160-pin memory module used in notebooks that uses Rambus technology.

South Bridge   That portion of the chipset hub that connects slower I/O buses (for example, an ISA bus) to the system bus. Compare to North Bridge.

spacers   *See* standoffs.

spam   Junk e-mail you don't ask for, don't want, and that gets in your way.

spanned volume   A type of dynamic volume used on two or more hard drives that fills up the space allotted on one physical disk before moving to the next.

SPI (SCSI Parallel Interface)   The part of the SCSI-3 standard that specifies how SCSI devices are connected.

spikes   Temporary surges in voltage, which can damage electrical components. Also called swells.

spooling   Placing print jobs in a print queue so that an application can be released from the printing process before printing is completed. Spooling is an acronym for simultaneous peripheral operations online.

spyware   Malicious software that installs itself on your computer to spy on you. It collects personal information about you that it transmits over the Internet to Web-hosting sites that intend to use your personal data for harm.

SSE (Streaming SIMD Extension)   A technology used by the Intel Pentium III and later CPUs and designed to improve performance of multimedia software.

SSL (secure socket layer)   A secure protocol developed by Netscape that uses a digital certificate including a public key to encrypt and decrypt data.

staggered pin grid array (SPGA)   A feature of a CPU socket whereby the pins are staggered over the socket in order to squeeze more pins into a small space.

standby time   The time before a "Green" system will reduce 92 percent of its activity. *See also* Green Standards.

standoffs   Round plastic or metal pegs that separate the motherboard from the case, so that components on the back of the motherboard do not touch the case.

star bus topology   A LAN that uses a logical bus design, but with all devices connected to a central hub, making a physical star.

star ring topology   A topology that is physically arranged in a star formation but is logically a ring because of the way information travels on it. Token Ring is the primary example.

star topology   A LAN in which all the devices are connected to a central hub.

start bits   Bits that are used to signal the approach of data.

startup BIOS   Part of system BIOS that is responsible for controlling the PC when it is first turned on. Startup BIOS gives control over to the OS once it is loaded.

startup disk   *See* rescue disk.

startup password   *See* power-on password.

stateless   Term for a device or process that manages data or some activity without regard to all the details of the data or activity.

static electricity   *See* electrostatic discharge.

static IP address   An IP address permanently assigned to a workstation.

static RAM (SRAM)   RAM chips that retain information without the need for refreshing, as long as the computer's power is on. They are more expensive than traditional DRAM.

static VxD   A VxD that is loaded into memory at startup and remains there for the entire OS session.

stealth virus   A virus that actively conceals itself by temporarily removing itself from an infected file that is about to be examined, and then hiding a copy of itself elsewhere on the drive.

stop error   An error severe enough to cause the operating system to stop all processes.

streaming audio   Downloading audio data from the Internet in a continuous stream of data without first downloading an entire audio file.

striped volume   A type of dynamic volume used for two or more hard drives that writes to the disks evenly rather than filling up allotted space on one and then moving on to the next. Compare to spanned volume.

subdirectory   A directory or folder contained in another directory or folder. Also called a child directory or folder.

subnet mask   A subnet mask is a group of four numbers (dotted decimal numbers) that tell TCP/IP if a remote computer is on the same or a different network.

subsystems   The different modules into which the Windows NT/2000/XP user mode is divided.

surge suppressor or surge protector   A device or power strip designed to protect electronic equipment from power surges and spikes.

Surround Sound   A sound compression standard that supports six separate sound channels using six speakers known as Front Left and Right, Front Center, Rear Left and Right, and Subwoofer. Surround Sound 7.1 supports two additional rear or side speakers. Also known Dolby AC-3, Dolby Digital Surround, or Dolby Surround Sound.

suspend time   The time before a "Green" system will reduce 99 percent of its activity. After this time, the system needs a warm-up time so that the CPU, monitor, and hard drive can reach full activity.

swap file   A file on the hard drive that is used by the OS for virtual memory. Also called a page file.

swells   *See* spikes.

switch   A device used to segment a network. It can decide which network segment is to receive a packet, on the basis of the packet's destination MAC address.

synchronization   The process by which files and programs are transferred between PDAs and PCs.

synchronous DRAM (SDRAM)   A type of memory stored on DIMMs that runs in sync with the system clock, running at the same speed as the motherboard.

synchronous SRAM   SRAM that is faster and more expensive than asynchronous SRAM. It requires a clock signal to validate its control signals, enabling the cache to run in step with the CPU.

SyncLink DRAM (SLDRAM)   A type of DRAM developed by a consortium of 12 DRAM manufacturers. It improved on regular SDRAM but is now obsolete.

Sysedit   The Windows 9x/Me System Configuration Editor, a text editor generally used to edit system files.

system BIOS   BIOS located on the motherboard.

system board   *See* motherboard.

system bus   The bus between the CPU and memory on the motherboard. The bus frequency in documentation is called the system speed, such as 400 MHz. Also called the memory bus, front-side bus, local bus, or host bus.

system clock   A line on a bus that is dedicated to timing the activities of components connected to it. The system clock provides a continuous pulse that other devices use to time themselves.

system disk   Windows terminology for a bootable disk.

system partition   The active partition of the hard drive containing the boot record and the specific files required to load Windows NT/2000/XP.

system resource   A channel, line, or address on the motherboard that can be used by the CPU or a device for communication. The four system resources are IRQ, I/O address, DMA channel, and memory address.

System Restore   A Windows Me/XP utility, similar to the ScanReg tool in earlier versions of Windows, that is used to restore the system to a restore point. Unlike ScanReg, System Restore cannot be executed from a command prompt.

system state data   In Windows 2000/XP, files that are necessary for a successful load of the operating system.

System Tray   An area to the right of the taskbar that holds the icons for running services; these services include the volume control and network connectivity.

System.ini   A text configuration file used by Windows 3.x and supported by Windows 9x/Me for backward-compatibility.

TAPI (Telephony Application Programming Interface)   A standard developed by Intel and Microsoft that can be used by 32-bit Windows communications programs for communicating over phone lines.

taskbar   A bar normally located at the bottom of the Windows desktop, displaying information about open programs and providing quick access to others.

TCP (Transmission Control Protocol)   Part of the TCP/IP protocol suite. TCP guarantees delivery of data for application protocols and establishes a session before it begins transmitting data.

TCP/IP (Transmission Control Protocol/Internet Protocol)   The suite of protocols that supports communication on the Internet. TCP is responsible for error checking, and IP is responsible for routing.

TDMA (time-division multiple access)   A protocol standard used by cellular WANs and cell phones.

technical documentation   The technical reference manuals, included with software packages and peripherals, that provide directions for installation, usage, and troubleshooting. The information extends beyond that given in user manuals.

telephony   A term describing the technology of converting sound to signals that can travel over telephone lines.

terminating resistor   The resistor added at the end of a SCSI chain to dampen the voltage at the end of the chain.

termination   A process necessary to prevent an echo effect of power at the end of a SCSI chain, resulting in interference with the data transmission.

thermal printer   A type of line printer that uses wax-based ink, which is heated by heat pins that melt the ink onto paper.

ThickNet   *See* 10Base5.

ThinNet   *See* 10Base2.

thread   Each process that the CPU is aware of; a single task that is part of a longer task or program.

TIFF (Tagged Image File Format)   A bitmapped file format used to hold photographs, graphics, and screen captures. TIFF files can be rather large, and have a .tif file extension.

time to live (TTL) Number of routers a network packet can pass through on its way to its destination before it is dropped. Also called hop count.

TLS (Transport Layer Security) A protocol used to secure data sent over the Internet. It is an improved version of SSL.

token ring An older LAN technology developed by IBM that transmits data at 4 Mbps or 16 Mbps.

top-level domain The highest level of domain names, indicated by a suffix that tells something about the host. For example, .com is for commercial use and .edu is for educational institutions.

touch screen An input device that uses a monitor or LCD panel as a backdrop for user options. Touch screens can be embedded in a monitor or LCD panel or installed as an add-on device.

tower case The largest type of personal computer case. Tower cases stand vertically and can be as high as two feet tall. They have more drive bays and are a good choice for computer users who anticipate making significant upgrades.

trace A wire on a circuit board that connects two components or devices.

track One of many concentric circles on the surface of a hard drive or floppy disk.

training *See* handshaking.

transceiver The component on a NIC that is responsible for signal conversion. Combines the words transmitter and receiver.

transformer A device that changes the ratio of current to voltage. A computer power supply is basically a transformer and a rectifier.

transistor An electronic device that can regulate electricity and act as a logical gate or switch for an electrical signal.

translation A technique used by system BIOS and hard drive controller BIOS to break the 504-MB hard drive barrier, whereby a different set of drive parameters are communicated to the OS and other software than that used by the hard drive controller BIOS.

Travan standards A popular and improved group of standards for tape drives based on the QIC standards and developed by 3M.

triad Three dots of color that make up one composite dot on a CRT screen.

Trojan horse A type of infestation that hides or disguises itself as a useful program, yet is designed to cause damage when executed.

TSR (terminate-and-stay-resident) A program that is loaded into memory and remains dormant until called on, such as a screen saver or a memory-resident antivirus program.

UART (universal asynchronous receiver-transmitter) chip A chip that controls serial ports. It sets protocol and converts parallel data bits received from the system bus into serial bits.

UDC (Universal Data Connector) *See* IDC (IBM Data Connector).

UDP (User Datagram Protocol) A connectionless protocol that does not require a connection to send a packet and does not guarantee that the packet arrives at its destination. UDP is faster than TCP because TCP takes the time to make a connection and guarantee delivery.

unattended installation A Windows NT/ 2000/XP installation that is done by storing the answers to installation questions in a text file or script that Windows NT/2000/XP calls an answer file so that the answers do not have to be typed in during the installation.

Universal Disk Format (UDF) file system A file system for optical media used by all DVD discs and some CD-R and CD-RW discs.

unshielded twisted-pair (UTP) cable A cable that is made of one or more twisted pairs of wires and is not surrounded by shielding.

upgrade install The installation of an OS on a hard drive that already has an OS installed in such a way that settings kept by the old OS are carried forward into the upgrade, including information about hardware, software, and user preferences.

upper memory In DOS and Windows 9x/Me, the memory addresses from 640 K up to 1024 K, originally reserved for BIOS, device drivers, and TSRs.

upper memory block (UMB) In DOS and Windows 9x/Me, a group of consecutive memory addresses in RAM from 640 K to 1MB that can be used by 16-bit device drivers and TSRs.

UPS (uninterruptible power supply) A device designed to provide a backup power supply during a power failure. Basically, a UPS is a battery backup system with an ultrafast sensing device.

URL (Uniform Resource Locator) An address for a resource on the Internet. A URL can contain the protocol used by the resource, the name of the computer and its network, and the path and name of a file on the computer.

USB (universal serial bus) port A type of port designed to make installation and configuration of

I/O devices easy, providing room for as many as 127 devices daisy-chained together.

USB host controller   Manages the USB bus. If the motherboard contains on-board USB ports, the USB host controller is part of the chipset. The USB controller uses only a single set of resources for all devices on the bus.

user account   The information, stored in the SAM database, that defines a Windows NT/ 2000/XP user, including username, password, memberships, and rights.

user component   A Windows 9x/Me component that controls the mouse, keyboard, ports, and desktop.

user mode   In Windows NT/2000/XP, a mode that provides an interface between an application and the OS, and only has access to hardware resources through the code running in kernel mode.

user profile   A personal profile about a user that enables the user's desktop settings and other operating parameters to be retained from one session to another.

User State Migration Tool (USMT)   A Windows XP utility that helps you migrate user files and preferences from one computer to another in order to help a user make a smooth transition from one computer to another.

V.92   The latest standard for data transmission over phone lines that can attain a speed of 56 Kbps.

value data   In Windows, the name and value of a setting in the registry.

VCACHE   A built-in Windows 9x/Me 32-bit software cache that doesn't take up conventional memory space or upper memory space as SMARTDrive did.

VESA (Video Electronics Standards Association) VL bus   An outdated local bus used on 80486 computers for connecting 32-bit adapters directly to the local processor bus.

VFAT (virtual file allocation table)   A variation of the original DOS 16-bit FAT that allows for long filenames and 32-bit disk access.

video card   An interface card installed in the computer to control visual output on a monitor. Also called display adapter.

video sharing   *See* shared memory.

virtual device driver (VxD or VDD)   A Windows device driver that may or may not have direct access to a device. It might depend on a Windows component to communicate with the device itself.

virtual machine   One or more logical machines created within one physical machine by Windows, allowing applications to make serious errors within one logical machine without disturbing other programs and parts of the system.

virtual memory   A method whereby the OS uses the hard drive as though it were RAM. Compare to RAM drive.

virtual real mode   An operating mode that works similarly to real mode and is provided by a 32-bit OS for a 16-bit program to work.

virus   A program that often has an incubation period, is infectious, and is intended to cause damage. A virus program might destroy data and programs or damage a disk drive's boot sector.

virus hoax   E-mail that does damage by tempting you to forward it to everyone in your e-mail address book with the intent of clogging up e-mail systems or by persuading you to delete a critical Windows system file by convincing you the file is malicious.

virus signature   A set of distinguishing characteristics of a virus used by antivirus software to identify the virus.

VMM (Virtual Machine Manager)   A Windows 9x/Me program that controls virtual machines and the resources they use including memory. The VMM manages the page table used to access memory.

volatile   Refers to a kind of RAM that is temporary, cannot hold data very long, and must be frequently refreshed.

volt (V)   A measure of potential difference in an electrical circuit. A computer ATX power supply usually provides five separate voltages: +12 V, -12 V, +5 V, -5 V, and +3.3 V.

voltage   Electrical differential that causes current to flow, measured in volts. *See* volt.

voltage regulator module (VRM)   A device embedded or installed on the motherboard that regulates voltage to the processor.

voltmeter   A device for measuring electrical AC or DC voltage.

volume   *See* logical drive.

VRAM (video RAM)   RAM on video cards that holds the data that is being passed from the computer to the monitor and can be accessed by two devices simultaneously. Higher resolutions often require more video memory.

VxD   *See* virtual device driver.

wait state   A clock tick in which nothing happens, used to ensure that the microprocessor isn't getting ahead of slower components. A 0-wait state is preferable to a 1-wait state. Too many wait states can slow down a system.

WAN (wide area network) A network or group of networks that span a large geographical area.

warm boot *See* soft boot.

watt (W) The unit used to measure power. A typical computer may use a power supply that provides 200 W.

wattage Electrical power measured in watts.

WDM (Win32 Driver Model) The only Windows 9x/Me Plug and Play component that is found in Windows 98 but not Windows 95. WDM is the component responsible for managing device drivers that work under a driver model new to Windows 98.

WEP (Wired Equivalent Privacy) A data encryption method used on wireless networks that uses either 64-bit or 128-bit encryption keys that are static keys, meaning the key does not change while the wireless network is in use.

WFP (Windows File Protection) A Windows 2000/XP tool that protects system files from modification.

wide SCSI One of the two main SCSI specifications. Wide SCSI has a 16-bit data bus. *See also* narrow SCSI.

Wi-Fi *See* IEEE 802.11b.

wildcard A * or ? character used in a command line that represents a character or group of characters in a filename or extension.

Win.ini The Windows initialization file that contains program configuration information needed for running the Windows operating environment. Its functions were replaced by the registry beginning with Windows 9x/Me, which still supports it for backward compatibility with Windows 3.x.

Win16 on Win32 (WOW) A group of programs provided by Windows NT/2000/XP to create a virtual DOS environment that emulates a 16-bit Windows environment, protecting the rest of the OS from 16-bit applications.

Win386.swp The name of the Windows 9x/Me swap file. Its default location is C:\Windows.

WINS (Windows Internet Naming Service) A Microsoft resolution service with a distributed database that tracks relationships between NetBIOS names and IP addresses. Compare to DNS.

WinSock (Windows Sockets) A part of the TCP/IP utility software that manages API calls from applications to other computers on a TCP/IP network.

wireless LAN (WLAN) A type of LAN that does not use wires or cables to create connections, but instead transmits data over radio or infrared waves.

word size The number of bits that can be processed by a CPU at one time.

workgroup In Windows, a logical group of computers and users in which administration, resources, and security are distributed throughout the network, without centralized management or security.

worm An infestation designed to copy itself repeatedly to memory, on drive space or on a network, until little memory or disk space remains.

WPA (WiFi Protected Access) A data encryption method for wireless networks that use the TKIP (Temporal Key Integrity Protocol) encryption method and the encryption keys are changed at set intervals while the wireless LAN is in use.

WPA2 (WiFi Protected Access 2) A data encryption standard compliant with the IEEE802.11i standard that uses the AES (Advanced Encryption Standard) protocol. WPA2 is currently the strongest wireless encryption standard.

WRAM (window RAM) Dual ported video RAM that is faster and less expensive than VRAM. It has its own internal bus on the chip, with a data path that is 256 bits wide.

zero insertion force (ZIF) socket A socket that uses a small lever to apply even force when you install the microchip into the socket.

zero-fill utility A utility provided by a hard drive manufacturer that fills every sector on the drive with zeroes.

zone bit recording A method of storing data on a hard drive whereby the drive can have more sectors per track near the outside of the platter.

INDEX

Note: Page numbers in **boldface** indicate pages where key terms appear.